Growth

Previous works by author

Growth

From Microorganisms to Megacities

Vaclav Smil

The MIT Press
Cambridge, Massachusetts
London, England

© 2019 Massachusetts Institute of Technology

All rights reserved. No part of this book may be reproduced in any form by any electronic or mechanical means (including photocopying, recording, or information storage and retrieval) without permission in writing from the publisher.

This book was set in Stone Serif and Stone Sans by Westchester Publishing Services. Printed and bound in the United States of America.

Library of Congress Cataloging-in-Publication Data

Names: Smil, Vaclav, author.
Title: Growth / Vaclav Smil.
Description: Cambridge, MA : The MIT Press, 2019. | Includes bibliographical references and index.
Identifiers: LCCN 2018059356 | ISBN 9780262042833 (hardcover : alk. paper)
Subjects: LCSH: Civilization, Modern—21st century. | Technology and civilization. | Growth. | Human ecology. | Population. | Energy development. | Economic development. | Cities and towns—Growth. | Urban ecology (Sociology).
Classification: LCC CB428 .S625 2019 | DDC 909.82—dc23
LC record available at https://lccn.loc.gov/2018059356

10 9 8 7 6 5 4 3

Contents

Preface

Growth is an omnipresent protean reality of our lives: a marker of evolution, of an increase in size and capabilities of our bodies as we reach adulthood, of gains in our collective capacities to exploit the Earth's resources and to organize our societies in order to secure a higher quality of life. Growth has been both an unspoken and an explicit aim of individual and collective striving throughout the evolution of our species and its still short recorded history. Its progress governs the lives of microorganisms as well as of galaxies. Growth determines the extent of oceanic crust and utility of all artifacts designed to improve our lives as well as the degree of damage any abnormally developing cells can do inside our bodies. And growth shapes the capabilities of our extraordinarily large brains as well as the fortunes of our economies. Because of its ubiquity, growth can be studied on levels ranging from subcellular and cellular (to reveal its metabolic and regulatory requirements and processes) to tracing long-term trajectories of complex systems, be they geotectonic upheavals, national or global populations, cities, economies or empires.

Terraforming growth—geotectonic forces that create the oceanic and continental crust, volcanoes, and mountain ranges, and that shape watersheds, plains, and coasts—proceeds very slowly. Its prime mover, the formation of new oceanic crust at mid-ocean ridges, advances mostly at rates of less than 55 mm/year, while exceptionally fast new sea-floor creation can reach about 20 cm/year (Schwartz et al. 2005). As for the annual increments of continental crust, Reymer and Schubert (1984) calculated the addition rate of 1.65 km^3 and with the total subduction rate (as the old crust is recycled into the mantle) of 0.59 km^3 that yields a net growth rate of 1.06 km^3.

That is a minuscule annual increment when considering that the continents cover nearly 150 Mm^2 and that the continental crust is mostly 35–40 km thick, but such growth has continued during the entire Phanerozoic eon, that is for the past 542 million years. And one more, this time

Figure 0.1
Slow but persistent geotectonic growth. The Himalayas were created by the collision of Indian and Eurasian plates that began more than 50 million year ago and whose continuation now makes the mountain chain grow by as much as 1 cm/year. Photo from the International Space Station (looking south from above the Tibetan Plateau) taken in January 2004. Image available at https://www.nasa.gov/multimedia/imagegallery /image_feature_152.html.

vertical, example of inevitably slow tectonic speeds: the uplift of the Himalayas, the planet's most imposing mountain range, amounts to about 10 mm/year (Burchfiel and Wang 2008; figure 0.1). Tectonic growth fundamentally constrains the Earth's climate (as it affects global atmospheric circulation and the distribution of pressure cells) and ecosystemic productivity (as it affects temperature and precipitation) and hence also human habitation and economic activity. But there is nothing we can do about its timing, location, and pace, nor can we harness it directly for our benefit and hence it will not get more attention in this book.

Organismic growth, the quintessential expression of life, encompasses all processes by which elements and compounds are transformed over time into new living mass (biomass). Human evolution has been existentially dependent on this natural growth, first just for foraged and hunted food, later for fuel and raw materials, and eventually for cultivated food and feed plants and for large-scale exploitation of forest phytomass as well as for the capture of marine species. This growing human interference in the biosphere has brought a large-scale transformation of many ecosystems, above all the conversion of forests and wetlands to croplands and extensive use of grassland for grazing animals (Smil 2013a).

Growth is also a sign of progress and an embodiment of hope in human affairs. Growth of technical capabilities has harnessed new energy sources, raised the level and reliability of food supply, and created new materials and new industries. Economic growth has brought tangible material gains with the accumulation of private possessions that enrich our brief lives, and it creates intangible values of accomplishment and satisfaction. But growth also brings anxieties, concerns, and fears. People—be it children marking their increasing height on a door frame, countless chief economists preparing dubious forecasts of output and trade performance, or radiologists looking at magnetic resonance images—worry about it in myriads of different ways.

Growth is commonly seen as too slow or as too excessive; it raises concerns about the limits of adaptation, and fears about personal consequences and major social dislocations. In response, people strive to manage the growth they can control by altering its pace (to accelerate it, moderate it, or end it) and dream about, and strive, to extend these controls to additional realms. These attempts often fail even as they succeed (and seemingly permanent mastery may turn out to be only a temporary success) but they never end: we can see them pursued at both extreme ends of the size spectrum as scientist try to create new forms of life by expanding the genetic code and including synthetic DNA in new organisms (Malyshev et al. 2014)—as well as proposing to control the Earth's climate through geoengineering interventions (Keith 2013).

Organismic growth is a product of long evolutionary process and modern science has come to understand its preconditions, pathways, and outcomes and to identify its trajectories that conform, more or less closely, to specific functions, overwhelmingly to S-shaped (sigmoid) curves. Finding common traits and making useful generalizations regarding natural growth is challenging but quantifying it is relatively straightforward. So is measuring the growth of many man-made artifacts (tools, machines, productive systems) by tracing their increase in capacity, performance, efficiency, or complexity. In all of these cases, we deal with basic physical units (length, mass, time, electric current, temperature, amount of substance, luminous intensity) and their numerous derivatives, ranging from volume and speed to energy and power.

Measuring the growth phenomena involving human judgment, expectations, and peaceful or violent interactions with others is much more challenging. Some complex aggregate processes are impossible to measure without first arbitrarily delimiting the scope of an inquiry and without resorting to more or less questionable concepts: measuring the growth of economies by relying on such variables as gross domestic product or national income are perfect examples of these difficulties and indeterminacies. But even when many attributes of what might be called social growth are readily measurable (examples range from the average living space per family and possession of household appliances to destructive power of stockpiled missiles and the total area controlled by an imperial power), their true trajectories are still open to diverse interpretations as these quantifications hide significant qualitative differences.

Accumulation of material possessions is a particularly fascinating aspect of growth as it stems from a combination of a laudable quest to improve quality of life, an understandable but less rational response to position oneself in a broader social milieu, and a rather atavistic impulse to possess, even to hoard. There are those few who remain indifferent to growth and need, India's loinclothed or entirely naked *sadhus* and monks belonging to sects that espouse austere simplicity. At the other extreme, we have compulsive collectors (however refined their tastes may be) and mentally sick hoarders who turn their abodes into garbage dumps. But in between, in any population with rising standards of living, we have less dramatic quotidian addictions as most people want to see more growth, be in material terms or in intangibles that go under those elusive labels of satisfaction with life or personal happiness achieved through amassing fortunes or having extraordinarily unique experiences.

The speeds and scales of these pursuits make it clear how modern is this pervasive experience and how justified is this growing concern about growth. A doubling of average sizes has become a common experience during a single lifetime: the mean area of US houses has grown 2.5-fold since 1950 (USBC 1975; USCB 2013), the volume of the United Kingdom's wine glasses has doubled since 1970 (Zupan et al. 2017), typical mass of European cars had more than doubled since the post–World War II models (Citroen 2 CV, Fiat Topolino) weighing less than 600 kg to about 1,200kg by 2002 (Smil 2014b). Many artifacts and achievements have seen far larger increases during the same time: the modal area of television screens grew about 15-fold, from the post–World War II standard of 30 cm diagonal to the average US size of about 120 cm by 2015, with an increasing share of sales taken by TVs with diagonals in excess of 150 cm. And even that impressive increase has been dwarfed by the rise of the largest individual fortunes: in 2017 the world had 2,043 billionaires (Forbes 2017). Relative differences produced by some of these phenomena are not unprecedented, but the combination of absolute disparities arising from modern growth and its frequency and speed is new.

Rate of Growth

Of course, individuals and societies have been always surrounded by countless manifestations of natural growth, and the quests for material enrichment and territorial aggrandizement were the forces driving societies on levels ranging from tribal to imperial, from raiding neighboring villages in the Amazon to subjugating large parts of Eurasia under a central rule. But during antiquity, the medieval period, and a large part of the early modern era (usually delimited as the three centuries between 1500 and 1800), most people everywhere survived as subsistence peasants whose harvest produced a limited and fluctuating surplus sufficient to support only a relatively small number of better-off inhabitants (families of skilled craftsmen and merchants) of (mostly small) cities and secular and religious ruling elites.

Annual crop harvests in those simpler, premodern and early modern societies presented few, if any, signs of notable growth. Similarly, nearly all fundamental variables of premodern life—be they population totals, town sizes, longevities and literacy, animal herds, household possessions, and capacities of commonly used machines—grew at such slow rates that their progress was evident only in very long-term perspectives. And often they were either completely stagnant or fluctuated erratically around dismal means, experiencing long spells of frequent regressions. For many of these phenomena we have the evidence of preserved artifacts and surviving descriptions, and some developments we can reconstruct from fragmentary records spanning centuries.

For example, in ancient Egypt it took more than 2,500 years (from the age of the great pyramids to the post-Roman era) to double the number of people that could be fed from 1 hectare of agricultural land (Butzer 1976). Stagnant yields were the obvious reason, and this reality persisted until the end of the Middle Ages: starting in the 14th century, it took more than 400 years for average English wheat yields to double, with hardly any gains during the first 200 years of that period (Stanhill 1976; Clark 1991). Similarly, many technical gains unfolded very slowly. Waterwheels were the most powerful inanimate prime movers of preindustrial civilizations but it took about 17 centuries (from the second century of the common era to the late 18th century) to raise their typical power tenfold, from 2 kW to

20 kW (Smil 2017a). Stagnating harvests or, at best, a feeble growth of crop yields and slowly improving manufacturing and transportation capabilities restricted the growth of cities: starting in 1300, it took more than three centuries for the population of Paris to double to 400,000—but during the late 19th century the city doubled in just 30 years (1856–1886) to 2.3 million (Atlas Historique de Paris 2016).

And many realities remained the same for millennia: the maximum distance covered daily by horse-riding messengers (the fastest way of long-distance communication on land before the introduction of railways) was optimized already in ancient Persia by Cyrus when he linked Susa and Sardis after 550 BCE, and it remained largely unchanged for the next 2,400 years (Minetti 2003). The average speed of relays (13–16 km/h) and a single animal ridden no more than 18–25 km/day remained near constant. Many other entries belong to this stagnant category, from the possession of household items by poor families to literacy rates prevailing among rural populations. Again, both of these variables began to change substantially only during the latter part of the early modern era.

Once so many technical and social changes—growth of railway networks, expansion of steamship travel, rising production of steel, invention and deployment of internal combustion engines and electricity, rapid urbanization, improved sanitation, rising life expectancy—began to take place at unprecedented rates during the 19th century, their rise created enormous expectations of further continued growth (Smil 2005). And these hopes were not disappointed as (despite setbacks brought by the two world wars, other conflicts, and periodic economic downturns) capabilities of individual machines, complicated industrial processes, and entire economies continued to grow during the 20th century. This growth was translated into better physical outcomes (increased body heights, higher life expectancies), greater material security and comfort (be it measured by disposable incomes or ownership of labor-easing devices), and unprecedented degrees of communication and mobility (Smil 2006b).

Nothing has embodied this reality and hope during recent decades as prominently as the growth in the number of transistors and other components that we have been able to emplace on a silicon wafer. Widely known as conforming to Moore's law, this growth has seen the number of components roughly double every two years: as a result, the most powerful microchips made in 2018 had more than 23 billion components, seven orders of magnitude (about 10.2 million times to be more exact) greater than the first such device (Intel's 4004, a 4-bit processing unit with 2,300 components for a Japanese calculator) designed in 1971 (Moore 1965, 1975; Intel

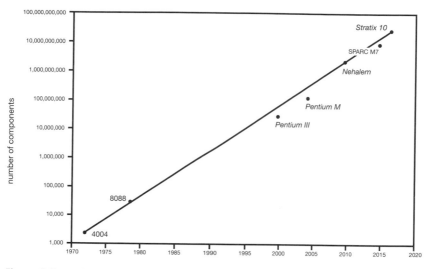

Figure 0.2
A quintessential marker of modern growth: Moore's law, 1971–2018. Semi-logarithmic graph shows steady exponential increase from 10^3 to 10^{10} components per microchip (Smil 2017a; IBM 2018b).

2018; Graphcore 2018). As in all cases of exponential growth (see chapter 1), when these gains are plotted on a linear graph they produce a steeply ascending curve, while a plot on a semilogarithmic graph transforms them into a straight line (figure 0.2).

This progress has led to almost unbounded expectations of still greater advances to come, and the recent rapid diffusion of assorted electronic devices (and applications they use) has particularly mesmerized those uncritical commentators who see omnipresent signs of accelerated growth. To give just one memorable recent example, a report prepared by Oxford Martin School and published by Citi claims the following time spans were needed to reach 50 million users: telephone 75 years, radio 38 years, TV 13 years, Internet four years, and Angry Birds 35 days (Frey and Osborne 2015). These claims are attributed to Citi Digital Strategy Team—but the team failed to do its homework and ignored common sense.

Are these numbers referring to global or American diffusions? The report does not say, but the total of 50 million clearly refers to the United States where that number of telephones was reached in 1953 (1878 + 75 years): but the number of telephones does not equal the total number of their users, which, given the average size of families and the ubiquity of phones in places of work, had to be considerably higher. TV broadcasting did not have just one but a number of beginnings: American transmission, and sales of first sets, began in 1928, but 13 years later, in 1941, TV ownership was still minimal, and the total number of TV sets (again: devices, not users) reached 50 million only in 1963. The same error is repeated with the Internet, to which millions of users had access for many years at universities, schools, and workplaces before they got a home connection; besides, what was the Internet's "first" year?

All that is just sloppy data gathering, and an uninformed rush to make an impression, but more important is an indefensible categorical error made by comparing a complex system based on a new and extensive infrastructure with an entertaining software. Telephony of the late 19th century was a pioneering system of direct personal communication whose realization required the first large-scale electrification of society (from fuel extraction to thermal generation to transmission, with large parts of rural America having no good connections even during the 1920s), installation of extensive wired infrastructure, and sales of (initially separate) receivers and speakers.

In contrast, Angry Birds or any other inane app can spread in a viral fashion because we have spent more than a century putting in place the successive components of a physical system that has made such a diffusion possible: its growth began during the 1880s with electricity generation and transmission and it has culminated with the post-2000 wave of designing and manufacturing billions of mobile phones and installing dense networks of cell towers. Concurrently the increasing reliability of its operation makes rapid diffusion feats unremarkable. Any number of analogies can be offered to illustrate that comparative fallacy. For example, instead of telephones think of the diffusion of microwave ovens and instead of an app think of mass-produced microwavable popcorn: obviously, diffusion rates of the most popular brand of the latter will be faster than were the adoption rates of the former. In fact, in the US it took about three decades for countertop microwave ovens, introduced in 1967, to reach 90% of all households.

The growth of information has proved equally mesmerizing. There is nothing new about its ascent. The invention of movable type (in 1450) began an exponential rise in book publishing, from about 200,000 volumes during the 16th century to about 1 million volumes during the 18th century, while recent global annual rate (led by China, the US, and the United Kingdom) has surpassed 2 million titles (UNESCO 2018). Add to this pictorial information whose growth was affordably enabled first by lithography, then by rotogravure, and now is dominated by electronic displays on mobile devices. Sound recordings began with Edison's fragile phonograph in 1878 (Smil 2018a; figure 0.3) and their enormous selection is now

Figure 0.3
Thomas A. Edison with his phonograph photographed by Mathew Brady in April 1878.
Photograph from Brady-Handy Collection of the Library of Congress.

effortlessly accessible to billions of mobile phone users. And information flow in all these categories is surpassed by imagery incessantly gathered by entire fleets of spy, meteorological, and Earth observation satellites. Not surprisingly, aggregate growth of information has resembled the hyperbolic expansion trajectory of pre-1960 global population growth.

Recently it has been possible to claim that 90% or more of all the extant information in the world has been generated over the preceding two years. Seagate (2017) put total information created worldwide at 0.1 zettabytes (ZB, 10^{21}) in 2005, at 2 ZB in 2010, 16.1 ZB in 2016, and it expected that the annual increment will reach 163 ZB by 2025. A year later it raised its estimate of the global datasphere to 175 ZB by 2025—and expected that the total will keep on accelerating (Reinsel et al. 2018). But as soon as one considers the major components of this new data flood, those accelerating claims are hardly impressive. Highly centralized new data inflows include the incessant movement of electronic cash and investments among major banks and investment houses, as well as sweeping monitoring of telephone and internet communications by government agencies.

At the same time, billions of mobile phone users participating in social media voluntarily surrender their privacy so data miners can, without asking anybody a single question, follow their messages and their web-clicking, analyzing the individual personal preferences and foibles they reveal, comparing them to those of their peers, and packaging them to be bought by advertisers in order to sell more unneeded junk—and to keep economic growth intact. And, of course, streams of data are produced incessantly simply by people carrying GPS-enabled mobile phones. Add to this the flood of inane images, including myriads of selfies and cat videos (even stills consume bytes rapidly: smartphone photos take up commonly 2–3 MB, that is 2–3 times more than the typescript of this book)—and the unprecedented growth of "information" appears more pitiable than admirable.

And this is one of the most consequential undesirable consequences of this information flood: time spent per adult user per day with digital media doubled between 2008 and 2015 to 5.5 hours (eMarketer 2017), creating new life forms of screen zombies. But the rapid diffusion of electronics and software are trivial matters compared to the expected ultimate achievements of accelerated growth—and nobody has expressed them more expansively than Ray Kurzweil, since 2012 the director of engineering at Google and long before that the inventor of such electronic devices as the charged-couple flat-bed scanner, the first commercial text-to-speech synthesizer, and the first omnifont optical character recognition.

In 2001 he formulated his law of accelerating returns (Kurzweil 2001, 1):

An analysis of the history of technology shows that technological change is exponential, contrary to the common-sense "intuitive linear" view. So we won't experience 100 years of progress in the 21st century—it will be more like 20,000 years of
progress (at today's rate). The "returns," such as chip speed and cost-effectiveness,
also increase exponentially. There's even exponential growth in the rate of exponential growth. Within a few decades, machine intelligence will surpass human
intelligence, leading to The Singularity—technological change so rapid and
profound it represents a rupture in the fabric of human history. The implications include the merger of biological and nonbiological intelligence, immortal
software-based humans, and ultra-high levels of intelligence that expand outward
in the universe at the speed of light.

In 2005 Kurzweil published *The Singularity Is Near*—it is to come in 2045, to
be exact—and ever since he has been promoting these views on his website,
Kurzweil Accelerating Intelligence (Kurzweil 2005, 2017). There is no doubt,
no hesitation, no humility in Kurzweil's categorical grand pronouncements
because according to him the state of the biosphere, whose functioning is a
product of billions of years of evolution, has no role in our futures, which
are to be completely molded by the surpassing mastery of machine intelligence. But as different as our civilization may be when compared to any
of its predecessors, it works within the same constraint: it is nothing but a
subset of the biosphere, that relatively very thin and both highly resilient
and highly fragile envelope within which carbon-based living organisms
can survive (Vernadsky 1929; Smil 2002). Inevitably, their growth, and for
higher organisms also their cognitive and behavioral advances, are fundamentally limited by the biosphere's physical conditions and (wide as it
may seem by comparing its extremes) by the restricted range of metabolic
possibilities.

Studies of Growth

Even when limited to our planet, the scope of growth studies—from ephemeral cells to a civilization supposedly racing toward the singularity—is too
vast to allow a truly comprehensive single-volume treatment. Not surprisingly, the published syntheses and overviews of growth processes and of
their outcomes have been restricted to major disciplines or topics. The great
classic of growth literature, D'Arcy Wentworth Thompson's *On Growth and
Form* (whose original edition came out it in 1917 and whose revised and
much expanded form appeared in 1942) is concerned almost solely with
cells and tissues and with many parts (skeletons, shell, horns, teeth, tusks)

of animal bodies (Thompson 1917, 1942). The only time when Thompson wrote about nonbiogenic materials or man-made structures (metals, girders, bridges) was when he reviewed the forms and mechanical properties of such strong biogenic tissues as shells and bones.

The Chemical Basis of Growth and Senescence by T. B. Robertson, published in 1923, delimits its scope in the book's title (Robertson 1923). In 1945, another comprehensive review of organismic growth appeared, Samuel Brody's *Bioenergetics and Growth*, whose content was specifically focused on the efficiency complex in domestic animals (Brody 1945). In 1994, Robert Banks published a detailed inquiry into *Growth and Diffusion Phenomena*, and although this excellent volume provides numerous examples of specific applications of individual growth trajectories and distribution patterns in natural and social sciences and in engineering, its principal concern is captured in its subtitle as it deals primarily (and in an exemplarily systematic fashion) with mathematical frameworks and applications (Banks 1994).

The subtitle of an edited homage to Thompson (with the eponymous title, *On Growth and Form*) announced the limits of its inquiry: *Spatiotemporal Pattern Formation in Biology* (Chaplain et al. 1999). As diverse as its chapters are (including pattern formations on butterfly wings, in cancer, and in skin and hair, as well as growth models of capillary networks and wound healing), the book was, once again, about growth of living forms. And in 2017 Geoffrey West summed up decades of his inquiries into universal laws of scaling—not only of organisms but also cities, economies, and companies—in a book titled *Scale* that listed all of these subjects in its long subtitle and whose goal was to discern common patterns and even to offer the vision of a grand unified theory of sustainability (West 2017).

Components of organic growth, be they functional or taxonomic, have received much attention, and comprehensive treatments deal with cellular growth (Studzinski 2000; Morgan 2007; Verbelen and Vissenberg 2007; Golitsin and Krylov 2010), growth of plants (Morrison and Morecroft 2006; Vaganov et al. 2006; Burkhart and Tomé 2012; Gregory and Nortcliff 2013), and animals (Batt 1980; Campion et al. 1989; Gerrard and Grant 2007; Parks 2011). As expected, there is an enormous body of knowledge on human growth in general (Ulijaszek et al. 1998; Bogin 1999; Hoppa and Fitzgerald 1999; Roche and Sun 2003; Hauspie et al. 2004; Tanner 2010; Floud et al. 2011; Fogel 2012).

Healthy growth and nutrition in children have received particular attention, with perspectives ranging from anthropometry to nutrition science, and from pediatrics and physiology to public health (Martorell and Haschke 2001; Hochberg 2011; Hassan 2017). Malthus (1798) and Verhulst (1845,

1847) published pioneering inquiries into the nature of population growth, whose modern evaluations range from Pearl and Reed (1920) and Carr-Saunders (1936) to Meadows et al. (1972), Keyfitz and Flieger (1991), Hardin (1992), Cohen (1995), Stanton (2003), Lutz et al. (2004), and numerous reviews and projections published by the United Nations.

Modern economics has been preoccupied with the rates of output, profit, investment, and consumption growth. Consequently, there is no shortage of inquiries pairing economic growth and income (Kuznets 1955; Zhang 2006; Piketty 2014), growth and technical innovation (Ruttan 2000; Mokyr 2002, 2009, 2017; van Geenhuizen et al. 2009), growth and international trade (Rodriguez and Rodrik 2000; Busse and Königer 2012; European Commission 2014), and growth and health (Bloom and Canning 2008; Barro 2013). Many recent studies have focused on links between growth and corruption (Mo 2001; Méndez and Sepúlveda 2006; Bai et al. 2014) and growth and governance (Kurtz and Schrank 2007; OECD 2016).

Publications are also dispensing advice on how to make all economic growth sustainable (WCED 1987; Schmandt and Ward 2000; Daly and Farley 2010; Enders and Remig 2014) and equitable (Mehrotra and Delamonica 2007; Lavoie and Stockhammer 2013). As already noted, the long life of Moore's law has focused interest on the growth of computational capabilities but, inexplicably, there are no comprehensive book-length studies on the growth of modern technical and engineering systems, such as long-term analyses of capacity and performance growth in extractive activities and energy conversions. And even when including papers, there is only a limited number of publications dealing explicitly with the growth of states, empires, and civilizations (Taagepera 1978, 1979; Turchin 2009; Marchetti and Ausubel 2012).

What Is (and Is Not) in This Book

The impossibility of a truly comprehensive account of growth in nature and society should not be an excuse for the paucity of broader inquiries into the modalities of growth. My intent is to address this omission by examining growth in its many natural, social, and technical forms. In order to cover such a wide sweep, a single volume must be restricted in both its scope and depth of coverage. The focus is on life on Earth and on the accomplishments of human societies. This assignment will take us from bacterial invasions and viral infections through forest and animal metabolism to the growth of energy conversions and megacities to the essentials of the global economy—while excluding both the largest and the smallest scales.

There will be nothing about the growth (the inflationary expansion) of the universe, galaxies, supernovas, or stars. I have already acknowledged inherently slow growth rates of terraforming processes that are primarily governed by the creation of new oceanic crust with spreading rates ranging between less than two and no more than about 20 cm/year. And while some short-lived and spatially limited catastrophic events (volcanic eruptions, massive landslides, tsunami waves, enormous floods) can result in rapid and substantial mass and energy transfers in short periods of time, ongoing geomorphic activities (erosion and its counterpart, sedimentary deposition) are as slow or considerably slower than the geotectonic processes: erosion in the Himalayas can advance by as much as 1 cm/year, but the denudation of the British Isles proceeds at just 2–10 cm in every 1,000 years (Smil 2008). There will be no further examination of these terraforming growth rates in this book.

And as the book's major focus is on the growth of organisms, artifacts, and complex systems, there will be also nothing about growth on subcellular level. The enormous intensification of life science research has produced major advances in our understanding of cellular growth in general and cancerous growth in particular. The multidisciplinary nature, the growing extent, and accelerating pace of these advances means that new findings are now reported overwhelmingly in electronic publications and that writing summary or review books in these fields are exercises in near-instant obsolescence. Still, among the recent books, those by Macieira-Coelho (2005), Gewirtz et al. (2007), Kimura (2008), and Kraikivski (2013) offer surveys of normal and abnormal cellular growth and death.

Consequently, there will be no systematic treatment of fundamental genetics, epigenetics and biochemistry of growth, and I will deal with cellular growth only when describing the growth trajectories of unicellular organisms and the lives of microbial assemblies whose presence constitutes significant, or even dominant, shares of biomass in some ecosystems. Similarly, the focus with plants, animals, and humans will not be on biochemical specificities and complexities of growth at subcellular, cellular, and organ level—there are fascinating studies of brain (Brazier 1975; Kretschmann 1986; Schneider 2014; Lagercrantz 2016) or heart (Rosenthal and Harvey 2010; Bruneau 2012) development—but on entire organisms, including the environmental settings and outcomes of growth, and I will also note some key environmental factors (ranging from micronutrients to infections) that often limit or derail organismic growth.

Human physical growth will be covered in some detail with focus both on individual (and sex-specific) growth trajectories of height and weight (as well as on the undesirable rise of obesity) and on the collective growth of populations. I will present long-term historical perspectives of population growth, evaluate current growth patterns, and examine possible future global, and some national, trajectories. But there will be nothing on psychosocial growth (developmental stages, personality, aspirations, self-actualization) or on the growth of consciousness: psychological and sociological literature covers that abundantly.

Before proceeding with systematic coverage of growth in nature and society, I will provide a brief introduction into the measures and varieties of growth trajectories. These trajectories include erratic advances with no easily discernible patterns (often seen in stock market valuations); simple linear gains (an hourglass adds the same amount of falling sand to the bottom pile every second); growth that is, temporarily, exponential (commonly exhibited by such diverse phenomena as organisms in their infancy, the most intensive phases in the adoption of technical innovation, and the creation of stock market bubbles); and gains that conform to assorted confined (restrained) growth curves (as do body sizes of all organisms) whose shape can be captured by mathematical functions.

Most growth processes—be they of organisms, artifacts, or complex systems—follow closely one of these S-shaped (sigmoid) growth curves conforming to the logistic (Verhulst) function (Verhulst 1838, 1845, 1847), to its precursor (Gompertz 1825), or to one of their derivatives, most commonly those formulated by von Bertalanffy (1938, 1957), Richards (1959), Blumberg (1968), and Turner et al. (1976). But natural variability as well as unexpected interferences often lead to substantial deviations from a predicted course. That is why the students of growth are best advised to start with an actual more or less completed progression and see which available growth function comes closest to replicating it.

Proceeding the other way—taking a few early points of an unfolding growth trajectory and using them to construct an orderly growth curve conforming to a specifically selected growth function—has a high probability of success only when one tries to predict the growth that is very likely to follow a known pattern that has been repeatedly demonstrated, for example, by many species of coniferous trees or freshwater fish. But selecting a random S-curve as the predictor of growth for an organism that does not belong to one of those well-studied groups is a questionable enterprise because a specific function may not be a very sensitive predictive tool for phenomena seen only in their earliest stage of growth.

The Book's Structure and Goals

The text follows a natural, evolutionary, sequence, from nature to society, from simple, directly observable growth attributes (numbers of multiplying cells, diameter of trees, mass of animal bodies, progression of human statures) to more complex measures marking the development and advances of societies and economies (population dynamics, destructive powers, creation of wealth). But the sequence cannot be exclusively linear as there are ubiquitous linkages, interdependencies, and feedbacks and these realities necessitate some returns and detours, some repetitions to emphasize connections seen from other (energetic, demographic, economic) perspectives.

My systematic inquiry into growth will start with organisms whose mature sizes range from microbes (tiny as individual cells, massive in their biospheric presence) to lofty coniferous trees and enormous whales. I will take closer looks at the growth of some disease-causing microbes, at the cultivation of staple crops, and at human growth from infancy to adulthood. Then will come inquiries into the growth of energy conversions and manmade objects that enable food production and all other economic activities. I will also look how this growth changed numerous performances, efficiencies, and reliabilities because these developments have been essential for creating our civilization.

Finally, I will focus on the growth of complex systems. I will start with the growth of human populations and proceed to the growth of cities, the most obvious concentrated expressions of human material and social advancement, and economies. I will end these systematic examinations by noting the challenges of appraising growth trajectories of empires and civilizations, ending with our global variety characterized by its peculiar amalgam of planetary and parochial concerns, affluent and impoverished lives, and confident and uncertain perspectives. The book will close with reviewing what comes after growth. When dealing with organisms, the outcomes range from the death of individuals to the perpetuation of species across evolutionary time spans. When dealing with societies and economies, the outcomes range from decline (gradual to rapid) and demise to sometimes remarkable renewal. The trajectory of the modern civilization, coping with contradictory imperatives of material growth and biospheric limits, remains uncertain.

My aim is to illuminate varieties of growth in evolutionary and historical perspectives and hence to appreciate both the accomplishments and the limits of growth in modern civilization. This requires quantitative treatment throughout because real understanding can be gained only by charting actual growth trajectories, appreciating common and exceptional growth rates, and setting accomplished gains and performance improvements (often so large that they have spanned several orders of magnitude!) into proper (historical and comparative) contexts. Biologists have studied the growth of numerous organisms and I review scores of such results for species ranging from bacteria to birds and from algae to staple crops. Similarly, details of human growth from infancy to maturity are readily available.

In contrast to the studies of organismic growth, quantifications of long-term growth trajectories of human artifacts (ranging from simple tools to complex machines) and complex systems (ranging from cities to civilizations) are much less systematic and much less common. Merely to review published growth patterns would not suffice to provide revealing treatments of these growth categories. That is why, in order to uncover the best-fitting patterns of many kinds of anthropogenic growth, I have assembled the longest possible records from the best available sources and subjected them to quantitative analyses. Every one of more than 100 original growth graphs was prepared in this way, and their range makes up, I believe, a unique collection. Given the commonalities of growth patterns, this is an unavoidably repetitive process but systematic presentations of specific results are indispensable in order to provide a clear understanding of realities (commonalities and exceptions), limits, and future possibilities.

Systematic presentation of growth trajectories is a necessary precondition but not the final goal when examining growth. That is why I also explain the circumstances and limits of the charted growth, provide evolutionary or historical settings of analyzed phenomena, or offer critical comments on recent progression and on their prospects. I also caution about any simplistic embrace of even the best statistical fits for long-term forecasting, and the goal of this book is not to provide an extended platform for time-specific growth projections. Nevertheless, the presented analyses contain a variety of conclusions that make for realistic appraisals of what lies ahead.

In that sense, parts of the book are helpfully predictive. If a century of corn yields shows only linear growth, there is not much of a chance for exponentially rising harvests in the coming decades. If the growth efficiency of broilers has been surpassing, for generations, the performance of all other terrestrial meat animals, then it is hard to argue that pork should be the best choice to provide more protein for billions of new consumers. If unit capacities, production (extraction or generation) rates, and diffusion of every energy conversion display logistic progress, then we have very solid ground to conclude that the coming transition from fossil fuels to renewables will not be an exceptionally speedy affair. If the world's population is getting inexorably urbanized, its energetic (food, fuels, electricity) and material needs will be shaped by these restrictive realities dictating the need for incessant and reliable, mass-scale flows that are impossible to satisfy from local or nearby sources.

Simply put, this book deals in realities as it sets the growth of everything into long-term evolutionary and historical perspectives and does so in rigorous quantitative terms. Documented, historically embedded facts come first—cautious conclusions afterward. This is, of course, in contradistinction to many recent ahistoric forecasts and claims that ignore long-term trajectories of growth (that is, the requisite energetic and material needs of unprecedented scaling processes) and invoke the fashionable mantra of disruptive innovation that will change the world at accelerating speed. Such examples abound, ranging from all of the world's entire car fleet (of more than 1 billion vehicles) becoming electric by 2025 to terraforming Mars starting in the year 2022, from designer plants and animals (synthetic biology rules) making the strictures of organismic evolution irrelevant to anticipations of artificial intelligence's imminent takeover of our civilization.

This book makes no radical claims of that kind; in fact it avoids making any but strongly justified generalizations. This is a deliberate decision resting on my respect for complex and unruly realities (and irregularities) and on the well-attested fact that grand predictions turn out to be, repeatedly, wrong. Infamous examples concerning growth range from those of unchecked expansion of the global population and unprecedented famines that were to happen during the closing decades of the 20th century to a swift takeover of the global energy supply by inexpensive nuclear power and to a fundamentally mistaken belief that the growth rate underlying Moore's law (doubling every two years) can be readily realized through innovation in other fields of human endeavor.

The book is intended to work on several planes. The key intent is to provide a fairly comprehensive analytical survey of growth trajectories in nature and in society: in the biosphere, where growth is the result of not just evolution but, increasingly, of human intervention; and in the man-made world, where growth has been a key factor in the history of populations and economies and in the advancement of technical capabilities. Given this scope, the book could be also read selectively as a combination of specific parts, by focusing on living organisms (be they plants, animals, humans, or populations) or on human designs (be they tools, energy converters, or transportation machinery). And, undoubtedly, some readers will be more interested in the settings of growth processes—in preconditions, factors, and the evolutionary and historical circumstances of natural, population, economic, and imperial growth—rather than in specific growth trajectories.

Yet another option is to focus on the opposite scales of growth. The book contains plenty of information about the growth of individual organisms, tools, machines, or infrastructures—as well as about the growth of the most extensive and the most complex systems, culminating in musings about the growth of civilizations. The book is also a summation of unifying lessons learned about the growth of organisms, artifacts, and complex systems, and it can be also read as an appraisal of evolutionary outcomes in nature and as a history of technical and social advances, that is as an assessment of civilizational progress (*record* might be a better, neutral, designation than progress)

As always in my writings, I stay away from any rigid prescriptions—but I hope that the book's careful reading conveys the key conclusion: before it is too late, we should embark in earnest on the most fundamental existential (and also truly revolutionary) task facing modern civilization, that of making any future growth compatible with the long-term preservation of the only biosphere we have.

1 Trajectories: or common patterns of growth

Growth attracts adjectives. The most common ones have been (alpha-betically) anemic, arithmetic, cancerous, chaotic, delayed, disappointing, erratic, explosive, exponential, fast, geometric, healthy, interrupted, linear, logistic, low, malignant, moderate, poor, rapid, runaway, slow, S-shaped, strong, sudden, tepid, unexpected, vigorous. Most recently, we should also add sustainable and unsustainable. Sustainable growth is, of course, a clear *contradictio in adjecto* as far as any truly long-run material growth is concerned (I am ignoring any possibilities of migrating to other planets after exhausting the Earth's resources) and it is highly doubtful that we can keep on improving such intangibles as happiness or satisfaction. Most of the adjectives used to describe growth are qualifiers of its rate: often it is not the growth per se that we worry about but rather its rate, either too fast or too slow.

Even a casual news reader knows about the constant worries of assorted chief economists, forecasters and government officials about securing "vigorous" or "healthy" growth of the gross domestic product (GDP). This clamoring for high growth rates is based on the most simplistic expectation of repeating past experiences—as if the intervening growth of GDP had nothing to do with the expected future rate. Put another way, economists have an implicit expectation of endless, and preferably fairly fast, exponential growth.

But they choose an inappropriate metric when comparing the outcomes. For example, during the first half of the 1950s the US GDP growth averaged nearly 5% a year and that performance translated roughly to additional $3,500 per capita (for about 160 million people) during those five years. In contrast, the "slow" GDP growth between 2011 and 2015 (averaging just 2%/year) added about $4,800/capita (for about 317 million people) during those five years, or nearly 40% more than 60 years ago (all totals are in constant-value monies to eliminate the effect of inflation). Consequently, in terms of actual average individual betterment, the recent 2% growth has been quite superior to the former, 2.5 times higher, rate. This is simple algebra, but it is repeatedly ignored by all those bewailing the "low" post-2000 growth of the US or European Union (EU) economies.

Results of the British referendum of June 23, 2016, about remaining in the EU or leaving it, provided another perfect illustration of how the rate of change matters more than the outcome. In 94% of the areas where the foreign-born population increased by more than 200% between 2001 and 2014, people voted to leave the European Union—even though the share of migrants in those regions had remained comparatively low, mostly less than 20%. In contrast, most regions where the foreign-born population was more than 30% voted to remain. As *The Economist* concluded, "High numbers of migrants don't bother Britons; high rates of change do" (Economist 2016).

Other adjectives used to qualify growth are precisely defined terms describing its specific trajectories that conform (sometimes almost perfectly, often fairly closely) to various mathematical functions. Those close, even perfect, fits are possible because most growth processes are remarkably regular affairs as their progress follows a limited array of patterns. Naturally, those trajectories have many individual and inter- and intraspecific variations for organisms, and are marked by historically, technically, and economically conditioned departures for engineered systems, economies, and societies. The three basic trajectories encompass linear growth, exponential growth, and various finite growth patterns. Linear growth is trivial to grasp and easy to calculate. Exponential growth is easy to understand but the best way to calculate it is to use the base of natural logarithms, a mystery to many. The principle of finite growth patterns, including logistic, Gompertz and confined exponential growth functions, is, again, easy to understand, but their mathematical solutions require differential calculus.

But before taking a closer look at individual growth functions, their solutions and resulting growth curves, I will devote two brief sections to time spans and to the figures of merit involved in growth studies. In their short surveys, I will note both common and less frequently encountered variables in whose growth we are interested, be it as parents, employees, or taxpayers, as scientists, engineers, and economists, or as historians, politicians, and planners. These measures include such universal concerns as the weight and height of growing babies and children, and the growth of national economies. And there are also such infrequent but scary concerns as the diffusion of potentially pandemic infections made worse by mass-scale air travel.

Time Spans

Growth is always a function of time and during the course of modern scientific and engineering studies their authors have traced its trajectories in countless graphs with time usually plotted on the abscissa (horizontal or x axis) and the growing variable measured on the ordinate (vertical or y axis). Of course, we can (and we do) trace growth of physical or immaterial phenomena against the change of other such variables—we plot the changing height of growing children against their weight or rising disposable income against the growth of GDP—but most of the growth curves (and, in simpler instance, lines) are what James C. Maxwell defined as diagrams of displacement and what Thompson called time-diagrams: "Each has a beginning and an end; and one and the same curve may illustrate the life of a man, the economic history of a kingdom ... It depicts a 'mechanism' at work, and helps us to see analogous mechanisms in different fields; for Nature rings her many changes on a few simple themes" (Thompson 1942, 139).

Growth of ocean floor or of mountain ranges, whose outcomes are driven by geotectonic forces and whose examination is outside of this book's already large scope, unfolds across tens to hundreds of millions of years. When dealing with organisms, the length of time span under consideration is a function of specific growth rates determined by long periods of evolution and, in the case of domesticated plant and animal species, often accelerated or enhanced by traditional breeding and, most recently, also by transgenic interventions. When dealing with the growth of devices, machines, structures or any other human artifacts, time spans under study depend both on their longevity and on their suitability to be deployed in new, enhanced versions under changed circumstances.

As a result, growth of some artifacts that were in use since the antiquity is now merely of historical interest. Sails are a good example of this reality, as their development and deployment (excepting those designed and used for fast yacht racing) ended fairly abruptly during the second half of the 19th century, just a few decades after the introduction of steam engines, and after more than five millennia of improving designs. But other ancient designs have seen spectacular advances in order to meet the requirements of the industrial age: construction cranes and dockyard cranes are perhaps the best example of this continued evolution. These ancient machines have seen enormous growth in their capacities during the past two centuries in order to build taller structures and to handle cargo of increasingly more voluminous ships.

Microbes, fungi, and insects make up most of the biosphere's organisms, and common time spans of interest in microbiology and invertebrate biology are minutes, days, and weeks. Bacterial generations are often shorter than one hour. Coccolithophores, single-celled calcifying marine algae that dominate oceanic phytomass, reach maximum cell density in nitrogen-limited environments in one week (Perrin et al. 2016). Commercially cultivated white mushrooms grow to maturity just 15–25 days after the growing medium (straw or other organic matter) is filled with mycelium. Butterflies usually spend no more than a week as eggs, two to five weeks as caterpillars (larval stage), and one to two weeks as chrysalis from which they emerge as fully grown adults.

In annual plants, days, weeks, and months are time spans of interest. The fastest growing crops (green onions, lettuces, radishes) may be harvested less than a month after seeding; the shortest period to produce mature staple grain is about 90 days (spring wheat, also barley and oats), but winter wheat needs more than 200 days to reach maturity, and a new vineyard will start producing only during the third year after its establishment. In trees, the annual deposition of new wood in rings (secondary growth originating in two cambial lateral meristems) marks an easily identifiable natural progression: fast-growing plantation species (eucalypts, poplars, pines) may be harvested after a decade of growth (or even sooner), but in natural settings growth can continue for many decades and in most tree species it can be actually indeterminate.

Gestation growth of larger vertebrates lasts for many months (from 270 days in humans to 645 days for African elephants), while months, or even just days, are of interest during the fastest spells of postnatal growth. That is particularly the case when meat-producing poultry, pigs, and cattle are fed optimized diets in order to maximize daily weight gain and to raise their mass to expected slaughter weight in the shortest possible time. Months and then years are the normal span of interest when monitoring growth of infants and children, and a pediatrician will compare age- and sex-specific charts of expected growth with actual individual growth to determine if a baby or a toddler is meeting its growth milestones or if it is failing to thrive fully.

Although the growth of some artifacts—be they sailing ships or construction cranes—must be traced across millennia, most of the advances have been concentrated in relatively brief growth spurts separated by long periods of no growth or marginal gains. Energy converters (engines, turbines, motors), machines, and devices characteristic of modern industrial civilization have much shorter life histories. Growth of steam engines lasted 200 years, from the early 18th to the early 20th century. Growth of steam turbines (and electric motors) has been going on since the 1880s, that of gas turbines only since the late 1930s. Growth of modern solid-state electronics began with the first commercial applications of the 1950s but it really took off only with microprocessor-based designs starting in the 1970s.

Studying the collective growth of our species in its evolutionary entirety would take us back some 200,000 years but our ability to reconstruct the growth of the global population with a fair degree of accuracy goes back only to the early modern era (1500–1800), and totals with small ranges of uncertainty have been available only for the past century. In a few countries with a history of censuses (however incomplete, with the counts often restricted to only adult males) or with availability of other documentary evidence (birth certificates maintained by parishes), we can recreate revealing population growth trajectories going back to the medieval period.

In economic affairs the unfolding growth (of GDP, employment, productivity, output of specific items) is often followed in quarterly intervals, but statistical compendia report nearly all variables in terms of their annual totals or gains. Calendar year is the standard choice of time span but the two most common instances of such departures are fiscal years and crop years (starting at various months) used to report annual harvests and yields. Some studies have tried to reconstruct national economic growth going back for centuries, even for millennia, but (as I will emphasize later) they belong more appropriately to the class of qualitative impressions rather than to the category of true quantitative appraisals. Reliable historical reconstructions for societies with adequate statistical services go back only 150–200 years.

Growth rates capture the change of a variable during a specified time span, with percent per year being the most common metric. Unfortunately, these frequently cited values are often misleading. No caveats are needed only if these rates refer to linear growth, that is to adding identical quantity during every specified period. But when these rates refer to periods of exponential growth they could be properly assessed only when it is understood that they are temporary values, while the most common varieties of growth encountered in nature and throughout civilization—those following various S-shaped patterns—are changing their growth rate constantly, from very low rates to a peak and back to very low rates as the growth process approaches its end.

Figures of Merit

There is no binding classification of the measures used to quantify growth. The most obvious basic division is into variables tracing physical changes and immaterial but quantifiable (at least by proxy if not in a direct manner) developments. The simplest entry in the first category is the increment of a studied variable counted on hourly, daily, monthly or annual basis. And when statisticians talk about quantifying the growth of assorted populations, they use the term beyond its strict Latin meaning in order to refer to assemblages of microbes, plants and animals, indeed to any quantifiable entities whose growth they wish to study.

As for the fundamental quantities whose growth defines the material world, the International System of Units (*Système international d'unités*, SI) recognizes seven basic entries. They are length (meter, m), mass (kilogram, kg), time (second, s), electric current (ampere, A) thermodynamic temperature (kelvin, K), amount of substance (mole, mol), and luminous intensity (candela, cd). Many growth measures deal with quantities derived from the seven basic units, including area (m^2), volume (m^3), speed (m/s), mass density (kg/m^3), and specific volume (m^3/kg). More complex quantity equations yield such common measures of growth as force, pressure, energy, power or luminous flux.

Most of these measures will be encountered repeatedly throughout this book (and their complete list, as well as the list of their multiples and submultiples, are available in Units and Abbreviations). The two basic units, length and mass, will be used to evaluate the growth of organisms (be they trees, invertebrates or babies), structures, and machines. Height has been always the most appreciated, admired and emulated among the linear variables. This preference is demonstrated in ways ranging from clear correlations between height and power in the corporate world (Adams et al. 2016) to the obsession of architects and developers with building ever taller structures. There is no international organization monitoring the growth of buildings with the largest footprint or the largest internal space—but there is the Council on Tall Buildings and Human Habitat, with its specific criteria for defining and measuring tall buildings (CTBUH 2018).

Their record heights rose from 42 m for the Home Insurance Building, the world's first skyscraper completed in 1884 in Chicago, to 828 m for Burj Khalifa in Dubai finished in 2009. Jeddah Tower (whose principal building contractor is Saudi Binladin company, whose family name will be always connected to 9/11) will reach 1,008 m by 2019 (CTBUH 2018). Length, as height, rather than mass, has been also a recurrent topic of comparative

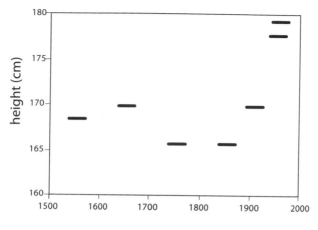

Figure 1.1
Evolution of average male body heights in Western Europe, 1550–1980. Data from Clio Infra (2017).

anthropometric studies, and Clio Infra (2017) and Roser (2017) provide convenient summaries of height measurements ranging from those of ancient skeletons to modern humans (figure 1.1). Height of European military recruits provides some of the most reliable testimonies of human growth during the early modern and modern eras (Ulijaszek et al. 1998; Floud et al. 2011).

Area appears in growth studies frequently on its own in instances as diverse as the average size of farms, expansion of empires, and annual installation of photovoltaic panels to generate solar electricity. Changes in housing development (average areas of houses or apartments) are measured in square meters (m^2), except for the nonmetric United States where square feet are still used. Square kilometers (km^2, 1,000 × 1,000 m) are used in tracing the growth of states and empires. Area is used even more commonly as the denominator to quantify productivity of photosynthetic output, that is yields and harvests in forestry and agriculture. Hectares (100 × 100 m or 10,000 m^2) are the most common areal unit in agricultural statistics (except, again, for the non-metric US, where acres are still used).

Volume is preferred to mass when surveying the growth of production and intake of both alcoholic and nonalcoholic beverages (usually in liters), and measuring annual cutting and industrial use of lumber and other wood products (usually in m^3). Volume has been also the indicator of choice when extracting and transporting crude oil—and it is also perhaps the best example of the endurance of a nonmetric measure. A steel container with the volume of 42 US gallons (or roughly 159.997 liters) was adopted by the US Bureau of the Census in 1872 to measure crude oil output, and barrel remains the standard output measure in the oil industry—but converting this volume variable to its mass equivalent requires the knowledge of specific densities.

Just over six barrels of heavy crude oil (commonly extracted in the Middle East) are needed to make up one tonne of crude oil, but the total may be as high as 8.5 barrels for the lightest crudes produced in Algeria and Malaysia, with 7.33 barrels per tonne being a commonly used global average. Similarly, converting volumes of wood to mass equivalents requires the knowledge of specific wood density. Even for commonly used species, densities differ by up to a factor of two, from light pines (400 kg/m^3) to heavy white ash (800 kg/m^3), and the extreme wood densities range from less than 200 kg/m^3 for balsa to more than 1.2 t/m^3 for ebony (USDA 2010).

The history of ubiquitous artifacts illustrates two opposite mass trends: miniaturization of commonly used components and devices on one hand (a trend enabled to an unprecedented degree by the diffusion of solid-state electronics), and a substantial increase in the average mass of the two largest investments modern families make, cars and houses, on the other. The declining mass of computers is, obviously, just an inverse of their growing capability to handle information per unit of weight. In August 1969, the Apollo 11 computer used to land the manned capsule on the Moon weighed 32 kg and had merely 2 kB of random access memory (RAM), or about 62 bytes per kg of mass (Hall 1996). Twelve years later, IBM's first personal computer weighed 11.3 kg and 16 kB RAM, that is 1.416 kB/kg. In 2018 the Dell laptop used to write this book weighed 2.83 kg and had 4 GB RAM, or 1.41 GB/kg. Leaving the Apollo machine aside (one-of-a-kind, noncommercial design), personal computers have seen a millionfold growth of memory/mass ratio since 1981!

As electronics (except for wall-size televisions) got smaller, houses and cars got bigger. People think about houses primarily in terms of habitable area but its substantial increase—in the US from 91 m^2 of finished area (99 m^2 total) in 1950 to about 240 m^2 by 2015 (Alexander 2000; USCB 2017)—has resulted in an even faster growth rate for materials used to build and to furnish them. A new 240 m^2 house will need at least 35 tonnes of wood, roughly split between framing lumber and other wood products, including plywood, glulam, and veneer (Smil 2014b). In contrast, a simple 90 m^2 house could be built with no more than 12 tonnes of wood, a threefold difference.

Moreover, modern American houses contain more furniture and they have more, and larger, major appliances (refrigerators, dishwashers, washing machines, clothes dryers): while in 1950 only about 20% of households had washing machines, less than 10% owned clothes dryers and less than 5% had air conditioning, now standard even in the northernmost states. In addition, heavier materials are used in more expensive finishes, including tiles and stone for flooring and bathrooms, stone kitchen counters and large fireplaces. As a result, new houses built in 2015 are about 2.6 times larger than was the 1950 average, but for many of them the mass of materials required to build them is four times as large.

The increasing mass of American passenger cars has resulted from a combination of desirable improvements and wasteful changes (figure 1.2). The world's first mass-produced car, Ford's famous Model T released in October 1908, weighed just 540 kg. Weight gains after World War I (WWI) were due to fully enclosed all-metal bodies, heavier engines, and better seats: by 1938 the mass of Ford's Model 74 reached 1,090 kg, almost exactly twice that of the Model T (Smil 2014b). These trends (larger cars, heavier engines, more accessories) continued after World War II (WWII) and, after a brief pause and retreat brought by the oil price rises by the Organization of the Petroleum Exporting Countries (OPEC) in the 1970s, intensified after the mid-1980s with the introduction of sport-utility vehicles (SUVs, accounting for half of new US vehicle sales in 2019) and the growing popularity of pick-up trucks and vans.

In 1981 the average mass of American cars and light trucks was 1,452 kg; by the year 2000 it had reached 1,733 kg; and by 2008 it was 1,852 kg (and had hardly changed by 2015), a 3.4-fold increase of average vehicle mass in 100 years (USEPA 2016b). Average car mass growth in Europe and Asia has

Figure 1.2
The bestselling American car in 1908 was Ford Model T weighing 540 kg. The bestselling vehicle in 2018 was not a car but a truck, Ford's F-150 weighing 2,000 kg. Images from Ford Motor Company catalogue for 1909 and from Trucktrend.

been somewhat smaller in absolute terms but the growth rates have been similar to the US rise. And while the worldwide car sales were less than 100,000 vehicles in 1908, they were more than 73 million in 2017, roughly a 700-fold increase. This means that the total mass of new automobiles sold globally every year is now about 2,500 larger than it was a century ago.

Time is the third ubiquitous basic unit. Time is used to quantify growth directly (from increased human longevity to the duration of the longest flights, or as time elapsed between product failures that informs us about the durability and reliability of devices). More importantly, time is used as the denominator to express such ubiquitous rates as speed (length/time, m/s), power (energy/time, J/s), average earnings (money/time, $/hour), or national annual gross domestic product (total value of goods and services/ time, $/year). Rising temperatures are encountered less frequently in growth studies, but they mark the still improving performance of turbogenerators, while growing total luminosity of illumination informs about the widespread, and intensifying, problem of light pollution (Falchi et al. 2016).

Modern societies have been increasingly concerned about immaterial variables whose growth trajectories describe changing levels of economic performance, affluence, and quality of life. Common variables that the economists want to see growing include the total industrial output, GDP, disposable income, labor productivity, exports, trade surplus, labor force participation, and total employment. Affluence (GDP, gross earnings, disposable income, accumulated wealth) is commonly measured in per capita terms, while the quality of life is assessed by combinations of socioeconomic variables. For example, the Human Development Index (HDI, developed and annually recalculated by the United Nations Development Programme) is composed of three indices quantifying life expectancy, educational level, and income (UNDP 2016).

And in 2017 the World Economic Forum introduced a new Inclusive Development Index (IDI) based on a set of key performance indicators that allow a multidimensional assessment of living standards not only according to their current level of development but also taking into account the recent performance over five years (World Economic Forum 2017). There is a great deal of overlap between HDI for 2016 and IDI for 2017: their rankings share six among the top 10 countries (Norway, Switzerland, Iceland, Denmark, Netherlands, Australia). Perhaps the most interesting addition to this new accounting has been the quantifications of happiness or satisfaction with life.

Small Himalayan Bhutan made news in 1972 when Jigme Singye Wangchuck, the nation's fourth king, proposed to measure the kingdom's progress by using the index of Gross National Happiness (GNH Centre 2016).

Turning this appealing concept into an indicator that could be monitored periodically is a different matter. In any case, for the post-WWII US we have a fairly convincing proof that happiness has not been a growth variable. Gallup pollsters have been asking Americans irregularly how happy they feel since 1948 (Carroll 2007). In that year 43% of Americans felt very happy. The measure's peak, at 55%, was in 2004, the low point came after 9/11 at 37%, but by 2006 it was 49%, hardly any change compared to more than half a century ago (47% in 1952)!

Satisfaction with life is closely connected with a number of qualitative gains that are not easily captured by resorting to simple, and the most commonly available, quantitative measures. Nutrition and housing are certainly the two best examples of this reality. As important as it may be, tracing the growth of average daily per capita availability of food energy may deliver a misleadingly reassuring message. Dietary improvements have lifted food supply far above the necessary energy needs: they may have delivered a more than adequate amount of carbohydrates and lipids and may have satisfied the minimum levels of high-quality protein—but could still be short of essential micronutrients (vitamins and minerals). Most notably, low intakes of fruit and vegetables (the key sources of micronutrients) have been identified as a leading risk factor for chronic disease, but Siegel et al. (2014) showed that in most countries their supply falls below recommended levels. In 2009 the global shortfall was 22% with median supply/need ratios being just 0.42 in low-income and 1.02 in affluent countries.

During the early modern era, the rise of scientific methods of inquiry and the invention and deployment of new, powerful mathematical and analytical tools (calculus during the mid-17th century, advances in theoretical physics and chemistry and the foundations of modern economic and demographic studies during the 19th century) made it eventually possible to analyze growth in purely quantitative terms and to use relevant growth formulas in order to predict long-term trajectories of studied phenomena. Robert Malthus (1766–1834), a pioneer of demographic and economic studies, caused a great of concern with his conclusion contrasting the means of subsistence that grow only at a linear rate with the growth of populations that proceeds at exponential rates (Malthus 1798).

Unlike Malthus, Pierre-François Verhulst (1804–1849), a Belgian mathematician, is now known only to historians of science, statisticians, demographers, and biologists. But four decades after Malthus's essay, Verhulst made a fundamental contribution to our understanding of growth when he published the first realistic formulas devised explicitly to express the progress of confined (bounded) growth (Verhulst 1838, 1845, 1847). Such growth governs not only the development of all organisms but also the improving performance of new techniques, diffusion of many innovations and adoption of many consumer products. Before starting my topical coverage of growth phenomena and their trajectories (in chapter 2), I will provide brief, but fairly comprehensive, introductions into the nature of these formal growth patterns and resulting growth curves.

Linear and Exponential Growth

These are two common but very different forms of growth whose trajectories are captured by simple equations. Relatively slow and steady would be the best qualitative description of the former, and increasingly rapid and eventually soaring the best of the latter. Anything subject to linear growth increases by the same amount during every identical period and hence the equation for linear growth is simple:

$$N_t = N_0 + kt$$

where a quantity at time t (N_t) is calculated by enlarging the initial value (N_0) by the addition of a constant value k per unit of time, t.

Analysis of a large number of stalagmites shows that these tapering columns of calcium salts created on cave floors by dripping water often grow for millennia in a near-linear fashion (White and Culver 2012). Even a relatively fast growth of 0.1 mm/year would mean that a stalagmite 1 meter tall would grow just 10 cm in thousand years ($1,000 \text{ mm} + 1,000 \times 0.1$). The plotted outcome of its linear growth shows a monotonously ascending line (figure 1.3). This, of course, means that the growth rate as the share of the total stalagmite height will be constantly declining. In a stalagmite growing at 0.1 mm/year for 1,000 years it would be 0.01% during the first year but only 0.009% a millennium later.

In contrast, in all cases of exponential growth the quantity increases by the same rate during every identical period. The basic functional dependence is

$$N_t = N_0 (1 + r)^t$$

where r is the rate of growth expressed as a fraction of unity growth per unit time, for example, for a 7% increase per unit of time, $r = 0.07$.

This exponential growth can be also expressed—after a trivial multiplicative unit-of-timekeeping adjustment—as

$$N_t = N_0 e^{rt}$$

where e ($e = 2.7183$, the base of natural logarithms) is raised to the power of rt, an easy operation to do with any scientific hand-calculator. We can

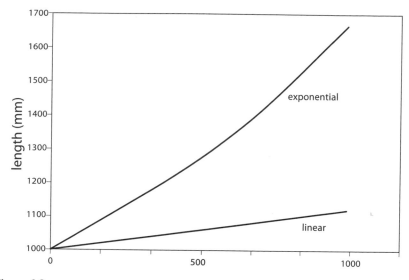

Figure 1.3
Millennium of stalagmite accretion illustrating linear and exponential growth trajectories.

imagine a cave where the amount of dripping water carrying the same fraction of dissolved salts keeps on increasing, resulting in an exponential growth of a stalagmite.

Assuming a very small 0.05% fractional length increase per year, this stalagmite would have lengthened by nearly 65 cm in 1,000 years $(1,000 \text{ mm} \times 2.718^{0.0005 \times 1000} = 1,648.6 \text{ mm}$ total length, or a length increase of 64.86 cm), about 50% more than its linearly growing counterpart, and the plotted exponential growth shows an upward-bending curve whose ascent is determined by the rate of increase (figure 1.3). After 10,000 years the linear stalagmite would double its height to 2 m while the exponentially growing stalagmite would need a giant cave as it would reach 148.3 m. As the exponent is the product of growth rate and time, equally large additions can come from lower growth rates over longer intervals of time or from shorter intervals of higher growth rates.

Another simple comparison shows how the trajectories of linear and exponential growth remain close only during the earliest stage of growth, when the product of growth rate and time interval is small compared to unity: soon they begin to diverge and eventually they are far apart. Gold (1992) assumed that bacterial colonies living deep underground fill up to 1% of all porous spaces in the topmost 5 km of the Earth's crust while Whitman et al. (1998) put the microbe-fillable volume at just 0.016% of the available porous space. That would still translate into enormous aggregate microbial mass—but one with exceedingly slow rates of reproduction. Let us assume (just for the sake of this simple example) that the physical and chemical constraints make it possible for a tiny colony of 100 cells (suddenly squeezed by a seismic event into a new rock pocket) to make the net addition of just five cells per hour; obviously, there will be 105 cells at the end of the first hour, after 10 hours of such linear growth the colony will have 150 cells, and the respective totals will be 350 and 600 cells after 50 and 100 hours.

In comparison to many common bacteria, *Mycobacterium tuberculosis*—a remarkably prevalent cause of premature mortality in the pre-antibiotic era, and still one of the single largest causes of human mortality due to infectious disease and the cause of what are now some of the most drug-resistant forms of such disease (Gillespie 2002)—reproduces slowly in most circumstances in infected human lungs. But when growing on suitable laboratory substrates, it will double its cell count in 15 hours, implying an hourly growth rate of roughly 5%. Starting, again, with 100 cells, there will be 105 cells at the end of the first hour, the same as with the linear growth of subterranean microbes; after 10 hours of exponential growth, the colony will have 165 cells (just 10% more than in the linear case), but the exponential totals will be 1,218 cells after 50 hours (roughly 3.5 times as much as in the linear case) and 14,841 cells after 100 hours, almost 25 times more. The contrast is obvious: without a priori knowledge, we could not tell the difference after the first hour—but after 100 hours the gap has become enormous as the exponential count is an order of magnitude higher.

Instances of linear (constant) growth are ubiquitous. Distance (length) travelled by light emitted by myriads of stars increases by 300,000,000 m (299,792,458 m to be exact) every second; distance covered by a truck averaging 100 km/h on a night-time freeway grows by 27.7 m during the same time. According to Ohm's law—voltage (volts, V) equals current (amperes, A) times the resistance (ohms, Ω) of the conducting circuit—when resistance remains constant, current increases linearly with increasing voltage. Fixed (and untaxed) hourly wage will bring a linear increase of salary with longer work time. Cellphone use charged per minute (rather than on an unlimited plan) will produce a linearly increasing monthly bill with linearly increasing chatter.

In nature, linear growth is often encountered temporarily during the early stages of postnatal development, be it of piglets or children. Increasing life expectancies in affluent countries have followed it for more than a century, and it is the only long-term growth trajectory for rising crop yields, be it of staple grains or fruits. Improvements in the ratings and capabilities of machines have been often linear, including the average power of American cars since the Ford Model T in 1908, maximum thrust and bypass ratio of jet engines since their origin, maximum train speed and boiler pressure of steam locomotives (since the beginning of regular service in 1830), and maximum ship displacements.

And sometimes simple linear growth is an outcome of complex interactions. Between 1945 and 1978, US gasoline consumption had followed an almost perfectly linear course—and after a brief four-year dip it resumed a slower linear growth in 1983 that continued until 2007 (USEIA 2017b). The two linear trajectories resulted from an interplay of nonlinear changes as vehicle ownership soared, increasing more than seven times between 1945 and 2015, while average fuel-using efficiency of automotive engines remained stagnant until 1977, then improved significantly between 1978 and 1985 before becoming, once again, stagnant for the next 25 years (USEPA 2015).

Some organisms, including bacteria cultivated in the laboratory and young children, experience periods of linear growth, adding the same number of new cells or the same height or the same mass increment, during specific periods of time. Bacteria follow that path when provided with a limited but constant supply of a critical nutrient. Children have spells of linear growth both for weight and height. For example, American boys have brief periods of linear weight growth between 21 and 36 months of age (Kuczmarski et al. 2002), and the Child Growth Standards of the World Health Organization (WHO) indicate a perfectly linear growth of height with age for boys between three and five years, and an almost-linear trajectory for girls between the same ages (WHO 2006; figure 1.4).

Exponential Growth

Exponential growth, with its gradual takeoff followed by a steep rise, attracts attention. Properties of this growth, formerly known as geometric ratio or geometric progression, have been illustrated for hundreds of years—perhaps for millennia, although the first written instance comes only from the year 1256—by referring to the request of a man who invented chess and asked his ruler-patron to reward him by doubling the number of grains of rice (or wheat?) laid on every square. The total of 128 grains (2^7) is still trivial at the end of the first row; there are about 2.1 billion grains (2^{31}) when reaching the end of the middle, fourth, row; and at the end, it amounts to about 9.2 quintillion (9.2×10^{18}) grains.

The key characteristic of advanced exponential growth are the soaring additions that entirely overwhelm the preceding totals: additions to the last row of the chessboard are 256 times larger than the total accumulated

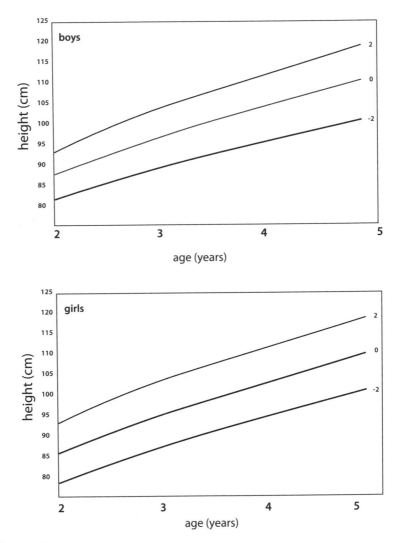

Figure 1.4
Graphs of expected height-for-age growth (averages and values within two standard deviations) for boys and girls 2–5 years old. Simplified from WHO (2006).

at the end of the penultimate row, and they represent 99.61% of all added grains. Obviously, undesirable exponential growth may be arrested, with various degrees of effort, in its early stages, but the task may quickly become unmanageable as the growth continues. When assuming an average rice grain mass of 25 milligrams, the grand total (all too obviously not able to fit any chessboard) would equal about 230 Gt of rice, nearly 500 times more than the grain's global annual harvest—which was just short of 500 Mt in 2015.

Over long periods even minuscule growth rates will produce impossible outcomes and there is no need to invoke any cosmic time spans—referring back to antiquity will do. When imperial Rome reached its apogee (in the second century of the common era), it needed to harvest about 12 Mt of grain (much of it grown in Egypt and shipped to Italy) in order to sustain its population of some 60 million people (Garnsey 1988; Erdkamp 2005; Smil 2010c). When assuming that Rome would have endured and that its grain harvest would have grown at a mere 0.5% a year its total would have now reached about 160 Gt, or more than 60 times the world's grain harvest of 2.5 Gt in 2015 used to feed more than 7 billion people.

Linear scale is a poor choice for charting exponential growth whose complete trajectory often encompasses many orders of magnitude. In order to accommodate the entire range on a linear y axis it becomes impossible to make out any actual values except for the largest order of magnitude, and the result is always a J-curve that has a nearly linear section of relatively slow gains followed by a more or less steep ascent. In contrast, plotting constant exponential growth on a semilogarithmic graph (with linear x axis for time and logarithmic y axis for the growing quantity) produces a perfectly straight line and actual values can be easily read off the y axis even when the entire growth range spans many orders of magnitude. Making a semilog plot is thus an easy graphic way of identifying if a given set of data has been a result of exponential growth. Figure 1.5 compares the two plots for such a phenomenon: it charts the growth of one of the key foundations of modern civilization, the almost perfectly exponential rise of global crude oil consumption between 1880 and 1970.

The fuel's commercial production began on a negligible scale in only three countries, in Russia (starting in 1846) and in Canada and the US (starting in 1858 and 1859). By 1875 it was still only about 2 Mt and then, as US and Russian extraction expanded and as other producers entered the market (Romania, Indonesia, Burma, Iran), the output grew exponentially to about 170 Mt by 1930. The industry was briefly slowed down by the economic crisis of the 1930s, but its exponential rise resumed in 1945 and,

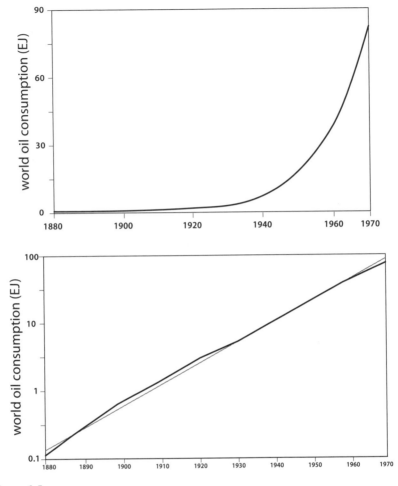

Figure 1.5
Growth of annual global crude oil consumption, 1880–1970: exponential growth plotted on linear and semilog scales. Data from Smil (2017b).

propelled by new huge Middle Eastern and Russian discoveries, by the mid-1970s the output was three orders of magnitude (slightly more than 1,000 times) higher than 100 years previous.

Temporary periods of exponential growth have not been uncommon in modern economies, where they have marked the rise of domestic product in such rapidly developing nations as Japan, South Korea, and post-1985 China, and where they characterized annual sales of electronic consumer goods whose mass appeal created new global markets. And, of course, fraudulent investing schemes (Ponzi pyramids) are built on the allure of the temporary exponential rise of make-believe earnings: arresting exponential growth in its early stages can be done in manageable manner, sudden collapse of Ponzi-like growth will always have undesirable consequences. Progress of technical advances has been also often marked by distinct exponential spells, but when the exponential growth (and its perils) became a major topic of public discourse for the first time it was in relation to rising sizes of populations (Malthus 1798).

That famous work—*An Essay on the Principle of Population*—by Thomas Robert Malthus had precedents in the work of Leonhard Euler, a leading scientist of the 18th century who left Switzerland to work in Russia and Prussia (Bacaër 2011). In Berlin, after his return from Russia, Euler published— in Latin, at that time still the standard language of scientific writing— *Introduction to Analysis of the Infinite* (Euler 1748). Among the problems addressed in the book was one inspired by Berlin's 1747 population census which counted more than 100,000 people. Euler wanted to know how large such a population, growing annually by one thirtieth (3.33% a year), would be in 100 years. His answer, determined by the use of logarithms, was that it could grow more than 25 times in a century: as $P_n = P_0 (1+r)^n$, the total in 100 years will be $100,000 \times (1 + 1/30)^{100}$ or 2,654,874. Euler then proceeded to show how to calculate the annual rate of population increase and the doubling periods.

But it was Malthus who elevated the powers of exponential growth to a major concern of the new disciplines of demography and political economy. His much-repeated conclusion was that "the power of population is indefinitely greater than the power in the earth to produce subsistence for man" because the unchecked population would be rising exponentially while its means of subsistence would be growing linearly (Malthus 1798, 8):

> Taking the population of the world at any number, a thousand millions, for instance, the human species would increase in the ratio of—1, 2, 4, 8, 16, 32, 64, 128, 256, 512, etc. and subsistence as—1, 2, 3, 4, 5, 6, 7, 8, 9, 10, etc. In two centuries and a quarter, the population would be to the means of subsistence as 512 to 10: in three centuries as 4096 to 13, and in two thousand years the difference would be almost incalculable, though the produce in that time would have increased to an immense extent.

Charles Darwin illustrated the process with references to Malthus and Linnaeus and with his own calculation of the consequences of unchecked elephant breeding (Darwin 1861, 63):

> There is no exception to the rule that every organic being increases at so high a rate, that if not destroyed, the earth would soon be covered by the progeny of a single pair. Even slow-breeding man has doubled in twenty-five years, and at

this rate, in a few thousand years, there would literally not be standing room for his progeny. Linnaeus has calculated that if an annual plant produced only two seeds—and there is no plant so unproductive as this—and their seedlings next year produced two, and so on, then in twenty years there would be a million plants. The elephant is reckoned to be the slowest breeder of all known animals, and I have taken some pains to estimate its probable minimum rate of natural increase: it will be under the mark to assume that it breeds when thirty years old, and goes on breeding till ninety years old, bringing forth three pairs of young in this interval; if this be so, at the end of the fifth century there would be alive fifteen million elephants, descended from the first pair.

As I will explain in detail in the chapters on the growth of organisms and artifacts, these specific calculations have to be understood with the right mixture of concern and dismissal, but they share two fundamental attributes. First, and unlike with linear growth where the absolute increment per unit of time remains the same, exponential growth results in increasing absolute gains per unit of time as the base gets larger. The US economy grew by 5.5% in 1957 as well as in 1970, but in the second instance the absolute gain was 2.27 times larger, $56 vs. $24.7 billion (FRED 2017). In most of the commonly encountered cases of exponential growth, the rate of increase is not perfectly constant: it either trends slightly over time or it fluctuates around a long-term mean.

A slowly declining growth rate will produce less pronounced exponential gains. Decadal means of US GDP growth since 1970 are a good example: they declined from 9.5% during the 1970s to 7.7% during the 1980s, 5.3% during the 1990s, and to just 4% during the first decade of the 21st century (FRED 2017). An increasing growth rate will result in a super-exponential pace of increase. Growth of China's real GDP between 1996 and 2010 was super-exponential: the annual rate was 8.6% during the first five years, 9.8% between 2001 and 2005, and 11.3% between 2006 and 2010 (NBS 2016). Fluctuating growth rates are the norm with the long-term expansion of economies: for example, US economic growth (expressed as GDP) averaged 7% a year during the second half of the 20th century, but that compounded mean rate of change hides substantial annual fluctuations, with the extreme rates at −0.3% in 1954 (the only year of GDP decline) and 13% in 1978 (FRED 2017).

Second, exponential growth, natural or anthropogenic, is always only a temporary phenomenon, to be terminated due to a variety of physical, environmental, economic, technical, or social constraints. Nuclear chain reactions end as surely (due to the limited mass of fissile material) as do Ponzi (pyramid investment) schemes (once the inflow of new monies sinks below the redemptions). But in the latter case it can take a while: think of Bernard Madoff, who was able to carry on his fraudulent activities—a Ponzi scheme so elaborate that it had eluded the oversight authorities who had repeatedly investigated his company (although certainly not as diligently as they should have)—for more than 30 years and to defraud about $65 billion from his investors before he was finally undone by the greatest post-WWII economic crisis in the fall of 2008 (Ross 2016).

That is why it can be so misleading to use exponential growth for longer-term forecasting. This could be illustrated by any number of examples based on actual histories, and I have chosen the impressive growth of America's post-1950 airline passenger traffic. During the 1950s its annual exponential growth averaged 11.1% and the rates for the 1960s and the 1970s were, respectively, 12.4% and 9.4%. A plot of the annual totals of passenger-kilometers flown by all US airlines between 1930 and 1980 produces a trajectory that is almost perfectly captured by a quartic regression (fourth-order polynomial with $r^2 = 0.9998$), and continuation of this growth pattern would have multiplied the 1980 level almost 10 times by 2015 (figure 1.6).

In reality, US airline traffic has followed a trajectory of declining growth (with average annual growth of just 0.9% during the first decade of the 21st century) and its complete 1930 to 2015 course fits very well into a four-parameter (symmetric) logistic curve, with the 2015 total only about 2.3 times higher than in 1980 and with only limited further gain expected by 2030 (figure 1.6). Taking temporarily high rates of annual exponential growth as indicators of future long-term developments is a fundamental mistake—but also an enduring habit that is especially favored by uncritical promoters of new devices, designs, or practices: they take early-stage growth rates, often impressively exponential, and use them to forecast an imminent dominance of emerging phenomena.

Many recent examples can illustrate this error, and I have chosen the capacity growth of Vestas wind turbines, machines leading the shift toward the decarbonization of global electricity generation. This Danish maker began its sales with a 55 kW machine in 1981; by 1989 it had a turbine capable of 225 kW; a 600 kW machine was introduced in 1995; and a 2 MW unit followed in 1999. The best-fit curve for this rapid growth trajectory of the last two decades of the 20th century (five-parameter logistic fit with R^2 of 0.978) would have predicted designs with capacity of nearly 10 MW in 2005 and in excess of 100 MW by 2015. But in 2018 the largest Vestas unit available for onshore installations was 4.2 MW and the largest unit suitable for offshore wind farms was 8 MW that could be upgraded to 9 MW (Vestas 2017a), and it is most unlikely that a 100 MW machine will be ever

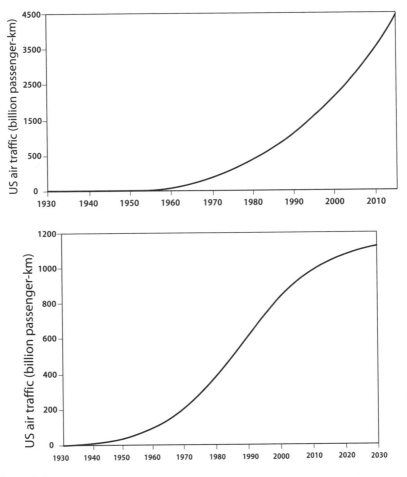

Figure 1.6
Predictions of growth of US air travel (in billions of passenger-kilometers) based on the period 1930–1980 (top, the best fit is quartic regression) and 1930–2015 (bottom, the best fit is a logistic curve with the inflection year in 1987). Data from various annual reports by the International Civil Aviation Organization.

built. This example of a sobering contrast between early rapid advances of a technical innovation followed by inevitable formation of sigmoid curves should be recalled whenever you see news reports about all cars becoming electric by 2025 or new batteries having impressively higher energy densities by 2030.

But the final, inescapable power of this reality may seem inapplicable in those cases where exponential growth has been underway for an extended period of time and when it keeps setting new record levels. More than a few normally rational people have been able to convince themselves—by repeating the mantra "this time it is different"—that performances will keep on multiplying for a long time to come. The best examples of these, often collective, delusions come from the history of stock market bubbles and I will describe in some detail just two most notable recent events, Japan's pre-1990 rise and America's New Economy of the 1990s.

Japan's economic rise during the 1980s provides one of the best examples of people who should know better getting carried away by the power of exponential growth. After growing 2.6 times during the 1970s, Nikkei 225 (Japan's leading stock market index and the country's equivalent of America's Dow Jones Industrial) increased by 184% between January 1981 and 1986, added 43% in 1986, nearly 13% in 1987, almost 43% in 1988, and a further 29% in 1989 (Nikkei 225 2017). Between January 1981 and December 1989, Nikkei 225 had more than quintupled, the performance corresponding to average annual exponential growth of 17% for the decade and 24% for its second half. Concurrently, Japan's GDP kept on growing at an annual rate surpassing 4%, as the yen's exchange rate strengthened from ¥239/US$ in January 1980 to ¥143/US$ by December 1989.

A sobering denouement had to come, and in chapter 6 I will trace that swift post-1989 unfolding. But exponential growth is a potent delusion-maker, and in 1999, 10 years after the Nikkei's peak, I was thinking about the Japanese experience as we were waiting to claim our rental car at San Francisco airport. Silicon Valley was years into its first dotcom bubble, and even with advance reservations people had to wait for the just-returned cars to get serviced and released again into the halting traffic on the clogged Bayshore freeway. Mindful of the Japanese experience, I was thinking that every year after 1995 might be the last spell of what Alan Greenspan famously called irrational exuberance, but it was not in 1996 or 1997 or 1998. And even more so than a decade earlier, there were many economists ready to assure American investors that this spell of exponential growth was really different, that the old rules do not apply in the New Economy where endless rapid growth will readily continue.

During the 1990s, the Dow Jones Industrial Average—driven by America's supposedly New Economy—posted the biggest decadal gain in history as it rose from 2,810 at the beginning of January 1990 to 11,497 at the end of December 1999 (FedPrimeRate 2017). The performance corresponded to annual exponential growth of 14% during the decade, with the peak gains of 33% in 1995 and 25% in 1996. Continuation of that growth pointed to a level around 30,000 by 2010. And the Nasdaq Composite Index—reflecting the rising computing and communication capabilities and, above all, the soaring performance of speculation-driven Silicon Valley companies—did even better during the 1990s: its exponential growth averaged almost 30% annually between April 1991, when it reached 500 points, and March 9, 2000, when it peaked at 5,046 points (Nasdaq 2017).

Even some normally cautious observers got swept away by this. Jeremy Siegel, at the Wharton School of Business, marveled: "It's amazing. Every year we say it can't be another year of 20 percent-plus (gains)—and then every year it's 20 percent-plus. I still maintain we have to get used to lower, more normal returns, but who knows when this streak is going to end?" (Bebar 1999). And the boosters made money by wholesaling the impossible: one bestseller saw an early arrival of Dow Jones at 40,000 (Elias 2000), another forecast the unstoppable coming of Dow 100,000 (Kadlec and Acampora 1999). But the end came and, again, it was fairly swift. By September of 2002, Dow Jones was down to 9,945, a nearly 40% decline from its 1999 peak (FedPrimeRate 2017), and by May 2002 Nasdaq Composite fell nearly 77% from its March 2000 peak (Nasdaq 2017).

Exponential growth has been common in many cases of technical advances and, as I will show in chapter 3, in some instances it has persisted for decades. The maximum power of steam turbines is a perfect example of this long-lasting exponential growth. Charles Algernon Parsons patented the first design in 1884 and almost immediately built a small machine—which can be seen in the lobby of the Parsons Building at Trinity College in Dublin—with power of just 7.5 kW, but the first commercial turbine was 10 times larger as the 75 kW machine began generating electricity in 1890 (Parsons 1936).

The subsequent rapid rise brought the first 1 MW turbine by 1899, a 2 MW machine just three years later, the first 5 MW design in 1907, and before WWI the maximum capacity reached 25 MW with the turbine installed at the Fisk Street station of the Commonwealth Edison Co. in Chicago (Parsons 1911). Between the year of the first commercial 75 kW model in 1890 and the 25 MW machine of 1912, maximum capacities of Parsons steam turbines were thus growing at an annual compounded exponential rate of more than 26%, doubling in less than three years. That was considerably faster than the growth of early steam engine capacities during the 18th century, or the rated power of water turbines since the 1830s when Benoît Fourneyron commercialized his first designs.

And some performances advance exponentially not by a constant improvement of the original technique but by a series of innovations, with the next innovation stage taking off where the old technique reached its limits: individual growth trajectories are unmistakably S-shaped but their envelope charts an exponential ascent. The history of vacuum tubes, briefly reviewed in chapter 4, is an excellent example of such an exponential envelope spanning nearly a century of advances. In chapter 4 (on the growth of artifacts), I will also look in detail at perhaps the most famous case of modern exponential growth that has been sustained for 50 years, that of the crowding of transistors on a silicon microchip described by Moore's law that has doubled the number of components every two years.

And before leaving the topic of exponential growth, this is an apposite place to note a simple rule for calculating the doubling period of quantities subject to it, be they cancerous cells, bank accounts or the processing capacity of computers, or, in reverse, to calculate a growth rate by using the known doubling time. Exact results are obtained by dividing the natural logarithm of 2 (that is 0.693) by the prevailing growth rate (expressed as a fraction of one, e.g. 0.1 for 10%), but a quite good approximation is dividing 70 by the growth rate expressed in percent. When the Chinese economy was growing at 10% a year, its doubling period was seven years ; conversely, the doubling of components on a microchip in two years implies an annual exponential growth rate of about 35%.

Hyperbolic Growth

Unbounded, and hence on Earth always only temporary, exponential growth should not be mistaken (as it sometimes is) for hyperbolic growth. While exponential progress is characterized by an increasing absolute rate of growth, it remains a function of time as it approaches infinity; in contrast, hyperbolic growth culminates in an absurdity as a quantity grows toward infinity in a finite time interval (figure 1.7). This terminal event is, of course, impossible within any finite confines and a moderating feedback will eventually exert a damping effect and terminate the hyperbolic progress. But when starting at low rates, hyperbolic trajectories may be sustained for relatively long periods of time before their progression stops and another form of growth (or decline) takes over.

Cailleux (1951) was the first to note what he called the *surexpansion*, the fact that the global population was growing at an ever-increasing rate, the process made possible by an accelerated evolution of civilizations: "Ainsi est-il normal de lier la surexpansion humaine à la présence de l'Esprit" (Cailleux 1951, 70). This process fits a quasi-hyperbolic equation: $P = a/(D-t)M$ where a, D and M are constants. Meyer and Vallee (1975, 290) thus concluded that the growth of human population, "far from tending 'naturally' toward an equilibrium state...exhibits a unique characteristic, that of self-acceleration."

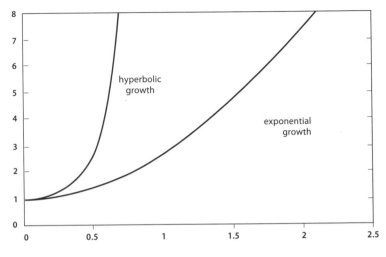

Figure 1.7
Hyperbolic growth curve in comparison with exponential growth.

But only temporarily, as the projection of this growth would eventually lead to infinite population. Von Foerster et al. (1960, 1291) had actually calculated that "Friday, 13 November, A.D. 2026" will be the doomsday when the "human population will approach infinity if it grows as it has grown in the last two millennia." Obviously, that could never happen, and just a few years after von Foerster et al. published their paper the annual growth of global population peaked and a transition to a new trajectory began.

Even so, Hern (1999) argued that global population growth had shown striking parallels with malignant growth because some cancers also display decreasing doubling times of cell proliferation during their most invasive phase. Starting the count 3 million years ago, he calculated that by 1998 the human population had undergone 32.5 doublings, with the 33rd (reaching 8.59 billion) to be completed in the early 21st century. When adding biomass of domestic animals to the anthropomass, the 33rd doubling was already completed. Some malignant tumors cause death of the host organism after 37–40 doublings, and (assuming the trend continues) the 37th doubling of the human population will be reached in a few hundred years.

Nielsen's (2015) analysis of world population growth showed that there were actually three approximately determined episodes of hyperbolic growth during the past 12,000 years: the first one between 10,000 and 500 BCE, the second one between 500 and 1200 CE, and the third one between 1400 and 1950, in total accounting for about 89% of total growth over the past 12 millennia. The first two transitions (500 BC to 500 CE and 1200–1400) were considerable slowdowns between two hyperbolic trajectories, while the current transition is to an unknown trajectory: will we see a relatively early leveling off followed by a prolonged plateau or a peak followed soon by a significant decline? I will have much more on the trajectories of population growth in chapters 5 and 6.

There is another class of notable examples of anthropogenic hyperbolic growth, one that has been noted by many authors pointing out the instances of accelerating developments in history. These writings have a long pedigree: they began in the latter half of the 19th century (Lubbock 1870; Michelet 1872), and their notable 20th-century additions include Henry Adams, French historians during the 1940s, and (starting during the 1950s) many American historians, physicists, technologists, and computer scientists. Adams wrote about a law of acceleration (Adams 1919) and about the "rule of phase applied to history" which would eventually see human thought brought to the limit of its possibilities (Adams 1920). Meyer (1947) and Halévy (1948) wrote about l'accélération évolutive and about l'accélération de l'histoire. Key contributions of the American wave, written from different perspectives, included Feynman (1959), Moore (1965), Piel (1972), Moravec (1988), Coren (1998), and Kurzweil (2005).

Many of these writings either imply or explicitly posit the arrival of singularity when the contributions of artificial superintelligence will rise to such a level that they will be transformed into an unprecedented runaway process. This implies not only artificial intelligence surpassing any human capabilities (imaginable) but also coming ever closer to an instantaneous rate of physical change. Obviously, such achievements would utterly reform our civilization. Adams predicted (as he understood it, that is excluding any computing dimensions) singularity's arrival sometime between 1921 and 2025 (Adams 1920), Coren (1998) put it off until 2140, and Kurzweil's latest prediction for artificial intelligence machines taking over is for 2045 (Galleon and Reedy 2017). While we are (as many of these writers assert) moving inexorably to that fantastic state, proponents of accelerating, that is hyperbolic, growth point to such unfolding processes as our ability to feed increasing populations, to use ever more powerful prime energy converters or to travel at ever higher speeds.

This is manifested as a sequence of logistic curves, a phenomenon well described by Derek J. de Solla Price (1963, 21):

> The newly felt constriction produces restorative reaction … If the reaction is successful, its value usually seems to lie in so transforming what is being measured that it takes a new lease on life and rises with a new vigor until, at last, it must meet its doom. One therefore finds two variants of the traditional logistic curve

that are more frequent than the plain S-shaped ogive. In both cases the variant sets in some time during the inflection, presumably at a time when the privations of the loss of exponential growth become unbearable. If a slight change of definition of the thing that is being measured can be so allowed as to count a new phenomenon on equal terms with the old, the new logistic curve rises phoenix-like on the ashes of the old...

Meyer and Vallee (1975) argued that this phenomenon of logistic escalation or accelerating growth has been underestimated and that hyperbolic, rather than exponential, growth is not uncommon when taking a long-term look at technical advances. Their examples of hyperbolic advances ranged from the number of individuals that could be supported by a unit of land, to growth of maximum power of prime movers, speed of travel, and best efficiencies of energy conversion techniques. Historical growth of specific advances conforms to S-curves (logistic or other with their inherent asymptotes) but the envelope of sequential gains makes the entire growth sequence temporarily hyperbolic. Echoing Price, Meyer and Vallee (1975, 295) saw this relay process as an automatic sequence: "as soon as it reaches its ceiling, another machine, in the sense of another qualitatively different technology, relays the previous one and goes through its ceiling, with the resulting effect of sustaining the acceleration of the quantitative variable." Closer looks reveal more complex realities.

Foraging practiced by early gatherers and hunters could support as few as 0.0001 people per hectare of land and typical rates in more hospitable environments were around 0.002 people/ha. Shifting agriculture elevated that density by up to two orders of magnitude to 0.2–0.5 people/hectare; the first societies practicing permanent agriculture (Mesopotamia, Egypt, China) raised it to 1 person/hectare. The best 19th-century traditional farming in such intensively cultivated places as southern China could support as many as five people/hectare while modern farming can feed more than 10 people/hectare and it does so by providing a much better average-quality diet than did the previous arrangements (Smil 2017a).

But this sequence does not describe any inexorably timed universal evolutionary progression, as in many regions foraging coexisted for millennia with settled farming (and still does today: think of collecting truffles and hunting wild pigs in Tuscany), as shifting agriculture was practiced even in parts of Europe (Scandinavia, Russia) well into the 20th century and as it still supports millions of families throughout Latin America, Africa, and Asia, and as such hybrid practices as agropastoralism have remained common in those environments where they help to reduce the risk of an exclusive reliance on cropping.

And, obviously, even if the best seeds are planted and when the crop receives optimum nutrients, moisture, and protection against weeds and pests, the maximum yield remains limited by light intensity, length of the growing period, minimum temperature tolerated by the species, and the vulnerability to many kinds of natural catastrophes. As I will show in chapter 2 (in the section on crop growth), many regions of previously rising productivities now have diminished returns with intensive inputs of fertilizers and enhanced irrigation and their yield trajectory has been one of minimal gains or outright stagnation. Clearly, there is no universal, superexponential progression toward superior harvests. Human ingenuity has brought more impressive gains when it did not have to reckon with the complexities of organisms whose life cycles are determined by assorted environmental constraints. Technical advances provide the best examples of self-accelerating development following hyperbolic growth trajectories, and the maximum unit power of prime movers and top travel speeds offer accurately documented illustrations.

The maximum unit power of modern prime movers (primary sources of mechanical power) shifted first from less than 1,000 W for steam engines in the early 17th century, to water turbines (between 1850 and 1900), and then to steam turbines, whose record ratings now surpass 1 GW (figure 1.8).

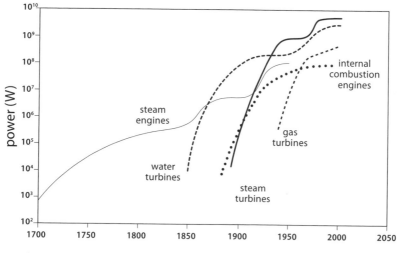

Figure 1.8
Relay growth of the largest stationary prime mover capacities (Smil 2017b). Overlapping logistic growth of unit ratings of steam engines, water turbines, and steam turbines produces a temporary hyperbolic growth trend with nearly seven-order-magnitude gain in 300 years.

Further extension could be made by including rocket engines deployed only for brief periods of time: power of the Saturn C 5 rocket that launched the Apollo mission to the Moon was about 2.6 GW (Tate 2012). Similarly, maximum travel speeds increased from endurance running (10–12 km/h sustained by messengers) and riders on good horses (average speed 13–16 km/h) to fast sailing ships (mid-19th century clippers averaging around 20 km/h with top speeds above 30 km/h), trains (maxima of around 100 km/h reached before 1900), to commercial airplanes powered by recip- rocating engines (speeds rising from 160 km/h in 1919 to 550 km/h in 1945) and, finally, to jetliners (more than 900 km/h since the late 1950s).

In both instances, the accelerating growth has been achieved by the relay phenomenon as the overlapping logistic (self-limiting) curves pro- duce an impressively ascending envelope. Obviously, this relay cannot con- tinue because it would eventually produce impossibly high growth rates, be it of unit power or speed.. As has been the case with global population growth, a temporary hyperbolic envelope will be eventually transformed to a logistic trajectory. In fact, this has already been the case when technical advances are considered in practical, realistic terms and not as sequences of maximum performances.

Obviously, constructing the maximum speed envelope by overlapping logistic curves of speeds for horses, sailing ships, trains, cars, airplanes, and rockets shows a progression of transportation modes that is not sequentially substitutable. High-volume urban transport progressed from horse-drawn vehicles to motorized road vehicles and subways but it will not progress to jet-powered flight. The opposite is true, as the average speed of urban traffic has declined in almost every major city since the 1960s, and just its dou- bling would be impossible even if every vehicle was part of a synchronized, automated urban system (unless all crossroads were eliminated, infrastruc- turally an impossible transformation in existing cities). The average speed of rapid trains has increased only marginally since their first deployment in 1964 and, once again, it is a very safe bet that billions of people traveling by train will not do so in a decade or two in a supersonic hyperloop fashion.

The typical speed of large container ships (30–40 km/h) is not radically higher than the typical speed of the 19th-century clippers; of course, their cargo capacities are orders of magnitude apart, but there has been no hyper- bolic growth of speeds in ocean shipping, and there is no realistic prospect that this fundamental mode of transport that enabled modern economic globalization will enter a new age of radically increased speeds. The cruising speed of the latest Boeing 787 (913 km/h) is nearly 7% lower than the cruis- ing speed of the company's first commercial jetliner, Boeing 707, in 1958

(977 km/h). Again, there is no realistic prospect that billions of passengers will be soon casually traveling at supersonic speeds. The seemingly hyperbolic envelope of maximum performances tells us little about the actual trajectories of speeds that have created modern economies by moving billions of people and billions of tonnes of raw materials, foodstuffs, and finished products.

The same is, inevitably, true about other envelopes of growing technical capabilities. The largest rockets may produce gigawatts of power during very brief periods of takeoff, but that is irrelevant as far as actual capacities of myriads of machines energizing modern civilization are concerned. Most electric motors in our appliances have power that is smaller than that delivered by a well-harnessed horse: washing machines need 500 W, a well-fed horse could easily sustain 800 W. The typical, or modal, capacity of steam turbines in large electricity-generating stations has been fairly stable since the 1960s, with units of 200–600 MW dominant in new plants fired by coal or natural gas, and with turbogenerators larger than 1 GW reserved mostly for the largest nuclear stations. And the power of typical road vehicles has gone up slightly only because they got heavier, not because they need to be more powerful to go from red light to red light or to cruise within posted speed limits on highways, for which a motive power of ~11 kW/t of vehicle weight is sufficient for 100 km/h travel on level roads (Besselink et al. 2011). Again, a synthetic rising trajectory is composed of disparate progressions that do not imply any unified rising trend of ever-ascending substitutions.

And there is no shortage of historical examples of technical advances that do not show any automatic, tightly sequenced acceleration of performance. Steelmakers continued to rely on open-hearth furnaces for nearly a century after they perfected their use, and the hard-wired rotary-dial telephone changed little between its adoption during the 1920s and the introduction of the push-button design in 1963 (Smil 2005 and 2006b). And there is no doubt about the long-term trajectory of hyperbolic growth on the Earth: it must either collapse or it must morph into a confined progression which might become a part of a homeostatic coexistence of humanity and the biosphere including an eventual upper limit on the information content in the external memory (Dolgonosov 2010).

Confined Growth Patterns

These are, above all, the trajectories of life: the biosphere's mass of recyclable nutrients allows for an enormous variety of specific genetic expressions and mutations but it puts fundamental limits on the performance of primary production (photosynthesis) and hence on the accumulation of secondary production (heterotrophic metabolism of organisms ranging from microbes to the most massive mammals). These limits unfold through intra- and interspecific competition of microorganisms, plants and animals for resources, through predation and viral, bacterial and fungal infections, and all multicellular organisms are subject to intrinsic growth limits imposed by apoptosis, programmed cell death (Green 2011).

No tree grows to heaven but neither does any artifact, structure or process, and confined (or constrained) growth patterns characterize the development of machines and technical capabilities as much as they describe the growth of populations and expansion of empires. And, inevitably, all diffusion and adoption processes must conform to that general pattern: no matter if their early trajectory shows rapid or slow progress, it is eventually followed by a substantial slowdown in growth rate as the process asymptotically approaches saturation and often reaches it (sometimes after many decades of diffusion) only a few percent, even only a fraction of a percent, short of the maximum. No households had electricity in 1880 but how many urban dwellings in Western cities are not connected to the grid today?

Given the ubiquity of phenomena exhibiting confined growth, it is not surprising that many investigators sought to fit them into a variety of mathematical functions. The two basic classes of trajectories of bounded growth are those of S-shaped (sigmoid) growth and of confined exponential growth. Scores of papers describe original derivations and subsequent modifications of these curves. There are also their extensive reviews (Banks 1994; Tsoularis 2001) and perhaps the best overview is table S1 in Myhrvold (2013) that systematically compares equations and constraints for more than 70 nonlinear growth functions.

S-shaped Growth

S-shaped functions describe many natural growth processes as well as the adoption and diffusion of innovations, be they new industrial techniques or new consumer items. Initially slow growth accelerates at the J-bend and it is followed by a rapid ascent whose rate of increase eventually slows down, forming the second bend that is followed by a slowing ascent as the growth becomes minimal and the total approaches the highest achievable limit of a specific parameter or a complete saturation of use or ownership. By far the best known, and the most often used function of the S-shaped trajectory is the one expressing logistic growth.

Unlike with exponential (unbounded) growth, whose rate of increase is proportional to the growing quantity, relative increments of logistic (limited) growth decrease as the growing quantity approaches its maximum possible level that in ecological studies is commonly called carrying capacity. Such growth seems to be intuitively normal:

> A typical population grows slowly from an asymptotic minimum; it multiplies quickly; it draws slowly to an ill-defined and asymptotic maximum. The two ends of the population-curve define, in a general way, the whole curve between; for so beginning and so ending the curve must pass through a point of inflection, it *must* be an S-shaped curve. (Thompson 1942, 145)

The origins of the formally defined logistic function go back to 1835 when Adolphe Quetelet (1796–1874; figure 1.9), Belgian astronomer and at that time Europe's leading statistician, published his pioneering analysis *Sur l'homme et le développement de ses facultés, ou Essai de physique sociale* in

Figure 1.9
Adolphe Quetelet and Pierre-François Verhulst. Steel engravings from the author's collection of 19th-century images.

which he pointed out the impossibility of prolonged exponential growth of any population (Quetelet 1835). Quetelet suggested that the forces opposing the indefinite development of the population increase proportionally to the square of the rate at which the population increases, and asked his pupil, mathematician Pierre-François Verhulst (1804–1849; figure 1.9), to come with a formal solution and then to apply it to the best available population statistics. Verhulst obliged and formulated the first equation expressing bounded population growth in his short notice in *Correspondance Mathématique et Physique* (Verhulst 1838; English translation was published by Vogels et al. 1975). The logistic model is described by the differential equation

$$\frac{dN}{dt} = \frac{rN(K-N)}{K}$$

with r being the rate of maximum growth and K the maximum attainable value, commonly known in ecology and population studies as carrying capacity.

To test the growth equation's utility, Verhulst compared expected outcomes with relatively short periods of census data available for France (1817–1831), Belgium (1815–1833), Essex county (1811–1831), and Russia (1796–1827), and although he found a "very accurate" fit for the French series he rightly concluded (given the brevity of the data series) that "the future alone will be able to reveal to us the true method of operation of the retarding force…" (Verhulst 1838, 116). Seven years later, in a more expansive paper, he decided to give "le nom *logistique* à la courbe" (Verhulst 1845, 9). He never explained why he chose the name but during his life the term was used in France to signify the art of computation, or he could have used it in the military sense of the word (provisioning the population) to suggest an arithmetical strategy (Pastijn 2006).

In his second paper, Verhulst illustrated the logistic curve by comparing it with exponential (*logarithmique*) growth (figure 1.10). The first part of the logistic curve, with *population normale* and when only good land is cultivated is exponential, then a slowdown of growth sets in. The relative growth rate declines as the population increases; the inflection point (at which the growth rate reaches its maximum) is always half of the ultimate limit, and eventually the *population surabondante* reaches its maximum. The instantaneous growth rate of the logistic function is symmetrically distributed about the inflection point at the middle of the trajectory (figure 1.11). Higher rates of growth will produce steeper growth curves that reach the maximum level faster (the curve will be compressed horizontally) while slower growth rates will produce curves extended horizontally.

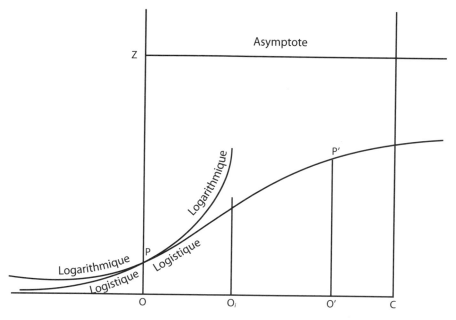

Figure 1.10
Verhulst's (1845) comparison of logistic and logarithmic (exponential) curves.

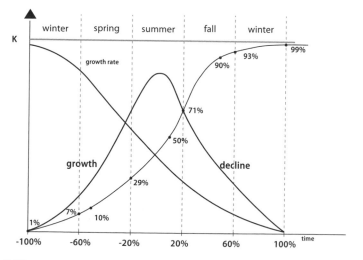

Figure 1.11
Qualitative characteristics of logistic growth.

In his 1845 paper, Verhulst assumed that the checks to further population growth would be proportional to the size of the excess population (*population surabondante*), and when he used this growth function to derive the ultimate limits of Belgian and French populations he set them, respectively, at about 6.6 and 40 million to be reached before the end of the 20th century. But in his last paper on population growth he concluded that the barriers to population growth are proportional to the ratio between the excess population and the total population (Verhulst 1847). That change resulted in a larger ultimate population or, as the asymptotic value became eventually known, in higher carrying capacities (Schtickzelle 1981).

Essentially, Verhulst's equation captures the shifting dominance between two feedback loops: a positive feedback loop (FBL) initiates growth that is eventually slowed down and brought into balance by a negative feedback that reflects the limits to growth prevailing in the finite world. As Kunsch (2006, 35) put it, logistic growth "is described as combining exponential growth embodied in (+) FBL, and goal-seeking growth, embodied in a (–) FBL." In that sense, Verhulst's function, with two feedback loops competing for dominance, can be seen as the very foundation of feedback-based systems dynamics developed by Jay Forrester at the Massachusetts Institute of Technology during the 1950s and 1960s (Forrester 1971) and applied by the study supported by the Club of Rome on the global *Limits to Growth* (Meadows et al. 1972).

This key systemic concept of constrained growth (a high density of organisms being the proximate constraining factor and resource availability being the complex causative driver) has been very useful when conceptualizing many natural, social, and economic developments involving series of feedbacks but its mechanistic application can result in substantial errors. Verhulst's original population forecasts are the earliest illustrations of such errors because population maxima are not preordained by any specific growth function but depend on changing a nation's, and ultimately the planet's, productive potential through scientific, technical, and economic development. How long such higher, evolving, maxima can be sustained is another matter. Verhulst eventually raised his Belgian population maximum by the year 2000 from 6.6 to 9.5 million—but by the end of the 20th century the Belgian and French populations were, respectively, at 10.25 and 60.91 million: for Belgium that was about 8% higher than Verhulst's adjusted maximum, but for France the error was 52%.

Although the second half of the 19th century saw an explosion of demographic and economic studies, Verhulst's work was ignored and it was rediscovered only during the 1920s and became influential only during the

1960s (Cramer 2003; Kint et al. 2006; Bacaër 2011). This was not the only instance of such forgetting: Gregor Mendel's fundamental experiments in plant genetics done during the 1860s were also ignored for nearly half a century (Henig 2001). Could the neglect of Verhulst's work be ascribed to Quetelet's reservations about his pupil's contributions published in the older man's eulogy after the younger man's premature death in 1849? Udny Yule had a better explanation: "Probably owing to the fact that Verhulst was greatly in advance of his time, and that the then existing data were quite inadequate to form any effective test to his views, his memories fell into oblivion: but they are classics on their subject" (Yule 1925a, 4).

The next appearance of logistic function (without using that name) was to quantify the progress of autocatalytic reactions in chemistry. While catalysis denotes the increasing rate of a chemical reaction caused by the presence of an additional element (notably, one of heavy metals) or a compound (often in minute quantities), autocatalysis describes a reaction that is catalyzed by its own products. Autocatalytic processes—reactions showing rate acceleration as a function of time followed by eventual saturation—are essential for the growth and maintenance of living systems and without them abiotic chemistry could not have given rise to replication, metabolism, and evolution (Plasson et al. 2011 Virgo et al. 2014).

After Wilhelm Ostwald (1853–1932, a leading chemist of the pre-WWI era) introduced the concept in 1890 (Ostwald 1890) it was quickly realized that the progress of the process follows a logistic function: the concentration of one reagent rises from its initial level, first slowly then more rapidly, but then, limited by the supply of the other reagent, it slows down while the concentration of the second reagent declines to zero. In 1908 T. Brailsford Robertson (1884–1930), an Australian physiologist at the University of California, noted that comparing the curve for monomolecular autocatalytic reaction with the increase of body weight of male white rats, "the resemblance between the curve of growth and that of an autocatalysed reaction is at once obvious" (figure 1.12)—but comparing the curve for autocatalyzed monomolecular reaction with the one showing the increase in body weight of a man showed that the latter trajectory has two superimposed curves (Robertson 1908, 586).

Both are sigmoid curves but Robertson did not mention Verhulst. Three years later, McKendrick and Kesava Pai (1911) used the function, again without naming Verhulst, to chart the growth of microorganisms, and in 1919 Reed and Holland (1919) made a reference to Robertson (1908) but did use the term logistic in their growth curve for the sunflower. That example of plant growth became later widely cited in biological literature on growth.

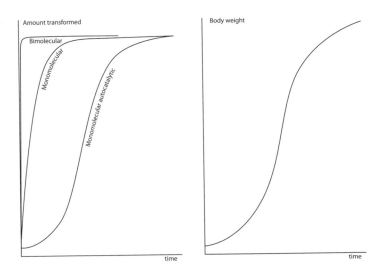

Figure 1.12
Robertson's (1908) comparison of the progress of an autocatalytic reaction with body weight increase of male white rats.

Observed growth of *Helianthus* height between planting and the 84th day follows closely a four-parameter logistic function with the inflection point falling on the 37th day (figure 1.13).

In 1920 the logistic function reappeared in demography when Raymond Pearl and Lowell Reed, professors at Johns Hopkins University, published a paper on the growth of the US population (Pearl and Reed 1920), but only two years later they briefly acknowledged Verhulst's priority (Pearl and Reed 1922). Much like Verhulst in the mid-1840s, Pearl and Reed used the logistic function to find the maximum population of the US supportable by the country's agricultural resources (Pearl and Reed 1920, 285):

> The upper asymptote … has the value 197,274,000 roughly. This means that … the maximum population which continental United States, as now areally limited, will ever have will be roughly twice the present population. We fear that some will condemn at once the whole theory because this number is not sufficiently imposing. It is so easy, and most writers on population have been so prone, to extrapolate population by geometric series, or by a parabola or some such purely empirical curve, and arrive at stupendous figures, that calm consideration of real probabilities is most difficult to obtain.

And as was the case with Verhulst's maxima for Belgium and France, Pearl and Reed also underestimated the supportable maximum of the US population. By 2018 its total had surpassed 325 million, nearly 65% above

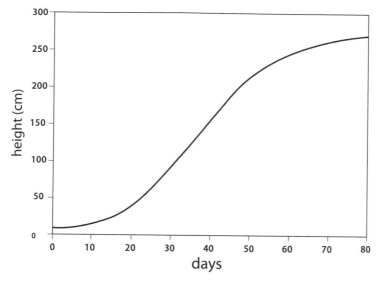

Figure 1.13

Logistic growth (inflection point at 37.1 days, asymptote at 292.9 cm) of a sunflower plant plotted by Reed and Holland (1919).

their calculation of the maximum carrying capacity (figure 1.14)—even as the country has been diverting 40% of its largest crop into corn-based fermentation of ethanol and still remains the world's largest food exporter. But Pearl had little doubt about the predictive power of his equation: in 1924 he compared the curve "in a modest way" with Kepler's law of planetary motion and with Boyle's law of gases (Pearl 1924, 585).

Applications of logistic growth function began to spread. Robertson used information about the growth of dairy cows, domestic fowl, frogs, annual plants and fruits in his voluminous survey of *The Chemical Basis of Growth and Senescence* (Robertson 1923). A year later, Spillman and Lang (1924) published a detailed treatment of *The Law of the Diminishing Returns* with many quantifications of bounded growth rates. Reed and Berkson (1929) applied the logistic function to several bimolecular reactions and to the proteolysis of gelation by pancreatin, and Bliss (1935) used it to calculate a dosage-mortality curve. And during the two decades before WWII, Pearl and his collaborators applied the logistic curve "to almost any living population from fruit flies to the human population of the French colonies in North Africa as well as the growth of cantaloupes" (Cramer 2003, 6).

In 1945 Hart published a comprehensive examination of logistic social trends with scores of examples classified as series reflecting the

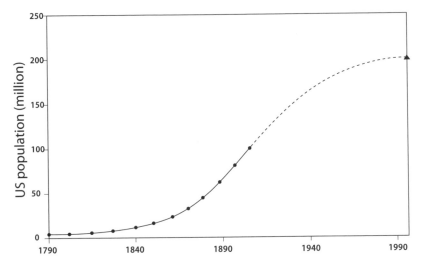

Figure 1.14
Forecast of US population growth based on the logistic curve (inflection point in 1919, asymptote at 197.3 million) fitted to decennial census data between 1790 and 1910 (Pearl and Reed 1920).

growth of specific social units (populations, cities, crop yields, output and consumption of industrial products, inventions measured by patenting, length of railways), the diffusion of specific cultural traits (school enrolments, car ownership, social and civic movements), and what he called indices of social efficiency, including life expectancy, speed records, and per capita incomes (Hart 1945). Two decades of rapid post-WWII population and economic growth driven by technical expansion were dominated by numerous instances of exponential growth, but the logistic function regained a greater prominence with the rise of modern ecological consciousness during the late 1960s and 1970s. Not surprisingly, there are many publications describing how to fit a logistic curve to data (Cavallini 1993; Meyer et al. 1999; Arnold 2002; Kahm et al. 2010; Conder 2016).

There is another fairly commonly used growth model, the Gompertz curve, whose origins are even older than the Verhulst function. The model was originally proposed in 1825 by Benjamin Gompertz (1779–1865), a British mathematician, in order to estimate the progress of human mortality (Gompertz 1825). It shares three constants, the asymptote and a fixed degree of skewness with the logistic function but, as already noted, the logistic function has the inflection point exactly halfway between the two asymptotes and its curve has a radial symmetry in relation to that inflection point; in contrast, the Gompertz function produces a skewed curve which has its inflection point at 36.78 percent of the asymptotic maximum and hence it is asymmetrical (Tjørve and Tjørve 2017). The curve offers a better choice than the logistic function for modeling sigmoid growth processes that slow down after reaching roughly the third of its maximum value (Vieira and Hoffmann 1977).

More than a century later, Winsor (1932, 1) noted that "the Gompertz curve was for long of interest only to actuaries. More recently, however, it has been used by various authors as a growth curve, both for biological and for economic phenomena." But he cited only three applications—the growth of body weight of cattle (but only after the animals reached about 70% of their mature mass), the growth in shell size of the razor clam, and the growth of the Pacific cockle—and concluded that because of the similar properties of logistic and Gompertz curves, neither "has any substantial advantage over the other in the range of phenomena which it will fit" (Winsor 1932, 7).

But that was before many subsequent studies found that the older function is, indeed, preferable in many cases. Natural phenomena that are best described by the Gompertz function include such fundamental biochemical processes as growth of normal and malignant cells, the kinetics of enzymatic reactions, and intensity of photosynthesis as a function of atmospheric CO_2 concentration (Waliszewski and Konarski 2005). As the use of the logistic equation became more common for studying the growth of organisms, many researchers noted the function's limitations in replicating the observed growth of animals and plants and its reliability in predicting gains based on the past performance. Nguimkeu (2014) provides a simple discriminatory test to choose between the Gompertz and the logistic growth models.

A key drawback of the latter is its symmetry: logistic growth has its kinetic analog in the motion of a pendulum as it progresses from rest to rest with the highest velocity at the midpoint of its trajectory. The inflection point of a logistic curve is at 50% of its maximum value, which means that the plot of its growth rates produces a symmetrical bell-shaped curve (Gaussian function) that will be covered in the next main section. Many organisms show faster growth rates in initial stages and curves of their growth reach inflection points well before getting to half of their asymptotic maximum. Similarly, many diffusion processes (be it adoption of new industrial techniques or spreading ownership of household appliances) follow asymmetric S-shaped trajectories.

And because the degree of skewness is also fixed in the asymmetric Gompertz function, many attempts to address these shortcomings led to the formulation of several additional logistic-type growth models. Tsoularis (2001) reviewed these derivative models—the principal ones being those introduced by von Bertalanffy (1938), Richards (1959), Blumberg (1968), Turner et al. (1976) and Birch (1999)—and he also offered his own generalized logistic function from which all of these modifications can be derived. There is no utility ranking: all of these functions belong to the same family (being variations on a theme of S-shaped growth) and none of them has a superior range of fitting power than other three-constant sigmoid curves.

Von Bertalanffy (1938) based his growth equation on the allometric relation between an animal's metabolic rate and body mass, with mass changing due to the difference of anabolic and catabolic processes. The function's maximum growth rate (inflection point) is at about 30% (8/27) of its asymptotic value and it has been used in growth and yield studies in forestry but above all in aquatic biology, for commercial fish species ranging from cod (Shackell et al. 1997) to tuna (Hampton 1991) and also for sharks (Cailliet et al. 2006) and even for polar bears (Kingsley 1979). But Roff (1980, 127) argued that the function "is at best a special case and at worst nonsense" and that it should be retired because it has outworn its usefulness in fishery studies. Similarly, Day and Taylor (1997) concluded that von Bertalanffy's equation should not be used to model age and size of organisms at maturity.

Richards (1959) modified von Bertalanffy's equation to fit empirical plant growth data. The function, also known as the Chapman-Richards growth model, has one more parameter than the logistic curve (needed to generate asymmetry) and it has been used widely in forestry studies but also for modeling the growth of mammals and birds and for comparing treatment effects on plant growth, but there are arguments against its use (Birch 1999). Its inflection points range from less than 40% to almost 50% of the asymptotic value. Turner et al. (1976) called their modified Verhulst equation the generic growth function. Blumberg's (1968) hyperlogistic function is also a modification of the Verhulst equation designed to model organ size growth as well as population dynamics.

And Weibull's distribution, originally developed to study the probability of material failure (Weibull 1951) and commonly used for reliability tests in engineering, is easily modified to produce a flexible growth function that can generate a wide variety of sigmoid growth curves; it has been used in forestry to model height and volume growth for single tree species as well as for volume and age of polymorphic tree stands (Yang et al. 1978; Buan and Wang 1995; Gómez-García et al. 2013). The last two additions to the still-growing family of sigmoid curves have been a new growth equation developed by Birch (1999) and, as already noted, a generalized logistic function by Tsoularis (2001). Birch (1999) modified Richards's equation to make it more suitable for generic simulation models, particularly for representing the growth of various plant species within mixed vegetation, while Tsoularis (2001) proposed a generalized logistic growth equation incorporating all previously used functions as special cases.

Logistic Curves in Forecasting

Logistic curves have been a favorite tool of forecasters because of their ability to capture, often very closely, growth trajectories of both living organisms and anthropogenic artifacts and processes. Undoubtedly, their use can provide valuable insights but, at the same time, I must caution against any overenthusiastic reliance on logistic curves as failure-proof forecasting tools. Noël Bonneuil's (2005, 267) verdict recalled the "golden age of the logistic curve, when Pearl enthusiastically applied the same function to any case of growth he could find, from the length of tails of rats to census data of the United States" and dismissed the claims of strikingly accurate applications of this model to historical data sets by tagging these "triumphs as shallow: most constrained growth processes do resemble the logistic, but to say so adds little understanding to dynamics in history… Curve fitting is too often an exercise that misleads in two fronts: not only should it not be taken as probative, but it can also conceal important detail."

Obviously, using these curves for long-range forecasting is no guarantee of success. Their application may be revealing and it can provide useful indications about coming limits, and throughout this book I will introduce retrospective fittings that are remarkably accurate and that may offer reliable indications of near-term growth. But in other cases, even highly accurate logistic fits of past trajectories may provide highly misleading conclusions about the coming advances and the forecasting errors may go far beyond those expected and acceptable ±10–25% deviations over a period of 10–20 years.

In one of the earliest surveys of logistic trends published at the end of WWII, Hart (1945) included speed records of airplanes between 1903 and 1938: that trajectory produces a very good logistic fit with the inflection point in 1932 and the maximum speed of close to 350 km/h—but technical innovation invalidated that conclusion twice within a dozen years. First, improvements in the performance of reciprocating engines (required to power wartime aircraft) brought their output to practical limits and they were soon adopted for commercial aviation. Lockheed L-1049 Super

Constellation, first flown in 1951, had a cruising speed of 489 km/h and maximum speed of 531 km/h, about 50% higher than the forecast of Hart's logistic ceiling.

Super Constellation became the fastest transatlantic airliner but its dominance was short-lived. The ill-fated British de Havilland Comet flew for the first time in January 1951 but was withdrawn in 1954, and the first scheduled jet-powered flight by an American company was Pan Am's Boeing 707 in October 1958 (Smil 2010b; figure 1.15). Turbojets, the first gas turbines in commercial flight, had more than doubled the pre-WWII cruising speeds of passenger aircraft (with the first service in 1919) and generated a new logistic curve with the inflection point in 1945 and asymptote around 900 km/h (figure 1.16). More powerful and more efficient turbofan engines, first introduced during the 1960s, enabled large aircraft and lower fuel consumption, but maximum cruising speeds have remained basically unchanged (Smil 2010b).

During the 1970s, it appeared that that the air speed trajectory might be raised yet again by supersonic airplanes, but Concorde (cruising at 2,150 km/h, 2.4 times faster than wide-body jetliners) remained an expensive exception until it was finally abandoned in 2003 (Glancey 2016. By 2018 several companies (Spark Aerospace and Aerion Corporation for Airbus, Lockheed Martin, and Boom Technology in Colorado) were working on designs of new supersonic aircraft and although any expectations of an early large-scale commercial operation would be highly premature, another eventual doubling of (at least some) cruising speeds cannot be excluded later in the 21st century.

One of the best extensive illustrations of excessive logistic enthusiasm is a book on predictions whose subtitle—*Society's Telltale Signature Reveal the Past and Forecasts the Future*—indicates the author's belief in the predictive efficacy of logistic fits. Modis (1992) used logistic curves to forecast trajectories of many modern techniques (ranging from the share of cars with catalytic converters to the performance of jet engines) and assorted economic and social phenomena (ranging from the growth of oil and gas pipelines to passenger air traffic). One of the agreements between data and curve that he singled out was the growth of world air traffic: he predicted that by the late 1990s it will reach 90% of the estimated ceiling. In reality, by 2017 air freight was 80% higher than in the year 2000, and the number of passengers carried annually had more than doubled (World Bank 2018).

In addition, Modis presented a long table of predicted saturation levels taken from Grübler (1990). Less than 30 years later some of these forecasts have become spectacularly wrong. A notable example of these failures is the prediction of the worldwide total of cars: their count was to reach 90% of

Figure 1.15
The plane that raised a logistic growth ceiling of the cruising speed: Boeing 707.
Image from wikimedia.

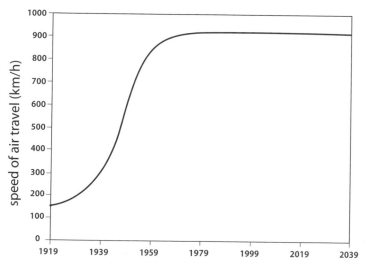

Figure 1.16
Logistic curve tracing the growth of cruising speed of commercial airliners 1919–
2039 (inflection point in 1945, asymptotic cruising speed of 930.8 km/h). Plotted
from data on speeds of specific airplanes, starting with KLM's de Havilland DH-16 in
1919 and ending with Boeing 787 in 2009.

the saturation level by 1988. At that time there were about 425 million car registrations, implying the eventual saturation at some 475 million cars— but one billion cars were registered by 2017, more than twice the supposed maximum, and their global count still keeps rising (Davis et al. 2018).

Marchetti (1985 and 1986b) brought the dictate of logistic growth "into one of the most defended strongholds of human ego, that of freedom, and in particular freedom in his creative acts" by concluding that "each of us has some sort of internal program regulating his output until death...and people die when they have exhausted 90–95% of their potential" (Marchetti 1986b, figure 42). After analyzing Mozart's cumulative output, he concluded that when the composer died at 35 "he had already said what he had to say" (Marchetti 1985, 4). Modis (1992) enthusiastically followed this belief but he carried it even further.

After fitting the cumulative number of Mozart's compositions into an S-curve, Modis (1992, 75–76) claimed not only that "Mozart was composing from the moment he was born, but his first eighteen compositions were never recorded due to the fact the he could neither write nor speak well enough to dictate them to his father." And he asserted, with accuracy on the order of 1%, that this logistic fit also indicates the total potential for 644 compositions and hence Mozart's creativity was 91% exhausted when he died and, echoing Marchetti, there was "very little left for Mozart to do. His work in this world has been practically accomplished."

I wonder what Bonneuil would have to say about these verdicts! I did my own fittings, using the enduring Köchel catalogue of 626 compositions listed between 1761 and 1791 (Giegling et al. 1964). When plotting the totals in five-year intervals, a symmetrical logistic curve with the inflection point in 1780 was the best fit ($R^2 = 0.995$): its saturation level was at 784 compositions and it predicted the total of 759 of them by 1806 when Mozart would have turned 50 (figure 1.17a). When I entered cumulative totals for every one of Mozart's productive years, I found that the best-fitting curve ($R^2 = 0.9982$) was an asymmetrical (five-parameter) sigmoid that predicted the total of 955 compositions by 1806 (figure 1.17b).

But quadratic regression (second order polynomial) is also a great fit for Mozart's three decades of productivity, as is quartic (fourth order polynomial) regression (both with R^2 of 0.99) and they would predict, respectively, just over 1,200 and more than 1,300 compositions completed by 1806 (figures 1.17c and 1.17d). The verdict is clear: various curves could be found to fit Mozart's composing trajectory, but none of them should be seen as revealing anything credible about the creativity of which Mozart was deprived by his early death (or, *pace* Modis, which he would have been

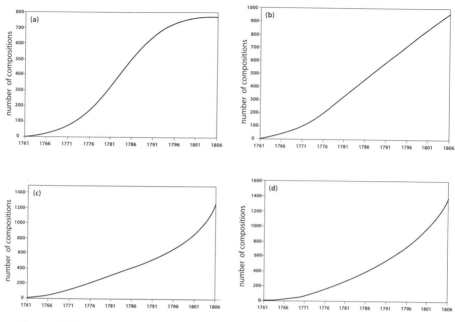

Figure 1.17

Fitting Mozart's oeuvre into growth curves: symmetrical (a) and asymmetrical (b) logistic functions and quadratic (c) and quartic (d) regression have all high degrees of fit ($R^2 = 0.99$) but predict substantially different long-term outcomes for the year 1806 when Mozart (who died in 1791) would have been 50 years old. Compositions by date listed in Giegling et al. (1964).

unable to realize even if he had lived much longer). Besides, all of this misses the most obvious point of such curve-fitting exercises based on cumulative numbers of creative acts (compositions, novels, or paintings): those analyzed numbers are mere quantities devoid of any qualitative content and they do not reveal anything about the course of a creative process or about the appeal and attractiveness of individual creations.

Marchetti has been also an enthusiastic user of logistic curves in forecasting technical developments in general and composition of global primary energy demand in particular. In his studies of energy transitions, he adopted a technique developed by Fisher and Pry (1971). Originally used to study the market penetration of new techniques, it assumes that the advances are essentially competitive substitutions which will proceed to completion (that is, to capturing most of the market or all of it) in such a way that the rate of fractional substitution is proportional to the remainder that is yet to be substituted.

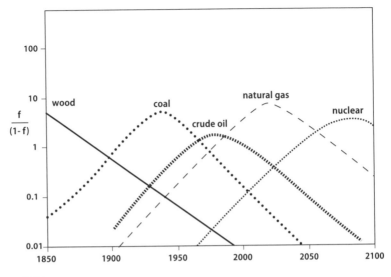

Figure 1.18
Marchetti's (1977) claim of predetermined shares of individual components of the world's primary energy supply: Fischer-Pry transforms show very regular substitutions.

Because their growth (market penetration rate) tends to follow a logistic curve, calculating the market fraction (f) of a new technique and expressing it as f/1–f produces a straight line when plotted on a semilogarithmic graph, and that makes it much easier to make medium- to long-range forecasts of technical advances than calculating their logistic functions. Fisher and Pry (1971) introduced this method to forecast the outcome of simple two-variable substitutions and applied it initially to competitions between synthetic and natural fibers, plastics and leather, open hearth furnaces and Bessemer converters, electric arc furnaces and open-hearth steelmaking, and water-based and oil-based paints (Fisher and Pry 1971).

When Marchetti began to apply Fisher-Pry transforms to historic shares of global primary energy supply (starting in 1850) he was impressed by "the extraordinary precision" of straight-line fit and that gave him the confidence to extend his forecasts all the way to 2100 (figure 1.18). His conclusion was absolutely solid:

> the whole destiny of an energy source seems to be completely predetermined in the first childhood … these trends … go unscathed through wars, wild oscillations in energy prices and depression. Final total availability of the primary reserves also seems to have no effect on the rate of substitution. (Marchetti 1977, 348)

Two years later he reiterated the perfection of historic fits and concluded that "it is as though *the system had a schedule, a will, and a clock*" and that it is capable of reabsorbing all perturbations "elastically without influencing the trend" (Marchetti and Nakicenovic 1979, 15). Marchetti's extreme techno-determinism had an unerring "system" in charge—except it was not. Even in the late 1970s, the proposed pattern did not appear as smooth as claimed, and during the 1970s powerful forces (changing prices and demand, new techniques) began to transform the global energy setup. Four decades later, the global energy system is far off its supposedly "completely predetermined" schedule (figure 1.19).

Clinging to a simplistic, mechanistic, deterministic model missed all key post-1980 realities: shares of coal and oil consumption have remained surprisingly flat rather than falling steadily, largely a result of vigorous demand for steam coal and transportation fuels in Asia in general and in China in particular. As a result, by 2015 the global share of crude oil was 30%, well above Marchetti's prediction of 25%, while coal, whose share was to sink to just 5%, still supplied nearly as much energy (about 29%) as oil. In contrast, natural gas, which was to be a new leading fuel with 60% share, delivered only about 24% of the world's primary energy in 2015. Moreover, Marchetti's (1977) clockwork transition forecast a complete disappearance of traditional biofuels (wood, charcoal, crop residues, and dried animal dung)

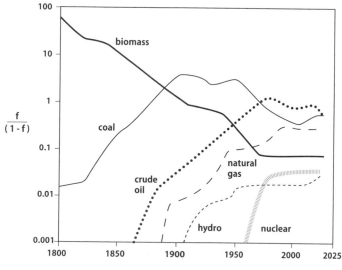

Figure 1.19
Actual trajectories of primary energy shares show that this has not been a system with an immutable "*schedule, a will, and a clock.*" Shares plotted from data in Smil (2017b).

before the year 2000—but by 2015 more than 2.5 billion people used them daily for cooking and heating; in absolute terms, the annual demand for these fuels is nearly twice as large as a century ago; and in 2015 they supplied at least 8% of all primary energy (Smil 2017a).

Curiously, Marchetti's original analysis of primary energy shares excluded hydroelectricity: in 2015 it delivered 55% more electricity than nuclear fission. But he included a rapid ascent of a new "solar/fusion" category whose contribution was to surpass coal's share around 2020—but in 2019 there is no commercially generated fusion electricity (indeed no fusion electricity and no prospects for any early breakthrough), while in 2018 solar photovoltaics produced an equivalent of less than 0.5% of the world's primary energy supply. Obviously, the unerring internal clock has failed and all of Marchetti's supposedly immutable growth trajectories departed substantially from their predetermined schedules.

The only correct conclusion of Marchetti's analysis is that global energy substitutions unfold slowly, but his specific timing—about 100 years to go from 1% to 50% of the market, what he called time constant of the system—has been an exception rather than a rule. Only coal has done that, going from 1% just before 1800 to 50% a century later—while crude oil's global share has never reached 50%. By 2015, more than a century after it surpassed 1% of global energy supply, natural gas was still just short of 25%, while wind- and solar-generated electricity have reached, after two decades of subsidized development, just 2% of global primary energy consumption by 2016. These lessons of failed forecasts should be kept in mind whenever I use logistic fits to indicate (not to forecast!) possible future developments: some may foretell specific levels fairly well, while others may turn out to be only rough indicators, and others yet may fail as unexpected superior solutions emerge.

But which ones will surpass our expectations? Since 1900, the maximum battery energy densities rose from 25 Wh/kg for lead-acid units to about 300 Wh/kg for the best lithium-ion designs in 2018, a 12-fold gain that fits a logistic curve predicting about 500 Wh/kg by 2050 (figure 1.20). We must hope that new discoveries will vault us onto a new logistic trajectory as even 500 Wh/kg is not enough for battery-powered machines to displace all liquid derived from crude oil: the diesel fuel used to power heavy machines, trains, and ships has energy density of 13,750 Wh/kg. In contrast, another (fairly mature) logistic curve has a much higher probability to provide useful guidance: the stock of US passenger vehicles—after growing from just 8,000 to 134 million during the 20th century and to 189 million by 2015—will most likely grow by no more than about 25% by 2050.

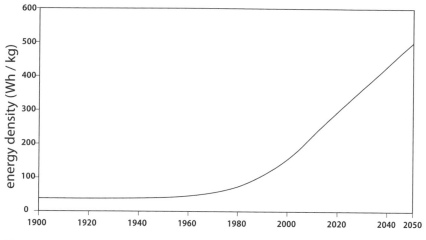

Figure 1.20
Logistic growth trajectory (inflection point in 2024, asymptote at 625.5 Wh/kg) of battery energy densities, 1900–2017. Plotted from data in Zu and Li (2011) and from subsequent news reports.

Confined Exponential Growth

Many growth phenomena do not follow S-shaped trajectories and belong to the other major class of finite growth patterns, confined exponential distributions. Unlike exponential growth, with its doubling time, these curves trace exponential decay, with its declining growth rates. Their maximum slope and curvature occur right at the beginning and hence they have no inflection point, and their concave shapes become more prominent with higher growth rates (figure 1.21). Such trajectories illustrate many phenomena of diminishing returns and are encountered with processes ranging from heat and mass transfer to tracing yield response to crop fertilization. The confined exponential function often used in these fertilizer application/crop response studies is also known as Mitscherlich equation (Banks 1994).

Confined exponential functions also capture well many diffusion processes, be it public interest in a news item, or adoption of technical innovations, often called technology transfer (Rogers 2003; Rivera and Rogers 2006; Flichy 2007). Comin and Hobijn (2004) concluded—after examining all major classes of technical innovations (including textiles, steelmaking, communications, information, transportation, and electricity) from the closing decades of the 18th century to the beginning of the 21st century—that a robust pattern of trickle-down diffusion dominates. Innovations originate

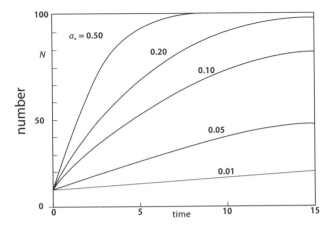

Figure 1.21
Examples of confined exponential growth curves (based on Banks 1994).

mostly in advanced economies and then get adopted elsewhere, with the quality of human capital, type of government, openness to trade, and adoption of predecessor innovations being the key factors that determine the rate of trickling down.

The spread of a technical innovation (adoption of new manufacturing processes or new prime movers), rising ownership of a new consumer product (share of families owning a microwave oven or air conditioning), or a displacement of an old product by a better version (color TV driving out black-and-white TV) are examples of diffusion processes that commonly follow a sigmoid function. But there are also instances of an immediate rapid takeoff followed by gradual slowdown, with the complete trajectory resembling a bow segment. This kind of confined exponential trajectory in innovation diffusion is also known as the Coleman model, and Sharif and Ramanathan (1981 and 1982) offered a comprehensive evaluation of binomial and polynomial innovation diffusion models.

The model applies to all situations where the population of potential adaptors (companies, customers) is both limited and constant, where all of them eventually adopt (there are no intercontinental flights powered by piston engines; there are no vacuum electronic computers) and where the diffusion proceeds independently of the number of adopters. Binomial models of confined exponential growth—limited to two variables representing the population that has already adopted an innovation and the potential adopters—have captured well such phenomena as the adoption of the fluoridation of the US water supply or the diffusion of credit card banking (Evans 2004).

Given the variety of growth processes, it is not surprising that even the two large categories of growth trajectories—S-shaped functions and confined exponential growth function—cannot subsume all variations of real-world growth. Ultimately, growth trajectories must be governed by first principles expressed through biochemical reactions, material limits, entropy change, and information decay, but actual nonlinear progressions will show irregularities and deviations from specific growth functions. As a result, some growth processes are best captured by a combination of growth functions: for example, California's post-1860 population growth followed an exponential path for 100 years until 1960 and then entered a confined exponential stage (Banks 1994). Brody (1945) found this combination useful for capturing the growth of livestock.

And the evolution of technical advances offers examples of very slow linear growth suddenly accelerating into an exponential expansion followed by confined exponential growth. And technical and economic advances get interrupted by extended performance plateaus caused by such external interventions as economic downturns or armed conflicts. Consequently, too much effort could be spent on fitting assorted growth phenomena into chosen growth models, or on seeking the "best" function for a particular growth trajectory. Doing that may have both heuristic and economic rewards—for example, a highly accurate model of body mass of an aqua-cultured fish species would help to optimize the consumption of relatively expensive protein feed—but this quest has been repeatedly subverted by moving the ultimate bar, that is by changing the maximum value whose level determines the trajectories of all S-shaped functions.

Staying with an aquacultural example, the growth rate of farmed salmon (produced since the late 1960s in offshore pens, now in Europe, North and South America and in New Zealand) has been doubled with the approval of AquaBounty genetically engineered fish (all sterile females) for human consumption in 2015 (AquaBounty 2017). A growth-promoting gene from Chinook salmon put into fertilized Atlantic salmon eggs makes them grow like a trout would, reaching the market weight of 2–3 kg in 18–24 months rather than in three years. The transferred gene also allows the fish to be grown in warmer waters and in complete containment.

Examples of such fundamental innovation-induced shifts in the asymptote abound, and I will cite just one more here, with many others to come in the topical chapters of this book. Waterwheels were the first inanimate

prime movers to provide stationary power for tasks ranging from grain milling and water pumping and from powering blast furnace bellows to forging
iron. For nearly two millennia they were wooden, and even by the early
18th century their average capacities were less than 4 kW, with only a few
machines approaching 10 kW. At that point, the trajectory of waterwheel
growth would have indicated future maxima of less than 100 kW—but by
1854, Lady Isabella, England's largest iron overshot wheel, reached a capacity of 427 kW (Reynolds 1970). Meanwhile, water turbines, derived from
horizontal water wheels, began to make their inroads. In 1832 Benoît Fourneyron installed his first low-head (2.4 m) small capacity (38 kW) reaction
turbine to power forge hammers in Fraisans, but just five years later he built
two 45 kW machines with water falling more than 100 m (Smith 1980).

Other turbine designs (by James B. Francis and Lester A. Pelton) followed
during the second half of the 19th century, and Viktor Kaplan patented his
axial flow machine in 1920. Turbines took over from waterwheels as the
prime movers in many industries but, above all, they enabled inexpensive
conversion of falling water into electricity, with capacities above 1 MW
by 1900, and by the 1930s, when America's largest hydro stations were
built on the Columbia and Colorado Rivers, turbine capacities surpassed
100 MW. The first technical innovation, moving from wood to iron, raised
the maximum power about fourfold, the second one (moving from wheels
to turbines) lifted that value by an order of magnitude, and since the early
20th century it has grown by two orders of magnitude as the largest water
turbines now rate 1,000 MW.

Collective Outcomes of Growth

A perceptive observer of organisms, artifacts, and achievements (be they
record running speeds or average incomes) is aware that collective outcomes
of their growth do not fit into a single category that could be characterized
(whether almost perfectly or with satisfactory approximation) by an all-
embracing mathematical function: growth of children and adolescents does
not end up with the same distribution as does the growth of towns and cities.
But many measured attributes do fall into two basic categories as they form
either a normal distribution or as they extend over a range of values conforming (more or less closely) to one of many specific power laws. The first
common category of growth outcomes includes species, objects, or properties whose distribution is dominated by a single quantity around which all
individual measurements are centered and this clustering produces a typical
value, and large deviations from this mean are relatively rare.

Normal and Lognormal Distributions

Normal distribution means that a plot of a large number (or of a complete set) of naturally occurring frequencies forms a symmetrical curve characterized by a continuous function approximating the binomial distribution of events (Bryc 1995; Gross 2004). The plot is often described as a bell-shaped curve. The second most common name besides normal is the Gaussian distribution, named after Carl Friedrich Gauss, although Gauss was not the first mathematician to identify its existence (figure 1.22). His first published work on that topic came more than three decades after Pierre-Simon Laplace published his *Mémoire sur la probabilité* which contains normal curve function (Gauss 1809; Laplace 1774). Laplace's distribution should have been a more accurate attribution—until Pearson (1924) discovered that the work of de Moivre antedates that of Laplace (figure 1.22).

In 1730 Abraham de Moivre published his *Miscellanea Analytica* and three years later attached a short supplement entitled *Approximatio ad Summam Terminorum Binomii (a+b)^n in Seriem expansi* which contains the first known treatment of what we now know as the normal curve and was included in the second edition of his *Doctrine of Chances* (de Moivre 1738). In his book on the theory of probabilities, Adolphe Quetelet, whose pioneering contributions to practical applications of the logistic curve were described earlier in this chapter, applied the distribution to two large-scale data sets, to his measurements of chest circumferences of 1,000 Scottish soldiers and to heights of 100,000 French conscripts (Quetelet 1846).

The distribution is continuous and symmetrical, its mean coincides with mode (the most frequent occurrence), and its shape is determined by its mean and standard deviation. The distribution subsumes 68.3% of the set

Figure 1.22
Carl Friedrich Gauss, Pierre-Simon Laplace, and Abraham de Moivre. Portraits from the author's collection.

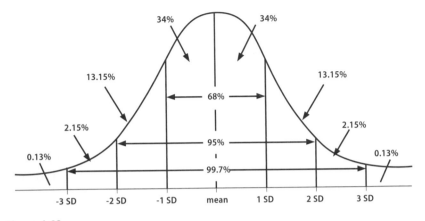

Figure 1.23
Characteristics of the normal distribution curve.

within one standard deviation of the mean, and 95.4% within two standard deviations (figure 1.23). Not surprisingly, the rare outliers at either end of the distribution spectrum (and particularly the right tails) have often received a disproportionate amount of attention. Virtually every outcome of organic growth—no matter if it concerns individual organs (height of sequoia trees, spans of butterfly wings, circumferences of newborn heads), entire organisms (their length and mass), or specific functional attributes (diffusion of viral infections, mammalian lung capacities)—is normally distributed.

From our daily interaction with people, it is easy to conclude that normal distribution applies to their height (most adults measure between 155 and 185 cm, adults smaller than 130 cm are very rare, as are those taller than 210 cm), and a brief consideration indicates that the same must be true also about virtually every functional attribute of our existence, be it resting adult heart rates (average of 70 beats per minute) or durations of pregnancies: not many people (except for endurance athletes) have fewer than 40 beats, and fewer than 5% of all births take place before the 36th or after the 42nd week of pregnancy.

This ubiquity has made the normal distribution the standard (and correct) choice for assuming its validity in the cases of organic growth that have not been quantified in detail (a good sample will suffice to deduce the most likely complete distribution) and for finding answers to probability questions. Once we know the mean and the standard deviation, answering such questions as what is the likelihood of a Pacific bluefin tuna weighing more than 600 kg (and thus commanding a record price in Japan) is fairly easy. But the distribution's common occurrence in nature has also led many to assume, falsely, that its fit is more universal than is justified by unruly realities.

Instances once thought to fit the normal pattern turned out to be better expressed by other distributions, and the long-standing explanation of normal distribution, invoking the central limit theorem (the sum of a numerous independent random variable tends to be normally distributed regardless of its underlying distribution) is not always (even approximately) satisfactory, while an alternative explanation, relying on the maximum entropy property, has its own problems (Lyon 2014). These caveats do not invalidate the commonality of normal distribution; they merely alert us to the fact that many distributions are more complicated than is suggested by sample averages.

After Quetelet, the normal distribution and the arithmetic mean became the norm for statistical analyses of many phenomena, but this changed once Galton (1876) and McAlister (1879) called attention to the importance of the geometric mean in vital and social statistics. Galton (1879, 367) pointed out the absurdity of applying the arithmetic mean (normal distribution) to wide deviations (as excess must be balanced by deficiency of an equal magnitude) and illustrated the point with reference to height: "the law is very correct in respect to ordinary measurements, although it asserts that the existence of giants, whose height is more than double the mean height of their race, implies the possibility of the existence of dwarfs, whose stature is less than nothing at all."

Skewed (nonnormal) distributions in nature are a common outcome of specific growth and interspecific competition. When the number of species in a community is plotted on a vertical axis and their abundance (numbers of individuals belonging to those species) are on a horizontal axis, the resulting asymmetric "hollow" curve has a long right tail—but the distribution will conform fairly closely to a normal curve when the horizontal values are expressed in decadic logarithms. Properties of this lognormal distribution have been well known since the mid-19th century: skewed to the left and characterized by its mean (or median) and a standard deviation (Limpert 2001). Lognormal distribution means that most species constituting a community will be present in moderate numbers, a few will be very rare and a few will be encountered in very high numbers.

Earlier studies of species abundance distribution (SAD) in ecosystems have identified lognormal abundance among 150 species of diatoms, hundreds of species of moths in England, Maine and Saskatchewan, and scores of species of fish and birds (Preston 1948; May 1981; Magurran 1988). Other interesting findings of lognormal SAD arising from the growth of organisms have included instances as dissimilar as airborne contamination by bacteria and fungi (Di Giorgio et al. 1996), abundance distribution of woody species in a fragment of *cerrado* forest in southeastern Brazil (Oliveira and Batalha 2005), and the length of terminal twigs on self-similar branches of Japanese elm trees (Koyama et al. 2017).

But lognormal SAD is not the norm in nature. Williamson and Gaston (2005) looked at three different distributions: the abundance of British breeding birds, the number of trees with breast-height diameter larger than 1 cm in a Panamanian forest plot, and the abundance of butterflies trapped at Jatun Sacha, Ecuador. The first two sets were complete enumerations and they showed left skew when the abundance was transformed to logarithms, while the third, incomplete, count showed right skew. They concluded that the lognormal distribution is placed uncomfortably between distributions with infinite variance and the log-binomial one, that a satisfactory species abundance distribution should have a thinner right-end tail than does the lognormal pattern, and that SAD for logarithmic abundance cannot be Gaussian.

Šizling et al. (2009) showed that lognormal-like species-abundance distributions (including the power-fraction model) cannot be universally valid because they apply only to particular scales and taxa, and the global species/range size distributions (measured in km^2) for raptors and owls are extremely right-skewed on untransformed axes, which means that when transformed they are not lognormally distributed (Gaston et al. 2005). Ulrich et al. (2010) found that completely censused terrestrial or freshwater animal communities tend to follow lognormal species abundance distributions more often than log-series or power-law types (and do so irrespective of species richness, spatial scale), but they also failed to identify a specific shape that should apply to a certain type of community and hence they strongly supported a pluralistic way of dealing with species abundances.

Baldridge et al. (2016) used rigorous statistical methods to compare different models of SAD and they found that in most cases several of the most popular choices (log-series, negative binomial, Poisson lognormal) provided roughly equivalent fits. By far the most comprehensive examination of lognormal distributions in ecosystems is by Antão et al. (2017), who analyzed 117 empirical data sets, all from intensely sampled communities, for plants, invertebrates, fish, and birds in marine, aquatic, and terrestrial habitats. They found excellent or good lognormal fits for many sets of fish, birds, and plants, but a significant share of species/abundance

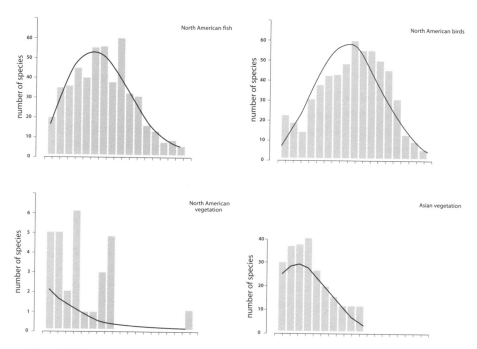

Figure 1.24

Lognormal species abundance distributions (x axes in log2 classes) of North American fish and birds and less regular distributions of North American and Asian vegetation. Simplified from Antão et al. (2017).

distributions (on the order of 20%, and including both vegetation and vertebrates) can also exhibit multiple modes. This multimodality appears to increase with ecosystemic heterogeneity, that is when the examined sets include a broader spatial scale and greater taxonomic range (figure 1.24).

Another commonly examined case of a lognormal distribution has become known as Gibrat's law (or Gibrat's rule of proportional growth), named after Robert Gibrat, a French engineer who realized that the proportional growth rate of companies within an industry is independent of their absolute size (Gibrat 1931). This produces a lognormal distribution—but an overview of about 60 published analyses (Santarelli et al. 2006) found that it is impossible either to confirm the general validity of the law or to reject it systematically. The rule appears to apply only in relation to certain sectors (particularly in the services) and to the largest size classes. This heterogeneous outcome across industries and size classes precludes seeing it, despite frequent references in economic literature, as a strictly valid law. But Eeckhout (2004) concluded that the size distribution for all US cities (based on the 2000 census) is lognormal rather than fitting the most commonly assumed power-law (Zipf) model (for more on this, see the growth of cities in chapter 5).

Asymmetrical Distributions

Asymmetrical distributions are commonly encountered when analyzing many natural and anthropogenic phenomena. Many of them are applicable to outcomes that have not been created by any gradual growth processes but rather by sudden, violent releases of energy. They include the intensity of solar flares, the size of lunar craters, the magnitude of earthquakes and volcanic eruptions, and the size of forest fires. But they also apply to the magnitude of terrorist attacks, to sudden and economically crippling losses (intensity of electricity outages), as well as to the constant flow of both numerical and verbal information, including frequencies of nine digits in assemblages of numbers ranging from logarithmic tables to newspapers and cost data, and word and surname frequencies in most languages (Clauset et al. 2009).

These, often highly asymmetrical, distributions vary over wide ranges, commonly spanning many orders of magnitude. They are a common outcome of inanimate growth processes, be it the height of mountains produced by tectonic uplift and subsequent erosion or the size of islands produced by plate tectonics, erosion, coral accretion and deposition processes. There is only one Qomolangma (Mount Everest) at 8,848 m (figure 1.25), just four mountains between 8.2 and 8.6 km, 103 mountains between 7.2 and 8.2 km, and about 500 mountains higher than 3.5 km (Scaruffi 2008). Similarly, there is only one Greenland (about 2.1 million km^2) and just three other islands larger than 500,000 km^2, more than 300 islands larger than 1,000 km^2, thousands of protuberances smaller than 100 km^2, and so on.

But highly asymmetric distribution is also a common outcome among anthropogenic growth processes. Towns have grown into cities and many cities have evolved into large metropolitan areas or conurbations in every country on every inhabited continent—but in 2018, there was only one Tokyo metro area with nearly 40 million inhabitants (figure 1.25), 31 cities had more than 10 million people, more than 500 cities had surpassed 1 million, and thousands of cities were larger than 500,000 (UN 2014 and 2016). On linear scales, plots of such distributions produce curves that are best characterized either by exponential functions or by a power-law function.

A perfect power-law function (approximating the form $f(x)=ax^{-k}$ where a and k are constant) produces a nearly L-shaped curve on a linear plot, and when both axes are converted to decadic logarithms, it produces a straight line. Obviously, neither exponential nor power-law functions can be well characterized by their modal or average values; in the real world

Figure 1.25
Peaks of two asymmetric distributions, one natural and one anthropogenic: there is only one Qomolangma and one Tokyo. Qomolangma image is available at wikimedia and Tokyo's satellite image is from NASA's Earth Observatory collection.

there are many deviations from the straight line, and the linear fit may not be always sufficient to identify true power-law behavior. Between 1881 and 1949 these asymmetric distributions were repeatedly and independently identified by observers in both natural and social sciences, and a number of these empirical observations earned their authors fame as they became known as eponymous laws.

But that was not so in the case of Simon Newcomb, an English mathematician and astronomer, who was the first to describe the first digit problem, chronologically the first suggestion of a widely applicable power law (Raimi 1976). Newcomb noticed that the first pages of frequently used logarithmic tables wear out much faster than the last ones and that "the first significant figure is oftener 1 than any other digit, and the frequency diminishes up to 9" (Newcomb 1881, 39). Only in 1938 did Frank Benford, an American physicist working for General Electric (GE), provide the quantitative backup for the (now eponymous) law of anomalous numbers by analyzing the percentage of times the natural numbers one to nine are used as first digits in numbers compiled from more than 20,000 observations of various physical and social phenomena (Benford 1938). The first digit came up 30.6% of the time, the second one 18.5%, and the last one just 4.7% (figure 1.26).

What has become perhaps the most famous power-law distribution (thanks to the influence of economics in public affairs) was described by

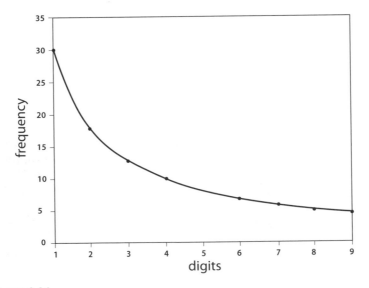

Figure 1.26
Benford's frequency distribution. Plotted from data in Benford (1938).

Vilfredo Pareto, an Italian economist (Pareto 1896). He noted that much like 20% of pea pods in his garden yielded 80% of all harvested peas, just 20% of rich Italians owned 80% of all land, and this principle turned out to be applicable to many natural, economic, and social phenomena. The second most cited power law was formulated by George Kingsley Zipf, an American linguist, and it is based on his observations of rank-frequency of words in natural languages (Zipf 1935).

He posited that the frequency of each word (Pn) is almost inversely proportional (exponent a being close to 1) to its rank in the frequency table: $Pn \propto 1/n^a$, which means that the most frequent word (*the* in English, accounting for about 7% of all occurrences) is used about twice as frequently as the second most common word (*of* in English, about 3.5% of all words), and so on. This relationship holds for up to about 1,000 words but breaks down for less frequently used words. As with so many intellectual and material discoveries, the observation of the regular rank-size rule was not Zipf's original idea (Petruszewycz 1973). Felix Auerbach, a German physicist, first called the attention to the phenomenon in his paper on the law of population concentration (Auerbach 1913), and three years later a French stenographer Jean-Baptiste Estoup published his frequency of French words with, predictably, *le*, *la*, *les* in the lead and, less predictably, *en* in 10th place (Estoup 1916).

By far the most enduring application of Zipf's law has been to study the ranking of cities by their population size: for any historical period, these distributions are approximated as a simple inverse power relationship where $x = r^{-1}$ (where x is city size and r is city rank) (Zipf 1949), and they are easily observed by plotting national or global data (figure 1.27). Zipf's law and the Pareto distribution are two kindred t generalizations of reality, one ranking the variables, the other one looking at the frequency distribution. As Adamic (2000, 3) put it,

> The phrase "The *r*th largest city has *n* inhabitants" is equivalent to saying "*r* cities have *n* or more inhabitants." This is exactly the definition of the Pareto distribution, except the x and y axes are flipped. Whereas for Zipf, *r* is on the x-axis and *n* is on the y-axis, for Pareto, *r* is on the y-axis and *n* is on the x-axis. Simply inverting the axes, we get that if the rank exponent is *b*, i.e. $n \sim r^{-b}$ in Zipf, (n=income, r=rank of person with income n) then the Pareto exponent is $1/b$ so that $r \sim n^{-1/b}$ (n=income, r=number of people whose income is *n* or higher).

Much like the Pareto distribution, Zipf's inverse law is applicable to rank-size distribution of many other phenomena besides word frequencies and city hierarchies, and since the 1950s it has been used to study

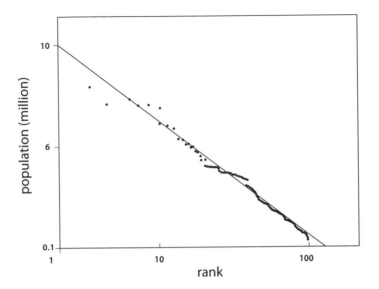

Figure 1.27 Ranking of the 100 largest US metropolitan districts based on 1940 census (Zipf 1949).

many social, economic, and physical phenomena ranging from company sizes (on national or global scales) to the characteristics of Internet traffic (Saichev et al. 2010; Pinto et al. 2012). Other inverse power laws are relatively less known in general, although they are much referred to within specific disciplines. In 1925 Udny Yule, based on the conclusions of J. C. Willis, presented almost perfect power-law frequency distribution of sizes of genera for a large family of plants (*Leguminosae*) and for two families of beetles, *Cerambycidae* and *Chrysomelidae* (Yule 1925b). In 1926 Alfred Lotka identified the inverse distribution in the frequency of scientific publications in a specific field (Lotka 1926).

In 1932 Max Kleiber, a Swiss biologist working in California, published his pioneering work on animal metabolism that challenged the nearly 50-year-old Rubner's surface law that expected animal metabolism to be proportional to two thirds of body mass (Rubner 1883; Kleiber 1932). Kleiber's law—simply stating that an animal's metabolic rate scales to the ¾ power of its mass and illustrated by the straight mouse-to-elephant line— has been one of the most important generalizations in bioenergetics. But Kleiber derived his exponent from only 13 data points (including two steers, a cow, and a sheep) and later extensive examinations have uncovered many significant departures from the ¾ power (for more, see the section on animals in chapter 2).

Jaromír Korčák called attention to the duality of statistical distribution, with the outcome of organic growth organized in normal fashion, while the distribution of the planet's physical characteristics—area and depth of lakes, size of islands, area of watersheds, length of rivers—follows inverse power law with distributions highly skewed leftward (Korčák 1938 and 1941). Korčák's law was later made better known, via Fréchet (1941), by Benoit Mandelbrot in his pioneering work on fractals (Mandelbrot 1967, 1975, 1977, 1982). But a recent reexamination of Korčák's law concluded that his ranked properties cannot be described with a single power-law exponent and hence the law is not strictly valid even for sets consisting of strictly similar fractal objects presented in his original publications (Imre and Novotný 2016).

The Gutenberg-Richter law—the second author's name is well known due to his classification system of earthquake magnitudes (Richter 1935)—relates the total number of earthquakes, N, to their magnitude, M (Gutenberg and Richter 1942). Ishimoto and Iida (1939) were the first authors to note this relationship. In the equation $N = 10^{a-bM}$ a indicates the activity rate (how many earthquakes of a given magnitude in a year) and b is usually close to 1 for interplate events but it is higher along oceanic ridges and lower for intra-plate earthquakes. Quincy Wright (1942) and Lewis F. Richardson (1948) used power law to explain the variation of the frequency of fatal conflicts with their magnitude.

And Benoit Mandelbrot's pioneering studies of self-similarity and fractal structures further expanded the applications of power laws: after all, the "probability distribution of a self-similar random variable X must be of the form $Pr(X>x) = x^{-D}$, which is commonly called *hyperbolic* or *Pareto* distribution" (Mandelbrot 1977, 320). Mandelbrot's D, fractal dimension, has many properties of a "dimension" but it is fractional (Mandelbrot 1967). Mandelbrot (1977) had introduced a more general power law—nearly the most general, as Gell-Mann put it—by modifying the inverse sequence, by adding a constant to the rank, and by allowing squares, cubes, square roots or any other powers of fractions (Gell-Mann 1994). Zipf's law is then just a special case with those two constants at zero. Fractal dimension equals 1 for smooth Euclidian shapes, between 1 and 2 for two-dimensional shapes—seacoast length has D of 1.25 (Mandelbrot 1967)—and as much as 2.9 (of possible 3) for such complex three-dimensional networks as human lungs (Turner et al. 1998).

Distributions of those collective outcomes where growth conforms to an inverse relationship have the negative exponent (constant scaling parameter) often close to one or ranging between one and three. Although power-law distributions appear to come up frequently in the studies of physical and social phenomena, it requires the deployment of standard statistical techniques to ascertain that an observed quantity does conform to a power-law distribution and that such a fit does not result merely from wishful thinking. Chen (2015) pointed out that while the inverse power function suggests a complex distribution and the negative exponential function indicates a simple distribution, a special type of the former function can be created through averaging of the latter.

And, almost always, linear fits on log-log scales do not persist across the entire range that is often spanning many orders of magnitude, but display noticeable curvatures. These heavy-tailed distributions are not exponentially bounded, and much more commonly they have a heavy right tail rather than left tail, but both tails may be heavy. Heavy-tailed scaling is obvious in the distribution of common natural events (including earthquake magnitudes, solar flux intensities, and size of wildfires), as well as information flows (distribution of computer file sizes, Web hits) and major socioeconomic phenomena resulting from population and economic growth, including the distribution of urban population and accumulated wealth (Clauset et al. 2009; Marković and Gros 2014; figure 1.28).

Jang and Jang (2012) studied the applicability of Korčák-type distribution for the size of French Polynesian islands. They found that above a certain value of island area in each sampling interval (scale), the double-log plot followed a straight line, but that it remained essentially constant below it: numbers of small islands do not vary with size. And power-law distributions are not the only ones with heavy tails: lognormal distribution and Weibull and Lévy distributions are also one-tailed, while the more complex Cauchy distribution is two-tailed. Consequently, when the sample size is limited and the data show large variance, it may be difficult to differentiate among these functions. Moreover, Laherrère and Sornette (1998) argued that a stretched exponential function (with an exponent smaller than one) provides a better fit in many commonly encountered probability distributions in nature and society and demonstrated the claim with data for French and American urban agglomerations. Tails of stretched exponential distributions are fatter than the exponential fit but much less fat than a pure power-law distribution.

Clauset et al. (2009) tested a large number of data sets describing real-world phenomena and claimed to follow power laws (figure 1.28). Their sets came from physics, earth and life sciences, computing and information sciences, engineering, and economics, with growth-related items including the numbers of distinct interaction partners in the metabolic network

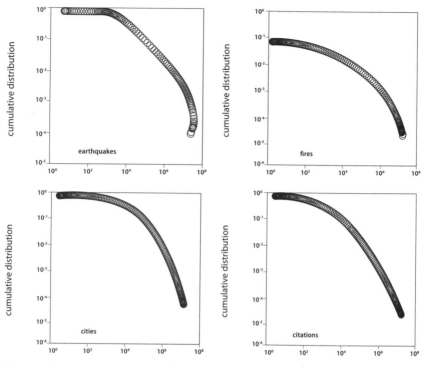

Figure 1.28
Heavy-tailed lognormal distributions of earthquake magnitudes, sizes of forest fires, cities, and the citations of academic papers. Simplified from Clauset et al. (2009).

of *Escherichia coli*, number of species per genus of mammals, and populations of US cities in the 2000 census. Their rigorous tests found that 17 of 24 data sets were consistent with power-law distribution—but, remarkably, they also concluded that the lognormal distribution could not be ruled out for any sets save one, because "it is extremely difficult to tell the difference between log-normal and power-law behavior. Indeed over realistic ranges of x the two distributions are very closely equal, so it appears unlikely that any test would be able to tell them apart unless we have an extremely large data set" (Clauset et al. 2009, 689).

Mitzenmacher (2004) came to the same conclusion as far as lognormal and power-law distributions are concerned, and Lima-Mendez and van Helden (2009) showed how an apparent power law can disappear when data are subjected to more rigorous testing. Most instances of power-law distributions do not even have strong statistical support, and any purely empirical fitting—while interesting, perhaps even remarkable—does not justify unsubstantiated suggestions of universality. Allometric scaling of metabolism is a rare exception as it finds strong statistical support across many orders of magnitude, from bacteria to whales (for details see chapter 2). And even if the law passes statistical muster, it commonly lacks a convincing generative mechanism. Long before the recent interest in complex systems and power-law scaling, Carroll (1982) listed five different classes of models that could explain city rank-size (Zipf) distributions but many of them had directly contradicted each other.

Similarly, Phillips (1999) listed 11 separate concepts to explain self-organization principles applied in earth and environmental sciences. Invariant behavior of many physical phenomena and their power-law distributions have been explained by various optimization schemes, cooperative effects, preferential attachment (most famously, rich get richer), self-similarity and fractal geometry, organized criticality, and by nonlinear dynamic behavior including multiplicative cascades (Mandelbrot 1982; Bak 1996; Pietronero et al. 2001; Yakovenko and Rosser 2009). But skepticism is in place, and on a closer examination power law does not appear to be either as ubiquitous or as fundamental as has been suggested by those who prefer to explain complex realities with simple models. Stumpf and Porter (2012, 665) considered the wide range of power-law occurrences and concluded that "the mechanistic insights are almost always too limited for the identification of power-law behavior to be scientifically useful."

But even if the statistics are convincing and even if there is empirical support for a theory explaining the generative process, "a critical question remains: What genuinely new insights have been gained by having found a robust, mechanically supported, and in-all-other-ways super power law? We believe that such insights are very rare" (Stumpf and Porter 2012, 666). Rather than demonstrating the existence of a universal principle, power laws illustrate that equifinality is common in complex open systems, as many different processes can lead to identical or very similar outcomes and hence these outcomes cannot be used to infer clear-cut causes (von Bertalanffy 1968).

What does this all mean for evaluating and understanding the distribution of many growth outcomes? Few things are incontestable: applications of power laws share the same fundamental relationship with one quantity varying as a power of another, the change being scale invariant and the direction positive or negative. Perhaps the most commonly applicable example in the first category was one of the fundamental breakthroughs in bioenergy, the discovery of metabolic scaling in animals (Kleiber 1932):

their basal metabolic rate varies approximately with ¾ power of body mass, no matter if the animal is a small rodent or a large ungulate. Understanding this law is, of course, very helpful for proper feeding of growing domestic animals, but as I will note in chapter 2, there are many notable departures from this general rule as well as lack of agreement about the energetic and physical imperatives that make it (albeit in far from perfects forms) so common.

This concludes my introduction into basic patterns and outcomes of growth and I will now turn to systematic, topical coverage of growth, starting with the smallest living organisms (unicellular microbes) and proceeding to plants (concentrating on trees and forests and on agricultural crops), animals (looking at both wild and domesticated species), and people (quantifying growth of their height and mass). Chapter 3 will deal with the growth of energy conversions; without them there would be no food production, no urbanization, no complex societies, economies, and civilizations, and I will also trace the growth of all-important prime movers, from the simplest waterwheels to extraordinarily complex turbines.

Then will come chapter 4 on the growth of artifacts, the world created by human ingenuity as simple inventions evolved into reliable, high-performance tools, machines, and machine assemblies whose growing reliabilities and capabilities improved our quality of life. Finally, I will turn to the growth of the most complex systems, population, societies, economies, empires and civilizations. They have been forming a new global superorganism whose continuation appears to be threatened not only by ancient enmities and by the human propensity for violence, but also by new anthropogenic phenomena of environmental degradation with its many environmental, economic, and social consequences. The book's sixth chapter will offer many facts to answer a fascinating question about what comes after growth, as well as musings, and more questions, concerning some fundamental uncertainties about the growth of modern civilization.

2 Nature: or growth of living matter

Perhaps the most remarkable attribute of natural growth is how much diversity is contained within the inevitable commonality dictated by fundamental genetic makeup, metabolic processes, and limits imposed by combinations of environmental factors. Trajectories of all organismic growth must assume the form of a confined curve. As already noted, many substantial variations within this broad category have led to the formulation of different growth functions devised in order to find the closest possible fits for specific families, genera or species of microbes, plants or animals or for individual species. S-shaped curves are common, but so are those conforming to confined exponential growth, and there are (both expected and surprising) differences between the growth of individuals (and their constituent parts, from cells to organs) and the growth of entire populations.

Decades-long neglect of Verhulst's pioneering growth studies postponed quantitative analyses of organismic growth until the early 20th century. Most notably, in his revolutionary book Darwin did not deal with growth in any systematic manner and did not present any growth histories of specific organisms. But he noted the importance of growth correlation—"when slight variations in any one part occur, and are accumulated through natural selection, other parts become modified" (Darwin 1861, 130)—and, quoting Goethe ("in order to spend on one side, nature is forced to economise on the other side"), he stressed a general growth principle, namely that "natural selection will always succeed in the long run in reducing and saving every part of the organization, as soon as it is rendered superfluous, without by any means causing some other part to be largely developed in a corresponding degree" (Darwin 1861, 135).

This chapter deals with the growth of organisms, with the focus on those living forms that make the greatest difference for the functioning of the biosphere and for the survival of humanity. This means that I will look at cell growth only when dealing with unicellular organisms, archaea and bacteria—but will not offer any surveys of the genetic, biochemical and bioenergetic foundations of the process (both in its normal and aberrative forms) in higher organisms. Information on such cell growth—on its genetics, controls, promoters, inhibitors, and termination—is available in many survey volumes, including those by Studzinski (2000), Hall et al. (2004), Morgan (2007), Verbelen and Vissenberg (2007), Unsicker and Krieglstein (2008) and Golitsin and Krylov (2010).

The biosphere's most numerous, oldest and simplest organisms are archaea and bacteria. These are prokaryotic organisms without a cell nucleus and without such specialized membrane-enclosed organelles as mitochondria. Most of them are microscopic but many species have much larger cells and some can form astonishingly large assemblages. Depending on the species involved and on the setting, the rapid growth of single-celled organisms may be highly desirable (a healthy human microbiome is as essential for our survival as any key body organ) or lethal. Risks arise from such diverse phenomena as the eruptions and diffusion of pathogens—be they infectious diseases affecting humans or animals, or viral, bacterial and fungal infestations of plants—or from runaway growth of marine algae. These algal blooms can kill other biota by releasing toxins, or when their eventual decay deprives shallow waters of their normal oxygen content and when anaerobic bacteria thriving in such waters release high concentrations of hydrogen sulfide (UNESCO 2016).

The second subject of this chapter, trees and forests—plant communities, ecosystems and biomes that are dominated by trees but that could not be perpetuated without many symbioses with other organisms—contain most of the world's standing biomass as well as most of its diversity. The obvious importance of forests for the functioning of the biosphere and their enormous (albeit still inadequately appreciated and hugely undervalued) contribution to economic growth and to human well-being has led to many examinations of tree growth and forest productivity. We now have a fairly good understanding of the overall dynamics and specific requirements of those growth phenomena and we can also identify many factors that interfere with them or modify their rates.

The third focus of this chapter will be on crops, plants that have been greatly modified by domestication. Their beginnings go back to 8,500 BCE in the Middle East, with the earliest domesticates being einkorn and emmer wheat, barley, lentils, peas, and chickpeas. Chinese millet and rice were first cultivated between 7,000 and 6,000 BCE and the New World's squash was grown as early as 8,000 BCE (Zohary et al. 2012). Subsequent millennia of traditional selection brought incremental yield gains, but only modern crop breeding (hybrids, short-stalked cultivars), in combination with improved agronomic methods, adequate fertilization, and where needed also irrigation and protection against pests and weeds, has multiplied the traditional crop yields. Further advances will follow from the future deployment of genetically engineered plants.

In the section on animal growth I will look first at the individual development and population dynamics of several important wild species but most of it will be devoted to the growth of domestic animals. Domestication has changed the natural growth rates of all animals reared for meat, milk, eggs, and wool. Some of these changes have resulted in much accelerated maturation, others have also led to commercially desirable but questionable body malformations. The first instance is illustrated with pigs, the most numerous large meat animals. In traditional Asian settings, animals were usually left alone to fend for themselves, rooting out and scavenging anything edible (pigs are true omnivores). As a result, it may have taken more than two years for them to reach slaughter weight of at least 75–80 kg. In contrast, modern meat breeds kept in confinement and fed a highly nutritious diet will reach slaughter weight of 100 kg in just 24 weeks after the piglets are weaned (Smil 2013c). Heavy broiler chickens, with their massive breast muscles, are the best example of commercially-driven body malformations (Zuidhof et al. 2014).

The chapter will close with the examination of human growth and some of its notable malfunctions. I will first outline the typical progress of individual growth patterns of height and body mass from birth to the end of adolescence and the factors that promote or interfere with the expected performance. Although the global extent of malnutrition has been greatly reduced, shortages of food in general or specific nutrients in particular still affect too many children, preventing their normal physical and mental development. On the opposite end of the human growth spectrum is the worrisome extent of obesity, now increasingly developing in childhood. But before turning to more detailed inquiries into the growth of major groups of organisms, I must introduce the metabolic theory of ecology. This theory outlines the general approach linking the growth of all plants and all animals to their metabolism, and it has been seen by some as one of the greatest generalizing advances in biology while others have questioned its grand explanatory powers (West et al. 1997; Brown et al. 2004; Price et al. 2012). Its formulation arises from the fact that many variables are related to body mass according to the equation $y = aM^b$ where y is the variable that is predicted to change with body mass M, a is a scaling coefficient and b is the slope of allometric exponent. The relationship becomes linear when double-logged: $log\ y = log\ a + b\ log\ M$.

The relationship of body size to metabolic characteristics has long been a focus of animal studies, but only when metabolic scaling was extended to plants did it become possible to argue that the rates of biomass production and growth of all kinds of organisms, ranging from unicellular algae to the most massive vertebrates and trees, are proportional to metabolic rate, which scales as the ¾ power of body mass M (Damuth 2001). Metabolic scaling theory for plants, introduced by West et al. (1997), assumes that the gross photosynthetic (metabolic) rate is determined by potential rates of resource uptake and subsequent distribution of resources within the plant through branching networks of self-similar (fractal) structure.

The original model was to predict not only the structural and functional properties of the vertebrate cardiovascular and respiratory system, but also those of insect tracheal tubes and plant vascular system. Relying on these assumptions, Enquist et al. (1999) found that annual growth rates for 45 species of tropical forest trees (expressed in kg of dry matter) scale as $M^{3/4}$ (that is, with the same exponent as the metabolism of many animals) and hence the growth rates of diameter D scale as $D^{1/3}$. Subsequently, Niklas and Enquist (2001) confirmed that a single allometric pattern extends to autotrophic organisms whose body mass ranged over 20 orders of magnitude and whose lengths (either cell diameter or plant height) spanned over 22 orders of magnitude, from unicellular algae to herbs and to monocotyledonous, dicotyledonous, and conifers trees (figure 2.1).

And a few years later Enquist et al. (2007) derived a generalized trait-based model of plant growth. The ¾ scaling also applies to light-harvesting capacity measured either as the pigment content of algal cells or as foliage phytomass of plants. As a result, the relative growth rate of plants decreases with increasing plant size as $M^{-1/4}$, and primary productivity is little affected by species composition: an identical density of plants with similar overall mass will fix roughly the same amount of carbon. The uniform scaling also means that the relative growth rate decreases with increasing plant size as $M^{-1/4}$. Light-harvesting capacity (chlorophyll content of algal cells or foliage in higher plants) also scales as $M^{3/4}$, while plant length scales as $M^{1/4}$.

Niklas and Enquist (2001) had also concluded that plants—unlike animals that have similar allometric exponents but different normalization constants (different intercepts on a growth graph)—fit into a single allometric pattern across the entire range of their body masses. This functional unity is explained by the reliance on fractal-like distribution networks required to translocate photosynthate and transpire water: their evolution

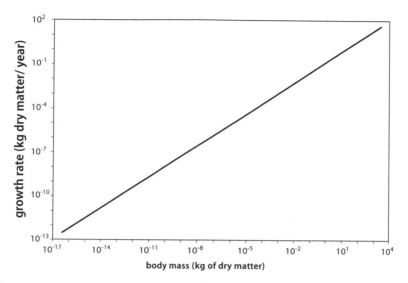

body mass (kg of dry matter)

Figure 2.1
Allometric pattern of autotrophic mass and growth rate. Based on Niklas and Enquist (2001).

(hierarchical branching and shared hydro- and biomechanics) had maximized metabolic capacity and efficiency by maximizing exchange surfaces and throughputs while minimizing transport distances and transfer rates (West et al. 1999).

But almost immediately ecologists began to question the universality of the metabolic scaling theory in general, and the remarkable invariance of exponents across a wide range of species and habitats in particular. Based on some 500 observations of 43 perennials species whose sizes spanned five of the 12 orders of magnitude of size in vascular plants, Reich et al. (2006) found no support for ¾-power scaling of plant nighttime respiration, and hence its overall metabolism. Their findings supported near-isometric scaling, that is exponent ~ 1, eliminated the need for fractal explanations of the ¾-power scaling and made a single size-dependent law of metabolism for plants and animals unlikely.

Similarly, Li et al. (2005), using a forest phytomass dataset for more than 1,200 plots representing 17 main forest types across China, found scaling exponents ranging from about 0.4 (for boreal pine stands) to 1.1 (for evergreen oaks), with only a few sites conforming to the ¾ rule, and hence no convincing evidence for a single constant scaling exponent for the phytomass-metabolism relationship in forests. And Muller-Landau et al.

(2006) examined an even large data set from ten old-growth tropical forests (encompassing more than 1.7 million trees) to show that the scaling of growth was clearly inconsistent with the predictions based on the metabolic theory, with only one of the ten sites (a montane forest at high elevation) coming close to the expected value.

Their results were consistent with an alternative model that also considered competition for light, the key photosynthetic resource whose availability commonly limits tropical tree growth. Scaling of plant growth that depends only on the potential for capturing and redistributing resources is wrong, and there are no universal scaling relationships of growth (as well as of tree mortality) in tropical forests. Coomes and Allen (2009) confirmed these conclusions by demonstrating how Enquist et al. (1999), by failing to consider asymmetric competition for light, underestimated the mean scaling exponent for tree diameter growth: rather than 0.33, its average across the studied Costa Rican forest species should be 0.44.

Rather than testing the metabolic theory's predictions, Price at al. (2012, 1472) looked at its physical and chemical foundations and at its simplifying assumptions and concluded that there is still no "complete, universal and causal theory that builds from network geometry and energy minimization to individual, species, community, ecosystem and global level patterns." They noted that the properties of distribution model are mostly specific to the cardiovascular system of vertebrates, and that empirical data offer only limited support for the model, and cited Dodds et al. (2001), who argued that ¾ scaling could not be derived from hydraulic optimization assumed by West et al. (1997). Consequently, these might be the best conclusions regarding the metabolic scaling theory: it provides only coarse-grained insight by describing the central tendency across many orders of magnitude; its key tenet of ¾ scaling is not universally valid as it does not apply to all mammals, insects or plants; and it is only a step toward a truly complete causal theory that, as yet, does not exist. Not surprisingly, the growth of organisms and their metabolic intensity are far too complex to be expressed by a single, narrowly bound, formula.

Microorganisms and Viruses

If the invisibility without a microscope were the only classification criterion then all viruses would be microorganisms—but because these simple bundles of protein-coated nucleic acids (DNA and RNA) are acellular and are unable to live outside suitable host organisms they must be classified separately. There are some multicellular microorganisms, but most microbes—including all archaea and bacteria—are unicellular. These single-celled organisms are the simplest, the oldest, and by far the most abundant forms of life—but their classification is anything but simple. The two main divisions concern their structure and their metabolism. Prokaryotic cells do not have either a nucleus or any other internal organelles; eukaryotic cells have these membrane-encased organelles.

Archaea and Bacteria are the two prokaryotic domains. This division is relatively recent: Woese et al. (1990) assigned all organisms to three primary domains (superkingdom categories) of Archaea, Bacteria, and Eucarya, and the division relies on sequencing base pairs in a universal ribosomal gene that codes for the cellular machinery assembling proteins (Woese and Fox 1977). Only a tiny share of eukaryotes, including protozoa and some algae and fungi, are unicellular. The basic trophic division is between chemoautotrophs (able to secure carbon from CO_2) and chemoheterotrophs, organisms that secure their carbon by breaking down organic molecules. The first group includes all unicellular algae and many photosynthesizing bacteria, the other metabolic pathway is common among archaea, and, of course, all fungi and animals are chemoheterotrophs.

Further divisions are based on a variety of environmental tolerances. Oxygen is imperative for growth of all unicellular algae and many bacteria, including such common genera as *Bacillus* and *Pseudomonas*. Facultative anaerobes can grow with or without the element and include such commonly occurring bacterial genera as *Escherichia*, *Streptococcus* and *Staphylococcus*, as well as *Saccharomyces cerevisiae*, fungus responsible for alcoholic fermentation and raised dough. Anaerobes (all methanogenic archaea and many bacterial species) do not tolerate oxygen's presence. Tolerances of ambient temperature divide unicellular organisms among psychrophilic species able to survive at low (even subzero) temperatures, mesophilic species that do best within a moderate range, and thermophiles that can grow and reproduce at temperatures above 40°C.

Psychrophiles include bacteria causing food spoilage in refrigerators: *Pseudomonas* growing on meat, *Lactobacillus* growing on both meat and dairy products, and *Listeria* growing on meat, seafood, and vegetables at just 1–4°C. Some species metabolize even in subzero temperatures, either in supercooled cloud droplets, in brine solutions or ice-laden Antarctic waters whose temperature is just below the freezing point (Psenner and Sattler 1998). Before the 1960s no bacterium was considered more heat-tolerant than *Bacillus stearothermophilus*, able to grow in waters of 37–65°C;

it was the most heat-tolerant known bacterium before the discoveries of hyperthermophilic varieties of *Bacillus* and *Sulfolobus* raised the maximum to 85°C during the 1960s and then to 95–105°C for *Pyrolobus fumarii*, an archaeon found in the walls of deep-sea vent chimneys spewing hot water; moreover, *Pyrolobus* stops growing in waters below 90°C (Herbert and Sharp 1992; Blöchl et al. 1997; Clarke 2014).

Extremophilic bacteria and archaea have an even larger tolerance range for highly acidic environments. While most species grow best in neutral (pH 7.0) conditions, *Picrophilus oshimae* has optimal growth at pH 0.7 (more than million times more acid than the neutral environment), a feat even more astonishing given the necessity to maintain internal (cytoplasmic) pH of all bacteria close to 6.0. Bacteria living in acidic environments are relatively common at geothermal sites and in acid soils containing pyrites or metallic sulfides and their growth is exploited commercially to extract copper from crushed low-grade ores sprinkled with acidified water.

In contrast, alkaliphilic bacteria cannot tolerate even neutral environments and grow only when pH is between 9 and 10 (Horikoshi and Grant1998). Such environments are common in soda lakes in arid regions of the Americas, Asia, and Africa, including Mono and Owens lakes in California. *Halobacterium* is an extreme alkaliphile that can tolerate pH as high as 11 and thrives in extremely salty shallow waters. One of the best displays of these algal blooms, with characteristic red and purple shades due to bacteriorhodopsin, can be seen in dike-enclosed polders in the southern end of San Francisco Bay from airplanes approaching the city's airport.

And there are also polyextremophilic bacteria able to tolerate several extreme conditions. Perhaps the best example in this category is *Deinococcus radiodurans*, commonly found in soils, animal feces and sewage: it survives extreme doses of radiation, ultraviolet radiation, desiccation and freeze-drying thanks to its extraordinary capacity to repair damaged DNA (White et al. 1999; Cox and Battista 2005). At the same time, for some bacterial growth even small temperature differences matter: *Mycobacterium leprae* prefers to invade first those body parts that are slightly cooler and that is why leprotic lesions often show up first in the extremities as well as ears. Not surprisingly, optimum growth conditions for common bacterial pathogens coincide with the temperature of the human body: *Staphylococcus aureus* responsible for skin and upper respiratory infections prefers 37°C as does *Clostridium botulinum* (producing dangerous toxin) and *Mycobacterium tuberculosis*. But *Escherichia coli*, the species most often responsible for the outbreaks of diarrhea and for urinary tract infections, has optimum growth at 40°C.

Microbial Growth

Microbial growth requires essential macro- and micronutrients, including nitrogen (indispensable constituent of amino acids and nucleic acids), phosphorus (for the synthesis of nucleic acids, ADP and ATP), potassium, calcium, magnesium, and sulfur (essential for S-containing amino acids). Many species also need metallic trace elements, above all copper, iron, molybdenum, and zinc, and must also obtain such growth factors as vitamins of the B group from their environment. Bacterial growth can be monitored best by inoculating solid (agar, derived from a polysaccharide in some algal cell walls) or liquid (nutrient broth) media (Pepper et al. 2011).

Monod (1949) outlined the succession of phases in the growth of bacterial cultures: initial lag phase (no growth), acceleration phase (growth rate increasing), exponential phase (growth rate constant), retardation phase (growth rate slowing down), and stationary phase (once again, no growth, in this case as a result of nutrient depletion or presence of inhibitory products) followed by the death phase. This generalized sequence has many variations, as one or several phases may be either absent or last so briefly as to be almost imperceptible; at the same time, trajectories may be more complex than the idealized basic outline. Because the average size of growing cells may vary significantly during different phases of their growth, cell concentration and bacterial density are not equivalent measures but in most cases the latter variable is of the greater importance.

The basic growth trajectory of cultured bacterial cell density is obviously sigmoidal: figure 2.2 shows the growth of *Escherichia coli* O157:H7, a commonly occurring serotype that contaminates raw food and milk and produces Shiga toxin causing foodborne colonic escherichiosis. Microbiologists and mathematicians have applied many standard models charting sigmoidal growth—including autocatalytic, logistic and Gompertz equations—and developed new models in order to find the best fits for observed growth trajectories and to predict the three key parameters of bacterial growth, the duration of the lag phase, the maximum specific growth rate, and the doubling time (Casciato et al. 1975; Baranyi 2010; Huang 2013; Peleg and Corradini 2011).

Differences in overall fit among commonly used logistic-type models are often minimal. Peleg and Corradini (2011) showed that despite their different mathematical structure (and also despite having no mechanistic interpretation), Gompertz, logistic, shifted logistic and power growth models had excellent fit and could be used interchangeably when tracing experimental isothermal growth of bacteria. Moreover, Buchanan et al. (1997) found that capturing the growth trajectory of *Escherichia coli* does not require curve

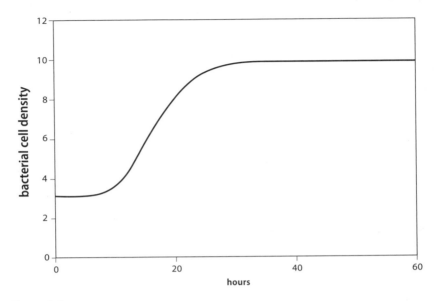

Figure 2.2
Logistic growth of *Escherichia coli* O157:H7. Plotted from data in Buchanan et al. (1997).

functions and can be done equally well by a simple three-phase linear model. A logical conclusion is that the simplest and the most convenient model should be chosen to quantify common bacterial growth.

Under optimal laboratory conditions, the ubiquitous *Escherichia coli* has generation time (the interval between successive divisions) of just 15–20 minutes, its synchronous succinate-grown cultures showed generation time averaging close to 40 minutes (Plank and Harvey 1979)—but its doubling takes 12–24 hours in the intestinal tract. Experiments by Maitra and Dill (2015) show that at its replication speed limit (fast-growth mode when plentiful nutrition is present) *Escherichia* duplicates all of its proteins quickly by producing proportionately more ribosomes—protein complexes that a cell makes to synthesize all of the cell's proteins—than other proteins. Consequently, it appears that energy efficiency of cells under fast growth conditions is the cell's primary fitness function.

Streptococcus pneumoniae, responsible for sinusitis, otitis media, osteomyelitis, septic arthritis, endocarditis, and peritonitis, has generation time of 20–30 minutes. *Lactobacillus acidophilus*—common in the human and animal gastrointestinal tract and present (together with other species of the same genus, *Lactobacillus bulgaricus*, *bifidus*, *casei*) in yoghurt and buttermilk—has generation time of roughly 70–90 minutes. *Rhizobium japonicum*, nitrogen-fixing symbiont supplying the nutrient to leguminous crops, divides slowly, taking up to eight hours for a new generation. In sourdough fermentation, industrial strains of *Lactobacillus* used in commercial baking reach their peak growth between 10–15 hours after inoculation and cease growing 20–30 hours later (Mihhalevski et al. 2010), and generation time for *Mycobacterium tuberculosis* averages about 12 hours.

Given the enormous variety of biospheric niches inhabited by microorganisms, it comes as no surprise that the growth of archaea, bacteria, and unicellular fungi in natural environments—where they coexist and compete in complex assemblages—can diverge greatly from the trajectories of laboratory cultures, and that the rates of cellular division can range across many orders of magnitude. The lag phases can be considerably extended when requisite nutrients are absent or available only in marginal amounts, or because they lack the capacity to degrade a new substrate. The existing bacterial population may have to undergo the requisite mutations or a gene transfer to allow further growth.

Measurements of bacterial growth in natural environments are nearly always complicated by the fact that most species live in larger communities consisting of other microbes, fungi, protozoa, and multicellular organisms. Their growth does not take place in monospecific isolation and it is characterized by complex population dynamics, making it very difficult to disentangle specific generation times not only *in situ* but also under controlled conditions. Thanks to DNA extraction and analysis, we came to realize that there are entire bacterial phyla (including *Acidobacteria*, *Verrucomicrobia*, and *Chloroflexi* in soils) prospering in nature but difficult or impossible to grow in laboratory cultures.

Experiments with even just two species (*Curvibacter* and *Duganella*) grown in co-culture indicate that their interactions go beyond the simple case of direct competition or pairwise games (Li et al. 2015). There are also varied species-specific responses to pulsed resource renewal: for example, coevolution with *Serratia marcescens* (an Enterobacter often responsible for hospital-acquired infections) caused *Novosphingobium capsulatum* clones (able to degrade aromatic compounds) to grow faster, while the evolved clones of *Serratia marcescens* had a higher survival and slower growth rate than their ancestor (Pekkonen et al. 2013).

Decomposition rates of litterfall (leaves, needles, fruits, nuts, cones, bark, branches) in forests provide a revealing indirect measure of different rates of microbial growth in nature. The process recycles macro- and micro-nutrients. Above all, it controls carbon and nitrogen dynamics in soil, and bacteria and fungi are its dominant agents on land as well as in aquatic eco-systems (Romaní et al. 2006; Hobara et al. 2014). Their degradative enzymes can eventually dismantle any kind of organic matter, and the two groups of microorganisms act in both synergistic and antagonistic ways. Bacteria can decompose an enormous variety of organic substrates but fungi are superior, and in many instances, the only possible decomposers of lignin, cellulose, and hemicellulose, plant polymers making up woody tissues and cell walls.

Decomposition of forest litter requires the sequential breakdown of dif-ferent substrates (including waxes, phenolics, cellulose, and lignin) that must be attacked by a variety of metallomic enzymes, but microbial decom-posers live in the world of multiple nutrient limitations (Kaspari et al. 2008). Worldwide comparison, using data from 110 sites, confirmed the expected positive correlation of litter decomposition with decreasing latitude and lignin content and with increasing mean annual temperature, precipita-tion, and nutrient concentration (Zhang et al. 2008). While no single factor was responsible for a high degree of explanation, the combination of total nutrients and carbon: nitrogen ratio explained about 70% of the variation in the litter decomposition rates. In relative terms, decomposition rates in a tropical rain forest were nearly twice as high as in a temperate broad-leaved forest and more than three times as fast as in a coniferous forest. Litter quality, that is the suitability of the substrate for common microbial metabolism, is clearly the key direct regulator of litter decomposition at the global scale.

Not surprisingly, natural growth rates of some extremophilic microbes can be extraordinarily slow, with generation times orders of magnitude lon-ger than is typical for common soil or aquatic bacteria. Yayanos et al. (1981) reported that an obligate barophilic (pressure-tolerant) isolate, retrieved from a dead amphipod *Hirondella gigas* captured at the depth of 10,476 meters in Mariana Trench (the world's deepest ocean bottom), had the opti-mal generation times of about 33 hours at 2°C under 103.5 MPa prevailing at its origin. Similarly, *Pseudomonas bathycetes*, the first species isolated from a sediment sample taken from the trench, has generation time of 33 days (Kato et al. 1998). In contrast, generation times of thermophilic and piezo-philic (pressure-tolerant) microbes in South Africa's deep gold mines (more than 2 km) are estimated to be on the order of 1,000 years (Horikoshi 2016).

And then there are microbes buried deep in the mud under the floor of the deepest ocean trenches that can grow even at gravity more than 400,000 times greater than at the Earth's surface but "we cannot estimate the generation times of [these] extremophiles…They have individual biological clocks, so the scale of their time axis will be different" (Horikoshi 2016, 151). But even the span between 20 minutes for average generation time of common gut and soil bacteria and 1,000 years of generation time for barophilic extremophiles amounts to the difference of seven orders of magnitude, and it is not improbable that the difference may be up to ten orders of magnitude for as yet undocumented extremophilic microbes.

Finally, a brief look at recurrent marine microbial growths that are so extensive that they can be seen on satellite images. Several organisms—including bacteria, unicellular algae and eukaryotic dinoflagellates and coccolithophores—can multiply rapidly and produce aquatic blooms (Smayda 1997; Granéli and Turner 2006). Their extent may be limited to a lake, a bay, or to coastal waters but often they cover areas large enough to be easily identified on satellite images (figure 2.3). Moreover, many of these blooms are toxic, presenting risks to fish and marine invertebrates. One of the most common blooms is produced by species of *Trichodesmium*, cyanobacteria growing in nutrient-poor tropical and subtropical oceans whose single cells with gas vacuoles form macroscopic filaments and fila-ment clusters of straw-like color but turning red in higher concentrations.

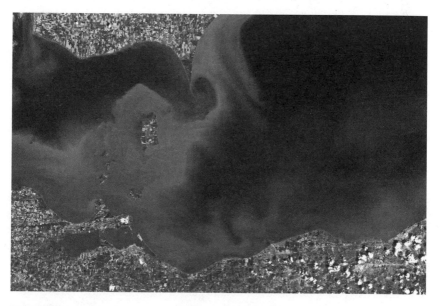

Figure 2.3
Algal bloom in the western part of the Lake Erie on July 28, 2015. NASA satellite image is available at https://eoimages.gsfc.nasa.gov/images/imagerecords/86000/86327/erie _oli_2015209_lrg.jpg.

The pigmentation of large blooms of *Trichodesmium erythraeum* has given the Red Sea its name, and recurrent red blooms have a relatively unique spectral signature (including high backscatter caused by the presence of gas vesicles and the absorption of its pigment phycoerythrin) that makes them detectable by satellites (Subramaniam et al. 2002). *Trichodesmium* also has an uncommon ability to fix nitrogen, that is to convert inert atmospheric dinitrogen into ammonia that can be used for its own metabolism and to support growth of other marine organisms: it may generate as much as half of all organic nitrogen present in the ocean, but because nitrogen fixation cannot proceed in aerobic conditions it is done inside the cyanobacteria's special heterocysts (Bergman et al. 2012). *Trichodesmium* blooms produce phytomass strata that often support complex communities of other marine microorganisms, including other bacteria, dinoflagellates, protozoa, and copepods.

Walsh et al. (2006) outlined a sequence taking place in the Gulf of Mexico whereby a phosphorus-rich runoff initiates a planktonic succession once the nutrient-poor subtropical waters receive periodic depositions of iron-rich Saharan dust. The availability of these nutrients allows *Trichodesmium* to be also a precursor bloom for *Karenia brevis*, a unicellular dinoflagellate infamous for causing toxic red tides. This remarkable sequence, an excellent example of complex preconditions required to produce high rates of bacterial growth, is repeated in other warm waters receiving more phosphorus-rich runoff from fertilized cropland and periodic long-range inputs of iron-rich dust transported from African and Asian deserts. As a result, the frequency and extent of red tides have become more common during the 20th century. They are now found in waters ranging from the Gulf of Mexico to Japan, New Zealand, and South Africa.

Pathogens

Three categories of microbial growth have particularly damaging consequences: common pathogens that infect crops and reduce their harvests; a wide variety of microbes that increase human morbidity and mortality; and microorganisms and viruses responsible for population-wide infections (epidemics) and even global impacts (pandemics). A few exceptions aside, the names of bacterial and fungal plant pathogens are not recognized outside expert circles. The most important plant pathogenic bacteria are *Pseudomonas syringae* with its many pathovars epiphytically growing on many crops, and *Ralstonia solanacearum* responsible for bacterial wilts (Mansfield et al. 2012). The most devastating fungal pathogens are *Magnaporthe oryzae* (rice blast fungus) and *Botrytis cinerea*, a necrophytic grey mold fungus attacking more than 200 plant species but best known for its rare beneficial role (producing noble rot, *pourriture noble*) indispensable in the making of such sweet (botrytic) wines as Sauternes and Tokaj (Dean et al. 2012).

Although many broad-spectrum and targeted antibiotics have been available for more than half a century, many bacterial diseases still cause considerable mortality, particularly *Mycobacterium tuberculosis* in Africa, and *Streptococcus pneumococcus*, the leading cause of bacterial pneumonia among older people. *Salmonella* is responsible for frequent cases of food contamination, *Escherichia coli* is the leading cause of diarrhea, and both are ubiquitous causes of morbidity. But widespread use of antibacterial drugs has shortened the span of common infections, accelerated recovery, prevented early deaths, and extended modern lifespans.

The obverse of these desirable outcomes has been the spread of antibiotic-resistant strains that began just a few years after the introduction of new antimicrobials in the early 1940s (Smith and Coast 2002). Penicillin-resistant *Staphylococcus aureus* was found already in 1947. The first methicillin-resistant strains of *Staphylococcus aureus* (MRSA, causing bacteremia, pneumonia, and surgical wound infections) emerged in 1961, have spread globally and now account for more than half of all infection acquired during intensive hospital therapy (Walsh and Howe 2002). Vancomycin became the drug of last resort after many bacteria acquired resistance to most of the commonly prescribed antibiotics but the first vancomycin-resistant staphylococci appeared in 1997 in Japan and in 2002 in the US (Chang et al. 2003).

The latest global appraisal of the state of antibiotics indicates the continuation of an overall decline in the total stock of antibiotic effectiveness, as the resistance to all first-line and last-resort antibiotics is rising (Gelband et al. 2015). In the US, antibiotic resistance causes more than 2 million infections and 23,000 deaths every year and results in a direct cost of $20 billion and productivity losses of $35 billion (CDC 2013). While there have been some significant declines in MRSA in North America and Europe, the incidence in sub-Saharan Africa, Latin America, and Australia is still rising, *Escherichia coli* and related bacteria are now resistant to the third-generation cephalosporins, and carbapenem-resistant Enterobacteriaceae have become resistant even to the last-resort carbapenems.

The conquest of pathogenic bacterial growth made possible by antibiotics is being undone by their inappropriate and excessive use (unnecessary self-medication in countries where the drugs are available without prescription and overprescribing in affluent countries) as well as by poor sanitation in hospitals and by massive use of prophylactic antibiotics in animal husbandry. Preventing the emergence of antibiotic-resistant mutations was never an option but minimizing the problem has received too little attention for far too long. As a result, antibiotic-resistance is now also common among both domestic and wild animals that were never exposed directly to antibiotics (Gilliver et al. 1999).

The quest to regain a measure of control appears to be even more urgent as there is now growing evidence that many soil bacteria have a naturally occurring resistance against, or ability to degrade, antibiotics. Moreover, Zhang and Dick (2014) isolated from soils bacterial strains that were not only antibiotic-resistant but that could use the antibiotics as their sources of energy and nutrients although they were not previously exposed to any antibiotics: they found 19 bacteria (mainly belonging to Proteobacteria and Bacteriodetes) that could grow on penicillin and neomycin as their sole carbon sources up to concentrations of 1 g/L.

The availability of antibiotics (and better preventive measures) have also minimized the much larger, population-wide threat posed by bacteria able to cause large-scale epidemics and even pandemics, most notably *Yersinia pestis*, a rod-shaped anaerobic coccobacillus responsible for plague. The bacterium causing plague was identified, and cultured, in 1894 by Alexandre Yersin in Hong Kong in 1894, and soon afterwards Jean-Paul Simond discovered the transmission of bacteria from rodents by flea bites (Butler 2014). Vaccine development followed in 1897, and eventually streptomycin (starting in 1947) became the most effective treatment (Prentice and Rahalison 2007).

The Justinian plague of 541–542 and the medieval Black Death are the two best known historic epidemics (not pandemics, as they did not reach the Americas and Australia) due to their exceptionally high mortality. The Justinian plague swept the Byzantine (Eastern Roman) and Sassanid empires and the entire Mediterranean littoral, with uncertain death estimates as high as 25 million (Rosen 2007). A similarly virulent infestation returned to Europe eight centuries later as the Black Death, the description referring to dying black skin and flesh. In the spring of 1346, plague, endemic in the steppe region of southern Russia, reached the shores of the Black Sea, and then it was carried by maritime trade routes via Constantinople to Sicily by October 1346 and then to the western Mediterranean, reaching Marseilles and Genoa by the end of 1347 (Kelly 2006).

Flea-infested rats on trade ships carried the plague to coastal cities, where it was transmitted to local rat populations but subsequent continental diffusion was mainly by direct pneumonic transmission. By 1350 plague had spread across western and central Europe, by 1351 it reached northwestern

Russia, and by 1853 its easternmost wave was reconnected to the original Caspian reservoir (Gaudart et al. 2010). Overall European mortality was at least 25 million people, and before it spread to Europe plague killed many people in China and in Central Asia. Between 1347 and 1351 it also spread from Alexandria to the Middle East, all the way to Yemen.

Aggregate mortality has been put as high as 100 million people but even a considerably smaller total would have brought significant depopulation to many regions and its demographic and economic effects lasted for generations. Controversies regarding the Black Death's etiology were definitely settled only in 2010 by identification of DNA and protein signatures specific for *Yersinia pestis* in material removed from mass graves in Europe (Haensch et al. 2010). The study has also identified two previously unknown but related *Yersinia* clades associated with mass graves, suggesting that 14th century plague reached Europe on at least two occasions by distinct routes.

Gómez and Verdú (2017) reconstructed the network connecting the 14th-century European and Asian cities through pilgrimage and trade and found, as expected, that the cities with higher transitivity (a node's connection to two other nodes that are also directly connected) and centrality (the number and intensity of connections with the other nodes in the network), were more severely affected by the plague as they experienced more exogenous reinfections. But available information does not allow us to reconstruct reliably the epidemic trajectories of the Black Death as it spread across Europe in the late 1340s.

Later, much less virulent, outbreaks of the disease reoccurred in Europe until the 18th century and mortality records for some cities make it possible to analyze the growth of the infection process. Monecke et al. (2009) found high-quality data for Freiburg (in Saxony) during its plague epidemics between May 1613 and February 1614 when more than 10% of the town's population died. Their models of the epidemic's progress resulted in close fits to the historical record. The number of plague victims shows a nearly normal (Gaussian) distribution, with the peak at about 100 days after the first deaths and a return to normal after about 230 days.

Perhaps the most interesting findings of their modeling was that introducing even a small number of immune rats into an otherwise unchanged setting aborts the outbreak and results in very few deaths. They concluded that the diffusion of *Rattus norvegicus* (brown or sewer rats, which may develop partial herd immunity by exposure to *Yersinia* because of its preference for wet habitats) accelerated the retreat of the 17th-century European plague. Many epidemics of plague persisted during the 19th century and localized plague outbreaks during the 20th century included those in India (1903), San Francisco (1900–1904), China (1910–1912) and India (Surat) in 1994. During the last two generations, more than 90% of all localized plague cases have been in African countries, with the remainder in Asia (most notably in Vietnam, India, and China) and in Peru (Raoult et al. 2013).

Formerly devastating bacterial epidemics have become only a matter of historic interest as we have taken preventive measures (suppressing rodent reservoirs and fleas when dealing with plague) and deployed early detection and immediate treatment of emerging cases. Viral infections pose a greater challenge. A rapid diffusion of smallpox, caused by variola virus, was responsible for well-known reductions of aboriginal American populations that lacked any immunity before their contact with European conquerors. Vaccination eventually eradicated this infection: the last natural outbreak in the US was in 1949, and in 1980 the World Health Organization declared smallpox eliminated on the global scale. But there is no prospect for an early elimination of viral influenza, returning annually in the form of seasonal epidemics and unpredictably as recurrent pandemics.

Seasonal outbreaks are related to latitude (Brazil and Argentina have infection peaks between April and September), they affect between 10% and 50% of the population and result in widespread morbidity and significant mortality among elderly. Annual US means amount to some 65 million illnesses, 30 million medical visits, 200,000 hospitalizations, 25,000 (10,000–40,000) deaths, and up to $5 billion in economic losses (Steinhoff 2007). As with all airborne viruses, influenza is readily transmitted as droplets and aerosols by respiration and hence its spatial diffusion is aided by higher population densities and by travel, as well as by the short incubation period, typically just 24–72 hours. Epidemics can take place at any time during the year, but in temperate latitudes they occur with a much higher frequency during winter. Dry air and more time spent indoors are the two leading promoters.

Epidemics of viral influenza bring high morbidity but in recent decades they have caused relatively low overall mortality, with both rates being the highest among the elderly. Understanding of key factors behind seasonal variations remains limited but absolute humidity might be the predominant determinant of influenza seasonality in temperate climates (Shaman et al. 2010). Recurrent epidemics require the continuous presence of a sufficient number of susceptible individuals, and while infected people recover with immunity, they become again vulnerable to rapidly mutating viruses as the process of antigenic drift creates a new supply of susceptible individuals

(Axelsen et al. 2014). That is why epidemics persist even with mass-scale annual vaccination campaigns and with the availability of antiviral drugs. Because of the recurrence and costs of influenza epidemics, considerable effort has gone into understanding and modeling their spread and eventual attenuation and termination (Axelsen et al. 2014; Guo et al. 2015).

The growth trajectories of seasonal influenza episodes form complete epidemic curves whose shape conforms most often to a normal (Gaussian) distribution or to a negative binomial function whose course shows a steeper rise of new infections and a more gradual decline from the infection peak (Nsoesie et al. 2014). More virulent infections follow a rather compressed (peaky) normal curve, with the entire event limited to no more than 100–120 days; in comparison, milder infections may end up with only a small fraction of infected counts but their complete course may extend to 250 days. Some events will have a normal distribution with a notable plateau or with a bimodal progression (Goldstein et al. 2011; Guo et al. 2015).

But the epidemic curve may follow the opposite trajectory, as shown by the diffusion of influenza at local level. This progression was studied in a great detail during the course of the diffusion of the H1N1 virus in 2009. Between May and September 2009, Hong Kong had a total of 24,415 cases and the epidemic growth curve, reconstructed by Lee and Wong (2010), had a small initial peak between the 55th and 60th day after its onset, then a brief nadir followed by rapid ascent to the ultimate short-lived plateau on day 135 and a relatively rapid decline: the event was over six months after it began (figure 2.4). The progress of seasonal influenza can be significantly modified by vaccination, notably in such crowded settings as universities, and by timely isolation of susceptible groups (closing schools). Nichol et al. (2010) showed that the total attack rate of 69% in the absence of vaccination was reduced to 45% with a preseason vaccination rate of just 20%, to less than 1% with preseason vaccination at 60%, and the rate was cut even when vaccinations were given 30 days after the outbreak onset.

We can now get remarkably reliable information on an epidemic's progress in near real-time, up to two weeks before it becomes available from traditional surveillance systems: McIver and Brownstein (2014) found that monitoring the frequency of daily searches for certain influenza- or health-related Wikipedia articles provided an excellent match (difference of less than 0.3% over a period of nearly 300 weeks) with data on the actual prevalence of influenza-like illness obtained later from the Centers for Disease Control. Wikipedia searches also accurately estimated the week of the peak of illness occurrence, and their trajectories conformed to the negative binomial curve of actual infections.

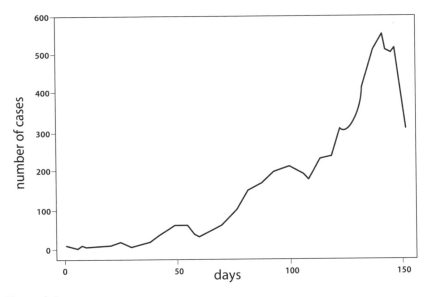

Figure 2.4
Progression of the Hong Kong influenza epidemic between May and September 2009.
Based on Lee and Wong (2010).

Seasonal influenza epidemics cannot be prevented and their eventual intensity and human and economic toll cannot be predicted—and these conclusions apply equally well to the recurrence of a worldwide diffusion of influenza viruses causing pandemics and concurrent infestation of the world's inhabited regions. These concerns have been with us ever since we understood the process of virulent epidemics, and it only got more complicated with the emergence of the H5N1 virus (bird flu) in 1997 and with a brief but worrisome episode of severe acute respiratory syndrome (SARS). In addition, judging by the historical recurrence of influenza pandemics, we might be overdue for another major episode.

We can identify at least four viral pandemics during the 18th century, in 1729–1730, 1732–1733, 1781–1782, and 1788–1789, and there have been six documented influenza pandemics during the last two centuries (Gust et al. 2001). In 1830–1833 and 1836–1837, the pandemic was caused by an unknown subtype originating in Russia. In 1889–1890, it was traced to subtypes H2 and H3, most likely coming again from Russia. In 1918–1919, it was an H1 subtype with unclear origins, either in the US or in China. In 1957–1958, it was subtype H2N2 from south China, and in 1968–1969 subtype H3N2 from Hong Kong. We have highly reliable mortality estimates only for the last two events, but there is no doubt that the 1918–1919 pandemic was by far the most virulent (Reid et al. 1999; Taubenberger and Morens 2006).

The origins of the 1918–1919 pandemic have been contested. Jordan (1927) identified the British military camps in the United Kingdom (UK) and France, Kansas, and China as the three possible sites of its origin. China in the winter of 1917–1918 now seems the most likely region of origin and the infection spread as previously isolated populations came into contact with one another on the battlefields of WWI (Humphries 2013). By May 1918 the virus was present in eastern China, Japan, North Africa, and Western Europe, and it spread across entire US. By August 1918 it had reached India, Latin America, and Australia (Killingray and Phillips 2003; Barry 2005). The second, more virulent, wave took place between September and December 1918; the third one, between February and April 1919, was, again, more moderate.

Data from the US and Europe make it clear that the pandemic had an unusual mortality pattern. Annual influenza epidemics have a typical U-shaped age-specific mortality (with young children and people over 70 being most vulnerable), but age-specific mortality during the 1918–1919 pandemic peaked between the ages of 15 and 35 years (the mean age for the US was 27.2 years) and virtually all deaths (many due to viral pneumonia) were in people younger than 65 (Morens and Fauci 2007). But there is no consensus about the total global toll: minimum estimates are around 20 million, the World Health Organization put it at upward of 40 million people, and Johnson and Mueller (2002) estimated it at 50 million. The highest total would be far higher than the global mortality caused by the plague in 1347–1351. Assuming that the official US death toll of 675,000 people (Crosby 1989) is fairly accurate, it surpassed all combat deaths of US troops in all of the wars of the 20th century.

Pandemics have been also drivers of human genetic diversity and natural selection and some genetic differences have emerged to regulate infectious disease susceptibility and severity (Pittman et al. 2016). Quantitative reconstruction of their growth is impossible for events before the 20th century but good quality data on new infections and mortality make it possible to reconstruct epidemic curves of the great 1918–1919 pandemic and of all the subsequent pandemics. As expected, they conform closely to a normal distribution or to a negative binomial regardless of affected populations, regions, or localities. British data for combined influenza and pneumonia mortality weekly between June 1918 and May 1919 show three pandemic waves. The smallest, almost symmetric and peaking at just five deaths/1,000, was in July 1918. The highest, a negative binomial peaking at nearly 25 deaths/1,000 in October, and an intermediate wave (again a negative binomial peaking at just above 10 deaths/1,000) in late February of 1919 (Jordan 1927).

Perhaps the most detailed reconstruction of epidemic waves traces not only transmission dynamics and mortality but also age-specific timing of deaths for New York City (Yang et al. 2014). Between February 1918 and April 1920, the city was struck by four pandemic waves (also by a heat wave). Teenagers had the highest mortality during the first wave, and the peak then shifted to young adults, with total excess mortality for all four waves peaking at the age of 28 years. Each wave was spread with a comparable early growth rate but the subsequent attenuations varied. The virulence of the pandemic is shown by daily mortality time series for the city's entire population: the second wave's peak reached 1,000 deaths per day compared to the baseline of 150–300 deaths (figure 2.5). When compared by using the fractional mortality increase (ratio of excess mortality to baseline mortality), the trajectories of the second and the third wave came closest to a negative binomial distribution, with the fourth wave displaying a very irregular pattern.

Very similar patterns were demonstrated by analyses of many smaller populations. For example, a model fitted to reliable weekly records of

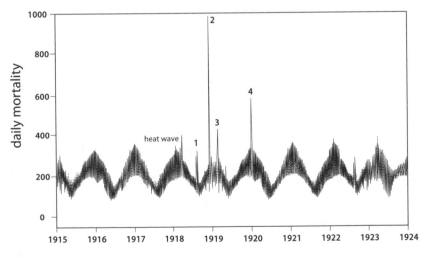

Figure 2.5
Daily influenza mortality time series in New York between February 1918 and April 1920 compared to baseline (1915–1917 and 1921–1923). Simplified from Yang et al. (2014).

incidences of influenza reported from Royal Air Force camps in the UK shows two negative binomial curves, the first one peaking about 5 weeks and the other one about 22 weeks after the infection outbreak (Mathews et al. 2007). The epidemic curve for the deaths of soldiers in the city of Hamilton (Ontario, Canada) between September and December 2018 shows a perfectly symmetrical principal wave peaking in the second week of October and a much smaller secondary wave peaking three weeks later (Mayer and Mayer 2006).

Subsequent 20th-century pandemics were much less virulent. The death toll for the 1957–1958 outbreak was about 2 million, and low mortality (about 1 million people) during the 1968–1969 event is attributed to protection conferred on many people by the 1957 infection. None of the epidemics during the remainder of the 20th century grew into a pandemic (Kilbourne 2006). But new concerns arose due to the emergence of new avian influenza viruses that could be transmitted to people. By May 1997 a subtype of H5N1 virus mutated in Hong Kong's poultry markets to a highly pathogenic form (able to kill virtually all affected birds within two days) that claimed its first human victim, a three-year-old boy (Sims et al. 2002). The virus eventually infected at least 18 people, causing six deaths and slaughter of 1.6 million birds, but it did not spread beyond South China (Snacken et al. 1999).

WHO divides the progression of a pandemic into six phases (Rubin 2011). First, an animal influenza virus circulating among birds or mammals has not infected humans. Second, the infection occurs, creating a specific potential pandemic threat. Third, sporadic cases or small clusters of disease exist but there are no community-wide outbreaks. Such outbreaks mark the fourth phase. In the next phase, community-level outbreaks affect two or more countries in a region, and in the sixth phase outbreaks spread to at least one other region. Eventually the infections subside and influenza activity returns to levels seen commonly during seasonal outbreaks. Clearly, the first phase has been a recurrent reality, and the second and third phases have taken place repeatedly since 1997. But in April 2009, triple viral reassortment between two influenza lineages (that had been present in pigs for years) led to the emergence of swine flu (H1N1) in Mexico (Saunders-Hastings and Krewski 2016).

The infection progressed rapidly to the fourth and fifth stage and by June 11, 2009, when WHO announced the start of an influenza pandemic, there were nearly 30,000 confirmed cases in 74 countries (Chan 2009). By the end of 2009, there were 18,500 laboratory-confirmed deaths worldwide but models suggest that the actual excess mortality attributable to the pandemics was between 151,700 and 575,400 cases (Simonsen et al. 2013). The disease progressed everywhere in typical waves, but their number, timing, and duration differed: there were three waves (spring, summer, fall) in Mexico, two waves (spring-summer and fall) in the US and Canada, three waves (September and December 2009, and August 2010) in India.

There is no doubt that improved preparedness (due to the previous concerns about H5N1 avian flu in Asia and the SARS outbreak in 2002)—a combination of school closures, antiviral treatment, and mass-scale prophylactic vaccination—reduced the overall impact of this pandemic. The overall mortality remained small (only about 2% of infected people developed a severe illness) but the new H1N1 virus was preferentially infecting younger people under the age of 25 years, while the majority of severe and fatal infections was in adults aged 30–50 years (in the US the average age of laboratory confirmed deaths was just 37 years). As a result, in terms of years of life lost (a metric taking into account the age of the deceased), the maximum estimate of 1.973 million years was comparable to the mortality during the 1968 pandemic.

Simulations of an influenza pandemic in Italy by Rizzo et al. (2008) provide a good example of the possible impact of the two key control measures, antiviral prophylaxis and social distancing. In their absence, the epidemic on the peninsula would follow a Gaussian curve, peaking about four months after the identification of the first cases at more than 50 cases per 1,000 inhabitants, and it would last about seven months. Antivirals for eight weeks would reduce the peak infection rate by about 25%, and social distancing starting at the pandemic's second week would cut the spread by two-thirds. Economic consequences of social distancing (lost school and work days, delayed travel) are much more difficult to model.

As expected, the diffusion of influenza virus is closely associated with population structure and mobility, and superspreaders, including healthcare workers, students, and flight attendants, play a major role in disseminating the virus locally, regionally, and internationally (Lloyd-Smith et al. 2005). The critical role played by schoolchildren in the spatial spread of pandemic influenza was confirmed by Gog et al. (2014). They found that the protracted spread of American influenza in fall 2009 was dominated by short-distance diffusion (that was partially promoted by school openings) rather than (as is usually the case with seasonal influenza) long-distance transmission.

Modern transportation is, obviously, the key superspreading conduit. Scales range from local (subways, buses) and regional (trains, domestic flights, especially high-volume connections such as those between Tokyo and Sapporo, Beijing and Shanghai, or New York and Los Angeles that carry millions of passengers a year) to intercontinental flights that enable rapid global propagation (Yoneyama and Krishnamoorthy 2012). In 1918, the Atlantic crossing took six days on a liner able to carry mostly between 2,000 and 3,000 passengers and crew; now it takes six to seven hours on a jetliner carrying 250–450 people, and more than 3 million passengers now travel annually just between London's Heathrow and New York's JFK airport. The combination of flight frequency, speed, and volume makes it impractical to prevent the spread by quarantine measures: in order to succeed they would have to be instantaneous and enforced without exception.

And the unpredictability of this airborne diffusion of contagious diseases was best illustrated by the transmission of the SARS virus from China to Canada, where its establishment among vulnerable hospital populations led to a second unexpected outbreak (PHAC 2004; Abraham 2005; CEHA 2016). A Chinese doctor infected with severe acute respiratory syndrome (caused by a coronavirus) after treating a patient in Guangdong travelled to Hong Kong, where he stayed on the same hotel floor as an elderly Chinese Canadian woman who got infected and brought the disease to Toronto on February 23, 2003.

As a result, while none of other large North American cities with daily flights to Hong Kong (Vancouver, San Francisco, Los Angeles, New York) was affected, Toronto experienced a taxing wave of infections, with some hospitals closed to visitors. Transmission within Toronto peaked during the week of March 16–23, 2003 and the number of cases was down to one by the third week of April; a month later, the WHO declared Toronto SARS-free—but that was a premature announcement because then came the second, quite unexpected wave, whose contagion rate matched the March peak by the last week of May before it rapidly subsided.

Trees and Forests

Now to the opposite end of the size spectrum: some tree species are the biosphere's largest organisms. Trees are woody perennials with a more or less complex branching of stems and with secondary growth of their trunks and branches (Owens and Lund 2009). Their growth is a marvel of great complexity, unusual persistence, and necessary discontinuity, and its results encompass about 100,000 species, including an extreme variety of forms, from dwarf trees of the Arctic to giants of California, and from tall straight stems with minimal branching to almost perfectly spherical plants with omnidirectional growth. But the underlying mechanisms of their growth are identical: apical meristems, tissues able to produce a variety of organs and found at the tips of shoots and roots, are responsible for the primary growth, for trees growing up (trunks) and sideways and down (branches). Thickening, the secondary growth, produces tissues necessary to support the elongating and branching plant.

As Corner (1964, 141) succinctly put it,

> The tree is organized by the direction of its growing tips, the lignification [i.e. wood production] of the inner tissues, the upward flow of water in the lignified xylem, the downward passage of food in the phloem, and the continued growth of the cambium. It is kept alive, in spite of its increasing load of dead wood, by the activity of the skin of living cells.

The vascular cambium, the layer of dividing cells and hence the generator of tree growth that is sandwiched between xylem and phloem (the living tissue right beneath the bark that transports leaf photosynthate), is a special meristem that produces both new phloem and xylem cells.

New xylem tissue formed in the spring has lighter color than the tissue laid down in summer in smaller cells, and these layers form distinct rings that make it easy to count a tree's age without resorting to isotopic analysis of wood. The radial extent of the cambium is not easy to delimit because of the gradual transition between phloem and xylem, and because some parenchymal cells may remain alive for long periods of time, even for decades. Leaves and needles are the key tissues producing photosynthate and enabling tree growth and their formation, durability, and demise are sensitive to a multitude of environmental factors. Tree stems have been studied most closely because they provide fuelwood and commercial timber and because their cellulose is by far the most important material for producing pulp and paper.

Roots are the least known part of trees: the largest ones are difficult to study without excavating the entire root system, the hair-like ones that do most nutrient absorption are ephemeral. In contrast, crown forms are easiest to observe and to classify as they vary not only among species but also among numerous varieties. The basic division is between excurrent and decurrent forms; the latter form, characteristic of temperate hardwoods, has lateral branches growing as long or even longer than the stem as they form broad crowns, the former shape, typical in conifers, has the stem whose length greatly surpasses the subtending laterals.

Massed trees form forests: the densest have completely closed canopies, while the sparsest are better classified as woodland, with canopies covering only a small fraction of the ground. Forests store nearly 90% of the biosphere's phytomass and a similarly skewed distribution applies on other scales: most of the forest phytomass (about three-quarters) is in tropical forests and most of that phytomass (about three-fifths) is in the equatorial rain forests where most of it is stored in massive trunks (often buttressed) of trees that form the forest's closed canopy and in a smaller number of emergent trees whose crowns rise above the canopy level. And when we look at an individual tree we find most of its living phytomass locked in xylem (sapwood) and a conservative estimate put its share at no more than 15% of the total (largely dead) phytomass.

Given the substantial differences in water content of plant tissues (in fresh tissues water almost always dominates), the only way to assure data comparability across a tree's lifespan and among different species is to express the annual growth rates in mass units of dry matter or carbon per unit area. In ecological studies, this is done in grams per square meter (g/m^2), t/ha or in tonnes of carbon per hectare (t C/ha). These studies focus on different levels of productivity, be it for an entire plant, a community, an ecosystem, or the entire biosphere. Gross primary productivity (GPP) comes first as we move from the most general to the most restrictive productivity measure; this variable captures all photosynthetic activity during a given period of time.

Primary Productivity

Total forest GPP is about half of the global GPP assumed to be 120 Gt C/year (Cuntz 2011). New findings have changed both the global total and the forest share. Ma et al. (2015) believe that forest GPP has been overestimated (mainly due to exaggerated forest area) and that the real annual total is about 54 Gt C or nearly 10% lower than previous calculations. At the same time, Welp et al. (2011) concluded that the global GPP total should be raised to the range of 150–175 Gt C/year, and Campbell et al. (2017) supported that finding: their analysis of atmospheric carbonyl sulfide records suggests a large historical growth of total GPP during the 20th century, with the overall gain of 31% and the new total above 150 Gt C.

A large part of this newly formed photosynthate does not end up as new tree tissue but it is rapidly reoxidized inside the plant: this continuous autotrophic respiration (R_A) energizes the synthesis of plant biopolymers from monomers fixed by photosynthesis, it transports photosynthates within the plant and it is channeled into repair of diseased or damaged tissues. Autotrophic respiration is thus best seen as the key metabolic pathway between photosynthesis and a plant's structure and function (Amthor and Baldocchi 2001; Trumbore 2006). Its intensity (R_A/GPP) is primarily the function of location, climate (above all of temperature), and plant age, and it varies widely both within and among species as well as among ecosystems and biomes.

A common assumption is that R_A consumes about half of the carbon fixed in photosynthesis (Litton et al. 2007). Waring et al. (1998) supported this conclusion by studying the annual carbon budgets of diverse coniferous and deciduous communities in the US, Australia, and New Zealand. Their net primary productivity (NPP)/GPP ratio was 0.47 ± 0.04. But the rate is less constant when looking at individual trees and at a wider range of plant communities: R_A at 50% (or less) is typical of herbaceous plants, and the actual rates for mature trees are higher, up to 60% of GPP in temperate forests and about 70% for a boreal tree (black spruce, *Picea mariana*) as well as for primary tropical rain forest trees (Ryan et al. 1996; Luyssaert et al. 2007).

In pure tree stands, R_A rises from 15–30% of GPP during the juvenile stage to 50% in early mature growth, and it can reach more than 90% of GPP in old-growth forests and in some years high respiration can turn the ecosystem into a weak to moderate carbon source (Falk et al. 2008). Temperature-dependent respiration losses are higher in the tropics but due to higher GPP the shares of R_A are similar to those in temperate trees. Above-ground autotrophic respiration has two major components, stem and foliar efflux. The former accounts for 11–23% of all assimilated carbon in temperate forests and 40–70% in tropical forests' ecosystems, respectively (Ryan et al. 1996; Chambers et al. 2004). The latter can vary more within a species than among species, and small-diameter wood, including lianas, accounts for most the efflux (Asao et al. 2015; Cavaleri et al. 2006).

The respiration of woody tissues is between 25% and 50% of the total above-ground R_A and it matters not only because of the mass involved but also because it proceeds while the living cells are dormant (Edwards and Hanson 2003). Because the autotrophic respiration is more sensitive to increases in temperature than is photosynthesis, many models have predicted that global warming would produce faster increases in R_A than in overall photosynthesis, resulting in declining NPP (Ryan et al. 1996). But acclimation may negate such a trend: experiments found that black spruce may not have significant respiratory or photosynthetic changes in a warmer climate (Bronson and Gower 2010).

Net primary productivity cannot be measured directly and it is calculated by subtracting autotrophic respiration from gross primary productivity ($NPP = GPP - R_A$): it is the total amount of phytomass that becomes available either for deposition as new plant tissues or for consumption

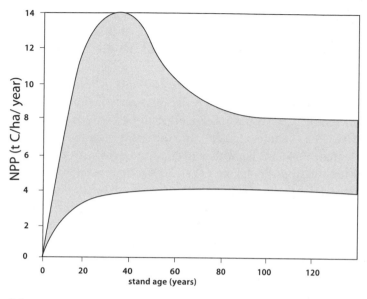

Figure 2.6

Bounds of age-related NPP for 18 major forest type groups in the US: the most common annual productivities are between 5 and 7 t C/ha. Modified from He et al. (2012).

by heterotrophs. Species-dependent annual forest NPP peaks early: in US forests at 14 t C/ha at about 30 years for Douglas fir, followed by a rapid decline, while in forests dominated by maple beech, oak, hickory, or cypress it grows to only 5–6 t C/ha after 10 years, when it levels off (He et al. 2012). As a result, at 100 years of age the annual NPP of American forests ranges mostly between 5 and 7 t C/ha (figure 2.6). Michaletz et al. (2014) tested the common assumption that NPP varies with climate due to a direct influence of temperature and precipitation but found instead that age and stand biomass explained most of the variation, while temperature and precipitation explained almost none. This means that climate influences NPP indirectly by means of plant age, standing phytomass, length of the growing season, and through a variety of local adaptations.

Heterotrophic respiration (R_H, the consumption of fixed photosynthate by organisms ranging from bacteria and insects to grazing ungulates) is minimal in croplands or in plantations of rapidly growing young trees protected by pesticides but considerable in mature forests. In many forests, heterotrophic respiration spikes during the episodes of massive insect invasions that can destroy or heavily damage most of the standing trees, sometimes across vast areas. Net ecosystem productivity (NEP) accounts for the photosynthate that remains after all respiratory losses and that enlarges the existing stores of phytomass (NEP=NPP-R_H), and post-1960 ecosystemic studies have given us reliable insights into the limits of tree and forest growth.

The richest tropical rain forests store 150–180 t C/ha above ground (or twice as much in terms of absolutely dry phytomass), and their total phytomass (including dead tissues and underground growth) is often as much as 200–250 t C/ha (Keith et al. 2009). In contrast, boreal forests usually store no more than 60–90 t C/ha, with above-ground living tissues of just 25–60 t C/ha (Kurz and Apps 1994; Potter et al. 2008). No ecosystem stores as much phytomass as the old-growth forests of western North America. Mature stands of Douglas fir (*Pseudotsuga menziesii*) and noble fir (*Abies procera*) store more than 800 t C/ha, and the maxima for the above-ground phytomass of Pacific coastal redwoods (*Sequoia sempervirens*) are around 1,700 t C/ha (Edmonds 1982). Another instance of very high storage was described by Keith et al. (2009) in an Australian evergreen temperate forest in Victoria dominated by *Eucalyptus regnans* older than 100 years: its maximum density was 1,819 t C/ha in living above-ground phytomass and 2,844 t C/ha for the total biomass.

Not surprisingly, the world's heaviest and tallest trees are also found in these ecosystems. Giant sequoias (*Sequoiadendron giganteum*) with phytomass in excess of 3,000 t in a single tree (and lifespan of more than 3,000 years) are the world's most massive organisms, dwarfing blue whales (figure 2.7). But the comparison with large cetaceans is actually misleading because, as with every large tree, most of the giant sequoia phytomass is dead wood, not living tissue. Record tree heights are between 110 m for Douglas firs and 125 m for *Eucalyptus regnans* (Carder 1995).

Net ecosystem productivity is a much broader growth concept than the yield used in forestry studies: it refers to the entire tree phytomass, including the steam, branches, leaves, and roots, while the traditional commercial tree harvest is limited to stems (roundwood), with stumps left in the ground and all branches and tree tops cut off before a tree is removed from the forest. New ways of whole-tree harvesting have changed and entire trees can be uprooted and chipped but the roundwood harvests still dominate and statistical sources use them as the basic wood production metric. After more than a century of modern forestry studies we have accumulated a great deal of quantitative information on wood growth in both pure and mixed, and natural and planted, stands (Assmann 1970; Pretzsch 2009; Weiskittel et al. 2011).

Figure 2.7
Group of giant sequoia (*Sequoiadendron giganteum*) trees, the most massive terrestrial organisms, in Sequoia National Park. National Park Service image is available at https://www.nps.gov/seki/planyourvisit/images/The-House-2_1.jpg.

There are many species-specific differences in the allocation of above-ground phytomass. In spruces, about 55% of it is in stem and bark, 24% in branches, and 11% in needles, with stumps containing about 20% of all above-ground mass, while in pines 67% of phytomass is in stem and bark, and the share is as high as 78% in deciduous trees. This means that the stem (trunk) phytomass of commercial interest (often called merchantable bole) may amount to only about half of all above-ground phytomass, resulting in a substantial difference between forest growth as defined by ecologists and wood increment of interest to foresters.

Patterns of the growth of trees over their entire lifespans depend on the measured variable. There are many species-specific variations but two patterns are universal. First, the rapid height growth of young trees is followed by declining increments as the annual growth tends to zero. Second, there is a fairly steady increase of tree diameter during a tree's entire life and initially small increments of basal area and volume increase until senescence. Drivers of tree growth are difficult to quantify statistically due to covarying effects of size- and age-related changes and of natural and anthropogenic environmental impacts ranging from variability of precipitation and temperature to effects of nitrogen deposition and rising atmospheric CO_2 levels (Bowman et al. 2013).

Tree Growth

Height and trunk diameter are the two variables that are most commonly used to measure actual tree growth. Diameter, normally gauged at breast height (1.3 m above ground) is easy to measure with a caliper, and both of these variables correlate strongly with the growth of wood volume and total tree phytomass, a variable that cannot be measured directly but that is of primary interest to ecologists. In contrast, foresters are interested in annual stem-wood increments, with merchantable wood growth restricted to trunks of at least 7 cm at the smaller end. Unlike in ecological studies, where mass or energy units per unit area are the norm, foresters use volumetric units, cubic meters per tree or per hectare, and as they are interested in the total life spans of trees or tree stands, they measure the increments at intervals of five or ten years.

The US Forest Service (2018) limits the growing stock volume to solid wood in stems "greater than or equal to 5.0 inches in diameter at breast height from a one-foot high stump to a minimum 4.0-inch top diameter outside bark on the central stem. Volume of solid wood in primary forks from the point of occurrence to a minimum 4-inch top diameter outside bark is included." In addition, it also excludes small trees that are sound but have a poor form (those add up to about 5% of the total living tree volume). For comparison, the United Nations definition of growing stock includes the above-stump volume of all living trees of any diameter at breast height of 1.3 m (UN 2000). Pretzsch (2009) gave a relative comparison of the ecological and forestry metrics for a European beech stand growing on a mediocre site for 100 years: with GPP at 100, NPP will be 50, net tree growth total 25, and the net stem growth harvested only 10. In mass units, harvestable annual net stem growth of 3 t/ha corresponds to GPP of 30 t/ha.

Productivity is considerably higher for fast-growing species planted to produce timber or pulp, harvested in short rotations, and receiving adequate fertilization and sometimes also supplementary irrigation (Mead 2005; Dickmann 2006). Acacias, pines, poplars, and willows grown in temperate climates yield 5–15 t/ha, while subtropical and tropical plantings of acacias, eucalypts, leucaenas, and pines will produce up to 20–25 t/ha (ITTO 2009; CNI 2012). Plantation trees grow rapidly during the first four to six years: eucalypts add up to 1.5–2 m/year, and in Brazil—the country with their most extensive plantations, mostly in the state of Minas Gerais, to produce charcoal—they are now harvested every 5–6 years in 15-year to 18-year rotations (Peláez-Samaniegoa 2008).

The difference between gross and net growth (the latter is reduced by losses and tree mortality) is particularly large in forests with turnover of high whole trees due to their advanced age. Foresters have studied long-term growth of commercially important species both as individual trees and as their pure or mixed stands and express them in terms of current annual increment (CAI) in diameter, height, and stem volume (Pretzsch 2009). The expansion of tree diameter at breast height is the most commonly monitored dimension of tree growth: not only is it easily measured but it also strongly correlates with the tree's total phytomass and with its wood volume.

Annual additions are commonly just 2–3 mm for trees in boreal forests and 4–6 mm for leafy trees in temperate forests, but slow-growing oaks add just 1 mm, while some coniferous species and poplars can grow by up to 7–10 mm (Teck and Hilt 1991; Pretzsch 2009). Annual diameter additions of tropical trees are strongly influenced by their growth stage, site, and access to light. Small, shade-tolerant species in a secondary forest can add less than 2 mm/year and annual growth of just 2–3 mm is common for tropical mangrove formations, while annual increments in rich natural forests range mostly between 10 and 25 mm (Clark and Clark 1999; Menzes et al. 2003; Adame et al. 2014).

Young poplars in temperate-climate plantations add more than 20 mm/year (International Poplar Commission 2016), and some species of commonly planted city trees also grow fast: urban plane trees (*Acer platanoides*) in Italy average about 12 mm/year up to 15 years after planting and about 15 mm/year during the next 10 years (Semenzato et al. 2011). For most trees, annual increments peak at a time when the trunks reach about 50 cm of breast-height diameter and decline by 40–50% by the time the trees measure 1 meter across. In terms of age, stem diameter CAI reach maxima mostly between 10 and 20 years and brief peaks are followed by exponential declines. But stem diameter can keep on expanding, albeit at much slower rates, as long as a tree is alive, and many mature trees continue to add phytomass for their entire life spans.

Excellent examples of this lifelong growth were provided by Sillett et al. (2010). His team climbed and measured crown structures and growth rates of 43 trees of the biosphere's two tallest species, *Eucalyptus regnans* and *Sequoia sempervirens*, spanning a range of sizes and ages. Measurements at ground level found expected declines in annual growth of diameters and ring width—but wood production of both the main stem and of the entire crown kept on increasing even in the largest and oldest studied trees. As expected, the two species have divergent growth dynamics: eucalyptus trees die at a relatively young age because of their susceptibility to fire and fungi, while sequoias attain a similar size more slowly and live much longer not only because they are more fire resistant but also because they channel more of their photosynthate into decay-resistant hardwood. Remarkably, not just individual old trees but even some old-growth forests continue to accumulate phytomass (Luyssaert et al. 2008).

Increases in tree height do not follow the indeterminate growth of tree mass: even where soil moisture is abundant, taller trees experience increasing leaf water stress due to gravity and greater path length resistance that eventually limit leaf expansion and photosynthesis for further height growth. Young conifers reach maxima of height CAI rate of growth (60–90 cm) mostly between 10 and 20 years; some slower growing deciduous trees (maxima of 30–70 cm) can reach maximum height rate of growth only decades later, followed (as in the case of diameter expansion) by exponential declines. Koch et al. (2004) climbed the tallest surviving northern California redwoods (*Sequoia sempervirens*, including the tallest tree on Earth, 112.7 m) and found that leaf length as well as the angle between the long axis of the leaf and the supporting stem segment decrease with height, with leaf length more than 10 cm at 2 m but less than 3 cm at 100 m. Their analysis of height gradients in leaf functional characteristics put the maximum tree height (in the absence of any mechanical damage) at 122–130 m, the range confirmed by the tallest recorded trees in the past.

Lianas, common in tropical rain forests and, to a lesser extent, in many temperate biomes, should grow faster than the host trees because they reduce biomass investment in support tissues and can channel more of their photosynthate in leaves and stem extension. Ichihashi and Tateno (2015) tested this obvious hypothesis for nine deciduous liana species in Japan and found they had 3–5 times greater leaf and current-year stem mass for a given above-ground mass and that they reached the canopy at the same time as the co-occurring trees but needed only 1/10 of the phytomass to do so. But this growth strategy exacts a high cost as the lianas lost about 75% of stem length during their climb to the canopy.

The addition of annual increments over the entire tree life span produces yield curves which are missing the earliest years of tree growth because foresters begin to measure annual increments only after a tree reaches a specified minimal diameter at breast height. Growth curves for both tree heights and stem diameters are available in forestry literature for many species from ages of five or ten to 30–50 years and for some long-lived species for a century or more, and they follow confined exponential trajectories with a species-specific onset of declining growth. All of the nonlinear growth models commonly used in the studies of other organisms or other growth processes have been used in forestry studies (Fekedulegn et al. 1999; Pretzsch 2009). In addition, several growth functions rarely encountered elsewhere (Hossfeld, Levakovic, Korf) were found to provide good fits when charting the growth of heights and volumes.

Confined exponential curves characterize the growth of such different trees as the tallest Douglas firs east of the Cascades in the Pacific Northwest between the ages of 10 and 100 years (Cochran 1979) and fast-growing poplars grown in plantations 10–25 years old on Swedish agricultural land (Hjelm et al. 2015). Growth equations are used to construct simple yield tables or to offer more detailed specific information, including mean diameter, height and maximum mean annual increment of tree stands, their culmination age, and the volume yield by species to several diameter limits. For example, natural stands of Douglas fir in British Columbia will reach their maximum volume (800–1200 m³/ha depending on the degree of crown closure) after about 140 years of growth (Martin 1991; figure 2.8). The maximum mean annual increment of planted Douglas fir stands is

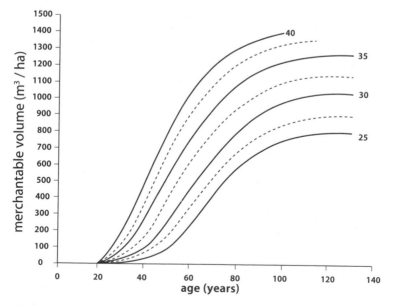

Figure 2.8
Age-related and site-dependent growth of merchantable volume for coastal Douglas fir in British Columbia. Based on Martin (1991).

reached (depending on the site) after 50–100 years of growth, but the merchantable volume of such stands keeps increasing even after 150 years of growth before it eventually saturates, or is reduced to marginal rates, at ages of 200–300 years.

But, as already noted, this well-documented growth decline of even-aged (nearly coeval) forest stands is not, contrary to commonly held assumption, applicable to individual healthy aged trees. Despite their declining growth efficiency (expressed as phytomass growth per unit mass of photosynthesizing tissues), annual growth increments of aging trees can increase until the tree dies due to external forces (ranging from drought to lightning). This continuing accumulation of carbon at increasing rates—a type of accelerating indeterminate mass growth—is well documented by studies of exceptionally large trees. For example, until it was killed by fire in 2003, an enormous 480-year-old *Eucalyptus regnans* tree in Tasmania had aboveground phytomass of about 270 t and an estimated annual growth increment of 1 t (Sillett et al. 2015).

A global analysis of 403 tropical and temperate tree species showed the widespread occurrence of the increasing annual additions of old tree phytomass (Stephenson et al. 2014). Such trees are not senescent reservoirs of phytomass but continue to fix large amounts of carbon when compared to smaller trees. The total annual phytomass addition of trees with 100 cm in trunk diameter is typically nearly three times the rate for trees of the same species with a diameter of 50 cm, and this rapid growth of old trees is the global norm rather than being limited to a few unusual species. At the extreme, a single old massive tree can add annually the same amount of carbon as is stored in an entire mid-sized tree, even as stand-level productivity is declining.

Stephenson et al. (2014) explain this apparent paradox by increases in a tree's total leaf area that are able to outpace decreasing productivity per unit of leaf area and by reductions in age-related population density. The younger trees grow faster in relative terms, older trees, having more leaves and more surface across which new wood gets deposited, grow faster in absolute terms. But to say that "tree growth never slows" (Tollefson 2014) is to leave out the critical qualifier: absolute growth (mass addition per year) may not slow but relative growth does as no group of organisms can keep on growing exponentially.

But some studies have questioned the validity of traditional asymptotic-size models. Bontemps et al. (2012) published an original non-asymptotic growth model formulated as a first-order four-parameter differential equation. They tested the resulting sigmoid curve on 349 old growth series of top height in seven temperate tree species growing in pure and even-aged stands, and it produced a better fit than asymptotic growth equations and hence it may have general relevance to tree growth modelling. The growth of individual trees—much like the growth of some animals and unlike the growth of annual crops and other herbaceous plants—will be indeterminate but the age-related decline in forest productivity is primarily a size-related decline as populations of trees, much like all the assemblages of all organisms, must follow sigmoidal growth curves (Weiner et al. 2001).

As a result, continuing growth of individual trees can be achieved only by reducing the number of stems per unit area: sooner or later, resources (nutrients, water) become insufficient to support all growing trees and self-thinning (plant mortality due to competition in crowded even-aged plant communities) begins to regulate the growth of tree stands. Many trees have to stop growing and have to die in order to make room for other, incessantly growing, survivors. The process lowers the stem density (ρ, numbers/m^2) and it limits the average mass per plant in a highly predictable way captured by the allometric relationship $M = k.\rho^{-a}$ with the exponent between -1.3 and -1.8 and an ideal value of -1.5 and with k at between 3.5 and 5.0 (Reineke 1933; Yoda et al. 1963; Enquist et al. 1998).

As growth gets concentrated in fewer trees, those larger-size trees require larger, long-lasting structures (heavy stems and branches) and effective protection (barks or defensive chemicals). The self-thinning rule means that time can be ignored (mortality depends only on phytomass accumulation) and that thinning proceeds more slowly under poor growing conditions. In terms of actual tree growth, it means (to give a specific example for a commonly planted tree) that in an even-aged monospecific stand of North American balsam fir (*Abies balsamea*) containing 100,000 stems/ha, the mass of an average sapling will be no more than 100 g and their total mass will add up to only about 10 t, while the same lot containing 10,000 (1/10 as many) stems will have trees averaging 10 kg and will hold the total of 100 t of phytomass (Mohler et al. 1978).

Much like in the case of metabolic scaling theory, the universality of the self-thinning rule exponent has been questioned. Lonsdale (1990) argued that it does not approximate to the -1.5 rule and that the straight lines delimiting maximum phytomass are exceptional. Hamilton et al. (1995) concluded that there is no theoretical or empirical evidence for a -1.5 slope. Competition for light is far from being the only cause of self-thinning stem mortality, the maximum supportable phytomass depends on the site quality, and thinning trajectories can be more or less steep than -1.5. Pretzsch (2006) confirmed this absence of narrow clustering as he tested both Reineke's

1.605 and Yoda's 1.5 rule against 120 years of growth in unthinned, even-age stands of deciduous trees spread across southern part of Germany. He found species-specific exponents ranging from −1.4 for common beech to −1.8 for common oak. There were also many nonlinear trajectories caused by storm damage and ice breakage.

Tree growth is strongly affected by the growing conditions, above all the quality of soils and climatic variables. That is why foresters almost invariably use the species-specific site index that measures potential site productivity and that is defined as the average height reached by freely growing (undamaged, unsuppressed) dominant (top height) trees in 50 years of growth above their breast height (Ministry of Forestry 1999). For example, British Columbia's Douglas fir with site index 40 (dominant trees at 40 m) and breast-height diameter of 12.5 cm will have a maximum annual increment of about 15 m^3, while the same species with site index 25 (and the same diameter) will add only 6.3 m^3.

This also means that tree growth can respond rapidly to changed conditions. Large interannual differences in growth rates are common and widely documented. To cite just one recent example, in English temperate broadleaf trees the growth rate was 40% lower in 2010 compared to 2011 and 2012, mostly because low temperature delayed the start of the growing season (Butt et al. 2014). Height increment is often the most sensitive variable affected by drought and annual mass growth can be affected by environmental variables ranging from nutrient shortages to fire damage. Tree rings provide convenient records of these growth fluctuations and their study (dendrochronology) has evolved into a sophisticated discipline (Vaganov et al. 2006; Speer 2011).

Forests can also experience vigorous regrowth and expansion following both natural and anthropogenic disruptions. For example, pollen analysis from the southeastern Netherlands enabled a clear reconstruction of the extent and timing of significant agricultural regression caused by population decline following the Black Death and notable forest regrowth in its aftermath between 1350 and 1440 (van Hoof et al. 2006). Preindustrial deforestation in Massachusetts reduced the state's extent of forest cover from about 85% in 1700 to only about 30% by 1870, but by the year 2000 tree cover had returned to about 70% of the state (Foster and Aber 2004).

And New England's forests, subject to recurrent (infrequent but enormously devastating) super-hurricanes, are also a perfect reminder of the fact that in some regions most trees are not able to live their maximum natural life span. The cyclone of 1938 downed about 70% of all timber in Harvard Forest in central Massachusetts (Spurr 1956). Regrowth has largely healed those losses (Weishampel et al. 2007), but one of the region's dominant trees is now on the verge of extinction. Before 2030, the eastern hemlock (*Tsuga canadensis*) might join the American chestnut as yet another species that has succumbed to a pest, in this case to the woolly adelgid (*Adelges tsugae*), a small aphid-like insect from East Asia that has been killing hemlock trees since the 1960s with no known defense against its depredations (Foster 2014).

Reforestation has been particularly impressive in Europe. First, the transition from wood to coal stopped large-scale forest cutting for fuel during the first half of the 20th century. Post-1950 gains came from a combination of natural reforestation of marginal farmland (made redundant by rising agricultural productivity) and extensive replanting. Between 1900 and 2005, Europe gained almost 13 Mha of forests (approximately the area of Greece), and the gains during the second half of the 20th century were in the order of 20% in Italy and 30% in both France and Germany, and they were even higher in terms of the growing stock (Gold 2003).

Extensive reforestation tied to the abandonment of marginal farmland has also taken place in eastern and southern parts of the US, but no other nation has supported such massive afforestation campaigns as modern China. Unfortunately, most of the Mao-era plantings have failed and only the post-1979 campaigns have been relatively successful (Liu et al. 2005). When using the definition of the Food and Agriculture Organization (FAO) of the United Nations, forests now cover up to 22% of the nation's territory (FAO 2015a), but most of these gains have been in monocultural plantings of fast-growing pines and poplars rather than in mixed stands that would at least somewhat resemble natural growth.

But deforestation continues to be a serious problem in Southeast and South Asia, throughout Africa, and in Latin America, with the largest absolute losses in the Amazon Basin: between 1990 and 2015, the lost forest area of 129 Mha has been almost equal to the territory of South Africa (FAO 2015a). Relative estimates of global deforestation depend on the definition of forests. There is, obviously, a large difference between defining forests only as closed-canopy growth (the ground 100% covered by tree crowns in perpendicular view) or allowing, as FAO does, as little as 10% canopy cover to qualify as a forest. As a result, different estimates imply losses of 15–25% of pre-agricultural (or potential) forest cover (Ramankutty and Foley 1999; Williams 2006), and Mather (2005) emphasized that it is impossible to compile reliable historical series of forested areas even for the 20th century.

Global deforestation estimates have become more reliable only with regular satellite monitoring (the first LANDSAT was launched in 1972). The best estimates see worldwide deforestation rising from 12 Mha/year between 1950 and 1980 to 15 Mha/year during the 1980s, to about 16 Mha/year during the 1990s, and then declining to about 13 Mha/year during the first decade of the 21st century. As already noted, the latest FAO account put the global loss at 129 Mha between 1990 and 2015 but during the same period the rate of net global deforestation had slowed down by more than 50% (FAO 2015a). This slowdown was helped by increasing protection of forests in national parks and other reservations. The beginnings of protected areas go to the closing decade of the 19th century (Yellowstone National Park was set up in 1891) but the process accelerated with the diffusion of environmental consciousness that started in the 1960s. In 2015 about 16% of the world's forested area was under some kind of protection (FAO 2015a).

No simple generalizations can capture the prospects of forest in the coming warmer biosphere with higher concentrations of atmospheric CO_2 (Bonan 2008; Freer-Smith et al. 2009; IPCC 2014). Currently there is no doubt that forests are a major net carbon sink on the global scale, sequestering annually on the order of 4 Gt C, but because of continuing deforestation, particularly in the tropics, the net storage is only about 1 Gt C/year (Canadell et al. 2007; Le Quéré et al. 2013). As with all plants, forest productivity (everything else being equal) should benefit from higher levels of atmospheric CO_2. Experience from greenhouses and a number of recent field tests have shown that higher levels of atmospheric CO_2 result in higher water use efficiency, particularly for C_3 plants (wheat, rice).

This response would be welcome in all those regions where global warming will reduce average precipitation or change its annual distribution. Moreover, Lloyd and Farquhar (2008) found no evidence that tropical forests (by far the most import contributors to annual phytomass growth) are already dangerously close to their optimum temperature range and concluded that enhanced photosynthetic rates associated with higher atmospheric CO_2 levels should more than offset any decline in photosynthetic productivity due to higher leaf-to-air water pressure deficits and leaf temperatures or due to ensuing increased autotrophic respiration rates.

Perhaps the most convincing evidence of positive consequences of higher CO_2 and higher temperatures for forest growth was provided by McMahon et al. (2010). They analyzed 22 years of data from 55 temperate forest plots with stands ranging from 5–250 years and found that the observed growth was significantly higher than the expected increase. Besides increased temperature (and hence an extended growing season) and higher atmospheric CO_2 levels, their explanation has also included nutrient fertilization (via atmospheric nitrogen deposition) and community composition (with some pioneering species growing faster than late-succession trees).

In contrast, an analysis of all major forest biome types (at 47 sites from boreal to tropical environments) showed that while the post-1960s increase of over 50 ppm CO_2 did result in 20.5% improvement of intrinsic water use efficiency (with no significant difference among biomes), the growth of mature trees has not increased as expected as the sites were evenly split between positive and negative trends and showed no significant trend within or among biomes (Peñuelas et al. 2011). Obviously, other factors (most likely periods of drought, nutrient shortages, and acclimation difficulties) negated a significantly positive improvement. In addition, several studies suggest (albeit with low confidence) that in many regions this stimulatory effect may have already peaked (Silva and Anand 2013).

Many forests will adapt to higher temperatures by migrating northward or to higher altitudes but the pace of these displacements will be highly specific to species, region, and site. Net assessments of coming productivity changes remain highly uncertain even for well-studied forests of Europe and North America as faster growth may be largely or entirely negated by a higher frequency of fires, cyclones, and pest damage (Shugart et al. 2003; Greenpeace Canada 2008). And Europe's managed forests have actually contributed to global warming during the past two centuries, not only because of the release of carbon that would have remained stored in litter, dead wood, and soil, but because the conversion of broadleaved forests to economically more valuable conifers increased the albedo and hence evapotranspiration, both leading to warming (Naudts et al. 2016).

Crops

In the preceding section, I explained the relationships between gross and net plant productivity and autotrophic and heterotrophic respiration. Using those variables, it is obvious that agriculture—cultivation of domesticated plants for food, feed, and raw materials—can be best defined as a set of activities to maximize NEP, the goal that is achieved by maximizing GPP while minimizing R_A and, above all, by reducing R_H. Maximized photosynthetic conversion and minimized autotrophic respiration are achieved largely through breeding; by supplying adequate plant nutrients and, where needed, water; by minimizing competition due to weed growth by applying herbicides; by limiting heterotrophic respiration of crops by a variety of defensive measures, now most prominently by applying insecticides and fungicides; and by timely harvesting and waste-reducing storage.

Although several species of mushrooms and of freshwater and marine algae are cultivated for food or medicinal uses, most crops are domesticated species of annual or perennial plants whose structure, nutritional value, and yield have been substantially modified by long periods of selective breeding and recently also by the creation of transgenic forms. Hundreds of plants have been cultivated to supply food, feed, fuel, raw materials, medicines, and flowers, with most species contributed by fruits and vegetables. Some of them include numerous cultivars, none more so than *Brassica oleracea* including various cabbages, collard greens, kales, broccoli, cauliflowers, brussels sprouts, and kohlrabi.

But the range of staples was always much smaller and it has been further reduced in modern mass-scale agriculture, with only a few cultivars providing most of the nutrition, be it in terms of overall energy, or as sources of the three macronutrients. This small group of staples is dominated by cereals. In the order of global harvest in 2015, they are corn (although in affluent countries it is used overwhelmingly not as food but as animal feed), wheat, and rice. These three crops account for more than 85% of the global cereal harvest (just over 2.5 Gt in 2015), the remainder being mostly coarse grains (millets, sorghum) and barley, oats, and rye.

The other indispensable categories of major crops are tubers (white and sweet potatoes, yams, cassava, all almost pure carbohydrates with hardly any protein), leguminous grains (now dominated by soybeans and including various beans, peas, and lentils, all high in protein), oil seeds (the principal sources of plant lipids, ranging from tiny rapeseed to sunflower seeds, with soybeans and oil palm being now major contributors) and the two largest sugar sources, cane and beets (but high-fructose syrup derived from corn has become a major sweetener in the US). Vegetables and fruits, rich in vitamins and minerals, are consumed mainly for these micronutrients, while nuts combine high protein and high lipid content. Major nonfood crops include natural fibers (with cotton far ahead of jute, flax, hemp, and sisal) and a wide variety of feed crops (most grains are also fed to animals, while ruminants require roughages, including alfalfa and varieties of hay and straw).

Our species has relied on domesticated plants for only about one-tenth of its evolutionary span (distinct *Homo sapiens* can be traced since about 200,000 years ago). The earliest dates (years before the present) for well-attested cultivation are as follows: 11,500–10,000 years for emmer (*Triticum dicoccum*), einkorn wheat (*Triticum monococcum*) and barley (*Hordeum vulgare*) in the Middle East, most notably in the upper reaches of the Tigris and Euphrates rivers (Zeder 2008); 10,000 years for millets (*Setaria italica*) in China and squash (*Cucurbita* species) in Mexico; 9,000 years for corn (*Zea mays*) in Central America; 7,000 for rice (*Oryza sativa*) in China and potatoes (*Solanum tuberosum* in the Andes (Price and Bar-Yosef 2011).

Tracing the growth of major crops can be done in several revealing ways. Their planted areas have been expanding or shrinking as new crops have been introduced and old ones have fallen out of favor and as new tastes and preferences have displaced old dietary patterns. The most notable example in the first category has been the diffusion of corn, potatoes, tomatoes, and peppers. Unknown outside Central and South America before 1492, these crops eventually became worldwide favorites of enormous economic and dietary importance. The most common example in the second category has been the declining consumption of legumes and rising intake of processed cereals. As modern societies have become more affluent, eating of leguminous grains (nutritious but often difficult to digest) has receded (with more affordable meat supplying high-quality protein), while intakes of white rice and white flour (increasingly in the form of convenience foods, including baked goods and noodles) have reached new highs.

Two variables have driven the increases in total crop harvests: growing populations that have required larger harvests for direct food consumption, and dietary transitions that have resulted in higher consumption of animal foodstuffs (meat, dairy foods, eggs) whose production has required greatly expanded cultivation of feed crops. As a result, in affluent countries crop production is not destined primarily for direct food consumption (wheat flour, whole grains, potatoes, vegetables, fruits) or for processing to produce sugar and alcoholic beverages, but for feeding meat and dairy mammals and meat and egg-laying birds (and in the US about 40% of all corn is now diverted to produce automotive ethanol).

But no growth indicator of crop cultivation has been more revealing than the increase in average yields. Given the finite amount of good-quality farmland, modern societies would not provide adequate diets to greatly expanded populations without rising yields. In turn, these rising yields have been made possible by the development of improved cultivars and by rising materials and energy inputs, most notably by more widespread irrigation, mass-scale fertilization by synthetic and inorganic compounds, and now nearly universal mechanization of field tasks enabled by growing consumption of liquid fuels and electricity.

Crop Yields

All crop yields have their productivity limits set by the efficiency of photosynthesis. Its maximum limit of converting light energy to chemical energy in new phytomass is almost 27% but as only 43% of the incoming radiation is photosynthetically active (blue and red parts of the spectrum), that rate is reduced to about 12%. Reflection of the light and its transmission through leaves make a minor difference, taking the overall rate down to about 11%. This means that an ideal crop, with leaves positioned at 90° angle to direct sunlight, would fix daily 1.7 t/ha of new phytomass or 620 t/ha if the growth continued throughout the year.

But inherently large losses accompany the rapid rates of photosynthetic conversion. Plant enzymes cannot keep up with the incoming radiation, and because chlorophyll cannot store this influx the incoming energy is partially reradiated, lowering the performance to roughly 8–9%. Autotrophic respiration (typically at 40–50% of NPP) lowers the best achievable plant growth efficiencies to around 5%—and the highest recorded short-term rates of net photosynthesis under optimum conditions are indeed that high. But most crops will not perform that well during the entire growing season because their performance will be limited by various environmental factors.

In addition, there are important interspecific differences. The photosynthetic pathway used by most plants, a multistep process of O_2 and CO_2 exchange energized by red and blue light, was first traced by Melvin Calvin and Andrew Benson during the early 1950s (Bassham and Calvin 1957; Calvin 1989). Because the first stable carbon compound produced by this process is phosphoglyceric acid containing three carbons plants deploying this carboxylation, reduction and regeneration sequences are known as C_3 plants and they include most of the staple grain, legume, and potato crops, as well all common vegetables and fruits. Their principal downside is photorespiration, daytime oxygenation that wastes part of the newly produced photosynthates.

Some plants avoid this loss by producing first four-carbon acids (Hatch 1992). Most of these C_4 plants are also structurally different from C_3 species, as their vascular conducting tissue is surrounded by a bundle sheath of large cells filled with chloroplasts. Corn, sugar cane, sorghum, and millets are the most important C_4 crops. Unfortunately, some of the most persistent weeds—including crab grass (*Digitaria sanguinalis*), barnyard grass (*Echinochloa crus-galli*), and pigweed (*Amaranthus retroflexus*)—are also C_4 species, presenting an unwelcome competition for C_3 crops. Although the C_4 sequence needs more energy than the Calvin-Benson cycle, the absence of photorespiration more than makes up for that and C_4 species are inherently better overall converters of sunlight into phytomass. Differences are around 40% when comparing the maximum daily growth rates, but daily maxima integrated and averaged over an entire growing season are up to 70% higher.

Moreover, photosynthesis in C_4 species proceeds without any light saturation, while C_3 plants reach their peak at irradiances around 300 W/m^2. And while C_3 crops do best in a temperature between 15° and 25°C, photosynthetic optima for C_4 crops are 30°–45°C, making then much better adapted for sunny, hot, and arid climates. Everything else being equal, typical yields of corn and sugar cane are thus well ahead of average yields of wheat and sugar beets, the two common C_3 species that have a similar nutritional composition. Peak daily growth rates actually measured in fields are more than 50 g/m^2 for corn, but less than 20 g/m^2 for wheat. Means for the entire growing season are obviously much lower: in 2015, a very good corn harvest of 10 t/ha corresponded (assuming total growth period of 150 days) to average daily growth of less than 10 g/m^2.

There can be no reliable reconstruction of prehistoric crop yields, only isolated approximations are available to quantify the harvests in antiquity, and even the reconstructions of medieval yield trajectories remain elusive. But if such data were available, they would not reveal any surprises because indirect agronomic and population evidence attests to low, barely changing and highly fluctuating staple grain yields. And the history of English wheat yields—a rare instance where we have nearly a millennium of evidence of reports, estimates and eventually of actual measurements that allows us to reconstruct the growth trajectory—illustrates how uncertain our conclusions are even regarding the early part of the early modern era.

There are two major reasons for these uncertainties. European yields were traditionally expressed in relative terms, as returns of planted seed, and poor harvests yielded barely enough to produce sufficient seed for the next year's planting. Up to 30% of all seed from below-average harvests had to be diverted to seed and only with higher yields during the early modern era did that share gradually decline to less than 10% by the mid-18th century. In addition, the original medieval measures (bushels) were volumetric rather than in mass units, and because premodern seeds were smaller than our high-yielding cultivars their conversions to mass equivalents cannot be highly accurate. And even some of the best (usually monastic) records have many gaps, and yields were also subject to considerable annual fluctuations caused by inclement weather, epidemics, and warfare, making even very accurate rates for one or two years hard to interpret.

Earlier studies of English wheat yields assumed typical wheat seed returns of between three and four during the 13th century, implying very low harvests of just above 500 kg/ha, with reported maxima close to 1 t/ha (Bennett 1935; Stanhill 1976; Clark 1991). Amthor's (1998) compilation of yields based on a wide range of manorial, parish, and country records show values ranging mostly between 280 and 570 kg/ha for the 13th to 15th centuries (with exceptional maxima of 820–1130 kg/ha) and 550–950 kg/ha for the subsequent two centuries. A permanent doubling of low medieval wheat yields took about 500 years, and discernible takeoff began only after 1600. But uncertainties mark even the 18th century: depending on the sources used, wheat yields did not grow at all—or as much as doubled by 1800 (Overton 1984).

More recent assessments produce a different trajectory. Campbell (2000) derived his average wheat yield for the year 1300—0.78 t/ha—from the assessments of demesne (land attached to manors) harvests and assumed the seeding rate of almost 0.2 t/ha. But in the early 14th century the demesnes accounted only about 25% of the cultivated land and assumptions must be made about the average output from peasant fields, with arguments made for both higher or lower outputs (and a compromise assumption of equal yields). Allen (2005) adjusted his 1300 mean to 0.72 t/ha and put the 1500 average about a third higher at 0.94 t/ha. There is little doubt that by 1700 the yields were much higher, close to 1.3 t/ha, but according to Brunt (2015), English wheat yields of the 1690s were depressed by unusually poor weather while those of the late 1850s were inflated by exceptionally good weather, and this combination led to overestimating the period's growth of yields by as much as 50%.

After a pause during the 18th century, the yields rose to about 1.9 t/ha by 1850, with the general adoption of regular rotations with legumes and improved seed selection accounting for most of the gain. According to Allen (2005), average English wheat yields thus increased almost threefold between 1300 and 1850. Subsequent yield rise was credited by Chorley (1981) primarily to the general adoption of rotations including legume cover crops, as in the common four-year succession of wheat, turnips, barley, and clover in Norfolk. These practices had at least tripled the rate of symbiotic nitrogen fixation (Campbell and Overton 1993), and Chorley (1981) concluded that the importance of this neglected innovation was comparable to the effects of concurrent industrialization.

Other measures that boosted English wheat yields included extensive land drainage, higher rates of manuring, and better cultivars. By 1850 many counties had harvests of 2 t/ha (Stanhill 1976), and by 1900 average British wheat yields had surpassed 2 t/ha. Dutch wheat yields showed a similar rate of improvement but average French yields did not surpass 1.3 t/ha by 1900. Even when opting for Allen's (2005) reconstruction (an almost threefold rise between 1300 and 1850), average annual linear growth would have been just 0.3% and the mean rate during the second half of the 19th century would have been just above 0.2%/year.

The long-term trajectory of English wheat yields is the first instance of a very common growth sequence that will be pointed out many times in the coming chapters of this book dealing with technical advances. Centuries, even millennia, of no growth or marginal improvements preceded an eventual takeoff that was followed by a period of impressive gains that began in a few instances already during the 18th century, but much more commonly during the 19th and 20th centuries. While some of these exponential trajectories continue (albeit at often attenuated rates), recent decades have seen many of these growth phenomena approaching unmistakable plateaus, some even entering a period of (temporary or longer-lasting) decline.

And wheat yields also represent one of those relatively rare phenomena where the US has not only not led the world in their modern growth but was a belated follower. This is due to the extensive nature of US wheat farming, dominated by vast areas of the Great Plains where the climate is much harsher than in Atlantic Europe. Recurrent shortages of precipitation preclude heavy fertilizer applications, and low temperatures limit the cultivation of winter wheat and reduce the average yield. Records from Kansas, the heart of the Great Plains wheat region, show nearly a century of stagnating (and highly fluctuating) harvests. Average yields (calculated as the mean of the previous five years) was 1 t/ha in 1870 as well as in 1900 and 1950 (1.04, 0.98 and 1.06, to be exact), and they rose above 2 t/ha only by 1970 (USDA 2016a). Nationwide wheat yield rose only marginally during the second half of the 19th century from 0.74 t/ha in 1866 to 0.82 t/ha in 1900, and it was still only 1.11 t/ha by 1950.

During the first half of the 20th century, plant breeders aimed at introducing new cultivars that would be more resistant to wheat diseases and whose shorter and stiffer stalks would reduce the lodging (falling over) of maturing crops and the resulting yield loss. Traditional cereal cultivars had a very low harvest index expressed as the ratio of grain yield and the total above-ground phytomass including inedible straw (stalks and leaves). This quotient, often called the grain-to-straw ratio, was as low as 0.2–0.3 for wheat (harvests produced three to five times as much straw as grain) and no higher than 0.36 for rice (Donald and Hamblin 1976; Smil 1999).

Short-stalked wheat varieties may have originated in Korea in the third or fourth century. They reached Japan by the 16th century and by the early 20th century the Japanese variety Akakomugi was brought to Italy for crossing. In 1917 Daruma, another Japanese short-straw variety, was crossed with American Fultz; in 1924 that cultivar was crossed with Turkey Red; and in 1935 Gonjiro Inazuka released the final selection of that cross as Norin 10, just 55 cm tall (Reitz and Salmon 1968; Lumpkin 2015). Two key genes produced semidwarf plants and allowed better nitrogen uptake and heavier grain heads without becoming top-heavy and lodging. Samples of Norin 10 were brought to the US by an American breeder visiting Japan after World War II, and Orville Vogel used the cultivar to produce Gaines, the first semidwarf winter wheat suitable for commercial production, released in 1961 (Vogel 1977). Vogel also provided Norin 10 to Norman Borlaug, who led Mexico's antilodging, yield-raising breeding program that has operated since 1966 as CIMMYT, the International Maize and Wheat Improvement Center.

CIMMYT released the first two high-yielding semidwarf commercial Norin 10 derivatives (Pitic 62 and Penjamo) in 1962 (Lumpkin 2015). These cultivars and their successors enabled the sudden yield growth that became known as the Green Revolution and resulted in a Nobel Prize for Norman Borlaug (Borlaug 1970). Their harvest indices were around 0.5, yielding as much edible grain as inedible straw, and their worldwide diffusion changed the yield prospects. Berry et al. (2015) offered a closer look at the long-term impact of short-stalked wheat by analyzing the height of UK winter wheat using data from national variety testing trials between 1977 and 2013. Overall average height reduction was 22 cm (from 110 to 88 cm) and annual yield increases attributable to new varieties were 61 kg/ha between 1948 and 1981 and 74 kg/ha between 1982 and 2007, amounting to a total genetic improvement of about 3 t/ha between 1970 and 2007.

Until the 1960s, wheat was the world's leading grain crop, but Asia's growing populations and high demand for meat pushed both rice and corn ahead of wheat. Corn has become the most important grain (with an annual global harvest just above 1 Gt), followed by rice, with wheat closely behind. China, India, US, Russia, and France are the world's largest wheat producers, Canada, US, Australia, France, and Russia are the crop's leading exporters. Wheat's global yield (depressed by crops grown in a semiarid environment without adequate irrigation and fertilization) rose from 1.2 t/ha in 1965 to 1.85 t/ha in 1980, a gain of nearly 55% in just 15 years, and in the next 15 years it increased by another 35%. The response was no less impressive in the most productive European agricultures where the yields of 3–4 t/ha reached during the early 1960s marked the limit of improved traditional cultivars grown under near-optimal environmental conditions with plenty of fertilizers. Western European wheat yields more than doubled from 3 t/ha during the early 1960s to 6.5 t/ha during the early 1990s (FAO 2018).

After the yields began to rise during the 1960s, progress remained linear but average growth rates were substantially higher (in some places up to an order of magnitude) than during the previous decades of marginal gains. Global wheat yields rose from the average of just 1.17 t/ha (mean of 1961–1965) to 3.15 t/ha (mean of 2010–2014), an annual gain of 3.2% or about 40 kg/year per hectare (FAO 2018). During the same period, the British harvest grew by 1.7% a year, the French by 3.2%, and growth rates reached 5% in India and 7% in China. The yield trajectories of other major wheat-producing countries show decades of stagnating low productivity pre-1960 followed by more than half a century of linear growth, including in Mexico (showing a fairly steep improvement), Russia, and Spain (Calderini and Slafer 1998).

Nationwide means of US wheat yields have been available annually since 1866 (USDA 2017a) and their trajectory closely fits a logistic curve with obvious plateauing since the 1980s and with the prospect for 2050 no higher than the record harvests of the early 2010s (figure 2.9). Will the stagnation persist this time? The introduction of modern cultivars raised the nationwide average yield from 1.76 t/ha in 1960 to 2.93 t/ha in 2015, a growth rate of 1.2% a year. A closer look reveals the continuation of substantial annual deviation from the long-term trends, with both above- and below-average yields fluctuating by more than 10% for winter wheat, and

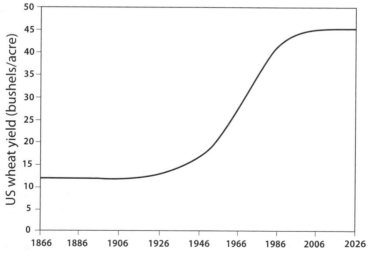

Figure 2.9
Logistic growth (inflection point in 1970, asymptote at 46.5 bushels/acre) of average American wheat yields, 1866–2015. Data from USDA (2017a).

much larger departures (up to about 40%) for Western Canadian spring wheat (Graf 2013).

And there are also clear regional differences. Harvests in the eastern (rainier) states grew a bit faster than those in the central (more arid) states, and western yields rose from just over 2 t/ha to nearly 4.5 t/ha by the early 1990s (an average annual growth rate of nearly 4%) before their linear growth reached a distinct plateau from 1993. Unfortunately, the western US is not the only region that has seen the arrival of wheat yield plateaus. Statistical testing by Lin and Huybers (2012) confirmed that average wheat yields have also leveled off not only in the high-yielding countries of the European Union—in Italy (since 1995), in France (since 1996), in the UK (since 1997)—but also in Turkey (since 2000), India (since 2001), Egypt (since 2004), Pakistan (since 2007), and most notably, since 2009 in China. In total, nearly half of the 47 regions they tested had transitioned from linear growth to level trajectories. Most of these yield plateaus are in affluent countries with large food surpluses where agricultural policies discourage further yield increases.

Brissona et al. (2010) took a closer look at the French decline and stagnation in the growth trend of wheat yields that has been evident in most of the country's regions mainly since 1996–1998. They concluded that this was not due to genetic causes, but that the continuing breeding progress was partially negated by a changing climate, mainly due to heat stress during grain filling and drought during stem elongation. Agronomic changes guided by economic considerations (decline of legumes in cereal rotations, expanded rapeseed cultivation, reduced nitrogen fertilization) had also contributed to the new trend since the year 2000. In any case, even a prolonged yield plateau would have no effect on domestic supply and a minor effect on exports, but the presence of China (with nearly stabilized population but rising meat demand) and India and Pakistan (with their still expanding populations) among the countries with wheat yield stagnation is worrisome.

Chinese crop yield stagnation has not been limited only to wheat. Between 1980 and 2005, when wheat yields increased on about 58% of the total harvest area but stagnated on about 16% of the area, rice and corn yields stagnated, respectively, on 50% and 54% of their total harvested areas (Li et al. 2016). Areas particularly prone to yield stagnation have included regions planted to lowland rice, upland intensive subtropical plantings with wheat, and regions growing corn in the temperate mixed system. The extent of these yield stagnations is high enough to raise questions about the country's long-term staple food self-sufficiency: unlike Japan or South Korea, China is too large to secure most of its grain by imports.

But not all major wheat-growing countries show the dominant trajectory of flat yield followed by rising (or rising and leveling-off) trajectories. The Australian experience has been perhaps the most idiosyncratic (Angus 2011). Yields fell from around 1 t/ha in 1860 to less than 0.5 t/ha by 1900 due to soil nutrient exhaustion, and although they recovered somewhat due to superphosphate fertilization, new cultivars, and fallowing, they remained below 1 t/ha until the early 1940s. Legume rotations boosted the yield above 1 t/ha after 1950, but the period of rapid yield increases brought by semidwarf cultivars after 1980 was relatively short as a millennium drought caused great fluctuations and depressed yields in the new century.

Global rice production is larger than the worldwide wheat harvest when measured in unmilled grain (paddy rice), smaller when compared after milling (extraction rates are about 85% for wheat but just 67% for white rice, with the voluminous milling residues use for feed, specialty foods, and for various industrial products). Average per capita rice consumption has been declining in all affluent countries where rice was the traditional staple (Japan, South Korea, Taiwan) and recently also in China. Global output is still rising to meet the demand in Southeast Asia and Africa. The long-term trajectory of rice yield has been very similar to changes in wheat productivity: centuries of stagnation or marginal gains followed by impressive post-1960 growth due to the introduction of short-stalked, high-yielding cultivars.

The best long-term record of rice yields is available for Japan (Miyamoto 2004; Bassino 2006). Average yields were above 1 t/ha already during the early Tokugawa period (1603–1867) period and by the end of the 19th century they rose to about 2.25 t/ha (as milled, 25% higher as unmilled paddy rice). Long-term linear growth during the 300 years from 1600 was thus less than 0.4%/year, similar to contemporary European rates for wheat harvests. But Japanese rice harvests (much like the English wheat yields) were exceptional: even during the 1950s, typical yields in India, Indonesia, and China were no higher than, respectively, 1.5, 1.7, and 2 t/ha (FAO 2018).

The development of short-stalked rice cultivars (crossing the short *japonica* variety with the taller *indica*) was begun by FAO in 1949 in India but the main work proceeded (concurrently with the breeding of high-yielding wheats) at the International Rice Research Institute (IRRI) at Los Baños in the Philippines, established in 1960. The first high-yielding semidwarf cultivar released by the IRRI was IR8, whose yields in field trials in 1966 averaged 9.4 t/ha and, unlike with other tested cultivars, actually rose with higher nitrogen fertilization (IRRI 1982; Hargrove and Coffman 2006). But

IR8 also had undesirable properties: its chalky grain had a high breakage rate during milling and its high amylose content made it harden after cooling.

But the cultivar launched Asia's Green Revolution in rice and it was followed by better semidwarf varieties that were also more resistant to major pests and diseases. IR36 in 1976 was the first rapidly maturing cultivar (in just 105 days compared to 130 days for IR8) producing preferred slender grain, and it was followed by other releases developed at the IRRI by teams led by Gurdev Singh Khush (IRRI 1982). The adoption of new cultivars has diffused rapidly from Southeastern Asia to the rest of the continent as well as to Latin America and Africa (Dalrymple 1986). Productivity results have been impressive: between 1965 and 2015, average rice yields in China rose 2.3 times to 6.8 t/ha (figure 2.10). Yields in India and Indonesia increased 2.8 times (to 3.6 and 5.1 t/ha, respectively), implying annual linear growth rates of 2.7–3.7%, while the mean global yield had improved from 2 to 4.6 t/ha (2.6%/year).

Corn, the dominant feed grain in affluent countries and an important staple food in Latin America and Africa, was the first crop whose yields benefited from hybridization. In 1908 George Harrison Shull was the first breeder to report on inbred corn lines showing deterioration of vigor and

Figure 2.10
Longsheng Rice Terraces in Guangxi province in China: even these small fields now have high yields thanks to intensive fertilization. Photo available at wikimedia.

yield that were completely recovered in hybrids between two inbred (homo-zygous) lines (Crow 1998). After years of experiments, American breeders developed crosses that produced consistently higher yields and introduced them commercially starting in the late 1920s. The subsequent diffusion of hybrid corn in the US was extraordinarily rapid, from less than 10% of all plantings in 1935 to more than 90% just four years later (Hoegemeyer 2014). New hybrids also produced more uniform plants (better for machine harvesting) and proved considerably more drought-tolerant, a more impor-tant consideration during the exceptional Great Plains drought of the 1930s than their higher yield under optimal conditions.

Yields of traditional pre-1930 open-pollinated corn varieties stayed mostly between 1.3 and 1.8 t/ha: in 1866 (the first recorded year), the US mean was 1.5 t/ha, in 1900 it was 1.8 and in 1930 just 1.3 t/ha, and while there were expected annual weather-induced fluctuations the yield trajectory remained essentially flat (USDA 2017a). Between 1930 and 1960, the adoption of new commercial double crosses improved the average yield from 1.3 t/ha to about 3.4 t/ha corresponding to an average yield gain of 70 kg/year and mean annual linear growth of 5.4%. Subsequent adoption of single-cross varieties (they became dominant by 1970) produced even higher gains, about 130 kg/year, from 3.4 t/ha in 1965 to 8.6 t/ha by the year 2000, imply-ing an average linear growth rate of 3.8%/year (Crow 1998; figure 2.11).

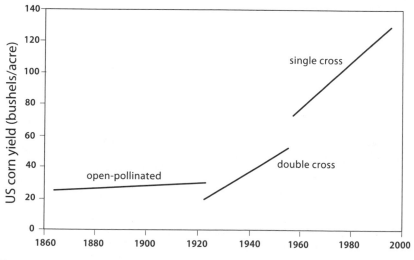

Figure 2.11
Trends of distinct stages of stagnation and growth of average American grain corn yields, 1866–1997. Based on Crow (1998).

And the growth continued in the early 21st century, with the 2015 crop setting a new record of 10.6 t/ha and linear growth rate of about 1.6% during the 15 years. But it would be wrong to credit that impressive yield growth (nearly an order of magnitude gain, from 1.3 t/ha in 1930 to 10.6 t/ha in 2015) solely to hybrid seeds. High yields would have been impossible without greatly expanded applications of nitrogenous fertilizers which allowed a far greater density of planting, widespread use of herbicides and insecticides, and complete mechanization of planting and harvesting that minimized the time needed for field operations and reduced grain losses (Crow 1998). The complete trajectory of average US corn yields (1866–2015) fits almost perfectly a logistic curve that would plateau around 2050 at about 12 t/ha (figure 2.12). That would be a challenging, but not an impossible achievement given that Iowa's record 2016 yield (in the state with the best growing conditions) was 12.7 t/ha.

Higher planting densities were made possible by hybrid improvements in stress tolerance but higher yields could not be achieved without requisite increases in fertilizer applications. During the past 30 years, average North American corn seeding rates have increased at a linear rate by about 750 seeds/ha every year; in 2015 they averaged about 78,000 seeds/ha and in that year almost 10% of the total corn area in the US and Canada was planted with more than 89,000 seeds/ha (Pioneer 2017). Nitrogen

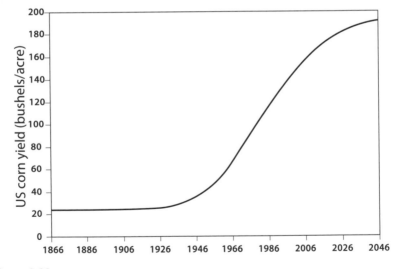

Figure 2.12
Logistic growth trajectory (inflection point in 1988, asymptote at 194.1 bushels/acre) of average American grain corn yields, 1866–2015. Data from USDA (2017a).

applications in US corn production nearly quadrupled between 1960 and 2015, while phosphate applications about doubled and potassium use more than doubled.

America's corn yields remain exceptionally high and they have kept on growing, from a higher base, more impressively than the global mean. Six decades after the widespread adoption of hybrids, American farmers were the first producers to grow transgenic corn. The first genetically modified variety was commercialized in 1996 by Monsanto as "Roundup Ready Corn": it incorporated genes from *Bacillus thuringiensis* that make corn plants tolerant to high levels of herbicide applications (initially to glyphosate, a broad-spectrum herbicide) (Gewin 2003). *Bacillus thuringiensis* transfers expressing toxins can be also used to combat insect infestations. Genetically modified cultivars should have increased yields by preventing the losses that would have taken place in the absence of insect and herbicide tolerance, and the actual gains depend on the efficacy of insect and weed control before the introduction of transgenic plants.

Transgenic corn conquered US production quite rapidly: starting from zero in 1996, the area planted to new cultivars rose to 25% in the year 2000, and in 2016 89% of all corn plantings had herbicide tolerance, 79% had insect tolerance, and 76% were stacked varieties, containing both traits (USDA 2016b). Genetically modified soybeans, rapeseed (and cotton) had followed soon afterward, but the adoption of transgenic crops has encountered a great deal of consumer as well as regulatory resistance (particularly in the EU). As a result, there is still no large-scale cultivation of transgenic wheat or rice. But the opposition is not based on solid scientific foundations. Klümper and Qaim (2014) examined all principal factors that influence outcomes of genetically modified cropping and their meta-analysis provided robust evidence of benefits for producers in both affluent and low-income countries. On average, the adoption of transgenic crops has reduced pesticide use by 37% while it increased crop yields by 22% and profits by 68%, and yield gains were larger for insect-resistant than for herbicide-tolerant crops, and they have been higher in low-income countries.

But there has been one worrisome trend. Lobell et al. (2014) analyzed corn yields in the most productive Corn Belt states (Iowa, Illinois, and Indiana) and found that between 1995 and 2012 agronomic changes translated into improved drought tolerance of plants but that corn yields remain sensitive to water vapor pressure deficit (VPD), a variable that was not included in the previous analyses of yields and climate change. Because VPD is expected to increase from 2.2 kPa in 2014 to 2.65 kPa by 2050, the unchanged annual rainfall across the study area (940 mm) would support an average yield about 10% lower, making production more vulnerable to even moderate droughts (Ort and Long 2014).

But neither short-stalked cultivars nor genetically modified plants have changed the fundamental nature of crop yield trajectories: linear growth has been the dominant long-term trend in increasing average global productivity of staple grains since the beginning of the green revolution of the 1960s. Exponential increase in crop yields is possible during relatively short time periods (10–20 years) but not over the long term because it must eventually approach a yield potential ceiling determined by biophysical limits: that is why projections assuming that future crop yields will increase at exponential rates have absolutely no justification in past experience (Grassini et al. 2013). Such a growth pattern would require unprecedented departures from the prevailing ways of crop breeding and from the best agronomic procedures. And while some astonishing advances in designing synthetic crops *de novo* cannot be absolutely excluded, such designs remain in the realm of science fiction and cannot be seen as plausible contributions to feeding the world in the coming few decades.

Moreover, it is important to reiterate that a wide variety of annual crop yield gains have begun to deviate from decades of linear growth. This has ranged from declines in the annual rate of yield gain (some fairly abrupt, others showing a gradual transition to reduced rates) to the establishment of clear yield plateaus. Grassini et al. (2013) showed that since the beginning of the Green Revolution of the 1960s the first pattern, linear piecewise growth with a decreasing growth rate, has applied to such crops as Indonesian rice and Chinese corn, while the second pattern (linear growth with upper plateau) is much more common, evident for Chinese, Korean, and Californian rice, wheat in northwestern Europe and India, and corn in Italy. Although these slowdowns and plateaus have not been worldwide phenomena extending to all major crops, some of these shifts have been worrisome because they have affected some key crops in major cropping regions.

Looking ahead, a warmer world with higher atmospheric CO_2 levels will have complex impacts on future crop productivity. Net outcome will depend on species- and environment-specific responses not only to higher average temperatures but also to changes in growing season and temperatures (and water availability) during critical phases of plant development. Even one of the least controversial expectations—that C_3 plants should benefit more from increasing concentrations of atmospheric CO_2 than C_4 species, mainly because of promoting stomatal closure and saving water (Bazzaz and Sombroek 1996; Körner et al. 2007)—will be greatly affected by nutrient availability and higher temperatures.

The extent of what has become known (inaccurately) as the CO_2 fertilization effect has been put at a 20–60% increase of gross primary productivity for land photosynthesis at large. Wenzel et al. (2016) constrained that uncertainty (by looking at annual amplitude of the CO_2 seasonal cycle) to $37 \pm 9\%$ for high-latitude ecosystems and 32% or extratropical ecosystems under a doubling of CO_2 concentrations. But such findings cannot be extrapolated to specific crops, net gains could be much lower, and some crops may see substantial yield declines. Most notably, an assessment based on 30 different wheat crop models concluded that warming is already slowing yield gains in most wheat-growing locations, with wheat yield declines with rising temperature likely to be larger than previously expected (falling by 6% for every degree of temperature increase) and becoming more variable (Asseng et al. 2014).

Moreover, even an unchanged trajectory or a clear new trend may be accompanied by greater yield variability and increased unpredictability of harvests. Analysis of changes in yield variability of major crops during the last two decades of the 20th century showed a decrease in 33% of the global harvested area for corn, in 21% of areas for wheat, and 19% of areas for rice, while significant variability increases were found in 11%, 22%, and 16% of the respective areas (Iizumi and Ramankutty 2016). Major agricultural regions with higher variability included Indonesia and South China for rice and Australia, France, and Ukraine for wheat.

Assessments of future crop harvests are on a safer ground when examining yield potential and quantifying the yield gap for specific crops in specific locations. Yield potential refers to a crop whose harvest is limited by the plant's genetic makeup, received solar radiation, temperature during the growing season, and atmospheric CO_2 concentration, and not by shortages of nutrients and water or by pests and weeds. The yield gap is the difference between yield potential (with different values for fully irrigated, partially irrigated, and rainfed crops) and actual yield. Record yields achieved during contests designed to maximize productivity realize 70–85% of the potential, and the difference between 85% of potential yields and actual prevailing crop yields is the exploitable yield gap (FAO 2015c). This value is perhaps the most revealing information about the prospects of long-term crop yield growth and ensuing food security in all regions where nutritional supply remains barely adequate or inadequate.

The best way to determine the yield potential is to use a variety of crop growth models primed with appropriate natural parameters. *Global Yield Gap and Water Productivity Atlas* uses them to provide what it terms "robust estimates of untapped crop production potential on existing farmland based on current climate and available soil and water resources" (GYGA 2017). In 2017 the atlas covered, respectively, 60%, 58%, and 35% of the world's rice, corn, and wheat production and it identifies the regions with the greatest potential for yield growth, allowing an appraisal of the likelihood of food self-sufficiency or the extent of future imports.

Average absolute nationwide yield gaps (all in t/ha) in the US are 2–3 for both rainfed and irrigated corn and 3–4 for irrigated rice (wheat coverage is not yet available), 1.6–2.4 for rainfed and 3.2–4 for irrigated wheat in India, and 2–3 for irrigated rice in China. As expected, absolute gaps are much larger in sub-Saharan Africa where inadequate nutrient supply and poor agronomic practices have kept yields far below their potential. For example, water-limited yields for corn are 12–13 t/ha in Ethiopia and 10–11 t/ha in Nigeria, and with actual harvest being, respectively, just 2–3 and 1–2 t/ha this creates huge yield gaps between 9 and 11 t/ha. This means that even with modest agronomic improvements crop yields in the sub-Saharan Africa could see the fastest growth rates during the coming decades. Yield gaps, quantified and mapped on large scales, are useful guides for assessing the extent of future crop yield growth.

In contrast, world record harvests achieved on small plots under optimal growing conditions should not be taken as indicators of the potential growth of national or regional yields but as demonstrations of how close some of these performances have come to achievable photosynthetic maxima. Remarkably, the US record corn yield rose from 23.5 t/ha in 1985 to 33.3 t/ha in 2015, which means that its average annual gain of 327 kg/ha was three times higher than the corresponding value for the nationwide mean (averages of 7.4 and 10.6 t/ha, that is annual yield gain of 107 kg/ha during those 30 years). Three decades before a Virginia farmer set the record corn harvest of just over 33 t/ha, Tollenaar (1985) calculated that the maximum theoretical yield with existing cultivars should be about 32 t/ha, but that plausible future changes in the plant's energy conversion and photosynthate partitioning might raise the theoretical level to just over 83 t/ha.

And 2015 saw new world records also for winter wheat and rice. Wheat yield of 16.52 t/ha harvested in Lincolnshire in eastern England was nearly twice the national mean of 8.8 t/ha and five time the global mean of 3.3 t/ha (AHDB 2015; FAO 2018). The record for rice of 22.4 t/ha, by a farmer in Nalanda district of India's Bihar state, was nearly five times the global mean of 4.6 t/ha and more than six times the Indian mean of 3.5 t/ha. For comparison, the yield potential of temperate direct-seeded high-yielding rice grown in a southern US state and in California (which now yields between 8.3 (long-grain) and 9.1 (medium-grain) t/ha) has been set at 14.5 t/ha, with actual top yields falling within 85% of the calculated value (Espe et al. 2016).

The best available long-term records for major crops other than staple grain follow the same general pattern of very long premodern yield stagnation followed by decades of linear growth made possible by better cultivars, adequate fertilization, use of pesticides and herbicides, mechanized harvesting and, in many cases, also by supplementary irrigation. In 2015 soybeans were the leading US crop by planted area (usually they are second only to corn) but their cultivation took off only during the 1930s. Yields rose from just 875 kg/ha in 1930 to 1.46 t/ha by 1950, 2.56 t/ha by the year 2000, and 3.2 t/ha in 2015 (USDA 2017a), a linear growth adding annually about 27 kg/ha.

Assessments of future global supply focus on staple crops and typically give little attention to fruits and vegetables. Harvests of these crops have also benefited from the combination of better cultivars, better agronomic practices, and enhanced protection against diseases and pests. During the 50 years between the early 1960s and the early 2010s, the American fruit crop had averaged an annual linear harvest increment of about 150 kg/ha (but apples did much better at 500 kg/ha and are now at about 40 t/ha) and during the same period the average annual gain for all vegetables (excluding melons) was nearly 400 kg/ha (FAO 2018).

But the gains in low-income countries have been much smaller, with annual fruit gains of less than 100 kg/ha. This lag matters, because low intakes of fruit and vegetables are a leading risk factor for chronic disease, and Siegel et al. (2014) showed that in most countries their supply falls below recommended levels. In 2009 the global shortfall was 22%, with median supply/need ratios being just 0.42 in low-income and 1.02 in affluent countries. This inadequacy could be eliminated only by a combination of rising yields and reduced food waste, but improving fruit and vegetable yields is often highly resource-intensive as many of these crops need high nitrogen fertilizer inputs and supplementary irrigation.

Animals

Animal growth has always fascinated many scientific observers, and modern contributions to its understanding have come both from theoretical biology studies and careful field observations, and from disciplines ranging from genetics and biochemistry to ecology and animal husbandry. Thompson (1942) and Brody (1945) remain the classic book-length treatments and they have been followed by volumes dealing with animal growth in general

(McMahon and Bonner 1983; Gerrard and Grant 2007), as well as by volumes on growth and its regulation in farm animals (Campion et al. 1989; Scanes 2003; Hossner 2005; Lawrence et al. 2013).

Animal growth begins with sexual reproduction, and embryonic growth in birds and mammals (much less studied than postnatal development) is well described by the Gompertz function (Ricklefs 2010). As expected, embryonic growth rates decline with neonate size as the –¼ power. Growth rates of neonates weighing 100 g (a typical kitten) are nearly an order of magnitude faster than those of neonates weighing 10 kg (red deer is a good example). The postnatal growth rate scales linearly with embryonic growth rates but it is, on the average, nearly five times more rapid in birds than in mammals.

Growth Imperatives
Extremes of animal growth are dictated by energetic and mechanical imperatives. The temperature limits of animal life are much narrower than those for unicellular organisms (Clarke 2014). Rare marine invertebrates associated with ocean hydrothermal vents can function in temperatures of 60–80°C and few terrestrial invertebrates can survive temperatures of up to about 60°C. Even the most resilient ectothermic vertebrates (cold-blooded organisms that regulate their body temperature by relying on external energy inputs) can manage only up to 46°C, and the cellular temperature of endothermic vertebrates ranges between 30° and 45°C.

Ectotherms can be microscopic (smaller than 50 μm) or, as is the case with hundreds of thousands of insect species, have body mass less than 1 milligram. Even beetles (Coleoptera) and butterflies (Lepidoptera) rarely go above 0.2 g (Dillon and Frazier 2013). In contrast, endotherms, warm-blooded organisms that maintain a steady body temperature, have minimum weights determined by the ratio of body area to body volume. Obviously, for any increase in size (height, length), body area goes up by the square of that increase and body volume by its cube. An endothermic shrew sized as a tiny insect would have too much body surface in relation to its body volume and its radiative heat loss (particularly during cooler nights) would be so high that it would have to eat constantly but that would require spending more energy on incessant searching for food. That is why we have no smaller mammal than the Etruscan pygmy shrew (*Suncus etruscus*) with average body mass of 1.8 (1.5–2.5) g and 3.5 cm long without its tail.

The same imperative limits the minimum bird size: there is no smaller bird that than the bee hummingbird (*Mellisuga helenae*)—endemic to Cuba and now near threatened (IUCN 2017b)—with average body mass of 1.8

(1.6–2.0) g and length of 5–6 cm. At the other extreme, the growth of endo-therms reduces the ratio of their surface area to their body volume (this would eventually lead to overheating), and massive animals would also encounter mechanical limits. Their volume and body mass will grow with the third power of their linear dimensions while the feet area needed to support that growing mass will scale up only with the second power, put-ting an extraordinary load on leg bones.

Other mechanical challenges can be alleviated by a better design, but still only within limits. For example, very long dinosaur necks reduced the need for moving around as they grazed the treetops within their reach, and hollow vertebrae (weighing only about a third of solid bones) made it pos-sible to support very long necks as well as tails (Heeren 2011). The largest sauropods also had additional sacral vertebrae connecting their pelvis and backbone and interlocking bones in forelimbs to enhance their stability. Calculating body masses of the largest known dinosaurs might not seem to be so difficult given the preservation of complete, or nearly complete, skeletons and given the well-established ways of relating skeletal mass to body mass.

That is particularly true with birds providing the clear evolutionary link to dinosaurs—and measurements of skeletal mass and total body mass of 487 extant birds belonging to 79 species have confirmed that the two vari-ables are accurate proxies for estimating one another (Martin-Silverstone et al. 2015). But there are large variabilities of both variables within a single species, and with phylogeny being the key controlling variable it may not be appropriate to use this relationship for estimating total body masses of extinct non-avian dinosaurs. Conceptual and methodological uncertainties in reconstructing dinosaur body masses are reviewed by Myhrvold (2013), who examined published estimates of dinosaur growth rates and reanalyzed them by improved statistical techniques.

The corrections have ranged from relatively small differences (the high-est growth rate for *Albertosaurus* at about 155 kg/year compared to the pub-lished value of 122 kg/year) to very large discrepancies (the highest growth rate for *Tyrannosaurus* at 365 kg/year compared to the published value that was more than twice as large). As for the total body mass, the weight of the largest known dinosaur, a Mesozoic *Argentinosaurus huinculensis* was estimated, on the basis of a preserved femur (using regression relationship between humeral and femoral circumferences) to be 90 t, with 95% predic-tion interval between 67.4 and 124 t (Benson et al. 2014). Other most likely totals for the animal have been given as 73, 83, 90, and 100 t (Burness et al. 2001; Sellers et al. 2013; Vermeij 2016).

For comparison, African male elephants grow to as much as 6 t. But all extraordinarily large mass estimates for extinct animals remain questionable. Bates et al. (2015) found that the value obtained for a newly discovered titanosaurian *Dreadnoughtus* by using a scaling equation (59.3 t) is highly implausible because masses above 40 t require high body densities and expansions of soft tissue volume outside the skeleton that are both several times greater than found in living quadrupedal mammals. On the other hand, reconstructions of total weights for *Tyrannosaurus rex* (6–8 t, with the largest preserved animal up to 9.5 t) are based on multiple specimens of well-preserved complete skeletons and hence have smaller margins of error (Hutchinson et al. 2011).

In addition, the decades-long debate about thermal regulation in dinosaurs remains unresolved. Benton (1979) argued that dinosaurian ectothermy would have been both distinctly disadvantageous and unnecessary, but ectothermic dinosaurs could have achieved endothermy inertially, simply by being large. Grady et al. (2014) believes that the animals were mesothermic, having a metabolic rate intermediate between endothermy and ectothermy, but Myhrvold (2015) questioned their analysis. Perhaps the best conclusion is that "the commonly asked question whether dinosaurs were ectotherms or endotherms is inappropriate, and it is more constructive to ask which dinosaurs were likely to have been endothermic and which ones ectothermic" (Seebacher 2003, 105). The biomechanics of running indicates that endothermy was likely widespread in at least larger non-avian dinosaurs (Pontzer et al. 2009).

Erickson et al. (2004) concluded that a *Tyrannosaurus rex* whose mature mass was 5 t had a maximal growth rate of 2.1 kg/day. This rate was only between a third and one half of the rates expected for non-avian dinosaurs of similar size—but a new peak growth rate resulting from a computational analysis by Hutchinson et al. (2011) largely erases that difference. In any case, it appears that the maximum growth rates of the largest dinosaurs were comparable to those of today's fastest growing animal, the blue whale (*Balaenoptera musculus*), whose reported gains are up to 90 kg/day. We may never know either the fastest growth rate or the greatest body mass of the largest dinosaur with a great degree of certainty, but there is no doubt that the body mass evolution spanning 170 million years produced many successful adaptations, including 10,000 species of extant birds (Benson et al. 2014).

Inevitably, animal growth will result in higher absolute metabolic rates but there is no simple general rule for this relationship. Allometric scaling has been used to quantify the link between body mass and metabolism across the entire range of heterotrophic organisms (McMahon and Bonner 1983; Schmidt-Nielsen 1984; Brown and West 2000). Because animal body mass is proportional to the cube and body area to the square of a linear dimension ($M \propto L^3$ and $A \propto L^2$), area relates to mass as $A \propto M^{2/3}$. Because of the heat loss through the body surface, it is then logical to expect that animal metabolism will scale as $M^{2/3}$. Rubner (1883) confirmed this expectation by relying on just seven measurements of canine metabolism and (as already noted in the introductory chapter) his surface law remained unchallenged for half a century until Kleiber (1932) introduced his ¾ law. His original exponent was actually 0.74 but later he chose to round it to 0.75 and the actual basal metabolic rates can be calculated as $70M^{0.75}$ in kcal/day or as $3.4M^{0.75}$ in watts (Kleiber 1961).

Biologists have not been able to agree on the best explanation. The simplest suggestion is to see it as a compromise between the surface-related (0.67) and the mass-related (1.0, required to overcome gravity) exponents. McMahon (1973) ascribed the 0.75 exponent to elastic criteria of limbs. West et al. (1997), whose work has already been noted in the section on plant growth, applied their explanation of allometric scaling—based on the structure and function of a network of tubes required to distribute resources and remove metabolites—also to animals. Terminal branches of these networks must be identically sized in order to supply individual cells. Indeed, mammalian capillaries have an identical radius and the animals have an identical number of heartbeats per lifetime although their sizes span eight orders of magnitude, from shrews to whales (Marquet et al. 2005). The entire system must be optimized to reduce resistance, and a complex mathematical derivation indicates that the animal metabolism must scale with the ¾ power of body mass.

Other explanations of the ¾ law have been offered (Kooijman 2000), and Maino et al. (2014) attempted to reconcile different theories of metabolic scaling. In retrospect, it seems futile to focus on a single number because several comprehensive reexaminations of animal metabolic rates ended up with slightly to substantially different exponents. White and Seymour's (2003) data set included 619 mammalian species (whose mass spanned five orders of magnitude) and they found that animal basal metabolic rate scales as $M^{0.686}$ and that the exponent is 0.675 (very close to Rubner's exponent) for the temperature-normalized rate. The inclusion of nonbasal metabolic rates and of too many ruminant species in older analyses were seen as the key misleading factor.

Among the major orders, Kozłowski and Konarzewski (2004) found the exponents close to 0.75 for carnivores (0.784) and for primates (0.772) but as low as 0.457 for insectivores and intermediate (0.629) for lagomorphs. The resting metabolic rate for mammals changes from around 0.66 to 0.75 as their body size increases (Banavar et al. 2010), while analysis of the best available avian metabolic data yielded 0.669, confirming Rubner's exponent (McKechnie and Wolf 2004). Bokma (2004) concluded that it is more revealing to focus on intraspecific variability and after analyzing 113 species of fish he found no support for any universal exponent for metabolic scaling.

Glazier (2006) supported that conclusion by finding that the metabolic rate of pelagic animals (living in open water) scales isometrically (1:1, for pelagic chordata actually 1:1.1) with their body mass during their development. The most obvious explanations are high energy costs of the continual swimming required to stay afloat and rapid rates of growth and reproduction due to high levels of mortality (predation). Ectothermic exponents vary widely, 0.57–1 in lizards, 0.65–1.3 in jellyfish and comb jellies, and as much as 0.18–0.83 in benthic cnidarians. Killen et al. (2010) found the full range of intraspecific allometries in teleost fishes between 0.38 and 1.29. Boukal et al. (2014) confirmed a wide variability of the exponent within various taxa.

Additional meta-analyses will confirm the findings just cited, but at least ever since White et al. (2007) published a meta-analysis of 127 interspecific allometric exponents there should have been no doubts about the absence of any universal metabolic allometry. The effect of body mass on metabolic rate is significantly heterogeneous and in general it is stronger for endotherms than for ectotherms, with observed mean exponents of 0.804 for ectotherms and 0.704 for endotherms. A range of exponents, rather than a single value, is thus the most satisfactory answer, and Shestopaloff (2016) developed a metabolic allometric scaling model that considers both cellular transportation costs and heat dissipation constraints and that is valid across the entire range, from torpid and hibernating animals to the species with the highest levels of metabolic activity.

The model does not explicitly incorporate the ¾ value, but considers it as a possible compromise when a body mass grows both through cell enlargement (exponent 0.667) and increase in cell number (isometric scaling, with the allometric exponent of 1). Alternatively, Glazier (2010) concluded that the unifying explanation for diverse metabolic scaling that varies between 2/3 and 1 will emerge from focusing on variation between extreme boundary limits (rather than from explaining average tendencies), on how the slope and elevation (metabolic level) are interrelated, and on a more balanced consideration of internal and external (ecosystemic) factors.

Growth Trajectories

Of the two possible growth trajectories—determinate growth ceasing at maturity and indeterminate growth continuing throughout life—the first one is the norm among the endotherms. The outermost cortex of their long bones has a microstructure (an external fundamental system) showing that they have reached skeletal maturity and hence the end of any significant growth in bone circumference or girth. Continued weight gain after maturity is not uncommon among mammals but that is different from continued skeletal growth. For example, most male Asian elephants (*Elephas maximus*) complete their growth by the age of 21 years but then they continue to gain weight (at reduced rates) for decades, reaching 95% of asymptotic mass by about 50 years of age (Mumby et al. 2015).

Indeterminate growers can accomplish most of their growth either before or after maturation. Kozłowski and Teriokhin (1999) originally concluded that in seasonal environments most of the growth should take place before maturation where winter survival is high and mainly after maturation (displaying highly indeterminate growth) where winter survival is low. But a model that incorporates the decrease in the value of newborns (devaluation of reproduction) with the approach of the end of the favorable season changes the outcome: the relative contribution of growth before and after maturation becomes almost independent of winter survival, and most of the growth comes only after maturation, conforming to a highly indeterminate pattern (Ejsmond et al. 2010). Indeterminate growth has been described in all major ectothermic taxa (Karkach 2006).

Among invertebrates, indeterminate growth is the norm for many benthic marine organisms, freshwater bivalves, clams and mussels and for sea urchins. Insects with indeterminate growth include species with no terminal mold and no fixed number of instars (apterygota: jumping bristletails, silverfish). Indeterminately growing crustaceans include tiny cladocerans (*Daphnia*) as well as shrimp, crayfish, and large crabs and lobsters. Short-lived fishes in warmer regions have determinate growth, long-lived species in colder waters—commercially important salmonids (Atlantic salmon, trout) and perch as well as sharks and rays—continue growing after maturity. As already noted, the growth of fish has been most often modeled with von Bertalanffy's function, but this choice has been problematic (Quince et al. 2008; Enberg et al. 2008; Pardo et al. 2013). The function fits better with growth after maturation but it does not do so well for the immature phase. Alternative models distinguish between the juvenile growth phase (often approaching linearity) and mature growth, where energy is diverted into reproduction (Quince et al. 2008; Enberg et al. 2008).

Evidence of indeterminate growth in reptiles has been equivocal and it is based on inadequate data (Congdon et al. 2013). Recent studies have questioned the existence, or at least the importance, of that growth pattern. The American alligator (*Alligator mississippiensis*) has parallel-fibered tissue that ends periosteally in an external fundamental system, confirming it as another instance of reptilian determinate growth (Woodward et al. 2011). Desert tortoises continue to grow past sexual maturity and into adulthood but their growth ends later in life (Nafus 2015). And while Congdon et al. (2013) concluded that indeterminate growth is a common feature among long-lived freshwater turtles, they found that nearly 20% of all adults of both sexes stopped growing for a decade or more and that the results of indeterminate growth are not a major factor in the evolution and longevity of those species. Indeterminate growth is uncommon among mammals, with examples including males of some kangaroo and deer species, of American bison, and of both African and Asian elephants.

Compensatory growth describes a spell of faster than usual growth rate that follows a period of reduced or arrested growth caused by inadequate nutrition (often precipitated by an extreme environmental event). Because of their determinate growth, birds and mammals invest more resources in such accelerated growth required to achieve their final size, while ectotherms with indeterminate growth remain relatively unaffected by periods of restricted nutrition (Hector and Nakagawa 2012). Fish in particular show little change in their growth rates because their lower metabolism makes them more resistant to short spells of starvation and depletion of their fat stores.

Animal growth spans a continuum of strategies delimited by a single reproductive bout (semelparity) at one end, and repeated successive breeding (iteroparity) at the other. The first extreme produces a large, in some cases truly prodigious, number of offspring; the second one results in single births or, at most, a few offspring spaced far apart. Iteroparity is favored in all cases where the juvenile survival rate varies more than an adult survival rate that is relatively high (Murphy 1968). Katsukawa et al. (2002) related these reproduction strategies to the two growth modes. Their model demonstrated that iteroparity with indeterminate growth is the best choice either when there is a nonlinear relationship between weight and energy production, or in fluctuating environments even with a linear relationship between weight and energy production. The optimal strategy in such environments is to maximize the long-term population growth rate, a goal that does not correspond with maximizing total fecundity.

Zoologists and ecologists now commonly call semelparity r selection (or strategy) and iteroparity K selection, the terms chosen first by MacArthur and Wilson (1967) and borrowed from growth-curve terminology (r being the rate of increase, K the maximum asymptotic size). Each strategy has its advantages and drawbacks. R-selected species (which include most insects) are opportunists *par excellence*, taking advantage of conditions that may be temporarily favorable for rapid growth. These include numerous water puddles after heavy rains to shelter mosquito larvae, trees damaged by fire presenting seemingly endless munching ground for wood-boring beetles, or a carcass of a large animal providing breeding ground for flesh flies. R-selected species produce large numbers of small offspring that mature rapidly and usually without any parental care. Such a strategy assures that more than a few will always survive, and it presents opportunities for rapid colonization of new (usually nearby but sometimes quite distant) habitats and creates problems with what are often bothersome and sometime destructive pests.

For obnoxious species that can spread rapidly over short distances, think of mosquitoes, bedbugs, or black flies; for the destructive ones traveling afar, think of migrating locusts (*Schistocerca gregaria*), whose largest swarms may contain billions of individuals and travel thousands of kilometers as they devour crops, tree leaves, and grasses. If environmental conditions are right, a few successive reproduction bouts can result in exponential increases that may cause a great deal of distress or harm. But because the r-selection parents must channel such large shares of their metabolism into reproduction, their life spans, and hence their reproductive chances, are limited and once the conditions enabling their exponential growth end, their numbers may crash.

They live long only if they have an assured steady supply of nutrients, as is the case with parasites, especially with some intestinal species. Pork tapeworm (*Taenia solium*), the most common tapeworm parasite in humans, can produce up to 100,000 eggs per worm and it can live for as long as 25 years. Parasites and insects are not the only r-selected forms of life: there are plenty of r-selected small mammals whose litters, while considerably smaller, can still translate into overwhelming growth rates. Brown rats (*Rattus norvegicus*) mature in just five weeks, their gestation period is just three weeks, and with at least six to seven newborns in a typical litter the number of females can increase by an order of magnitude in just 10 weeks. If all offspring were to survive, the increase would be about 2,000-fold in a year (Perry 1945).

K-selected species have adapted to a specific range of more permanent resources and maintain their overall numbers fairly close to the carrying capacity of their environment. They reproduce slowly, they have a single offspring that requires prolonged maternal care (direct feeding of regurgitated biomass for birds, suckling by mammals), take long to mature, and have long life expectancy. African elephants (*Loxodonta africana*) and the smaller, and now more endangered, Asian *Elephas maximus* are perfect examples of that reproductive strategy: African elephants start reproducing only at 10–12 years of age, pregnancy lasts 22 months, a newborn is cared for by females of an extended family, and they can live for 70 years. All of the largest terrestrial mammals, as well as whales and dolphins, reproduce in the extreme K-selected mode (twin births are rare, one in 200 births for cattle) but there are also many smaller mammals with a single offspring.

Sibly and Brown (2009) concluded that mammal reproductive strategies are driven primarily by offspring mortality/size relationships (preweaning vulnerability to predation). In order to minimize the chances of predation, animals which give birth in the open on land or in the sea produce one, or just a few precocial offspring (born relatively mature and instantly mobile) at widely separated intervals. These mammals include artiodactyls (even-toed ungulates including cattle, pigs, goats, sheep, camels, hippos, and antelopes), perissodactyls (odd-toed ungulates, including horses, zebras, tapirs, and rhinos), cetaceans (baleen and toothed whales), and pinnipeds (seals, sea lions). And those mammals which carry the young until weaning—including primates, bats, and sloths—must also have a single (or just two) offspring. In contrast, those mammals whose offspring are protected in burrows or nests—insectivores (hedgehogs, shrews, moles), lagomorphs (rabbits, hares), and rodents—produce large litters of small, altricial (born in an undeveloped state) newborns.

Efficiency of animal growth is a function of feed quality, metabolic functions, and thermoregulation (Calow 1977; Gerrard and Grant 2007). Assimilation efficiency (the share of consumed energy that is actually digested) depends on feed quality. Carnivores can extract 90% or more of available energy from their protein- and lipid-rich diets, digestibility rates are between 70–80% for insectivores and for seed-eating animals, but only 30–40% for grazers, some of which can (thanks to symbiotic protozoa in their gut) digest cellulose that remains indigestible for all other mammals.

Net production efficiency (the share of assimilated energy diverted into growth and reproduction) is highly correlated with thermoregulation. Endotherms keep diverting large shares of digested energy for thermoregulation and have low net production efficiencies: just 1–2% for birds (whose internal temperature is higher than in mammals) and for small mammals (whose large surface/volume ratio cause faster heat loss) and less than 5% for larger mammals (Humphreys 1979). In contrast, ectotherms can divert much larger shares of assimilated energy into growth and reproduction. The rates are more than 40% for nonsocial insects, more than 30% for some aquatic invertebrates, and 20–30% for terrestrial invertebrates but (due to their much higher respiration rates) only about 10% for social insects (ants, bees). The earliest growth is often linear, with the published examples including such different species as young Angus bulls and heifers in Iowa (Hassen et al. 2004) and New Zealand sea lion pups (Chilvers et al. 2007).

Growth Curves

As expected, studies of many terrestrial and aquatic species have shown that their growth was best described by one of the confined-growth functions. The Gompertz function represents well the growth of the broiler chicken (Duan-yai et al. 1999) as well as of the domestic pigeon (Gao et al. 2016) and goose (Knizetova et al. 1995). The logistic function describes very accurately the growth of a traditional Chinese small-sized Liangshan pig breed (Luo et al. 2015) as well as of modern commercial pigs, including those reared to heavy weights (Vincek et al. 2012; Shull 2013).

The von Bertalanffy equation has been used to express the growth of many aquatic species, including aquacultured Nile tilapia (de Graaf and Prein 2005) and the shortfin mako shark in the North Atlantic (Natanson et al. 2006). It also captured well the central growth tendency of polar bears collared in the Canadian Arctic—but this study also illustrated significant variance among wild animals which tends to increase with age. Weights of five-year-old bears clustered tightly; for ten-year-old bears averaging about 400 kg, the extremes were between just over 200 kg and more than 500 kg (Kingsley 1979).

Fitting sigmoidal growth curves to 331 species of 19 mammalian orders has shown that the Gompertz equation was superior to von Bertalanffy and logistic function for capturing the complete growth history of mammals (Zullinger et al. 1984). This large-scale analysis also confirmed numerous deviations from expected trajectories. Notable departures include ground squirrels (having faster-than-expected growth rates) and seals (growing slower than expected by the Gompertz function). Chimpanzee (*Pan troglodytes*) growth displayed both negative and positive deviation from the expected growth both in infancy and near maturity; for comparison, human growth appears faster than expected in both of these cases. In contrast, Shi et al. (2014) concluded that the logistic equation, rather than a modified von Bertalanffy equation with a scaling exponent of ¾, is still the best model for describing the ontogenetic growth of animals.

West and his colleagues introduced a general growth equation (universal growth curve) that is applicable to all multicellular animals. The equation is based on the observation that all life depends on hierarchical branching networks (circulatory systems) which have invariant terminal units, fill available space, and have been optimized by evolution (West and Brown 2005). As organisms grow, the number of cells that have to be supplied with energy grows faster than the capacity of branching networks required to supply them and, inevitably, this translates into S-shaped growth curves. When growth data for invertebrates (represented by shrimp), fish (cod, guppy, salmon), birds (hen, heron, robin) and mammals (cow, guinea pig, pig, shrew, rabbit, rat) are plotted as dimensionless mass ratio $(m/M)^{1/4}$ against a dimensionless time variable, they form a confined growth curve with rapid gains followed by a relatively prolonged asymptotic approach (figure 2.13).

Early growth gains are often linear and their daily maxima can be expressed as power functions of adult mass (in grams per day it is $0.0326M^{0.75}$ for placental mammals). The two animal groups that depart from this general rule are primates with their much slower growth, and pinniped carnivores with their very fast growth. Maximum vertebrate growth scales with mass as about 0.75: larger species acquire their mass by proportional acceleration of their maximum growth rate but there are important differences among thermoregulatory guilds and major taxa (Grady et al. 2014; Werner and Griebeler 2014). As expected, endotherms grow faster than ectotherms. Lines of the best fit show an order of magnitude difference between mammals

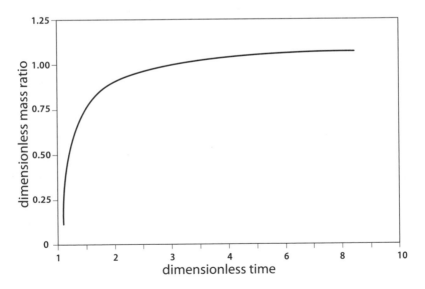

Figure 2.13
Universal growth curve, a plot of the dimensionless mass ratio and the dimensionless time variable. Based on West et al. (2001).

and reptiles, and two orders of magnitude difference between fishes and altricial birds.

Actual maximum gains (all in g/day, rounded) for a few common species with similar final body mass (all about 1 kg) are as follows: rock cod 0.2; cottontail rabbit 8; black grouse (a precocial bird) 14; common raven (an altricial bird) 50. Pinnipeds (walruses and seals) have the highest daily growth rates, with the largest animals (large male walrus, *Odobenus rosmarus* weighing 1–1.5 t) adding maxima of well over 1 kilogram a day (Noren et al. 2014). Growth rates increase with the rate of metabolism, but there are exceptions to this rule. Juvenile altricial birds, brooded by their parents, have lower metabolic rates but higher growth rates than thermoregulating, juvenile precocial birds (McNab 2009). Actual maxima for terrestrial animals range from nearly 2 kg/day for rhinoceros and more than 700 g/day for horse to about 1 g/day for small possums and 0.01 g/day for the smallest skinks and geckos. The African elephant manages only less than 400 g/day, chimpanzees add up to 14 g/day, gorillas about twice as much (human maxima are 15–20 g/day).

One of the most remarkable cases of avian growth is that of the wandering albatross (*Diomedea exulans*), and not only because this bird has the largest wingspan (2.5–3.5 m) as well as the longest postnatal growth period: it also loses up to almost 20% of its body mass before fledging (Teixeira et al. 2014; figure 2.14). The wandering albatross needs 280–290 days to grow

Figure 2.14
Wandering albatross (*Diomedea exulans*) in flight. Photo available at wikimedia.

from hatchling to fledgling, and then 6–15 years before it becomes sexually mature. After 80 days of incubation, single hatchlings are brooded by adults for just 21–43 days and then they are left alone, with a parent returning at progressively longer intervals for brief periods of feeding. This results in a declining amount of food a chick receives during its growing season, and after its body mass peaks in August (at about 1.5 times the adult weight) the chick loses about half of the weight difference from adults before it fledges in November or December, when it still weighs more than the adult.

Finally, a brief clarification of a supposed evolutionary trend in animal growth. According to Cope's rule, animal lineages should evolve toward larger body size over time. Increased body mass has been seen to offer several competitive advantages (increased defense against predation, more successful inter- and intraspecific competition, higher longevity, and more generalized diet) that should outweigh inevitable downsides, above all lower fecundity, longer gestation and development, and higher food and water needs (Schmidt-Nielsen 1984; Hone and Benton 2005). Although he researched evolutionary trends, Edward D. Cope, a much-published 19th-century American paleontologist, never made such a claim. Charles Depéret, a French geologist, favored the notion in his book about the transformations of the animal world (Depéret 1907) but the rule got its name only after WWII (Polly and Alroy 1998) and its thorough examinations began only during the closing decades of the 20th century.

The verdict has been mixed. Alroy's (1998) analysis of Cenozoic mammalian fossils found that the descendant species were, on the average, about 9% larger than their ancestors. Kingsolver and Pfennig (2004) concluded that such key attributes as survival, fecundity, and mating success were positively correlated with larger body size not only in animals but also in insects and plants. Perhaps most impressively, Heim et al. (2015) tested the hypothesis across all marine animals by compiling data on body sizes of 17,208 genera since the Cambrian period (that is during the past 542 million years) and found the minimum biovolume declining by less than a factor of 10 but the maximum biovolume growing by more than a factor of 100,000, a pattern that cannot be explained by neutral evolutionary drift and that has resulted from differential diversification of large-bodies classes.

Another seemingly convincing confirmation came from Bokma et al. (2016). They found no tendency for body size increase when using data from more than 3,000 extant mammalian species, but when they added 553 fossil lineages they found decisive evidence for Depéret's rule. Naturally, they stressed the importance of a long-term perspective, and their findings also indicated that the tendency toward larger body size is not due to gradual increase over time in established species, but that it is associated with the formation of new groups of organisms by evolutionary divergence from their ancestral forms.

In contrast, reconstruction of the evolution of different carnivore families (using both fossil and living species) found that some have acquired larger body sizes while others have become smaller (Finarelli and Flynn 2006). Such a mixed finding was also the result of Laurin's (2004) study of more than 100 early amniote species, and he suggested that the rule's applicability depends largely on the data analyzed and on the analytical method. The most convincing refutation of Cope's rule has come from Monroe and Bokma (2010), who tested its validity by Bayesian analyses of average body masses of 3,253 living mammal species on a dated phylogenetic tree. Difference in natural log-transformed body masses implied that descendant species tend to be larger than their parents, but the bias is negligible, averaging only 0.4% compared to 1% when assuming that the evolution is a purely gradual process.

Smith et al. (2016) offered the most comprehensive review of body size evolution for the three domains of life across the entire Geozoic (3.6 billion years) as organisms had diversified from exclusively single-celled microbes to large multicellular forms. Two major jumps in body sizes (the first in the mid-Paleoproterozoic about 1.9 billion years ago, the second during the late Neoproterozoic to early Paleozoic 600–450 million years ago) produced the variation seen in extant animals. The maximum length of bodies increased from 200 nm (*Mycoplasma genitalium*) to 31 m (blue whale, *Balaenoptera musculus*), that is eight orders of magnitude, while the maximum biovolume (for the same two species) grew from 8×10^{-12} mm^3 to 1.9×10^{11} mm^3, an evolutionary increase of about 22 orders of magnitude. There has been an obvious increase in typical body size from Archaea and Bacteria to Protozoa and Metazoa, but average biovolumes of most of the extinct and extant multicellular animals have not shown similar evolutionary growth.

Average biovolumes of marine animals (Mollusca, Echinodermata, Brachiopoda) have fluctuated mostly within the same order of magnitude, and only marine Chordata have shown a large increase (on the order of seven magnitudes). Average biovolumes of Dinosauria declined during the early Cretaceous period but at the time of their extinction they were nearly identical to the early Triassic sizes. Average biovolumes of arthropods have shown no clear growth trend for half a billion years, while the average biovolumes of Mammalia grew by about three orders of magnitude during the past 150 million years (figure 2.15). Several animal groups (including marine animals, terrestrial mammals, and non-avian dinosaurs) show size increase

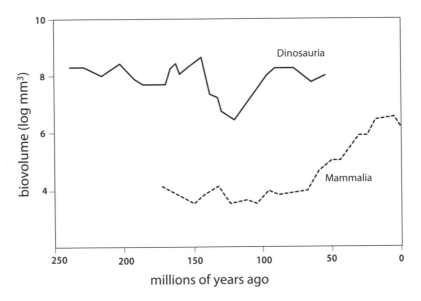

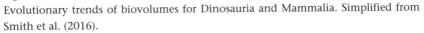

millions of years ago

Figure 2.15
Evolutionary trends of biovolumes for Dinosauria and Mammalia. Simplified from
Smith et al. (2016).

over their evolution (confirming Cope's rule) but statistical analyses make
it clear that unbiased random walk is the best evolutionary trend for five
animal phyla (Brachipoda, Chordata, Echinodermata, Foraminifera, Mollusca), while stasis captures best the evolution of arthropod sizes.

Growth of Domesticated Animals
By far the greatest changes of animal growth have resulted from domestication, whose origins go back more than 10 millennia. Archaeological evidence allows reliable dating of animal domestication: first goats and sheep
(about 11,000 years ago), then pigs and cattle (10,500–10,000 years ago), all
in the Middle Eastern region where today's Turkey, Iraq, and Iran meet (Zeder
2008). Domestication of horses on the Eurasian steppes came much later,
about 2,500 BCE (Jansen et al. 2002). These five species (and dogs) eventually
achieved a global distribution, while an additional eight species of domesticated mammals—water buffaloes, yaks, dromedary and Bactrian camels,
donkeys, alpacas, rabbits, and guinea pigs—remain spatially restricted. Why
just these species, why have we not domesticated dozens of other mammals?

Proclivity to taming, ability to reproduce in captivity, low or no aggres-
siveness and, with large species, easy herding were obvious selection criteria

for domestication (Russell 2002). The growth cycle (time to reach sexual maturity), the rate of reproduction, the length of pregnancy and lactation, and the time to reach the slaughter weight were other key considerations. Extremes were excluded. Small mammals with a high rate of metabolism grow fast but yield very little: this puts 1–2 kg rabbits and guinea pigs at the bottom of domesticates. Very large mammals grow too slowly and require large amounts of feed. As McCullough (1973) observed, animals raised for meat can be thus seen as compromise mammals, combining relatively fast growth with the capacity to accumulate mass, and that limits their body weights mostly to 40–400 kg. Not surprisingly, the largest domesticates are ruminants that can (because of the protozoa in their gut) digest roughages indigestible by other mammals and can survive only by grazing.

Most birds are far too small (and hence their basal metabolism is far too high) to be rewardingly domesticated for meat or egg production and the body weight of wild species that were eventually adopted ranges from less than 500 g for pigeons to about 10 kg for wild turkeys. Southeast Asia's wild fowl were domesticated already some 8,000 years ago and chickens have become by far the most important domesticated birds. Domesticated turkeys (in Mesoamerica) date back to about 7,000 years ago, ducks (in China) to about 6,000 years ago (in China), and geese were domesticated about a millennium later, most likely in Egypt.

Both the pace of maturation and the final slaughter weights were elevated to unprecedented levels by the combination of modern breeding (genetic selection), better feeding in confinement, and the use of prophylactic medications. This combination has worked particularly well for pigs and broilers (Whittemore and Kyriazakis 2006; Boyd 2003; Havenstein 2006; Zuidhof et al. 2014; NCC 2018). Extensive studies of nutritional requirements for cattle, pigs, and poultry have established optimum ratios of macronutrients and supplements for different stages of growth, and periodic updates of guidelines prepared by expert committees of the US National Research Council offer their best summaries (NRC 1994, 1998, 1999, 2000b). Modern practices have also relied on growth enhancers, on widespread preventive use of antibiotics, and on extreme confinement of animals, practices seen by the meat-producing industries as economically imperative but judged from other perspectives, regarded as definitely undesirable (Smil 2013c).

No domesticated mammal can produce meat as efficiently as a pig, not because of its omnivory but because its basal metabolism is almost 40% lower than would be expected for its adult body weight. During the fastest phase of its growth, a healthy pig converts almost two-thirds of all metabolized energy in feed to grow new tissues, a performance more than 40% better than in cattle and even slightly ahead of chickens. Pig growth is also exceptionally rapid and starts from an unusually low birth weight. Human newborns (average 3.6 kg) weigh about 5% of the adult mass, pigs less than 2% (birth weight about 1.5 kg, slaughter weight of 90–130 kg). Piglets grow linearly after birth, doubling their weight during the first week and more than quintupling it by the end of the third week (Chiba 2010). Piglets are weaned in just 25 days (compared to 56 days 50 years ago) and receive supplementary (creep) feeding before weaning. Faster weaning makes it possible to raise the number of piglets per sow from 20 to 25 a year.

Wild pigs, who have to spend a great deal of energy on searching for food and on rooting, reach their maximum adult weight only after three years for males and two years for females (they live 8–15 years). The postweaning growth of domesticated pigs has been compressed into a fraction of that span due to a combination of better feeding in confinement. Landless "confined animal feeding operations" have become the norm in modern meat production and the limits for pigs, normally widely roaming animals, are particularly severe. In the EU they are confined within 0.93 m^2, in Canada the minimum allotment is just 0.72 m^2, both for a mature 100-kg animal on a slatted floor (Smil 2013c).

While the proportions of human and pig bodies differ, adult masses are similar, and for Western men (whose normal body masses range mostly between 65 and 85 kg, in the same range as maturing pigs) it might be an instructive exercise trying to spend a day confined even to 2 m^2, to say nothing about a third of that space! Usually more than 1,000 pigs are now kept under one roof in small stalls and pig production is highly concentrated. Iowa, North Carolina, and Minnesota now produce nearly 60% of all marketed animals (USDA 2015). The growth of confined animal feeding operations has thus created unprecedented concentrations of organic waste.

Newborn piglets grow by about 200 g/day, young pigs add 500 g/day, and mature pigs approaching slaughter weight gain 800 g/day. Modern breeds reach slaughter weight just 100–160 days after weaning, or less than half a year after birth. As always, growth efficiency declines with age, from 1.25 units of feed per unit of gain for young piglets to as many as four units for heavy mature animals (NRC 1998). The US has a unique long-term record of nationwide feeding efficiencies thanks to the calculations regularly published by the Department of Agriculture (USDA 2017c). Data for pigs and beef cattle start in 1910, for chickens 25 years later, and they include all feedstuffs (grain, legumes, crop residues, forages) converted to corn feeding units (containing 15.3 MJ/kg).

In 1910 the average feed/live weight efficiency of American pigs was 6.7; it declined only marginally during the 20th century (fluctuating between 5.9 and 6.2 during the 1990s) but since 2009 it has been just below 5.0 (USDA 2017c). There is a simple explanation for this relatively limited progress: modern pigs have been bred to meet the demand for leaner meat and the animals are significantly less fatty than their predecessors of three or four generations ago and hence less efficient in converting feed to added body mass. For fat the conversion can exceed 70%, for protein (lean muscle) it does not go above 45% (Smil 2013c).

Modern breeding and feeding in confinement has also compressed the growth of domesticated birds, and altered their body size (largest male turkeys now weight more than 20 kg, double the mass of their wild ancestors), composition, and proportions. South Asian red jungle fowl (*Gallus gallus*), the wild ancestor of modern chickens, took up to six months to reach its maximum weight. Traditional free-running chicken breeds (mostly fending for themselves and only occasionally receiving some grain feed) were slaughtered when four to five months old while today's free-range chicken (fed high-quality commercial feed mixtures) are slaughtered in 14 weeks (about 100 days).

In 1925 American broilers commercially produced in confined spaces were marketed after 112 days and their live weight was just 1.1 kg. By 1960, when broiler production began to take off, the market age was 63 days and weight rose to 1.5 kg. By the century's end, the age declined to 48 days (just short of seven weeks) and the weight rose to 2.3 kg; by 2017, the marketing age had not changed, but the weight was just over 2.8 kg (Rinehart 1996; NCC 2018). In 90 years, the feeding span was thus reduced by 57%, the final weight had risen 2.5-fold, and the number of days required to add 500 g of weight was cut from 49 to 8.5. And while during the 1920s it was no more efficient to feed a chicken than to feed a pig, with feed/live weight gain close to five, subsequent improvements lowered the ratio to three by 1950, to two by 1985 and 1.83 by 2017 (NCC 2018), and the USDA series gives even slightly lower values with a minimum at 1.53 in 2012 (USDA 2017c).

Consequently, no terrestrial animal can now grow meat as efficiently as chickens, while ducks need about 50% more feed per unit weight gain, and the recent ratios for American turkeys have been between 2.5 and 2.7. This reality explains the extraordinary rise of chicken production from a relatively minor share of total meat output right after WWII to its recent dominance in many markets. The US output of chicken meat has risen more than 20-fold since 1950, from 1.1 to 23.3 Mt in 2015, and the worldwide growth has been even more impressive, from less than 4 Mt in 1950 to just over 100 Mt in 2015 (FAO 2018). But this growth has subjected modern broilers to a great deal of stress, even to outright suffering.

Increasing growth through confinement has led to such restrictions on bird movement (both for broilers and egg-laying hens) that detestable would be the right adjective to label this practice. There are no legally binding density restrictions for American broilers but guidelines by the National Chicken Council specify just 560–650 cm^2 per bird. The smaller area is easy to visualize, it is smaller than the standard A4 paper sheet, which measures 602 cm^2, or a square with sides just short of 25 cm. Canada's national regulations are only relatively more generous: 1,670 cm^2 on slat or wire flooring is a square of 41 cm (CARC 2003). And turkeys, much larger birds, get no more than 2,800 cm^2 (53 cm square) for lighter individuals.

This crowding is also a perfect illustration of how maximization of profit drives growth even as that growth is not optimal. Studies have shown that broilers convert feed more efficiently, grow heavier, and have lower mortality when given more space (Thaxton et al. 2006), but as Fairchild (2005) noted broiler farmers cannot afford low densities because they would not achieve a satisfactory return. Similarly, feeding efficiency and daily weight gain of pigs improve with lower stocking density, but the overall return (total meat sold) is marginally higher with the highest density.

American broiler houses are large rectangles (typically 12×150 m) that house more than 10,000 birds at a time and produce up to 135,000 birds a year, with some large growers operating as many as 18 houses and marketing about 2 million birds from a single operation. Waste disposal of chicken waste is not helped by the extraordinary concentration of broiler operations. Georgia, Arkansas, and Alabama produce nearly 40% of birds, and Delaware, Maryland, and Virginia (Delmarva) Peninsula have the highest US concentrations of broiler chickens per unit of farmland (Ringbauer et al. 2006). Inside the houses, broilers spend their short lives not only in extreme crowding but also in near darkness.

Hart et al. (1920) discovered that the addition of vitamin D (dispensed in cod liver oil) prevents leg weakness caused by the absence of outdoor ultraviolet light and this made it possible to grow the birds indoors under artificial lighting and in increasingly smaller spaces. Light intensity up to seven days of age is 30–40 lux but afterwards the prescribed broiler house lighting delivers just 5–10 lux (Aviagen 2014). For comparison, 10 lux is an equivalent of twilight and illuminance on a very dark overcast day is about 100 lux. Not surprisingly, this practice affects the bird's normal circadian rhythm, dampens behavioral rhythms, and has possible health effects (Blatchford et al. 2012).

Selection for excessively enlarged breast has been particularly painful as it shifts the bird's center of gravity forward, impairing its natural movement and stressing its legs and heart (Turner et al. 2005). This, in sum, is the growth of modern broilers: abbreviated lives with malformed bodies in dark crowded places that preclude normal activity of what are, after all, social birds, forced to live on a layer of excrement that damages feet and burns skin. Of course, this unprecedented growth causing a great deal of suffering has its ultimate commercial reward, inexpensive lean meat. And there is yet another common feeding practice that carries the risks of white meat production beyond the broiler house.

Soon after the discovery that antibiotics boost broiler weight gain by at least 10%, the US Food and Drug Administration allowed the use of penicillin and chlortetracycline as commercial feed additives in 1951. The two compounds, and oxytetracycline added in 1953, became common growth enhancers in the broiler industry. Half a century later, American poultry producers were feeding more antibiotics than were pig or cattle farmers, a practice that has undoubtedly contributed to the spread of antibiotic-resistant bacterial strains in the modern world (NRC 1994; UCS 2001; Sapkota et al. 2007). Of course, many people have argued that without antibiotics the modern meat industry would collapse, but the recent Danish experience with a more than halving of the use of antibiotics in livestock demonstrates otherwise (Aarestrup 2012).

Unlike in the case of broilers and pigs, the natural cattle cycle leaves much less room for accelerating the growth of animals reared for beef. Heifers, the young females before their first pregnancy, become sexually mature at 15 months of age, are inseminated when two years old, and after nine months of pregnancy a calf stays with the mother for 6–8 months. After weaning, most male calves are castrated and the steers (castrated males) and heifers (except for small numbers set aside to maintain the herd) are fed to market weight. After 6–10 months of stocker phase (summer pasture or roughage), they are moved for the finishing to feedlots where they spend usually three to six months (NCBA 2016).

During the finishing period, American beef animals are fed rations composed of optimized carbohydrate-protein and roughage mixtures (70–90% grain) and nutritional supplements and they gain 1.1–2 kg of live weight a day, with a dry feed-to-liveweight ratio between 6:1 to 8:1. Finishing periods, rations, and maximum gains are similar in two major beef-producing countries, in Canada and Australia. In Canada, finishing animals average 200 days on feed and gain about 1.6 kg/day, in Australia the average weight gain for both the domestic and Japanese market is 1.4 kg/day (BCRC 2016; Future Beef 2016).

For more than 50 years, America's cattlemen have been accelerating this growth by using steroid hormones implanted under the skin on the back of an ear. They dissolve in 100–120 days and promote the growth in finishing beef lots (NCBA 2016). Four out of five of beef animals in US feedlots receive the treatment, and three naturally occurring hormones (estradiol, progesterone, and testosterone) and three synthetic compounds (Zeranol, Trenbolone, and Melengestrol) are approved for use. Depending on the implant used and on the age and sex of the animal, the growth rate will increase by 10–120%, reducing production costs by 5–10%, but the implants do not change the need to reach a certain degree of fatness before the meat marbles and can be awarded a higher quality grade.

Growth hormones used in cattle have been approved as safe not only by the US regulatory bodies but also by the World Health Organization and Food and Agriculture Organization. Beef produced with growth promotants has minuscule amounts of estrogen residue compared to many natural foods and faster growth also translates into reduced demand for feed and hence to reduced greenhouse gas emissions (Thomsen 2011). Nevertheless, the use of hormones in meat production has been prohibited in the European Union since 1981 and the ban survived a US and Canadian challenge (European Commission 2016).

Cattle crowding in large feedlots is, necessarily, less extreme than with smaller animals. American minima are just 10–14 m^2 in unpaved lots and the Canadian allotment is just 8 m^2 on unpaved lots and only 4.5 m^2 on paved ground in a shed (Hurnik et al. 1991). And large beef feedlots are also the extreme illustrations of how the unprecedented agglomerations of animals create inevitable environmental problems, with objectionable odors, waste removal, and water contamination. The country's largest beef cattle feedlots used to finish the animals contain more than 50,000 heads, with the record operations confining 75,000 animals (Cactus Feeders 2017; JBS Five Rivers Cattle Feeding 2017) or a total living zoomass on the order of 30 Mt.

While all those widely cited USDA feed/live weight gain ratios are good indicators of overall growth, they cannot provide comparable data for assessing the energy and protein costs of actually consumed meat. That is why I have recalculated all feeding ratios in terms of feed to edible product (Smil 2013c). This adjustment is particularly important for proteins because collagen (protein present mostly in bones, tendons, ligaments, skin, and connective tissues) accounts for about a third of all protein in mature animals. That is, as Blaxter (1986, 6) put it, "a sobering thought in view of its abysmal nutritive value as food. It is indeed disturbing to think that animal scientists spend so much time and treasure in producing animal protein when a third of it has been recognized since the times of the Paris soup kitchens to be of very poor nutritive worth."

The protein digestibility corrected amino acid score (PDCAAS) is the best way to evaluate protein quality and while in lean meat (be it red meat, poultry, or fish) it ranges between 0.8 and 0.92 (and it is a perfect 1.0 in ovalbumin in eggs or in milk protein), PDCAAS for pure collagen is zero. While only feathers, beak, and bones (all high collagen tissues) may remain uneaten after cooking a chicken in some traditional Asian cuisines, less than 40% of live weight in heavy beef cattle may be edible even when most organ meats have been consumed (in protein terms, the rest is again largely collagen in heavy bones, ligaments, and skin). That is why I have not only recalculated all feeding ratios in terms of feed to edible product but also calculated separate conversion rates for energy (using gross feed input and average energy content of edible tissues) and protein (as direct ratios of feed protein units needed to produce a unit of edible protein as well as in terms of gross feed energy per unit of food protein).

These adjustments show that in mass terms (kg of feed/kg of edible meat and associated fat), the recent American feeding efficiency ratios have averaged about 25 for beef (but it must be remembered that most of it is phytomass indigestible by nonruminants), nine for pork and more than three for chicken, implying respective energy conversion efficiencies of less than 4%, nearly 10% and 15%, and protein conversion efficiencies of 4%, 10% and 30%, while about 25 MJ of feed energy are needed to produce a gram of beef protein and the rates are about10 MJ/g for pork and 2.5 MJ/g for chicken (Smil 2013c). These comparisons show (even more convincingly than the feed/live weight ratios) that chicken growth produces meat protein with by far the highest efficiency and hence with relatively the lowest environmental impact, and the combination explains why chicken became the modern world's most popular meat.

Humans

Long periods of gestation and of helpless infancy, growth during childhood and subsequent spurt during adolescence have been always matters of keen human interest and endless wonder, and eventually subjects of detailed inquiry by a number of scientific disciplines and interdisciplinary studies (Ulijaszek et al. 1998; Bogin 1999; Hoppa and Fitzgerald 1999; Roche and Sun 2003; Hauspie et al. 2004; Karkach 2006; Tanner 2010; Cameron and Bogin 2012). Those inquiries have focused on the one hand on normal, healthy development—whose outward manifestation, besides height and weight, are all those notable and timely developmental milestones: first smile, first words, first walk, naming things, counting (CDC 2016). Extensive research has also looked at retarded and stunted growth, at the failure to thrive caused by malnutrition and poor sanitation, and at the long-term consequences of such deprivations (Jamison et al. 2006; WaterAid 2015). I will review the progress of normal growth, and its secular changes (for both height and body mass) and note the extent of two opposite undesirable conditions, stunting and excessive weight.

Growth in stature is a complex trait involving the interaction of many genes—which are moderately to strongly determinative with overall heritability of 0.5–0.8 (Visscher 2008)—with available nutrition, disease, and other exogenous factors. In its entirety the process is distinctly nonlinear, biophysically driven by selective hormonal stimulation of bone epiphyses. The most important factor is human growth hormone, whose secretion by the adenophysis (pituitary gland) is controlled by the hypothalamus (the brain section governing the production of many hormones) via various stimulating mediators (Bengtsson and Johansson 2000). Sex hormones (above all estrogens) stimulate secretion of growth hormone and insulin-like growth factor.

The growth curves of humans differ substantially from the pattern shared by other placental mammals regardless of their size, a fact first recognized by Brody (1945) and confirmed by von Bertalanffy (1960) and Tanner (1962). Bogin (1999) identified five ways in which human growth differs from that of all other placental mammals. First, human growth velocity, both in mass and length, peaks during gestation and postnatal growth decelerates during infancy, while other placental mammals, be they mice or cattle, have the highest growth velocities during their infancy. Second, sexual maturation of mammals occurs soon after their weaning, but in humans there is, on average, a delay for more than a decade between gestation and puberty.

Third, puberty in mammals occurs while their growth rates are in decline but still close to maxima, while in humans it takes place while growth in both height and mass are at their lowest postnatal points. Fourth, human puberty is marked by an adolescent growth spurt, while mammalian growth rates continue to decline: this growth spurt in stature and skeletal maturation is uniquely human, absent even in the closest primate species. Lastly, other mammals begin to reproduce soon after puberty but humans delay their reproduction. Moreover, this postponement of reproduction has recently lengthened in virtually all affluent societies, as marriage age has risen above 25 in some countries and as first births to older women, including those above 35 years of age, continue to rise (Mathews and Hamilton 2014).

Embryonic growth (up to eight weeks after conception) and fetal development usually end in term delivery (38 weeks from conception, with a range of 37–42 weeks). Survival of prematurely born babies (gestation shorter than 37 weeks, now comprising more than 10% of all American births) has been improving even in the case of very (29–34 weeks) and extremely (24–28 weeks) premature deliveries—but significant shares of surviving infants pay a high price for that survival. About 10% of all premature babies develop a permanent disability, but half of those born before the 26th weeks are disabled in some way, and at six years of age roughly one of every five prematurely born children remains severely affected (Behrman and Butler 2007).

The growth of our brain is a key consideration for the length of pregnancy (longer than in other primates, both in absolute and relative terms) and the need for intensive postnatal feeding and care. The brain of a mature chimpanzee (*Pan troglodytes*) averages less than 400 cm^3, *Australopithecus afarensis* (3 million years ago) had brains of less than 500 cm^3, *Homo erectus* (1.5 million years ago) averaged less than 900 cm^3—while modern adult brains average close to 1,300 cm^3 (Leonard et al. 2007). The human encephalization quotient (the ratio of actual to expected brain mass for a given body weight) is thus as much as 7.8 compared to 2.2–2.5 in chimpanzees and 5.3 in dolphins (Foley and Lee 1991; Lefebvre 2012).

Humans are born with less-developed brains than chimpanzees but at the time of delivery human brain size is a larger percentage of maternal body mass than for primates (Dunsworth et al. 2012). This means that the baby's head size is more likely limited by the mother's metabolic cost of carrying a large fetus rather than (as believed previously) by the width of the birth canal. The subsequent growth of the human brain is rapid, reaching 80% of adult size by age four and nearly 100% by age seven, while the body continues to grow for at least another decade (Bogin 1999). Moreover, the combination of a large active brain (and its need for further substantial growth) and an inept body requires a prolonged period of feeding and maternal care (Shipman 2013).

How we could afford such large brains was a puzzle as long as it was believed that our metabolic rate was very similar to that of other large primates. The best explanation of that paradox was the expensive-tissue hypothesis (Aiello and Wheeler 1995): it posits the need for a tradeoff, a reduction in the mass of another metabolic organ. That would be difficult with heart, liver, and kidneys but it has been accomplished with the human gastrointestinal tract thanks to an improved quality of diet (Fish and Lockwood 2003). Unlike in nonhuman primates that have nearly half of their gut mass in the colon and 14–29% in the small intestine, the reverse is true in humans, with the small intestine accounting for nearly 60% and the colon for 17–25%. In turn, this shift was obviously related to eating more foods of better quality and higher energy-density, including the meat, nutrient-rich innards and fat that began to enter hominin diets with higher frequency in contrast to grasses, leaves, fruits, and tubers that dominate simian diets. Improved walking efficiency was another explanatory ingredient.

But a new study of total energy expenditure in humans and large primates—using the doubly labelled (with isotopes of hydrogen and oxygen) water method (Lifson and McClintock 1966; Speakman 1997)—shows that the key to our high encephalization has been metabolic acceleration. The total energy expenditure of humans exceeds that of chimpanzees (and bonobos), gorillas, and orangutans by, respectively, about 400, 635, and 820 kcal/day, and this difference (averaging 27% more energy per day than chimpanzees) readily accommodates the cost of growth and maintenance of our greater brain and reproductive output (Pontzer et al. 2016). High encephalization is thus supported by hypermetabolic existence.

Height and Mass

Human height is a highly heritable but also a highly polygenic trait: by 2017 researchers had identified 697 independent variants located within 423 loci but even those explain only about 20% of the heritability of height (Wood et al. 2014). As with so many quantitative inquiries, the first systematic monitoring of human growth was done in prerevolutionary France, between 1759 and 1777, by Philibert Guéneau de Montbeillard, who measured his son every six months from birth to his 18th birthday, and the Comte de Buffon published the table of the boy's measurements in the supplement to his famous *Histoire naturelle* (de Buffon 1753).

De Montbeillard's height chart shows a slightly undulating curve, while the plot of annual height increments displays a rapidly declining rate of growth until the fourth year of age followed by the slower decline that precedes the pubertal growth spurt (figure 2.16). These spells of accelerated growth are not unique to our species: sub-adult growth spurts are the norm in both New World and Old World anthropoid primates, more commonly in males (Leigh 1996). This saltatory growth often takes place during small

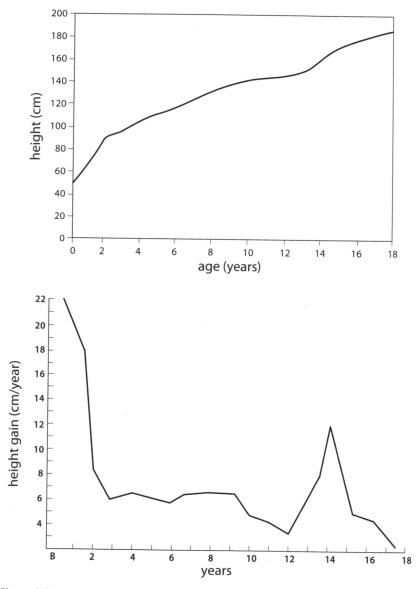

Figure 2.16

Growing height and height gain (cm/year) of de Montbeillard's son. Height data from de Buffon (1753).

intervals of time and because it is detectable only by appropriately detailed sampling and it easily missed by infrequent measurements of large populations (Lampl et al. 1992; Lampl 2009; Gliozzi et al. 2012).

Montbeillard's pioneering observations of a single boy were revealing but they did not, by chance, catch the process close to its statistical mean. As I will show shortly, his son was tall even by the standards of the early 21st century: as a young adult he matched today's average young Dutchman, who belongs to the world's tallest national male group. In 1835 Edouard Mallet applied the concept of normal distribution (for its origins see chapter 1) to his pioneering study of heights of Genevan conscripts (Staub et al. 2011). But the most famous contribution to early studies of human stature was published by Adolphe Quetelet, who related weight and height (body mass index) and, inspired by work linking poverty and the height of French recruits (Villermé 1829) and his own surveys of child growth (in 1831 and 1832), prepared growth tables (for both height and weight of children and adolescents (Quetelet 1835; figure 2.17). After Francis Galton introduced percentile grading (Galton 1876), everything was in place to produce the first charts of human growth (Davenport 1926; Tanner 2010; Cole 2012).

Bowditch (1891) pioneered the practice based on the growth of Massachusetts children, and during the 20th century this was followed by a number of national and international standard curves based on large-scale monitoring of birth weights and heights and of subsequent infant, child, and adolescent growth. We now have many detailed weight-for-age, height-for-age, weight-for-height standards, as well as velocity charts assessing changes in the rate of growth with age. In the US, recommendations are to use the WHO growth charts to monitor growth for infants and children up to two years of age and CDC growth charts for children older than two years (WHO 2006; CDC 2010).

These charts confirm that human ontogeny (the pattern of growth and development) differs substantially not only from that of other similarly massive mammals (pigs are one of the closest examples) but also from other primate species, including chimpanzees, our genetically closest animal predecessors. Growth curves are complex for both body mass and stature (containing sinuous as well as linear intervals); there are dramatic changes of many proportions between infancy and adolescence, and high levels of parental care and a long time between birth and maturation are ontogenetic traits as distinctive among human attributes as a large brain and language (Leigh 2001).

Early linear growth is due to endochondral ossification taking place at the end of long bones and subject to complex regulation by endocrine,

AGES.	TAILLE observée.	TAILLE calculée.	DIFFÉRENCE.
Naissance.	0^{m}490	0^{m}490	0^{m}000
1 an.		0,690	
2 ans.	0,780	0,781	—0,001
3	0,853	0,852	+0,001
4	0,913	0,915	—0,002
5	0,978	0,974	+0,004
6	1,035	1,031	+0,004
7	1,091	1,086	+0,005
8	1,154	1,141	+0,013
9	1,205	1,195	+0,010
10	1,256	1,248	+0,008
11	1,286	1,299	—0,013
12	1,340	1,353	—0,013
13	1,417	1,403	+0,014
14	1,475	1,453	+0,022
15	1,496	1,499	—0,003
16	1,518	1,535	—0,017
17	1,553	1,555	—0,002
18	1,564	1,564	0,000
19	1,570	1,569	+0,001
20	1,574	1,572	+0,002
Croissance terminée.	1,579	1,579	0,000

Figure 2.17
Quetelet's loi de le croissance de la femme (law of women's growth) shows a final average height of 1.58 m. Reproduced from Quetelet (1835), 27.

nutritional, paracrine, and inflammatory factors and also by other cellular mechanisms (Millward 2017). This growth proceeds most rapidly during the first 1,000 days after conception, and in malnourished children it can be postponed until they are better fed and catch-up growth takes place. And when Lampl et al. (1992) measured (semiweekly and daily) 31 infants aged 3 days to 21 months they found that 90–95% of the normal development during infancy is growth-free and that the body length accretion is a distinctly saltatory process as brief incremental bursts punctuate much longer periods of stasis. These saltations get less frequent as children age and are governed by maternal and environmental factors.

WHO standards start with average birth weights of 3.4 kg for boys (98th and 2nd percentiles at, respectively, 4.5 and 2.5 kg) and 3.2 for girls (the same percentiles at 4.4 and 2.4 kg). They show, for both sexes, a brief span of linear growth during the first two months (by that time male infants add about 2 kg and female infants about 1.8 kg), followed by accelerated growth until six or seven months of age, and then slightly declining growth rates until the first year of age when boys reach about 9.6 kg and girls about 9 kg (WHO 2006). Afterwards comes a period of an almost perfectly linear growth until 21–22 months of age, then a longer period of accelerating childhood growth until the age of 14–15 years when American boys add 5 kg and girls about 3 kg a year, and finally an asymptotic approach to the mature weight (figure 2.18).

The growth curves of body mass charted by these standards approximate Gompertz or logistic functions, but even an early study noted that it might be better analyzed as a combination of curves (Davenport 1926). The growth, in terms of both height and mass, is best seen as a growth curve divided into three separate, additive, and partially overlapping components expressed by three separate growth curves, and, inevitably, modeling the velocity curve of human growth also requires three mathematical functions (Laird 1967). The stature growth curve in infancy is an exponential function that lasts for a year and it fades away during the next two years. The childhood curve slows down gradually; it includes a period of near-linear growth between the ages of four and nine (when American boys add 6–7 cm every year), and its best fit is a second-degree polynomial. Pubertal growth is a hormonally induced acceleration that slows down when reaching genetic limits and that is well described by a logistic growth function: annual additions peak at 8–9 cm between the ages of 13 and 14 and slow down to 1 cm between 17 and 18. Each of these curves is determined by the three parameters of the dynamic phenotype: initial length at birth, genetic limits of body length, and maximum velocity of length growth.

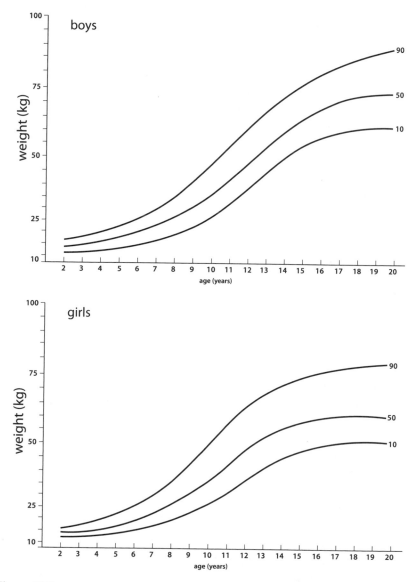

Figure 2.18
Expected weight-for-age growth of American boys and girls. Based on Kuczmarski et al. (2002).

Not surprisingly, examinations of specific populations show nonnegligible deviations from WHO's global growth standards. A recent study in the world's most populous nation—based on the growth of nearly 95,000 Chinese urban children and young adults (0–20 years of age)—showed that all measured variables differed from those standards at nearly all ages, with the most notable differences in height and body mass index (BMI) (Zong and Li 2013). Chinese boys aged 6–10 years are strikingly heavier than the WHO standard, those younger than 15 years (and girls younger than 13 years) are taller, but both genders are significantly shorter when older. BMI is higher for boys of 6–16 years but appreciably lower for girls of 3–18 years. The authors proposed to base a new Chinese growth standard on these findings but inclusion of nonurban children would certainly shift the outcomes: China's population, unlike in the overwhelmingly urban EU or North America, is still about 45% rural.

And we now have a worldwide examination (albeit with inadequate number of observations for Africa) of these departures from WHO standards. When Natale and Rajagopalan (2014) compared them with the worldwide variation in human growth, they concluded that both height and weight curves are not optimal fits in all cases. Height variations were generally within 0.5 of a standard deviation of WHO's means, weights varied more than heights, and for the mean head circumference many groups had means consistently between 0.5 and 1 standard deviation above the WHO standard. Using WHO charts would thus put many children at risk for misdiagnosis of macrocephaly or microcephaly. That is why in the future we may rely on more specific curves not only for different populations but also for various stages of childhood (Ferreira 2012).

Growth (formation of new body tissues and their energy content) requires major shares of total energy expenditure in infants and children: approximately 40% in a newborn, with 35% the mean for the first three months of life. Exponential decline halves it during the next three months, and the share is just 3% at the end of the first year. Subsequent growth claims only 1–2% of total energy expenditure until the end of adolescence. And the share in all individuals who maintain steady body mass is only a small fraction of 1% afterwards, used for the renewal and replacement of short-lived tissues (intestinal lining, epidermis, nails, hair).

But the share of energy intakes claimed by growth has been obviously slightly higher for many adults in modern societies whose body mass keeps on increasing throughout their entire life. The first study that followed a small number of Americans from birth to 76 years of age for weight and stature showed a small decline in height starting in late middle age but continuous (albeit fluctuating) increase in body weight into old age (Chumlea et al. 2009). By age 70, the studied men gained about 20 kg compared to their weight at age 20, while women had a slightly smaller increase. As a result, the BMI (defined as the quotient of weight in kilograms and height in meters squared, kg/m^2) of these individuals rose from desirable levels below 25 to overweight level (25–30).

Adequate energy intake is only a part of human growth requirements. Infants and children could have a surfeit of energy supplied as carbohydrates and lipids and would fail to thrive because humans cannot synthesize nine essential amino acids, required to build body tissues (muscles, internal organs, bones) and to maintain the necessary levels of metabolic and control compounds (enzymes, hormones, neurotransmitters, antibodies), and must digest them preformed in plant and animal proteins. Moreover, these amino acids must be present in adequate proportions: while all common plant foods have incomplete proteins, all animal proteins have the desirable amino acid ratios and are also almost completely digestible (digestibility of legume proteins is less than 80%).

That is why milk and egg proteins are used as the standards to which the quality of all dietary protein is compared, and why the growth of stunted children and acutely malnourished children is best promoted by dairy protein (Manary et al. 2016). Stunting—poor (linear) growth that produces a low height for age in young children—remains common in many low-income countries and it has a number of causes ranging from antenatal and intra-uterine development to postnatal malnutrition. For example, stunting from birth to 10 years of age in a rural district in Bangladesh (with 50% of children affected at age two, 29% at age 10) was independently correlated with maternal height, maternal educational level, and season of conception; the highest probability of stunting was for children born to short, uneducated mothers who were conceived in the pre-monsoon season (Svefors et al. 2016). In more pronounced cases, stunting is linked to such long-lasting consequences as poor cognition, low educational performance, low adult wages, and lost productivity.

De Onis et al. (2011) analyzed nearly 600 representative national surveys in nearly 150 countries and estimated that in 2010 stunting (defined as height less than two standard deviations below the WHO growth targets) affected 171 million children (167 million in low-income countries). The good news was that the global prevalence of stunting had declined from about 40% in 1990 to about 27% in 2010 and was expected to fall to about 22% by 2020, largely due to impressive improvements in Asia (mostly in China). Unfortunately, the share of African stunting has stagnated during the past generation, and if the current trends remain, it would increase by 2025 (Lartey 2015). Improved eating can eliminate stunting fairly rapidly through the process of catch-up growth.

One of the most impressive illustrations of this phenomenon is the growth history of American slave children documented by measurements during the early part of the 19th century in the country's cotton states (Steckel 2007). The growth of those children who received inadequate nutrition was depressed to such an extraordinary degree that even by ages 14 or 15 their height was less than the fifth percentile of modern height standards—but the adult heights of American slaves were comparable to those of the contemporary European nobility, only 1.25 cm shorter than the Union Army soldiers, and less than 5 cm below the modern height standard.

Social inequality, manifested through inferior nutrition, has been a common cause of stunting in societies ranging from relatively rich 19th-century Switzerland (Schoch et al. 2012) to China of the early 21st century, where even the rapid pace of modernization had still left many children behind. Data extracted from the China National Nutrition and Health Survey in 2002 showed that, according to China's growth reference charts, 17.2% of children were stunted and 6.7% severely so, both shares being significantly higher than when using the WHO growth standards (Yang et al. 2015). And in 2010 a survey by the Chinese Center for Disease Control and Prevention found that 9.9% of children younger than five years were stunted (Yuan and Wang 2012).

Advances in economic development can erase such growth differences quite rapidly: stunting is much less common in China's richest coastal cities than in the country's poorest interior provinces, and the growth of children born and growing outside the countries of their parents' birth can become rapidly indistinguishable from the new normal. For example, there is now a sizable Chinese immigrant population in Italy, and a study of Chinese children born and living in Bologna showed that their body length was greater than that of children born and living in China and that their weight and height were higher than those of Italian children during the first year of life and comparable afterwards (Toselli et al. 2005).

Because human height is easy to measure, it has become widely accepted as a simple but revealing marker of human welfare that is linked to health status, wages, and income and gender inequality (Steckel 2008, 2009). Modern societies, whose improved nutrition resulted in a steady increase in average heights, see normal stature as highly desirable and above-normal height as welcome, if not preferable: there is no widespread yearning for growing up short and correlations confirm why. Sohn (2015, 110) summed it well: "It has long been understood that tall people generally exhibit a variety of positive attributes: they are healthier, stronger, smarter, more educated, more sociable, more liked, and more confident than short people. Hence, it is not surprising that they are richer, more influential, more fertile, happier, and longer-lived than short people."

These conclusions now rest on a multitude of quantitative confirmations. Continuation of robust childhood growth into adulthood has been associated with better cognitive function, better mental health, and better conduct of daily activities (Case and Paxson 2008). Being taller correlates with a surprisingly large number of other positives, including such critical physical factors as higher life expectancy, lower risk of cardiovascular and respiratory diseases, and lower risk of adverse pregnancy outcomes, and such socioeconomic benefits as higher cognitive ability, higher probability of getting married, higher education, higher lifetime earnings, and higher social status. The correlation between height and earnings has been known for a century (Gowin 1915) and it has been demonstrated for both physical and intellectual occupations. Choosing just a few of many studies, taller men earn more as coalminers in India (Dinda et al. 2006), as farmers in Ethiopia (Croppenstedt and Muller 2000), and in all categories of occupation in the US, UK, and Sweden (Case and Paxson 2008; Lundborg et al. 2014).

Perhaps the most comprehensive study of this link, a comparative examination by Adams et al. (2016) of 28,000 Swedish men who acted as CEOs between 1951 and 1978, showed not only that they were taller than the population mean but that their height increased in firms with larger assets. CEOs managing companies worth more than 10 billion Swedish kronor average 183.5 cm compared to 180.3 cm for those running companies worth less than 100 million Swedish kronor. And in Western societies, taller bodies win even female beauty contests: the preferred height range of female fashion models (172–183 cm) is significantly above their cohort average of 162 cm (CDC 2012). Top of the female range is thus 13% higher than the mean, while for the men the difference (188 vs. 176 cm) is only about 7%.

Excessive height is a different matter. A reasonably nimble man can leverage his 2 meter height as a basketball star. In 2015 the average height of players in the top teams of the National Basketball Association was exactly 200 cm, with the two tallest players ever measuring 231 cm (NBA 2015). Otherwise there is not much value in exceptional height, and runaway growth that characterizes gigantism, acromegaly, and Marfan syndrome often carries other serious health risks. Pituitary malfunction in children, taking place before the fusion of the epiphyseal growth plates, leads to gigantism that makes young bodies exceptionally large for their age (heights in excess of 2.1 m) and produces extremely tall adults (Eugster 2015). Excessive production of growth hormone by the pituitary gland in middle age, after complete epiphyseal fusion, does not increase stature but it causes acromegaly, abnormal enlargement of bones, especially evident in larger-than-usual sizes of hands, feet, and face. Fortunately, both of these conditions are rather rare. Gigantism is extremely rare and acromegaly affects one out of every 6,250 people.

Marfan syndrome is a slightly more common instance of excessive growth, affecting roughly one out of every 5,000 people. In this genetic disorder a mutation affects the gene controlling the production of fibrillin-1, a connective tissue protein, and results in an excess of another protein, transforming growth factor beta (Marfan Foundation 2017). The resulting features, individually quite different, include generally taller bodies, curved spine, long arms, fingers and legs, malformed chest, and flexible joints—but the heart (aortic enlargement), blood vessels, and eyes may be also affected. Abraham Lincoln is the most famous American who lived with the syndrome, but it is much less known that the mutation affected two virtuoso players and composers of classical music, Niccolò Paganini and Sergei Rachmaninov. Heart complications are relatively common.

Because human height is easy to measure, we can use skeletal remains (femur length has the best correlations with body height) and data from diverse historical sources to trace long-term trends in human growth (Floud et al. 2011; Fogel 2012). Steckel's (2004) millennial perspective used data on more than 6,000 Europeans from the northern part of the continent (ranging from Icelanders in the 9th–11th centuries to 19th-century Britons) and it indicated a significant decline of average heights from about 173.4 cm in the early Middle Ages to about 167 cm during the 17th and 18th centuries, and a return to the previous highs only during the early 20th century.

Both the high early level and a broadly U-shaped time trend are remarkable. The early highs could be explained by a warmer climate during those centuries, and subsequent declines by a cooler climate and medieval warfare and epidemics, while the post-1700 recovery was driven by improved farming methods, new crops, and food imports from the colonies (Fogel 2004). But another long-term European study, extending over two millennia, did not replicate the decline. Koepke and Baten (2005) assembled measurements of 9,477 adults who lived in all major areas of Europe between the 1st and the 18th centuries, and their most surprising finding was one of stagnant heights and no progress even during the early modern centuries (1500–1800) when economic activity was increasing (Komlos 1995) or during Roman times. The latter conclusion contradicts the common view of improving living standards due to the effects of the *pax Romana*: according to Kron (2005), the average male height during the Roman period equaled that of the mid 20th-century European man.

Weighted averages for European males fluctuated narrowly between 169 and 171 cm, with only two significant departures, one of a slight increase above 171 cm during the 5th and 6th centuries, and one of a slight dip below 169 cm during the 18th century. Moreover, average heights were very similar in central, western and southern Europe, and climate and social and gender inequality were also of marginal significance. Clark's (2008) much smaller pre-1867 global data set (with nearly 2,000 skeletons from Norway, and about 1,500 from locations ranging from Mesolithic Europe to Edo Japan) spans heights from 166 to 174 cm with an average of 167, very similar to Koepke and Baten's (2005) mean. Evidence becomes much more abundant for the 19th and 20th centuries and Baten and Blum's (2012) anthropometric set includes 156 countries between 1810 and 1989; it is now also readily accessible in a graphic form (Roser 2017). The authors also published an informative summary of worldwide height trends between 1820 and the 1980s (Baten and Blum 2014).

By far the best analysis of heights for the 20th century was published by the NCD Risk Factor Collaboration (2016) that reanalyzed 1,472 population-based studies, with height data on more than 18.6 million people born between 1896 and 1996 in 200 countries. These analyses documented post-1850 growth throughout Europe, and widespread, but not universal, gain in adult height during the 20th century. Onsets of European growth cluster between the 1830s for the Netherlands—until that time the Dutch, now the world's tallest population, were not exceptionally tall (de Beer 2004)—and the 1870s for Spain, and for men the process resulted in increases of 12–17 cm before the end of the 20th century.

The average gain in adult height for cohorts born between 1896 and 1996 was 8.3±3.6 cm for women and 8.8±3.5 cm for men. When plotted for all studied countries, these increases were largely linear until the 1950s, but afterwards there has been clear plateauing in the tallest populations among both men and women in high-income countries, and Marck et al. (2017) point to this trend as another example of reaching the limits of *Homo sapiens*. This conclusion is strengthened by the fact that the mid 20th-century height plateau is found in all major US sports which select for tall individuals. The average National Football League player gained 8.1 cm between 1920 and 2010, but his height has remained constant at 187 cm since 1980 (Sedeaud et al. 2014).

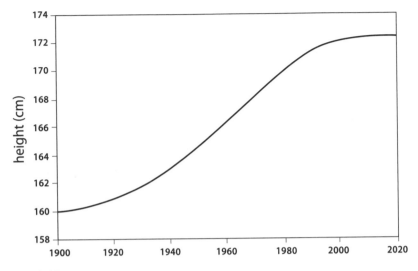

Figure 2.19
Average height of 18-year-old Japanese males, 1900–2020. Plotted from data in SB (1996). Logistic curve has R^2 of 0.98, inflection point in 1961, and asymptote height is 172.8 cm.

The largest 20th-cenury increases were in South Korean women (they gained 20.2 cm on average) and Iranian men (average increase of 16.5 cm). Every population in Europe has grown taller, and perhaps the best long-term record of height increases is available for Japan where the government has been recording the height of both sexes at 5, 6, 8, 10, 12, 14, 15, 16, 18, 20, 22, and 24 years of age since 1900 (SB 2006). The trajectory for 18-year-old males shows an average gain of 11.7 cm and, a brief post–WWII period aside, a good logistic fit with inflection point in 1961 and only marginal gains ahead (figure 2.19). Data for females and for other ages show generally similar trajectories with steadily rising trends interrupted during WWII and a few hungry postwar years, renewed growth at faster rates afterwards, and peak heights reached during the 1990s followed by two decades of stagnation (SB 2017a). The overall 1900–2015 gain was 13 cm for young men and 11 cm for young women.

The gains have been much smaller in the US and Australia. Even during the colonial times (thanks to an abundance of good farmland and low population density) Americans were taller than any contemporary population whose average heights are known, but there was actually a slight dip in average male height between 1830 and 1890, followed by a more than 10 cm gain by the year 2000 (Komlos 2001; Chanda et al. 2008). Australia has closely matched that rise. And a study of 620 infants born in Ohio between 1930 and 2008 (the Fels Longitudinal Study) showed that the most pronounced differences in growth occurred in the first year of life (Johnson et al. 2012). Boys and girls born after 1970 were 1.4 cm longer, and about 450 g heavier but during their first year of life their growth was slower than that of infants born before 1970 ("catch-down growth").

Chinese gains were briefly interrupted by the world's largest famine (1959–1961) but growth of the country's youth in 16 major cities over the period of half a century between the 1950s and 2005 shows that the average height at 18 years of age increased from 166.6 to 173.4 cm for males and from 155.8 to 161.2 cm for females, gains of 1.3 and 1.1 cm/decade (Ji and Chen 2008). And there was no, or very little change, in adult height in some sub-Saharan countries as well as in South Asia: minimal gains in India and Nigeria, no gain in Ethiopia, slight decrease in Bangladesh, but Indonesia has managed a 6 cm gain for its males since the 1870s.

The five nations with the tallest males are now the Netherlands, Belgium, Estonia, Latvia, and Denmark, the female ranking is led by Latvia, Netherlands, Estonia, Czech Republic, and Serbia, and the tallest cohort ever born (average surpassing 182.5 cm) are the Dutch men of the last quarter of the 20th century. The height differential between the tallest and shortest populations was 19–20 cm in 1900 and despite substantial changes in the ranking of countries it has remained the same a century later for women and it increased for men. The lowest average male height is now in Timor-Leste, Yemen (both less than 160 cm), Laos, Madagascar, and Malawi, while the list of shortest adult women is headed by Guatemala (less than 150 cm), Philippines, Bangladesh, Nepal, and Timor-Leste (NCD Risk Factor Collaboration 2016).

Rates of average consumption of high-quality animal proteins are the best explanation of significant height differences through history. The smaller statures of Mediterranean populations during the Roman era reflected limited intakes of meat and fresh dairy products that were consumed often only by high-income groups (Koepke and Baten 2005). Extensive cattle grazing was only a limited option in seasonally arid Mediterranean environments and in all traditional agricultures whose low (and highly fluctuating) cereal and legume yields made it impossible to divert a significant share of grains to animal feeding (available feed went primarily to draft animals). As a result, cow milk—one of the best sources of protein for human growth and a staple food among many northern European populations—was consumed much less in the Mediterranean countries.

Koepke and Baten (2008) investigated the link between height and availability of protein-rich milk and beef by analyzing a data set of more than 2 million animal bones in central-western, northeastern and Mediterranean

Europe. Their indices of agricultural specialization for these three regions during the first and the second millennia of the common era confirm that the share of cattle bones was a very important determinant of human stature. The Germanic, Celtic, and Slavic populations of northern and eastern Europe were not taller than the Mediterranean populations for genetic reasons but because of their higher, and more egalitarian intakes of high-protein foodstuffs (milk, unlike meat, could not be traded easily and was consumed locally).

Improved nutrition—above all the increased supply of high-quality animal protein in general and of dairy products in particular—and a reduced burden of childhood and adolescent diseases have clearly been the two key drivers of the modern growth of average stature. The effect of dairy products on stature is evident from national comparisons and it has been quantified by meta-analysis of modern controlled trials (de Beer 2012). The most likely result of dairy product supplementation is 0.4 cm of additional growth per year per 245 mL (US cup is about 237 mL) of daily intake. The nationwide effect is clearly seen by diverging US and Dutch height trends. American milk consumption was stable during the first half of the 20th century and steadily declined afterwards, while Dutch consumption was increasing until the 1960s and, despite its subsequent decline, is still above the US level; Dutch males, smaller than Americans before WWII, surpassed their American peers after 1950.

There may be other important explanatory variables. Perhaps most intriguingly, Beard and Blaser (2002) have suggested that the human microbial environment played a substantial role in determining the increase of average human height during the 20th century. Its change has included both exogenous and indigenous biota (now the much-researched human microbiome), and particularly microbial transmission of *Helicobacter pylori* in childhood. The recent slowdown of this secular increase (especially among better-off population groups) indicates that we have become increasingly specific pathogen-free.

We do not have as much historical information on changing body weights as we do on growth in height. Skeletal studies of hominins and early humans yielded two general, and opposite, trends, while the modern, and virtually universal, body mass trend is obvious even without any studies. Archaeological evidence (derived from regressions on femoral head size) shows a marked increase of body size with the appearance of genus *Homo* some 2 million years ago (reaching between 55 and 70 kg), and in higher latitudes this was followed about half a million years ago by a further increase of hominin body masses (Ruff 2002). The body masses of Pleistocene *Homo* specimens (reaching up to 90 kg) were, on average, about 10% larger than the averages for humans now living in the same latitudes. The decline of average body masses began about 50,000 years ago and continued during the Neolithic period, undoubtedly associated with the declining selective advantage of larger body weights.

Obesity

The obvious modern trend has been "from growth in height to growth in breadth" (Staub and Rühli 2013, 9). There are sufficient long-term data to show that entire populations as well as such specific groups as Swiss conscripts, US major league baseball players, or Chinese girls (Staub and Rühli 2013; Onge et al. 2008; O'Dea and Eriksen 2010) have been getting heavier, and that this process has accelerated since the 1960s to such an extent that large shares of them are now overweight and obese. These undesirable trends are best measured not in terms of absolute mass gains but as changes of BMI, and this quotient has been used to gauge relative adiposity among all ages. WHO categorization puts people with BMI above 25 kg/m^2 into the overweight category and those with BMI>30 are classified as obese (WHO 2000)—but these cutoffs may not be the best choice for every adult population and for children and adolescents (Pietrobelli et al. 1998). These are important concerns because obesity, traditionally a condition of mature and old age, has become a major adolescent and even childhood problem.

US data make it clear that large-scale obesity is not a new type of disease but a consequence of overeating and insufficient activity. Until the late 1970s, the two excesses were holding steady, with about a third of Americans being overweight and about 13% obese. By the year 2000, the share of overweight people remained steady but the prevalence of obesity among adults older than 20 years had more than doubled and by 2010 it reached 35.7%, and the share of extremely obese adults has surpassed 5% of the total (Ogden et al. 2012). This means that by 2010 three in four American men (74% to be exact) were either overweight or obese. Among American children and adolescents, almost as many as among adults (one in three) were overweight and 18.2% were obese, with the latter share rising to nearly 23% among Hispanic and 26% among black youth.

Disaggregated statistics show that since 1990 adult obesity has increased in every state. Weight gains have been highest among adults with less than completed high school education but they have affected all socioeconomic groups. Progression of the prevalence was linear between 1990 and 2010 (with frequency gain averaging 0.8%/year and the range mostly 0.65–0.95%/year) and the growth rate has slowed down since 2010. S-shaped

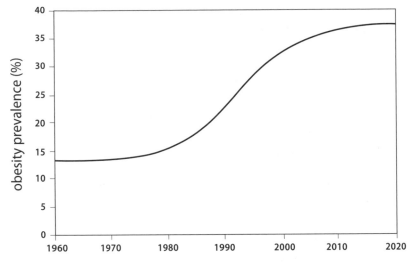

Figure 2.20
Growing prevalence of obesity in the US. Data from Ogden et al. (2012) and The State
of Obesity (2017). The logistic curve had its inflection point in 1993 and its asymptote
is at 37.5% of the total population.

trajectories are tending to very different asymptotic prevalence levels: in
Mississippi to around 35–36%, in Colorado, the least obese state, to just
20%. A longer nationwide data series (1960–2015) supports that conclusion, with its logistic curve saturating at about 37.5% (figure 2.20). Unfortunately, by 2015 the adult obesity prevalence in Louisiana, now number one
at just over 36%, was still increasing (The State of Obesity 2017).

British growth has been nearly as bad. Between 1993 and 2013, the percentage of obese males doubled and that of obese women rose by nearly
half, and in 2013 67.1% of British men, and 57.2% of women, were overweight or obese, rates only slightly lower than in the US (HSCIC 2015).
And China's rapid post-1980 economic advances—making the country the
world's largest economy (in terms of purchasing power parity) and lifting its
average daily per capita food availability above that in Japan (FAO 2018)—
have resulted in notable increases of childhood and adolescent overweight
and obesity, from just 4.4% for the cohort born in 1965 to 9.7% by 1985
and 15.9% in the year 2000 (Fu and Land 2015).

The first global analysis of trends in BMI looked at 28 years of data
(1980 to 2008) for adults 20 years of age and older in 199 countries, and it
found an increase in male BMI in all but eight countries, with the global
mean rising by 0.4 kg/m^2/decade, and female BMI rising slightly faster at

0.5 kg/m^2/decade (Finucane et al. 2011). The globally standardized mean reached 23.8 kg/m^2 for males and 24.1 kg/m^2 for women, with the highest rates in the Pacific islands (Nauru, Tonga, Samoa, Palau) in excess of 30 kg/m^2, and the worldwide prevalence of obesity (9.8%) being more than twice the 1980 rate. As a result, an estimated 205 million men (highest share in North America) and 297 million women (highest share in Southern Africa) were obese. Japanese women have been the only notable exception to the global trend of rising BMI and spreading obesity (Maruyama and Nakamura 2015). Not only is their BMI significantly lower than in other affluent countries, but for women at age 25 it decreased from 21.8 in 1948 to 20.4 kg/m^2 in 2010, while the BMI of Japanese men had increased concurrently from 21.4 to 22.3 kg/m^2.

The most worrisome component of this global epidemics is the early onset of the condition because childhood obesity tends to persists into adult age. As a result, we are now seeing an increasing frequency of individuals spending nearly entire life spans as overweight or obese. Khodaee and Saeidi (2016) estimated that in 2013 the worldwide total of overweight children under the age of five years had surpassed 42 million. According to WHO, the total of obese children and adolescents has increased tenfold in four decades and by 2016 there were about 124 million (7%) obese youngsters, with another 213 million overweight (WHO 2017). And WHO predicted that the number of obese children will surpass the total of undernourished ones as soon as 2022. The most comprehensive nationwide US study showed that between 2011and 2014 the obesity rate among children and adolescents aged 2–19 years was 17% (nearly 6% extremely obese), and that among children aged 2 to 5 years it was nearly 10% (Ogden et al. 2016). The only hopeful sign is that the obesity of young children (2–5 years) increased until 2003–2004 and then it began to decline slowly.

Recent trends in human growth are marked by a great contradiction. On one hand, there is excessive growth that actually worsens the quality of life and reduces longevity, on the other hand there is insufficient growth that weakens proper development during childhood and reduces the likelihood of realizing life's full physical and mental potential. The first failure is entirely preventable by a combination of moderate eating (and there is a surfeit of information about how to manage that) and active lifestyle (and that does not require any strenuous exercises, just frequent quotidian activity). A few most impoverished African countries aside (where a foreign intervention would be required), the problem of childhood stunting and malnutrition can be effectively addressed by national resources: it is not the food supply that falls short but adequate access to food that could be much improved by limited redistribution and supplementary feeding, steps that get repaid manifold by avoiding, or minimizing, physical and mental disabilities stemming from inadequate nutrition in the early years of life.

This concludes my surveys of natural growth on the organismic level and the next two chapters will be devoted to the growth of inanimate objects. Chapter 3 deals with the long-term advances in the capabilities and efficiencies of energy converters (whose deployment is an indispensable precondition of any complex human activities), while chapter 4 surveys the growth of artifacts, man-made objects ranging from the simplest tools (levers, wheels) to complex machines, structures, and infrastructures. As in nature, the ultimate patterns of these classes of growth conform to various confined growth functions, but the qualitative growth of artifacts (their increased durability, reliability, safety) has been no less important than many quantitative gains marking their rising capacities and performance.

3   Energies: or growth of primary and secondary converters

The growth of any organism or of any artifact is, in fundamental physical terms, a transformation of mass made possible by conversion of energy. Solar radiation is, of course, the primary energizer of life via photosynthesis, with subsequent autotrophic and heterotrophic metabolism producing an enormous variety of organisms. Inevitably, our hominin ancestors, relying solely on somatic energies as hunters and gatherers, were subject to the same energetic limits. The boundaries of their control were expanded by the mastering of fire: burning of phytomass (whose supply was circumscribed by photosynthetic limits) added the first extrasomatic energy conversion and opened the way to better eating, better habitation, and better defense against animals. Cooking was a particularly important advance because it had greatly enlarged both the range and quality of consumed food (Wrangham 2009). Prehistoric human populations added another extrasomatic conversion when they began to use, about 10,000 years ago, domesticated animals for transport and later for field work.

The subsequent history of civilization can be seen as a quest for ever higher reliance on extrasomatic energies (Smil 2017a). The process began with the combustion of phytomass (chemical energy in wood, later also converted to charcoal, and in crop residues) to produce heat (thermal energy) and with small-scale conversions of water and wind flows into kinetic energy of mills and sails. After centuries of slow advances, these conversions became more common, more efficient, and available in more concentrated forms (larger unit capacities), but only the combustion of fossil fuels opened the way to modern high-energy societies. These fuels (coals, crude oils, and natural gases) amount to an enormous store of transformed biomass produced by photosynthesis over the span of hundreds of millions of years and their extraction and conversion has energized the conjoined progression of urbanization and industrialization. These advances brought unprecedented levels food supply, housing comfort, material affluence, and personal mobility and extended expected longevity for an increasing share of the global population.

Appraising the long-term growth of energy converters (both in terms of their performance and their efficiency) is thus the necessary precursor for tracing the growth of artifacts—anthropogenic objects whose variety ranges from the simplest tools (lever, pulley) to elaborate structures (cathedrals, skyscrapers) and to astonishingly complex electronic devices—that will be examined in chapter 4. I use the term energy converter in its broadest sense, that is as any artifact capable of transforming one form of energy into another. These converters fall into two basic categories.

The primary ones convert renewable energy flows and fossil fuels into a range of useful energies, most often into kinetic (mechanical) energy, heat (thermal energy), light (electromagnetic energy), or, increasingly, into electricity. This large category of primary converters includes the following machines and assemblies: traditional waterwheels and windmills and their modern transformations, water and wind turbines; steam engines and steam turbines; internal combustion engines (gasoline- and diesel-fueled and gas turbines, either stationary or mobile); nuclear reactors; and photovoltaic cells. Many forms of electric lighting and electric motors are now by far the most abundant secondary converters that use electricity to produce light and kinetic energy for an enormous variety of stationary machines used in industrial production as well as in agriculture, services, and households, and for land-based transportation.

Even ancient civilizations relied on a variety of energy converters. During antiquity, the most common designs for heating in cold climates ranged from simple hearths (still in common use in Japanese rural households during the 19th century) to ingenious Roman hypocausts and their Asian variants, including Chinese *kang* and Korean *ondol*. Mills powered by animate labor (slaves, donkeys, oxen, horses) and also by water (using wheels to convert its energy to rotary motion) were used to grind grains and press oil seeds. Oil lamps and wax and tallow candles provided (usually inadequate) illumination. And oars and sails were the only two ways to propel premodern ships.

By the end of the medieval era, most of these converters saw either substantial growth in size or capacity or major improvements in production quality and operational reliability. The most prominent new converters that became common during the late Middle Ages were taller windmills (used for pumping water and for a large variety of crop processing and industrial tasks), blast furnaces (used to smelt iron ores with charcoal and limestone to produce cast iron), and gunpowder propelled projectiles (with chemical energy in the mixture of potassium nitrate, sulfur and charcoal instantly converted into explosive kinetic energy used to kill combatants or to destroy structures).

Premodern civilizations also developed a range of more sophisticated energy converters relying on gravity or natural kinetic energies. Falling water powered both simple and highly elaborate clepsydras and Chinese astronomical towers—but the pendulum clock dates from the early modern era: it was invented by Christiaan Huygens in 1656. And for wonderment and entertainment, rich European, Middle Eastern and East Asian owners displayed humanoid and animal automata that included musicians, birds, monkeys and tigers, and also angels that played, sang, and turned to face the sun, and were powered by water, wind, compressed air, and wound springs (Chapuis and Gélis 1928).

The construction and deployment of all traditional inanimate energy converters intensified during the early modern period (1500–1800). Water-wheels and windmills became more common and their typical capacities and conversion efficiencies were increasing. Smelting of cast iron in charcoal-fueled blast furnaces reached new highs. Sail ships broke previous records in displacement and maneuverability. Armies relied on more power-ful guns, and manufacturing of assorted automata and other mechanical curiosities reached new levels of complexity. And then, at the beginning of the 18th century, came, slowly, the epochal departure in human energy use with the first commercial installations of steam engines.

The earliest versions of the first inanimate prime mover energized by the combustion of coal—fossil fuel created by photosynthetic conversion of solar radiation 10^6–10^8 years ago—were extremely wasteful and delivered only reciprocating motion. As a result, they were used for decades only for water pumping in coal mines, but once the efficiencies improved and once new designs could deliver rotary motion, the engines rapidly conquered many old industrial and transportation markets and created new indus-tries and new travel options (Dickinson 1939; Jones 1973). A greater vari-ety of new energy converters was invented and commercialized during the 19th century than at any other time in history: in chronological sequence, they include water turbines (starting in 1830s), steam turbines, internal combustion engines (Otto cycle), and electric motors (all three during the 1880s), and diesel engines (starting in the 1890s).

The 20th century added gas turbines (first commercial applications dur-ing the 1930s), nuclear reactors (first installed in submarines in the early 1950s, and for electricity generation since the late 1950s), photovoltaic cells (first in satellites during the late 1950s), and wind turbines (modern designs starting during the 1980s). I will follow all of these advances in a thematic, rather than chronological order, dealing first with harnessing wind and water (traditional mills and modern turbines), then with steam-powered converters (engines and turbines), internal combustion engines, electric light and motors, and, finally, with nuclear reactors and photovoltaic (PV) cells.

Harnessing Water and Wind

We cannot provide any accurate timing of the earliest developments of two traditional inanimate prime movers, waterwheels (whose origins are in Mediterranean antiquity) and windmills (first used in early Middle Ages). Similarly, their early growth can be described only in simple qualitative terms and we can trace their subsequent adoption and the variety of their uses but have limited information about their actual performance. We get on a firmer quantitative ground only with the machines deployed during the latter half of the 18th century and we can trace accurately the shift from waterwheels to water turbines and the growth of these hydraulic machines.

In contrast to the uninterrupted evolution of water-powered prime movers, there was no gradual shift from improved versions of traditional windmills to modern wind-powered machines. Steam-powered electricity generation ended the reliance on windmills in the early 20th century, but it was not until the 1980s that the first modern wind turbines were installed in a commercial wind farm in California. The subsequent development of these machines, aided both by subsidies and by the quest for the decarbonization of modern electricity generation, brought impressive design and performance advances as wind turbines have become a common (even dominant) choice for new generation capacity.

Waterwheels

The origins of waterwheels remain obscure but there is no doubt that the earliest use of water for grain milling was by horizontal wheels rotating around vertical axes attached directly to millstones. Their power was limited to a few kW and larger vertical wheels (Roman *hydraletae*), with millstones driven by right-angle gears, became common in the Mediterranean world at the beginning of the common era (Moritz 1958; White 1978; Walton 2006; Denny 2007). Three types of vertical wheels were developed to match best the existing water flow or to take advantage of an artificially enhanced water supply delivered by stream diversions, canals, or troughs (Reynolds 2002). Undershot wheels (rotating counterclockwise) were best suited for faster-flowing streams, and the power of small machines was often less than 100 W, equivalent to a steadily working strong man. Breast wheels (also rotating counterclockwise) were powered by both flowing and falling water, while gravity drove overshot wheels with water often led by troughs. Overshot wheels could deliver a few kW of useful power, with the best 19th-century designs going above 10 kW.

Waterwheels brought a radical change to grain milling. Even a small mill employing fewer than 10 workers would produce enough flour daily to feed more than 3,000 people, while manual grinding with quern stones would have required the labor of more than 200 people for the same output. Waterwheel use had expanded far beyond grain milling already during the Roman era. During the Middle Ages, common tasks relying on water power ranged from sawing wood and stone to crushing ores and actuating bellows for blast furnaces, and during the early modern era English waterwheels were often used to pump water and lift coal from underground mines (Woodall 1982; Clavering 1995).

Premodern, often crudely built, wooden wheels were not very efficient compared to modern metal machines but they delivered fairly steady power of unprecedented magnitude and hence opened the way to incipient industrialization and large-scale production. Efficiencies of early modern wooden undershot wheels reached 35–45%, well below the performance of overshots at 52–76% (Smeaton 1759). In contrast, later all-metal designs could deliver up to 76% for undershots and as much as 85% for overshots (Müller 1939; Muller and Kauppert 2004). But even the 18th-century wheels were more efficient than the contemporary steam engine and the development of these two very different machines expanded in tandem, with wheels being the key prime movers of several important pre-1850 industries, above all textile weaving.

In 1849 the total capacity of US waterwheels was nearly 500 MW and that of steam engines reached about 920 MW (Daugherty 1927), and Schurr and Netschert (1960) calculated that American waterwheels kept supplying more useful power than all steam engines until the late 1860s. The Tenth Census showed that in 1880, just before the introduction of commercial electricity generation, the US had 55,404 waterwheels with a total installed power of 914 MW (averaging about 16.5 kW per wheel), which accounted for 36% of all power used in the country's manufacturing, with steam supplying the rest (Swain 1885). Grain milling and wood sawing were the two leading applications and Blackstone River in Massachusetts had the highest concentration of wheels in the country, prorating to about 125 kW/ha of its watershed.

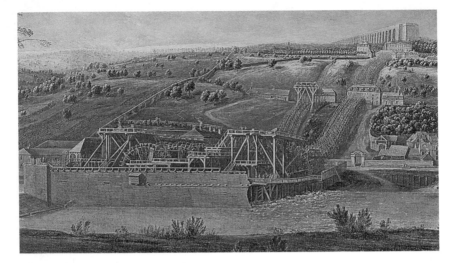

Figure 3.1
Machine de Marly, the largest waterwheel installation of the early modern era, was completed in 1684 to pump water from the River Seine to the gardens of Versailles. Detail from a 1723 painting by Pierre-Denis Martin also shows the aqueduct in the background. The painting's reproduction is available at wikimedia.

There is not enough information to trace the growth of average or typical waterwheel capacities but enough is known to confirm many centuries of stagnation or very low growth followed by steep ascent to new records between 1750–1850. The largest installations combined the power of many wheels. In 1684 the project designed to pump water for the gardens of Versailles with 14 wheels on the River Seine (*Machine de Marly*) provided about 52 kW of useful output, but that averaged less than 4 kW/wheel (Brandstetter 2005; figure 3.1). In 1840 the largest British installations near Glasgow had a capacity of 1.5 MW in 30 wheels (average of 50 kW/wheel) fed from a reservoir (Woodall 1982). And Lady Isabella, the world's largest waterwheel built in 1854 on the Isle of Man to pump water from Laxey lead and zinc mines, had a theoretical peak of 427 kW and actual sustained useful power of 200 kW (Reynolds 1970).

Installations of new machines dropped off rapidly after 1850 as more efficient water turbines and more flexible heat engines took over the tasks that had been done for centuries by waterwheels. Capacity growth of a typical installation across the span of some two millennia was thus at least 20-fold and perhaps as much as 50-fold. Archaeological evidence points to common unit sizes of just 1–2 kW during the late Roman era; at the beginning of the 18th century most European waterwheels had capacities of 3–5 kW and only few of them rated more than 7 kW; and by 1850 there were many waterwheels rated at 20–50 kW (Smil 2017a). This means that after a long period of stagnation (almost a millennium and a half) or barely noticeable advances, typical capacities grew by an order of magnitude in about a century, doubling roughly every 30 years. Their further development was rather rapidly truncated by the adoption of new converters, and the highly asymmetrical S-curve created by pre-1859 development had, first gradually and then rapidly, collapsed, with only a small number of waterwheels working by 1960.

Water Turbines

Water turbines were conceptual extensions of horizontal waterwheels operating under high heads. Their history began with reaction turbine designs by Benoît Fourneyron. In 1832 his first machine, with 2.4 m rotor operating with radial outward flow and head of just 1.3 m, had rated capacity of 38 kW, and in 1837 its improved version, installed at Saint Blaisien spinning mill, had power of 45 kW under heads of more than 100 m (Smith 1980). A year later, a better design was patented in the US by Samuel B. Howd and, after additional improvements, introduced in Lowell, MA by a British-American engineer, James B. Francis, in 1849; it became widely known as the Francis turbine. This design remains the most commonly deployed large-capacity hydraulic machine suitable for medium to high generating heads (Shortridge 1989). Between 1850 and 1880 many industries located on streams replaced their waterwheels by these turbines. In the US, Massachusetts was the leading state: by 1875, turbines supplied 80% of its stationary power.

With the introduction of Edisonian electricity systems during the 1880s, water turbines began to turn generators. The first small installation (12.5 kW) in Appleton, Wisconsin, began to operate in 1882, the same year Edison's first coal-powered station was completed in Manhattan (Monaco 2011). By the end of 1880s, the US had about 200 small hydro stations and another turbine design to deploy. An impulse machine, suitable for high water heads and driven by water jets impacting the turbine's peripheral buckets, was developed by Lester A. Pelton. The world's largest hydro station, built between 1891 and 1895 at Niagara Falls, had ten 5,000 hp (3.73 MW) turbines.

In 1912 and 1913, Viktor Kaplan filed patents for his axial flow turbine, whose adjustable propellers were best suited for low water heads. The first small Kaplan turbines were built already in 1918, and by 1931 four 35 MW units began to operate at the German Ryburg-Schwörstadt station on the Rhine. Although more than 500 hydrostations were built before WWI, most of them had limited capacities and the era of large projects began in the 1920s in the Soviet Union and in the 1930s in the US, in both countries led by a state policy of electrification. But the largest project of the Soviet program of electrification was made possible only by US expertise and machinery: Dnieper station, completed in 1932, had Francis turbines rated at 63.38 MW, built at Newport News, and GE generators (Nesteruk 1963).

In the US, the principal results of government-led hydro development were the stations built by the Tennessee Valley Authority in the east, and the two record-setting projects, Hoover and Grand Coulee dams, in the west (ICOLD 2017; USDI 2017). The Hoover dam on the Colorado River was completed in 1936 and 13 of its 17 turbines rated 130 MW. Grand Coulee construction took place between 1933 and 1942 and each of the 18 original turbines in two power houses could deliver 125 MW (USBR 2016). Grand Coulee's total capacity, originally just short of 2 GW, was never surpassed by any American hydro station built after WWII, and it was enlarged by the addition of a third powerhouse (between 1975 and 1980) with three 600 MW and three 700 MW turbines. Just as the Grand Coulee upgrading was completed (1984–1985), the plant lost its global primacy to new stations in South America.

Tucuruí on Tocantins in Brazil (8.37 GW) was completed in 1984. Guri on Caroní in Venezuela (10.23 GW) followed in 1986, and the first unit of what was to become the world's largest hydro station, Itaipu on Paraná, on the border between Brazil and Paraguay, originally 12.6 GW, now 14 GW, was installed in 1984. Itaipu now has 20 700 MW turbines, Guri has slightly larger turbines than Grand Coulee (730 MW), and Tucuruí's units rate only 375 and 350 MW. The record unit size was not surpassed when Sanxia (Three Gorges) became the new world record holder with 22.5 GW in 2008: its turbines are, as in Itaipu, 700 MW units. A new record was reached only in 2013 when China's Xiangjiaba got the world's largest Francis turbines, 800 MW machines designed and made by Alstom's plant in Tianjin (Alstom 2013; Duddu 2013).

The historical trajectory of the largest water turbine capacities forms an obvious S-curve, with most of the gains taking place between the early 1930s and the early 1980s and the formation of a plateau once the largest unit size approaches 1,000 MW (figure 3.2). Similarly, when the capacity of generators is expressed in megavolt amperes (MVA), the logistic trajectory of maximum ratings rises from a few MVA in 1900 to 200 MVA by 1960 and to 855 MVA in China's Xiluodu on the Jinsha River completed in

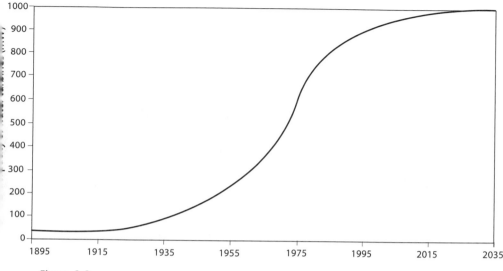

Figure 3.2
Logistic growth of maximum water turbine capacities since 1895; inflection point was in 1963. Data from Smil (2008) and ICOLD (2017).

2013 (Voith 2017). The trajectory forecast points to only marginal gains by 2030 but we already know that the asymptote will be reached due to the construction of China's (and the world's) second-largest hydro project in Sichuan: Baihetan dam on the Jinsha River (between Sichuan and Yunnan, under construction since 2008) will contain 16 1,000 MW (1 GW) units when completed in the early 2020s.

There is a very high probability that the unit capacity of 1 GW will remain the peak rating. This is because most of the world's countries with large hydro generation potential have either already exploited their best sites where they could use such very large units (US, Canada) or have potential sites (in sub-Saharan Africa, Latin America, and monsoonal parts of Asia) that would be best harnessed with the 500–700 MW units that now dominate record-size projects in China, India, Brazil, and Russia. In addition, Baihetan aside, environmental concerns make the construction of another station with capacity exceeding 15 GW rather unlikely.

Windmills and Wind Turbines

The earliest Persian and Byzantine windmills were small and inefficient but medieval Europe eventually developed larger wooden post mills which had to be turned manually into the wind. Taller and more efficient tower mills became common during the early modern era not only in the Netherlands but in other flat and windy Atlantic regions (Smil 2017a). Improvements that raised their power and efficiency eventually included canted edge boards to reduce drag on blades and, much later, true airfoils (contoured blades), metal gearings, and fantails. Windmills, much as waterwheels, were used for many tasks besides grain milling: oil extraction from seeds and water pumping from wells were common, and draining of low-lying areas was the leading Dutch use (Hill 1984). In contrast to heavy European machines, American windmills of the 19th century were lighter, more affordable but fairly efficient machines relying on many narrow blades fastened to wheels and fastened at the top of lattice towers (Wilson 1999).

The useful power of medieval windmills was just 2–6 kW, comparable to that of early waterwheels. Dutch and English mills of the 17th and 18th centuries delivered usually no more than 6–10 kW, American mills of the late 19th century rated typically no more than 1 kW, while the largest contemporary European machines delivered 8–12 kW, a fraction of the power of the best waterwheels (Rankine 1866; Daugherty 1927). Between the 1890s and 1920s, small windmills were used in a number of countries to produce electricity for isolated dwellings, but cheap coal-fired electricity generation brought their demise and wind machines were resurrected only during the 1980s following OPEC's two rounds of oil price increases.

Altamont Pass in northern California's Diablo Range was the site of the first modern large-scale wind farm, built between 1981 and 1986: its average turbine was rated at just 94 kW and the largest one was capable of 330 kW (Smith 1987). This early experiment petered out with the post-1984 fall in world oil prices, and the center of new wind turbine designs shifted to Europe, particularly to Denmark, with Vestas pioneering larger unit designs. Their ratings rose from 55 kW in 1981 to 500 kW a decade later, to 2 MW by the year 2000, and by 2017 the largest capacity of Vestas onshore units reached 4.2 MW (Vestas 2017a). This growth is captured by a logistic growth curve that indicates only limited future gains. In contrast, the largest offshore turbine (first installed in 2014) has capacity of 8 MW, which can reach 9 MW in specific site conditions (Vestas 2017b). But by 2018 neither of the 10 MW designs—SeaTitan and Sway Turbine, completed in 2010 (AMSC 2012)—had been installed commercially.

Average capacities have been growing more slowly. The linear increase of nameplate capacities of American onshore machines doubled from 710 kW in 1998–1999 to 1.43 MW in 2004–2005 but subsequent slower growth raised the mean to 1.79 MW in 2010 and 2 MW in 2015, less than tripling the average in 17 years (Wiser and Bollinger 2016). Averages for European onshore machines have been slightly higher, 2.2 MW in 2010 and about 2.5 MW in 2015. Again, the growth trajectories of both US and EU mean ratings follow sigmoidal courses but ones that appear much closer to saturation than does the trajectory of maximum turbine ratings. Average capacities of a relatively small number of European offshore turbines remained just around 500 kW during the 1990s, reached 3 MW by 2005, 4 MW by 2012, and just over 4 MW in 2015 (EWEA 2016).

During the 28 years between 1986 and 2014, the maximum capacities of wind turbines were thus growing by slightly more than 11% a year, while the Vestas designs increased by about 19% a year between 1981 and 2014, doubling roughly every three years and eight months. These high growth rates have been often pointed out by the advocates of wind power as proofs of admirable technical advances opening the way to an accelerated transition from fossil fuels to noncarbon energies. In reality, those gains have not been unprecedented as other energy converters logged similar, or even higher, gains during early stages of their development. In the 28 years between 1885 and 1913, the largest capacity of steam turbines rose from 7.5 kW to 20 MW, average annual exponential growth of 28% (figure 3.3). And while the subsequent growth of steam turbine capacities pushed the

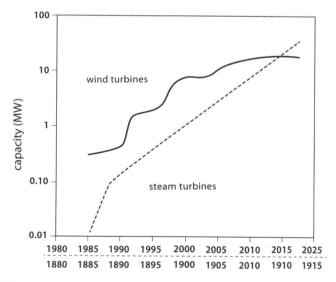

Figure 3.3
Comparison of early growth stages of steam (1885–1913) and wind (1986–2014) turbines shows that the recent expansion is not unprecedented: maximum unit capacities of steam turbines were growing faster (Smil 2017b).

maximum size by two orders of magnitude (to 1.75 GW by 2017), wind turbines could never see similar gains, that is, unit capacities on the order of 800 MW.

Even another two consecutive doublings in less than eight years will be impossible: they would result in a 32 MW turbine before 2025. The Upwind project published a predesign of a 20 MW offshore turbine based on similarity scaling in 2011 (Peeringa et al. 2011). The three-bladed machine would have a rotor diameter of 252 m (more than three times the wing span of the world's largest jetliner, an Airbus A380), hub diameter of 6 m, and cut-in and cut-out wind speeds of 3 and 25 m/s. But doubling turbine power is not a simple scaling problem: while a turbine's power goes up with the square of its radius, its mass (that is its cost) goes up with the cube of the radius (Hameed and Vatn 2012). Even so, there are some conceptual designs for 50 MW turbines with 200 m long flexible (and stowable) blades and with towers taller than the Eiffel tower.

Of course, to argue that such a structure is technically possible because the Eiffel tower reached 300 m already in 1889 and because giant oil tankers and container ships are nearly 400 m long (Hendriks 2008) is to commit a gross categorical mistake as neither of those structures is vertical and topped by massive moving parts. And it is an enormous challenge to design actual blades that would withstand winds up to 235 km/h. Consequently, it is certain that the capacity growth of wind turbines will not follow the exponential trajectory established by 1991–2014 developments: another S-curve is forming as the rates of annual increase have just begun, inexorably, declining.

And there are other limits in play. Even as maximum capacities have been doubling in less than four years, the best conversion efficiencies of larger wind turbines have remained stagnant at about 35%, and their further gains are fundamentally limited. Unlike large electric motors (whose efficiency exceeds 99%) or the best natural gas-fired furnaces (with efficiencies in excess of 97%), no wind turbine can operate with similarly high efficiency. The maximum share of the wind's kinetic energy that can be harnessed by a turbine is 16/27 (59%) of the total flow, a limit known for more than 90 years (Betz 1926).

Steam: Boilers, Engines, and Turbines

Harnessing steam generated by the combustion of fossil fuel was a revolutionary shift. Steam provided the first source of inanimate kinetic energy that could be produced at will, scaled up at a chosen site, and adapted to a growing variety of stationary and mobile uses. The evolution began with simple, inefficient steam engines that provided mechanical energy for nearly two centuries of industrialization, and it has reached its performance plateaus with large, highly efficient steam turbines whose operation now supplies most of the world's electricity. Both converters must be supplied by steam generated in boilers, devices in which combustion converts the chemical energy of fuels to the thermal and kinetic energy of hot (and now also highly pressurized) working fluid.

Boilers

The earliest boilers of the 18th century were simple riveted copper shells where steam was raised at atmospheric pressure. James Watt was reluctant to work with anything but steam at atmospheric pressure (101.3 kPa) and hence his engines had limited efficiency. During the early 19th century, operating pressures began to rise as boilers were designed for mobile use. Boilers had to be built from iron sheets and assume a horizontal cylindrical shape suitable for placement on vessels or wheeled carriages. Oliver Evans and Richard Trevithick, the two pioneers of mobile steam, used such high-pressure boilers (with water filling the space between two cylindrical shells and a fire grate placed inside the inner cylinder) and by 1841 steam pressure in Cornish engines had surpassed 0.4 MPa (Warburton 1981; Teir 2002).

Better designs were introduced as railroad transportation expanded and as steam power conquered shipping. In 1845, William Fairbairn patented a boiler that circulated hot gases through tubes submerged in the water container, and in 1856 Stephen Wilcox patented a design with inclined water tubes placed over the fire. In 1867, Wilcox and George Herman Babcock established Babcock, Wilcox & Company to make and to market water tube boilers, and the company's design (with numerous modifications aimed at improving safety and increasing efficiency) remained the dominant choice for high-pressure boilers during the remainder of the 19th century (Babcock & Wilcox 2017). In 1882 Edison's first electricity-generating station in New York relied on four coal-fired Babcock & Wilcox boilers (each capable of about 180 kW) producing steam for six Porter-Allen steam engines (94 kW) that were directly connected to Jumbo dynamos (Martin 1922). By the century's end, boilers supplying large compound engines worked with pressures of 1.2–1.5 MPa.

Growth of coal-fired electricity generation required larger furnace volumes and higher combustion efficiencies. This dual need was eventually solved by the introduction of pulverized coal-fired boilers and tube-walled furnaces. Before the early 1920s, all power plants burned crushed coal (pieces of 0.5–1.5 cm) delivered by mechanical stokers onto moving grates at the furnace's bottom. In 1918, the Milwaukee Electric Railway and Light Company made the first tests of burning pulverized coal. The fuel is now fine-milled (with most particles of less than 75 μm in diameter, similar to flour), blown into a burner, and burns at flame temperatures of 1600–1800°C. Tube-walled furnaces (with steel tubes completely covering the furnace's interior walls and heated by radiation from hot combustion gases) made it easier to increase the steam supply demanded by larger steam turbines.

The large boilers of the late 19th century supplied steam at pressures of no more than 1.7 MPa (standard for the ships of the Royal Navy) and temperature of 300°C; by 1925, pressures had risen to 2–4 MPa and temperatures to 425°C, and by 1955 the maxima were 12.5 MPa and 525°C (Teir 2002). The next improvement came with the introduction of supercritical boilers. At the critical point of 22.064 MPa and 374°C, steam's latent heat is zero and its specific volume is the same as liquid or gas; supercritical boilers operate above that point where there is no boiling and water turns instantly into steam (a supercritical fluid). This process was patented by Mark Benson in 1922 and the first small boiler was built five years later, but large-scale adoption of the design came only with the introduction of commercial supercritical units during the 1950s (Franke 2002).

The first supercritical boiler (31 MPa and 621°C) was built by Babcock & Wilcox and GE in 1957 at Philo 6 unit in Ohio, and the design rapidly diffused during the 1960s and 1970s (ASME 2017; Franke and Kral 2003). Large power plants are now supplied by boilers producing up to 3,300 t of steam per hour, with pressures mostly between 25 and 29 MPa and steam temperatures up to 605°C and 623°C for reheat (Siemens 2017a). During the 20th century, the trajectories of large boilers were as follows: typical operating pressures rose 17 times (1.7 to 29 MPa), steam temperatures had doubled, maximum steam output (kg/s, t/h) rose by three orders of magnitude, and the size of turbogenerators served by a single boiler increased from 2 MW to 1,750 MW, an 875-fold gain.

Stationary Steam Engines

Simple devices demonstrating the power of steam have a long history but the first commercially deployed machine using steam to pump water was patented by Thomas Savery in England only in 1699 (Savery 1702). The machine had no piston, limited work range, and dismal efficiency (Thurston 1886). The first useful, albeit still highly inefficient, steam engine was invented by Thomas Newcomen in 1712 and after 1715 it was used for pumping water from coal mines. Typical Newcomen engines had power of 4–6 kW, and their simple design (operating at atmospheric pressure and condensing steam on the piston's underside) limited their conversion efficiency to no more than 0.5% and hence restricted their early use only to coal mines with ready on-site supply of fuel (Thurston 1886; Rolt and Allen 1997). Eventually John Smeaton's improvements doubled that low efficiency and raised power ratings up to 15 kW and the engines were also used for water pumping in some metal mines, but only James Watt's separate condenser opened the way to better performances and widespread adoption.

The key to Watt's achievement is described in the opening sentences of his 1769 patent application:

> My method of lessening the consumption of steam, and consequently fuel, in fire engines consists of the following principles: First, that vessel in which the powers of steam are to be employed to work the engine, which is called the cylinder in common fire engines, and which I call the steam vessell, must during the whole time the engine is at work be kept as hot as the steam that enters it... Secondly, in engines that are to be worked wholly or partially by condensation of steam, the steam is to be condensed in vessels distinct from the steam vessells or cylinders, although occasionally communicating with them. These vessels I call condensers, and whilst the engines are working, these condensers ought at least to be kept as cold as the air in the neighbourhood of the engines by application of water or other cold bodies. (Watt 1769, 2)

When the extension of the original patent expired in1800, Watt's company (a partnership with Matthew Boulton) had produced about 500 engines whose average capacity was about 20 kW (more than five times that of typical contemporary English watermills, nearly three times that of the late 18th-century windmills) and whose efficiency did not surpass 2.0 %. Watt's largest engine rated just over 100 kW but that power was rapidly raised by post-1800 developments that resulted in much larger stationary engines deployed not only in mining but in all sectors of manufacturing, from food processing to metal forging. During the last two decades of the 19th industry, large steam engines were also used to rotate dynamos in the first coal-fired electricity-generating stations (Thurston 1886; Dalby 1920; von Tunzelmann 1978; Smil 2005).

The development of stationary steam engines was marked by increases of unit capacities, operating pressures, and thermal efficiencies. The most important innovation enabling these advances was a compound steam engine which expanded high-pressure steam first in two, then commonly in three, and eventually even in four stages in order to maximize energy extraction (Richardson 1886). The designed was pioneered by Arthur Woolf in 1803 and the best compound engines of the late 1820s approached a

Figure 3.4
Corliss steam engine at America's Centennial Exposition in Philadelphia in 1876.
Photograph from the Library of Congress.

thermal efficiency of 10% and had slightly surpassed it a decade later. By
1876 a massive triple-expansion two-cylinder steam engine (14 m tall with
3 m stroke and 10 m flywheel) designed by George Henry Corliss was the
centerpiece of America's Centennial Exposition in Philadelphia: its maximum power was just above 1 MW and its thermal efficiency reached 8.5%
(Thompson 2010; figure 3.4).

   Stationary steam engines became the leading and truly ubiquitous
prime movers of industrialization and modernization and their widespread
deployment was instrumental in transforming every traditional segment
of the newly industrializing economies and in creating new industries,
new opportunities, and new spatial arrangements which went far beyond
stationary applications. During the 19th century, their maximum rated
(nameplate) capacities increased more than tenfold, from 100 kW to the
range of 1–2 MW and the largest machines, both in the US and the UK,
were built during the first years of the 20th century just at the time when
many engineers concluded that low conversion efficiencies made these

machines an inferior choice compared to rapidly improving steam turbines (their growth will be addressed next).

In 1902, America's largest coal-fired power plant, located on the East River between 74th and 75th Streets, was equipped with eight massive Allis-Corliss reciprocating steam engines, each rated at 7.45 MW and driving directly a Westinghouse alternator. Britain's largest steam engines came three years later. First, London's County Council Tramway power station in Greenwich installed the first of its 3.5 MW compound engines, nearly as high as it was wide (14.5 m), leading to Dickinson's (1939, 152) label of "a megatherium of the engine world." And even larger steam engines were built by Davy Brothers in Sheffield. In 1905, they installed the first of their four 8.9 MW machines in the city's Park Iron Works, where it was used for hot rolling of steel armor plates for nearly 50 years. Between 1781 and 1905, maximum ratings of stationary steam engines thus rose from 745 W to 8.9 MW, nearly a 12,000-fold gain.

The trajectory of this growth fits almost perfectly a logistic curve with the inflection point in 1911 and indicating further capacity doubling by the early 1920s—but even in 1905 it would have been clear to steam engineers that this not going to happen, that the machine, massive and relatively inefficient, had reached its performance peak. Concurrently, operating pressures increased from just above the atmospheric pressure of Watt's time (101.3 kPa) to as much as 2.5 MPa in quadruple-expansion machines, almost exactly a 25-fold gain. Highest efficiencies had improved by an order of magnitude, from about 2% for Watt's machines to 20–22% for the best quadruple-expansion designs, with the reliably attested early 20th-century records of 26.8% for a binary vapor engine in Berlin and 24% for a cross-compound engine in London (Croft 1922). But common best efficiencies were only 15–16%, opening the way for a rapid adoption of steam turbines in electricity generation and in other industrial uses, while in transportation steam engines continued to make important contributions until the 1950s.

Steam Engines in Transportation

Commercialization of steam-powered shipping began in 1802 in England (Patrick Miller's *Charlotte Dundas*) and in 1807 in the US (Robert Fulton's *Clermont*), the former with a 7.5 kW modified Watt engine. In 1838, *Great Western*, powered by a 335 kW steam engine, crossed the Atlantic in 15 days. Brunel's screw-propelled *Great Britain* rated 745 kW in 1845, and by the 1880s steel-hulled Atlantic steamers had engines of mostly 2.5–6 MW and up to 7.5 MW, the latter reducing the crossing to seven days (Thurston 1886).

The famous pre-WWI Atlantic liners had engines with a total capacity of more than 20 MW: *Titanic* (1912) had two 11.2 MW engines (and a steam turbine), *Britannic* (1914) had two 12 MW engines (and also a steam turbine). Between 1802 and 1914, the maximum ratings of ship engines rose 1,600-fold, from 7.5 kW to 12 MW.

Steam engines made it possible to build ships of unprecedented capacity (Adams 1993). In 1852 *Duke of Wellington*, a three-deck 131-gun ship of the line originally designed and launched as sail ship *Windsor Castle* and converted to steam power, displaced about 5,800 t. By 1863 *Minotaur*, an iron-clad frigate, was the first naval ship to surpass 10,000 t (10,690 t), and in 1906 *Dreadnought*, the first battleship of that type, displaced 18,400 t, implying post-1852 exponential growth of 2.1%/year. Packet ships that dominated transatlantic passenger transport between 1820 and 1860 remained relatively small: the displacement of Donald McKay's packet ship designs grew from the 2,150 t of *Washington Irving* in 1845 to the 5,858 t of *Star of Empire* in 1853 (McKay 1928).

By that time metal hulls were ascendant. Lloyd's Register approved their use in 1833, and in 1849 Isambard Kingdom Brunel's *Great Britain* was the first iron vessel to cross the Atlantic (Dumpleton and Miller 1974). Inexpensive Bessemer steel was used in the first steel hulls for a decade before the Lloyd's Register of Shipping accepted the metal as an insurable material for ship construction in 1877. In 1881 Concord Line's *Servia*, the first large transatlantic steel-hull liner, was 157 m long with 25.9 m beam and a 9.8:1 ratio unattainable by a wooden sail ship. The dimensions of future steel liners clustered close to that ratio: *Titanic's* (1912) was 9.6. In 1907 Cunard Line's *Lusitania* and *Mauritania* displaced each nearly 45,000 t and just before WWI the White Star Line's *Olympic*, *Titanic*, and *Britannic* had displacements of about 53,000 t (Newall 2012).

The increase of the maximum displacement by an order of magnitude during roughly five decades (from around 5,000 to about 50,000 t) implies an annual exponential growth rate of about 4.5% as passenger shipping was transformed by the transition from sails to steam engines and from wooden to steel hulls. Only two liners that were launched between the two world wars were much larger than the largest pre-WWI ships (Adams 1993). The *Queen Mary* in 1934 and *Normandie* in 1935 displaced, respectively, nearly 82,000 t and almost 69,000 t, while Germany's *Bremen* (1929) rated 55,600 t and Italy's *Rex* 45,800 t. After WWII, the *United States* came at 45,400 t in 1952 and *France* at 57,000 t in 1961, confirming the modal upper limit of great transatlantic liners at between 45,000 t and 57,000 t and forming another sigmoid growth curve (figure 3.5), and also ending, abruptly, more

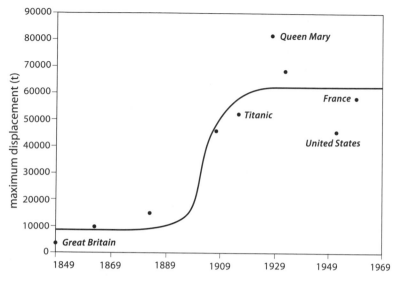

Figure 3.5
Logistic curve of the maximum displacement of transatlantic commercial liners, 1849–1961 (Smil 2017a).

than 150 years of steam-powered Atlantic crossings. I will return to ships in chapter 4, where I will review the growth of transportation speeds.

Larger ships required engines combining high power with the highest achievable efficiency (in order to limit the amount of coal carried) but inherent limits on steam engine performance opened the way for better prime movers. Between 1904 and 1908 the best efficiencies recoded during the British Marine Engine Trials of the best triple- and quadruple-expansion steam engines ranged between 11% and 17%, inferior to both steam turbines and diesels (Dalby 1920). Steam turbines (which could work with much higher temperatures) and Diesel engines began to take over marine propulsion even before WWI. For diesel engines, it was the first successful niche they conquered before they started to power trucks and locomotives (during the 1920s) and automobiles (during the 1930s).

But decades after they began their retreat from shipping, steam engines made a belated and very helpful appearance: they were chosen to power 2,710 WWII Liberty (EC2) class ships built in the US and Canada that were used to carry cargo and troops to Asia, Africa, and Europe (Elphick 2001). These triple-expansion machines were based on an 1881 English design, worked with inlet pressure of 1.5 MPa (steam came from two oil-fired boilers), and could deliver 1.86 MW at 76 rpm (Bourneuf 2008). This important development illustrates a key lesson applicable to many other growth phenomena: the best and the latest may not be the best in specific circumstances. Relatively low-capacity, inefficient, and outdated steam engines were the best choice to win the delivery war. Their building did not strain the country's limited capacity to produce modern steam turbines and diesel engines for the Navy, and a large number of proven units could be made by many manufacturers (eventually by 18 different companies) inexpensively and rapidly.

Experiments with a high-pressure steam engine suitable to power railroad locomotives began at the same time as the first installations of steam engines in vessels (Watkins 1967). Richard Trewithick's simple 1803 locomotive was mechanically sound, and many designs were tested during the next 25 years before the commercial success of Robert Stephenson's *Rocket* in the UK (winner of 1829 Rainhill locomotive trails to select the best machine for the Liverpool and Manchester Railway) and *The Best Friend of Charleston* in the US in 1830 (Ludy 1909). In order to satisfy the requirements of the Rainhill trials of a locomotive weighing 4.5 tons needed to pull three times its weight with a speed of 10 mph (16 km/h) using a boiler operating at a pressure of 50 lbs/in^2 (340 kPa). Stephenson's *Rocket*, weighing 4.5 t, was the only contestant to meet (and beat) these specifications by pulling 20 t at average speed of 16 mph.

The approximate power (in hp) of early locomotives can be calculated by multiplying tractive effort (gross train weight in tons multiplied by train resistance, equal to 8 lbs/ton on steel rails) by speed (in miles/h) and dividing by 375. *Rocket* thus developed nearly 7 hp (about 5 kW) and a maximum of about 12 hp (just above 9 kW); *The Best Friend of Charleston* performed with the identical power at about 30 km/h. More powerful locomotives were needed almost immediately for faster passenger trains, for heavier freight trains on the longer runs of the 1840s and 1850s, and for the first US transcontinental line that was completed in May 1869; these engines also had to cope with greater slopes on mountain routes.

Many improvements—including uniflow design (Jacob Perkins in 1827), regulating valve gear (George H. Corliss in 1849), and compound engines (introduced during the 1880s and expanding steam in two or more stages)—made steam locomotives heavier, more powerful, more reliable, and more efficient (Thurston 1886; Ludy 1909; Ellis 1977). By the 1850s the most powerful locomotive engines had boiler pressures close to 1 MPa and power above 1 MW, exponential growth of close to 20%/year spanning two orders of magnitude in about 25 years. Much slower expansion continued for another 90 years, until the steam locomotive innovation ceased by the mid-1940s. By the 1880s the best locomotives had power on the order of 2 MW and by 1945 the maximum ratings reached 4–6 MW. Union Pacific's *Big Boy*, the heaviest steam locomotive ever built (548 t), could develop 4.69 MW, Chesapeake & Union Railway's *Allegheny* (only marginally lighter at 544 t) rated 5.59 MW, and Pennsylvania Railroad's *PRR Q2* (built in Altoona in 1944 and 1945, and weighing 456 t) had peak power of 5.956 MW (E. Harley 1982; SteamLocomotive.com 2017).

Consequently, the growth of maximum power ratings for locomotive steam engines—from 9 kW in 1829 to 6 MW in 1944, a 667-fold gain—was considerably slower than the growth of steam engines in shipping, an expected outcome given the weight limits imposed by the locomotive undercarriage and the bearing capacity of rail beds. Steam boiler pressure increased from 340 kPa in Stephenson's 1829 *Rocket* to more than 1 MPa by the 1870s, and peak levels in high-pressure boilers of the first half of the 20th century were commonly above 1.5 MPa—record-breaking in its speed (203 km/h in July 1938), *Mallard* worked with 1.72 MPa—and reached 2.1 MPa in *PRR Q2* in 1945, roughly a 6.2-fold gain in 125 years. That makes for a good linear fit with average growth of 0.15 MPa/decade. Thermal efficiencies improved from less than 1% during the late 1820s to 6–7% for the best late 19th and the early 20th-century machines. The best American pre-WWI test results were about 10%, and the locomotives of the Paris-Orleans Railway of France, rebuilt by André Chapelon, reached more than 12% thermal efficiency starting in 1932 (Rhodes 2017). Efficiency growth was thus linear, averaging about 1% per decade.

Steam Turbines

Charles Algernon Parsons patented the first practical turbine design in 1884 and immediately built the first small prototype machine with capacity of just 7.5 kW and low efficiency of 1.6% (Parsons 1936). That performance was worse than that of 1882 steam engine that powered Edison's first power plant (its efficiency was nearly 2.5%) but improvements followed rapidly. The first commercial orders came in 1888, and in 1890 the first two 75 kW machines (efficiency of about 5%) began to generate electricity in Newcastle. In 1891, a 100 kW, 11% efficient machine for Cambridge Electric Lighting was the first condensing turbine that also used superheated steam (all previous models were exhausting steam against atmospheric pressure, resulting in very low efficiencies).

The subsequent two decades saw exponential growth of turbine capacities. The first 1 MW unit was installed in 1899 at Germany's Elberfeld station, in 1903 came the first 2 MW machine for the Neptune Bank station near Newcastle, in 1907 a 5 MW 22% efficient turbine in Newcastle-on-Tyne, and in 1912 a 25 MW and roughly 25% efficient machine for the Fisk Street station in Chicago (Parsons 1911). Maximum capacities thus grew from 75 kW to 25 MW in 24 years (a 333-fold increase), while efficiencies improved by an order of magnitude in less than three decades. For comparison, at the beginning of the 20th century the maximum thermal efficiencies of steam engines were 11–17% (Dalby 1920). And power/mass ratios of steam turbines rose from 25 W/kg in 1891 (five times higher than the ratio for contemporary steam engines) to 100 W/kg before WWI. This resulted in compact sizes (and hence easier installations) and in large savings of materials (mostly metals) and lower construction costs.

The last steam engine-powered electricity-generation plant was built in 1905 in London but the obvious promise of further capacity and efficiency gains for steam turbines was interrupted by WWI and, after the postwar recovery, once again by the economic crisis of the 1930s and by WWII. Steam turbogenerators became more common as post-1918 electrification proceeded rapidly in both North America and Europe and US electricity demand rose further in order to supply the post-1941 war economy, but unit capacities of turbines and efficiencies grew slowly. In the US, the first 110 MW unit was installed in 1928 but typical capacities remained overwhelmingly below 100 MW and the first 220 MW unit began generating only in 1953.

But during the 1960s average capacities of new American steam turbogenerators had more than tripled from 175 MW to 575 MW, and by 1965 the largest US steam turbogenerators, at New York's Ravenswood station, rated 1 GW (1,000 MW) with power/mass ratio above 1,000 W/kg (Driscoll et al. 1964). Capacity forecasts anticipated 2 GW machines by 1980 but reduced growth of electricity demand prevented such growth and by the century's end the largest turbogenerators (in nuclear power plants) were the 1.5 GW Siemens at Isar 2 nuclear station and the 1.55 GW Alstom unit at Chooz B1 reactor.

The world's largest unit, Alstom's 1.75 GW turbogenerator, was scheduled to begin operation in 2019 at France's Flamanville station, where two 1,382 MW units have been generating electricity since the late 1980s (Anglaret 2013; GE 2017a). The complete trajectory of maximum steam turbine capacities—starting with Parsons's 7.5 kW machine in 1884 and ending in 2017 shows an increase by five orders of magnitude (and by three orders of magnitude, from 1 MW to 1.5 GW during the 20th century) and a near-perfect fit for a four-parameter logistic curve with the inflection year in 1963 and with unlikely prospects for any further increase (figure 3.6).

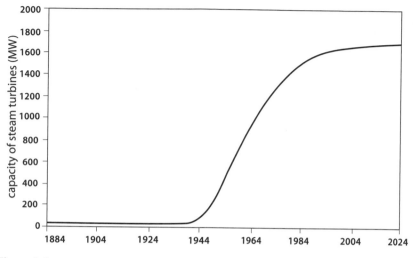

Figure 3.6

Growth of maximum steam turbine capacities since 1884. Five-parameter logistic curve, inflection year in 1954, asymptote has been already reached. Data from Smil (2003, 2017a).

As already noted in the section describing the growth of boilers, working steam pressure rose about 30-fold, from just around 1 MPa for the first commercial units to as high as 31 MPa for supercritical turbines introduced in the 1960s (Leyzerovich 2008). Steam temperatures rose from 180°C for the first units to more than 600°C for the first supercritical units around 1960. Plans for power plants with ultra-supercritical steam conditions (pressure of 35 MPa and temperatures of 700/720°C) and with efficiency of up to 50% were underway in 2017 (Tumanovskii et al. 2017). Coal-fired units (boiler-turbine-generator) used to dominate the largest power plants built after WWII, and at the beginning of the 20th century they still generated about 40% of the world's electricity. But after a temporary increase, caused by China's extraordinarily rapid construction of new coal-fired capacities after the year 2000, coal is now in retreat. Most notably, the share of US coal-fired generation declined from 50% in the year 2000 to 30% in 2017 (USEIA 2017a).

US historical statistics allow for a reliable reconstruction of average conversion efficiency (heat rates) at thermal power plants (Schurr and Netschert 1960; USEIA 2016). Rates rose from less than 4% in 1900 to nearly 14% in 1925, to 24% by 1950, surpassed 30% by 1960 but soon leveled off and in 2015 the mean was about 35%, a trajectory closely conforming to a logistic

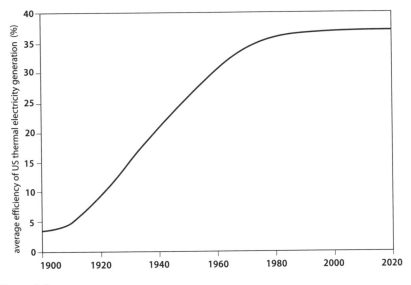

Figure 3.7
Logistic growth (inflection year in 1933, asymptote at 36.9%) of average efficiency
of US thermal electricity-generating plants. Data from Schurr and Netschert (1960)
and USEIA (2016).

curve with the inflection point in 1931 (figure 3.7). Flamanville's 1.75 GW
Arabelle unit has design efficiency of 38% and its power/mass ratio is
1,590 W/kg (Modern Power Systems 2010). Further substantial growth of
the highest steam turbine capacities is unlikely in any Western economy
where electricity demand is, at best, barely increasing or even declining,
and while the modernizing countries in Asia, Latin America, and Africa
need to expand their large-scale generating capacities, they will increasingly rely on gas turbines as well as on new PV and wind capacities.

Although diesel engines have dominated shipping for decades, steam
turbines, made famous by powering record-breaking transatlantic liners
during the early decades of the 20th century, have made some contributions to post-1950 waterborne transport. In 1972 Sea-Land began to use
the first (SL-7 class) newly built container ships that were powered by GE
45 MW steam turbines. Diesels soon took over that sector, leaving tankers
transporting liquefied natural gas (LNG) as the most important category of
shipping relying on steam turbines. LNG tankers use boil-off gas (0.1–0.2%
of the carrier's capacity a day; they also use bunker fuel) to generate steam.
America's large aircraft carriers are also powered by turbines supplied by
steam from nuclear reactors (ABS 2014).

Internal Combustion Engines

Despite their enormous commercial success and epoch-making roles in creating modern, high-energy societies, steam engines, inherently massive and with low power/mass ratio (the combination that could be tolerated for stationary designs and with low fuel costs), could not be used in any applications that required relatively high conversion efficiency and high power/mass ratio, limiting their suitability for mobile uses to rails and shipping and excluding their adoption for flight. High efficiency and high power/mass ratio were eventually supplied by steam turbines, but the requirements of mechanized road (and off-road) transport were met by two new kinds of the 19th-century machines, by internal combustion engines. Gasoline-fueled Otto-cycle engines power most of the world's passenger cars and other light-duty vehicles and diesel engines are used for trucks and other heavy machinery and also for many European automobiles.

Reciprocating gasoline-fueled engines were also light enough to power propeller planes and diesels eventually displaced steam in railroad freight and marine transport. Gas turbines are the only 20th-century addition to internal combustion machines. These high power/mass designs provide the only practical way to power long-distance mass-scale global aviation, and they have become indispensable prime movers for important industrial and transportation systems (chemical syntheses, pipelines) as well as the most efficient, and flexible, generators of electricity.

Gasoline Engines

Steam engines rely on external combustion (generating steam in boilers before introducing it into cylinders), while internal combustion engines (fueled by gasoline or diesel fuel) combine the generation of hot gases and conversion of their kinetic energy into reciprocating motion inside pressurized cylinders. Developing such machines presented a greater challenge than did the commercialization of steam engines and hence it was only in 1860, after several decades of failed experiments and unsuccessful designs, that Jean Joseph Étienne Lenoir patented the first viable internal combustion engine. This heavy horizontal machine, powered by an uncompressed mixture of illuminating gas and air, had a very low efficiency (only about 4%) and was suitable only for stationary use (Smil 2005).

Fifteen years later, in 1877, Nicolaus August Otto patented a relatively light, low-power (6 kW), low-compression (2.6:1) four-stroke engine that was also fueled by coal gas, and nearly 50,000 units were eventually bought by small workshops (Clerk 1909). The first light gasoline-fueled engine suitable for mobile use was designed in Stuttgart in 1883 by Gottlieb Daimler and Wilhelm Maybach, both former employees of Otto's company. In 1885 they tested its version on a bicycle (the prototype of a motorcycle) and in 1886 they mounted a larger (820 W) engine on a wooden coach (Walz and Niemann 1997). In one of the most remarkable instances of independent technical innovation, Karl Benz was concurrently developing his gasoline engine in Mannheim, just two hours by train from Stuttgart. By 1882 Benz had a reliable, small, horizontal gasoline-fueled engine, and then proceeded to develop a four-stroke machine (500 W, 250 rpm, mass of 96 kg) that powered the first public demonstration of a three-wheeled carriage in July 1886 (figure 3.8).

And it was Benz's wife, Bertha, who made, without her husband's knowledge, the first intercity trip with the three-wheeler in August of 1888 when she took their two sons to visit her mother, driving some 104 km to Pforzheim. Daimler's high-rpm engine, Benz's electrical ignition, and Maybach's carburetor provided the functional foundations of automotive

© Daimler AG

Figure 3.8
Carl Benz (with Josef Brecht) at the wheel of his patent motor car in 1887. Photograph courtesy of Daimler AG, Stuttgart.

engines but the early motorized wooden carriages which they powered were just expensive curiosities. Prospects began to change with the introduction of better engines and better overall designs. In 1890 Daimler and Maybach produced their first four-cylinder engine, and their machines kept improving through the 1890s, winning the newly popular car races. In 1891 Emile Levassor, a French engineer, combined the best Daimler-Maybach engine with his newly designed, car-like rather than carriage-like, chassis. Most notably, he moved the engine from under the seats in front of the driver (crankshaft parallel with the vehicle's long axis), a design helping later aerodynamic body shape (Smil 2005).

During the last decade of the 19th century, cars became faster and more convenient to operate, but they were still very expensive. By 1900 cars benefited from such technical improvements as Robert Bosch's magneto (1897), air cooling, and the front-wheel drive. In 1900 Maybach designed a vehicle that was called the "first modern car in all essentials" (Flink 1988, 33): Mercedes 35, named after the daughter of Emil Jellinek who owned a Daimler dealership, had a large 5.9 L, 26 kW engine whose aluminum block and honeycomb radiator lowered its weight to 230 kg. Other modern-looking designs followed in the early years of the 20th century but the mass-market breakthrough came only in 1908 with Henry Ford's Model T, the first truly affordable vehicle (see figure 1.2). Model T had a 2.9 L, 1 -kW (20 hp) engine weighing 230 kg and working with a compression ratio of 4.5:1.

Many cumulative improvements were made during the 20th century to every part of the engine. Beginning in 1912, dangerous cranks were replaced by electric starters. Ignition was improved by Gottlob Honold's high-voltage magneto with a new spark plug in 1902, and more durable Ni-Cr spark plugs were eventually replaced by copper and then by platinum spark plugs. Band brakes were replaced by curved drum brakes and later by disc brakes. The violent engine knocking that accompanied higher compression was eliminated first in 1923 by adding tetraethyl lead to gasoline, a choice that later proved damaging both to human health and to the environment (Wescott 1936).

Two variables are perhaps most revealing in capturing the long-term advances of automotive gasoline engines: their growing power (when comparing typical or best-selling designs, not the maxima for high-performance race cars) and their improving power/mass ratio (whose rise has been the result of numerous cumulative design improvements). Power ratings rose from 0.5 kW for the engine powering Benz's three-wheeler to 6 kW for Ford's Model A introduced in 1903, to 11 kW for Model N in 1906, 15 kW for Model T in 1908, and 30 kW for its successor, a new Model A that enjoyed record sales between 1927 and 1931. Ford engines powering the models introduced a decade later, just before WWII, ranged from 45 to 67 kW.

Larger post-1950 American cars had engines capable mostly of more than 80 kW and by 1965 Ford's best-selling fourth-generation Fairlane was offered with engines of up to 122 kW. Data on the average power of newly sold US cars are available from 1975 when the mean was 106 kW; it declined (due to a spike in oil prices and a sudden preference for smaller vehicles) to 89 kW by 1981, but then (as oil prices retreated) it kept on rising, passing 150 kW in 2003 and reaching the record level of nearly 207 kW in 2013, with the 2015 mean only slightly lower at 202 kW (Smil 2014b; USEPA 2016b). During the 112 years between 1903 and 2015 the average power of light-duty vehicles sold in the US thus rose roughly 34 times. The growth trajectory was linear, average gain was 1.75 kW/year, and notable departures from the trend in the early 1980s and after 2010 were due, respectively, to high oil prices and to more powerful (heavier) SUVs (figure 3.9).

The principal reason for the growing power of gasoline engines in passenger cars has been the increasing vehicle mass that has taken place despite the use of such lighter construction materials as aluminum, magnesium, and plastics. Higher performance (faster acceleration, higher maximum speeds) was a secondary factor. With few exceptions (German *Autobahnen* being the best example), speed limits obviate any need for machines

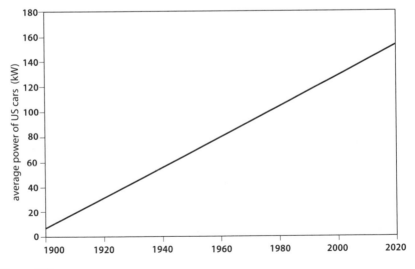

Figure 3.9
Linear growth of average power of US passenger vehicles, 1903–2020. Data from Smil (2014b) and USEPA (2016b).

capable of cruising faster than the posted maxima—but even small cars (such as Honda Civic) can reach maxima of up to or even above 200 km/h, far in excess of what is needed to drive lawfully.

Weight gains are easily illustrated by the long-term trend of American cars (Smil 2010b). In 1908 the curb weight of Ford's revolutionary Model T was just 540 kg and three decades later the company's best-selling Model 74 weighed almost exactly twice as much (1,090 kg). Post-WWII weights rose with the general adoption of roomier designs, automatic transmissions, air conditioning, audio systems, better insulation, and numerous small servo-motors. These are assemblies made of a small DC motor, a gear-reduction unit, a position-sensing device (often just a potentiometer), and a control cir-cuit: servomotors are now used to power windows, mirrors, seats, and doors.

As a result, by 1975 (when the US Environmental Protection Agency began to monitor average specifications of newly sold vehicles) the mean inertia weight of US cars and light trucks (curb weight plus 200 lbs, or 136 kg) reached 1.84 t. Higher oil prices helped to lower the mean to 1.45 t by 1981, but once they collapsed in 1985 cars began to gain weight and the overall trend was made much worse by the introduction of SUVS and by the increasing habit of using pickups as passenger cars. By 2004 the average mass of newly sold passenger vehicles reached a new record of 1.86 t, that was slightly surpassed (1.87 t) in 2011, and by 2016 this mean declined only marginally to 1.81 t (Davis et al. 2016; USEPA 2016b). The curb weight of the average American light-duty vehicle had thus increased roughly three times in a century.

Until the 1960s both European and Japanese cars weighed much less than US vehicles but since the 1970s their average masses have shown a similarly increasing trend. In 1973 the first Honda Civic imported to North America weighed just 697 kg, while the 2017 Civic (LX model, with auto-matic transmission and standard air conditioning) weighs 1,247 kg, that is about half a tonne (nearly 80%) more than 44 years ago. Europe's popular small post-WWII cars weighed just over half a tonne (Citroen 2 CV 510 kg, Fiat Topolino 550 kg), but the average curb weight of European compacts reached about 800 kg in 1970 and about 1.2 t in the year 2000 (WBCSD 2004). Subsequently, average mass has grown by roughly 100 kg every five years and the EU car makers now have many models weighing in excess of 1.5 t (Cuenot 2009; Smil 2010b). And the increasing adoption of hybrid drives and electric vehicles will not lower typical curb weights because these designs have to accommodate either more complicated power trains or heavy battery assemblies: the Chevrolet Volt hybrid weighs 1.72 t, the electric Tesla S as much as 2.23 t.

The power/mass ratio of Otto's heavy stationary horizontal internal combustion engine was less than 4 W/kg, by 1890 the best four-stroke Daimler-Maybach automotive gasoline engine reached 25 W/kg, and in 1908 Ford's Model T delivered 65 W/kg. The ratio continued to rise to more than 300 W/kg during the 1930s and by the early 1950s many engines (including those in the small Fiat 8V) were above 400 W/kg. By the mid-1950s Chrysler's powerful Hemi engines delivered more than 600 W/kg and the ratio reached a broad plateau in the range of 700–1,000 W/kg during the 1960s. For example, in 1999 Ford's Taunus engine (high performance variant) delivered 830 W/kg, while in 2016 Ford's best-selling car in North America, Escape (a small SUV), was powered by a 2.5 L, 125 kW Duratec engine and its mass of 163 kg resulted in a power/mass ratio of about 770 W/kg (Smil 2010b). This means that the power/mass densities of the automotive gasoline engine have increased about 12-fold since the introduction of the Model T, and that more than half of that gain took place after WWII.

Before leaving the gasoline engines I should note the recent extreme ratings of high-performance models and compare them to those of the car that was at the beginning of their evolution, Maybach's 1901 Mercedes 35 (26 kW engine, power/mass ratio of 113 W/kg). In 2017 the world's most powerful car was the Swedish limited-edition Megacar Koenigsegg Regera with a 5 L V8 engine rated at 830 kW and electric drive rated at 525 kW, giving it the actual total combined propulsion of 1.11 MW—while the top Mercedes (AMG E63-S) rated "only" 450 kW. This means that the maximum power of high-performance cars has risen about 42-fold since 1901 and that the Regera has more than eight times the power of the Honda Civic.

Finally, a brief note about the growth of gasoline-fueled reciprocating engines in flight. Their development began with a machine designed by Orville and Wilbur Wright and built by their mechanic Charles Taylor in 1903 in the brothers' bicycle workshop in Dayton, Ohio (Taylor 2017). Their four-cylinder 91 kg horizontal engine was to deliver 6 kW but eventually it produced 12 kW, corresponding to a power/mass ratio of 132 W/kg. Subsequent improvement of aeroengines was very rapid. Léon Levavasseur's 37 kW *Antoinette*, the most popular pre-WWI eight-cylinder engine, had a power/mass ratio of 714 W/kg, and the American Liberty engine, a 300 kW mass-produced machine for fighter aircraft during WWI, delivered about 900 W/kg (Dickey 1968). The most powerful pre-WWII engines were needed to power Boeing's 1936 Clipper, a hydroplane that made it possible to fly, in stages, from the western coast of the United States to East Asia. Each of its four radial Wright Twin Cyclone engines was rated at 1.2 MW and delivered 1,290 W/kg (Gunston 1986).

High-performance aeroengines reached their apogee during WWII. American B-29 (Superfortress) bombers were powered by four Wright R-3350 Duplex Cyclone radial 18-cylinder engines whose versions were rated from 1.64 to 2.76 MW and had a high power/mass ratio in excess of 1,300 W/kg, an order of magnitude higher than the Wrights' pioneering design (Gunston 1986). During the 1950s Lockheed's L-1049 Super Constellation, the largest airplane used by airlines for intercontinental travel before the introduction of jetliners, used the same Wright engines. After WWII spark-ignited gasoline engines in heavy-duty road (and off-road) transport were almost completely displaced by diesel engines, which also dominate shipping and railroad freight.

Diesel Engines

Several advantageous differences set Diesel's engines apart from Otto-cycle gasoline engines. Diesel fuel has nearly 12% higher energy density compared to gasoline, which means that, everything else being equal, a car can go further on a full tank. But diesels are also inherently more efficient: the self-ignition of heavier fuel (no sparking needed) requires much higher compression ratios (commonly twice as high as in gasoline engines) and that results in a more complete combustion (and hence a cooler exhaust gas). Longer stroke and lower rpm reduce frictional losses, and diesels can operate with a wide range of very lean mixtures, two to four times leaner than those in a gasoline engine (Smil 2010b).

Rudolf Diesel began to develop a new internal combustion engine during the early 1890s with two explicit goals: to make a light, small (no larger than a contemporary sewing machine), and inexpensive engine whose use by independent entrepreneurs (machinists, watchmakers, repairmen) would help to decentralize industrial production and achieve unprecedented efficiency of fuel conversion (R. Diesel 1913; E. Diesel 1937; Smil 2010b). Diesel envisaged the engine as the key enabler of industrial decentralization, a shift of production from crowded large cities where, he felt strongly, it was based on inappropriate economic, political, humanitarian, and hygienic grounds (R. Diesel 1893).

And he went further, claiming that such decentralized production would solve the social question as it would engender workers' cooperatives and usher in an age of justice and compassion. But his book summarizing these ideas (and ideals)—*Solidarismus: Natürliche wirtschaftliche Erlösung des Menschen* (R. Diesel 1903)—sold only 300 of 10,000 printed copies and the eventual outcome of the widespread commercialization of Diesel's engines was the very opposite of his early social goals. Rather than staying small and serving decentralized enterprises, massive diesel engines became one of the principal enablers of unprecedented industrial centralization, mainly because they reduced transportation costs, previously decisive determinants of industrial location, to such an extent that an efficient mass-scale producer located on any continent could serve the new, truly global, market.

Diesels remain indispensable prime movers of globalization, powering crude oil and LNG tankers, bulk carriers transporting ores, coal, cement, and lumber, container ships (the largest ones now capable of moving more than 20,000 standard steel containers), freight trains, and trucks. They move fuels, raw materials, and food among five continents and they helped to make Asia in general, and China in particular, the center of manufacturing serving the worldwide demand (Smil 2010b). If you were to trace everything you wear, and every manufactured object you use, you would find that all of them were moved multiple times by diesel-powered machines.

Diesel's actual accomplishments also fell short of his (impossibly ambitious) efficiency goal, but he still succeeded in designing and commercializing an internal combustion engine with the highest conversion efficiency. He did so starting with the engine's prototype, which was constructed with a great deal of support from Heinrich von Buz, general director of the Maschinenfabrik Augsburg, and Friedrich Alfred Krupp, Germany's leading steelmaker. On February 17, 1897, Moritz Schröter, a professor of theoretical engineering at Technische Universität in Munich, was in charge of the official certification test that was to set the foundation for the engine's commercial development. While working at its full power of 13.5 kW (at 154 rpm and pressure of 3.4 MPa), the engine's thermal efficiency was 34.7% and its mechanical efficiency reached 75.5 % (R. Diesel 1913).

As a result, the net efficiency was 26.2%, about twice that of contemporary Otto-cycle machines. Diesel was justified when he wrote to his wife that nobody's engine had achieved what his design did. Before the end of 1897 the engine's net efficiency reached 30.2%—but Diesel was wrong when he claimed that he had a marketable machine whose development would unfold smoothly. The efficient prototype required a great deal of further development and the conquest of commercial markets began in 1903, and it was not on land but on water, with a small diesel engine (19 kW) powering a French canal boat. Soon afterwards came *Vandal*, an oil tanker operating on the Caspian Sea and on the Volga with three-cylinder engines rated at 89 kW (Koehler and Ohlers 1998), and in 1904 the world's first diesel-powered station began to generate electricity in Kiev.

The first oceangoing ship equipped with diesel engines (two eight-cylinder four-stroke 783 kW machines) was the Danish *Selandia*, a freight and passenger carrier that made its maiden voyage to Tokyo and back to Copenhagen in 1911 and 1912 (Marine Log 2017). In 1912 *Fionia* became the first diesel-powered transatlantic steamer of the Hamburg-American Line. Diesel adoption proceeded steadily after WWI, got really underway during the 1930s, and accelerated after WWII with the launching of large crude oil tankers during the 1950s. A decade later came large container ships as marine diesel engines increased both in capacity and efficiency (Smil 2010b).

In 1897 Diesel's third prototype engine had capacity of 19.8 bhp (14.5 kW), in 1912 *Selandia's* two engines rated 2,100 bhp. In 1924 Sulzer's engine for ocean liners had a 3,250 bhp engine, and a 4,650 bhp machine followed in 1929 (Brown 1998). The largest pre-WWII marine diesels were around 6,000 bhp, and by the late 1950s they rated 15,000 bhp. In 1967 a 12-cylinder engine was capable of 48,000 hp, in 2001 MAN B&W-Hyundai's machine reached 93,360 bhp and in 2006 Hyundai Heavy Industries built the first diesel rated at more than 100,000 bhp: 12K98MC, 101,640 bhp, that is 74.76 MW (MAN Diesel 2007).

That machine held the record of the largest diesel for just six months until September 2006 when Wärtsilä introduced a new 14-cylinder engine rated at 80.1 MW (Wärtsilä 2009). Two years later modifications of that Wärtsilä engine increased the maximum rating to 84.42 MW and MAN Diesel now offers an 87.22 MW engine with 14 cylinders at 97 rpm (MAN Diesel 2018). These massive engines power the world's largest container ships, with *OOCL Hong* Kong, operating since 2017, the current record holder (figure 3.10). Large-scale deployment of new machines saw efficiencies approaching 40% after WWI, in 1950 a MAN reached 45% efficiency, and the best two-stroke designs now have efficiencies of 52% (surpassing that of gas turbines at about 40%, although in combined cycle, using exhaust gas in a steam turbine, they now go up to 61%) and four-stroke diesels are a bit behind at 48%.

On land, diesels were first deployed in heavy locomotives and trucks. The first diesel locomotive entered regular service in 1913 in Germany. Powered by a Sulzer four-cylinder two-stroke V-engine, it could sustain speed of 100 km/h. After WWI yard switching locomotives were the first railroad market dominated by diesels (steam continued to power most passenger trains) but by the 1930s the fastest trains were diesel-powered. In 1934 streamlined stainless-steel *Pioneer Zephyr* had a 447 kW, eight-cylinder, two-stroke diesel-electric drive that made it possible to average 124 km/h on the Denver-Chicago run (Ellis 1977; ASME 1980).

By the 1960s steam engines in freight transport (except in China and India) were replaced by diesels. Ratings of American locomotive diesel

Figure 3.10
OOCL Hong Kong, the world's largest container ship in 2019, carries an equivalent of 21,413 twenty-foot standard units. Diesels and container vessels have been the key prime movers of globalization. Photo available at wikimedia.

engines increased from 225 kW in 1924 for the first US-made machine to 2 MW in 1939, and the latest GE Evolution Series engines have power ranging from 2.98 to 4.62 MW (GE 2017b). But modern locomotive diesels are hybrids using diesel-electric drive: the engine's reciprocating motion is not transmitted to wheels but generates electricity for motors driving the train (Lamb 2007). Some countries converted all of their train traffic to electricity and all countries use electric drive for high-speed passenger trains (Smil 2006b).

After WWII diesels had also completely conquered markets for off-road vehicles, including agricultural tractors and combines, and construction machinery (bulldozers, excavators, cranes). In contrast, diesels have never conquered the global passenger car market: they account for large shares of all cars in much of Europe, but remain rare in North America, Japan, and China. In 1933 Citroën offered a diesel engine option for its Rosalie and in 1936 Mercedes-Benz, with its 260D model, began the world's most enduring series of diesel-powered passenger cars (Davis 2011). Automotive diesels eventually became quite common in post-WWII Europe thanks to their cheaper fuel and better economy.

In 2015 about 40% of the EU's passenger cars were diesel-powered (with national shares as high as about 65% in France and 67% in Belgium), compared to only 3% of all light-duty vehicles in the US (Cames and Helmers 2013; ICCT 2016). The largest recent SUV diesels (the Audi Q7 offered between 2008 and 2012) rate 320 kW, an order of magnitude more powerful than the engine (33 kW) in the pioneering 1936 Mercedes design. The power of diesels in most popular sedans (Audi 4, BMW 3, Mercedes E, VW Golf) ranges mostly between 70 and 170 kW. The power of diesel cars produced by Mercedes-Benz rose from 33 kW in 1936 (260D) to 40 kW in 1959 (180D), 86 kW in 1978 (turbo-charged 300SD), 107 kW in 2000 (C220 CDI), and 155 kW in 2006 (E320 BlueTec), a fivefold gain for the company's designs in seven decades.

Diesel's engines are here to stay because there are no readily available mass-scale alternatives that could keep integrating the global economy as conveniently and as affordably as do diesels powering ships, trains, and trucks. But the engine's advantages in passenger vehicles have been declining as prices of diesel fuel have risen, as the efficiency gap between diesel and gasoline engines has narrowed (the best gasoline engines are now only about 15% behind), and as new environmental regulations require much cleaner automotive fuels. Stricter regulations for marine shipping will also have an impact on the future growth of heavy diesel engines.

Gas Turbines

Gas turbines have a long history of conceptual and technical development, with the idea patented first before the end of the 18th century and with the first impractical designs (using more energy than they produced) dating to the beginning of the 20th century (Smil 2010b). Their first working versions were developed for military use, concurrently and entirely independently, during the late 1930s and the early 1940s in the UK by Frank Whittle and in Nazi Germany by Hans Pabst von Ohain (Golley and Whittle 1987; Conner 2001; Smil 2010b). Serial production of jet engines began in 1944 and the first British and German fighter jets began to fly in August of that year, too late to affect the war's outcome. Continuous improvements of both military and civilian versions have continued ever since (Gunston 2006; Smil 2010b).

The performance of jet engines is best compared in terms of their maximum thrust and thrust-to-weight (T/W) ratio (the ideal being, obviously, the lightest possible engine developing the highest possible thrust). HeS 3, von Ohain's first engine powering an experimental aircraft (Heinkel-178) in August 1937, had thrust of just 4.9 kN. Whittle's W.1A engine that powered the first Gloster E.28/29 flight in April 1941 developed 4.6 kN and had T/W 1.47:1 (Golley and Whittle 1987). Because of its development of early British military jet engines, Rolls-Royce was able to introduce in 1950 the world's first axial flow jet engine, the 29 kN (5.66:1 T/W) Avon that was used first in a bomber and later in various military and commercial airplanes. But the British Comet, the world's first jetliner, was powered by low-thrust (22.3 kN) and very low thrust/weight ratio de Havilland Ghost Mk1 engines. In 1954, just 20 months after it began, the project was suspended after two major fatal accidents following takeoffs from Rome, later attributed to stress cracks around the plane's square windows leading to catastrophic decompression of the fuselage.

By the time a redesigned version of the Comet was ready in October 1958 it had two competitors. The Soviet Tupolev Tu-104 (with 66.2 kN Mikulin engines) began commercial service in September 1956, and Boeing 707 (with four Pratt & Whitney JT3 turbojets rated at 80 kN, thrust/weight ratio of 3.5–4.0) launched Pan Am's transatlantic service in October 1958; a year later the airline deployed the Boeing for its round-the-world series of flights.

All of the early engines were turbojets derived from military designs that were not the most suitable choice for commercial aviation due to their relatively low propulsion efficiencies. Whittle realized this limitation of turbojets during the earliest days of his work on jet propulsion when he talked about replacing a low-mass high-velocity jet by a high-mass low-velocity (understood in relative terms) jet (Golley and Whittle 1987). This was eventually accomplished by turbofan engines, using an additional turbine to tap a part of the propulsive power and deploy it to rotate a large fan placed in front of the main compressor to force additional air (compressed to only twice the inlet pressure) to bypass the engine and exit at speed only about half as fast (450 vs. 900 m/s) as the compressed air forced through the engine's combustor.

Unlike turbojets, whose thrust peaks at high speeds, turbofans have peak thrust during low speeds, a most desirable property for takeoffs of heavy passenger jets. Moreover, turbofans are also much quieter (as bypass air envelopes the fast-moving hot exhaust) and higher bypass ratios lower specific fuel consumption, but this improvement is limited due to the diameter of fans and mounting of engines (very large engines would have to be mounted on elevated wings). Frank Whittle patented the bypass idea already in 1936, and in 1952 Rolls-Royce built the first jet engine with a bypass, albeit just 0.3:1. By 1959, P&W's JT3D (80.1 kN) had a bypass ratio of 1.4:1 and in 1970 the company introduced the first high-bypass engine, JT9D (initially 210 kN, bypass ratio 4/8:1, T/W 5.4–5.8) designed to power the Boeing 747 and other wide-body jetliners (Pratt & Whitney 2017).

GE demonstrated an engine with an 8:1 bypass ratio already in 1964 and it became available as TF39 in 1968 for military C-5 Galaxy planes. The first engines of the GE90 family, designed for the long-range Boeing 777, entered service in 1996: they had thrust of 404 kN and a bypass ratio of 8.4. A larger variant followed, and the world's most powerful turbofan engine—GE90–115B rated initially at 512 kN, with bypass ratio 9:1, and thrust-to-weight ratio of 5.98—was deployed commercially for the first time in 2004. The engine with the highest bypass ratio in 2017 (12.5:1) was P&W's PW1127G, a geared turbofan powering Bombardier's CSeries and Airbus 320neo, while the Rolls-Royce Trent 1000 (used by Boeing 787) has a 10:1 ratio.

Technical advances of gas turbines in flight have been well documented and hence we can follow the growth trajectories of jet engines in detail (Gunston 2006; Smil 2010a). Maximum engine thrust went from 4.4 kN (von Ohain's He S3B in 1939) to 513.9 (and in tests up to 568) kN (GE's GE90–115B certified in 2003, in service a year later). This has resulted in an almost perfectly linear growth trajectory with an average annual gain of nearly 8 kN (figure 3.11). Obviously, other critical specifications rose in tandem. Overall pressure ratio (compression ratio) was 2.8 for HE S3B and 4.4

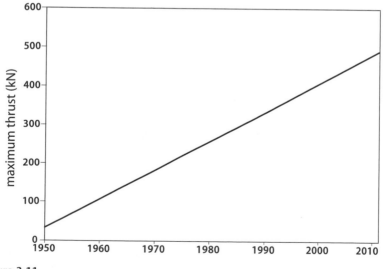

Figure 3.11
Linear fit of the maximum thrust of jet engines. Data from Smil (2010b).

for Whittle's W.2. British Avon reached 7.5 by 1950, P&W's JT9D surpassed 20 in 1970, and in 2003 GE90–115B set a new record of 42, an order of magnitude larger than Whittle's engine. Similarly, total air mass flow rose by an order of magnitude, from about 12 kg/s for the earliest Whittle and von Ohain designs to 1,360 kg/s for GE90–115B.

The dry mass of jet engines rose from 360 kg for HE S3B to nearly 8.3 t for GE90–115B (that is almost as much as the DC3, the most popular propeller commercial aircraft introduced in 1936), and thrust-to-weight ratio increased from just 1.38 for HE S3B and 1.6 for W.2 to about 4.0 by the late 1950s, to 5.5 during the late 1980s with GE90–11B at about 6, and maximum bypass ratios went from 0.3:1 in 1952 to 12.5:1 in 2016 (figure 3.12). Larger fans have been required to produce high bypass ratios, with their diameters growing from 1.25 m for Conway in 1952 to 2.35 m for JT9D in 1970 and 3.25 m for GE90–115B in 2004. Increases in operating efficiency (declines in specific fuel consumption per unit of thrust, per km or per passenger-km flown) have been impressive: early turbofans were 20–25% more efficient than the best turbojets, by the 1980s the efficiency of high-bypass turbofans was up to 35% better, and the best designs of the early 21st century

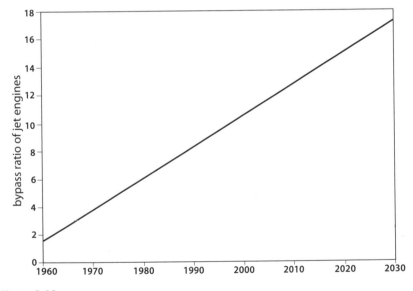

Figure 3.12
Evolution of the bypass ratio in commercial jetliners. Data from specifications for GE, P&W, and Rolls-Royce engines and from Ballal and Zelina (2003). Maximum ratios have seen linear growth that averaged about 2.2 units per decade.

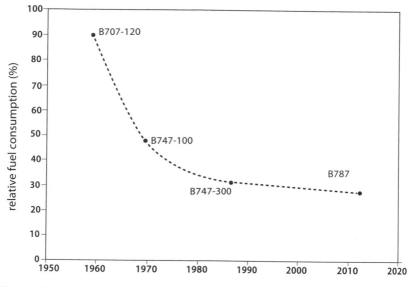

Figure 3.13
Evolution of jetliner efficiency in terms of relative fuel consumption from Boeing 707 (1958) to Boeing 787–10 (2017). Data from Ballal and Zelina (2003) and from www.com positesworld.com.

consume only about 30% as much fuel for every seat-kilometer as did the engines of the late 1950s (figure 3.13).

Much as in the case of diesel engines in shipping and heavy land transport, gas turbines in flight are here to stay as there is no alternative to powering jetliners flying hundreds of people on routes ranging from commuter hops to intercontinental journeys (the record one now lasting more than 17 hours). At the same time, turbofans are not expected to grow substantially in terms of their thrust, thrust-to-weight ratio, or bypass ratio. Capacities are also not expected to rise more than 800 people (the maximum for Airbus A380 double-decker, although in existing configurations it boards typically between 500 and 600). Moreover, preferred point-to-point flights (rather than channeling the traffic through a limited number of hubs using the largest-capacity planes) creates higher demand for efficient jetliners capable to transport 200–400 people on long flights (a niche now exploited by Boeing's 787).

The development of the gas turbine achieved its first great commercial applications in flight, but stationary units have eventually become highly successful as flexible, highly efficient and affordable means of generating electricity or delivering rotary power (especially for compressors). Commercial uses of stationary gas turbines began with electricity generation by the Swiss Brown Boveri Corporation at the municipal power station in Neuchâtel in 1939 (ASME 1988). The world's first operating gas turbine had nameplate capacity of 15.4 MW (3,000 rpm, inlet temperature 550°C) and its low efficiency (merely 17.4%, and hence generating just 4 MW_e) was due to high energy consumption (75% of the input) by its compressor and to the absence of any heat recovery. But the design worked so reliably that the machine failed only after 63 years, in 2002!

A post-WWII preference for large central stations slowed down the expansion of relatively small gas turbine units (their total capacity grew to just 240 MW by 1960, less than a single typical steam turbogenerator installed in a coal-fired station). Strong takeoff came only in reaction to the November 1965 blackout that left about 30 million people in the northeastern US without electricity for as long as 13 hours (US FPC 1965). Obviously, small gas-fired units could be rapidly deployed in such emergencies and the US utilities ordered 4 GW of new capacity in 1968, and 7 GW in 1971. As a result, the stationary gas turbine capacity owned by the utilities increased from 1 GW in 1963 to nearly 45 GW by 1975, the largest unit size rose from 20 MW in 1960 to 50 MW in 1970, and GE produced its first 100 MW machine in 1976 (Hunt 2011).

The subsequent slowdown (caused by a combination of rising natural gas prices and falling electricity demand following OPEC's two rounds of oil price increases) was reversed by the late 1980s and by 1990 almost half of all new US generating capacity was installed in gas turbines (Smock 1991). By the 1990s it also became less common to use gas turbines alone and in most new installation they are now combined with a steam turbine: hot exhaust leaving gas turbines produces steam (in a heat recovery generator) that is used to power a steam turbine, and power plants generating electricity with these combined-cycle gas turbine arrangements have recently set new records by surpassing 60% efficiency (Siemens 2017a; Larson 2017).

By 2017 the world's largest gas turbines were offered by GE and Siemens. SGT5–8000H is the most powerful 50-Hz gas turbine produced by Siemens; its gross output is 425 MW in simple cycle and 630 MW in combined cycle operation, with overall efficiency of 61% (Siemens 2017b). The world's largest machines are now made by GE: 9HA.2 delivers 544 MW (with efficiency of 43.9%) in simple cycle, and in combined cycle it rates 804 MW, with overall efficiency up to 63.5% and with start-up time of less than 30 minutes (GE 2017c). Gross output of stationary gas turbines has thus progressed from 15.4 MW in 1939 to 544 MW in 2015, or roughly a 35-fold increase in 76 years. But there is no doubt that the growth of stationary gas turbines will not follow the course suggested by the continuation of the best logistic fit because that would bring enormously powerful machines with capacities in excess of 2 GW by 2050.

The growing capacity of the largest stationary units has met the needs of utilities as they shift from coal toward more efficient, and more flexible, ways of generation, but since the 1960s smaller gas turbines have also become indispensable in many industrial applications. Most notably, they power compressors used to move natural gas in pipelines. Compressor stations are sited at regular intervals (typically on the order of 100 km on major trunk lines) and they use machines of 15–40 MW capacity. Gas turbine-driven centrifugal compressors are common in the oil and gas industry, in refineries and in chemical syntheses, most notably in Haber-Bosch ammonia plants.

Nuclear Reactors and PV Cells

I have put these two completely different modes of modern energy conversion into the same section simply as a matter of convenience: after investigating the growth of external (steam) and internal (gasoline, diesel) combustion engines and water, wind, steam, and gas turbines, these are the only remaining converters of major economic consequence in the early 21st century. Nuclear fission, proceeding in several types of reactors, has already made a significant contribution to the global primary energy supply since its commercial beginnings during the late 1950s, while land-based conversion of sunlight by photovoltaic modules to transmit electricity into national and international grids is the latest addition to large-scale generation. Besides the differences in their longevity and modes of operation, the two conversions also have very different prospects.

Regardless of its actual rates of future expansion, it is obvious that direct conversion of solar radiation to electricity—natural energy flow that could be harnessed with a much higher power density than any other renewable resource—has an assured and expansive future. In contrast, fission-based electricity generation has been in retreat in all Western economies (and in Japan), and although new reactors are being built in a number of countries (above all in China, India, and Russia) pending retirement of reactors built during the decades of rapid nuclear expansion (1970–1990), will not make nuclear generation relatively more important than in the past. In 1996 fission supplied nearly 18% of the world's electricity, by 2016 the share was down to 11% and even the best scenario for 2040 does not see it rising above 12% (WNA 2017).

Nuclear Reactors

Nuclear reactors could be put into the same energy converter category as boilers: their role is to produce heat that is used to generate steam whose expansion rotates turbogenerators to produce electricity. Of course, the heat production rests on an entirely different conversion: instead of combustion (rapid oxidation) of carbon in fossil fuels that could be done in simple metallic vessels, nuclear reactors proceed by controlled fission of an isotope of uranium, the heaviest stable element, and they are among the most complex and technically demanding engineering assemblies. But their growth has been always constrained by economic and technical imperatives (Mahaffey 2011).

In order to operate as economically as possible and to meet the new capacity requirements during the decades of rising electricity demand, the minimum unit capacities of nuclear reactors had to be above 100 MW. Only the first British Magnox reactors at Calder Hall (construction started in 1953) and Chapelcross (construction started in 1955) stations were smaller, with gross capacity of 60 MW, while the subsequent early units installed at Bradwell, Berkeley, and Dungeness ranged from 146 to 230 MW (Taylor 2016). British reactors commissioned during the 1970s had gross unit capacities between 540 and 655 MW and during the 1980s the largest unit rated 682 MW.

The French decision to develop large nuclear capacity as the best way to reduce dependence on imported crude oil was based on an economically optimal repetition of standard, and relatively large, reactor sizes (Hecht 2009). Most French reactors have capacities of 900 MW_e (951–956 MW gross), the second most common class is rated at 1,300 MW_e (1,363 MW gross), and there are also four reactors capable of 1,450 MW_e (1,561 MW gross). Commissioning of the first reactor of the 1,650 MW_e class at Flamanville has been repeatedly delayed. Many US reactors built during the 1970s and 1980s have capacities in excess of 1 GW, with the largest units between 1,215 and 1,447 MW_e.

Development of nuclear reactor capacities has been obviously constrained by overall electricity demand and by the evolution of steam turbine capacities (covered earlier in this chapter). Operational reliability, minimized cost, and the need to conform to regional or national requirements for base-load generation (capacity factors of nuclear reactors are commonly above 90%) have been more important considerations than the quest for higher unit capacities. But the average size of reactors has grown larger: only two reactors commissioned during the 1960s had capacity in excess of 1 GW and the mean rating was just 270 MW—while 60 reactors under construction in 2017 ranged from 315 MW in Pakistan to 1.66 GW in China, with a modal rating (17 reactors) of 1 GW_e, the capacity of the most commonly built Chinese unit (WNA 2017).

PV Modules

Photovoltaics has been—together with nuclear reactors and gas and wind turbines—one of the four post-WWII additions to commercial means of large-scale electricity generation. The photovoltaic principle (generation of electric current in a material exposed to sunlight) was discovered by Antoine Henri Becquerel in 1839, the PV effect in selenium was identified in 1876 and in cadmium sulfide in 1932, but the first practical applications came only after researchers at Bell Laboratories invented a silicon PV cell in 1954 (Fraas 2014). Their cells initially converted just 4% of incoming radiation to electricity but subsequent improvements during the remainder of the decade, mainly thanks to the work of Hoffman Electronics, pushed efficiency to 8% by 1957 and 10% by 1959 (USDOE 2017).

The first installation of very small PV cells (~1 W) came in 1958 on the Vanguard satellite, and other space applications followed soon: very high price of the cells was a small portion of the overall cost of a satellite and its launch. In 1962 Telstar, the world's first telecommunications satellite, carried a 14 W array and progressively larger modules have followed. For example, Landsat 8 (an Earth-observation satellite) carries an array of triple-junction cells with capacity of 4.3 kW. Land-based PV generation got its first stimulus with the two rounds of rapid increases of world oil prices during the 1970s and the world's first 1 MW PV facility was installed in Lugo, California in 1982, followed two years later by a 6 MW plant. The return to low oil prices postponed any new large commercial uses, but development of more efficient monocrystalline silicon cells, and introduction of new cell types, continued.

The best research cell efficiencies have unfolded as follows (NREL 2018; figure 3.14). Single silicon cells without a concentrator reached 20% in 1986 and 26.1% by 2018, while the Shockley–Queisser limit restricts the maximum theoretical efficiency of a solar cell to 33.7% (Shockley and

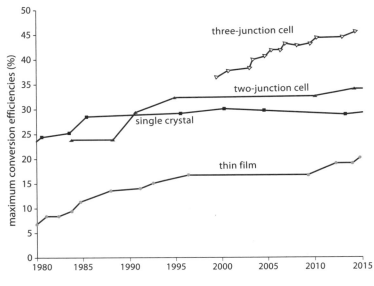

Figure 3.14
Record conversion efficiencies of research PV cells. Simplified from NREL (2018).

Queisser 1961). The cheapest amorphous silicon cells began during the late 1970s with efficiencies of just 1–2%, reached 10% by 1993, and 14% by 2018. In contrast, the efficiency of copper indium gallium selenide amorphous cells rose from about 5% in 1976 to 22.9% by 2018, nearly matching that of monocrystalline silicon. Currently the most efficient research cells are single junction gallium arsenide and multijunction cells (figure 3.14). These cells are made of two to four layers of different semi-conducting materials that absorb solar radiation in different wavelengths and hence boost the conversion efficiency: three-junction cells with a concentrator were the first to surpass the 40% efficiency mark (in 2007), and four-junction cells with a concentrator reached 46% in 2015 (NREL 2018).

The modular nature of photovoltaics makes it possible to install units ranging from a few square centimeters to large power plants whose peak power is now in hundreds of MW. As a result, growth of large PV installations has been primarily limited by the cost of modules (which has been steadily declining) and the expense of providing the requisite high-voltage transmission from those sunny places that do not have an existing connection to a national grid. As already noted, a California solar farm already aggregated 1 MW in 1982, but the first installation reaching 10 MW followed only in 2006 (Germany's Erlasee Park with 11.4 MW_p), and in 2010

Ontario's Sarnia (97 MW$_p$) came close to 100 MW. In 2011 China's Golmud Park reached 200 MW and in 2014 California's Topaz Farm was the first to aggregate 500 MW.

The largest PV solar park on grid in 2017 was Tengger Desert in Nigxia with 1.547 GW$_p$ while China's Datong in Shanxi province and India's Kurnool Ultra Mega Solar Park in Andhra Pradesh had 1 GW each but the Datong plant is to be eventually expanded to 3 GW$_p$ (SolarInsure 2017). This means that between 1982 and 2017 capacities of the largest solar park grew by three orders of magnitude (1,500 times to be exact), with recent rapid increases made possible by the declining costs of PV panels. Naturally, the location of these plants (latitude, average cloud cover) determines their capacity factors: for fixed panels they range from only about 11% for German plants to about 25% for the facilities in the US Southwest.

Electric Lights and Motors

All electric lights and motors are, obviously, secondary energy converters turning electricity produced by steam turbogenerators or water, wind and gas turbines and PV cells into illumination or into mechanical energy (motors as inverse generators). Electric lights are now by far the most numerous energy converters and more than 130 years after their introduction we do not even notice their truly revolutionary consequences for human development and modern civilization. But electric motors, too, have become ubiquitous; however, as they are nearly always hidden—built into an enormous variety of electrical and electronic devices, ranging from washing machines and dough mixers to laptop computers, mounted behind metal and plastic panels in cars, and rotating incessantly behind the walls of industrial enterprises—most people are not even aware of the multitude of their now indispensable services.

And while there are some needs for extraordinarily powerful lights and very large electric motors, the growth of these energy converters should be traced primarily in terms of their improving efficiency, durability, and reliability rather than in terms of increasing unit capacity. Indeed, the two markets with rapidly growing demand for electric motors—electronic devices and cars—need, respectively, devices of tiny or small-to-moderate capacities. For example, a brushless DC 5V/12V electric motor energizing a CD-ROM in a laptop operates mostly with power of just 2–7 W, while the power of DC window lift motors (now installed in every car, together with other motors needed to lock doors and adjust seats) ranges mostly from 12 to 50 W (NXP Semiconductors 2016).

Electric Lights

In order to appreciate the revolutionary nature of even the first, highly inefficient, electric lights it is necessary to compare their performance with that of their common predecessors. Burning candles converted as little as 0.01% and no more than 0.04% of the chemical energy in wax, tallow or paraffin into dim, unstable, and uncontrollable light. Even Edison's first light bulbs, with filaments of carbonized paper, were 10 times more efficient than candles. But by the early 1880s less convenient gas lights (introduced just after 1800 and burning coal gas made by distillation of coal) had a slight edge with efficiencies up to 0.3%. That changed soon when osmium filaments were introduced in 1898 and raised efficiency to 0.6%; that was doubled by 1905 with tungsten filaments in a vacuum, and doubled again when light bulbs were filled with inert gas (Smil 2005). Fluorescent lights, introduced during the 1930s, raised efficiency above 7%, above 10% after 1950, and close to 15% by the year 2000.

The best comparison of light sources is in terms of their luminous efficacy, the ratio expressing the generation of visible light per unit of power, lumens per watt (lm/W), with a theoretical maximum of 683 lm/W. The history of lighting has seen luminous efficacies (all data in lm/W) rising from 0.2 for candles to one to two for coal-gas light and less than five for early incandescent light bulbs to 10–15 for the best incandescent lights and up to about 100 for fluorescent lights (Rea 2000). High-intensity discharge lights were the most efficacious source of indoor lighting at the beginning of the 21st century, with maxima slightly above 100 lm/W. Efficacy improvements of nearly all of these light sources have seen long periods of stagnation or slow linear growth but the future belongs to light emitting diodes (LED) whose light spectrum is suitable for indoor or outdoor applications (Bain 2015; figure 3.15. Their use began as small lights in electronics and cars and by 2017 their efficacies had surpassed 100 lm/W, and by 2030 they are expected to save 40% of US electricity used for lighting (Navigant 2015).

Gains in efficiency of electricity conversion and generation have combined to deliver a unit of light at a tiny fraction of its traditional costs. By the end of the 20th century the average cost of US lighting was just 0.0003% of its 1800 rate; inversely, this meant that for the same price consumers received about 3,300 times more illumination (Nordhaus 1998), definitely one of the highest overall performance gains for an energy converter. Fouquet (2008) ended up with a similar long-term fraction: his calculations show that in the year 2000 a lumen of British light cost just 0.01% of its value in 1500, a 10,000-fold gain in 500 years (with virtually all of it taking place

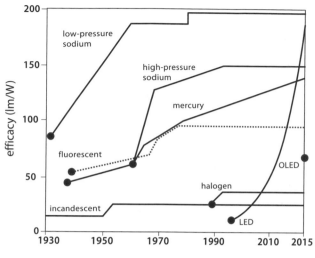

Figure 3.15
Light efficacy (lm/W) since 1930. Based on Osram Sylvania (2009) and subsequent efficacy reports.

during the last 150 years of the period), and 1% of its value in 1900, a 100-fold gain in a century.

Electric Motors

Electric motors had a protracted evolution. Michael Faraday discovered electromagnetic induction in 1839 (Faraday 1839), but it took more than four decades before the first small DC motors became commercialized and nearly 60 years before the introduction of AC motors (Pope 1891). As long as batteries remained the only means of reliable electricity supply, direct current motors remained small and uncommon. A stencil-making pen used in duplicating documents powered by Edison's small DC motor sold several thousand units during the late 1870s (Burns 2018), but the real beginnings of commercial diffusion (in industry, for streetcars) came only with the first central electricity-generating plants (starting in 1882) and with the production of polyphase motors in the late 1880s.

Tesla dated his original electric motor idea to 1882 but his design for a polyphase motor was first patented only in 1888 after he had spent several years in the US (Tesla 1888). Tesla patented a two-phase machine, and the first three-phase motor, a design that quickly became dominant, was built by a Russian engineer, Mikhail Osipovich Dolivo-Dobrowolsky, working in Germany for AEG. Tesla sold all of his motor patents to Westinghouse, whose small fan-powering motor (125 W) sold almost 10,000 units during the 1890s (Hunter and Bryant 1991). Rapid adoption of electric motors in industry also began during the last decade of the 19th century and accelerated after 1900. As already noted in the introduction to this section, variables that are commonly used to trace the growth of many energy converters and other artifacts—their capacity, size, mass, or efficiency—are not the most appropriate measures for appraising the advances in design, production, and deployment of electric motors.

In the first place this is due to the fact that this category of secondary energy converters (all motors are essentially generators running backward) includes different operating modes: the basic divides are between DC and AC motors, and between induction and synchronous motors within the latter category (Hughes 2006). In addition, electric motors are inherently highly efficient, particularly when they work at or near their full capacity. Although there are several pathways lowering the overall performance (due to friction, windage and hysteresis and eddy and ohmic losses), full-load efficiencies of electric motors were around 70% even for the early commercial models made at the end of the 19th century; that left a limited range for further improvement and by the beginning of the 21st century we came close to practical performance limits. The latest standards adopted by the National Electrical Manufacturers Association in the US specify minimum full-load efficiencies of 95% for motors rated at more than 186.4 kW (250 hp) and 74–88.5% for small motors of 750 W to 7.5 kW (Boteler and Malinowski 2015).

But the most important reason why tracing growth in unit capacity or mass are not the most revealing variables to quantify is that the physical attributes of electric motors are determined by the specific requirements of their deployment and that the miniaturization and mass-production of small-capacity motors for uses in electronics and mechatronics have been as (if not more) important than the growth of capacities for industrial or transportation applications demanding higher power. Improving the ability to meet a specific functionality—be it extended durability in a dusty environment or underwater, long-term delivery of steady power, or the ability to provide sudden high-torque requirements—as well as a rapid expansion of global demand for electric motors used in new applications (especially in household and electronic consumer products and in cars where the motor size is inherently limited) are thus more revealing attributes than a secular increase in power ratings.

As a result, the two most notable growth phenomena marking the post-1890 history of electric motors have been their unusually rapid conquest of the industrial market during the early decades of the 20th century and their mass-scale nonindustrial deployment during recent decades. In North America and in Western Europe the electrification of industrial processes in general, and manufacturing in particular, was accomplished in a matter of three to four decades (in the US the process was essentially over by the late 1920s), while nonindustrial uses of electric motors expanded slowly for many decades before their deployment accelerated during the closing decades of the 20th century and then reached unprecedented heights—with worldwide annual unit additions now exceeding 10 billion units—from the year 2000.

Data derived from censuses of manufacturing illustrate the rapid diffusion of electric motors and the retreat of steam (Daugherty 1927; Schurr et al. 1990). In 1899, 77% of all power installed in the country's manufacturing enterprises was in steam engines and 21% in waterwheels and turbines. During the next three decades the total mechanical power installed in US manufacturing increased 3.7-fold but the aggregate capacity of electric motors grew nearly 70-fold and the converters whose share of manufacturing power was less than 5% in 1900 supplied 82% of all power in US factories. The share rose further during the 1930s to reach 90% in 1940, with the growth trajectory following closely a sigmoid course (figure 3.16). But

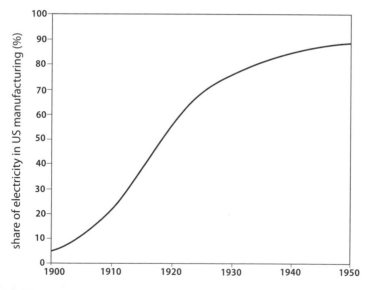

Figure 3.16
Logistic fit (inflection point in 1916, asymptote of 89.9%) of the share of power in US manufacturing supplied by electric motors, 1909–1950. Data from Daugherty (1927) and Schurr et al. (1990).

a long-term plateau had formed at a slightly lower level: by 1954 the share had declined to 85% and stayed close to that high share for the remainder of the 20th century as other efficient converters (gas turbines and diesel engines) claimed the rest.

But this rapid shift to electric motors was far from being just a transition to a new kind of energy converter. Moving from shafts to wires had profound consequences for factory organization, quality and safety of the working environment, and labor productivity (Devine 1983). Reciprocating motion produced by steam engines was transferred from the converter (waterwheel, water turbine, or steam engine) first by mainline shafts, running the length of a building under factory ceilings, and then by parallel countershafts and belts. Obviously, these arrangements were inconvenient and dangerous. They were inefficient (due to frictional losses), unsafe (slipping belts), and noisy and they did not allow any individual precision adjustment of rotation or torque. Moreover, any problem with the main converter or with any part of an elaborate transmission setup (easily caused by a slipped belt) necessitated a temporary outage of the entire system.

Electric motors changed all that. They were first used to power shorter shafts serving a small number of machines, but soon the unit drive became the norm. As a result, ceilings were opened to natural light or to installation of electric lighting and adequate heating and (later) air conditioning; highly efficient motors also allowed individualized precision control, machines and workstations could be switched on and off without affecting the entire system, and expansion or machine upgrading could be handled easily by requisite rewiring. Electric drive was a key factor in the near-doubling of US manufacturing productivity during the first 30 years of the 20th century, as well as in another doubling that was accomplished by the late 1960s (Schurr 1984). Small and efficient servomotors are now deployed not only in such common industrial tasks as metal cutting and forming, woodworking, spinning, and weaving but also to power conveyor belts (now also indispensable for preparing the rising volume of e-commerce orders), position PV panels (solar tracking for maximum efficiency), and open doors automatically.

The second notable growth trajectory associated with the adoption of nonindustrial electric motors began slowly with the diffusion of major household appliances (white goods), first in the US already before WWII, then in post-1950 Europe and Japan. In 1930 almost 10% of US households had a small refrigerator, 90% penetration was reached by 1955, and the rate was close to 100% by 1970 (Felton 2008). To run their compressors, refrigerators need durable, low-vibration, low-noise electric motors (now typically 550–750 W) and the demand for these devices increased further with rising ownership of freezers. Clothes washers (whose market penetration was much slower and reached about 80% of US households by the year 2000) have electric motors now rating mostly between 500 and 1,000 W.

Other commonly owned appliances powered by small electric motors include clothes dryers, dishwashers, and heating, ventilation and air-conditioning equipment (including heat recovery ventilators that run non-stop in highly insulated homes, as do natural gas furnace fans when the heating cycle is on). Electric motors in some kitchen appliances are also fairly powerful, 1,000–1,200 W in some food processors, although 400–600 W is the most common range. New markets for small electric motors have been created by growing ownership of electric tools and garden tools (including electric lawnmowers and trimmers).

Again, some of these tools must be fairly powerful (drills up to 1 kW, saws well over 1 kW), others have tiny electric motors. But by far the largest surge in demand for small electric motors has been due to the rapid sequential adoption of new electronic devices. Mass production and low prices of these consumer goods were made possible by the rise of transistors, then integrated circuits and, eventually, of microprocessors, but most of these devices still need mechanical (rotary) energy (for turntables, assorted drives, and cooling fans), with electric motors as the only viable choice to meet that demand (desktop and laptop computers have three to six small motors to run disk drives and ventilation fans).

The electrification of cars powered by internal combustion engines began just a few years after the introduction of the first mass-made commercial automobile. Ford's Model T, introduced in 1908, had no electric motors (starting the engine required laborious, and sometimes dangerous, cranking) but in 1911 Charles F. Kettering patented the first electric starter, in 1912 GM ordered 12,000 of these labor-saving devices for its Cadillacs, and by 1920 electric starters became common, with Model T switching to them in 1919 (Smil 2006b). Power steering became common in the US during the 1960s and small electric motors have eventually taken over functions (ranging from opening windows to lifting gates) that relied for generations on human power.

In cars, small electric motors start engines, enable power steering, run water pumps, operate antilock brakes, seatbelt retractors and windshield wipers, adjust seats, run heating and air-conditioning fans, open and close windows, door locks, and now also sliding doors, lift gates, and fold in side mirrors. Electric parking brakes are the latest addition to these applications. Nonessential electric motors became common first in luxury cars but their use has been steadily percolating downwards, with even basic North American, European and Japanese sedans having about 30 of them, while the total can be three to four times as many in upscale models. The total weight of luxury car motors is on the order of 40 kg, with seat control, power steering and starter motors accounting for about half of the total mass (Ombach 2017). Global sales of automotive electric motors surpassed 2.5 billion units in 2013 and with the demand growing by 5–7% a year they were to reach 3 billion in 2017 (Turnbough 2013).

In aggregate, Turnbough (2013) estimated that global sales of small non-industrial motors would rise from 9.8 billion units in 2012 to 12 billion in 2018, and their cumulative operating total would be far larger than the aggregate number of all (larger, and longer-lasting) industrial units. The smallest electric motors are now also the most ubiquitous because almost every cell phone has a vibration alert produced by the spinning of an eccentrically mounted tiny (typically 1 cm long and 4 mm in diameter) motor that now wholesales for as little as 50 cents apiece. These mini-motors use linear voltage regulators and constant voltage supply. Global sales of cell phones rose from 816 million in 2005 to 1.42 billion in 2016, creating an unprecedented demand for those tiny motors. Small vibrator motors are also commonly included in toys.

Finally, a few numbers to trace the trajectory of the largest industrial motors. In rail transportation, maximum power rose from 2.2 kW capacity of the first electric mini-railway (just a 300 m long circular track) built in 1879 at the Berlin Trade Fair by Werner von Siemens, to 6.45–12.21 MW of asynchronous motors installed in two pairs of power cars powering French rapid trains (TGV, Thalys, Eurostar), an increase of three orders of magnitude. Synchronous motors, best suited for constant speed applications and commonly used to power pipeline and refinery compressors, pumps, fans, and conveyors have seen exponential growth during the second half of the 20th century, from only about 5 MW in 1950 to more than 60 MW in 2000; the highest voltages stayed at between 10 and 15 kV for decades and only early in the 21st century did they rise suddenly to nearly 60 kV (Kullinger 2009).

4 Artifacts: or growth of man-made objects and their performances

Surveying the growth of artifacts in a single chapter can be done only in the most truncated manner and by concentrating on the most important items. An analogy might be a good way to indicate the challenge. Even after decades of trying to narrow down the most likely grand total of living species we still have no definite answer, but catalogued terrestrial organisms now amount to almost 1.25 million, including about 950,000 animals, 215,000 plants and almost 45,000 fungi, with nearly 200,000 species (mostly animals) identified in the ocean (Mora et al. 2011). Even cursory attempts at parallel classifications of man-made objects (ranging from smallest tools to massive structures) indicate that the diversity of artifacts is at least comparable to the diversity of organisms—and, although such a comparison is obviously one of apples and automobiles, it is not indefensible to conclude that the total of anthropogenic "species" is actually far larger.

I will illustrate the point by constructing corresponding taxonomic hierarchies (necessarily arbitrary in the case of artifacts) and by making parallel comparisons descending from all organisms to dolphins, and from all artifacts to mobile phones. The vast domain of artifacts (equivalent to all Eukarya, organisms with nuclei in their cells) would contain the kingdom (equivalent to Animalia) of multi-component man-made objects (as opposed to single-component artifacts made solely of metal or wood or plastic) in which we would find the phylum (equivalent of Chordata) of electricity-powered devices, one of whose classes (equivalent to Mammalia) would be portable designs, containing an order of devices (equivalent to Cetacea) used for communication, within which would be the family of phones (equivalent to Delphinidae) composed of many genera of mobile phones (Alcatel, Apple, Huawei, Motorola … equivalent to *Delphinus, Orcinus, Tursiops* …), some of which contain a single species (equivalent to *Orcinus orca*, killer whale), others (most notably Samsung, and dolphins belonging to genus *Lagenorhynchus*) are species-rich.

Using this (inevitably contestable) taxonomy, there were at least 8,000 "species" of mobile phones in 2018, that is more than the total number of described mammals or amphibians, belonging to more than 100 genera (GSMArena 2017). And it makes surprisingly little difference if this taxonomy is dismissed as unrealistic and if an argument is made that modern mobile phones are just varieties of a single species. The richness of the manmade world is undeniable, and the growth of artifact diversity has been one of the formative trends of modern history. The World Steel Association recognizes about 3,500 grades of steel, that is more than all described species of rodents, the largest mammalian order. In terms of macroscopic components, complex machines are easily as "species-rich" as complex ecosystems: the average Toyota car has 30,000 parts, Boeing 737 (the smallest plane of the 700 series) has about 400,000 parts (excluding wiring, bolts, and rivets), the new Boeing 787 has 2.3 million, and Boeing 747–8 has 6 million parts (Boeing 2013).

Of course, the functioning of living systems (be they rain forests or human bodies) depends on assemblages of microbial species (microbiomes), and the numbers of bacteria, archaea, and microscopic fungi in a unit mass of forest will be vastly larger than the total of the smallest functional components in a unit mass of even the most complicated machine. And, obviously, there can be no true comparison between biomass, the mass of living (and, in wood, dead) cells that form the bodies of organisms, and the mass of metals, composite materials, plastics, and glass that form the bodies of complex machines. Functional differences, and hence the impossibility of making any simple comparisons, are self-evident but so is the astounding complexity of human artifacts whose most accomplishment designs must fit and function so perfectly that they can operate faultlessly for extended periods of time under the most demanding conditions. My small electronic calculator is an excellent example of convenient longevity.

I bought Texas Instruments TI-35 Galaxy Solar when it came out in 1984 because it was the first design powered by four small (total of about 7 cm^2) PV cells. They, as well as the display and all keys, have now worked for 35 years as I have done nearly all calculations for all of my post-1984 books on this tiny machine. On a large scale, there is no better example than jet engines (gas turbines). Their improved reliability allowed the extended-range operation with two-engine airplanes to go from 90 minutes in 1976

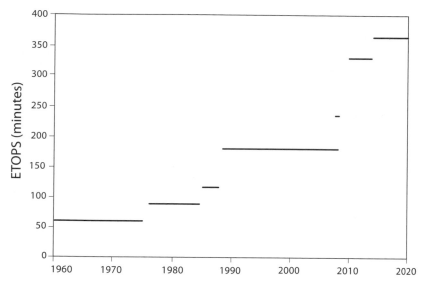

Figure 4.1
Growth of ETOPS for jetliners. In 1988 the three-hour limit opened 95% of the Earth's surface for commercial air transport, and the longest permissible single-engine operation of 370 minutes in 2018 is just 53 minutes shorter than the flight time from New York to London.

to 120 minutes in 1985 (this opened almost all North Atlantic routes to crossing by twin-engine jetliners) and three hours in 1988, opening not only the North Pacific routes to twin-engine planes, but 95% of the Earth's surface for ETOPS, Extended-range Twin-engine Operational Performance Standards (Smil 2010b). Extension to 240 minutes followed in 2009, to 330 minutes in 2010 (first for Boeing 777–200ER), and in 2014 the Airbus 350XWB was given the maximum ETOPS of 370 minutes (Airbus 2014), which means that the transatlantic crossing between New York and London could almost be made with a single engine (figure 4.1)!

The richness applies also to the range of artifacts measured by performance capacity, size, or mass. Electric motors, whose development was charted in chapter 3, are an excellent example of this diversity (Hughes 2006). The largest ones (with capacities around 60 MW) are used to power huge compressors, the tiniest ones (micro-ultrasonic motors with one mm^3 stator) are designed for minimally invasive surgical operations (Kullinger 2009; Phys.org 2015). Other artifacts have even greater performance and mass ranges, matching the range of living organisms. There is a 100 million-fold difference in the mass of mammals between the smallest (Etruscan shrew 1.3–2.5 g) and the largest (blue whale, 180 t), but there is an even larger mass difference between the lightest flying object (miniature photo drone at 5 g) and fully loaded Airbus 380 (560 t).

Consequently, no matter if we compare overall diversity (species through evolution, artifacts through deliberate design) or the ranges of mass, capacity or typical performance, the universe of man-made objects and structures is as rich, and in some ways even richer, than the variety contained within the biosphere. Tracing the growth of this immense diversity can be done only in a highly selective manner and I have chosen to concentrate on a few fundamental classes of objects. I will look first at those whose design and use have separated us from our hominin ancestors. The growth of major structures and infrastructure deserves special attention, as does the growth of our transportation capabilities and of electronics, the most recent class of designed objects that have affected, and in so many ways truly revolutionized, our mobility and communication, as well as our productive capacities, leisure, and social interactions.

Tools and Simple Machines

Systematic study of simple tools and machines began in ancient Greece and eventually Greek engineers listed five devices that provided significant mechanical advantage, that is, expanding the scope of human action by deploying smaller forces over longer distances. They were wheel and axle, lever, a system of pulleys, wedge (inclined plane), and endless screw. Modern definitions would be different: Wheel and axle actually form a circular lever, and screws are circular inclined planes wrapped around a cylindrical or conical shaft. Levers (to lift and move heavy loads, also common as oars, crowbars, scissors, pliers, and wheelbarrows) and inclined planes (ramps to lift loads, to erect heavy stones, also as wedges to exert larger sideways forces, axes, adzes, and screws in presses) were used by many prehistoric societies (otherwise they could not have built their megalithic monuments), while a simple pulley is first documented during the 9th century BCE and ancient Greeks and Romans used compound pulleys (Needham 1965; Burstall 1968; Cotterell and Kamminga 1990; Winter 2007).

Many devices and machines combine basic mechanical principles in order to achieve otherwise impossible performances. Construction cranes—machines as indispensable for modern megaprojects as they were for building medieval cathedrals and antique temples—are excellent examples of such combinations as they rely on pulleys and levers to lift as well as to move heavy loads. I will trace the progress of their maximum performances (the process that began nearly three millennia ago and whose main steps are fairly well documented) in order to illustrate slow, but eventually impressive, growth of basic artifact capabilities achieved primarily by ingenious design and only secondarily by deploying more powerful prime movers.

Pulleys, Winches, Capstans

The single pulley—used first (as early as the 9th century BCE) to draw water from wells (ancient Egyptian *shaduf*)—has no mechanical advantage (expressed as the multiplier of the input force applied over a commensurately longer distance) but it makes it possible to accomplish the work faster and with less exertion because pulling on a rope is easier and generates a greater force than lifting an object by hand. The oldest crane designs used in Greece starting in the 6th century BCE were simple wooden jibs with single pulleys with mechanical advantage gained by winding rope with a winch, but by the 3rd century BCE compound pulleys were used to multiply maximum loads (Wilson 2008).

Perhaps the most impressive ancient illustration of the capability of compound pulleys was recorded by Plutarch, who described how Archimedes demonstrated their action to Hiero II, the king of Syracuse:

> Archimedes therefore fixed upon a three-masted merchantman of the royal fleet, which had been dragged ashore by the great labours of many men, and after putting on board many passengers and the customary freight, he seated himself at a distance from her, and without any great effort, but quietly setting in motion with his hand a system of compound pulleys, drew her towards him smoothly and evenly, as though she were gliding through the water. (Plutarch 1917, 473).

In the absence of any reported masses involved in this stunt it is impossible to estimate the actual mechanical advantage, but the calculation can be done readily for the two kinds of common Roman cranes. *Trispastos* had three pulleys, two in the upper and one in the lower block, and it offered a threefold mechanical advantage: in an ideal case, the force required to lift a load was a third of its weight. The actual mechanical advantage was smaller due to the friction between the axle and the pulley and also due to internal friction of the rope. Cotterell and Kamminga (1990) used 18th-century studies of rope stiffness to calculate the actual efficiency of *trispastos* as 87%, that is a mechanical advantage of 2.61. *Pentaspastos* supported the load by five ropes and its efficiency was less than 80%. Roman builders were aware of this inevitable efficiency deterioration and did not use machines with more than five pulleys: if they needed more power, they placed two machines in series and such a *polyspastos* had a roughly sevenfold actual mechanical advantage.

Further increases in maximum lift were achieved by deploying the combined forces of several workers turning winches or capstans (a winch with a vertical axis whose radial spokes can be pushed horizontally) or walking in treadwheels. The mechanical advantage of a winch or a capstan is the quotient of the radii of its handspikes and axle. A winch with a 10 cm axle and 30 cm handspikes will produce, ideally, a threefold gain. Theoretically, a single worker using such a winch to power a *pentaspastos* could lift 750 kg (50 kg×5×3). A capstan with a 10 cm axle and 60 cm spikes will double that advantage and four workers pushing such a capstan connected to the same machine could produce a theoretical lift of up to 6 t (50 kg×4×5×6). In practice, the first performance was reduced by friction and stiffness to no more than 600 kg, the second one to still an impressive lift if close to 4 t! Moreover, large capstans could be powered by animals.

Cranes
The most powerful cranes relied on treadwheels. The earliest preserved illustration of this machine (*magna rota* used to build a temple) is shown in a funerary bas-relief in the Roman tomb of the Haterii, a family of builders, dating to about 100 CE (figure 4.2). The difference between the radius of the axle drum and that of the trodden wheel provided a large mechanical advantage. A drum radius of 20 cm and wheel radius of 2.25 m resulted, even after subtracting friction losses, in a ninefold gain, and a large *polyspastos* with a treadwheel powered by two people had actual maximum lift of more than 5 t (60 kg×2×5×9). This ancient design reappeared in France in the early 13th century and in England a century later (Matthies 1992). These machines, installed inside cathedrals and sometimes powered by oxen rather than by men, were used to lift massive timbers, heavy stones, and bells (Klein 1978).

Treadwheels used to power these cranes had diameters up to 4.8 m and were operated by one or two people. The latter option, as confirmed by the experience with the wheel at Canterbury Cathedral that still worked during the 1970s, was rather uncomfortable as the two men had to hold on to struts and kept jostling each other in the confined space. Medieval cranes—with man-powered winches, capstans, and treadwheels—were not, in general, more capable than their antique predecessors, and even a harnessed ox turning a whim would have power equivalent no more than three or four

Figure 4.2
Roman crane depicted on a marble relief in the tomb of the Haterii (ca. 100 CE) discovered in 1848 near Porta Maggiore in Rome. The crane is powered by five people treading inside a large wooden wheel. Image available at www.museivaticani.va.

steadily working men. This stagnation persevered until the 18th century: Glynn (1849, 30) described that era's English cranes as "rude and clumsy devices borrowed from the Dutch."

Before 1850 that changed rapidly as William Fairbairn designed the first hand-operated harbor cranes able to lift up to 12 t to a height of 9 m and to sweep that load in a circle of 20 m in diameter. Eventually, his colossal crane could lift 60 t up to 18 m and to move the load suspended from the extreme point of the jib over a circle of 32 m in diameter. Here is the description of the crane's operation (Fairbairn 1860, 293–294):

> Four men, each working a winch of 18 inches radius. Act by two 6 inch pinions upon a wheel 5 feet 3.75 inches diameter, this in turn moves the spur wheel, 6 feet 8 inches diameter, by mean of an 8 inch pinion, and on the axle of the former the chain barrel, 2 feet in diameter, is fixed. Hence the advantage gained by the gearing will be $W/P = 18 \times 63.75 \times 80 / 6 \times 8 \times 12 = 158$ or taking the number of cogs in each wheel $W/P = 18 \times 95 \times 100 / 12 \times 9 \times 10 = 158$ and as this result is quadrupled by the fixed and moveable pulleys, the power of the men applied to the handles is multiplied 632 times by the gearing and blocks.

The capabilities of mid 19th-century cranes powered by human power were thus up to an order of magnitude higher than those of Roman machines (10–60 t, compared to 1–6 t) but we cannot compute any meaningful long-term growth rate. The process was one of some 1,500 years of performance stagnation followed by rapid growth within just a few decades as industrialization during the latter half of the 19th century demanded many new crane designs. By 1900, factories and loading operations used not only traditional small hand, wall, and pillar cranes but also large wharf and overhead travelling machines of unprecedented capacity powered by steam power and, starting in the 1890s, by electric motors (Marks 1904). The largest overhead traveling cranes in iron and steel mills had capacities of 125–150 t, and after WWII Hans Liebherr invented his tower crane in order to speed up Germany's reconstruction, a machine that could swing its loads horizontally and be easily assembled from parts transported to the construction site (Liebherr 2017).

The tower top is the fulcrum of a lever formed by the crane's jib arm (used to lift loads) and balance arm (with a counterweight), the lift capacity is potentiated by using pulleys, and a mobile crane moves into position on multiple wheels and relies on an inclined plane to reach a higher elevation: a compound machine indeed. The lifting capacities of tower cranes visible on many urban and industrial construction sites are mostly between 12 and 20 t, while the most powerful design, the Danish K-10000, can lift up to 94 t at 100 m radius and 120 t at standard (82 m) radius (Krøll Cranes 2017; figure 4.3). Gantry (portal or ship-to-shore) quay cranes used to unload large containers ships have capacities up to 90 t, the largest mobile crane (Liebherr 11200–9 on an 18-wheeler truck) can lift 1,200 t, and the world's most powerful shipbuilding gantry crane in Yantai (Shandong, China) has capacity of up to 22,000 t.

Many tools, devices, and simple machines followed the pattern exemplified by the growth of crane capacity, with long periods (in some cases more

Figure 4.3
K-10000, the world's largest crane. Maximum hook radius is 100 m, height under the hook is 85 m and capacity is 94 t. Image available at http://www.towercrane.com /tower_cranes_Summary_Specs.htm.

than a millennium and a half) of stagnation or marginal growth followed by a rapid expansion that started at different times between 1700 and 1850. I will introduce two additional examples to illustrate this common trajectory. They were chosen because of their fundamental importance for the development of civilization; they come from two very different economic activities but both of them are products of combined (concurrent or sequential) deployment of many tools and simple machines. The first refers to an entire suite of techniques used in producing wheat, the staple grain of Western civilization. The second example traces gradual improvements in the performance of sail ships that arose primarily from better designs and from more effective combinations of their basic components, including sails and rigging and keel, hull and rudder shapes, and secondarily from better navigation procedures.

Tools of Grain Production
Historical sources provide enough basic agronomic information to reconstruct the productivities of ancient and medieval grain farming, and much more detailed records allow us to make accurate calculations for the 19th century. The complete sequence of wheat cultivation in Roman Italy

during the early third century of the common era took about 180 hours of human labor per hectare (and about the same time of animal labor), and the grain yield was just 0.4 t/ha (Smil 2017a). Field preparation was done by wooden plows and harrows pulled by oxen, seeding was by hand, harvesting was by sickles, transportation from fields was by people and animals, threshing was done by animals treading the crop spread on hard ground or with flails, and grain was stored in bulk in *horrea*, stone granaries common throughout the empire (Rickman 1971).

A millennium later, English peasants and their oxen, performing a sequence of operations in ways very similar to the Roman practice, had to spend nearly as much time (about 160 hours) to produce 0.5 t/ha. By 1800 Dutch farmers were investing slightly more time (about 170 hours, and 120 hours of animal labor) to grow their wheat but they produced 2 t/ha. When expressed as mass of grain produced per unit of human labor (kg/h), average productivity rose from about 2.2 kg/h in the Roman Empire to roughly 3.2 kg/h in medieval England and to nearly 12 kg/h for an exceptionally productive early 19th-century Dutch cultivation.

Then came the great mechanization gains. Prime movers remained the same (humans and horses) but new machines speeded up the work. First came better plows: in 1838 John Lane made them from saw-blade steel, in 1843 John Deere used wrought iron, and by 1868 they were made from newly available inexpensive Bessemer steel. By the century's end, large gang plows (drawn by as many as 12 horses) had up to 10 steel shares (Smil 2017a). Mass-produced affordable reapers were introduced during the 1830s by Cyrus McCormick and Obed Hussey, the first harvester was patented in 1858, the first practical twine knotter, discharging tied sheaves, came in 1878. By 1850 American productivity was around 15 kg of wheat per hour of human labor, and by 1875 the rate rose to about 25 kg/h (Rogin 1931).

Once again, there was an order of magnitude difference between antiquity and the late 19th century (from average productivity of 2.2 kg/h to 25 kg/h), and, once again, we cannot use those two productivities to calculate a long-term rate of growth because centuries of stagnation or marginal growth were followed by rapid gains during the 19th century. And further major productivity gains took place during the last three decades of the 19th century. Gang plows, larger seeders, better mechanical harvesters, and the first horse-drawn wheat combines reduced the total of human labor in American wheat farming to just nine hours per hectare and boosted average productivity to more than 100 kg of grain per hour of labor (Rogin 1931). America's first tractor factory opened up in 1905 but the machines became important only after WWI, and only after WWII in Europe (Dieffenbach and Gray 1960).

Sail Ships

My second specific illustration of the historical trend of long-term stagnation or very slow advances of the capacities of basic mechanical designs quantifies the performance of sail ships. The three most obvious components that can be traced across the millennia of sailing ship history are their sails, their masts and rigging, and the shape of their hulls. Sails inflated by wind are simple but effective aerofoils, shapes that maximize lift force and minimize drag. Their action must be combined with the balancing force of the keel in order to prevent drifting (Anderson 2003). Sails, much like airplane wings, exploit the Bernoulli principle: wind moving around the downwind side of the sail (an equivalent of the upper surface of a wing) travels a longer path and hence moves faster than the air passing along the upwind side. But the physics of sailing is complex and the pressure difference that generates the lift are not entirely from the Bernoulli effect (Anderson 2003).

Before the advent of modern aerodynamics sail design was guided by experience, and despite a great variety of sail shapes and sizes there is one general measure that could be used to quantify the progress and trace the improvements of sail performance: ability to sail against the wind. According to a vessel's heading (course) and the direction of wind, a ship can be running (with wind from astern), reaching (beam reach, wind from the side), or beating (close-hauled, wind from ahead). A vessel will not reach the highest speed when running because with wind astern it can never move faster than the wind, but it can do so when moving abeam, with wind from the side. At the same time, sailing very close to the wind (just 10° or 20° off from its direction) is impossible even for today's best racing yacht designs.

The earliest preserved depiction of a vessel with a mast is on a ceramic disc from the 6th to 5th millennium BCE excavated at as-Sabiyah in Kuwait: it shows a two-footed mast that had to be used on vessels made of reed whose frame could not support a socket mast (Carter 2006). Later Egyptian depictions also show bipod masts, placed about one-third of the waterline length from the bow, with square sails. The adjective square actually refers to the mounting of such sails that are set at right angles to the vessel's keel. The sails are four-cornered and could be square but usually they were rectangular (low-aspect ratio, broader than tall) or trapezoidal.

As Campbell (1995, 1) remarked, "sails as an artifact have not demonstrated very great human inventiveness," and their square forms continued to propel ships until the very end of the sail era. But between antiquity and the late 19th century many changes included the number of square sails, their placement and their specific shapes, the addition of other sail designs and different rigging (Block 2003). Greeks relied on a single square sail placed amidships, and later came a second, smaller, square sail on a foremast and a third sail on a mizzen mast. Roman ships used similar low-aspect rectangular sails placed at right angles across the ship's long axis. Obviously, square sails performed well with the wind astern (180°) and they could manage wind at an angle of 150°.

Caravelas latinas, the first Portuguese ships that accomplished the voyages of discovery around the African coast (*caravelas dos descobrimentos*), had three lateen sails (Gardiner and Unger 2000; Schwarz 2008). These triangular sails were neither as radical nor as helpful an innovation as was previously believed but they did improve the ship's maneuverability (Campbell 1995). When Columbus sailed to America in 1492 his *Pinta* was a *caravela redonda*, a three-mast vessel whose foremast and mainmast were square-rigged with the mizzenmast carrying a lateen sail, and *Niña*, originally a lateen rig, was re-rigged the same way. These caravels could proceed with the wind on their beam (90°), and their post-Renaissance successors could move at an angle of about 80° into the wind.

The next stage saw the adoption of some fore-and-aft rigging, with sails set along the keel-line rather than at the right angle to it. These asymmetrically mounted sails, capable of swiveling around their masts, made sailing closer to the wind possible. During the 18h century this was most commonly done by substituting fore-and-aft jib sails for the square spritsail and spritsail topsail, and the deployment of square and fore-and-aft sails resulted in an improved ability to sail closer to the wind (McGowan 1980). Some ships combining the two kinds of rigging could manage 62°, and fore-and-aft rigs could come as close as 45° to the wind. This means that the ability to sail close to the wind improved by about 100° in two millennia. If it was a steady improvement it would imply a minuscule average gain of half a degree per decade. But the overall gain was not actually that significant because fore-and-aft rigging was never adopted either for the heaviest war ships or for the largest clippers, the fastest ships of the last decades of the sailing era.

Other simple devices and design improvements were needed to enhance the performance of sail ships. Sternpost-mounted rudders first replaced steering oars (levers) about two millennia ago in Han China and hulls and keels had seen significant dimensional increases and cross-section changes. An important indicator to trace the evolution of ship hulls is their length-to-width (beam) ratio. Roman ships had a ratio of only about 3:1 and this proportion prevailed throughout the Middle Ages, but it had nearly doubled by the end of sailing era. Large late medieval caravels had ratios up to around 3.3 and with their rounded hulls and tall fore- and after-castles their profiles almost resembled spherical sections. This was followed by gradual

Figure 4.4

Flying Cloud became the most famous clipper ship built by Donald McKay after it clocked the world's fastest time (89 days and 8 hours) for sailing from New York to San Francisco in 1853. Image available at wikimedia.

elongation. In 1492 the *Santa Maria* came at 3.7:1, in 1628 the preserved Swedish warship *Vasa* reached 4.4:1, by the 1840s packet ships that carried European immigrants had ratios around 4:1. In 1851 *Flying Cloud*, Donald McKay's speediest clipper (figure 4.4) was 5.4:1, and McKay's *Great Republic* (the largest clipper ever built, launched in 1853) had a record beam ratio of 6.1:1, albeit with iron bolts and steel reinforcements (McKay 1928).

An original French design of a large two-decked battleship carrying 74 guns and crewed by up to 750 men became the dominant class of naval vessels during the late 18th and the early 19th centuries, with the British Royal Navy commissioning nearly 150 of these ships of the line (Watts 1905). Clippers, used mostly by US and British companies and important between 1843 and 1869, were built for fast sailing on long intercontinental routes (Ross 2012). Both of these designs were fully rigged ships—with three or more square-rigged masts and with additional headsails (jibs), some also with staysails and a spanker—whose ability to sail close to the wind was greatly restricted: for example, with a northerly wind the best they could manage was east-northeast or west-northwest, or about 67°.

The only way to tackle these sailing limits was to steer the ship close to its best capability while changing course: ships with fore-and-aft rigs were tacking (coming about) by turning their bows into the wind and eventually catching it on the opposite side of the sail, while square-rigged ships did so by a slower process of wearing, making a complete downwind turn and coming back for another turn. Efficient execution of these turns required great skill at the helm and was also determined by the hull's design. Kelly and Ó Gráda (2018) attribute the notable speed increase of East India ships during the 1780s to the copper plating of hulls which had largely eliminated fouling with weeds and barnacles. But frequently nothing could help and ships could not proceed against a strong prevailing wind for days and had to give up after tiresome but fruitless tacking and wait for the wind to shift its directions (Willis 2003).

Finally, some basic facts about the growth of ship sizes in terms of their displacement tonnage, that is the mass of the ship. This measure is greatly preferable to tonnage, a ship's capacity to carry cargo. Tonnages have been quantified in a number of different ways (and specific choices are not always explicitly noted) and measured in various old nonmetric units, making long-term worldwide comparisons both complex and uncertain (Vasudevan 2010). But if displacements are not directly available they can be approximated for major categories of wooden ships by using basic vessel dimensions to calculate their mass. Hulls, masts, and spars of sailing ships typically accounted for 65–70% of their total displacement, and the rest was a combined mass of sails, ballast, supplies, armaments, and crew.

According to Homer's description of Odysseus building his boat: "Twenty trees in all did he fell, and trimmed them with the axe; then he cunningly smoothed them all and made them straight to the line" (*Odyssey*, 5.244). A generous assumption of 1 m^3 of trimmed wood per tree sets the maximum timber mass for the Greek Bronze Age ship at about 20 m^3. With 600 kg/m^3 the timber mass would be about 12 t, and about 15 t after adding mast, sail, seats, and oars. Triremes, large ancient Greek ships with three lines of rowers and bronze-sheathed battering rams, displaced as much as 50 t. The Romans built some very large cargo ships, with capacities of more than 1,000 t, capable of transporting up to 10,000 amphoras and bringing massive Egyptian obelisks to Rome.

But typical cargo vessels during the early centuries of the common era were much smaller, carrying about 70 t of grain and displacing no more than 200 t (Casson 1971). A Viking Gokstad ship (built around 890 CE and discovered in 1880) displaced only 20 t, and the ships used for the late medieval intercontinental voyages by Portuguese and Spanish sailors were smaller than typical merchant vessels of the Roman era (Smil 2017a). Columbus's *Santa Maria* displaced about 150 t and Magellan's *Victoria* only

120 t (Fernández-González 2006). A quarter of a millennium later, displacements of colonial merchant ships in the American northeast were similar (ranging between 100 and 120 t) but colliers, at 100–170 t, were much larger.

Wooden vessels reached record sizes (an order of magnitude larger than their predecessors) during the 18th and 19th centuries with the construction of large triple-deck naval ships of the line. In 1670 *Prince* displaced 2,300 t; in 1839 *Queen* had a mass of 5,100 t (Lavery 1984). The total mass of wood (almost always seasoned, high-density oak) required to build a 74-gun ship of the line during the early 19th century ranged from less than 3,000 to nearly 4,000 t, requiring wood from a small forest of more than 6,000 oak trees. Clippers, built for speed, were considerably lighter: the *Cutty Sark* displaced 2,100 t.

These totals, ranging over nearly two millennia of sail ship history, indicate slow, linear growth of maximum displacements. But because they refer to different types of ships they preclude any meaningful calculation of average gains. But records for English and then British ships of the line compare naval vessels in the same category and they confirm that between 1650 and 1840 the growth of their maximum displacement was linear, with maxima rising from 2,300 t to just over 5,000 t (Lavery 1984). This implies average growth of nearly 200 t per decade. Centuries of linear increases were followed by steep exponential enlargements made possible by the introduction of steam power and metal hulls for both naval and merchant vessels.

Structures

The growth of capacities and performances of some essential energy-related structures were traced in chapter 3. In this section I will concentrate on the growth of structures ranging from ancient pyramids, basilicas, and castles to modern skyscrapers, and especially on the advances in housing. The brevity of most of these surveys is owing to the fact that no category of remarkable structures built during antiquity, the Middle Ages, and the early modern era (1500–1800) shows any lasting growth trajectory. This is obviously true of pyramids, temples, churches, and cathedrals as well as of castles. Famously, the diameter of the Pantheon's cupola (43.4 m, completed in 125 CE) was not surpassed until the 19th century.

No matter which relevant dimensions are used to chart their progress (footprint, volume, internal area, length, height, capacity), growth of these structures was characterized mostly by relatively rapid advances followed by long periods of stagnation and decline (Europe's grand basilicas and cathedrals are excellent examples of this trend) or by complete abandonment of a particular form of construction (Egyptian pyramids and Europe's gothic cathedrals and castles are perhaps the most memorable examples of this truncated trajectory). In contrast, skyscrapers became possible only with the affordable availability of structural steel during the 1880s, and sizes of average houses began to increase only when populations became more affluent: even in the US this was only after WWII.

Pyramids

Construction of Egyptian pyramids went from the first structures of that shape, clearly demonstrating their experimental nature and learning process as projects grew larger, to the unsurpassed peaks of cut stone assembly in a single century (Lepre 1990; Wier 1996; Lehner 1997). Djoser's step pyramid in Saqqara (3rd dynasty, ~2650 BCE), 330,000 m^3, apparently a somewhat cautious test for larger structures, was followed by Sneferu's three pyramids (4th dynasty), the first one in Meidun (640,000 m^3), the other two (the bent pyramid of about 1.2 Mm^3 and the red pyramid of nearly 1.7 Mm^3) in Dahshur.

Khufu's great pyramid at Giza, with volume of 2.58 Mm^3 and rising to a height of 139 m, was built during the 4th dynasty and completed around 2560 BCE. Khafre's neighboring Giza pyramid was nearly as large (2.21 Mm^3) but the third Giza structure (Menkaure's pyramid) was, at 235,000 m^3, smaller than Djoser's pyramid built more than a century earlier—and so were all other Egyptian pyramids built during the subsequent dynasties as well as pyramids built in the neighboring Kushite kingdom of Nubia. Completely unrelated, and structurally different, Mesoamerican pyramids, particularly those at Teotihuacan dated to the 2nd century CE, were also smaller and their construction was much easier because their cores were made of packed earth, rubble, and adobe bricks, with only the exterior of stone (Baldwin 1977). Stone pyramids are thus megastructures whose peak achievements came shortly after their ancient origins and that were never surpassed, not even equaled, by any later projects.

Churches and Cathedrals

Christian churches had a much more gradual trajectory than Egyptian pyramids, but major basilicas (derived from such large Roman civic structures as Trajan's Basilica Ulpia) had large dimensions even from the earliest period of Rome's new official religion (Ching et al. 2011). The Old St. Peter's, completed around 360 CE, was about 110 m long, with interior area of about 9,000 m^2 and volume of about 180,000 m^3 created by the main central nave (about 30 m tall), two smaller aisles on each side, and a transept (Kitterick et al. 2013). Less than two centuries later, the interior area of Hagia Sophia (completed under Justinian I in 537) had a nearly identical size but its volume (thanks to its enormous dome) had surpassed 250,000 m³; this record was doubled only by the completion of Seville cathedral in 1507 (interior area of 11,500 m²).

But just before Seville cathedral's consecration, Julius II began the construction of the new St. Peter's Basilica in Rome and ever since its completion in 1626 it has remained the world's largest church both in terms of its total interior area of about 15,000 m² and volume of 1.6 Mm³ (Scotti 2007). Both dimensions are well ahead of the Basílica do Santuário Nacional de Nossa Senhora da Conceição Aparecida in Brazil's Aparecida, a Romanesque Revival building resembling a hotel or an office complex, completed in 1980. Contrasts between the old and the new St. Peter's Basilica are impressive (Kitterick et al. 2013). The interior area of the new buildings is 66% larger but the interior volume is nearly nine times larger, with the new structure able to accommodate 60,000 people. Again, the time elapsed between their completions (1,266 years apart) and the saltatory nature of construction progress (with centuries-long periods that saw no new dimension records) make it impossible to derive any meaningful long-term growth rate.

And we can do no better when focusing on the history of Europe's gothic cathedrals, whose overall appearance, innovative design, and appropriate adornments mattered far more than surpassing any specific dimension, be it the total area, the longest nave, or the tallest spire (Erlande-Brandenburg 1994; Gies and Gies 1995; Recht 2008). And even if we were to ignore those unique designs and focus only on maximum spire height we would see no obvious growth trend. Malmesbury Abbey had a spire of 131.3 m already in 1180, London's Old Saint Paul's reached 150 m in 1240, and in 1311 Lincoln cathedral got the 159.7 m spire that was the world's tallest structure until its collapse in 1549. Ulm Minster's spire, at 161.5 m the world's highest, was completed only in 1890—but it was just 1.1% taller than the medieval Lincoln spire.

Castles

Similarly, there can be no meaningful comparison of the growth of medieval and early modern castles, whose siting, size, and fortifications were determined by their unique locations, the availability of nearby materials, wealth of the builders, and the degree of strategic importance that would justify their continued maintenance and even enlargement. And the largest castle complexes that are still inhabited, house various institutions, or are open to the public as tourist attractions (some combine all of these functions) are almost invariably amalgams of buildings, towers, chapels, churches, fortifications, moats, and walls whose construction has spanned centuries. The world's largest castle, Hradčany in Prague occupying nearly 7 ha, is a perfect example of such an architectural amalgam, containing structures built between 920 and 1929 (Pokorný 2014). Windsor and Salzburg castles (each occupying about 5.5 ha) and Buda (4.5 ha) and Edinburgh (about 3.5 ha) are other notable examples of the same centuries-long agglomeration process.

Skyscrapers

As far as buildings are concerned, we get to designs explicitly seeking to break new records only with modern skyscrapers (high-rise buildings). Their construction was made possible by a combination of late 19th-century innovations: by inexpensive structural steel—first produced during the 1860s by the Bessemer process, soon afterward in open hearth furnaces (Smil 2016b)—and by elevators (initially steam-powered, with the first electric elevator in 1887, the first Otis design in 1889), central heating, electric plumbing pumps, telephones, and the use of reinforced concrete (Smil 2005). Chicago's Home Insurance Building, ten stories and 42 m tall, which was designed by William Le Baron Jenney, completed in 1885 and replaced in 1931 by a taller Field Building, was the world's first high-rise structure whose weight-bearing steel columns resulted in larger floor space and allowed the installation of large windows.

Subsequent record heights remained in the US, and after 1890 in New York, until 1998. The first skyscraper to reach 100 m was the Manhattan Life Insurance Building in 1894 (106 m, 18 stories), and the first one above 200 m was Metropolitan Life Insurance in 1909 (213 m, 50 stories). The introduction of long rolled H-beams eliminated on-site riveting and the structures with their higher tensile strength could make buildings rise even higher (Hogan 1971). The Woolworth Building, finished in 1913, remained the world's tallest skyscraper (241 m, 57 stories; figure 4.5) until April 1930, when the Manhattan Company Building took the record with 283 m, only to be surpassed in May 1930 by the Chrysler Building, whose roof was at 282 m but the addition of antenna spire brought it to 318.9 m (Stravitz 2002). In turn, this record was surpassed by the Empire State Building with 381 m and 102 stories (Landau and Condit 1996; figure 4.5).

The Empire State's height was surpassed only in 1972 by the World Trade Center's prismatic twin towers (417 m, 110 stories) and two years later by Chicago's Sears Building (now Willis Tower, 443 m, 108 floors). The US lost its skyscraper primacy only in 1998 with the completion of the Petronas

Figure 4.5
Four record-holding skyscrapers: Woolworth Building (1913–1930); Empire State Building (1930–1972); Petronas Towers (1998–2004); and Burj Khalifa (2010–2020). All photos available at wikimedia.

twin towers in Kuala Lumpur (452 m, 88 stories; figure 4.5). In 2004 came Taiwan's Taipei 101 (508 m, 101 floors), and in 2017 the world's tallest building was Burj Khalifa (828 m, 163 floors) in Dubai that was completed in 2010 (CTBUH 2018; figure 4.5). This growth in height corresponds to the following annual exponential rates: from 1972 to 2010 (World Trade Center to Burj) 1.8%, from 1998 to 2010 (Petronas to Burj) 5%.

The Council on Tall Buildings and Urban Habitat used to label all buildings over 300 m "supertall" but in 2011 it created a new category of megatall for structures over 600 m. Such buildings did not exist before the completion of Burj Khalifa in 2010 (CTBUH 2011a). As a result, the average height of the 20 tallest buildings increased from 375 m in 2000 to 439 m in 2010 and it will be 598 m in 2020, almost reaching the threshold for the megatall category. After decades of slow growth there has been an exponential increase of the number of supertall buildings since the mid-1990s, from 15 in 1995 to 51 in 2010 and in 2020 there will be 185 of them and 13 megatall structures. This corresponds to an exponential gain of 10.3%/year. At the same time, the number of such buildings completed annually shows clear signs of saturation.

Long periods between successive record heights (17 years from Woolworth to Manhattan Company building, 41 years from Empire State to World Trade Center, and 24 years from Sears to Petronas) followed by a quick succession of new record heights mean that a four-parameter logistic curve does not provide a very good fit. Polynomial regression provides a much closer fit but it cannot be used for any plausible long-range forecasting of coming elevations (figure 4.6). A new record will be reached when Kingdom Tower in Jeddah is finished in 2020: its 167 floors should reach 1 km (Skyscraper Center 2017), and the annual growth rates will then be 1.8% (World Trade Center to Kingdom Tower) and 3.6% (Petronas to Kingdom Tower).

As of 2017, none among the scores of other skyscrapers under construction or proposed to be built during the early 2020s was higher than 739 m (H700 Shenzhen Tower) which means that once it is completed the Kingdom Tower may remain the world's tallest building for some time to come. Structural engineers are confident that buildings taller than 1 km are possible, and that even a mile-high (1,609 m) structure could be built with the existing know-how and available materials (CTBUH 2011b). A building of that size would use the buttressed core principle that made Burj Khalifa possible, and an even taller structure could rest on hollow bases (resembling giant Eiffel towers). But buildings of extraordinary height face challenges beyond structural design: transporting people by elevators, ensuring the

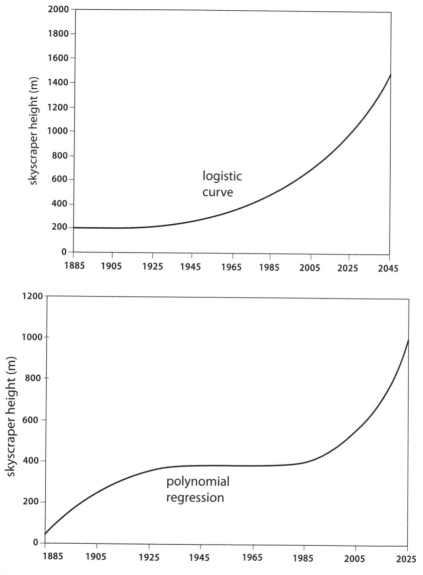

Figure 4.6

Logistic curve and polynomial regression of the growth of maximum skyscraper height. Data from Landau and Condit (1996) and Skyscraper Center (2017).

building's safety (making such buildings earthquake- and cyclone-proof), providing good indoor air quality, and keeping up with the requisite maintenance would become a vastly more complex task with a structure rising 1,600 m from the ground.

In the final analysis, the extraordinary cost of megatall buildings may be the most important consideration limiting their height. For those who might see skyscraper numbers as a proxy of economic power, the latest distribution offers convincing proof of Asia's rise, American decline, and Europe's near-total absence in the rankings. Since the end of the 20th century, skyscrapers have become disproportionately concentrated in a small number of countries and cities. Since 2008 China has led the count with the largest number of skyscrapers 200 m or taller and in 2016 70% of all such high-rises under construction were in the Chinese cities.

New York, with 722 skyscrapers in 2017, now ranks a distant second behind Hong Kong (which had 1,302 such structures in 2017), with Tokyo in third place with 484 structures (Emporis 2017). Chicago is still number four (311 skyscrapers) but the next US city, Houston, ranked 39th. Sixteen of the top 20 cities with most skyscrapers are now in Asia, with nine in China, and Moscow (17th) the only European city in the group. The total number of buildings exceeding 200 m rose from six in 1930 to 1,175 in 2016 and the exponential fit (an early stage of an inevitable logistic trajectory) implies a continuing strong rate of future additions and no inflection point appears to be imminent in the near future (figure 4.7).

To end this section on tall structures I must note an even less explicable quest for height that has led to new records set in building the world's tallest statues. In 1843 London's Nelson's Column in the middle of the Trafalgar Square reached 52 m, New York's Statue of Liberty (a French gift to the US dedicated in 1886) rises to 93 m—but the massive Spring Temple Buddha built between 1997 and 2008 in the Zhaocun township in China's Henan province is 208 m tall. India's Chhatrapati Shivaji Maharaj Memorial (under construction in 2018) honoring the 17th-century founder of the Maratha Empire, plans to top the Buddha by two meters, reaching 210 m to the top of the horse rider's upright spear.

Housing

Finally, a brief look at family houses, structures in which most people spend most of their lives. The current range of their sizes is greater than for any common structural artifacts, from flimsy corrugated metal, plywood, and plastic sheet shacks of the poorest slums in the megacities of Africa and Asia to obscenely sized mansions (many in excess of 1,000 m^2) built in assorted

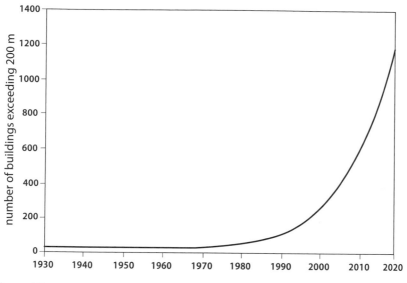

Figure 4.7
Growth of the total number of buildings taller than 200 m. Logistic curve in its early stage of ascent. Data from Emporis (2017).

pseudo-styles, particularly in California and Texas. Once again, long historical perspectives show that even in relatively well-off places ordinary houses remained small, primitively built, and sparsely furnished well into the early modern era. For example, even in 17th-century France many rural houses were simple mud huts covered with straw or rushes, a shared bed was often the only substantial piece of furniture, and small rooms also stored farming tools (Roche 2000).

Within many European urban houses, stores or workshops were adjacent to (or often below) the living areas, all cramped and uncomfortable. To give an example from another continent, in the imperial capital of Tokugawa Japan, Kyoto's elongated *machiya* houses (with stores facing the street and living quarters in the back) had footprints as small as 50 m^2 (5×10 m rectangles, with a smaller second floor) and side-by-side crowding made them very dark inside (Kyoto-machisen 2017). And small preindustrial houses had no, or inadequate, heating in many places where winter temperatures come close to, or below, freezing: most notably, no houses in Jiangnan (China south of the Yangzi) had any heating.

Better quality urban housing (albeit still limited to higher-income families) arrived in Europe during the Dutch Golden Age (1581–1701) and the famous painters of that period (Jan Molenaer, Pieter de Hooch, Jan Vermeer) left behind pictorial testimonials of relatively spacious houses in Amsterdam, Delft, and Haarlem (NGA 2007). These houses also included such quality finishes as large windows, tiled floors, well-built furniture, and wall decorations (paintings, maps), a combination deserving the label of bourgeois dwellings. But these were exceptions, not the norm, for a long time to come. During the 18th and 19th centuries, better-off European urbanites came to enjoy sturdier, more spacious, and more comfortable housing, but, concurrently, growing migration to industrializing cities resulted in dismal housing conditions for millions of new arrivals from the countryside.

Parisian contrasts provide an excellent illustration of this dichotomy. The city saw its first wave of new and better construction between 1715 and 1752 with the addition of some 22,000 sturdily built houses using the lightly colored limestone from Saint-Maximin quarries about 40 km north of the city's center. A century later, George-Eugène Haussmann's bold renovation of the city added 40,000 new houses between 1853 and 1870, with well-built multistory structures replacing old, even medieval, small decrepit buildings (Brice 1752; des Cars 1988). This initial rebuilding wave was followed by decades of urban transformation that put in place a large stock of spacious, and often elegant, apartment buildings. At the same time, rapid immigration increased the crowding in the poorest quarters, yet the annual rents per m^2 of small (habitable area of less than 50 m^2) and unhygienic apartments were often higher than for spacious modern housing (Faure 1998), and the city's periphery became surrounded by extensive areas of irregular substandard (slum-like) housing built on the open land (Bertillon 1894; Shapiro 1985).

Overcrowding (defined as more than two people per room) was common. In 1906 26% of all French people in cities with populations of more than 50,000 lived in such conditions, with the shares of families living in just one room between 15–20% (Prost 1991). This combination of overcrowding, lack of basic hygienic amenities, and frequency of infectious diseases initiated attempts to formulate minimum acceptable housing standards. Once in place, the norms that applied to French dwellings for low rent (*habitations à loyer modique*) changed very slowly during the 20th century: the minimum area specified for a two-room apartment was 35 m^2 in 1922, 34–45 m^2 during the 1950s, and 46 m^2 in 1972 (Croizé 2009). Nationwide statistics for the average size of French housing became available only after WWII and they show the mean rising from 64 m^2 in 1948 (equivalent to a three-room apartment for low-rent lodging) to 68 m^2 in 1970, 84 m^2 in 1984, and 91 m^2 in 2013 (INSEE 1990; FNAIM 2015).

The latter mean was composed of 112 m^2 for detached houses (this area, slightly higher than in 2003, is similar to the average US houses of the early 1950s) and 65 m^2 for apartments, whose area was marginally down since the year 2001. These changes imply a slow linear gain of about 2 m^2/decade for the minimum size of low-rent housing during the 50 years between 1922 and 1972, and a linear gain of about 4 m^2/decade for the size of all post-WWII dwellings. Qualitative changes were even slower in coming: the 1954 census found only 26% of French homes with an indoor toilet and only 10% with a bathtub, shower, or central heating, while 42% still did not have even running water (Prost 1991).

American statistics for the average size of newly built houses are available for the entire 20th century (USBC 1975; USCB 2013). They show a typical size of 90 m^2 in 1900, with only 8% of all households connected to electricity or telephone and only one in seven having a bathtub and indoor toilet. Average housing size began to grow only after WWII. The first mass-built postwar housing developments were still quite modest: the standard house in what was perhaps the most famous planned development of that time, Levittown in Nassau County, New York, built between 1947 and 1951 by Abraham Levitt and his two sons, was just short of 70 m^2 (Ferrer and Navarra 1997; Kushner 2009).

The nationwide mean of newly built houses reached 100 m^2 in 1950, and the 1950s also saw substantial growth in housing quality. In 1950 45% of all dwellings lacked complete plumbing (84% in Arkansas), but in 1960 that share was reduced to less than 17% (USCB 2013). The post-1950 combination of larger baby-boom families and rising incomes brought steady increases of living space, and this trend survived even the decline of average household size after the baby-boom, from 3.7 in 1950 to 2.54 by 2015. Crowded housing (defined in the US as more than 1.5 people/room) declined from 9% of all units in 1940 to 3.6% in 1960 and to the low of 1.4% in 1980 (USCB 2013).

The average floor area of a new single-family American house surpassed 150 m^2 in 1970, 200 m^2 in 1998, and it reached 234 m^2 in 2008; for comparison, the average floor space area of single-family houses in Japan was just above 120 m^2 in 2015 (SB 2017a). The Great Recession of 2008–2009 brought a slight temporary reduction but by 2012 the mean surpassed the 2008 record, and by 2015 the average size of a new American house set a new record at 254.6 m^2, followed by a slight decline by 2017 (NAHB 2017). Post-1950 linear growth thus added nearly 2.4 m^2 of additional living space per year, a pace six times higher than in France. This is a stunning reminder

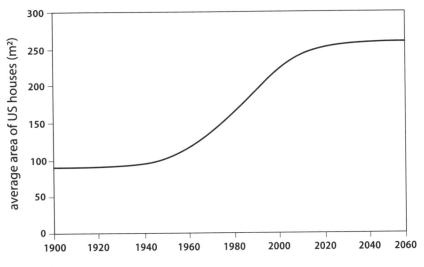

Figure 4.8
Growth of the average area of American houses since 1900. Logistic curve had the inflection year in 1979 and its asymptote is about 260 m². Data from Wilson and Boehland (2005) and USCB (2016a).

of the housing differential between the EU and the US, where the average area of a newly built house increased 2.5 times in 65 years. And when put in per capita terms, habitable area had nearly quadrupled from 27 m²/capita in 1950 to almost exactly 100 m²/capita in 2015 (Wilson and Boehland 2005; USCB 2016a). The growth trajectory of the average area of American houses between 1900 and 2015 has an almost perfect logistic fit that indicates only a marginal size gain to about 260 m² by 2050 (figure 4.8).

The average increase in the total mass of a family house during the 20th century was even higher because almost all new American houses have air conditioning (92.5% in 2015), better windows and doors, and more bathrooms (nearly 40% had three or more in 2015). New houses contain more furniture and appliances, use heavier finishing materials (ranging from granite and composite stone kitchen countertops to marble bathrooms), have larger garages and driveways and more extensive outdoor additions (patios, decks, porches, storages). Two extremes illustrate the difference. A typical Japanese *minka* (people's house), characteristic of the late Tokugawa, Meiji, and Taisho eras (1800–1926), measuring 100 m² and using traditional post and beam construction, clay walls, earthen floors, sliding doors, and paper partitions, required no more than 5 t of pine wood—while a new North American house of 200 m² (smaller than the average) requires about 28 t of structural lumber and other wood products, mostly plywood (Kawashima 1986; Smil 2014b).

And there has been important additional growth beyond the standard, mass-scale housing developments as an increasing share of American houses has been custom-built, and the average size of those structures has surpassed 450 m^2 (nearly double the size of mass-built housing) and almost five times the size of a typical Japanese house. Moreover, since the 1980s there has been a discernible trend toward even larger, ostentatious so-called McMansions, with living area in excess of 500 or even 600 m^2. Although expensive, they are often poorly built, odd looking, and esthetically offensive. In contrast to this American excess, the recent growth of average living space has remained subdued in both Europe and Japan, but no other country has seen such a rapid growth of living space (albeit from a very low base) as China (including some imitations of American styles).

China's pent-up demand for better housing (indeed better everything, as all forms of private consumption were depressed by decades of Maoist economic mismanagement) resulted in the greatest construction boom in history. The best estimates for 1900 indicate average per capita living space of 4 m^2 in rural areas and 3 m^2 in cities and little changed during the first half of the 20th century. The urban mean of living space was 4.5 m^2 during the 1950s and by 1978 it had actually fallen to 3.6 m^2; moreover, the new housing was of exceedingly poor quality and all housing was poorly maintained (Hu et al. 2010). Publication of Chinese statistics resumed in 1978 and in that year the country constructed 38 Mm^2 of urban and 100 Mm^2 of rural residential space; a decade later the two totals had, respectively, increased 5.3- and 8.4-fold, and while the rate of rural construction leveled off, urban building had more than doubled by the century's end (NBS 2000).

Rapid growth of urban housing continued during the first decade of the 21st century, when China's cities added twice the total of houses in the UK and Spain and roughly the equivalent of Japan's total housing stock (EIU 2011). As a result, by the century's end average per capita provision of living space reached 20 m^2 in urban and 25 m^2 in rural areas, and by 2015 the two rates rose, respectively, to about 35 m^2 and 40 m^2, that is roughly tenfold compared to the late 1970s before the economic reforms took off (Mao died in 1976). This means that China's average urban living space is now roughly the same as in the UK and marginally above the Japanese mean. And it also means that the post-1978 growth of Chinese housing provides a rare example of a temporary exponential increase in housing construction, sustaining roughly 3% annual growth for 35 years.

Even so, given the mass immigration to China's rapidly expanding cities, urban overcrowding continues, and the new rules for rental apartments (where many temporary workers often share a single room) now specify a minimum of 5 m²/capita. Despite China's rapidly aging population, a combination of this urban overcrowding and continued migration from the countryside is expected to keep up significant growth of residential stock at least until 2020. During the second decade of the 21st century, many large Chinese municipalities are expected to add as much new residential building area as the total stock in many smaller-sized European countries, with Beijing adding more than Switzerland and Chengdu more than Sweden (EIU 2011).

Infrastructures

Societies have usually had much better success in building the essential infrastructures than maintaining them, and regular American assessments clearly demonstrate that chronic shortcoming. In 2017 the biennial Infrastructure Report Card published by the American Society of Civil Engineers awarded D+ as the overall grade, with individual categories ranging from B for railroads to D for drinking water, inland waterways, levees, and roads, and D– for public transit (ASCE 2017). This deficit is, of course, partly a function of the enormous cumulative extent of modern infrastructures and I will indicate some of their growth trajectories in societies with the requisite statistics. The ASCE report has 16 categories, including two items that usually do not come first to mind, namely the disposal of hazardous waste and public parks. I will focus first on the three groups of artifacts with very long histories, aqueducts (both ancient and modern), tunnels, and bridges. Then I will follow growth trajectories of indispensable transportation infrastructures, roads, railroads, and long-distance pipelines and also high-voltage transmission lines.

Aqueducts

Aqueducts were perhaps the most admirable ancient engineering structures as they combined many structural elements into remarkable systems of reliable water delivery to towns and cities. They appeared first in Mesopotamian societies, and the Romans became eventually their most accomplished builders. Maintaining suitable gradients in stone water channels (at least 1:200, that is 1 meter drop for every 200 m of horizontal distance) may have necessitated cuts in mountain sides. Once that became impossible, the builders had to resort to tunnels and bridges, including some consisting of multilevel arches. In valleys that were too deep to be spanned by stone bridges (taller than 50–60 m) they built heavy-duty inverted siphons with lead pipes connecting a header tank on one side of the valley with a receiving tank built a bit lower on the opposite side (Hodge 2001; Schram 2017). Not surprisingly, in his *Historia naturalis* Pliny (Gaius Plinius Secundus) called the Roman aqueducts "the most remarkable achievement anywhere in the world."

But information on scores of ancient aqueducts, mainly in Mediterranean societies, does not indicate any growth trajectory: length, capacity, and obstacles that had to be overcome during aqueduct construction were the results of specific natural conditions and the water demand of cities financing their construction. Rome's aqueducts do not indicate any growth (either in maximum length or annual throughput) during the more than half a millennium that elapsed between the first and the last line water conduit built to supply the growing, and then stagnating, city. The first link, Aqua Appia, in service by 312 BCE, was 16 km long with 11 km underground.

The second-oldest aqueduct (completed in 269 BCE) was a 64 km channel cut underground; Aqua Marcia (finished in 140 BCE) was 90 km long (80 km underground), while the last ancient Roman supply link, Aqua Alexandrina completed in 266 CE, was just 23 km long with less than 7 km underground, very much in the same category as the pioneering Appia (Ashby 1935; Hodge 2001). Although we have no accurate account of the total volume delivered reliably by ancient Rome's aqueducts, it was most likely at least 1 million cubic meters (a billion liters) a day during the second century, when it supplied the needs of 1 million people. Daily per capita flow of at least 1 cubic meter of water was twice as high as the city's supply at the end of the 20th century (Bono and Boni 1996).

Tokyo provides another example of a traditional water supply system that delivered impressively large volumes of water for nearly three centuries. In July 1590, even before he arrived in Edo, his new capital (today's Tokyo), the first shōgun, Tokugawa Ieyasu, sent one of his retainers to assess the city's water needs and to design a replacement for the supply of drawing water from local springs and deep wells. First, a relatively short aqueduct from Koishikawa was replaced by 1629 by the nearly 66 km long Kanda canal that fed more than 3,600 subsidiary ducts distributing water around the city (Hanley 1987). As the population increased, construction of a new system was completed in 1653.

Water from the Tama River was diverted by a dam and a 43 km canal brought it to Yotsuya at the city's northwestern edge, from where it was distributed (gravity-fed) by underground stone and bamboo pipes, and during the 18th century it supplied the world's largest city with about 1.1 million people (Hanley 1997). The new supply also fed the city's numerous samurai and temple gardens and it was in use until 1965, when it was replaced by the Tonegawa system. Modern megacities (with more than 10 million inhabitants) have the most elaborate water supply systems and New York's Delaware aqueduct, completed in 1945, is not only the longest, 137 km, but it also has a large, 4.1 m, diameter and extensive repairs are needed to reduce substantial water losses from some of its sections (Frillmann 2015).

Tunnels
Tracing the growth of tunneling capabilities is a rather complicated matter because tunnels make up a very heterogeneous category of structures. Among the longest (and oldest) are underground aqueducts of relatively limited diameter, but New York's Delaware aqueduct has a diameter larger than that of the notoriously claustrophobic early lines of London's Underground dating to the latter half of the 19th century. Conduits to remove sewage (again, mostly of limited diameters, with some of them also of antique origin, going back to Rome's remarkable *cloaca maxima*) form extensive urban networks.

The traffic problems of large modern cities would be incomparably worse without subway tunnels (although many underground tubes, both early and modern, were not opened by tunneling but by the cheaper cut-and-cover process), which in some cities (London, New York, Tokyo, and Shanghai being the best examples) form networks of exceptional density and complexity. The other two categories of tunnels built for high throughputs are those for road and rail traffic, the latter group ranging from single-track lines to large-diameter parallel twin tunnels able to accommodate modern high-speed electric trains. Moreover, modern tunnels have excellent lighting, ventilation, and safety features that were largely, or entirely, absent generations ago, and are built by using advanced boring machines (with diameter rising from about 6 m in 1975 to 15 m by 2010) and precast concrete segmental linings (Clark 2009).

Consequently, looking at increases of record tunnel diameters or lengths is just the most readily quantifiable way to trace the growth of these structures—but one that ignores specific construction methods and fails to capture concurrent qualitative improvements. And unlike in the case of skyscrapers—where the quest for record height has been a very important, if not decisive, design consideration—the expense of tunneling has traditionally led to minimizing the length of tunnels or avoiding them altogether (Beaver 1972). The transcontinental Canadian Pacific Railway is the best example of such deliberate avoidance (Murray 2011).

As this line proceeded west from Toronto, a series of short tunnels along the northern shore of Lake Superior was unavoidable, but the line (in operation since 1885) crossed the Rocky Mountains and the coastal ranges to reach the Pacific Coast without any mountain tunnels. But ascending steep grades (up to 4%) was both challenging and costly and in 1909 Spiral Tunnels between Hector and Field reduced the maximum grade to 2.3%, and in 1916 Connaught Tunnel under Rogers Pass also eliminated frequent avalanche risks. Similarly, the great pioneering links under the Alps in Switzerland tried to minimize the tunneling distance.

The northern portal of the 15 km long Gotthard tunnel, opened in 1882, was at an altitude of 1.1 km, while the current world record holder for the longest tunnel, Gotthard Base Tunnel, completed in 2016, starts at just 549 m above sea level (SBB 2017). And the Lötschberg tunnel (14.6 km), completed in 1913, started at 1,200 m above sea level, while the Lötschberg Base Tunnel, opened in 2007, begins at 780 m. Record Swiss achievements in tunneling thus show a great discontinuity between early projects (Gotthard 15 km in 1882, Simplon I 19.803 km in 1906, Simplon II 19.824 km in 1922) and the recent base tunnels (Gotthard 57.1 km in 2016, Lötschberg 34.6 km in 2007). Because of the long interval between the Swiss tunneling records (101 years between Simplon and Lötschberg), it does not make any sense to calculate average growth rates.

Similar discontinuities could be seen elsewhere. Some relatively long tunnels were built during the earliest decades of railroad expansion in the UK, most notably the Box Tunnel on the Great Western Main Line (2.88 km, completed in 1841) and the trans-Pennine Woodhead tunnels, 4.8 km, on the line linking Manchester and Sheffield and opened in 1845 (Beaver 1972). Box Tunnel held the record for the longest railroad link until 1871, when the Mont Cenis tunnels between France and Italy spanned 12.234 km, to be surpassed just 11 years later by the St. Gotthard tunnel (Onoda 2015). All of the 10 longest railway tunnels that were in operation in 2017 had been completed since 1988 when Japan opened the 53.85 km long Seikan Tunnel crossing Tsugaru Strait.

Despite the long gap between record tunnel length (82 years between Simplon and Seikan), the growth trajectory for the world's longest railway tunnels fits rather closely a logistic curve with the inflection point already in 1933 but the indicated protraction to the maximum length of 80 km by 2050 rather uncertain (figure 4.9). The longest road tunnels are shorter (they can start at much higher elevations than railroad links (Laerdar in Norway goes for 24.5 km) and, again, most them are of recent construction. Ten of

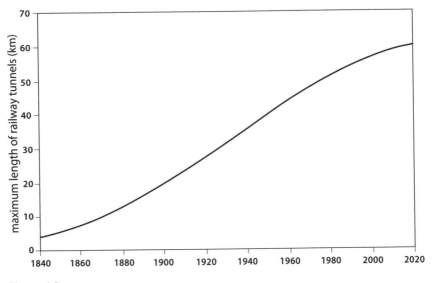

Figure 4.9
Growth of the longest railway tunnels, 1840–2020. Data mostly from Beaver (1972) and Onoda (2015).

the world's longest road tunnels have been completed since 1980, when the two longest Alpine tunnels, St. Gotthard and Fréjus, opened for traffic.

Bridges
Bridges are also a rather heterogeneous category of infrastructural artifacts, especially when any elevated aqueduct, road, or railroad is put into that category. According to this classification, the world's longest bridges are high-speed rail viaducts in China, led by Danyang-Kunshan (164.8 km) on the Beijing-Shanghai route (History of Bridges 2017). Taiwan's Changhua-Kaohsiung, running above farmed and inhabited countryside, is 157.3 km long. Some bridges across shallow water bodies use closely spaced concrete piers: Lake Ponchartrain Causeway runs for 38.4 km. Increasing the length of such structures is not a major engineering challenge, rather a matter of cost or of long term cost-benefit accounting.

Suspension bridges belong to a category of structures that perhaps best exemplifies the gradual growth of a critical dimension due to technical advances and not just due to repetitive emplacement of mass-produced piers. Cable-stayed bridges—the other common solution to cross great spans that relies on supporting cables running directly from tall towers to bridge decks—are similarly dependent on special materials and ingenious designs, but the record length of their main span (distance between the tall suspension towers, maximum of 1,104 m for the Russian Bridge in Vladivostok) is only slightly more than half of the distances spanned by suspension structures.

The origins of suspension bridges go back to the Middle Ages, when short spans were supported by wrought-iron chains (and suspension ropes), including some daring structures across Himalayan river gorges in Tibet and Nepal. Construction of European and American chain cable bridges took off in the early 19th century (Drewry 1832). Thomas Telford's chain-cable bridge across the Menai Strait to Anglesey had the longest span of 176 m in 1826 (Jones 2011), and by 1864 the Clifton Bridge across the Avon gorge, using three separate wrought-iron chains for every side, had a main span of 214 m (Andrews and Pascoe 2008).

The first wire cable supported structure in the US was a narrow footbridge across Schuylkill in Philadelphia in 1816 (main span of 124 m) and the first major suspension bridge, spanning 109 m, crossed the same river in 1842 in Philadelphia (Bridgemeister 2017). Afterward, the US remained the leader until 1981 thanks to a succession of famous structures. The first one was John A. Roebling Bridge (322 m) in Cincinnati in 1866, followed by Brooklyn Bridge (486.3 m) in 1883, Benjamin Franklin Bridge in Philadelphia (533.7 m) in 1926, Ambassador Bridge in Detroit (564 m) in 1929, the double-decked George Washington Bridge in New York (1,067m) in 1931, the Golden Gate Bridge in San Francisco (1,280 m) in 1937, and Verazzano Narrows Bridge in New York (1,298 m) in 1964. The Humber Bridge, connecting Yorkshire and Lincolnshire in the UK, held the record for the longest span (1,410 m) between 1981 and 1998, when Akashi Kaikyo bridge from Kobe to Awaji Island spanned the still unsurpassed distance of 1,991 m (HSBEC 2017).

The longest span of wire suspension bridges grew from 109 m in 1842 to 1,280 m in 1937, nearly a 12-fold gain in 96 years, implying an annual exponential growth rate of about 2.6%. Gains during the next 44 years were marginal (Humber in 1981 was just 10% longer than Golden Gate in 1937) and then Akashi jumped ahead with a 40% longer span. The entire 1842–1998 trajectory conforms to a logistic curve with the inflection point in 1975 and with further growth potential to about 2,500 m by 2050 (figure 4.10). By 2017 no suspension bridge under construction had a longer central span than Akashi Kaikyo, but there have been proposals to bridge the Strait of Messina from Italy to Sicily and the Strait of Sunda from Java to Sumatra with structures having central spans of 3,000 m, and even longer distances (3,700–4,000 m) have been under consideration for

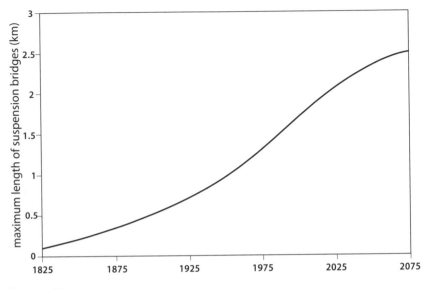

Figure 4.10
Growth of the longest suspension bridges since 1825. Data mostly from History of Bridges (2017).

Norwegian fjord bridges. The limits of the eventual longest span will be dictated not only by the tensile capacity of steel but also by the bridge's aerodynamic (and in earthquake-prone regions also by its seismic) stability.

Modern suspension bridges are designed to withstand environmental onslaughts by using massive anchorage towers, hinged stiffening girder systems (to cope with hurricane-strength winds and earthquakes), and cables of large diameter containing tens of thousands of strands of wire (Akashi has a diameter of 112 cm, 36,830 strands). Structural engineers also must make allowance for repeated thermal expansion and shrinkage (Akashi Kaikyo can lengthen up to 2 m on a hot day), and dehumidification extends the lifespans of bridges by minimizing corrosion in humid environments. This is done by protecting both cable anchorages and main cables as metal-clad enclosures; dehumidification systems are built around anchorages and cables are loosely wrapped with rubber covers and inside these rubber jackets release dry air and maintain relative humidity of 40% (Mahmoud 2013; Kiewit 2017).

Roads
The history of European roads is perhaps the best example of not only prolonged stagnation but actual long-term regression following the early

advances under the Roman Empire. Starting in 312 BCE with the Via Appia between Rome and Capua (a distance of nearly 200 km in a southeastern direction), Romans spent centuries investing considerable amounts of labor and materials in building and maintaining their *cursus publicus*, an extensive system of hard-top roads (Sitwell 1981). Roman *viae* were well founded and drained and they were topped with gravel, large stones set in mortar, or concrete mixed with broken stones or bricks. By the beginning of the 4th century CE, their total length reached about 85,000 km and I have calculated that the task required as much as 1.2 billion labor days, or an annual equivalent of some 20,000 full-time workers during more than 600 years of expansion and maintenance (Smil 2017a).

But beyond the *cursus publicus*, Roman road transport remained primitive. The existing paved network helped to speed up the movements of armies but provisioning of inland cities not situated on a navigable river remained challenging as poor roads, limited draft power, inefficient harnessing, and heavy wagons made cheap land transport impossible. The difficulties of road transport in antiquity are best illustrated by a price comparison in Diocletian's *edictum de pretiis*. In the early 4th century CE, the cost of moving Italian grain 120 km by road was higher than bringing it from Egypt to Ostia, Rome's harbor, reloading it onto barges, and hauling it by ox-draft to Rome. In one of greatest technical stagnations of history, these realities remained unchanged for more than a millennium.

Even during the first half of the 18th century, it was cheaper to ship goods from overseas than to transport domestic inland products to ports, and in such a rainy country as England roads were often impassable and justly described as barbarous, execrable, abominable, and infernal (Savage 1959). Improvements during the century's second half brought wider lanes, better drainage, and more common surfacing with gravel (Ville 1990). Further improvements came in the early 19th century with roads first built in Scotland according to designs by Thomas Telford and John McAdam (McAdam 1824). Telford used paving stones covered with gravel, McAdam had a cheaper solution with a foundation layer (20 cm deep) of coarser gravel (up to 7.5 cm) and top layer (5 cm deep) of smaller (2.5 cm) stones.

But after 1830 most of the construction effort in all industrializing countries went into the rapid expansion of railroads. The first modern pavements did not appear until the 1870s, when asphalt-covered roads were constructed with material extracted from the tar lakes of Trinidad. The concurrent rise of the new oil industry and the expansion of crude oil refining began to produce enough asphalt (amounting typically to 1.5–2% of total crude input) to make it a common urban paving material by the beginning of the 20th century. But intercity roads remained mostly unpaved: even the famous Route 66 connecting Chicago and Santa Monica since 1921 was mostly gravel, with stretches including bricks and wooden planks, and asphalted stretches as narrow as 3 m (Wallis 2001).

The first concrete highway in the US was built in 1913 (in Arkansas) and the practice became more common after 1919 as the federal government began to help the states with road financing (PCA 2017). Pennsylvania Turnpike, opened in 1940, was the first major all-concrete highway in the US, but Germany was the first country to build a network of concrete-surfaced, limited-access, multilane, high-speed roads (Zeller 2007). Construction of *Autobahnen*, begun during the Weimar republic and accelerated under Hitler, was interrupted by the war and the post-WWII expansion (following a logistic course) brought the total to nearly 13,000 km by 2015 (figure 4.11). Post-WWII technical advances in roadbuilding included air-entrained concrete (to reduce scaling damage) and slip-form pavers. Construction of America's largest road-building program (now officially known as the Dwight D. Eisenhower System of Interstate and Defense Highways) was authorized in 1956, the originally planned routes were completed by 1991, and by 2017 the entire system surpassed 77,000 km (USDOT 2017a).

Given the enormous range of road qualities (numbers of lanes, their width, adjacent shoulders, and year-round access are other qualitative

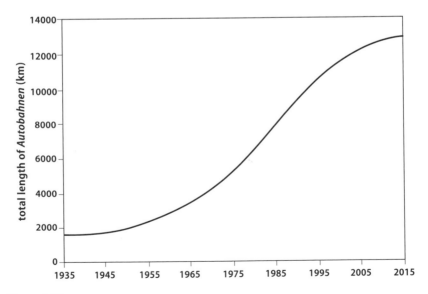

Figure 4.11
Growth curve of German *Autobahnen*, 1935–2015. Data from Zeller (2007) and Bundesamt für Statistik.

variables to consider in addition to the kind of road surfacing), tracing the growth of total road length in a country is the most obvious, most readily available but not the most revealing measure to follow. Data are available for this all-inclusive category for many Western countries during the entire 20th century and, as expected, they follow sigmoid courses. For example, the total length of American roads grew from about 3.7 to 6.5 million km and the trajectory fits well a logistic curve with very limited prospect for further extension.

US data on paved roads include an irreconcilable difference between the historical series by the US Bureau of the Census and the modern series (beginning in 1960) by the US Department of Transport. Even this category is still quite heterogeneous, ranging from low-quality surfaces (an earth, gravel, or stone roadway with less than 2.5 cm of bituminous cover) to well-founded concrete multilane highways with shoulders. The best merging of the two series indicates roughly a 16-fold expansion of paved road length during the 20th century, and the complete trajectory fits closely a logistic curve that indicates an additional 10% extension by the middle of this century (figure 4.12).

Similar patterns prevail in most high-income countries that already have dense road networks, while China is the best example of recent (post-1980) rapid expansion. The total length of its highways (Chinese statistics do not

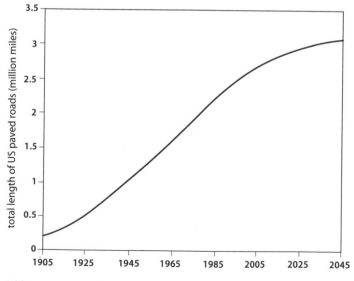

Figure 4.12
Growth of the total length of paved US roads since 1905. Plotted from data in USBC (1975) and subsequent volumes of US *Statistical Abstract*.

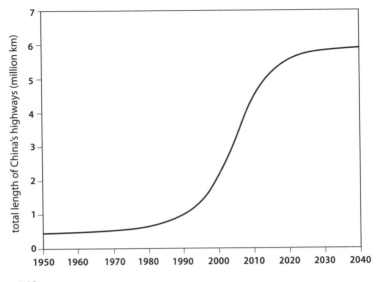

Figure 4.13
Growth of the total length of highways in China. Logistic curve with the inflection point in 2007 and asymptote about 30% above the 2015 total. Data from NBS (2000, 2016).

offer any quality-related definitions) increased from just 127,000 km in 1952 (the first year of available data) to nearly 900,000 km by 1980. Then China began to build an interprovincial multilane network, the National Trunk Highway System, whose length surpassed the total length of US interstate highways (77,000 km) in 2011 and reached 123,000 km in 2015 (NBS 2016). China has also vastly expanded its secondary and tertiary roads in cities and in rural areas. As a result, total highway length grew to nearly 1.7 million km by the year 2000 and then, in an unprecedented leap, to almost 4.6 million km by 2015. The growth trajectory fits well a logistic curve that indicates a further 30% expansion by 2050 (figure 4.13).

Railroads
As with the roads, the most obvious variable used to trace the growth of railroads is the total length of tracks in operation. But unlike the overall road length, which still continues to grow or has reached peak plateaus in most countries, the aggregate length of railway tracks has receded from its peak in all European countries as well as in North America as competing modes of transportation (cars, buses, airplanes) have taken over major shares of passenger travel previously dominated by railroads. Railroads in today's

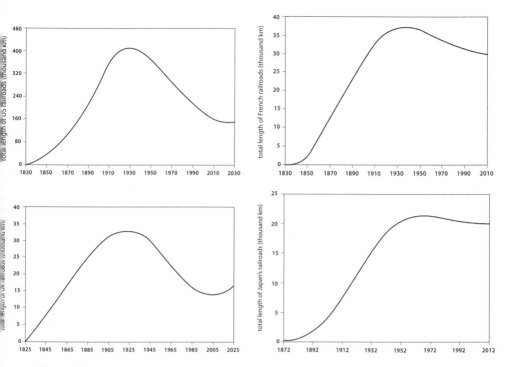

Figure 4.14
Growth curves of the total length of railroads in the US, UK, France, and Japan with some short-term extensions. Plotted from data in Mitchell (1998).

high-income countries reached their national maxima at different times during the 20th century (figure 4.14). The total length of British railroads grew exponentially from 43 km in 1825 (Stockton & Darlington Railway connecting coal mines near Shildon with Stockton-on-Tees and Darlington) to nearly 10,000 km by 1850 and 30,000 km in 1900 (Mitchell 1998).

The British railway peak was followed first by a decline that nearly mirrored the ascent but in 1963 the report on *The Reshaping of British Railways* outlined a cut of nearly 10,000 km (British Railways Board 1963) and by 1970 the total length had been reduced by almost 40%. The French trajectory has been different, with rapid growth after 1850 and with the record length reached in 1930. In the US, exponential growth (annual average rate of 7.5% between 1830 and 1916) was followed by decades of decline with a new, low plateau beginning to form after the year 2000 when the total extent was a bit less than 40% of the peak length. The growth trajectory of Japan's railroads has followed fairly closely a sigmoid course, with a new plateau only less than 15% below the peak (figure 4.14). China, thanks to its rapid post-2000 expansion of high-speed rail lines, is still in the ascending part of its railroad length growth curve, with considerable potential for further extensions (NBS 2016).

Long-Distance Pipelines and High-Voltage Transmission Lines

Without pipelines, consumption of liquid and gaseous fuels would have to be either restricted to the immediate vicinity of hydrocarbon fields or their shipments would have to rely on much more expensive, and much more risky, rail and road transport. Without high-voltage transmission lines, electricity supply would require a multitude of smaller stations serving limited areas. That was, indeed, the case during the 1880s when commercial electricity generation began with small plants using direct current transmission. The long-term growth of both of these infrastructures is marked by increased distances spanned by new projects as well as higher capacities (mass throughput for pipelines, rising voltage for transmission lines).

Pipelines are compact (a 1 m diameter line can transport annually 50 Mt of crude oil) and relatively inexpensive to build and to operate (using centrifugal compressors powered by electricity or gas turbines), and no other form of mass transportation is as environmentally safe as large trunk lines (Smil 2017c). The pace of their construction was dictated by the progress of new oil and gas discoveries and by the development of suitable markets. The US pioneered both oil and gas links. The first short American pipelines during the 1860s and early 1870s were wooden (hollowed-out white pine logs), and then came wrought-iron pipes: in 1878 a 152.4 mm (6 inch) diameter line was laid on the ground (later buried) between Coryville and Williamsport in Pennsylvania and later extended to New Jersey (hence its Tidewater name).

Large-scale construction was made possible thanks to the new way of producing inexpensive steel (the Bessemer process, followed by open-hearth furnaces) and by the invention of the pierce-rolling process to make seamless steel pipes by Reinhard and Max Mannesmann in 1885. But no less important was the Hepburn Act of 1906, which made all US interstate pipelines common carriers with guaranteed service to all customers at equal cost. Growth of diameters and distances followed to meet the rising output and demand. In 1897 came the first 762 mm (30 inch) diameter lap-welded oil pipe, two years later a 50.8 cm (20 inch) seamless oil pipe, and in 1904 a 40.6 cm (16 inch) diameter natural gas pipe (Johnson 1956). Large-diameter (61 cm) seamless pipes became available in 1925, and the Big Inch and Little Inch, the two longest lines built between 1942 and 1944 from Texas to New Jersey (to avoid German submarine attacks on coastal tankers), had diameters of 61 and 50.8 cm (Casella and Wuebber 1999). Most crude oil pipelines built in the US after WWII shared those diameters, with the Trans-Alaska Pipeline being one of a few exceptions at 106.68 cm.

Russians built the first short 3 inch line (from the Baku fields to Nobel's refinery) in 1878 and the first long-distance (835 km) product pipeline (for kerosene from Baku to Batumi on the Black Sea) in 1906. By 1950 the Soviet Union had only about 5,400 km of oil pipelines but that changed with the construction of record-breaking projects bringing Siberian oil to Russian and European markets (Transneft' 2017). The Trans-Siberian line (3,662 km) from Tuymazy to Irkutsk was completed in 1964. The Druzhba pipeline from Almetievsk in Tatarstan to Central Europe, built mostly with 102 cm pipes, was eventually extended (with spurs) to about 8,000 km. The Ust'-Balik-Kurgan-Almetievsk line, 2,120 km long and with a diameter of up to 122 cm, was completed in 1973 to carry up to 90 Mt of crude oil annually from the supergiant Western Siberian Samotlor oilfield.

By the time of its demise in 1990, the Soviet Union held the records for both the longest and the largest-diameter crude oil pipelines, while the US still had the world's densest network of crude and refined product lines. The latest wave of pipeline megaprojects is bringing crude oil to China from Kazakhstan and Russia. The Kazakhstan (Atyrau) to China (Xinjiang) line, completed in 2009, spans 2,229 km and brings annually 20 Mt through 81.3 cm pipes. The Eastern Siberia-Pacific Ocean pipeline, built between 2006 and 2012, is a 4,857 km long link from Taishet in Irkutsk region to Kozmino port near Nakhodka on the Pacific coast, and it was built with 122 cm pipes.

Large-scale expansion of natural gas pipelines (compared to oil lines, larger diameters are needed to move the same total of energy per year) began only after 1950 and new record-length projects were completed after the year 2000. The first 30 inch (76.2 cm) gas line was laid in 1951 and long-distance gas trunk lines now have diameters up to 152 cm (60 inches). Rockies Express from Colorado to Ohio (1,147 km) measures 107 cm (Tallgrass Energy 2017), while Russia's massive Yamal-Europe line (4,107 km) has a diameter of 142 cm. By 2014 China had completed three stages of its extensive west-east gas pipeline project (with total lengths of about 4,000, 8,700, and 7,300 km) using pipes of up to 122 cm in diameter (Hydrocarbon Technology 2017). Turkmen gas began to flow to China in 2009 through a 1,833 km 106.7 cm line, and a nearly 3,000 km long 1.42 m diameter line from East Siberia to China should be completed in 2019.

The growth of pipeline specifications has been dictated by many unique national, market, and policy considerations and hence there has been no gradual organic growth of either the largest diameters or the longest distances. Since the mid-1920s, when large-diameter seamless oil pipes became available, the maximum diameter has only doubled. As expected, the longest lines have been laid either in oil-rich nations with large territories (Russia, US) or to bring crude oil to the most important markets that cannot be supplied by cheaper seaborne shipments (China importing from Central Asia and Siberia being the most obvious example). This has increased the maximum distances from 10^1 km during the 1870s to 10^3 km.

The very first electricity transmission links in the early 1880s were short underground lines, but before the end of the 19th century these direct current (DC) links were superseded by high-voltage alternating current (AC) transmission that minimizes losses over long distances before it is reduced by transformers to voltages suitable for industrial, commercial, and household use (Melhem 2013). The well-documented history of transmission in North America began with simple wooden poles and cross arms carrying solid copper wires at 3.3 kV, and it progressed through a series of multiplications to 60 kV by 1900; the highest pre-WWI voltage was 150 kV in 1912. The record had risen to 287 kV by 1936, the first 345 kV line came into operation only in 1953, a 500 kV line in 1964 (all AC), and in 1965 Hydro-Québec installed the world's first 765 kV DC link from large hydro stations in the province's north to Montreal (USEIA 2000; Hydro-Québec 2017).

Limited attempts at higher voltages were made in the Soviet Union during the 1980s and in Japan, but the first long-distance 800 kV lines (both AC and DC) began operating in China in 2009, and in 2016 ABB earned a contract for the world's first 1,100 kV DC line for China (ABB 2016). This line, completed in 2018, runs 3,324 km from Xinjiang to Anhui and has a transmission capacity of 12 GW. The complete historic progress of the highest North American transmission voltages between 1891 and 1965 conforms fairly closely to a logistic curve that is still in its early phase—while in reality the highest voltage has remained unchanged for half a century and while it is most unlikely that we will see even just its doubling in the near future. Similarly, Chinese developments may not go above the maximum voltage (1,100 kV DC) for decades to come.

Transportation

Transportation—defined in the most general way as any activity moving individuals, groups of people, and cargo over any desired distance—has been a notable component of human evolution and premodern technical advances and an even more important factor of modern economic development. This range of activities, energized by a variety of animate and inanimate prime movers, has been always closely linked with food and industrial production, with construction, and more recently also with the leisure industry. The growth trajectories of all key inanimate prime movers that enable transportation of people and goods (engines and turbines) were described in chapter 3, and this section will have a different focus as it traces the growth of the processes rather than the growth of artifacts by focusing on the speed and capacity trajectories of all key modern mass transportation conveyances, that is ships, trains, automobiles, and airplanes. But in order to recount the complete history of transportation advances, I will begin with the records of animate locomotion, with transportation powered by people and animals.

Speeds of walking and running are, of course, fundamentally constrained by the forms of human and animal bodies and by the maximum rate of their metabolism. Speed gains among racing animals (most notably horses) have resulted from their better feeding and selective breeding. Records in human foot races undoubtedly reflect optimized training regimes, nutrition, and mental support. But the search for factors responsible for the dominance of North and East African runners in middle- and long-distance events (and of athletes of West African origin in sprints) has yet to identify an incontrovertible set of physical qualities (Onywera 2009).

Walking and Running

As I showed in chapter 2, there have been some significant long-term changes in human size but higher statures and heavier bodies have not resulted in any appreciable increase in human capacities to transport loads. Moreover, during the most recent three generations, humans have ceased to perform nearly all transport duties in affluent societies and carrying, pushing, and pulling of loads is becoming less common even in low-income countries. But there have been some notable gains in the fastest times for both sprints and long distances, and their progression has been well documented thanks to detailed record-keeping in athletics.

People switch voluntarily from walking to running at speeds of 1.9–2.1 m/s (6.8–7.6 km/h) and healthy but untrained adults run at 3–4 m/s (10.8–14.4 km/h). The latter speed was good enough for the best marathon time (distance of 42,195 m) in 1910, when the record time for the 100 m sprint was 10.6 seconds. The long-term trajectories of the fastest times show steadily improving record speeds for both sprints and long distances during the 20th century. Higher speeds are achieved by applying greater support forces to the ground, not by a more rapid repositioning of legs. Support forces to the ground (which may exceed the body mass fivefold in sprints) increase with speed, while the time taken to swing the leg into position for the next step does not vary (Weyand et al. 2000).

The best indication of long-term speed improvements during the past two centuries comes from analysis of long-distance foot races that were popular in the UK during the 18th and 19th centuries (Radford and Ward-Smith 2003). Times for running 10 and 20 miles were 10% and 15% better during the 20th century than during the 19th century, while the latter performances were only about 2% faster than in the 18th century. Steady post-1900 gains were examined in the mid-1970s by Ryder et al. (1976) and they concluded that the historic rate of improvements of running times could continue for decades to come: this turned out to be correct.

Analyses done by Marc et al. (2014) show that during the 20 years preceding 2011 marathon speeds improved at every level (measured by deciles) of performance. These gains were accompanied by decreases in the stature, body mass, and BMI of record-breaking athletes, with 94% of the 100 best male runners and 52% of the best female runners being African. Hamilton (2000) reviewed the possible reasons for this dominance. Top speeds for men increased from 5.45 m/s in 1990 to 5.67 m/s in 2011, and with expected improvements of 10 s/year the marathon could be run in less than two hours by about 2021 (Joyner et al. 2011). On the other hand, Whipp and Ward (1992) predicted that before the end of the 20th century women might run the marathon as fast as men, but by 2015 the respective record speeds were still about 12% apart. And the marathon is now a modest distance compared to endurance races of more than 100 km, and Rüst et al. (2013) found that between 1998 and 2011 the best time for 100-mile ultramarathon races improved by 14%, a much faster gain than for the marathon, whose record time was reduced by just 2% during the same period.

Historical comparisons of the world's fastest sprints have been affected by the 1975 switch from manual to automatic electronic recording but the overall trends since 1900, as well as the post-1975 records, show almost perfectly linear gains in speed. Some minuscule gains are still possible. Barrow (2012) argued that Usain Bolt could cut his record of 9.58 seconds without any additional effort if he combined realistic improvement in his relatively poor reaction time with running helped by the maximum permissible wind (2 m/s) at the maximum altitude (1,000 m) allowed for setting world records. That combination would reduce the run to 9.45 seconds and to an average speed of 10.58 m/s.

The most comprehensive analyses of running records for the entire 20th century (1900–2007) result in several clear conclusions (Lippi et al. 2008; Denny 2008; Desgorces et al. 2012). First, as expected, improvements in race times were highly correlated with the race distance for both men and women. Women's improvements were significantly higher for shorter distances as well as for the marathon. The gain for a world record 100 m sprint was 8.1% for men and 22.9% for women, with the respective increases of 9.7% and 25.7% for 400 m, 12.4% and 10.3% for 1,500 m, 15.1% and 8.5% for 10 km, and 21.5% and 38.6% for the marathon. Second, there was a consistent linear progression of records with time.

Recalculating the speed gains in average terms yields long-term linear increases of 0.11% a year for the 100 m sprint and 4% a year for the marathon. Times for short events (100–800 m) fit logistic curves for both men and women, but while the fastest speeds for women have reached plateaus after 1980, men's speeds are still increasing but have come very close to the predicted maxima of 10.55 m/s for 100 m, 10.73 m/s for 200 m, and 9.42 m/s for 400 m runs (Denny 2008). And Desgorces et al. (2012), after modeling the best performances in 200, 400, 800, and 1,500 m races between 1891 and 2009 by fitting them to Gompertz curves, concluded that these human running speeds have already reached their asymptotic values.

An analysis of men's record long-distance runs between 1980 and 2013 confirmed continued gains for marathon speed but noted that from the late 1990s there were only limited improvements in the 5 km and 10 km records, with the longest spell of time between new records since the early 1940s (Kruse et al. 2014). The study offers three explanations for this apparent end of growth. First, better antidoping measures have limited the ability to enhance oxygen transport. Second, the performances have reached a physiological limit for 5 and 10 km runs, and continued marathon gains are merely catching up by comparison. Finally, prize money for marathon runs has increased from the maximum of $50,000 in 1980 to 1 million dollars just over two decades later, providing a great incentive for long-distance runners to compete in the longer run.

The most comprehensive long-term analyses of record performances in 800 m races (between 1896 and 2016 for men and 1921 and 2016 for women) show clear plateaus after the mid-1980s that are also present for other athletic endeavors and that "may now indicate the potential upper limits" of our species (Marck et al. 2017, 4; figure 4.15). A combination of the three possibilities adds up to a limited outlook for further gains. Many explanations have been offered to explain the limit of running speeds: body mass, locomotory musculature, the rate of energy supply to legs, the ground force produced by muscles, leg stiffness, bone, ligament and tendon strength, and aerobic capacity—but it is unlikely that the limit could be explained by a single mechanical or metabolic factor. Denny (2008, 3846)

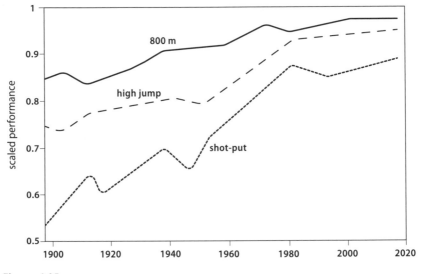

Figure 4.15
Limits of human performance: the world's 10 best performances annually between 1896 and 2016 in men for the 800 m run, high jump, and shot-put show clear plateaus since the early 1980s. Simplified from Marck et al. (2017).

concluded that the "distance-independent scope for increase suggests that some sort of higher order constraint may act" on the suite of these factors to limit running speed.

Animate transportation capacities are also inherently restricted by the structure of human and animal bodies but limited gains can be obtained by deploying mechanical advantage or less taxing ways of carrying loads. Wheelbarrows are perhaps the best example of the first strategy. On better roads they allowed men to push as much as 150 kg with the Chinese barrows (centrally mounted wheel with the load above the axle) and up to 100 kg with European barrows (with wheel at or near the front). Better ways of carrying loads include placing their center of gravity above the carrier's own (but balancing may be difficult) using shoulder- or head-straps or shoulder-borne yokes or poles.

All of these uses have been known since antiquity and documented maxima are 30–35 kg (or roughly half of the adult body mass) carried by individuals and up to 40 kg per man when walking (at speeds of no more than 5 km/h) with litters (sedan chairs) borne by four men. The only (marginal) growth of human carrying performance has been associated with slightly higher average body mass, better nutrition resulting in improved endurance, and better shoes and apparel in extreme terrain, a combination best exemplified by modern Nepali Sherpas carrying heavy loads for the Himalayan mountain expeditions.

Maximal human-powered transportation capabilities have been multiplied by deploying massed labor using ropes, sledges and rollers, also aided by ramps, pulleys and capstans when erecting massive stones. The most massive statues and megalithic structures in Europe, Africa, and Latin America attest to ancient abilities to routinely move loads of 50–100 t. The extant evidence makes it clear that there was only very slow growth in this kind of massed transportation capabilities before the introduction of inanimate prime movers and that Neolithic and preindustrial builders could move stones whose mass was of the same order of magnitude. The Er Grah menhir at Locmariaquer in Brittany (now broken on the ground) weighed 330 t when it was moved and erected (by means that can be only surmised) by a Neolithic society in about 4700 BCE (Niel 1961). In 1832 Alexander's 700 t granite column was transported by ship from Virolahti in Finland to Saint Petersburg, moved to the Palace Square and erected with the help of levers, inclined planes and capstans, the final operation involving 1,700 soldiers (Luknatsskii 1936).

Horses

During the 19th century—before their services were displaced by inanimate prime movers—horses became better performers than they had been in the past. This was true both in terms of average speed (daily distance covered by a single rider with the same animal or changing horses, as well as by horse teams harnessed to coaches) and typical loads (draft horses pulling heavy wagons)—but those gains could be only partially attributed to the larger size of animals: better feeding (with more grains), better harnessing, better wagon and coach designs, and better roads (compacted or paved surfaces) accounted for most of the difference.

A hand, the traditional English unit of horse height, is equal to four inches or 10.16 cm, and it was measured from the ground to the horse's withers, the ridge between the shoulder blades below the animal's neck and head. During antiquity, horses were no higher than 11–13 hands, while the heaviest breeds in late early modern and 19th century Europe—Brabançons in Belgium, Boulonnais and Percherons in France, Clydesdales in Scotland, Suffolks and Shires in England, and Rheinlanders in Germany—reached, or even surpassed 17 hands and weighed up to around 1,000 kg (Silver 1976). A pair of such animals harnessed to a wagon with rubber wheels moving on a macadamized road could pull loads an order of magnitude heavier than a typical medieval horse pair harnessed to a heavy wooden wagon on a soft-surface road, and do so at speeds twice as high.

But there were only marginal long-term gains in the speed of fast horse riding. Unlike sheep and cattle that were among the earliest domesticated species (together with wheat, rice and beans) some 8,000 years ago, the domestication of horses for riding took place no sooner than around 4,000 BCE on the steppes of today's Ukraine, and perhaps only around the middle of the second millennium BCE (Anthony 2007). Horse gaits beyond four-beat walking (comparable to human walking and averaging about 6.5 km/h) are trotting (at 13–19 km/h), cantering (up to 24–25 km/h) and galloping, which ranges typically between 40 and 48 km/h (that is up to about 13.3 m/s) but can reach brief maxima of more than 80 km/h (Reisner 2017). Naturally, a gallop cannot be sustained for many hours but strong animals and experienced riders could cover 50–60 km in a day and significantly more (in excess of 100 km/h) when changing horses.

William F. Cody (1846–1917) claimed that when he rode for the Pony Express (mail service) as a young man he set the record of 515 km in 21 hours and 40 minutes by using 21 fresh horses and averaging nearly 24 km/h (Carter 2000). But such feats and speeds would not be compatible with everyday usage of the animals for a regular messenger or postal service. Minetti (2003) concluded that the performance of long-distance riding was carefully optimized at relatively modest speeds of 13–16 km/h in order to reduce the risk of injury and exhaustion. This optimum performance was adhered to by the famous Persian courier service set up by Cyrus between Susa and Sardis after 550 BCE, by Genghis Khan's Mongolian *yam* (messenger system) riders of the 13th century, as well as by the Overland Pony Express that served California before the telegraphs and railways.

Long-term improvements in horse racing speeds are closely modeled by a logistic equation (Denny 2008). Winning speeds for the American Triple Crown races (Kentucky Derby, Preakness Stakes, and Belmont Stakes) show slow, steady gains followed by unmistakable plateaus: there has been no significant correlation between year and top speed in the Kentucky Derby since 1949, and apparent plateaus in the Preakness and Belmont Stakes were reached, respectively, in 1971 and 1973, while predicted maximum speed (almost exactly 17 m/s) is only marginally higher than actual records.

Alternatively, the record trajectories can be seen as linear progressions an order of magnitude lower than those for human foot races with a distinct leveling off after the 1970s. For example, the Belmont Stakes, run annually at Belmont Park in Elmont, New York on a course of 1.5 miles (2,400 m), was won in 1926 (the first year at that distance) with a time of 2:32:20

and the record was set in 1974 by Secretariat at 2:24:00 or 16.66 m/s (Belmont Stakes 2017): that translates to an average gain of 0.2% during those 48 years. Similarly, the Kentucky Derby (1.25 miles, 2,012 m) was won in 1875 with 2:37:75 and Secretariat holds the 1973 record at 1:59:40 with an average speed of 16.82 m/s and average gain of 0.32% in 98 years (Kentucky Derby 2017). Similarly, Desgorces et al. (2012) modeled maximum thoroughbred horse speeds with a Gompertz curve and found they are already at 99% of their asymptotic limit and that the progression of maximal running speed will not continue despite the genetic selection of animals.

In contrast, any speed gains of horse-drawn passenger transport were not only inherently limited by the performance of the horse teams harnessed to carriages and coaches but also by the quality of the roads and by the design and durability of the vehicles. Larger teams of better fed and well-harnessed horses could make only a marginal difference in the absence of well-paved roads and well-designed carriages with light but durable wheels. In antiquity, the daily progress of heavy wagons and carriages (with the earliest designs having massive wooden wheels) on soft, muddy, or sandy roads was limited to just 10–20 km, and even in 18th-century England the best passenger coaches traveling between major cities averaged about 50 km/day in winter and 60 km/day in summer (Gerhold 1996).

The growth of inanimate transportation—traced above all by its typical and maximum speeds and by its passenger and cargo capacities—offers yet another illustration of very slow premodern gains followed by exponential increases that began at various times during the 19th and the early 20th centuries. But as I will quantify these well-known phenomena, it will become clear how rapidly those modern improvements reached saturation levels, and how these new plateaus were dictated mostly not by technical barriers but by economic or environmental considerations. Consequently, recent advances have concentrated on making long-distance transport cheaper and more reliable rather than faster, but some sectors have still seen important but questionable attempts to raise overall capacity (larger container ships, cruise ships of unprecedented size, the double-decked Airbus 380).

Sail Ships

When tracing the increases in the speed of long-distance movement on water, be it for passenger and cargo transport or for naval forces, it is necessary to use comparable records. Perhaps the best way to compare the highly variable speeds of sail ships is to calculate average (or typical) speeds for an entire voyage and also note the maximum daily runs under favorable conditions. Greek and Roman writings contain numerous references confirming that when pushed by northwesterly winds, Roman vessels travelling between Italy and Egypt might take as few as six days from Messina to Alexandria, while the return voyage to Rome (Ostia) took typically 53 and up to 73 days (Duncan-Jones 1990). A compilation of many extant references shows that Mediterranean sailing in antiquity averaged 8–10 km/h with favorable winds (maxima around 11 km/h) and about 4 km/h in unfavorable conditions (Casson 1951). A millennium later, the daily mean for European caravels was around 7 km/h and top speeds reached about 15 km/h.

Peak sailing speeds were reached by the mid 19th-century clippers. The first clipper, *Rainbow*, designed by John Griffiths and launched in New York in 1845, was followed by scores of sleek ships deployed on the long-distance routes from the US East Coast to California and Asia and from the UK to Australia and China. *Flying Cloud*, designed built by Donald McKay in East Boston and launched in 1851, set a new record on its first voyage from New York to San Francisco around Cape Horn when it completed the trip that had previously lasted more than 200 days in 89 days and 21 hours (averaging 15 km/h for the entire journey) and when it set the fastest speed for a consecutive 24 hours at 33 km/h (Nautical Magazine 1854; see figure 4.4).

In 1853 *Flying Cloud* bested her sailing time from New York to San Francisco by 13 hours and this record stood until 1989 when it was surpassed by a modern ultralight sloop crewed by three people. In 1854 McKay's *Sovereign of the Seas* reached 41 km/h on its way to Australia, one of the 12 known instances when ships surpassed a speed of 33 km/h (McKay 1928). The most impressive sustained speeds were achieved by *Champion of the Seas* (861 km in one day, averaging 35.9 km/h) and by the British *Cutty Sark* (1869) which in 1890 ran 6,000 km in 13 consecutive days, averaging 19 km/h (Armstrong 1969). These comparisons imply an approximate tripling of sailing speeds (from close to 10 to about 30 km/h) during the course of 18 centuries, once again a minuscule average annual gain if it were seen as a steady process of improvement, and even the doubling from 15 to 30 km/h took about 400 years.

Steam-Powered Ships

Steam engines—initially powering large paddlewheels placed amidships and, since 1845, rotating large metal propellers (invented in 1827)—eventually more than doubled the highest sustained clipper speeds. In 1838 Brunel's *Great Western*, the pioneering paddlewheel liner, averaged 16.04 km/h when it crossed the Atlantic to New York in 15.5 days (Doe 2017). By the early 1860s the combination of compound steam engines, screw propulsion, and

Figure 4.16
Four-masted paddlewheel liner *Great Western* designed by Isambard Kingdom Brunel and launched in 1837. Image available at Wikipedia.

iron hulls cut the time on the slower westward journey (against the prevailing winds) to less than nine days: in 1863 *Scotia* claimed the Blue Riband for the fastest westward crossing with 26.78 km/h (eight days and three hours), and in October 1907 *Lusitania* averaged 44.43 km/h during its westward crossing from Irish Queenstown to New Jersey's Sandy Hook.

In September 1909 *Mauretania* surpassed that record by averaging 48.26 km/h, an average that was bested only in 1929 by *Bremen* at 51.71 km/h (Kludas 2000). The *United States* became the fastest ever liner in July 1952 with westbound speed of 63.91 km/h and eastbound average of 65.91 km/h. Plotting the speeds produces the expected sigmoidal curve with a long segment of slow growth followed by rapid ascent and terminating in the 1950s when the great transatlantic liners were superseded by jetliners. The speed gain for record transatlantic crossings was thus about 32 km/h between 1838 and 1909, and 47.87 km/h for more than a century between 1838 and 1952.

Maximum speeds for naval vessels show the same expected boost with the transition to steam power, but unlike in the case of passenger liners (whose services were eliminated by inexpensive flying), naval propulsion has seen many post-WWII advances that allowed faster speeds for ships launched during the second half of the 20th century. With favorable winds the ships of the line that dominated European sail-powered navies just before the intro-duction of steam propulsion had a maximum speed of around 20 km/h. In 1850 *Le Napoléon*, the first steam-powered gunship, could average 22 km/h, and in 1906 the famous *Dreadnought* could reach 39 km/h. The maximum speeds of today's naval vessels range from about 60 km/h for aircraft carriers (America's Nimitz class relies on nuclear reactors to produce steam for its turbines) and between 63 and 65 km/h for the fastest cruisers and destroy-ers. Fast attack boats reach as much as 75 km/h and small patrol boats can go 100 km/h.

Railroads

Train speeds, both maxima and typical operating performances, have grown by an order of magnitude in about 150 years. To be more precise, the high-est average speed on frequently traveled runs rose about 15-fold between 1830 and the beginning of the 21st century. In 1804 Trevithick's pioneering locomotive covered 8 km/h. In 1830 the specification for the 1830 Rain-hill Trials to select the best locomotive for the new Manchester-Liverpool railway included an average speed of 16 km/h; the winner, Stephenson's *Rocket*, averaged 19 km/h and its top speed was (for that time) an astonish-ing 48 km/h (Gibbon 2010). Larger engines brought rapid improvements. In 1848 trains on the Boston and Maine line reached 60 mph (97 km/h), and by the early 1850s several British trains had broken the 100 km/h bar-rier, reaching perhaps as much as 131 km/h by 1854. Obviously, average speeds remained far lower and a speed of 100 mph (161 km/h) by a steam-locomotive powered train was reached only in 1934 by the *Flying Scots-man* on the east-coast main line connecting England and Scotland (Flying Scotsman 2017).

Substantial improvements came only with the introduction of high-speed electricity-powered trains. Japan was their pioneer: the first *shinkan-sen* (new trunk line) between Tokyo and Osaka opened in 1964. It reached its 50th anniversary in 2014 (after transporting 5.3 billion people) with-out a single fatal accident (Smil 2014a). Centralized traffic control enabled the trains to be run at short intervals with a maximum speed of 250 km/h (Noguchi and Fujii 2000). Later train designs became slightly faster and the latest *nozomi* trains travel at 300 km/h. French *trains à grand vitesse* (TGVs) have been running since 1983, with the fastest scheduled journey at nearly 280 km/h, and with a record-setting test run (with only a couple of cars and on a modified track) of 574.8 km/h in 2007.

Europe's other, similarly fast, high-speed train services are Spain's Alta Velocidad Española (AVE), Italy's Frecciarossa, and Germany's Intercity, but

China now has by far the most extensive network of rapid trains with more than 20,000 km in 2016 (Xinhua 2016). The fastest recorded speed is a test run of Japan's magnetic levitation train prototype in 2015 at 603 km/h. But so far, the only operating maglev train is in Shanghai, traveling just 30.5 km, and despite frequent forecasts of widespread adoption, the cost of this propulsion makes it an unlikely candidate for large-scale commercialization. Leaving these maglev exceptions aside, maximum train speeds rose from 45–48 km/h in 1830 to about 130 km/h by the mid-1850s, 160 km/h in 1934, 250 km/h in 1964, and 280–300 km/h by the beginning of the 21st century, a slightly fluctuating but generally linear growth trajectory corresponding to a mean growth rate of nearly 15 km/h for every decade.

The capacity of all trains is obviously limited by the power of their prime movers, be they locomotives pulling the trains or, as in *shinkansen*, multiple electric motors in carriages. And the most obvious economic consideration determining the capacity of passenger trains is the frequency of connections. That is, in turn, heavily dependent on the population density of the regions served by trains and by the compromise between passenger comfort, accessibility, and operating cost (Connor 2011). As a result, Japanese rapid trains, connecting the regions with some of the world's highest population densities, have relatively high capacities. *Tōkaidō shinkansen* between Tokyo and Osaka has capacity of just above 1,300 passengers and 342 trains are dispatched every day; given high load factors, this results in a daily ridership of 424,000 people (JR Central 2017). And the world's largest high-speed train, *Jōetsu shinkansen* between Tokyo and Niigata, can accommodate 1,634 people. In contrast, Europe's rapid trains have much more limited capacities, typically fewer than 500 people: the German iCE 460; the French TGV Atlantique 485; and Thalys between Paris and Brussels 377.

Total ridership (millions of passengers served per year) experienced the expected exponential growth during the early decades of railroad expansion (Mitchell 1998). The American total rose from 12.4 billion pkm in 1882 (the earliest available datum) to 25.8 billion by 1900 and to the peak of 76.2 billion by 1920. Subsequent decline (to 38 billion by 1940) was reversed, sharply but temporarily, during WWII and it resumed immediately afterwards; by 1970 the level was back to that reached during the late 1880s. Only if leaving aside both the decline caused by the economic crisis of the 1930s and the boom brought by WWII traffic would the century-long trajectory come close to a Gaussian curve.

The British experience has been quite unique. After peaking around 1910 at more than 1.5 billion passengers, ridership had declined by nearly 60% by the early 1980s (with 40% of that fall taking place during the decades

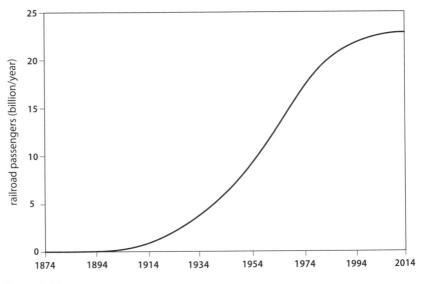

Figure 4.17
Passengers on Japan's trains, 1874–2014. Plotted from data available at SB (1996, 2017a). Logistic curve with the inflection year in 1958 and with the 2015 total only a fraction of 1 percent below the asymptotic level.

of nationalization between 1945 and 1995) but since the 1995 privatization the total rose 2.3-fold, from 750 million to a new record of nearly 1.75 billion by 2015. In contrast, the complete trajectory of Japanese railroad ridership since 1873 (SB 2017a) conforms very closely to a four-parameter symmetrical logistic curve with a plateau forming at close to 25 billion passengers a year (figure 4.17).

Automobiles
As in the case of steam-powered trains, we have to distinguish between maximum speeds attained by vehicles designed to set new records and typical speeds in urban and intercity traffic. In the latter case, other, more important, considerations (above all costs and safety) restrict the maximum speeds to levels that were first reached during the early stages of automotive development. The relation between speed and fuel consumption is distinctly U-shaped, with cars operating less efficiently at both very low and high speeds. There is a relatively narrow optimum range of speed, centered on 60 km/h, for the most economic driving. As for fatality rates, they increase exponentially for occupants of vehicles travelling faster than 100 km/h (going 120 km/h increases the chance of death fourfold), while

the risk of death for pedestrians struck by a car increases exponentially with speeds above 30 km/h (Richards 2010).

Increasing speed beyond the optimum range of 60–80 km/h is thus highly undesirable from the safety point of view. Moreover, once the evaluation is done in an all-encompassing manner, the realities of modern economies have resulted in the very opposite outcome. Illich (1974) showed that after accounting for the time required to earn money for buying (or leasing) the car, fueling, maintaining, and insuring it, the average speed of American car travel shrank to less than 8 km/h in the early 1970s, and I have calculated that by the year 2000 the speed declined to less than 5 km/h, no faster than walking or of horse-drawn omnibuses more than a century ago.

Consequently, a far more meaningful variable tracing the advances in automotive transportation—especially given its ubiquity, its demand for refined liquid fuels, and its atmospheric emissions—is the prevailing fuel conversion efficiency (fuel economy). The first years for which we can calculate the average fuel consumption of the American passenger car fleet is 1936 when the performance was 15 mpg but—in a rare instance of long-term performance retrogression during the decades that have seen many admirable technical advances—by 1973 the mean had declined to 13.4 mpg (Sivak and Tsimhoni 2009).

This dismal trend was reversed only thanks to OPEC's oil price increase in 1973–1974; in response, the US Congress mandated Corporate Average Fuel Economy (CAFE) rates (efficiency standards for new vehicles), with the first increase taking place in 1978. Their success was impressively rapid (made easier by starting from a very poor level), with the pre-1975 performance of new cars doubled to 27.5 mpg by 1985, when the mean for all cars rose to 23 mpg (Sivak and Tsimhoni 2009). But the new trend did not survive the steep oil price decline (from nearly $40 per barrel in 1980 to only about $15 per barrel by 1986) and no new CAFE mandates were legislated until 2008, when the average for the car fleet was 24.3 mpg and for SUVs (accounting for nearly 11% of all new cars) just 21.2 mpg (USEPA 2016b). By 2015 the average fuel economy of new cars rose to 29.3 mpg and that of SUVs to 24.9 mpg.

Four decades of American automotive development thus show two discouraging trajectories and a mildly encouraging trend. By 2015 average body mass had increased by 27% compared to its low in 1982, and during the same time average power rose nearly 2.3 times, while adjusted fuel economy had nearly doubled since 1975, with most of the gain achieved by 1988 (USEPA 2016b). The trajectories of national growth of car ownership in all affluent economies have followed the expected sigmoidal curves. In the US the passenger car fleet rose from just 8,000 vehicles in 1900 to 25 million by the late 1930s and 190 million by 2010, with obvious signs of saturation. Coming shifts are even harder to predict: cars (including SUVs) are now just short of 60% of all US light-duty vehicles, with trucks just above 40%. Hybrid vehicles have made some significant inroads, but the greatest uncertainty concerns the market penetration of new electric cars, with available forecasts ranging from imminent rapid adoption to a gradual introduction.

Airplanes

The first 40 years of commercial aviation had seen the quest for higher cruising speeds but once we got close to the speed of sound other considerations, above all the maximum carrying capacity and the cost per passenger-kilometer, became more important. Dutch KLM, the world's oldest and still operating commercial airline (set up in October 1919), began its flight with De Havilland planes (Airco DH.9A) carrying four passengers and cruising at 161 km/h (maximum speed of 219 km/h) and in 1929 it launched the first multistop intercontinental service to Batavia (Jakarta) using Fokker F.VII planes whose cruising speed was just a bit higher at 170 km/h (Allen 1978). In 1936 Douglas produced its DC-3, the most successful propeller aircraft in history, capable of carrying 32 passengers at a cruising speed of 333 km/h (maximum of 370 km/h) with a ceiling of 7.1 km (McAllister 2010).

In many ways, this was the first modern passenger plane, but its maximum range of 3,421 km was still far too short for transatlantic flights (New York-London is 5,572 km and New York-Paris 5,679 km), and the first intercontinental passenger airplane was Boeing 314 (Trautman 2011). This four-engine hydroplane (known as the Clipper) was relatively slow (cruising speed of 314 km/h, maximum of 340 km/h) but its maximum range with up to 74 passengers (half that many in a sleeping configuration) was 5,896 km, enough for Pan American Airways to use it, starting in 1939, for a regular trans-Pacific service to Hong Kong—with stops at Honolulu, Midway, Wake Island, Guam, and Manila, and the one-way trip taking more than six days—as well as to Europe, with stops in New Brunswick, Newfoundland, and Ireland.

Lockheed Constellation, the largest four-engine propeller passenger plane used after WWII (1945–1958), had a cruising speed of 550 km/h. That reciprocating-engine record was surpassed in 1952 by about 30% by the British jet-powered Comet cruising at 725 km/h before its withdrawal from service in 1954, and then by more than 70% with the introduction of jetliners in the late 1950s. Cruising speeds for the first generation of these planes were set about 15% lower than the speed of sound (Mach, M) which is 1,062 km/h between 10.7 and 12.2 km (35,000–40,000 feet) above ground, where most long-distance flights take place. Speed of 0.85 M thus means cruising at just over 900 km/h. There has been no substantial change in the subsequent generations of jetliners, with cruising speeds at 0.86 M for Boeing 747, 0.84 M for the long-distance 777, and 0.85 M for both the newest Boeing (787) and for the double-decker Airbus 380 (see chapter 1, figure 1.16).

All of these planes could be engineered to fly faster but additional drag generated as they surpass 1 M would make them significantly more expensive to operate: a speed plateau dictated by the economics of commercial operation has been thus in place ever since the beginning of the jetliner era. The British-French Concorde was the only jetliner that broke the sound-speed barrier when it cruised at 2,158 km/h on select intercontinental (mostly transatlantic) flights between 1976 and 2003 (Darling 2004). But the planes were never profitable and no other attempts to introduce supersonic aircraft have succeeded. A new attempt to revive supersonic commercial flight is underway: Boom Technology of Colorado is developing a 2.2 M plane for 45–55 passengers, promising actual service certification by 2023 (Boom Technology 2017).

The introduction of jetliners brought also a similarly early capacity plateau. Boeing 747–100, the first version of the first wide-body jet introduced in 1969, could carry 452 passengers in two classes and up to 500 in economy only. The latest version, 747–400, can carry up to 660 passengers in a single-class configuration, but typical three- or two-class seating accommodates 416–524 passengers. The double-decker Airbus 380 is certified for up to 853 people but airlines using it fly two- or three-class configurations for 379–615 (typically 544) passengers. Consequently, the world's most capacious plane usually carries no more than 20% more passengers than did the 747 two generations ago. The growth of passenger capacity in commercial aviation—from four people in 1919 to 544 in 2007—has followed a typical sigmoidal shape (figure 4.18) and it is unlikely that the existing capacity plateau will be raised by the middle of the 21st century.

But there is one variable describing the growth of global aviation that is still following an exponential ascent. Reliable totals of passenger-kilometers flown by the world's airlines begin in 1929, just a decade after the beginning of scheduled commercial flight. In that year, all flights (excluding those in the Soviet Union) added up to 96.3 million pkm, and this low total was not due only to the relative novelty and expense of flying but also to the fact that most scheduled flights were just domestic intercity connections spanning short or medium distances. By 1939 the combination of more spacious

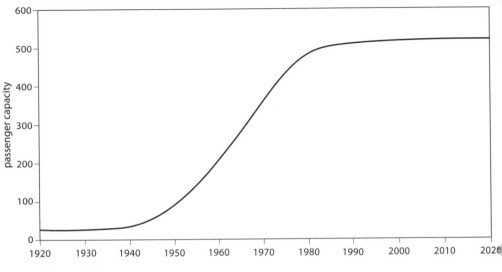

Figure 4.18
Logistic fit of the maximum passenger capacity of commercial airplanes: from KLM's
de Havilland DH.16 (four passengers) in 1920 to Airbus 380 (544 passengers in three
classes, 868 maximum) in 2007. Plotted from individual airplane specifications.

airplanes, more frequent flights, and the first intercontinental routes raised
the total rapidly to nearly 1.4 billion pkm, more than 14 times in 10 years.
Rapid expansion resumed after WWII as the totals rose to 28 billion pkm in
1950, and the introduction and rapid adoption of jetliners lifted it to 2.8
trillion pkm in the year 2000. Passenger air traffic was thus growing exponentially at about 9%/year, doubling in less than eight years.

The terrorist attacks of 9/11 brought only a temporary downturn. By 2003
the worldwide level was back to the record set in the year 2000 and then,
largely thanks to high growth rates of air traffic in Asia in general and China
in particular, new records were set every year except for a minimal dip in
2009 caused by the global economic crisis. Between 2010 and 2015 the total
of passengers carried rose from 2.69 to 3.53 billion (average annual growth of
about 5.5%), total departures increased from 29.6 to nearly 33 million, and
passenger-kilometers grew from 4.9 to 6.6 trillion, averaging 6%/year (ICAO
2016). The logistic curve of global flying is thus still very much in its ascending phase (figure 4.19). The International Air Transport Association expects
7.2 billion passengers in 2035 (compared to 3.8 billion in 2016) or roughly a
90% increase resulting from annual average growth rate of 3.7%, with total
pkm rising to about 15 trillion (logistic fit points to about 17 trillion in 2035).
China is likely to surpass the US by 2024 (the US passenger total appears

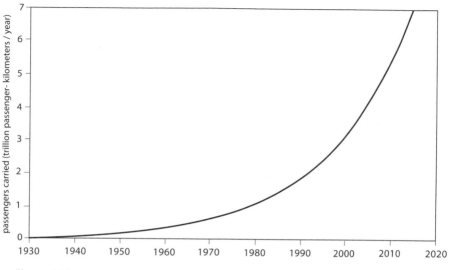

Figure 4.19

Growth of global civil aviation traffic (domestic and international flights) measured in terms of passenger-kilometers. Logistic curve in its early stage indicates further substantial growth in the decades ahead. Data from ICAO (2016) and from earlier annual reports.

close to saturation), and India will have the fastest growth rate in air travel (IATA 2016). Mail tonne-km total has been also growing recently at about 6%/year but freight increased by only about 1%/year.

Improvements in energy efficiency are usually expressed in measures charting the decline of fuel use per pkm. The first version of the turbojet-powered Boeing 707 needed about 6 MJ/pkm in 1958, and the greatest reduction resulted from the introduction of turbofans. In 1969 the Boeing 747 required only about 2 MJ/pkm, by 1984 the rate for the Boeing 757–200 was about 1.5 MJ/rpm, and by 2009 the rate declined to just 1 MJ/pkm for the Boeing 787 built largely of light carbon composite materials and powered by the most efficient engines (Lee and Mo 2011; ATAG 2010). The trajectory calculated by reversing the ratio and tracing how many pkm an airliner could travel on 1 MJ of kerosene (1958 0.17, 1969 0.5, 1984 0.66, 2009 1) shows half a century of linear increase, with further gains anticipated in the future. Another published comparison, using the Comet 4 (first flight in 1949) as the performance baseline (100%) for fuel burned per seat (100%) shows a decline to 50% by 1970, 30% by 1990, and just short of 20% by 2010 (ATAG 2010). Again, reversing the ratio shows an almost perfect linear gain for the 50 years preceding 2010.

The growth of commercial aviation could be thus summarized by the following four growth curves. Passenger capacity and the cruising speed of airplanes display clear sigmoidal (saturation) curves. Improvements in operating efficiency of jetliners (energy required per pkm or per seat) show linear improvements with the shift from early turbojets to the latest turbofans. And the growth of worldwide air traffic (in pkm) has seen exponential growth averaging 5.4%/year between 1970 and 2016, with a significantly slower rate (3.7%) expected between 2016 and 2035. Most people still want to fly more, but, inevitably, another S-curve is forming.

Before closing this section about infrastructures, I should note that their national growth trajectories have been often presented as competitive substitution waves (Grübler 1990; Nakicenovic and Grübler 1991)—but such an interpretation is too general and hence often misleading. In some cases, the competitive displacement label is quite justified in functional terms. For example, construction of canals was an important economic activity in the 18th century and the early 19th century in Europe and the US, but it ended not because there were no more opportunities for canal building but because the advancing railways took over long-distance land transport: a 90% saturation level of canal construction was reached in the UK by 1824, in the US by 1851.

Subsequently, railway construction began to decline as road construction took off, but in this case the apparent switch was a matter of genuine spatial saturation. By 1900 both Western Europe and most of the US had very dense railroad networks and, while during the coming decades railroad freight transport had to compete with both short- and long-distance trucking, moving goods by rail (unlike moving goods through canals) has always retained a large share of the total market. In the US the share carried on roads has increased during the past two generations and by 2017 truck and rail totals were nearly equal (USDOT 2017b). Clearly, highways have not substituted railways: both systems have advanced in a new synergy driven by containerization of transport (Smil 2010b). And to add airways as the fourth competitive wave is correct for moving people but not for moving goods: between 1980 and 2015 the share of US freight moved by air rose from 0.1% to 0.2% of the total, and the high cost of airborne transportation will prevent it from any real mass-scale competition with land- or waterborne shipping.

Electronics

The history of electronics has one theoretical and many practical beginnings. James Clerk Maxwell, building on findings by Michael Faraday, formulated his theory of electromagnetic waves propagating at the speed of light in 1865 and developed it in detail eight years later (Maxwell 1865, 1873). But neither he nor any other physicist began their immediate investigation. And the first two actual demonstrations of such waves did not lead to anything practical either. The first one came in late 1879 and early 1880 in London where David Edward Hughes was able not only to transmit but also to receive invisible waves first indoors and later outdoors for distances up to 450 m—but he was unable to convince the Royal Society experts "of the truth of these aërial electric waves" and did not submit any paper summarizing his work (Hughes 1899).

And in 1883 Thomas Edison filed a patent for an apparatus "showing conductivity of continuous currents through high vacuo" and displayed it at the International Electrical Exhibition in Philadelphia in 1884 (Edison 1884). The device was called a tripolar incandescent lamp and the "etheric force" became known as the Edison effect, a mere curiosity for which the great inventor failed to find any practical application. The breakthrough came between 1886 and 1888 when Heinrich Hertz deliberately generated and received electromagnetic waves whose frequencies he accurately placed "in a position intermediate between the acoustic oscillations of ponderable bodies and the light-oscillations of the ether" (Hertz 1887, 421). Honoring his invention, the unit of frequency (cycles/second) was named the hertz.

Hertz's motivation was to confirm Maxwell's theory and his findings were soon translated into wireless telegraphy (first short-range trials by Oliver J. Lodge and Alexander S. Popov in 1894 and 1895, the first transatlantic transmission by Guglielmo Marconi in 1901) and broadcasts of voice and music (first long-distance transmissions by Reginald A. Fessenden in 1906). After WWI came public radio broadcasts (first licenses in the early 1920s), black and white television (experimental broadcast in 1929, scheduled broadcasts in the US and the UK during the 1930s), and radar (Robert Watson-Watt in 1935), and after WWII into the first electronic computers, color TV, satellite telecommunications, cellular telephony, and the World Wide Web (Smil 2005, 2006b).

Vacuum Tubes

Until the 1950s vacuum tubes were at the heart of all electronics, but eventually they ceded virtually all those niches to solid-state devices. Cathode ray tubes in TVs and desktop computer monitors were one of their last mass-scale applications but during the late 1990s and the early 2000s they were replaced by flat panel displays, starting with liquid crystal and followed by light emitting diodes. Vacuum tubes (magnetrons) still power microwave ovens but alternatives using solid-state radio frequencies and offering enhanced power control, frequency accuracy, and a longer lifetime have become available (Wesson 2016).

The diode, the simplest vacuum tube based on Edison's effect (basically a light bulb with an added electrode), was invented in 1904 by John A. Fleming. A diode is a sensitive detector of Hertzian waves and a converter of AC to DC. In 1907 Lee de Forest created a triode by fixing a metal plate near a bulb's carbon filament and placing a grid between the plate and the filament (Fleming 1934). This current modulator can be adapted for reception, amplification, and transmission. Tetrodes and pentodes (with four and five electrodes) followed during the 1920s. Work on magnetrons (generating microwaves through the interaction of electrons with a magnetic field) proceeded during the 1920s. A multicavity magnetron was first patented in Germany in 1935 and deployed in the UK in 1940 in early radars (Blanchard et al. 2013). The klystron (used in radar, later in satellite communication and high-energy physics) was patented in 1937, and gyrotrons (the prime sources of high power in the mm-wave part of the spectrum, and used for rapid heating of materials and plasmas) were introduced first in the Soviet Union during the early 1970s (Osepchuk 2015).

Comparing the performance of vacuum tubes and calculating the growth rate of their capabilities requires a suitable common metric. Power density, the maximum power that can be transported through a device, is proportional to the circuit's area, which is inversely proportional to the device's frequency. Granatstein et al. (1999) calculated power densities for all types of vacuum tubes and the advancing rates for each device follow a logistic curve as each design approaches its limits. The performance of the major types of vacuum tubes progressed at impressive rates. Between 1935 and 1970 the power density of gridded tubes (triode and higher) rose by four orders of magnitude, and so did the power density of cavity magnetrons between 1935 and 1960. And between 1944 and 1974 the maximum power density of klystrons rose by six orders of magnitude and, between 1970 and the year 2000, so did the power density of gyrotrons (Granatstein et al. 1999).

As a result, the post-1930 envelope of the maximum power density of vacuum devices forms a straight line on the semilog graph, gaining nearly 1.5 orders of magnitude every decade and corresponding to an average annual exponential growth of about 35% (figure 4.20). And that turns out to be exactly the average annual rate of growth for the post-1965 crowding of transistors, solid-state devices performing the function previously done by vacuum tubes. To be clear, this is not a comparison of identical measures of merit (the rates are calculated for the power density of vacuum tubes

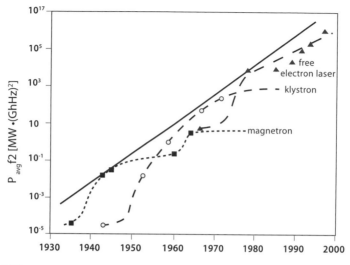

Figure 4.20
The growing power density of successive families of vacuum tubes forms a hyperbolic growth envelope similar to that of Moore's law. Data from Granatstein et al. (1999).

and for the number of transistors on a silicon chip) but one looking at key properties of vacuum and solid-state devices and showing that high rates of performance growth (roughly doubling every two years) characterized successive vacuum devices before they became associated with the increasing capacities of microprocessors, whose growth has conformed to Moore's law. Simply put, vacuum electronics had seen gains anticipated by Moore's law for decades before that growth rule was formulated by Gordon Moore in 1965.

Other ways to judge the improving performance of vacuum tubes is to look at their falling prices and at the ownership of new electronic consumer products that their advances made possible. Price declines are commonly highest during the early stages of commercial diffusion and, according to Okamura (1995), prices of Japanese receiving tubes (the country was an early pioneer of mm-wave power generation) dropped by more than 90% between 1925 and 1940. In 1924, four years after the beginning of licensed US radio broadcasting, a high-quality best-selling model, RCA AR-812, was priced at $220, just $45 less than the Runabout version of the dependable Ford Model T (Radiomuseum 2017).

As vacuum tube prices fell, the ownership of radios rose. By 1931 half of US households had radio and the share reached 95% by 1949, when the logistic growth curve had only a few points to gain to level off a few points short of 100%. Ownership of black-and-white TVs rose even faster, from a small fraction of 1% in 1945 to 90% of all households by 1964. And the S-curve of the growing microwave oven ownership in the US had an almost identical rate of the ascent, with annual sales rising from just 10,000 units in 1960 to more than a million units by the mid-1970s and with 80% of households owning the device by 1990 (Osepchuk 2015).

And vacuum tubes were used to build the first electronic computers (British Colossus in 1943, American ENIAC in 1946), and they remained indispensable for large, mainframe machines until transistors began taking over during the late 1950s. Transistors soon prevailed due to their unprecedented combination of low mass and high reliability. Vacuum tubes are excellent amplifiers and switching devices, but with tubes having volumes of mostly between 20 and 60 cm^3 and mass of 50–100 g, even small computers were bulky and heavy, and frequent overheating shortened their life spans to as little as 50–100 hours to begin with. Nothing illustrates these vacuum tube drawbacks better than a comparison of America's first electronic computer and its later transistorized re-creation (Kempf 1961; Van der Spiegel et al. 2000).

ENIAC had 17,648 vacuum tubes of 16 different kinds (as well as tens of thousands of resistors, capacitors, manual switches, and relays), total volume of about 80 m^3 (footprint of 167 m^2 or roughly two badminton courts), and with power supply and air cooling it weighed about 30 t. About 90% of operating interruptions were due to recurrent tube failures necessitating laborious maintenance and replacement (the checking routine alone took about eight hours). Half a century later, ENIAC was reconstructed on a 7.4×5.3 mm silicon microchip that contained 174,569 transistors: their total was ten times larger than the original count for vacuum tubes because the transistors also replaced all resistors, capacitors, and other components (Van der Spiegel et al. 2000). ENIAC was more than 5 million times heavier, it consumed about 40,000 more electricity but its speed was no more than 0.002% that of the reconstructed processor (100 kHz vs. 50 Mhz), all of it thanks to solid-state electronics and its continuous advances.

Solid-State Electronics and Computers
Although Julius Edgar Lilienfeld patented the concept of a field-effect transistor already in 1925, the first useful designs emerged only in the late 1940s at Bell Laboratories. First, in 1947, came the field-effect transistor designed by Walter Brattain and John Bardeen, and then, in 1948, William Shockley's more useful bipolar junction transistor (Smil 2006b). Texas Instruments began to sell the first silicon transistors in 1954, but early performance gains

in solid-state electronics remained relatively slow before the invention of integrated circuits in 1958 and 1959 by Jack Kilby at Texas Instruments and Robert Noyce at Fairchild Semiconductor, and their limited commercialization in the early 1960s. In 1965 the number of transistors on a most complex microchip rose to 64 after doubling every 18 months since 1959.

In 1965 Gordon Moore, who was at that time the director of research at Fairchild Semiconductor, made one of the boldest and ultimately also one of the most far-reaching and most consequential forecasts in modern technical history. In a short paper in *Electronics* he concluded, not surprisingly, that "the future of integrated electronics is the future of electronics itself," and he predicted that "certainly over the short term this rate can be expected to continue" (Moore 1965, 114). He was less certain about looking a decade ahead but predicted that by 1975 an integrated circuit would have at least 65,000 components.

In 1968 Burroughs began to sell the first computers based on integrated circuits and in the same year Moore and Robert Noyce, one of the inventors of the integrated circuit, cofounded Intel (Integrated Electronics), the company that more than any other has extended the life of Moore's law. The company's first profitable product was a RAM (random access memory) chip and in 1969 Intel contracted with Japan's Busicom to design a customized LSI (large-scale integration) microchip for a programmable calculator. Federico Fagin, Marcian Hoff, and Stanley Mazor were the principal designers of 4004, the world's first universal microprocessor, with 2,300 transistors. This capability was equivalent to that of the room-size ancestor in 1945 (Mazor 1995; Intel 2018a). Before Busicom went bankrupt, Intel bought back the design and marketing rights to the microchip that became the foundation of their decades-long growth of microprocessor capacities.

In 1974 Intel's 8080 had 4,500 transistors and a year later Moore reconsidered the length of the doubling time for crowding components on a chip and raised it to two years (Moore 1975). That implies an annual compounded growth rate of 35%, the pace that became known as Moore's law and that prevailed for four decades after 1975. Intel 8088, with 29,000 transistors, was released in 1979 and after IBM chose it as the central processing unit for its first personal computer Intel saw demand rising to more than 10 million units a year. Subsequent fabrication moved from large-scale integration (up to 100,000 transistors on a chip) to very large-scale integration (with up to 10 million transistors), and then to ultra large-scale integration (up to a billion transistors) by 1990.

Sustained high exponential growth raised the number of components on a microchip above 100,000 by 1982 and to millions during the 1990s.

In the year 2000, Intel's Pentium III Coppermine had 21 million transistors, in 2001 Pentium III Tualatin reached 45 million, and soon afterward Moore (by that time Intel's chairman emeritus) noted his amazement that "we can design and manufacture the products in common use today. It is a classic case of lifting ourselves up by our bootstraps—only with today's increasingly powerful computers can we design tomorrow's chips" (Moore 2003, 57). And growth was far from over. The component total surpassed 100 million in 2003 (AMD K8 with 105.9 million transistors). In 2010 Sparc T3 was the first design to reach 1 billion components on a chip, Intel's Xeon Phi had 5 billion transistors in 2012, Oracle's SPARC M17 reached 10 billion in 2015, and Intel's Stratix 10 surpassed 30 billion components in 2018 (Intel 2018b; see figure 0.2). The overall growth between 1971 and 2018 had spanned seven orders of magnitude and resulted in average annual exponential growth of about 35%, that is, in doubling in just over two years (750 days).

Large mainframe computers were the first beneficiaries of advances in solid-state electronics, and their history is best summarized by the growth of their maximum computational performance. The variable is usually expressed in terms of floating point operations per second (flops). In order to set the baseline, the head-hand-paper calculations will (depending on their complexity) range between 0.01 and one flop, and even the best electromechanical calculators used by the US and UK military during the early 1940s did not average more than one flop. By 1951 UNIVAC, the first commercially available computer, reached about 1,900 flops and by the early 1960s UNIVAC's transistorized Livermore Advanced Research Computer was the first machine to reach one megaflop. Seymour Cray's designs made the greatest advances in supercomputing during the 1970s, with CRAY-1 capable of 160 megaflops in 1976, and by 1985 CRAY-2 approached two gigaflops.

The next three-orders-of-magnitude gain to one teraflop was reached in 1996 by IBM's ASCI Red at Sandia Laboratory in New Mexico. The race to a petaflop progressed from IBM's ASCI White (at the Lawrence Livermore National Laboratory) with 7.2 teraflops in 2000 to Japan's NEC Earth Simulator with 35.86 teraflops in 2002, IBM Blue Gene/L at 70.7 teraflops in 2004 and IBM Roadrunner (at Los Alamos National Laboratory) at 1.026 petaflops in 2008. Chinese designs rose rapidly to top ranks after the year 2000, with new records set by Tianhe-IA (2.56 petaflops) in 2008, Tianhe-2 (33.86 petaflops with 32,000 Xeon and 48,000 Xeon Phi chips) in 2013 and by Sunway TaihuLight (in Wuxi) in 2016 with 93 petaflops (Top 500 2017). Growth trajectory from one megaflop in 1960 to 93.01 petaflops in 2016 conforms to exponential growth averaging 45%/year, that is doubling in

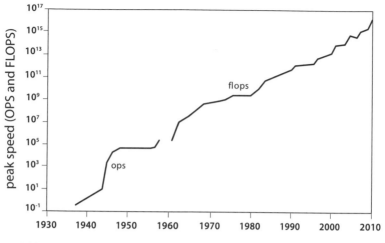

Figure 4.21
Computing speed records in operations per second and floating point operations per second. Data from Top 500 (2017).

less than 19 months at the rate that is, as expected, very similar to Moore's law (figure 4.21).

Obviously, mass-produced computers have seen smaller capability gains than the fastest one-of-a-kind supercomputer designs whose top performance was nearly 14 orders of magnitude (almost 100 trillion times) higher in 2017 than in it was in 1950. Perhaps the best appreciation of advancing computing performance during the 20th century is gained by comparing its progress with manual calculations (the only option available until the closing decades of the 19th century) and with the capabilities of the first mechanical calculators.

Measured in the simplest possible way, by comparing additions per second, the trajectory leads from 0.07 for manual operations, 0.53 for Hollerith's 1890 tabulator and 2–3 for the earliest prototypes of electronic computers (Harvard Mark, Zuse) to 5,000 for the massive ENIAC in 1946, 100,000 for the mainframe IBM 704 in 1955, 250,000 for IBM's first PC in 1982, and eventually to tens and hundreds of millions of additions per second in desktops of the late 1990s. The two most common variables used to trace the progress of computing are in terms of million instructions per second (MIPS, to capture a computer's central processing unit capability) and cycle speed (in Hz, to measure the celerity of execution). The first variable progressed from just 0.002 MIPS for the 1951 UNIVAC to 0.092 20 years later for Intel's first microprocessor, 4004, and the relentless rise brought the record levels to more than 1,000 MIPS during the 1990s and to over 300,000 MIPS by 2017 (Singularity.com 2017).

This trajectory corresponds to average annual exponential growth of 28.5%, that is doubling every 2.5 years, slower than the growth of transistor density. Obviously, cycle speed can be compared only for electronic machines, and it rose from 0.1 kHz for ENIAC to 2 MHz for the transistorized designs of the late 1950s and to more than 5 MHz for computers with early microprocessors during the 1980s. Speeds in excess of 1 GHz were reached by the beginning of the 21st century and the peak speed in 2017 was 4.2 GHz with Intel Core i7–7700K (Nordhaus 2001; techradar.com 2018). This gain of seven orders of magnitude implies an average annual exponential growth of about 25% (doubling every 2.8 years), being, as expected, fairly close to the pace anticipated by Moore's law. Gains of many orders of magnitude (resulting in annual exponential growth rates of 25–35%) were also made in terms of random access memory and magnetic data storage.

This growth of computing performance has been made possible by correspondingly impressive declines in the cost of fabricating transistors and microprocessors. Their prices had a halving time of just over 1.5 years and their power requirement per MIPS fell by six orders of magnitude between the introduction of the first microprocessor in 1971 and 2015. This has resulted in an unprecedented reduction in the total cost of computing measured as expenditure per million standardized operations per second equivalent (MSOPS; one-MSOPS device can add 20 million 32-bit integers in a second). This latter measure enables comparison of manual, mechanical, vacuum tube, and solid-state devices. Nordhaus (2001) calculated its values (in 1998 dollars) for the entire 20th century: early mechanical devices cost 2.77×10^4/MSOPS; by 1950 vacuum tubes cut it down to $57.8/MSOPS; transistors lowered it by another order of magnitude (to $2.61 by 1960); by 1980 microprocessors lowered the cost to half a cent/MSOPS; and in 2001 the cost was vanishingly small at 4.3×10^{-8}.

The total cost reduction of computing thus amounted to 11 orders of magnitude during the 20th century, with the post-1970 cut responsible for six orders of magnitude. Cost reductions were, inevitably, smaller for commercially available devices but comparisons require proper adjustments for quality change. The first PCs available in 1976 had only several kilobytes of RAM, no hard disk, and clock speed of less than 1 MHz, but they cost several thousand dollars. By 1999 a PC had megabytes of RAM, gigabytes of hard-disk memory, clock speed exceeding 1 GHz, and many designs cost less than $1,000. Berndt and Rappaport (2001) calculated that when adjusted for quality change the price of 1999 desktops was three orders of magnitude below that of the pioneering models in 1976 (depending on the price index used the actual figure was as large as 1/3,700).

This combination of performance, information storage gains, and price declines has had transformative effects far beyond research, commercial, and personal computing. Transistors, integrated circuits, and microprocessors made it possible to design and produce new kinds of affordable electronic devices whose mass-scale ownership, growing capabilities, and increasing reliabilities resulted in unprecedented personal access to information, to a still expanding range of services and entertainment, and eventually allowed instant global communication and sharing of knowledge—while also enabling new forms of criminality and fostering a ubiquitous loss of privacy.

Consumer Electronics and Mobile Phones

This great innovation cluster began with transistorized radios during the early 1950s, continued with successive waves of music recording and reproduction (first with cassettes displacing vinyl singles and long-playing records, and then compact discs displacing cassettes, for those only to succumb to music downloads) and data storage and retrieval, and it has reached an unprecedented extent with the mass ownership of mobile phones. Waves of audio dominance offer excellent examples of rapid market penetration followed by brief peaks and precipitous retreats (I return to these specific life-cycle trajectories in chapter 6). Sales of vinyl records (singles and long-playing recordings introduced in 1948) reached their US peak in 1978 with 531 million units, the totals declined to less than 10 million units by 1999 and 5 million units by 2004 but then a partial revival boosted the demand to 17.2 million records in 2016 (RIAA 2017).

Compact cassettes were introduced in 1963 in Europe and in 1964 in the US; their sales peaked in 1988 and essentially ceased by 2005. CD sales began in 1984, peaked in 1999, and the last one of these three successive audio techniques became dwarfed by music downloading. But dominance of that new audio mode became even more fleeting. American downloads (of singles and albums) rose from 144 million in 2004 to a peak of just over 1.5 billion units in 2012 before retreating to just over 800 million by 2016: another unmistakable Gaussian trajectory has formed unusually rapidly as downloading has been replaced by streaming. By 2016 revenues from US music sales were more than twice as high for streaming as for downloading and they also surpassed the combined earnings from downloads and physical sales (RIAA 2017).

But during the first two decades of the 21st century the most far-reaching electronically mediated mass-scale innovation was not confined to listening to music but involved a multifaceted experience of using portable electronic devices in general and smartphones in particular. Smartphones are now by far the most abundant devices belonging to what is a relatively diverse category of portable, small-sized electronic gadgets, with items ranging from noise-cancelling headphones to electronic readers and from cameras to handheld games. One thing that nearly all of these devices have in common has been an extraordinarily rapid growth of their ownership, with the earlier designs diffusing first in affluent economies, but with mobile phones making a swift global sweep including even some of the poorest economies in sub-Saharan Africa.

US data allow us to trace rising ownership of electrical and electronic household products: as expected, all completed diffusions form S-shaped trajectories, but not all can be captured by the same function. Most of them form asymmetrical logistic curves, the diffusion of refrigerators is very close to a symmetrical logistic function, some pre-1950 progressions (of electric stoves and clothes washers) were interrupted by the economic crisis of the 1930s and by WWII, and some product diffusions contain spells of almost perfect linear increase: clothes washers between 1950 and 1975, color TVs between 1965 and 1975, and dishwashers between 1975 and 1995 (figure 4.22).

During the first decade of the 21st century the list of products that most Americans claimed they could not live without included mostly electrical and electronic gadgets ranging from microwave ovens and home computers

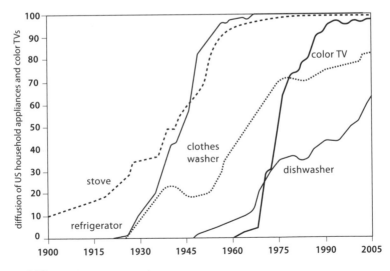

Figure 4.22
Adoption rates of electric stoves, refrigerators, clothes washers, color TVs, and dishwashers. Based on Taylor et al. (2006).

to dishwashers, clothes dryers, and home air conditioning (Taylor et al. 2006). And although it is easy to get the impression that the diffusions work progressively faster—it took more than 60 years for telephones (landlines) to go from 10% to 90%, but radio ownership achieved the same penetration rate after 22 years, color television after 20 years, and cellphones in only 13 years—that generalization is not without exceptions as some older spreads of ownerships had periods of diffusion as fast as the most recent processes. Between 1925 and 1930 radio ownership grew as fast as did cellphone ownership between 1995 and 2000, and that rate was slightly lower than the adoption of VCRs between 1984 and 1989 (figure 4.23).

As with computers, widespread ownership of mobile phones would not have been possible without their steadily declining mass combined with rising performance. In 1973, Motorola's first experimental portable unit weighed 1.135 kg. In 1984 the company's first commercially available device, DynaTAC 8000X, weighed 900 g and a decade later Nokia's units still averaged about 600 g. Devices lighter than 200 g came on the market by 1998 and since 2005 typical mass has reached a plateau at between 110 and 120 g as units became thinner but screens got larger (GSMArena 2017). Worldwide statistics for all mobile phone sales show that 1997 was the first year with the total above 100 million; in 2009 the shipments reached more than 1 billion, and by 2017 they were close to 2 billion units. Plotting the worldwide sales of mobile phones since 1997 conforms to a logistic curve

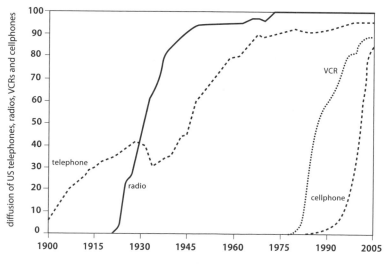

Figure 4.23
Adoption rates of telephones, radios, VCRs, and mobile phones in the US. Based on Taylor et al. (2006).

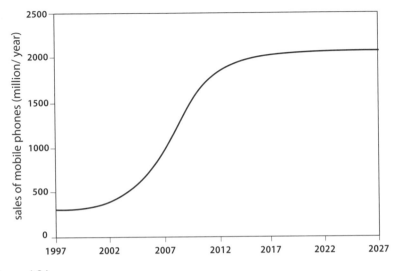

Figure 4.24

Growth of annual sales of all mobile phones since 1997. The trajectory fits a logistic curve that inflected in 2008 and that is now approaching its asymptotic value. Data from GSMArena (2017).

with the inflection point in 2008 and a ceiling of about 2.1 billion units compared to more than 1.96 billion sold in 2018 (figure 4.24).

Most of these devices are now smartphones, essentially hand-held high-performance minicomputers using touch screens and advanced operating systems to access the Internet and to run a still-increasing range of specific applications. During the second decade of the 21st century, no complex manufactured product has come even close to the annual sales of these miniaturized portable electronic devices whose popularity has been due not only to their use for inexpensive instant communication but also to the fact that their smart variants subsume services that were previously provided by a number of function-specific objects and gadgets. Tupy (2012) claimed that 16 devices or functions were replaced by applications available on smartphones: camera, personal computer that was used largely for e-mail, radio, fixed phone, alarm clock, newspaper, photo album, video recorder, stereo, map, white-noise generator, DVD player for movies, rolodex, TV, voice recorder, and compass.

And we could also add dictionaries, calendars, notebooks, appointment books, and convenient banking. Some of these claims are quite true. Today's mobile phones produce photos with resolution much higher than good electronic cameras commonly used a decade ago, and the devices make excellent alarm clocks, rolodexes, compasses and, of course, phones. But others are easily disputable: a tiny screen is hardly an equivalent of watching large-size high-definition TV, and scanning truncated news items is not an equivalent of reading a newspaper. Even so, there is no doubt that the growth of mobile phones has been marked, along with easily quantifiable market penetration and annual sales levels, by impressive growth of not so easily quantifiable overall utility and functionality.

American ownership of mobile phones went from 10% to 50% in just seven years and to the near-saturation level of 95% in just additional six years, while smartphones rose from 10% to 90% ownership in less than a decade. The first smartphone (connected to the Internet) was introduced by NTT DOCOMO in Japan in 1999, followed by Nokia and Sony Ericsson, and 56 million units had been sold worldwide by 2005 (Canalys 2007). Apple brought out its iPhone 2G in June 2007, when the global sales reached 122 million units. The subsequent rise in the annual global sales of smartphones—to just over 1 billion units in 2013 and 1.49 billion units in 2016 (Meeker 2017)—conforms almost perfectly to a four-parameter logistic curve whose projection indicates that the recent shipments have come close to the saturation level of 1.6 billion devices (figure 4.25).

Where the global saturation levels are for the use of the most common services accessed by modern electronic devices in general, and by mobile

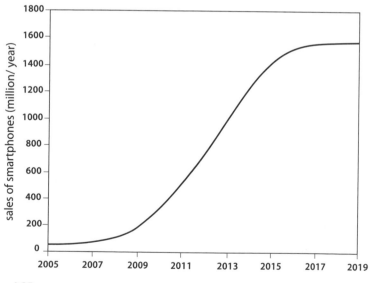

Figure 4.25
The growth of annual sales of smartphones since the year 2005 has followed perfectly a logistic curve with the inflection year in 2012 and with the asymptote less than 10% above 2016 sales. Data from Canalys (2007) and Meeker (2017).

phones in particular, is less clear. Obviously, in many affluent countries, Internet access is already at its maximum or has closely approached saturation levels. By 2015 84% of American adults used the Internet (compared to 52% in the year 2000) and the rates were as high as 96% for people 18–29 years old (their participation was already at 70% in the year 2000), 93% for ages 30–49 years, and 97% for families earning in excess of $75,000 (Pew Research Center 2015). In contrast, global opportunities would appear to be far from exhausted but the available data show decelerating growth and a formation of another S-curve.

Already in 2005, Modis (2005) wrote about the end of the Internet rush and although he did not exclude the arrival of a new growth phase, he calculated that the worldwide total of Internet users could reach a ceiling as low as 14% of the global population (that would be close to 1.1 billion people in 2017), a discouragingly low figure in his judgment. Devezas et al. (2005) found that in 2005 the Internet was coming to the end of the 4th Kondratiev wave downswing (innovation structural phase) and predicted that it would then embark on the 5th Kondratiev upswing, or consolidation structural phase. In 2012 Miranda and Lima (2012) analyzed the cumulative growth of Internet hosts since 1989, putting the logistic asymptote at about 1.4 billion by 2030, and forecast the Internet penetration index peaking at about 80% of global population by 2040. They also concluded that the growth of software has been powered by bursts of creativity with periods close to Kuznets and Kondratiev economic cycles.

I have reanalyzed the growth of Internet hosts by using the Domain Survey of the Internet Systems Consortium, which aims to discover every host on the Internet by searching the allocated address space and following links to domain names (ISC 2017). Its regular surveys have been available since January 1995 and the trajectory of domain growth fits perfectly a symmetrical logistic curve with the inflection point in 2008 and with a 2030 asymptote only some 7% above the 2017 level of 1.06 billion hosts in 2017 (figure 4.26). Curiously, the host series conforms no less perfectly ($R^2 = 0.999$) to a Gaussian curve peaking in 2016 and returning by 2030 to the level it attained first in 2002 (figure 4.27). Neither of these functions may turn out to be a reliable indicator of the future trend but both of them strongly support the conclusion of approaching saturation and a low probability of any further rapid growth.

Internet traffic presents a different trajectory: its global total saw very steep growth, from 100 GB/day (that is 1.15 MB/s) in 1992 to 26.6 TB/s in 2016 (CISCO 2017). This exponential growth, averaging about 63%/year (doubling every 13 months), is much faster than the rate predicted by Moore's law, and the growth curve (including the anticipated 2021 total

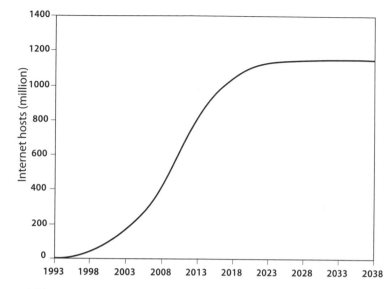

Figure 4.26
The post-1993 growth of Internet hosts has followed a logistic curve with the inflection year in 2008 and with the asymptotic value less than 10% above the 2017 total. Data from ISC (2017).

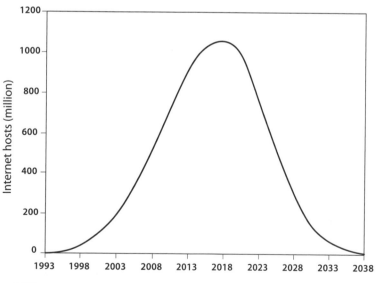

Figure 4.27
The growth of Internet hosts also fits a Gaussian curve peaking in 2016 and returning to negligible values before 2040. Such a development seems quite unlikely—unless a new mode of hosting takes over. Data from ISC (2017).

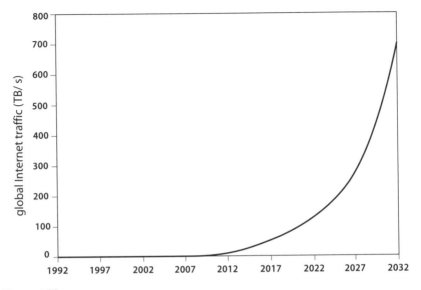

Figure 4.28
Post-1992 growth of Internet traffic in TB/s fits a logistic curve in its early stages of growth indicating further substantial gains in decades ahead. Data from CISCO (2017).

of 105.8 TB/s) fits best a five-parameter logistic curve indicating roughly a sevenfold increase during the 2020s (figure 4.28). Concurrently, maximum speed for modems was rising by 40%/year and capacity of submarine fiber-optic cables was growing by 33%/year: the record holder in 2018 was the 13,000-km long submarine cable between Los Angeles and Hong Kong whose six fiber-optic pairs will be able to transmit 144 terabits in both directions (Hecht 2018). Per capita Internet traffic rose from about 10 MB/month in 2000 to 10 GB/month in 2016 and it is expected to reach 30 GB/month by 2021 (CISCO 2017). Other forecasts for 2021 include smartphone traffic exceeding PC traffic and number of devices connected to IP networks being more than three times the global population.

Finally, a look at the growth of what is now known as social media, a new mass phenomenon that has made it nearly effortless to gossip, boast and to prove convincingly that the volume of communication must be inversely related to its quality (and, all too often, to a regrettable loss of privacy). Facebook has emerged as the leader of the social pack with the total number of accounts (only one is allowed per person) passing 1 million in 2004, 1 billion in 2012, and reaching 2.27 billion by the end of 2018 (Facebook 2018). This ascent points to about 4.27 billion users by 2030. With an expected global population of 8.5 billion, that would amount to a penetration rate of 50%, a plausible share given the fact that in 2018 the North American Facebook penetration rate reached 66%, and the global rate was about 29%.

The vastly enlarged scope of information flows (with text now taking up a minuscule share of the global traffic dominated by streaming music and video) has been much admired for its unprecedented transformative (socially and economically) repercussions but, inevitably, the new benefits also carry many negative consequences. These include increased loss of privacy, threats of hacking and information theft, new means for covert criminal activities, as well as an enormous waste of valuable, highly energy-intensive and often environmentally damaging materials. Makers of mobile phones have been directly promoting this waste by introducing new models at unnecessarily short intervals and by brainwashing gullible masses into paying for barely changed copycat devices, a reality best attested by the volume of patent-infringement lawsuits involving major firms.

A 2014 study reported the average life span of smartphones as 4.7 years (Ely 2014) but a later survey put smartphone life span at about 22 months in the US and 20 months in China (Kantar World Panel 2015). Taking an average of 22 months means that some 800 million units are discarded annually, and the addition of laptops, tablets, notebooks, and netbooks would bring the annual total close to 900 million abandoned devices. Yet the best estimates show that recycling rates for all smartphone metals (including rare earth elements) must improve: in 2015 the shares were still mostly below 1%, although the rates for precious metals (silver, gold) as well as for copper, lead, and tin are above 50% (Compoundchem 2015).

5 Populations, Societies, Economies: or growth of the most complex assemblies

Terms always need clarifying in order to avoid misunderstandings and ambiguities. This book deals with nothing but the growth of systems, that is, entities consisting of connected and interdependent parts that make up specific structures and provide desired functions. Most of them—including organisms, energy converters, machines, and other artifacts—are complex according to even the most restrictive definition of that term. But there is a clear hierarchy of complex systems with, to use the organismic sequence, tissues above cells, organs above tissues, complete functioning species above organs, and populations above species. The highest levels of systemic complexity will be the subject of this chapter, focusing on the growth of human populations and their grand-scale creations, cities, states and empires, economies and civilizations.

The growth of human populations can be examined by focusing on several key variables ranging from basic vital statistics (birth- and death rates) and fertility rates (all of them could be studied as aggregates or in age-specific form) to natural growth (births minus deaths) and overall population growth (natural rate plus net migration). The spatial resolution of such inquiries can range from small communities to the global population, and time spans can go from a single generation to the entire sweep of human evolution, and I will include most of these diverse aspects in my systematic examination of population growth.

I will start with tracing the long-term growth of the global population and contrast its lengthy span of very low increments with rapid gains during the 20th century, and I will also look at possible outcomes by the middle and the end of the 21st century. Inevitably, this long-term reconstruction will also consider some notable past fears and forecasts and follow their subsequent fate. Then I will present population growth trajectories of the world's most populous nations (including China, India, and the United States) and conclude the section by looking at the unfolding population aging and decline that is now the norm in most of the world's affluent countries, with Japan leading the trend.

Starting the chapter with population growth is an obvious choice, but the further order is necessarily arbitrary as the growth of cities, empires, and economies has progressed through dynamic interaction of all of these complex systems. Following the evolutionary sequence, cities (drawing their energies and materials from their expanding hinterlands) were the first complex anthropogenic creations. Their growth during antiquity and the Middle Ages was limited by inherent difficulties in securing sufficient food, energy, and raw materials in societies relying on traditional modes of crop production (with yields remaining low and stagnant for centuries), resource extraction (overwhelmingly dependent on animate labor), and transportation (in the absence of strong prime movers, good roads and vehicles, it was slow and expensive on land, cheaper but unreliable by shipping).

As a result, large cities were uncommon and, in addition, many relatively large ancient cities were relatively short-lived, victims of environmental change, neighborly aggression or dynastic exhaustion. Urban growth became more common only during the early modern era (1500–1800), but it was only the 19th century's industrialization that brought an unprecedented acceleration of urbanization in Europe and North America. The second, post-WWII, urbanization wave has been much more extensive, affecting Latin America and Asia, with China being a notable late starter due to the three decades of retarding Maoist policies.

But the ancient growth of concentrated settlements, slow and limited as it was, led eventually to the establishment of larger governance units whose persistence was based on personal loyalties to a ruler, on shared history and religion, and on economic interests driving their defense and expansion. Growth that began more than 5,000 years ago with Mesopotamia's clay-built cities led, relatively early, to the emergence of city-states followed by more extensive centrally controlled entities and, surprisingly soon, the formation of the first territorially expansive empires. Empires are, by definition, substantially sized entities encompassing smaller political units and different nationalities, religions and economic practices, and they have shared a key attribute across millennia of history: a high, often absolute, degree of central control.

After WWII the term empire was used not only for the Soviet Union (an entity with several imperial characteristics) but also for the US-dominated system of alliances and military bases abroad. By any reasonable definition, the United States has never been an empire, although since 1945 the country has exercised a peculiar form of global hegemony (Smil 2010a). American hegemony was threatened but not decisively shaken by the Soviet empire (which had collapsed by 1991), and it is now facing further, and apparently more intractable, challenges arising from the economic and military ascent of China (a modern reincarnation of the world's oldest existing empire that fits all the key requirements to be defined as such), from militant Islam, and from internal discord.

Some notable exceptions aside, nation-states, now the dominant form of political organization, are of relatively recent origin and their foundations are being weakened by new trends ranging from supranational allegiances to mass migration. Unlike many empires, many states reached their maximum extent relatively early in their history as they encountered physical barriers (mountain ranges, major rivers, sea coasts) that, although certainly not insurmountable, were formidable enough to restrict further expansion. On the other hand, many modern states were created by the partition of formerly larger entities and hence they are products of diminution rather than of any organic growth.

Few modern preoccupations have been as widespread and as incessant as concerns about economic growth. A revealing perspective is offered by Google Ngram, which counts the frequency of words or terms in a corpus of English-language books during the 19th and 20th centuries. The terms population growth and economic growth both came into more common use during the 1920s but while the references to population growth peaked during the late 1970s, the frequency of using the term economic growth in books (although forming a clear S-shaped curve) was still rising by the end of the 20th century, when it was twice as popular as the former term.

Moreover, a key qualifier is in order: those incessant concerns about economic growth are, as already noted in chapter 1, not just about any growth. No matter what size the economy and level of average prosperity, annual rates of less than 1% are seen as disappointing, if not worrisome. Only gains on the order of 3–4% are seen as "healthy," while analysts and commentators are mesmerized by the utterly unsustainable rates approaching, even surpassing, double digits that were characteristic of the growth of the Japanese economy between 1955 and 1969, of the South Korean economy between the late 1960s and the late 1980s, and of the Chinese economy since the beginning of Deng Xiaoping's reforms in 1980 (World Bank 2018).

Japanese annual GDP growth was above 10% for most of the late 1950s and 1960s, with 1969 (at 12%) being the last year of double-digit gain (SB 1996). During the 20 years between 1968 and 1988 the South Korean economy experienced 12 years of double-digit growth, with a peak of almost 15% in 1973, and between 1980 and 2015 official Chinese statistics claimed

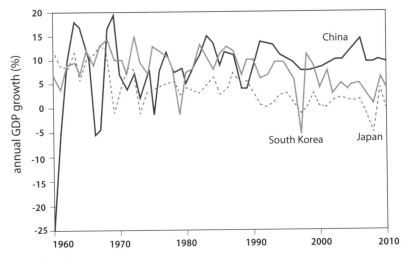

Figure 5.1
Annual rates of GDP growth in Japan, South Korea, and China, 1960–2010. Plotted from World Bank data (World Bank 2018).

13 years of annual GDP growth in excess of 10%, with peaks of 14–15% in 1984, 1992, and 2007 (World Bank 2018). But when comparing these trajectories (figure 5.1) we must keep in mind that the actual Chinese rates have been substantially smaller. One giveaway was the fact that annual GDP growth rates were reported to surpass 7% even as electricity generation (considered a good proxy of economic growth) was flat or barely increasing, but finding a widely acceptable correction factor has been elusive (Koch-Weser 2013; Owyang and Shell 2017).

Tracing the growth of economies can be done by focusing on some key proxy measures of key inputs (total energy or electricity demand, food supply), products (steel, cars) or product groups (total manufacturing output) but by far the most revealing commonly used indicator, gross domestic product, is also one that is questionable, both because of how it is accounted for and what it omits. In any case, this measure (particularly in an internationally comparable form) has become widely available only after WWII although some ingenious reconstructions have quantified it for some countries as far back as the late early modern era (late 1700s) and attempts were even made to estimate it for select years in the Middle Ages and in antiquity (Maddison 2007).

I will start my coverage by reviewing these grand historic contours of the growth of the global economy and of its key national (or imperial) actors.

Then I will proceed with a more detailed coverage of modern economic growth, focusing first on its major sectoral constituents before concentrating on longer historic trends for the leading countries with the best statistical coverage (US, UK, France, Japan) and on the recent rise of China. I will also address the most obvious weaknesses of the standard GDP approach and look at some additional or alternative ways to assess economic growth and its wider impacts, including the Human Development Index and recent efforts to measure subjective satisfaction with life and to compare self-assessed happiness on the global scale.

Populations

Interest in population growth has a long history and there is no shortage of comprehensive analyses at the global level (McEvedy and Jones 1978; Keyfitz and Flieger 1971, 1991; Livi-Bacci 2012; Bashford 2014), as well as those focusing on continents (Livi-Bacci 2000; Liu et al. 2001; Groth and May 2017; Poot and Roskruge 2018) and on major nations (Poston and Yaukey 1992; Dyson et al. 2005). Rising numbers of people have had many inevitable impacts on national and global capacities to supply adequate nutrition and to sustain desirable levels of global economic growth, as well on the state of the Earth's environment and on the strategic options of major world powers. The first linkage, addressed just before the end of the 18th century by Thomas Robert Malthus, has remained a matter of concern ever since (Malthus 1798; Godwin 1820; Smith 1951; Meynen 1968; Cohen 1995; Dolan 2000).

During the early 1970s this concern was potentiated by claims of imminent resource scarcities and a perilously deteriorating state of the global environment (Meadows et al. 1972). In turn, these claims were challenged by those who saw growing populations as the ultimate resource (Simon 1981; Simon and Kahn 1984). More recently, population growth has been seen as part of a much larger challenge of coping with anthropogenic global warming, particularly in African countries which will experience the largest population increments during the 21st century while many of them already face serious environmental degradation and recurrent droughts.

The declining importance of physical labor—due to advancing mechanization, automation, robotization, and the large-scale adoption of computerized controls in modern agriculture, extractive industries, manufacturing, and transportation, and most recently also in a wide range of services—has helped to weaken the link between a nation's population and economic might, but size still matters. That is why even some populous countries are concerned about their future status as their populations will continue to decline. Standard projections show that by 2050 Japan will have fewer people than the Philippines, and that Russia's population might be smaller than that of Vietnam (UN 2017).

The basic dynamics of population growth is simple. Natural increase (growth of a population) is the difference between natality and mortality and these vital statistics are expressed as births and deaths per 1,000 people. But their dominant levels, prolonged trends, or relatively sudden shifts result from complex interplays of factors ranging from nutrition and life expectancy to economic status and attitudes to marriage and family. As a result, high accuracy of long-range forecasts of population growth remains elusive, but a relative abundance of historical information allows us to reconstruct past growth trends with a high degree of confidence as well as to identify all major factors responsible for epochal shifts in global and national population trajectories.

In premodern societies, birth rates were very high but so were death rates, due to inadequate nutrition, recurrent epidemics, pandemics, and violent conflicts. As a result, natural population growth was very low. Modern health care, industrialization, and urbanization transformed the premodern pattern as both rates declined, with birth rate declines preceding the reduction in mortalities and resulting in a temporary acceleration of natural growth before both rates found new, much lower, equilibria in modern affluent societies. In some European countries this demographic transition took a few centuries to run its course; in a few East Asian countries it was completed in just two generations.

The birth rate is a function of fertility, the number of children born to a woman during the course of her fertile years. Some premodern societies took steps to reduce fertility but in most traditional settings the rate was close to its biological maximum (about seven). Slightly lower total fertility rates, on the order of 5–6 births per female's fertile span, are still found in some sub-Saharan countries, notably in Burkina Faso, Niger, Nigeria, Mali, and Somalia. In contrast, total fertility rates in many affluent countries, including Japan, Germany, and Italy, are just around 1.4, far below the replacement rate of 2.1. In most national cases, natural increase captures all but a small fraction of total population growth but net migration (the difference between immigration and emigration) has been an important factor in the history of many countries and regions.

History of Population Growth

My inquiry into global population growth will start in prehistory when the bottlenecks in population size, caused by environmental changes, shaped the evolution of hominins far more than any periods of accelerated growth.

Paleontological findings support the occurrence of a population size bottleneck at the very origin of the evolution of the *Homo sapiens* lineage some 2 million years ago (Hawks et al. 2000). Anatomically modern humans first appeared around 190,000 years ago, and mitochondrial DNA studies indicate that during the next 100,000 years their numbers in small and isolated African groups remained close to extinction (Behar et al. 2008). Beyond Africa, the first fossil evidence of the species is as early as 100,000 years ago in the Middle East, 80,000 years ago in China, and 65,000 years ago in Australia (Clarkson et al. 2017) and the ancestors of all contemporary non-African people met and admixed with Neanderthals, with the hybridization taking place about 50,000 years ago, in some places even much earlier (Harris and Nielsen 2017).

And the very existence of humans was imperiled by a super-eruption of Sumatra's Toba volcano about 74,000 years ago (Chesner et al. 1991). The eruption produced about 2,700 km^3 of ejecta (second only to La Garita that deposited the Fish Canyon Tuff in Colorado 27.8 million years ago), which covered at least 1% of the Earth's surface with more than 10 cm of ash, with far greater impact in Southeast Asia. Studies of mitochondrial DNA have identified a severe population shrinkage that took place between 80,000 and 70,000 years ago: Toba's megavolcanic eruption is the best explanation of this late Pleistocene population bottleneck that reduced the global total to fewer than 10,000 individuals and brought the species close to extinction and ending its evolution (Harpending et al. 1993; Ambrose 1998). Ambrose (2003) concluded that the bottleneck would not have been shorter than 20 generations and may have been longer than 500 but that it was not, like other Cenozoic explosive volcanic eruptions of comparable magnitude, accompanied by a mass extinction of animal species.

Once the human migrations resumed, they proceeded to settle all of the planet's habitable environments. The date of the first wave that reached North America remains uncertain. Available archaeological evidence suggests that the first peopling of the continent took place about 14,000 years ago, long after the last glacial maximum—but new radiocarbon dating on cut-marked bones from of the Bluefish Caves in Yukon shows that humans occupied the site as early as 24,000 years before the present (Bourgeon et al. 2017). In any case, there is no doubt that a few thousand years before the end of the Pleistocene epoch (it came 11,700 years ago) all non-glaciated land masses were sparsely inhabited.

The Holocene epoch, with its warmer temperatures and higher CO_2 levels, was conducive to settled agriculture: as Richerson et al. (2001) put it, agriculture was impossible during the Pleistocene but mandatory during the Holocene. The adoption and diffusion of settled farming during the Neolithic era—starting 11,000–12,000 years ago in the Middle East and eventually spreading to all continents with the exception of Australia— was credited with the first notable population increase. This is ascribed to an expanded and more reliable food supply. This Neolithic demographic transition (also called, inaccurately because it was a long process, Neolithic or agricultural revolution) was seen as the first notable period of population growth and its extent has been documented by a variety of linguistic, anthropological, and archaeological evidence (Barker 2009).

One of the convincing archaeological studies based on cemetery sequences has shown an abrupt increase in the proportion of juvenile skeletons as an indicator of an increase in the total fertility rate, a shift seen as one of the fundamental structural processes of human history (Bocquet-Appel and Bar-Yosef 2008; Bocquet-Appel 2011). A study based on 217 skeletons of foragers and 262 skeletons of Neolithic farmers who succeeded them in the southern Levant after 8,300 BCE showed very slight increases of life expectancy at birth and an increase in maternal mortality as a result of a concomitant increase in fertility (Eshed et al. 2004).

But as is the case with many grand generalizations, both the intensity and the unprecedented nature of the Neolithic demographic transition are arguable (as is the revolutionary description of a process that was clearly evolutionary, extending across millennia). A recent sequencing of 36 diverse Y chromosomes from Africa, Europe, Asia, and the Americas indicates a previously unknown period of relatively rapid population expansion that took place 40,000 to 50,000 years ago, that is between the migration out of Africa and the later Neolithic growth (Wei et al. 2013). This extreme population increase is seen as the result of an eventual adaptation to new mountainous and forested environments of the inner continents.

And after analyzing 910 random samples of mitochondrial DNA (collected by the 1000 Genome Project) from 11 populations in Africa, Europe, and the Americas, Zheng et al. (2012) found that in all cases most major lineage expansions (11 out of 15 in Africa, all autochthonous lineages in Europe and the Americas) coalesced before the first appearance of agriculture and that major population expansions took place after the Last Glacial Maximum but before the Neolithic era; they suggested that the rising temperatures and growing populations actually provided the stimulus for the introduction of agriculture. And a new approach to studying the growth of prehistoric populations indicates that contemporaneous foragers and agriculturalists had very similar population growth rates. This approach uses the summed probability distribution of calibrated radiocarbon measurements (with large populations producing more datable material) as a proxy for the relative size of a population as a function of time (Zahid et al. 2016).

The study compared European societies that were either already farming or transitioning to agriculture with the foraging societies in Wyoming and Colorado during the period of 800 to 13,000 years before the present and their findings challenge the common impression that the advent of farming was linked to higher population growth. They discovered the same rate of population growth, 0.04% per year, that was sustained at near-equilibrium levels for millennia, and they concluded that population growth was governed primarily by the global climate and species-specific factors rather than by the regional environment or particular subsistence practices.

But the evidence for rapid global population expansions after the adoption of agriculture is quite convincing and analysis of 425 globally distributed whole mitochondrial genomes (separating lineages associated with agricultural populations from those associated with foragers) also reveals important differences in its regional onset and rate (Gignoux et al. 2011). The timing of population growth based on genetic data corresponds well to dates of agricultural origins established by archaeological evidence, and comparisons of population growth rates show that they were five times higher after the adoption of agricultural practices than during the preceding periods of foraging subsistence.

In West Africa, where the first evidence of agriculture dates to about 5,000 years ago, population growth began about 4,600 years ago and its annual rate averaged 0.032%, or nearly five times the rate the region experienced during the Upper Paleolithic about 40,000 years ago. In Europe, where the first evidence of agriculture dates to about 7,800 years ago, the average annual growth rate reached 0.058% (with maxima up to about 0.25%) compared to 0.021% during the last glacial period, while the difference between the Holocene and Upper Paleolithic population growth rates for Southeast Asia is nearly sixfold (0.063 vs. 0.011%).

Gignoux et al. (2011) set the Neolithic growth rate on the order of 0.06%. This growth rate implied a doubling of the population in more than a millennium, 1,167 years to be exact. Carneiro and Hilse (1966) came to the same order-of-magnitude conclusion by considering the dynamics of the Near Eastern population growing from a base of 100,000 people in 8,000 BCE: only rates between 0.08% and 0.12% would give a plausible result. Claims of a rapid Neolithic growth rate are thus valid only in relation to some (but not all) periods of the preceding growth of foraging societies. But it is one thing to identify periods of accelerated prehistorical population growth and quite another to come up with defensible aggregate counts on regional, continental, or global levels.

All published totals must be seen merely as indicators of relative progress rather than markers of actual growth. Prehistoric population sizes have been

calculated by assuming average hunter-gatherer densities across the estimated totals of inhabited areas; obviously, both of these numbers have wide
error margins. A model by Hawks et al. (2000) has the total passing through
half a million 777,000 years ago and 1.3 million about 480,000 years ago.
In contrast, Harpending et al. (1993), basing their estimate on archaeological site distributions and a low assumed population density, put the global
total as low as 125,000 between one and half a million years ago.

Permanent settlements of emerging and expanding agricultural societies have left behind a great deal of physical evidence, and for later periods (starting around 3,000 BCE) we can reconstruct population totals and
growth rates from a variety of indicators ranging through the size of settlements, intensity of crop cultivation, skeletal analyses, and written records.
The history of population censuses begins in antiquity but these irregular
activities were not in the same category as the periodic modern efforts: they
counted, for taxation or military purposes, only certain segments of population, usually adult males. As a result, even the best available population
estimates for the most important antique empires are highly uncertain.
There is no better illustration of this reality than our understanding of the
Roman population.

Early imperial censuses in Egypt provide the best information but preserved records are quite marginal (just hundreds of individuals in a population estimated to be in millions) and hence their use to derive population
totals and to apply them to other parts of the empire is questionable
(Bagnall and Frier 1994; Smil 2010c). Analyses of tombstone inscriptions
and burial grounds are no less problematic (Parkin 1992). Not surprisingly,
"our ignorance of ancient population is one of the biggest obstacles to our
understanding of Roman history" (Scheidel 2007, 2). As for the imperial
totals, Beloch's (1886) much-cited estimate was 54 million people in 14
CE, McEvedy and Jones (1978) estimated 40.25 million at the beginning
of the 1st century CE, Frier's (2000) total for the same period is 45.5 million, and Maddison (2007) used 44 million. Beloch (1886) put the empire's
population at 100 million people in the 2nd century CE, McEvedy and
Jones (1978) set it at 45 million in 200 CE, and Frier (2000) at 61.4 million
in 164 CE.

With the exception of China, there are no systematic and consistent
series of population estimates going back for more than a millennium.
Thanks to China's exceptional censuses, its population growth can be reconstructed since the beginning of the common era and estimates are available for most of the preceding millennium (Cartier 2002). The trajectory
extending over nearly three millennia shows periods of growth (peace and

prosperity) alternating with significant population declines and an overall rise from about 20 million in 800 BCE to 60 million at the beginning of CE, 100 million by the year 1100, 140 million in 1700, and 1.26 billion in the year 2000.

Medieval European population data are largely lacking, and the coverage improves only during the early modern era (Biraben 2003). Historical population estimates (starting in antiquity) and eventual census data for major countries aggregated on continental, regional, and global scales were collected by McEvedy and Jones (1978), and (with the emphasis on the past three centuries) by Reinhard et al. (1988). Global series (some going back to 10,000 BCE) were also published by Durand (1974), Thomlinson (1975), Haub (1995), the United Nations (UN 1999), and Biraben (2003), and all series are compared in USCB (2016b). Not surprisingly, agreement among the estimates declines as we move further into the past: differences between lower and upper values are two- to fourfold for 5000 BCE, more than twofold at the beginning of the common era, still nearly 40% in 1800, less than 20% in 1900, and only about 5% by 1950.

Very large uncertainties regarding the trajectory of all prehistoric populations make it impossible to come up with a reliable total of people who ever lived on earth. Kaneda and Haub (2018) applied changing birth rates to different periods and ended up with 108.5 billion births by 2017. That would mean that about 7% of all people ever born are alive today, a lot less than has been claimed in the media during the past 50 years, but still a fairly high share considering the longevity of our species.

Inaccuracies in historic estimates have a much smaller effect on calculating the correct magnitudes of average growth rates. During the first millennium of the common era they remained below 0.05% a year, during some centuries amounting to less than half of that rate. The next 500 years, between 1000 and 1500, saw the average more than doubling to about 0.1% a year and then doubling again during the 16th century. A growth dip during the 17th century was followed by a recovery to around 0.2% during the 18th century; global population increments averaged 0.8% during the 19th and about 1.35% a year during the 20th century.

Plotting estimated global population growth during the past 50,000 years on a linear scale yields an essentially flat line for 99% of the time followed by a near-vertical ascent. On a semilogarithmic scale the same ascent will appear as a series of stepwise rises interspersed with periods of rapid gains, with the last one resulting in the near-quadrupling of the total during the 20th century (figure 5.2). Restricting the trace to the last three centuries when more reliable data can be plotted shows a very high fit into

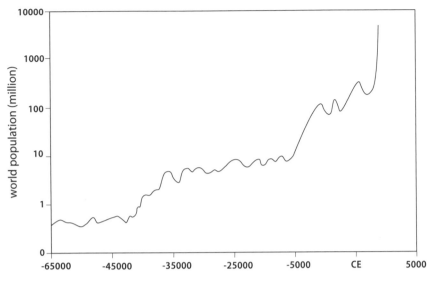

Figure 5.2
World population growth during the past 65,000 years plotted on a semi-logarithmic graph based on Biraben (2003).

a symmetrical four-parameter logistic curve still ascending in 2015 and pointing to about 10 billion people by 2050.

Other interpretations are possible. As already noted in chapter 1, Cailleux (1951) was the first demographer to realize that pre-1960 global population growth followed a hyperbolic function, and von Foerster et al. (1960, 1291) calculated that continuation of that growth would lead to a singularity (reaching infinite growth) by November 13 of 2026. One may think this was done more in jest—but von Foerster et al. strenuously defended themselves when Shinbrot (1961, 940) suggested that their article "would be too ridiculous to comment on if it were not such an outstanding example of the inadmissible use of mathematics to prop up a manifestly absurd conclusion."

Of course, what would be ridiculous would be to assume that such growth can come even close to reaching a singularity—but there is no doubt that the pre-1960 rise of global population did fit a hyperbolic growth pattern and several studies examined that historic progression and its implications (von Hoerner 1975; Kapitsa 1992; Kremer 1993; Korotayev et al. 2006; R. W. Nielsen 2015; R. Nielsen et al. 2017). Fears generated by this accelerating growth were a major factor in the emergence of the Western environmental movement of the 1960s. In 1968 Paul Ehrlich, an entomologist (specializing in butterflies) at Stanford University, published *The Population Bomb*, whose utterly dystopic predictions were given wide publicity by mass media eager to disseminate more bad news: "The battle to feed all of humanity is over. In the 1970s the world will undergo famines—hundreds of millions of people are going to starve to death in spite of any crash programs embarked on now" (Ehrlich 1968, 132). That was a spectacularly wrong prediction. Between 1968 and 2017 the world's population more than doubled (from 3.5 to 7.5 billion) and yet by 2015 the total number of malnourished people had declined to fewer than 800 million or just below 13% of the world population compared to more than 23% a quarter century before, and the Food and Agriculture Organization set its sights on the virtual eradication of that debilitating condition (FAO 2015b).

Coincidentally, it was also during the 1960s that the unprecedented growth rate began to moderate (as it had to) and the unmistakable beginnings of yet another S-curve began to form. Different data bases give different years of peak annual growth, all between 1962 and 1969. According to World Bank's annual growth rate series, the first peak was 2.107% in 1966 and then a marginally higher rate of 2.109% in 1969 (World Bank 2018). Given the inherent uncertainties of global population counts, accuracy to the third decimal place should be discounted, and the best conclusion is that relative growth peaked at about 2.1% during the mid-1960s, nearly an order of magnitude higher than three centuries earlier when it was no higher than 0.22% (figure 5.3). This was followed by a relatively rapid decline to

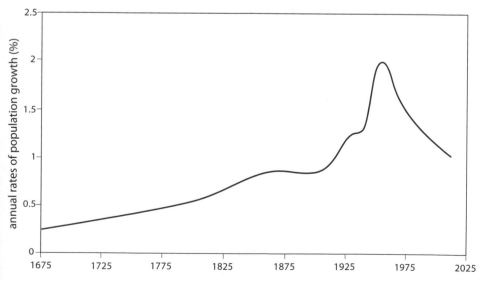

Figure 5.3
Annual rates of world population growth, 1675–2018. Calculated from data in USCB (2016a) and World Bank (2018).

1.75% by 1980, 1.32% by the year 2000, 1.23% by 2010, and 1.09% by 2018 (World Bank 2018). Decadal averages were 1.84% for the 1970s, 1.69% for the 1980s and 1.42% during the 1990s, and then the rate dropped to 1.23% during the first decade of the 21st century, altogether a 40% decline in five decades (by 2016 it was just 1.18%).

Absolute annual increments rose from 50 million in 1950 to the peak growth of the human population at about 87 million between 1985 and 1990, and the combination of a declining growth rate and a larger population base means that in 2015 the world population increased still by about 84 million people. This combination has also resulted in declining time spans required to add a billion people. The first billion was reached in 1804, some 200,000 years following the emergence of *Homo sapiens*; 123 years were needed to reach 2 billion (in 1927), 33 years to get to 3 billion (in 1960), 14 years to 4 billion (in 1974), 13 years to 5 billion (in 1987), 12 years to 6 billion (in 1999), and another 12 years to 7 billion (in 2011), and it will have taken 13 years to reach 8 billion (in 2024).

What would Thomas Robert Malthus say if he could see this phenomenal rise to more than 7 billion people from less than 1 billion at the time he wrote his famous essay on the principle of population in 1798? His has been certainly the most often quoted and paraphrased verdict regarding the long-term growth of any variable and hence it is worth citing at length. Malthus based his conclusions on two postulates:

> First, That food is necessary to the existence of man. Secondly, That the passion between the sexes is necessary and will remain nearly in its present state…Assuming then my postulata as granted, I say, that the power of population is indefinitely greater than the power in the earth to produce subsistence for man. Population, when unchecked, increases in a geometrical ratio. Subsistence increases only in an arithmetical ratio…By that law of our nature which makes food necessary to the life of man, the effects of these two unequal powers must be kept equal. This implies a strong and constantly operating check on population from the difficulty of subsistence. (Malthus 1798, 4–5)

Malthus drew an unforgiving conclusion from what he saw as an unbridgeable gap between an exponentially growing population and its linearly growing means of subsistence.

> I see no way by which man can escape from the weight of this law…No fancied equality, no agrarian regulations in their utmost extent, could remove the pressure of it even for a single century. And it appears, therefore, to be decisive against the possible existence of a society, all the members of which should live in ease, happiness, and comparative leisure: and feel no anxiety about providing the means of subsistence for themselves and families. (Malthus 1798, 5)

Malthusian fears proved to be quite resilient but he himself hinted at a possibility of a different outcome. As he closed the fourth edition of his essay, Malthus argued that his inquiry should not

> make us give up the improvement of human society in despair ... And although we cannot expect that the virtue and happiness of mankind will keep pace with the brilliant career of physical discovery; yet, if we are not wanting to ourselves, we may confidently indulge the hope, that, to no unimportant extent, they will be influenced by its progress and will partake in its success. (Malthus 1807, 426–427)

The extent of that progress was impressive indeed. As I have shown in chapter 2, after centuries of stagnation and very slow increments, crop yields of staple grains doubled, or even more than doubled after WWII, food waste (although still unacceptably high) was reduced by better storage methods, and improved nutrition could not only support much enlarged populations but do so by supplying unprecedented average per capita intakes of high-quality protein. As also described in chapter 2, these nutritional improvements were promptly translated into significant gains in the average height and body mass of new generations.

Malthus's basic assumption is unassailable: the power of population growth is indeed much greater than the capacity to produce adequate subsistence—but that applies only when, as he correctly stated, the population growth is unchecked. But he was obviously wrong to believe that it will be "the difficulty of subsistence" that will always provide "a strong and constantly operating check." Instead, population growth has undergone a fundamental transformation through the process of demographic transition, and our abilities to support a larger population (and with better nutrition) have been transformed no less fundamentally by reliance on high direct and indirect energy subsidies (mechanization, irrigation, fertilization, pesticides) that have resulted in increasing harvests.

Demographic Transition

The unprecedented population growth of the past two centuries is explained by the gradual progress of the demographic transition, the outcome of a complex process of declining death rates (mortality) and birth rates (natality) that was conceptualized by Warren Thompson (1929), called first a "demographic transition" by Landry (1934), and received its standard (classic) formulations from Notestein (1945) and Davis (1945). After WWII it became a subject of increasing attention not only among demographers but also among economists and sociologists. Closer looks have included not only theoretical analyses and general process summaries (Chesnais 1992; Kirk

1996; Caldwell 2006) but also specific regional and national studies (Lee and Reher 2011; Canning et al. 2015) and critical deconstructions of the concept (Szreter 1993).

Traditional, pretransition, societies had both high birth rates and high death rates (with death rates prone to spikes caused by epidemics and warfare) and this combination produced fluctuating, but always very low annual rates (less than 0.1% or even below 0.05%) of natural increase. During the earliest stage of demographic transitions, the death rate begins to fall, in some cases relatively rapidly (as a result of better nutrition and better health care), while birth rates remain at traditionally high levels and this combination results in high rates of population growth (commonly in excess of 1%, that is an order of magnitude higher than in pretransition societies). Eventually birth rates begin to fall as well (and, again, rather precipitously in some cases) and population increase decelerates. A society that has undergone a demographic transition finds itself at a new equilibrium as low birth rates and low death rates result in low natural increases, or even in no growth and absolute population decline.

The process of demographic transition began first in European countries, where it took up to two centuries. For example, Finland's crude death rates fell from about 30/1,000 people in 1750 to 10 in 1950, while during the same two centuries crude birth rates declined from more than 40 to just over 20; while Swedish birth rates stayed between 30 and 35 until the early 1860s, death rates began to decline from their longstanding rates of 25–30 after 1820, and both rates were lowered to just above 10 by the late 1970s (CSO 1975). Somewhat faster transitions, but still generations long, are statistically well documented for a number of other European countries. Japan was the first populous Asian country to undergo the process of demographic transition. Crude death rates remained above 20 until the early 1920s and were more than halved in just 30 years, while birth rates fell from about 35 in the early 1920s to just above 10 by the early 1980s.

Declining mortalities were accompanied by rising life expectancies. During the century and a half between 1850 and the year 2000 the highest life expectancies in most European countries, the US, and Japan increased in an almost perfectly linear manner, doubling from about 40 to almost 80 years (averages for both sexes, with women in all societies living longer), with the Japanese female life span (the longest in the world) gaining a decade between 1970 and the year 2000 and surpassing 85 years by the year 2010 (SB 2017a). The flu pandemic of 1918 and WWII were the only periods of large-scale temporary reversals of life expectancy.

Bongaarts (2006) decomposed the life expectancy trends of 16 high-income countries into juvenile, background (adult), and senescent mortality and showed that gains came in all of these categories. After he removed the first two trends plus smoking-induced mortality, he concluded that senescent life expectancy had increased almost linearly between 1950 and 2000 at a combined (male and female) rate of 0.15 years per year, and thought it plausible that this trend might continue for a few more decades. Recent Japanese female life expectancies have gone above the previously forecast limits of the maximum average life and this has led some demographers to argue that further substantial extensions are to come (Oeppen and Vaupel 2002).

An alternative way to quantify the process of demographic transition is to focus on changing fertility. The total fertility rate (TFR) is the average number of children that would be born per woman if all women were to live through their entire reproductive lives (with menopause setting in at different ages, mostly between 45 and 50) and bore children according to their age-specific fertility. The total fertility rate of most premodern societies was around five and its global average was still nearly that high during the early 1950s. Subsequently, it fell to three in the early 1990s and to less than 2.5 (2.36) during 2010–2015, approaching the replacement fertility rate, which is an average of 2.1 children per women. An additional 0.1 is needed to compensate for girls who will not survive to fecund age in modern societies but the increment has to be higher in countries where infant and childhood mortality remains unacceptably high.

High fertilities began to fall first in Europe and their earliest estimated declines can be dated to 1827 in France, with many western and central European countries following during the second half of the 19th century—Sweden in 1877, Belgium in 1881, Switzerland in 1887, Germany in 1888, UK in 1893, Netherlands in 1897, Denmark in 1898. In all but a few European countries, fertility began to drop before the onset of WWI (Newson and Richerson 2009). The trend continued in Europe, as well as in North America and Japan, during the 1920s and, mostly, also during the 1930s—but then came one of the most remarkable periods of population growth, which has become known as the baby boom. This spell of demographic resurgence was especially evident in the countries that participated in WWII. Its duration is delimited sometimes quite precisely (1945–1964), sometimes a bit more loosely (mid to late 1940s to mid to late 1960s).

The baby boom followed decades of declining birth rates dating back to the late 19th century. Its simplistic explanation was as a recuperation of childbearing postponed due to the economic depression of the 1930s and WWII in the first half of the 1940s. But that could explain only a birth rate spike of a short duration, not a phenomenon that lasted a generation. As Van Bavel and Reher (2013) noted, fertility recovery began in many countries during the late 1930s and early 1940s, and the high fertility of the 1950s and 1960s resulted from a combination of larger average family size in cohorts born during the Depression and higher nuptiality, due both to higher shares of married people and marriages at a young age.

The baby boom was followed by a pronounced resumption of low fertility, in many countries sinking far below the replacement level, the boom's end as unexpected as its onset. This new combination of interrelated trends began in some northern and western European countries during the late 1960s, and in 1986 it was labeled the second demographic transition (Lesthaeghe and van de Kaa 1986; Lesthaeghe and Neidert 2006). This shift in values has weakened the traditional family, bringing widespread postponement of marriages, much lower marriage rates, and much higher shares of nonmarital births. The reduction of fertility to long-term sub-replacement level has been linked to several social, behavioral, and economic features characteristic of modern postindustrial states. These include growing individualism (stress on self-actualization and autonomy) and secularization, rising symmetry in sex roles, availability of welfare, wider access to higher education, and changes brought by the rise of the service economy and electronic communication (Sobotka 2008; Lesthaege 2014).

As with all broad generalizations, the concept of the second demographic transition has been criticized (after all, in some affected countries cohort fertility rates have remained fairly close to the replacement level) and some observers questioned its validity beyond non-European (or non-Western) cultures. But there is no doubt about the direction of the fertility change, and about the presence of the second demographic transition in non-European settings, including parts of East Asia and Latin America (Lesthaege 2014). Reliable statistics document Europe's rapid fertility declines once the post-WWII baby boom was over. During the 1950s Europe's highest fertilities (close to or even above 3.0) were throughout the Catholic south, but by the century's end Spaniards and Italians shared the continent's lowest fertility rates with Czechs, Hungarians, and Bulgarians (Kohler et al. 2002).

By the mid-1970s most of the EU's total fertility rates had declined below the replacement level, by the century's end they had declined to less than 1.5 for the union's largest countries, and the post-2000 accession of new members made little difference with the EU-28 mean at just 1.58 in 2015 (Eurostat 2017b). What Kohler et al. (2002) called the lowest-low fertility (TFR below 1.3) had emerged for the first time in Europe during the 1990s. By the decade's end, 14 countries in eastern, central and southern Europe (with a total population of more than 370 million) were in that category. The EU-28 average has been somewhat higher but still far below replacement level: 1.58 in 2015, with 13 countries at or below 1.5, Portugal at the bottom with 1.31, and France at the top with 1.96 (Eurostat 2017b). Moreover, by 2016, 12 of the 28 EU states had already seen more than one year of absolute population decline, while the EU as a whole had a total population about 2.8% larger in 2016 than it had a decade earlier (Eurostat 2017a).

With the exception of Japan, where fertility rates began to decline in 1950, the fertility transition in East and Southeast Asia dates only to the 1960s and 1970s: the first year of declining fertility was 1962 in South Korea, 1963 in Philippines, 1966 in Thailand, 1969 in China, 1972 in Indonesia, and 1975 in Vietnam (Newson and Richerson 2009). In contrast to Europe, the East Asian transitions were accomplished just in a matter of one or two generations: by 2017 Indonesia had fertility at the replacement level while South Korea, China, Thailand, and Vietnam had fertilities far below it, as low as 1.25 in South Korea (CIA 2017).

When fertilities began to decline in East Asia, they remained high throughout the Middle East. By 2016 they were still above three in Egypt, Jordan, and Iraq, but at, or below, the replacement level in Saudi Arabia, Libya, and Iran. In fact, Iran has been through one of the fastest demographic transitions ever, as the average fertility fell rapidly from close to seven during the late 1970s (when the Shah was exiled and Khomeini took control) to below replacement level (1.8) by 2016. In most Latin American countries, fertility declines began, as in East Asia, during the 1960s and 1970s, leaving sub-Saharan Africa as the only major part of the world with recalcitrantly high fertilities (Winter and Teitelbaum 2013).

Opinion surveys show that the number of children seen as ideal in Asia's, and the world's, two largest countries (China and India) is now (at just two) slightly lower than in the US and UK, but a study of the number of children desired by married woman based on interviews done between 1999 and 2008 showed West and Central Africa far above any other regions. Ideal totals were as incredibly high as 9.2 in Chad and 9.1 in Niger, and no lower than 4.6 in Ghana, with the region's mean above six (USAID 2010). Those numbers have declined a bit, but fertility estimates for 2016 remain high, at 6.6 for Niger, 6 for Mali, and 5.1 for Nigeria (CIA 2017). And fertilities remain very high throughout most of East and Southern Africa: above five in Ethiopia, Somalia, Burundi, Uganda, Tanzania, Mozambique, Malawi, and Zambia (Canning et al. 2015).

But even an immediate drop to replacement fertility in formerly high-fertility populations will be still followed by decades of population growth because the previous period of high fertility gave rise to a high proportion of women of reproductive age: age-specific fertility may decline but total births keep rising. Keyfitz and Flieger (1971) called this phenomenon population momentum and Blue and Espenshade (2011) studied its trajectories across the demographic transitions. A new equilibrium is established only after the population momentum gets spent, but how stable that equilibrium will be has been highly country-specific. In some countries, declining fertilities have continued to go far below the replacement level and this trend must bring, even with record life expectancies, absolute population declines.

Future Population Growth
Long-range forecasting of population growth has been recently receiving an unprecedented amount of attention (Keyfitz and Flieger 1991; Cohen 1995; de Gans 1999; Bongaarts and Bulatao 2000; Newbold 2006; de Beer 2013)—but it remains an inherently uncertain enterprise. Three institutions (the United Nations, the World Bank, and the International Institute for Applied Systems Analysis) have been publishing projections that extend for many decades and even more than a century into the future. Standard deterministic projections of long-term population growth attempt to capture the uncertainties by presenting three scenarios (high-medium-low). The Department of Social and Economic Affairs of the United Nations has been their most cited producer. Its forecasts for the global total in 2050 (all for the medium variant) changed from 9.36 billion in 1996 to 8.91 billion in 1998, then up again to 9.32 billion in the year 2000 and 9.73 in 2015 (UN 2001, 2017).

Standard forecasts are based on outlining the future paths of vital rates by constructing scenarios of cohort-specific mortalities and fertilities, but Goldstein and Stecklov (2002) suggest that it may be better to use simple calculations based on an analytical model. Because the outcomes of standard cohort-specific scenarios are driven by assumptions about the total fertility rate and life expectancy, it might appear that the task has actually become easier since the worldwide demographic transition has been marked by demonstrable similarities. Raftery et al. (2012) argued in favor of Bayesian probabilistic predictions and the result of their modeling led them to conclude that the current United Nations high and low variants greatly underestimate the number of very old people in 2050 and also underestimate the uncertainty for high-fertility countries while overstating the uncertainty for countries that have already completed the demographic transition. Using cumulative probabilities is a much less misleading option—but one still affected by model assumptions.

The notable exception of most sub-Saharan countries aside, the fertility transition has been a truly global process, as has been rising life expectancy, and this means that the majority of the world's population has been taking part in a demographic convergence (Wilson 2011). But a closer look reveals that neither fertility nor life expectancy are easy to forecast in the very long run. The 20th-century growth rate of the maximum life span may not continue during the 21st century, parts of Africa (from where most of the future growth will come, in any case) have seen a slower fertility decline than in other regions, and temporary recoveries of regional fertility cannot be excluded.

Undoubtedly, the key uncertainty about the coming size of the global population concerns the future course of fertilities. For the richest countries, the uncertainty is about the extent of decline: will they remain close to where they are today, that is well below the replacement ratio, will they decline even more, or will they, at least partially, rebound? The same questions can be asked for the still much poorer but much more populous East Asian countries that have undergone a rapid demographic transition. The possibility of further fertility declines has been conceptualized by Lutz et al. (2006) as the low fertility trap: once a country's fertility declines to a very low level, three self-reinforcing mechanisms can prevent it from ever rising again.

The demographic component is the negative momentum of the established decline, as delayed childbirths and long spells of low fertility produce sequentially smaller and smaller infant cohorts. The normative component (with fewer and fewer children around) changes the perception of the ideal family size and sets it well below the replacement level. And the economic component arises from the altered relationship between personal aspirations and expected income: an aging population and shrinking labor force bring reduced social benefits, higher taxes, and lower disposable income, conditions when not only having children but even getting married becomes an unaffordable option.

Will sub-Saharan fertilities follow a long slow decline or will some countries experience rapid reductions akin to shifts that took place in Iran or South Korea? Even optimistically expected moderation will not be enough to reduce the absolute rate of Africa's population growth and it will rise from about 30 million a year in 2017 to at least 42 million a year by 2050, and nearly 55% of the world's population growth during the first half of the 21st century will come from the continent. Moreover, the latest assessments show that (for deep-seated cultural and kinship reasons) most African societies still harbor resistance (not evident in other major regions) to lowering fertilities below moderate levels (TFR<4) and hence the future course of fertility transition in sub-Saharan Africa remains highly uncertain (Casterline and Bongaarts 2017).

Uncertainties concerning the lengthening of life expectancies will make a much smaller difference to any eventual global aggregates. Recent studies provide convincing evidence that the room for further gains in maximum life expectancy (at birth) is diminishing. US data for both sexes and all races show a linear gain of 21 years (153 days per year, from 47.3 to 68.2 years) during the first half of the 20th century and only 8.6 years (63 days per year, from 68.2 to 76.8 years) during the second half (CDC 2011). This makes for a very close logistic fit pointing to a maximum of about 79 years by 2050. Disaggregated data show the fastest improvement among African American women, from 33.5 years in 1900 to 62.5 years in 1950 (212 days per year) followed by a much slower extension to 75.1 years in the year 2000 (only 92 days a year).

Zijdeman and de Silva (2014) compiled a global survey starting in 1820 and extending to the early years of the 21st century. High-quality Swedish data available for the entire studied period show a near-doubling of average life expectancy, from 41.6 in the 1820s to 80.5 years in the 2000s. The growth trajectory fits closely a symmetrical logistic curve with the inflection point in 1922 and indicating the gain of another year by 2050 (figure 5.4). Trajectories for France and the UK are very similar. Those countries whose life expectancy record covers the entire 20th century (UK, Iceland, Norway, Finland, Netherlands, Spain, Switzerland) experienced two distinct periods of rising longevity, with faster linear gains (about two decades in half a century) up to 1950, and slower gains afterwards (Dong et al. 2016).

That study also considered maximum reported ages of death in France, Japan, US, and UK, the four countries with the largest number of supercentenarians (Dong et al. 2016). If there were no upper limit to the human life span, the largest increases in survival should be seen in ever-older age groups—and that, indeed, was the case between the 1970s and early 1990s but by the mid-1990s the gains began to level off at about 99 years. A further slight gain has followed but a newly forming plateau is clear: improvements in survival age decline after age 100, and the age at death of the world's oldest person has not risen since Jeanne Calment died at 122.4 years in 1997.

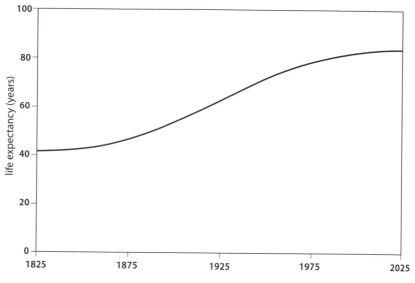

Figure 5.4

Average Swedish life expectancy since 1825. Curve fitted from data in Zijdeman and Silva (2014).

And I should note that her longevity and identity have been questioned (Zak 2018) and that the indisputably documented longevity records are all short of 120 years.

That is why Dong et al. (2016, 257) argue "that the maximum lifespan of humans is fixed and subject to natural constraints." This is not because there is a genetic program limit to the life span: as Olshansky (2016, 176) stresses,

> there is no fixed limit beyond which humans cannot live, but … there are, nevertheless, limits on the duration of life that are imposed by other genetically determined life-history traits. Think of constraints on running speed as an analogy. No genetic program specifically limits how fast humans can run, but biomechanical constraints on running speed are imposed by a fixed body design that evolved for other purposes.

The aging of elastin appears to be one of these biochemical constraints (Robert et al. 2008). This highly elastic protein is indispensable for the proper functioning of the cardiovascular system (mediating pressure wave propagation), lungs, ligaments, bladder, and skin. Age-related alterations of elastin include calcium accumulation, lipid deposition, and proteolytic degradation and quantitative evaluations of these processes indicate that the protein can maintain the elastic properties of the cardiorespiratory systems for up to about 120 years. This evidence makes it possible to forecast the highest female life expectancies at or slightly above 90 years by the middle of the 21st century, but it makes it highly unlikely that in the coming decades we will see a society whose average maximum life span will approach 100 years.

These conclusions would be disputed by those who point to experiments to rejuvenate human cells by extending telomeres, nucleotide sequences at the ends of a chromosome whose deterioration progresses with age, by reactivating telomerase (Jaskelioff et al. 2011) or by pursuing a life-expanding strategy of caloric restriction. But the former has been shown (as so many other great claims) only in laboratory mice, and the latter is easily conducted and very effective with laboratory invertebrates but ineffective with primates (Mattison et al. 2012) and it would be very difficult to maintain for a lifetime in humans. In any case, life span is controlled by so many genes that no single-variable intervention could make a decisive difference.

Long-Term Forecasts and Trajectories

Uncertainties about future fertility and, to a much lesser extent, about life expectancy explain why some leading demographers write about the end of world population growth coming in the foreseeable future, with a 60% probability that the global count will not exceed 10 billion people before 2100 (Lutz et al. 2001)—and other leading demographers in another leading journal can conclude that world population stabilization is unlikely during the 21st century, with an 80% probability that the global count will grow to 9.6–12.3 billion by 2100 (Gerland et al. 2014). Given the differences among major regions, a disaggregated probability forecast is more revealing. According to Scherbov et al. (2011), by 2100 there is a near-certainty that the population in western Europe will reach a peak followed by a decline, but such probabilities are only about 60% for both North America and sub-Saharan Africa.

The US National Research Council analyzed past errors in national projections by the United Nations and found that for horizons up to 10 years the largest source of error was the base population estimate, that migration made the greatest difference for spans up to 25 years, and that fertility assumptions were the main source of error in the longer term, while different mortality assumptions had only marginal effects (NRC 2000a). The latter is true even on the global level where migration is not a forecast variable and where fertility projections will drive the outcome. The medium variant of the 2015 edition of the UN's *World Population Prospects* forecasts 8.5 billion people in 2030, 9.725 billion in 2050 (with more than half of the growth taking place in Africa), and 11.123 billion in 2100, with a 95% degree of confidence that at the end of the 21st century the population will not be less than 9.5 or more than 13.3 billion (UN 2017). The last total would imply more than doubling (from 6.082 billion) during the 21st century.

The UN also carried its forecasts to 2300 (UN 2004), an effort whose utility is akin to forecasting today's global population in the early years of the 18th century. Nevertheless, the exercise is useful to remind us of the large uncertainties of any long-term forecasts and to reinforce an obvious, but still sometime ignored, notion that continuation of recent population growth rates cannot persist even for just a couple of centuries. The range of plausible forecasts spans an order of magnitude, from 2.3 billion for the low version (less than a third of 2019 total) to 36.4 billion for the high estimates, with the median at 9 billion and a zero-population-growth outcome of 8.3 billion. The idea of zero population growth became popular during the late 1960s (Davis 1967) but that goal has never been given serious consideration either by demographers in their future forecasts or by economists envisaging constantly growing output and consumption.

Keeping growth rate constant at the 1980–2000 level would increase the global population more than tenfold by 2150 and lead to an inconceivable aggregate of some 540 billion by the year 2300. The latter total would imply average population density of about 40 people for every hectare of the Earth's ice-free land. Such totals are easily dismissed as meaningless mechanical calculations devoid of any real-world constraints. At the same time, a high total of 36 billion by 2300 is not entirely implausible. Demeny (2004) made the point that in the long run the force of material incentives (that has been keeping fertility very low in all affluent and now also in many rapidly modernizing countries) may weaken and that we may see a return to above-replacement fertility. If so, an average fertility rate of 2.35 would yield a global total of 36 billion in 2300: "Welcome to the world of growth, preserving historical continuity. Good-bye to the brave new world of stasis and depopulation" (Demeny 2004, 517).

But even if we had the capability to make narrowly constrained forecasts far into the future, they would not be the most helpful quantifications we could get. The most useful number we would like to know in order to manage planetary affairs in a responsible manner is the most likely world population limit, the aggregate compatible with maintaining a long-term balance between the preservation of essential biospheric services and the provision of a good quality of life. Obviously, this definition is open to interpretation and to the setting of alternative boundaries, but reasonable arguments and in-depth studies of constraining factors could narrow the most acceptable range.

Van den Bergh and Rietveld (2003) performed a meta-analysis of 94 studies of the limits of global populations published between 1679—when Antonie van Leeuwenhoek, of microscopy fame, extrapolated the Dutch population density to the world and ended up with 13.4 billion people (Cohen 1995)—and 1999. Most of the estimates (75%) considered land and food as the key limiting factor and their mean total was about 62 billion people, while limits due to the synergy of multiple factors were less than 6 billion people. The best point estimate was 7.7 billion people, and lower and upper bounds supportable by current human capabilities were as low as 0.65 and as high as 98 billion people. That is an unhelpfully wide range and we hope to narrow the difference to less than a factor of two: otherwise it would be much more difficult to agree on a course of effective global action. But, as could be illustrated by the recent search for a sustainable population maximum, doing so anytime soon is not very likely.

The first study, which attempted to identify the population maximum based on what the authors call the ecological overshoot of the global economy (Wackernagel et al. 2002), explains why. The authors used maximum productivities and sets of assumptions to calculate the Earth's 1999 biological capacity to cope with growing crops, grazing animals, harvesting timber, fishing, accommodating infrastructures, and converting fossil fuels and nuclear energy. They concluded that in 1961 global demand created a load equivalent to about 70% of the biosphere's regenerative capacity and that by 1999 it was equivalent to 120% of the sustainable level. But even assuming their reasoning and assumptions were flawless, there is no simple way to translate them into global population limits.

The most obvious conclusion is to say that in order to stay within regenerative limits the Earth could have supported 4.8 billion people in 1999 (20% smaller than the 6 billion reached in that year) given the same level and the same inequities in resource demand. But if the entire global population were to consume at the American level, we would need 4–5 more Earths (Wackernagel and Rees 1996; Global Footprint Network 2017)—and further population growth will make such accounts even scarier. Conversely, we could argue that the total sustainably supported population could be raised to 6 billion people by reducing overconsumption in affluent countries, or to 8 billion people by being willing to live in a globally more equitable, low-waste, high-efficiency society. Alternatively, Taagepera (2014) proposed a model of the Earth's carrying capacity and technological-organizational skills in order to project the millennial trend toward a stable population of 10 billion people by 2100.

And looking further ahead, some of the constraining factors can become significantly more relaxed. Genetic modification of crops and animals, and eventually their *de novo* design (synthetic biology), could result in substantial productivity increases per unit of land. Fishing is being already replaced by aquaculture. Future advances in large-scale electricity storage might allow us to rely on intermittent energy flows (wind, solar) even for high base-load demand. Obviously, any calculation of the maximum global population—be it delimited in terms of carrying or regenerative capacity—depends on serial assumptions concerning the level of prevailing comfort and typical consumption and on a civilization's longevity: even modest demands might turn out to be excessive over the very long term, but rational adjustments and new scientific breakthroughs might relax the constraint boundaries.

As a result, large uncertainties concerning the future national and global trajectories of population growth will remain. The key question is what comes after sigmoid curves reach their maxima, and it has many different answers not only on the national level (as must be expected given the peculiarities of specific population histories) but also on the global level. While we do know the least likely outcome to take place (maintenance of the peak population level with only minimal fluctuations for centuries to come), we do not know if the post-peak decline will be gradual or steep, linear or exponential, or if the complete curve of global population history will come close to a symmetrical (normal) distribution or if it will be highly skewed.

Do these long-term trends—millennia of low population growth, demographic transitions resulting first in unprecedented increases and eventually in below-replacement fertilities, and persisting differences between affluent nations and many low-income countries—translate into orderly growth patterns, or are the population trajectories too irregular? As already explained in chapter 1, a pioneering attempt to find a pattern for a long-term trajectory of population growth on a national level concluded that a sigmoid curve offers an excellent fit (Verhulst 1838, 1845). And using Verhulst's two original examples, Belgium and France, I have also already shown the limits of this approach for long-range forecasting: it could work well in some cases, while in other instances it will result in large errors, and there is, obviously, no a priori way to decide into which category a specific forecast might fall. By the end of the 20th century, the Belgian population (at 10.25 million) was only about 8% higher than it would have been according to Verhulst's function, but the French population of 60.91 million was 52% higher than predicted by Verhulst's curve in 1845.

As already noted, Verhulst's findings were inexplicably ignored for decades, and began to receive widespread attention and application only during the 1920s, above all thanks to the work of Pearl and Reed (1920). The close correspondence between the actual numbers of the US population and its logistic growth model made Pearl and Reed confident in stating that the country's population growth curve had already passed the point of inflection: they put it, with great accuracy, at about April 1, 1914 at 98.637 million. They concluded that relatively lower gains lie ahead "unless there comes into play some factor not now known and which has never operated during the past history of the country to make the rate of growth more rapid"—but immediately they noted that "this latter contingency is improbable" (Pearl and Reed 1920, 284). As a result, the country's asymptotic population was to reach (as already noted in chapter 1) 197.274 million or roughly twice the total of the early 1920s (Pearl and Reed 1920, 285).

In reality, more than one improbable contingency came to pass, proving yet again that growth curve fitting is a safe and interesting retrospective exercise but a highly uncertain way to assess future long-term developments. Birth rates declined during the economic depression of the 1930s but the post-WWII baby boom (1945–1965) increased the population by a third in a single generation and by 1970 the total reached 203.2 million, just above the supposed maximum forecast in 1920. The subsequent combination of relatively high fertility (in comparison with Europe and Japan) and strong (legal and illegal) immigration added more than 100 million people in four decades and the 2010 total reached 308.7 million, 56% above Pearl's 1920 maximum.

Reviewing *The Biology of Population Growth* by Raymond Pearl, Wright correctly noted:

> If, nevertheless, it turns out that nations really grow by superposition of cycles, as Pearl describes them, it would tend to indicate that the growth of human populations is not, after all, comparable to that of fruit flies in a bottle. It is possible that the form of the population curve is, in the main, merely a reflection of progress in the ability of man to deal with nature. The development of the industrial applications of a new idea may well be conceived as something superimposed upon the previous state of industry. From the biologic viewpoint, such changes are changes in the upper limit of the population curve. The question is whether we are to consider populations as growing toward more or less remote limits, which

change only occasionally, or whether we are to consider them as always close to their upper limits which, however, are themselves continually changing in more or less definitely cyclical fashion. It is not necessary to hold either view to the complete exclusion of the other. In any case it appears very doubtful whether predictions are justified that are based on extrapolation for more than a few years. (Wright 1926, 495)

Could the accuracy of long-term population forecasts using the logistic function be improved by using the longest reliable series of actual population growth? I have used such series for the US (since 1790), Japan (since 1872), and France (since 1700), and all of these trajectories fit closely symmetrical logistic curves ($R^2 = 0.99$ for the US and Japan, 0.96 for France) and forecasts of 2050 populations produce, in all cases, totals that are higher than the best recent forecasts based on standard demographic models. That is not surprising: as already noted, starting with Verhulst's prediction even the best-fitting logistic curves tend to miss the targets in the long run.

The largest difference (at least 20% or as much as 30%) would be for Japan: the logistic trajectory would have its population rising to well above 130 million by 2050, while the population has been declining since 2008, the best Japanese forecasts are for about 100 million by 2050, and the UN foresees about 107 million. At the beginning of the 21st century, Japan was the world's 10th most populous nation, by 2050 it will be, at best, 15th, behind Vietnam and ahead of Turkey (UN 2004). The French population following the logistic curve would surpass 75 million compared to the UN forecast of 71 million, and the US total would be about 422 million while the US Census Bureau forecasts 398 million: in absolute terms, this difference of about 6% higher would be equal to the 2015 population of Australia.

Given the very slow growth of the premodern population and the enormous post-1850 growth spurt, all long-term plots of global population (no matter if they start in 10,000 BCE or at the beginning of the common era) are essentially extended nearly flat lines that change suddenly into a steep J shape and whose best fit is a logistic function—but one that is still far from reaching its inflection point. Extension of the logistic curve based on the growth between 1700 and 2015 indicates 12 billion people by 2050 and 22 billion by 2100. The inflection point comes only in 2105, and the asymptotic value of about 45 billion would be reached just before the year 2300 (figure 5.5). But, as already noted, this is just a calculating exercise and (should we be around in 2300) the actual total will be very different, almost certainly much lower.

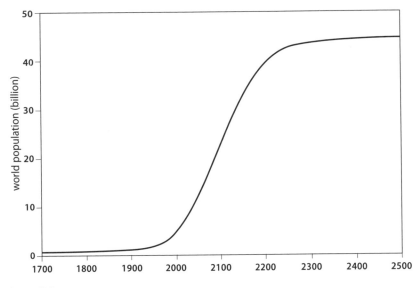

Figure 5.5
Global population growth, 1700–2500. Logistic curve with a distant inflection point (in 2105) and asymptote of 45.2 billion.

Cities

Cities were established and were able to grow thanks to agricultural surpluses produced first in their immediate surroundings. But already during antiquity some cities engaged in long-distance trade and today the energy and material metabolism of large modern cities rests on truly global foundations, with fuels, food, raw materials, and finished products traded worldwide. In turn, cities have been repaying this growing energy and material dependence by providing first manufacturing and now, most importantly, commercial, financial, managerial, educational, and recreational services that generate significant income and extend their reach and appeal on levels ranging from regional and nationwide to continental and global. Cities have also had a disproportionate influence on creating culture, setting commercial priorities, influencing political development, supplying an educated labor force, determining tastes and fashions, and fostering innovation (Geddes 1915; Chandler 1987; Modelski 2003; Norwich 2009; Lees 2015).

The first cities began to emerge in the Fertile Crescent of the Near East some 6,000 years ago during the time when the region's atmospheric moisture was relatively high and enabled sedentary cropping (Lawrence et al.

2016). The progression began with the Sumerian civilization whose oldest city, Eridu, predated 5,000 BCE and was followed by Larsa, Bad-tibira, Sippar, Shuruppak, Uruk, Kish, Ur, Nippur, and Lagash. But after the Early Bronze Age some agglomerations grew rather rapidly even as the moisture declined and urbanization and climate decoupled after 2000 BCE. And it was from these cities, starting around 3200 BCE in Sumerian Uruk, that we have the oldest cuneiform characters imprinted on wet clay tablets with a stylus, the first written records in history. After 1900 BCE the center of Mesopotamian power shifted to Babylon, whose rulers conquered most of the cities in southern Mesopotamia and eventually extended their power even further into today's Turkey, across the Levant and into Egypt. Similarly, the rise and evolution of Indian, Chinese, or (much later) Mesoamerican and South American civilizations were closely tied with their growing cities (Chandler 1987).

But when looking at the cities in antiquity we should keep Davis's (1955, 429) admonitions in mind:

> Because the archeological evidence is fragmentary, the role of cities in antiquity has often been exaggerated. Archeologists in particular are inclined to call any settlement a "city" which had a few streets and a public building or two. Yet there is surely some point in not mistaking a town for a city. Moreover, what is important is not only the appearance of a few towns or cities but also their place in the total society of which they were a part. Thus, even though in particular regions around the Mediterranean and in southern and western Asia many towns and a few cities arose prior to the Christian Era, there were severe limitations both on the size that such cities could reach and on the proportion of the total population that could live in them.

And while quantifying the growth of cities might seem to be a much easier challenge than tracing the growth of national populations, this relative advantage is of surprisingly recent origin as any urban censuses were no more common during antiquity or the Middle Ages than overall population counts. While it is true that reconstructions of population totals based on areas delimited by city walls must have much smaller margins of error than estimating nationwide populations, major uncertainties remain and trajectories of historical urban growth (and decline) are only approximate even for the cities for which we possess relatively rich written records and abundant archaeological evidence (Pasciuti and Chase-Dunn 2002).

There is no universally accepted quantitative divide between cities and towns, or (more fundamentally) between cities and nonurban settlements. Cutoffs used by national statistical services are hardly helpful as they range across an order of magnitude, being as low as 1,000 people in Canada or centers with 100 or more dwellings in Peru—and as high as 50,000 people in Japan, with China choosing to have a specific density threshold of places having more than 1,500 people/km^2 (UN 2016). The earliest populous settlements were no larger than today's small towns, with about 1,000 people in Çatalhöyük, one of the first Neolithic proto-cities in Turkey, in 7000 BCE and some 5,000 people in Sumerian Uruk in 4,000 BCE (Davis 1955; Çatalhöyük Research Project 2017). Numbers go up an order of magnitude during the Chalcolithic (Bronze) Age (3500–1700 BCE), with the largest cities having tens of thousands of people—Mohenjo-daro in the Indus Valley 40,000 and Uruk as many as 80,000 people in 2600 BCE—and another order of magnitude during classical antiquity: the sequential appearance of cities is mapped at Metrocosm (2017).

Morris (2005) examined the growth of Greek cities during the first millennium BCE and concluded that in good years even major centers like Athens (with about 20,000 people at that time) and Corinth could still feed themselves from their hinterlands up to about 525–500 BCE and afterwards required food imports in most years. The cities of classical Greece were administrative centers whose growth often depended on benefits derived from faraway conquests and this reality limited their eventual enlargement without undergoing the social and economic transformations that later supported the growth of European producer cities (Morris 2005). The Athenian walls enclosed only 215 ha (with slightly more than half used for housing, with little evidence for a significant population outside the walls), and during the classical era the city's population peaked around 430 BCE at around 40,000 inhabitants.

During the Hellenistic era, Alexandria was the largest city: Diodorus (60 BCE) reported 300,000 free citizens, Strabo (24 BCE) claimed a total of 500,000 (and hence larger than Rome), and even larger numbers are given for the early 1st century CE. Rome's area (within the Aurelian walls) was 15 km^2 and Hermansen (1978) assumed that half of it was taken by residential buildings. Nearly 1,800 *domus* structures of the rich Romans averaging 675 m^2 occupied 1.2 km^2, leaving 6.25 km^2 for *insulae*, dwellings of the poor (Smil 2010c). With 250 m^2 per *insula* there would be some 25,000 structures, and with 8 m^2/person they could accommodate 800,000 people, confirming that the often-cited estimate of 1 million people during the first century of the common era might be close to the actual (and, in the absence of any reliable census, unknown) count.

Low staple crop yields, large interannual harvest fluctuations, and the absence of any inexpensive large-scale land transport of food and raw materials limited the growth of all early settlements and it is no coincidence that the largest cities of classical antiquity (Athens, Corinth, Syracuse, Agrigento, Carthage, Rome) were those that could be supplied by boats and ships. Rome's 1 million people needed about 30 million *modii* or 200,000 t of grain every year (Garnsey 1988) and nearly all of it was delivered from Egypt and North Africa (Rickman 1980; Temin 2001). Adding imported olive oil and wine, the annual shipments of comestibles were on the order of 250,000 t, a mass too large to be transported from distant parts of Italy.

Chang'an (Xi'an), the capital of China's 10 imperial dynasties—including the Han (206 BCE–220 CE), contemporary with the late Roman republic and the early empire—rivaled Rome in size but the only city that might have surpassed 1 million inhabitants during the first millennium of the common era was Baghdad under the Abbasid Caliphate, with a peak of 1.2 million people during the 10th century before its decline and eventual destruction by invading Mongols in 1258. Even after Europe began to reorganize itself into relatively more prosperous political entities, the size of its cities remained limited.

The continent's most populous cities at the beginning of the 14th century were Paris (more than 200,000), Milan (more than 150,000), and Genoa (about 100,000), while the world's largest cities during the late Middle Ages were Hangzhou and Beijing in China (both at least 400,000), Cairo (of a similar size), and Sarai (as many as 600,000 people), a short-lived city established by Batu Khan after 1240 in the lower Volga region of Russia as the capital of the Golden Horde. Beijing retained its primacy for another five centuries but by 1800 its population of 1.1 million was rivaled by Edo (now Tokyo), the capital of the Tokugawa shogunate (1600–1868), and London's first official census showed 1,011,157 people in 1801 (Naito 2003).

Batty's (2006) rank clocks (long-term monitoring of changing ranks for the world's top 100 cities) offer an excellent tool to follow the rise, persistence, and decline (and sometimes yet another unforeseen rise) of humanity's largest agglomerations of population. In the global ranking, no city that was in the top 50 in 430 BCE was in that category by the year 2000. Following the Ottoman conquest of Constantinople in 1453, only six cities from that late medieval era remained in the top 50 half a millennium later. Chinese cities are prominent among the small number of large settlements that remained in the top 50 for very long periods of time after 430 BCE: Suzhou for 2,158 years, Nanking for 2,080 years, and Wuchang for 1,850 years; Rome stayed in that group for 1,530 years and Paris for 525 years as its population grew exponentially.

Between 1790 and 2000, 266 different American cities belonged to the top 100 but from 1840, when the number of cities first reached 100, only

21 remained in 2000, and rank clocks show that it has taken 105 years for half of the cities to appear or disappear from the top 100, with an average shift of seven ranks in each decade. And while in 1790 only 5% of the US population lived in the original 24 cities, in the year 2000 the top 100 metropolitan areas housed 20% of the country's population. The British urban growth has been much more stable: of the top 100 cities in 1901, 73 still belonged to the set a century later, and Batty (2006) concluded that the UK was essentially locked into its current urban pattern by 1901, with the greatest shifts during the 1950s and 1960s, the decades of rapid suburbanization.

The form of government had a strong influence on the growth of premodern cities. De Long and Shleifer (1993) analyzed the growth of the largest western European cities from 1000 to 1800 and presented statistical evidence that absolutist monarchies had a stunting effect on urban development as they imposed high rates of taxation which hindered the development of commerce and industry. European historians may have celebrated the imposition of princely authority in Spain, France, and Prussia because it provided the foundation of the 19th-century nation-states, but "for the people of Belgium, their incorporation into the Habsburg Empire was no benefit; for the people of Iberia, the marriage of Ferdinand and Isabella was no cause for rejoicing" (De Long and Shleifer 1993, 35), while the urban boom following the setting up of constitutional English monarchy resulted in an addition of more than 300,000 city inhabitants in 1650–1800 compared to what could have been expected under absolutist governments.

Urbanization
Urbanization, the process of mass-scale migration from the countryside to cities, began tentatively in some countries during the 18th century. Most notably, London grew from about 600,000 people in 1700 to 1.1 million in 1801—but the process became truly transformative only during the 19th century: by 1901 London's population had reached 6.5 million, sextupling in 100 years (Demographia 2001). Concurrently, Paris grew even faster, from 548,000 to about 4 million, New York increased from just over 60,000 in 1800 to 3.43 million in 1900 (nearly a 60-fold gain), and Edo (Tokyo) more than doubled from 0.685 to about 1.5 million. But the world at the beginning of the 20th century was still overwhelmingly rural as only about 9% of the world's population lived in cities with more than 20,000 people, and only about 5% were in cities with more than 100,000 inhabitants.

The subsequent growth of the global urban population has followed very closely a logistic trajectory with the inflection point in 1968. By 1960

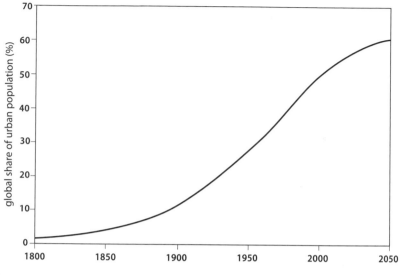

Figure 5.6

Global share of the urban population, 1800–2050. Plotted from various UN statistics. Logistic curve with the inflection point in 1969 and asymptote of 70.9%.

a third of all people lived in cities, the share surpassed 50% just before the end of 2007, it was about 54% by 2015, and a logistic curve (with inflection point in 1969) points to 61% by the year 2050, while the UN projects the rate at 66% (figure 5.6). The post-1790 growth of the US urban population has also followed very closely a logistic curve with the inflection point already in 1910, with a 50% share surpassed by 1919, a 75% share reached by 1975, and with the 2015 share of 81.6% very close to the asymptotic level as the trajectory points to about 84% by 2050 (figure 5.7). Most countries have been on urbanization trajectories that took many decades to go from 20% to 50% of the total population living in cities: on the global level, it took nearly 90 years and even in the US, one of the most rapidly urbanizing societies, it took nearly 60 years.

China has been the greatest exception. Before the Communist takeover in 1949 only 9% of its population (about 50 million) was urban and 27 years later, when Mao Zedong died in 1976, the share had just doubled to 18% (UN 1969; NBS 2000). Deng Xiaoping's post-1980 economic modernization allowed poor peasants to move to cities in search of new factory, construction, and service jobs and that radical departure from Maoist policies of tightly controlled internal migration resulted in an exceptionally rapid flight from the countryside to cities. By the year 2000, 36% of China's

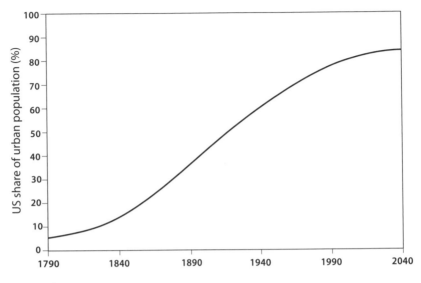

Figure 5.7
Share of the urban population in the US since 1790. Plotted from data in USBC (1975) and subsequent volumes of US *Statistical Abstract*. With the logistic curve inflected already in 1910, its asymptotic value is 87.2%.

population was urban, 57.6% was urban by 2015, and going from an urban share of 20% to 50% took just 20 years. This process also amounted to the most massive population shift in history (figure 5.8). In 1980 the total was 190 million city dwellers and in 2017 it had risen to almost exactly 800 million, the absolute gain of 610 million people being slightly larger than the combined populations of the US and Brazil, the world's third and fourth most populous countries.

Urbanization has been seen universally as synonymous with economic development and its rates and absolute city sizes have been used as proxies for estimating economic growth and levels of per capita economic product where such data are lacking. But urbanization without economic growth (or with very low economic gains for most of the new urban inhabitants) also took place in premodern history and recently it became evident in many low-income countries during the closing decades of the 20th century when very large cities (Dacca and Kinshasa being excellent examples) increasingly emerged in some of the world's poorest areas (Jedwab and Vollrath 2014).

But in general, the economic importance of large cities (and their concomitant social and environmental problems) has been indisputable and this strong link has led to suggestions that the key economic variables

Figure 5.8
The growth of Shanghai's Lujiazui financial district epitomizes the rapid urbanization of post-1990 China. Photo available at wikimedia.

could be predicted due to urban scaling effects. When Bettencourt and Lobo (2016) used new harmonized definitions for functional urban areas of cities in France, Germany, Italy, Spain, and the UK, they found that double-log plots of total populations (x axis) against total urbanized area, total GDP, total employment, and patents granted followed approximately the theoretical expectations (fairly good fits for straight lines with exponents ranging mostly between 0.9 and 1.1) but because of the relatively small number of large cities in each nation they could not draw strong scaling conclusions.

Because Europe's history was splintered among many small states (its most populous modern polity, united Germany, has existed only since 1871) the continent has a shortage of very large cities, but (as on all other continents) the largest cities have claimed a disproportionate amount of economic activity, inventiveness, and influence far beyond their expanding boundaries. In 2016 the UN listed 512 cities with a population of more than 1 million (UN 2016). About 85% of them (436 cities) had populations between 1 and 5 million, 45 were between 5 and 10 million, and there were 31 megacities of more than 10 million people (more about them later in this section). In addition, there were also 551 cities with populations between 500,000 and 1,000,000, and worldwide nearly half of all urbanites live in cities smaller than half a million. And while the populations of smaller cities have been growing, some very rapidly, throughout Africa and Asia, they have been declining in many European countries, in the Asian part of Russia, and in Japan.

But national concerns about the economic and social consequences of urban depopulation still affect much smaller populations than do the benefits and downsides resulting from the continuing expansion of smaller cities and from the rise of megacities. Urban growth has many quantifiable consequences and (using the term not in the strict physical sense) some of them have become known as laws (Batty 2013). I will take brief looks at Marshall's, von Thünen's, and Tobler's laws, and later in this section I will focus in more detail on Zipf's (1949) inverse power law relating city ranks and their population sizes.

Growing cities enjoy disproportionate increases in productivity, average income, and accumulated wealth that can be attributed to the phenomenon of agglomeration whose importance—in terms of transport cost savings, customer-supplier interactions, labor pooling, and exchange of knowledge allowing companies, regardless of their size, to take advantage of economies of scale and scope—was first recognized by Marshall (1890). Marshall's law has been examined and elaborated by many economic analyses that have focused on transportation costs, and the sharing, matching and learning opportunities so uniquely afforded by growing cities (Krugman 1991; Glaeser 2010; Behrens et al. 2014; Duranton and Kerr 2015).

These realities are far more important than any natural advantages (such as a deep port or a location in a heavily frequented valley) that might have played some role in the past but that now appear to explain no more than about one-quarter of existing industrial concentrations (Ellison and Glaeser 1997). Agglomeration economies show strong links between population density and high wages, per capita gross economic product and labor productivity (Ciccone and Hall 1996). Links to high housing prices, pronounced in some cities, have not been seen to the same general extent. Urban agglomerations have always had an outsize role in the incubation and transmission of ideas, the process that eventually resulted in the rise of the knowledge economy (Mokyr 2002). As Marshall (1890, 271) noted on the importance of these information spillovers in his classic treatment, in cities "the mysteries of the trade become no mysteries; but are as it were in the air" as firms learns from their collaborators and competitors by introducing better practices and sharing their knowledge.

This process has been examined from many perspectives (Jacobs 1970; Romer 1986; Krugman 1991; Glaeser et al. 1992; Mokyr 2002, 2017). Studies have focused on the accumulation of knowledge whose benefits also accrue to companies outside the original inventing outfit or even to different industries; on the importance of investment in human capital, and on the synergy of physical capital and disembodied knowledge; on the role of innovation spillovers in generating economic growth; and on the critical role of cities in fostering and diffusing these changes. But the specifics of this process will change with the stages of agglomeration. For example, an analysis of 170 US cities between 1956 and 1987 showed that interindustry knowledge spillovers were less important than the adoption of an innovation by additional sectors, particularly in fairly mature cities (Glaeser et al. 1992).

Coagglomeration (or collocation) of firms has been also an important part of the concentration process, first with industrial firms and later particularly with service enterprises. Wall Street (financial services), Silicon Valley (electronics and software), and Hollywood (entertainment) are the three best-known examples of the economic rewards of collocation and spatial concentration, with opportunities for changing jobs without changing residences and with more efficient labor market pooling being among its important advantages. Shenzen, the Chinese hub of electronic assembly industries on Hong Kong's border in Guangdong province, is perhaps the best example of modern, globally important collocation benefits in manufacturing.

Remarkably, even the post-1950 rise of inexpensive long-distance transportation (first large bulk carriers and tankers, then container ships in maritime trade; containerized diesel or electric railway shipments; long-distance trucking) and the rapid post-1980 diffusion of highly affordable instant communication, information and data sharing have not weakened the process of agglomeration. Urbanization has spread across Latin America, Asia, and parts of Africa and some old industrial-and-service agglomerations have made notable comebacks as global hubs of financial activities, with New York and London being the two prime examples. And no less remarkably, a well-known array of congestion costs accompanying agglomeration (crowding, cost of living, traffic, noise, pollution) has not been costly enough to curtail the growth even in the cities notorious for their combination of such problems, including Beijing, New Delhi, Mumbai, or Karachi in Asia, and Cairo, Lagos, and Kinshasa in Africa.

Preindustrial cities dependent on food and fuel from their surrounding areas created zones of various densities and economic activities determined (nonlinearly) by the distance and transportation cost from their centers. The German economist Johann Heinrich von Thünen (1826) was the first observer to formulate this relationship in a rigorous way. But his model has some fundamental limitations: it applied only to agriculture and to harvesting of other biomass (wood, grazing) in a preindustrial society dependent on fuelwood, and he posited a centrally located isolated city in a completely flat land with consistent soil quality and surrounded by wilderness.

Such a simplified idealized model resulted in four concentric rings of economic activity, with dairying and vegetable cultivation in the first zone nearest to the city, timber and firewood in the second, grain crops in the third, and animal grazing in the fourth zone. Few vestiges of these agricultural zones remain in the modern world, where inexpensive mass-scale transportation largely eliminated the importance of distance and where even dairy products and fresh vegetables come not only from faraway regions within a country but commonly from different continents. But the principle of a nonlinear decline of urban attributes with distance or transportation cost from a city's core or central business district remains readily discernible as far as declining population densities and average rents are concerned.

And as cities grow, their interaction with other cities is dependent both on their increasing size and on the distance between them, with the second variable subject to Tobler's law that "everything is related to everything else, but near things are more related than distant things" (Tobler 1970, 236). But like von Thünen's law, this apparent truism has undergone many modifications in the globalized economy, where two cities on different continents may have economic, communication and travel interactions whose intensity may rival the links they have with other metropolitan areas located in relative proximity within their own countries.

Batty (2013) also claims that as cities get bigger they get "greener," that is they become more sustainable. That may be true in the sense that higher densities make it more economical to introduce more efficient transportation solutions (dense networks of subways within cities and rapid train transport between large cities) that would be entirely uneconomical in smaller places with a low-density sprawl. And Glaeser (2011) presents the urban advantages in purely positive terms, as the title of his book piles up the benefits: *Triumph of the City: How Our Greatest Invention Makes Us Richer, Smarter, Greener, Healthier, and Happier.*

This enthusiastic generalization is also a misleading simplification. Above all, it does not offer even a hint of the fact that cities are our civilization's most complex and most intensive dissipative (entropy-producing) structures (Bristow and Kennedy 2015). Unprecedented agglomerations of people and economic activities must be supplied incessantly with enormous, and rising, amounts of energy in order to satisfy their high power-density demand, food to sustain record-size concentrations of humanity, and raw materials to build, maintain and renew many required infrastructures, ranging from water supply and wastewater treatment to roads and garbage collection. Resource demands created by urbanization have been enormous as virtually all per capita consumption rates always rise, and some soar, with the migration to cities (Smil 2015c).

Compared to average rural rates, food consumption of resource-intensive meat and fruit is commonly at least 50% higher in the cities. Water consumption increase must be often expressed in multiples. A single toilet flushing, consuming 20 L, surpasses the daily per capita use for drinking and cooking in arid rural settings without sanitation, and even in water-poor but rapidly modernizing China's urban consumption of water is double the rural use (Yu et al. 2015). Multiples are also needed to express higher demands for household appliances (ranges and refrigerators being standard in modern high-rise apartments) and consumer goods.

Overall per capita energy demand in cities—driven by energy-intensive multistory housing, domestic, industrial and transportation electricity demand, much higher car ownership, and necessarily extensive public transportation—is significantly higher than in small towns or villages (Parikh and Shukla 1995; Zhao and Wang 2015). Urbanization also changes the composition of energy use. In India, nearly 90% of rural households use firewood for cooking, but only 30% do so in the cities. Moreover, only 10% of rural households have access to electricity in Bihar but more than 90% in the highly urbanized states of Haryana (surrounding New Delhi) and Punjab, and India's per capita urban electricity consumption is nearly double the rural use (Woodbridge et al. 2016).

At the beginning of China's modernization, average urban demand for energy was five times the rural use, and even though the country's unequaled multiplication of primary energy use lowered the difference, urbanites still averaged 50% more energy in 2010 (Chu et al. 2016). But the diversity of megacities makes generalizations concerning energy and material flows elusive: Kennedy et al. (2015) found that in terms of per capita use the difference between the lowest- and highest-consuming megacities in 2010 was 35-fold for steel, 28-fold for energy, 23-fold for water, and sixfold for cement, while the greatest difference in per capita generation of waste was 19-fold. But generally high residential and power densities are the two attributes that all large cities have in common.

Urban crowding reached incredible densities already in the walled cities of antiquity and the medieval era. A reliable figure from the 1365 Paris census puts the density at more than 60,000 people/km^2 and even after the city had spread beyond its walls it remains among the world's most densely populated areas, averaging about 21,000 people/km^2 compared to Napoli's 25,000, Mumbai's 30,000, and Manila's 40,000 people/km^2. And high concentrations on the order of 50,000 people/km^2 are commonly found in the most densely populated parts of Asian megacities, while Los Angeles, the most densely populated metropolitan area in the US, averages just over 1,000 people/km^2. Assuming an age- and sex-weighted conservative body mass mean of 45 kg/capita, densities of more than 50,000 people/km^2 correspond to a live weight human biomass (anthropomass) of more than 2 kg/m^2, a rate that is unmatched by any other social mammal and that is three orders of magnitude higher than the peak seasonal biomass of large herbivorous ungulates (antelopes, wildebeest, giraffes, zebras) grazing on East Africa's richest grasslands (Smil 2013a).

The energy demand of modern cities requires unprecedented amounts of fuels and electricity delivered with the very high reliability needed to cover not only household and industrial demands but also to power vital infrastructures that operate incessantly (electricity supply, sewage pumping) or are needed for more than 18 hours a day (subways and commuter trains typically shut down only for a few early morning hours). What sets modern cities apart are the scale and highly concentrated nature of their energy demand. Power density consumption (energy flow per year per unit of area, usually expressed as W/m^2) of overall energy in modern buildings (most of it being electricity and natural gas) ranges from less than 10 W/m^2 for energy-efficient detached single-story houses in mild climates, to post-1990 (that is better-built) American two-story houses averaging 30–40 W/m^2 of their foundation area, while older (pre-1980) 20-story office buildings in temperate climates will need 800 W/m^2 (Smil 2015c). A city-wide mapping of New York showed that some mid-Manhattan blocks with high numbers of high-rises have power densities up to 900 W/m^2, while 400–500 W/m^2 is common in the financial district, Greenwich Village, Midtown South, and East Side (Howard et al. 2012).

Residential high-rise buildings in hot climates, now the norm in growing cities in Asia and Latin America, have similar power densities (Smil 2015c). Hong Kong has been building such housing for decades and Kwai Chung, its largest public housing estate including16 towers of 38 floors, has (with nearly 25 W/m^2 of habitable floor area) a power density of roughly 950 W/m^2 of the building foundations. The highest densities are now in the Persian Gulf countries where high-rise hotels have densities up to 2,000 W/m^2, and Burj Khalifa, the world's tallest building (828 m, 160 floors), in Dubai requires 6,250 W/m^2 of its foundation area (Smil 2015c). For comparison, even in Dubai the annual mean of incoming solar radiation is about 215 W/m^2 (Islam et al. 2009). The only way to meet such a highly concentrated energy demand in a reliable fashion is to electrify everything.

And although most of the tens of millions of rural migrants who continue to arrive every year at growing cities live in substandard temporary shelters (and often in the worst imaginable slums), accommodating the new urban residents has inevitably resulted in unprecedented rates of new housing construction. This requires a commensurate extension of engineering networks (water and electricity supply, sewage removal, transportation infrastructure) and the establishment of new factories, offices, and health and social services. China, due to its delayed urbanization, has seen the most intensive wave of this new construction and, rather than quoting statistics about the number of newly completed houses or about annual additions of living area, the intensity of that urbanization effort is perhaps best illustrated by the astonishing fact that China has been recently emplacing every three years more concrete than the United States used in construction of its infrastructure, housing, and transportation during the entire 20th century (Smil 2014b).

Inevitably, urbanization demanding concentrated higher levels of per capita resource consumption creates commensurate environmental burdens. Urban growth has resulted in the inevitable urban sprawl, a universal phenomenon whose progress can be profitably studied (now virtually in real time) from satellite imagery (Bhatta 2010) and whose impact takes places mostly in ecosystems that we can least afford to lose. The very beginnings of settled human existence aside, a disproportional share of large cities has been always in coastal areas, and the advantages of such locations have been only strengthened with the rise of modern inexpensive mass-scale marine transportation. In 2017, 14 of the 20 largest megacities were in coastal lowlands, and McGranahan et al. (2005) calculated that at the beginning of the 21st century cities in coastal ecosystems housed nearly 15% of all urban dwellers even though such ecosystems accounted for only about 3% of the continental area. The highest share of the urban population (more than a third) is living in cities surrounded by cultivated ecosystems where their expansion reduces the area of arable land.

Urban sprawl causes extensive loss of natural plant cover, erases biodiversity, fragments habitats, reduces the area of high-quality arable land, and disrupts streams (as they are forced into concrete troughs or even disappear), and in arid areas results in overuse of groundwater. Beijing's growth has been a particularly worrisome example of a city that had an inadequate water supply even a generation ago but whose population more than doubled between 1990 and 2015, further straining its groundwater resources (Zhou et al. 2012). The worst forms of water pollution have been mostly eliminated due to now common primary and secondary wastewater treatment. And, except for China and India with their continuing high reliance on coal combustion, heavy particulate air pollution is largely gone, replaced by seasonally high levels of photochemical smog. North China still has both forms of air pollution, and between 2010 and 2015 Beijing's levels of fine particulates (with diameters smaller than 2.5 μm) were repeatedly up to 50 times higher than the World Health Organization's recommended maxima (Chen et al. 2015).

Urban heat islands are created by energy emanating from buildings, industries, and transportation and are potentiated by large areas of impervious surfaces (roofs, roads, parking lots) whose high thermal capacity and low albedo help to generate stronger convective flows. In addition, restricted circulation (particularly in high-rise parts of a city) reduces radiative cooling and produces sensible heat loss larger than latent heat flux (Stewart 2011). Urban heat islands average often 2°C more than the surrounding countryside, with peak differences up to 8°C higher. Their impacts include local and downwind increases in cloudiness, precipitation and thunderstorms and reductions of relative humidity, wind speed and horizontal insolation due to shading. Heat islands also promote the formation of photochemical smog and increase premature mortality during summer heat waves (Wong et al. 2013). Nearly 15,000 people died during a heat wave in Paris in August 2003, and forecasts indicate a rising threat for most of the Middle East as summer temperatures will increasingly reach 50°C and stay at that level for days or even weeks (Lelieveld et al. 2016).

Urban growth has also created impervious surface areas (ISAs)—that is roofed and paved surfaces (roads, sidewalks, and parking lots) and aboveground storages of materials—that are devoid of any vegetation and prevent water absorption. These areas contribute to excessive runoff during major precipitation events and reduce the diversity and abundance of aquatic organisms. Available ISA estimates for the US (48 contiguous states) range from just over 90,000 km^2 (USGS 2000) to as much as 141,000 ± 40,000 km^2 for the year 2000 (Churkina et al. 2010). The latter mean is larger than the total area of Greece. A global inventory of ISAs relied on the brightness of satellite-observed nighttime lights and came up with a total of about

580,000 km^2 (0.43% of the land surface, an equivalent of Kenya or Madagascar) at the beginning of the 21st century (Elvidge et al. 2007).

Some of these undesirable environmental consequences will ease with further development. For example, China's rapid pace of opening new subways and expanding the older networks will reduce traffic congestion, while conversion from coal to natural gas and electricity will improve air quality. But many negative social impacts—ranging from speculation with housing prices and expectation of land appreciation, to immigration surpassing the capacity to accommodate new arrivals in decent conditions (a problem particularly acute in Africa's growing cities with their extensive slums) and lack of affordable housing for lower-income families—will only increase in many new megacities.

The most likely outcome is that by 2050 there will be 2.5 billion people added to the world's urban population, with just three countries (India, China, and Nigeria) responsible for nearly 40% of that gain. Considering the state of the urban environment (density of dwellings, near-permanent traffic gridlock, air and water pollution) now prevailing in Lagos, Nigeria's largest city, it is hard to image the consequences of the city's expected population doubling between 2015 and 2050. The growth of Lagos exemplifies a key trend within the urbanization trend, as an ever-higher share of the urban population lives in cities that do not seem to end, encompassing areas equivalent to, or larger than, many small countries and with populations larger than those of most EU countries. These aggregations of humanity are known as megacities, while the extended urban area whose growth has eventually resulted in several merging cities is best described as an agglomeration or, pace Geddes (1915), as a conurbation. The Boston-Washington corridor in the northeastern US was the first, and is still perhaps the most famous, example of a megalopolis (Gottmann 1961).

Megacities

The usual dividing line between a large city and a megacity is put at 10 million inhabitants. But wherever that divide might be, megacities must be studied as functional units, not according to any official administrative delimitations. The distinction is illustrated by focusing on New York and Tokyo, the two original megacities. New York City (encompassing five boroughs centered on Manhattan) has a total area of 789 km^2 and in 2016 it had a population of 8.54 million people. New York Metropolitan Statistical Area covers 17,405 km^2, with a population of about 20.5 million, and the wider Combined Statistical Area (CSA) extends over 34,493 km^2 (larger than Belgium, slightly smaller than Taiwan), with a population in 2016 close to 24 million (USDC 2012). And New York's CSA—including the five largest cities in New Jersey, six in Connecticut, and five counties in Pennsylvania—is a key part of the Northeast megalopolis that includes four CSAs in 11 states, covers about 130,000 km², has nearly 50 million people, and produces a fifth of the country's GDP (Scommegna 2011).

Tokyo's case is much more complex, with as many as eight definitions to consider, some administrative, others functionally defined for planning purposes or by the reach of transportation used for daily commuting. The most restrictive concept is the area of 23 special wards (*ku*, that used to form the old city) that cover 621.9 km² and housed 9.256 million people in 2016. Tokyo prefecture (not counting small and distant islands in the Pacific) covers 1,808 km² and in 2015 it had 13.491 million people. When excluding the WWII population dip, the prefectural population has followed a symmetrical logistic growth trajectory with the inflection point already in 1932 and it has reached its asymptotic level (figure 5.9).

The most expansive definition is that of the National Capital Region, which includes the entire Kanto plain (between the Pacific and Nagano province in the west, and north of Izu peninsula and south of Fukushima prefecture) with an area of about 36,900 km² and almost 44 million people in 2015. I plotted the history of population growth of the Tokyo Major Metropolitan Region (*Tōkyō daitoshi ken*) defined by commuting links and including municipalities (or their parts) within 70 km of the city's government buildings in Shinjuku (TMG 2017). Its population grew from nearly 10 million people in 1920 to 12.7 million by 1940, and since WWII it has been expanding continuously, reaching 33 million by the year 2000 and nearly 39 million in 2017: a symmetrical logistic trajectory inflected in 1971 and the curve indicates that the total is now very close to its asymptotic level. But it is also possible that Japan's population decline will soon become evident even in Tokyo and instead of seeing a further slight growth the metropolitan region's population will be a few percent lower by 2030.

China added to these confusing delineations by elevating Sichuan's Chongqing to one of the country's four directly controlled municipalities (the other three are Beijing, Tianjin, and Shanghai) and creating, *de jure*, the world's largest city with an area of more than 82,000 km², slightly larger than the Czech Republic and just a bit smaller than Austria (Chongqing Municipal Government 2017). But most of this area in eastern Sichuan is rural, comprised of 25 districts, 13 counties, and more than 1,200 towns and townships. The municipality's population has surpassed 30 million, but the city itself covers less than 500 km² and contains fewer than 9

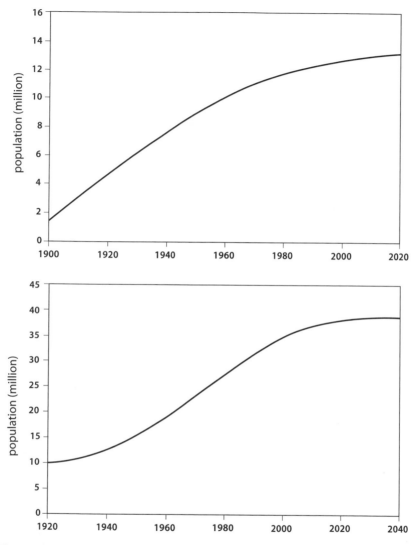

Figure 5.9
Tokyo's population within prefectural boundaries (1900–2020)—a logistic curve with
the inflection point in 1932 and asymptote at 13.8 million—and within the Tokyo
Major Metropolitan Region since 1920: logistic curve inflection point in 1971 and
asymptote at 38.8 million. Data from SB (1996) and TMG (2017).

million people. But China has a better claim to having the world's largest urban conglomeration in Guangdong's Pearl River Delta, just north of Hong Kong, where some 65 million people lived in 2015 spread across an area of about 56,000 km^2 (HKTDC 2017).

Before the rise of megacities, most of the world's largest cities during the preindustrial era were in Asia: eight out of ten in 1500 and still six out of ten in 1825, but then the Western urbanization shifted the order and by 1900 nine out of the ten largest cities were in Europe and the US (Jedwab and Vollrath 2014). But this shift was short-lived. By 1950 only five out of the top ten cities were in Europe and US, and only one (New York) remained by 2010. When using an extended functional definition, New York and Tokyo were the world's only two megacities in 1950, and a quarter of a century later they were joined by Mexico City. The next 25 years saw the fastest additions to the global list, with 18 megacities by the year 2000, 29 by the end of 2015, and 31 in 2016 (UN 2016).

Tokyo remained in the lead, and its exceptional size can be appreciated by making a few global comparisons. In 2017 the metropolitan region, with nearly 39 million people, would have been the world's 36th-largest country (out of the total of 233 states and territories), nearly 60% larger than Australia, a few million people ahead of Canada, and almost half the size of Turkey. Tokyo's 2017 population was also slightly larger than the total of six of Germany's southern and central states, whose area totals about 166,000 km^2 compared to just 13,572 km^2 of metropolitan Tokyo, making its average population density roughly 12 times higher. And no other city generates as much economic product (New York comes second with about 20% less), which contributes nearly 40% of Japan's GDP, equivalent to nearly half of the economic product of all of Germany!

The city has its negatives: high cost of living; a high share of cramped housing; long and crowded commutes from distant suburbs; polluted soil and groundwater in some of its formerly heavy industrial wards; and challenges of solid waste disposal and recycling. But, fortunately, Tokyo is exceptional in that it has avoided or solved other problems common in megacities, some in truly exceptional ways: its criminal rate is lower than in any other megacity, its air (significantly polluted until the late 1970s) is relatively clean thanks to highly efficient vehicles, imports of LNG and generation of nuclear electricity, and the density, frequency, and reliability of its subway system and of its rail links with other cities is outstanding.

In the global ranking, the city is followed by New Delhi, Shanghai, Mumbai, São Paulo, Beijing, and Mexico City. In 2015, 24 of the 31 megacities were in low-income countries (the global "South," as the UN calls it), with Asia having 18, China six, and India five. New York, the largest Western city, was relegated to 10th place, and Moscow, the largest European city, ranked 22nd and Paris 25th, another clear indicator of Europe's diminishing global importance. Given their size, it is not at all surprising that the annual growth of most megacities was slower than that of the whole urban population, which slowed down to about 2% between 2010 and 2015 (from more than 3% in the early 1950s) and ranged from just 0.76% in affluent countries to almost 4% in the poorest nations. Karachi, New Delhi, Dhaka, Guangzhou, and Lagos have been the fastest growing megacities since the 1990s, all in excess of 3%/year, followed by Mumbai, Istanbul, Beijing, and Manila (Canton 2011). The UN expects 10 additional megacities by 2030, six in Asia (including Pakistani Lahore, and Hyderabad and Ahmedabad in India), three in Africa (Johannesburg, Dar es Salaam, Luanda), and Colombia's Bogotá.

The resulting crowding has been as much the consequence of specific environmental and historical circumstances as it has been the result of universal forces of modern urbanization. When prorated over the entire metropolitan area (and measured in people/km^2), population density is surprisingly low in New York (below 2,000), fairly low in Tokyo and Beijing (around 5,000), high in Jakarta and Istanbul (about 10,000), very high not only in Lagos (around 15,000) but also (as already noted) in Paris (>20,000), and extremely high in Mumbai (>30,000) and Dhaka with about 45,000 people/km^2. Of course, all of these cities contain many smaller sections, wards, or districts where population densities reach even higher levels, and such densities can be found also in many cities smaller than 10 million people: Kwun Tong, Hong Kong's most densely populated district in Kowloon (east of the former airport's runway), houses more than 57,000 people/km^2 (ISD 2015).

Megacities span a wide range of developmental stages, from such mature metropolitan areas as London and New York to rapidly expanding agglomerations of housing and economic activity as New Delhi, Karachi, or Lagos. All megacities, regardless of their developmental stage, face the challenges of worrisome income inequality, poor living conditions for their low-income families, and inadequate and decaying infrastructures (most often evident in the state of public transportation). In addition, emerging megacities in low-income countries share serious to severe environmental problems (including crowding, air pollution, water pollution, and solid waste disposal), high unemployment levels (alleviated by extensive black economy sectors), and public safety concerns. And megacities also face what Munich Re, one of the world's leading reinsurance companies, calls megarisks, as the unprecedented accumulations of population, infrastructures, economic activities, and wealth also pose the possibility of unprecedented payoffs in the case of major natural catastrophes, terrorist attacks, or war (Munich Re 2004; Allianz 2015).

Companies welcome the opportunities presented by the need to insure all high-rises, subways, industries, and extensive real estate devoted to services. But they must consider the risks arising from loss potentials that are far higher in megacities than in any other settings, because even a single and time-limited failure (a serious accident closing down major subway lines, a high-rise fire, structural collapse) can rapidly create extensive chaos and translate into large economic losses whose aggregate is far beyond any insured total: damage caused by 1995 Kobe earthquake in Japan exceeded $100 billion but the insured losses covered only about $3 billion. Moreover, as Munich Re (2004, 4) also notes, long-term risks are much more serious due to "many megacities being virtually predestined to suffer major natural disasters."

Earthquakes and cyclones (hurricanes, typhoons) are the most widespread risks, but in some megacities a considerable number of fatalities could be also caused by heat waves and by storm surges (aggravated by the rising sea level) and volcanic eruptions. Increasing numbers of tall buildings also raise the risk of skyscraper conflagrations: as London's 2017 Grenfell Tower destruction demonstrated, they are very difficult to control once the fire begins to spread. And given the interconnectedness of the modern global economy (be it in terms of goods, travel, information, or financial flows), there can no longer be any just strictly local megacity failure. A major earthquake in Tokyo or in Beijing (cities relatively prone to such events) may trigger a global recession. The necessity to minimize the spread of a potentially pandemic infection (leading to severed air links) may cripple the everyday life and economic performance of closely linked megacities on different continents.

And it now appears to be only a matter of time before the world sees its first gigacity with more than 50 million people. Such a city would be larger than all but 27 of the world's 233 countries and territories were in 2015, larger than Spain or Colombia and comparable to South Korea, in 2016 the world's 11th-largest economy. But we need better terms to describe such agglomerations of people and economic activity. Conurbations consist of ever-larger contiguously built-up areas (or transportation and material- and product-handling districts and corridors) but they are not (indeed they cannot be) classic cities with single centers that are true hubs of urban life and that include a central business district, government offices, and major cultural amenities. Tokyo already works as such a multifocal arrangement. Although Ginza may be still seen as the traditional city center, Shinjuku has a far higher concentration of skyscrapers, and Shinjuku, Shibuya, and Ikebukuro have the city's (and the world's) busiest railway stations, with the main Tokyo station only in 8th place (Japan Today 2013).

Cities and the Rank-Size Rule

One attribute common to cities of any historical period is that their ranking by population size displays a surprisingly regular distribution that can be expressed (not perfectly but in many instances highly accurately) by a simple mathematical formula: population of the n-th largest city is 1/n times that of the largest city, which means that the city size distribution is governed by a power law with a coefficient very close to −1. Zipf's original plot of the ranks of US metropolitan districts (based on the 1940 census) had city ranks on the horizontal axis and city populations on the vertical axis (Zipf 1949, 375; see chapter 1, figure 1.27).

On a linear graph, the perfect inverse power relationship produces a smooth curve that turns into a straight line on a double-log graph. I should note that plots in many subsequent power-law publications reverse this original Zipfian placement and put log of population on horizontal axis. Some publications also use natural (ln) rather than decadic (log) logarithms and hence the totals between 10,000 and 10 million are not plotted between 4 and 7 (their respective decadic logarithm values) but (approximately) between 9 and 16 (their natural logarithm values), and there are even published misleading plots that show values in natural logarithms labeled as decadic logarithms of charted populations.

Analyses of many national, continental, and global data sets have been done in order to find out how Zipfian the urban rank-size distributions really are. Perhaps the best proof of how well the law holds for the cities on the global scale was published by Jiang et al. (2015), because rather than using conventional population statistics (that are inevitably affected by imposed census or administrative definitions), the authors used nighttime satellite images to extract about 30,000 of what they call naturally delineated settlements for the years 1992, 2001, and 2010. They found that the law holds remarkably well on the global level, that (with the exception of Africa) it is almost valid at the continental level, but that it is violated at the country level, either from country to country or from time to time.

But they argued that in a global world the law applies to the complete city set and hence continental or national observations are not appropriate for testing its validity. In addition, they found that the law is also reflected in the city numbers in individual countries, with the number of cities in the largest country being twice as large as that in the second-largest country and so on. In a similar study (using a version of the City Clustering Algorithm to derive urban land cover from satellite images and combining it with pointwise information on population), Fluschnik et al. (2016) found that at the global scale Zipf's law holds to a greater extent for the areas of urban clusters and to a lesser extent for their corresponding populations.

But when the global analysis is done in a standard fashion, that is on the basis of published urban population data rather than on the size of natural agglomeration identified by nighttime images, the extreme upper tail of the distribution does not follow Zipf's law (Luckstead and Devadoss 2014). With the Tokyo agglomeration at nearly 39 million people, the next largest city should be less than 20 million—but in 2017 there were two cities (Jakarta and Shanghai) with more than 30 million, and at least three metropolitan areas with around 25 million people (New Delhi, Karachi, and Beijing). But for cities with less than about 20 million people (log 7.3), Zipf's law applies quite well.

On a national level, Jiang et al. (2015) only confirmed what many other analyses have uncovered before or since. Soo (2005) analyzed city size data for 73 countries and found that Zipf's law had to be rejected for 53 of them. Major countries whose city size rankings were closest to Zipf's law included Iran, Mexico, Nigeria, Pakistan, Philippines, and Vietnam, while those that deviated most from it included Belgium, France, Kenya, Netherlands, Saudi Arabia, and Switzerland. When he tested the fit in 26 countries for urban agglomerations rather than for cities, Soo found near-perfect correspondence to inverse ranking for Brazil, Mexico, India, Indonesia, and the UK, and the lowest adherence to the −1 exponent for Australia and South Africa.

Chauvin et al. (2017) analyzed data for metropolitan areas with more than 100,000 people in the US, Brazil, China, and India. Following Gabaix and Ibragimov (2011), they used log of rank −0.5 in order to get a better estimate of the coefficient on the power-law distribution. The fit for the US was pretty good (coefficient −0.91) and for Brazil it was even better. In contrast, the coefficient for China was the same as for the US but it masked a strong nonlinearity at both ends, with the country having in particular fewer very large cities than Zipf's law would suggest, an example of a commonly encountered heavy-tail distribution (data below the expected exponential line) in power-law sets. In this particular case, it might be a consequence of deliberate Chinese measures to limit the growth of large cities in the past and to regulate their post-1990 expansion. The Indian frequency plot is also bent at both ends but the fit is better than in China's case.

Not surprisingly, Bettencourt and Lobo (2016) confirmed that none of the largest western European urban systems (German, France, UK, Italy, Spain) follows Zipf's law. Germany has a shortage of sufficiently large cities due to its long history of splintered governance, while the history of centralized rule in France and the UK explains the dominance by one very large city (Paris, London) and the presence of much smaller secondary cities. Spanish cities come closer to power-law expectations but Madrid and Barcelona are too big to fit. Power law fails also on an all-European level: if it were to apply, the largest EU city would have to have a population of 58 million, followed by cities of 29 and 19 million. But creating such cities by the accelerated growth of existing metropolitan areas is both most unlikely and undesirable. Even if population dynamics were to allow for these increases, such growth would only aggravate already significant regional inequalities within the EU.

Batty (2006) provided a useful corrective to urban power-law distribution studies by introducing long-term historical perspectives through his diagrammatic rank clocks. Successive plots of American city rankings and population sizes between 1790 and 2000 show relatively stable negative exponential fits—but they completely hide the underlying growth-and-decline dynamics as cities enter and leave the top 100. Batty (2006, 592) rightly concludes that the apparent stability of power-law distributions at different times masks often turbulent changes of rank order that "destroy any notion that rank–size scaling is universal: at the micro-level, these clocks show cities and civilizations rising and falling in size at many times and on many scales."

Why the power-law distribution arises in the first place has yet to be satisfactorily answered (Ausloos and Cerquetti 2016). A preferential-attachment process is perhaps the most obvious explanation: a rich-get-richer mechanism, with the largest cities attracting disproportionately large inflows, produces the Yule-Simon distribution (Simon 1955) which follows a power law (Newman 2005). Shyklo (2017) argues that the observed Zipf's curve is caused by specifics of a ranking process itself, and is not seriously influenced by an underlying system. Gabaix (1999, 760) is convinced that the outcome is an inevitable result of following similar growth processes—and hence "the task of economic analysis is reduced from explaining the quite surprising Zipf's law to the investigation of the more mundane Gibrat's law."

Its formal definition is that the probability distribution of the growth process is independent of the initial absolute size of an entity, be it a firm—as originally described by Gibrat (1931)—or a city, and that this fits a log-normal pattern (Saichev et al. 2010). According to Gabaix (1999), most growth-affecting shocks decline with city size (due to higher economic resilience, better education and policing, and higher taxes) and hence variance of city growth reaches a positive floor in the upper tail of the size distribution. Conversely, the growth of smaller cities is more vulnerable to various shocks and this produces a larger variance and lower Zipf exponents.

This reasoning appears highly plausible but I have already cited a number of studies that found the departure from the −1 exponent to be as pronounced for the largest cities as it is for those in the lower tail of the distribution. Zipf's law and the hierarchical scaling law are thus valid only within a certain range of scales (Chen 2016), and Ausloos and Cerquetti (2016) concluded that such a simple hyperbolic law as the Zipf's law power function is often inadequate to describe rank-size relationships, and that it cannot be viewed as a universal law even when applied to city ranking where many of its applications are persuasive; they proposed an alternative theoretical distribution based on theoretical arguments. But I think there is no better way to approach a complex matter of urban growth conforming to Zipf's law than to accept the conclusions made by Cristelli et al. (2012).

As already explained, the criteria used to define an analyzed set have a critical effect on the analytical outcome, and Cristelli et al. (2012, 1) conclude that "many real systems do not show true power law behavior because they are incomplete or inconsistent with the conditions under which one might expect power laws to emerge." Coherence of the sample (its proper scale) is thus decisive because in general Zipf's law does not hold for subsets of a true Zipfian set nor for a union of such sets. Splitting and disaggregating (or merging and aggregating) objects changes their order, and this can easily take place when objects are human artifacts (such as cities) subject to variable definitions.

As a result, the law largely holds (approximately) for the city sizes of each EU country but fails completely for the entire EU set, while the reverse is true for the US, where the complete national set is nearly Zipfian but individual state sets fail to conform. This difference reflects the fact that European cities grew for centuries as parts of national systems, while US expansion took place more rapidly within the confines of an economically united state. On the global level, Cristelli et al. (2012) concluded that the system of cities has yet to reach the point where the metropolitan areas will be truly competing with one another for limited resources. To put it differently, world populations are not yet sufficiently globalized to form a coherent integrated system where the rank-size distribution would follow the power law rather than, as it does now, deviating significantly from it.

Empires

The earliest states were little more than extended hinterlands of major cities that gradually took more or less direct control of territories required for economic survival or for defense. Some of these entities, most notably in Mesopotamia and in northern China, were relatively long-lived (for centuries) but within rather constrained (and very loosely defined) boundaries, showing little or no territorial growth beyond their early expansion stage. In contrast, some later city-states (such as those established by the Phoenicians and ancient Greeks) were able to project their power across considerable distances by establishing coastal colonies hundreds of kilometers away from their core areas, but such extensions of punctiform commercial presence did not fall into the category of territorially expanding states.

The coexistence, rivalries, and conflicts of neighboring cities and, later, small city-states during the early eras of Greek, Chinese, or Mesoamerican history offer—with their protracted enmities and often prolonged stalemates—similarly poor opportunities for studying the long-term growth of organized societies. But it did not take long before significantly larger organized entities began to assert themselves, or before their often remarkably long histories of expansion and conquest provided fascinating records of growth. They go under the label of empires, and while that designation may appear intuitively straightforward, it requires clarification before trying to assess their growth: What are they and how to gauge them? Which states, or nonstate entities, can be called empires, and what are the best variables, or their combinations, to measure their growth?

Defining empire as a state ruled by an emperor or empress (as some dictionaries suggest) offers an unsatisfactory tautology. Taagepera's (1978, 113) definition is "Any large sovereign political entity whose components are not sovereign, irrespective of this entity's internal structure or official designation." That might, arguably, make Canada an empire because Quebec was recognized by the federal parliament as a nation within Canada but it does not have exclusive control over its own affairs. I think Schroeder (2003, 1) got it right: "Empire means political control exercised by one organized political unit over another unit separate from it and alien to it...its essential core is political: the possession of final authority by one entity over the vital political decisions of another." This definition also makes it clear that an empire does not need an emperor, or even a single strongman: in many Communist countries, the Party's politburo exercised more power than its leading member.

The noun's origins were straightforward: *imperium*, the right to command (or to govern), was held by the Roman kings and later by the republic's consuls and praetors. Only by the second half of the 1st century CE did it come to be understood as it is now, a powerful state in control of extensive territories: *imperium populi Romani* "was the power Romans exercised over other peoples" (Lintott 1981, 53). Political entities satisfying that understanding existed millennia before the rise of the *imperium Romanum* and included various Mesopotamian, Egyptian, Indian, and Chinese empires. The Parthian, Sassanid, Qin, and Han empires were Rome's contemporaries (and the first two its enemies), and among many empires that followed, Byzantium became a byword for its bureaucratic opacity and durability, the Muslim and Mongol empires for their rapid ascent, the Ottoman Empire for its long decline, the Russian Empire for its eastward expansion, the British Empire for its thalassocratic might, and the Soviet empire for its relentless suppression of dissent.

Barfield (2001) introduced a useful hierarchy into the classification of empires. Primary empires, exemplified by Rome or China's dynasties, are established by conquest of large (subcontinental or continental-size) territories and encompass large (at least millions) and diverse populations. Secondary (shadow) empires assume forms ranging from those pressuring neighboring primary empires for tributes (nomad states on China's steppe and desert borders excelled in this for millennia) to maritime trade empires relying on relatively small forces and limited territorial control to lever great economic benefit; nobody mastered this strategy better than the Dutch (Ormrod 2003; Gaastra 2007).

Imperial Origins and Expansion

Empires have been around since the very beginning of written records, allowing Blanken to conclude that "most of human history has been characterized by large formal empires" (Blanken 2012, 2)—and historians have certainly paid a great deal of attention to the formation and expansion, as well as the decline and disappearance, of more than a score of major empires. This is not a new interest. The last volume of the most celebrated history of the decline and fall of the Roman Empire was published more than 200 years ago (Gibbon 1776–1789)—and the most commonly examined aspects of the imperial history have included its origins, ideologies, military operations, interactions with neighbors (be it through conflicts or commercial exchanges), and cultural and technical influences.

A representative selection of more recent general writings should include works by Alcock et al. (2001), Stoler et al. (2007), Darwin (2008), Parson (2010), Blanken (2012), and Burbank and Cooper (2012), with many more books exploring the history of individual empires. Not surprisingly, this attention has been unevenly distributed. The Roman Empire keeps receiving far more attention—recent works include those of Heather (2006) and Beard (2007, 2015)—than its two great eastern enemies, the Parthian and the Sassanian empires. Asian empires have been studied far more extensively than the American ones; and both the British and the Russian empires, whose rise and fall have shaped the modern world, have been subjects of many more inquiries than the Spanish and Portuguese empires whose might peaked before 1800.

There have been many attempts to formulate general principles behind the rise of empires and the identified prime movers have ranged from deliberate aggression to preemptive expansion, and from economic exploitation to cultural and civilizational motives (including religious and political justifications). Imperial retreats and falls have been no less common topics of inquiry, with explanations ranging from an inability to resist external pressures (not only outright armed assaults but also overwhelming influxes of immigrants), to internal decay (with both economic and moral components), and environmental degradation (favored by those looking for a clear deterministic story) as the three most common—but Rollins (1983) and Demandt (1984) have compiled lists of more than 200 reasons advanced to explain Rome's demise. I will note only a few major findings concerning the genesis, maintenance, and demise of empires.

Turchin (2009) claims that his model of imperiogenesis explains the formation of more than 90% of more than 60 mega-empires that arose between 3000 BCE and 1800 CE. His "mirror-empires" model is based on imperial dynamics observable in eastern Asia, the region that has had the highest concentration of empires. Its prime mover is antagonistic interactions between nomadic pastoralists and settled agriculturalists that force both nomadic and farming polities to scale up their size, and hence expand their military power. Location near a steppe frontier is the most important determinant driving the formation of large empires: more than nine out of ten of them arose in Old World regions extending from the Sahara to the Gobi.

China provides the most convincing (also unique) case of this process with its continuous sequence of rise and fall of empires from the Bronze Age's Shang dynasty (starting 1766 BCE) to the 20th-century reconstitution of most of the Qing (China's last dynastic) empire by the Communists (proclamation of the People's Republic of China in October 1949, takeover of Tibet in 1950). Remarkably, all but one of the 15 unifications (establishment of Ming dynasty in Nanjing in 1368) originated in the north, where the capital remained (close to the invasion-prone frontier) even after most of the economic activity had shifted south of the Yangzi early in the 2nd millennium CE.

Turchin's model is helpful in explaining the rise of the premodern empires of Eurasia but it does not have any universal validity. The most obvious exceptions to Turchin's model of ancient imperiogenesis are the tropical empires of Asia (South India, Khmer), and the Inca empire spanning high mountain plains (Altiplano) and Amazonian tropical forests, and the model is also of no use in explaining the rise of the great European empires or the 20th-century expansionist states. Turchin's study ignores all thalassocratic empires; the most plausible explanation would be that while all of those empires (Spanish, Portuguese, Dutch, French, British) arose much earlier than 1800 (the cutoff date of his study), their peak extent came after 1800—but that is not true for the Spanish empire, which began to unravel right after 1800 (independence of Mexico, Colombia, and Chile in 1810, Venezuela and Paraguay in 1811).

The mirror-empires model of imperiogenesis has nothing to offer in explaining the rise of Nazi Germany, expansionist Japan in the 1930s and early 1940s, and the formation of the Soviet empire. Alessio (2013) reminds us that territory purchase or lease (rather than armed conflicts) have been important, but often overlooked, methods of imperial expansion. Moreover, not all empires were led by states. The East India Company, set up in London in 1600, and the Dutch VOC (Vereenigde Oost-Indische Compagnie, chartered in 1602) carved out major spheres of control to rule, respectively, over large parts of the Indian subcontinent (between 1757 and 1858) and today's Indonesia (Keay 1994; Gaastra 2007).

Inoue et al. (2012) focused on medium-term sequences of growth and decline in order to identify the periods that experienced significant changes of scale. These upward sweeps (or upsweeps) are defined as periods of sustained growth that produce a new peak that is at least a third higher than the earlier high. In contrast, an upcycle is a smaller upturn in a cyclical trend, and a temporary upsweep followed by a return to the old lower norm is seen as a surge. Analogically, a downswing is part of the normal growth-and-decline sequence, while a downsweep goes significantly below previous troughs, a sustained collapse brings a new deep low that becomes the norm for at least two further cycles, and a downsurge follows the collapse of an upsurge.

These analyses were done within the framework of the world-system— an international system, a network of polities making war and allying with one another (Chase-Dunn and Hall 1994; Wallerstein 2004)—and concentrated on four world-regional political/military networks, Mesopotamia, Egypt, South Asia, and East Asia, and the expanding Central System which includes the Persian, Roman, Islamic, Mongol, and British empires (Inoue et al. 2012). After comparing the frequencies of cycles and sweeps across these five interpolity networks, they found, surprisingly, more similarities than differences and identified a total of 22 upsweeps and 19 downsweeps.

But they found only three instances of sustained system-wide collapses: the post-Islamic Caliphate collapse in the Central System, the post-Eastern Han collapse in East Asia, and the post-Guptan collapse in the South Asian system. The number of collapses is so low because the studied sets are interacting polities (international systems) rather than individual polities. Comparisons also found that the frequency of cycles increased over the long run but the frequencies of upsweeps and downsweeps showed no long-term trends: no downward trend in downsweeps implies that, contrary to a common assumption, resilience has not grown with sociocultural complexity and size.

Empires become large centrally controlled entities by growing from their limited core areas to encompass distant territories inhabited by populations speaking different languages and belonging to different cultures. This definition encompasses a wide range of political entities, ranging from such explicitly established imperial structures as the *imperium Romanum* or the British Empire to a *de facto* empire reassembled by the Soviet Union after the Russian Empire's dissolution during WWI and expanded after the Soviet victory in WWII by both direct and indirect control of half a dozen eastern and central European countries.

Central control could be exercised in different ways. What might be seen as a default mode is the sanctioned (and often inherited) rule of an individual, sometimes in an openly dictatorial fashion, at other times guided by the arguments of close advisors, or by various degrees of consensus arrived at by bargaining with other powerful actors (a common way of arranging the affairs of Europe's medieval and early modern Holy Roman Empire). Prolonged rule was common, be it by a family (the Habsburgs were the rulers of the Holy Roman Empire between 1438 and 1740 and ruled the Austrian, and later Austro-Hungarian Empire from Vienna until 1918) or by a small number of individuals belonging to a ruling elite (after Stalin's death in

1953, the politburo of the Soviet Communist Party was perhaps the best example of this mode of governance until the state's dissolution in 1991).

Growth of Empires

The most revealing measure that could be used to trace the growth and endurance of empires would be to quantify their economic might but, as I will show in the next section on the growth of economies, such information is arguable even in the case of the most recent accounts prepared by national and international statistical services. National accounts are fragmentary and generally inadequate even for industrializing countries prior to WWII; they have been reconstructed (with various degrees of success) for some nations going back to the 19th and, in a few instances, even to the latter part of the 18th century, but they are entirely absent for any polity during all earlier eras. The next best choice to trace imperial growth would be to use population data: there are two reasons why the power of premodern empires was defined more by their population than by their territory.

In all preindustrial societies—even in those with a relatively high reliance on draft animals and on the three converters of preindustrial inanimate power, that is on sails, waterwheels, and windmills—human muscles were by far the most important prime movers. Consequently, their aggregate capacity determined the extent of peacetime crop cultivation, mining, artisanal production and construction, and the wartime mobilization of attacking or defending forces, and while an empire's potential power was not determined solely by the size of its population, it was very closely related to it. The second reason why population mattered more than territory was the limited capability of premodern societies to identify many valuable natural resources, to extract them in affordable ways and to convert them into useful products.

Larger territories increased the likelihood that such resources would be under their control but, for millennia, their presence conferred no benefits, while larger populations could be readily exploited. But, as already noted, there is virtually no reliable, periodical, census-type information about the growth of premodern populations, not even at intervals as long as a century, and hence we are unable to provide time series reliable enough to use changing population totals to trace the trajectories of imperial growth. We are left with the measure of imperial growth that is most readily available—and we follow the rise (and the demise) of empires by their territorial extent, a metric that is problematic in many ways.

Uncertain lines of control (the term describing a range of actions from effective direct governance to a rule by proxy to a periodically reinforced pacification followed by a withdrawal) and the ephemeral nature of many conquests are perhaps the two most common complicating factors. Controls exercised at many imperial margins ranged from defended natural or man-made barriers (major rivers and mountain ranges, Chinese and Roman stone or earthen walls) to porous zones of uncertain dominance. And in many cases, imperial control was deliberately exercised only over towns and cities connected by major trade routes rather than over their trackless hinterlands, be they in the African or Central Asian interiors. Roman borders offer excellent illustrations of these uncertainties.

Examples of ephemeral maximum conquests are common in both ancient and modern history. Perhaps the best known and much-admired ancient case was the lightning foray of Alexander's armies all the way to Punjab followed by the retreat to Persia. Alexander's army advanced as far east as the Beas River (Hyphasis) in 326 BCE before it mutinied. Even the straight-line distance is nearly 5,000 km from the Macedonian base of his Argead dynasty, more than twice as far as the direct line from Berlin to Stalingrad, where Hitler's army met its defining defeat. The most obvious medieval example is the Mongol expansion: maps of its greatest extent in 1279 show contiguous area from the Pacific coast of Siberia to the Baltic Sea, but we can only guess what share of this vast territory beyond several core areas and main communication and trade routes was actually governed by Genghis Khan's heirs.

The best modern example is the ephemeral reach of the Japanese empire following its attack on Pearl Harbor in December 1941. Japan occupied Manchuria between 1933 and 1945, large parts of eastern China between 1937 and 1945, and today's Vietnam, Cambodia, Thailand, Myanmar, and nearly all Indonesia between different months of 1942 and September 1945, but its northeastern foray was particularly short-lived. In June 1942 Japanese troops occupied Attu and Kiska islands of the Aleutian chain (Morrison 1951). The two islands became the easternmost outposts of the empire with a toehold on US territory and a justification for drawing exaggerated maps of maximum control. But the Japanese occupation lasted just over a year: after the US forces destroyed the Attu garrison, the Kiska troops were evacuated by the Japanese navy on 28 July, 1943.

Slow, expensive, and unreliable means of long-distance transportation and communication during antiquity made distant territories difficult to govern and the longer borders (or transition zones) resulting from larger territories made them more taxing to defend. Such tenuously controlled territories were of no discernible economic benefit but posed the burden of difficult defense, a reality well illustrated by the near-continuous border

Figure 5.10
For nearly three centuries Hadrian's wall, built after 122 CE and crossing from the River Tyne to Bowness-on-Solvay, was the northernmost outpost of the Roman Empire. Photo by English Heritage.

conflicts that weakened the late Roman Empire for several centuries before its dissolution. The challenges of governing the northernmost territories in Britannia (figure 5.10), defending the border with Germania, and resisting incursions into Dacia (today's Romania) and Syria are the best examples.

And many areas claimed by ancient empires were only under nominal control as they continued to be ruled by local hierarchies. Some might see the irregular temporary presence of imperial armies. The history of Tibet—the territory seen by the Chinese as an ancient integral part of their empire and by the Tibetans as an independent entity forced into temporary accommodations with its more powerful eastern neighbor—is an excellent example of this uncertainty that ended only in 1950 with the Communist occupation of Lhasa and the imposition of strong central rule from Beijing.

The weaknesses of using territorial extent as the metric of imperial growth can be also illustrated by comparing empires that claimed nearly identical territories. The maximum areas of both the British and the Mongol empires were about 33 million km^2 but even those with only a basic knowledge of the nature and duration of those two empires would immediately sense how misleading it is to make anything out of that spatial equivalence. After more than 250 years of gradual enlargement, the British Empire reached its largest extent right after WWI with the addition of former German colonies in Africa, and although the numbers of civilians and military were often very small in relation to the governed populations, the central government exercised effective control, and was able to maintain it and restore it even after serious attempts at its defeat (Williamson 1916; Ferguson 2004; Brendon 2008). India was, of course, the best example of these abilities, with about 1,000 members of the Indian Civil Service controlling about 300 million people (Dewey 1993), and with a large-scale mutiny put down fairly swiftly in just over two years between May 1857 and July 1859 (David 2003).

In contrast, the Mongol Empire was the world's largest contiguous state-like entity for just a few decades but it exercised effective, prolonged control over a much smaller area than the greatest territorial extent of its westward and southward forays (Curtis 2005). Its maximum size was reached in less than 60 years after Genghis Khan unified the Mongolian tribes in 1206, but many of its rapid, arrow-like advances were followed by equally rapid retreats, and the empire split into four large, separate entities (Golden Horde, Chagatai Khanate, Ilkhanate, and China's Yuan dynasty) before the 13th century's end, in just three generations after its founding. Charting the growth of the British Empire, all of it eventually maintained by centralized administration, thus means studying a very different phenomenon than chronicling the spasmodic advance and retreat of Mongolian riders marking the extent of an ephemeral empire in gallop.

All of this means that some territorial expansions can be traced quite accurately, with likely aggregate errors no larger than 10–15%. The Roman conquest of Italy in the 3rd and 4th centuries BCE and its subsequent expansion to Iberia and Gallia, the spread of militant Islam during the 7th century, and the Qing dynasty's push into Central Asia during the late 17th and 18th centuries (Perdue 2005) are excellent examples of this well-documented growth. In many other cases, reconstructions of expanding (and shrinking) territories may reproduce general trends quite satisfactorily, but aggregate errors regarding the extent of controlled (be it effectively governed or merely pacified) territory are larger, while in other instances the inclusion of some territories becomes not only approximate, but even arbitrary.

And a peculiar problem arises when a large empire makes further acquisitions that may be strategically and economically highly important but whose total area amounts to a small fraction of the original territory. Plotted growth will show a negligible areal bump but the expansion will have had many profound consequences. The post-1945 extension of the Soviet empire (itself a slightly smaller replication of the ancient Russian Empire) is the best example of such growth. In 1945, after reclaiming the Baltic republics and a substantial share of pre-1939 Poland, the victorious Soviet Union was by far the world's largest state occupying 22.4 million km². Subsequent extension of political and economic control over Poland, East Germany, Czechoslovakia, Hungary, Romania, Bulgaria, and Albania enlarged the Communist empire by less than 5% (almost exactly 1 million km²)—but pushed Russian control further into the heart of Europe (both Berlin and Prague are west of Vienna) than at any time in the continent's history and added significant economic and technical capabilities.

The most revealing comparison of the largest imperial territories is in terms of the share of the Earth's ice-free land (about 134 million km²) controlled by an empire. By 1900 the British Empire claimed about 23% of that total, while the Russian Empire and Qing, China's last imperial dynasty, each claimed about 10%. In contrast, the Roman Empire at its largest extent controlled only about 3% of the total and it was surpassed by its great contemporary, China's Han dynasty, whose maximum area was about 6.5 million km² by 100 CE, or nearly 5% of the total. And the Parthian Empire, early Rome's most powerful eastern adversary, had a larger territory until the middle of the last century BCE, and before the end of the 4th century the extent of the territory controlled by late imperial Rome, as well as that ruled by the Qin dynasty (Han's successor), was surpassed by the expanding Sassanid Empire. Clearly, Rome's territorial extent has not been the most important reason either for the enduring fascination with the *imperium Romanum* or for its lasting multifaceted impact on subsequent Western and global history.

In overall global comparisons, its maximum area does not lift it even into the top 20, and it does not come on top even when the comparison is limited to its contemporaries. While keeping such caveats in mind, it should be also admitted that tracing the territorial growth of empires is far from being just another category of curve-fitting exercises. Relatively extensive territorial control was a key feature of antique empires that created the first great civilizational advances and, later, of centrally controlled polities that integrated large areas on unprecedented (even semicontinental) scales during the Middle Ages, the early modern era, and during the age of industrialization. Simplistic conclusions must be avoided—but a great deal of the world's historical dynamics can be captured by focusing on the rise and fall of empires traced by their territorial extent as the relatively most reliable indicator of imperial strength.

Quantitative studies of imperial growth and decline are only of relatively recent origin. In 1931 Hart included a chapter on the accelerating growth of empires in his book on the techniques of social progress (Hart 1931).

He based his claim of exponential growth of imperial size by comparing questionably appraised areas of just half a dozen empires, beginning with Egypt and ending with the British Empire. More sensibly, in 1945, in his paper on logistic social trends, he presented a curve for the record-breaking land-based empires of Asia (Hart 1945). A year later Keller published a more detailed inquiry into the growth curves of nations which concentrated on the rise and retreat of the Roman Empire (Keller 1946). At this point of my inquiry into the patterns of growth in nature and society, it comes as no surprise that the trajectories of imperial rise identified by these pioneering papers and by all subsequent analyses conform to a pattern of sigmoid growth.

The first systematic examination of the growth curves of several major empires was done by Taagepera, who cited Hart (1945) but was unaware of Keller's (1946) more analytical work. Taagepera traced the expansion of the Roman, Ottoman, and Russian empires as well as the territorial enlargement of the United States (Taagepera 1968). He followed a decade later with more extensive inquiries that examined growth-decline curves of 41 empires between 3000 and 600 BCE (Taagepera 1978) and 600 BCE and 600 CE (Taagepera 1979). The territorial data gathered for these assessments have been repeatedly used by later researchers in their analyses (Chase-Dunn et al. 2006; Turchin 2009; Arbesman 2011; Marchetti and Ausubel 2012; Yaroshenko et al. 2015). This has perpetuated some exaggerations and approximations present in the original sets (with areas measured by using maps in historical atlases, and hence of relatively low spatial resolution).

Such (often unavoidable) inaccuracies may affect parts of some growth trajectories but they do not change the fundamental conclusions regarding the dynamics of imperial growth. Taagepera (1968, 174) put it best when explaining why the growth of empires, expressions of extreme complexity, follows the same rules as the growth of bacteria or plant seedlings:

> we may overestimate the additional complexity involved in humans, as compared to cells in a sunflower. The reason why the simple logistic curve can apply to sunflowers and empires is that not all aspects of a complex system need to be complex. In particular, the simpler laws of physics and biology are not suspended for political science and history...

While there is no doubt about the general S-shaped trajectory of the territorial growth of empires, there have been many expected and substantial differences in the rate of expansion. Durations of growth periods (measured either from the formation of a new polity or from its first expansive actions) were as brief as a few decades. The Persian Empire (the Achaeme-nid dynasty) conquered most of its lands between the Indus and Greece in less than 60 years (580 to 525 BCE), and most of the westward expansion under Genghis Khan and his successors was also accomplished in about six decades, between 1200 and 1260. The early Muslim conquests that created the extensive caliphate (from Afghanistan to Portugal and from the Caspian Sea to Yemen) took just over a century, between 622 and 750. But growth periods of several centuries have not been uncommon.

The longevity of empires is obviously a far better measure of their historic success than is the rapidity of their expansion, but long-lasting empires able to combine vigorous control over large territories with gradual improvement of economic strength are a thing of the distant past. Arbesman's (2011) analysis of 41 empires showed that life spans of less than two centuries have been most common, the frequency of survival was nearly halved for those lasting 200–400 years, it declined by more than 80% for empires lasting 400–600 years, and the expected mean imperial lifetime was about 220 years. All of three most durable empires were in early antiquity: Mesopotamian Elam (lasting 10 centuries) and Egypt's New and Old Kingdoms (each lasting five centuries) reached their adulthood phases before 1000 BCE (Elam around 1600 BC, the two Egyptian kingdoms at, respectively, 2800 and 1500 BCE).

And the two aggressive totalitarian empires of the 20th century had a relatively short duration. The Soviet empire lasted almost exactly 74 years, from the Bolshevik revolution of November 7, 1917 to the final dissolution of the Soviet Union in December 1991. And the Third Reich—intended by Hitler, as he claimed at a Nuremberg rally in September 1934, to determine the German form of life "for the next thousand years"—lasted just 12 years and three months when we count from January 30, 1933 when Hitler became Reichskanzler to May 8, 1945 when Germany signed the definitive act of surrender in Berlin (Kershaw 2012).

I will close this inquiry into imperial growth and retreat by comparing the two empires that have had perhaps the greatest influence on world history. The multifaceted legacy of the Roman Empire has been a key factor in forming, maintaining, and changing Western civilization, while the Chinese empire (despite its many upsweeps and downturns) offers a remarkable example of durability, adaptability, and continuity. Its latest reincarnation, in the form of the People's Republic of China established in 1949, demonstrates many enduring continuities whose consequences—thanks to China's new economic might—have a greater global impact than ever before in the country's long history.

Roman and Chinese Empires

The Romans themselves had few doubts about the empire's importance—and about its extent. In the *Aeneid* (vol. 1, line 278) Virgil describes Jupiter's mythical promise to the Romans: *imperium sine fine dedi* (I have granted empire without end). Remarkably, some observers came to find this hyperbolic poetic license persuasive. Even before the Romans conquered Macedonia and Aegyptus, Polybius asked in his *Histories* who would not want to know how the Romans "have succeeded in subjecting nearly the whole inhabited world to their sole government—a thing unique in history?" And "Res gestae divi Augusti" ("The deeds of divine Augustus," engraved on two bronze pillars in Rome in 14 CE) affirmed that "he subjected the whole wide earth to the rule of the Roman people." And in the 2nd century CE, Antoninus Pius styled himself as the *dominus totius orbis* (lord of the whole world). The reality was much less impressive—and also much more difficult to ascertain with a high degree of accuracy.

Modern maps of Roman provinces show contiguous bands of color sweeping across North Africa, reaching far inland from the Mediterranean coast, but their southernmost extremes are nothing but largely arbitrary lines cutting through the interior of today's Algeria, Tunisia, Libya, and Egypt. In reality, Roman control extended further inland only in parts of Numidia (today's easternmost coastal Algeria and Tunisia), where centuration (the settlements allocated to retired Roman legionnaires) extended the contiguously inhabited areas up to 200 km inland from the Mediterranean coast (Smil 2010c).

Further inland, the Sahara remained a largely impenetrable barrier until the introduction of camels from the Arabian Peninsula, a process that began in Egypt and Sudan during the 2nd and 1st centuries BCE and then spread very slowly westward, with the West African trans-Saharan trade coming only centuries later (Bulliet 1975). Centuration areas and some forward fortified positions aside, actual Roman control extended only to narrow coastal plains, and in remote provinces such settlements and outposts provided mostly just punctiform and linear control, limited to the Roman bases and the roads connecting them and excluding most of the surrounding countryside. The Roman province of Mauretania Tingitana—which covered the coastal parts of today's Algeria and northern and central Morocco north of the Atlas Mountains, rather than the modern country of Mauretania—is an excellent example of another control caveat at the empire's fringes: most of the territory was "Roman" only because of alliances with local rulers, not because of any widespread Roman settlements or direct military occupation.

Similar exaggerations of territorial extent arise due to the inclusion of substantial chunks of Egypt beyond the Delta and the Nile Valley, or to choosing highly uncertain, and fluid, lines of control in the empire's easternmost territories. Romans set up a Mesopotamian province in today's eastern Syria on at least four occasions but they never gained permanent control of the area (Millar 1993). And although maps of the Roman Empire in 117 CE show a broad swath of imperial control all the way to the northernmost end of the Persian Gulf, the Romans never possessed lower Mesopotamia (today's southern Iraq). True, in 116 CE Trajan reached the shores of Sinus Persicus and, according to Dio Cassius, regretted (when watching a ship departing for India) that he was not young anymore in order to follow Alexander's great eastward thrust, but a client state he set up in southern Mesopotamia ceased to exist the very next year.

As a result, the empire's maximum area at the beginning of the 2nd century CE is commonly put at about 5 million km^2, Taagepera (1968) and his followers used a total of 4.6 million km^2, while my most generous measurement is 4.5 m million km^2. I have also calculated that even a conservative estimate of Roman knowledge of the world's inhabited area, *oikoumene*, was at least 32 million km^2, which means that the greatest extent of the *imperium Romanum* was less than 15% of the area known by the Mediterranean civilizations in antiquity (Smil 2010c). Its great East Asian contemporary, China's Han dynasty, controlled as much as 6.5 million km^2 by 100 CE and a century later it still covered about 4.5 million km^2.

That was far from making the Romans the rulers of their *totius orbis*, and while the Roman Empire and Han China were roughly matched in total populations—perhaps as many as 60 million people (Hardy and Kinney 2005)—Han China was undoubtedly more technically innovative and economically more powerful. And the Roman Empire's longevity was not that much greater than the durability of its contemporaries: its 503 years compare to 427 years of Han rule and 425 years of the Sassanid Empire. But these realities do not detract from Rome's historic achievement in unifying the Mediterranean world in a centrally governed state. A combination of written records and archaeological findings allow us to reconstruct the growth of the empire and its farthest reach with a high degree of certainty (Talbert 2000).

The northernmost line of control was just north of the Vallum Antonini that spanned Scotland along the Forth-Clyde isthmus (Fields 2005). An enduring continental border was established along the rivers Rhine and Main (Rhenus and Moenus) and then along the Ister (Danube), with most of Germania, and all Bohemia and Slovakia beyond the empire's control. The easternmost provinces included Pannonia (today's Hungary) and Dacia (today's western and central Romania, conquered by Trajan by 106) and the imperial borders reached the Black Sea (Pontus Euxinus) just north of the Danube delta. Anatolia (Asia Minor, today's Turkey) was Roman but while the Romans tried repeatedly to incorporate northern Mesopotamia they succeeded only temporarily as they were checked, again and again, first by the Parthian and then the Sassanid Empire.

Syria was a province, but Roman control of the Arabian Peninsula was limited to a narrow coastal strip along the Red Sea. In Egypt beyond the Nile delta and the Nile valley the Romans controlled several oases and the roads between the Nile and the Red Sea ports of Myos Hormos (close to today's al-Qusair in southern Egypt) and Berenike, the departure points for sailing to India. In today's Libya, control was limited to the coastal plain, while in parts of Tunisia and Algeria some Roman settlements were further inland, and the westernmost province, Mauretania Tingitana, was never strongly held. But trying to delimit clear borders is an ahistorical effort as the Romans tried to control populations and towns rather than enforcing their domination along precisely delimited lines (Isaac 1992).

There were some famous walls (*limes*; see figure 5.10) but the empire's territorial limits were commonly indicated only by vague descriptions or by a few impermanent markers. The goal was not to control entire territories but to assure enough oversight by deploying limited forces stationed in a few garrison towns or, commonly, by relying mostly on allied forces. But the opposite was also true in a few regions where the Roman legions ventured far beyond a border zone and stayed in such forward positions for long periods of time. One of the most notable examples of such a penetration was in the inhospitable environment of Arabia's northern Hijaz: inscriptions left by the Legio III Cyrenaica, the Cyrenean Third Legion, were found in Medain Saleh (Hegra), about 900 km southeast from its main base in Bostra, in today's northeastern Jordan (Bowersock 1983; Millar 1993; Young 2001).

The Roman road to empire began slowly during the 5th century BCE (the republic's first war was waged between 437 and 426 BCE) with expansion into Etruscan territories and only a century later, after victories in the Latin war, did the republic gained the control of central Italy. After victory in the Samnite war (298 to 290 BCE), it extended control to the southeastern coastal region, with Calabria, Sicilia, and the Po valley still out of its reach. The first great territorial surge came as a result of the Punic wars. By their end in 146 BCE Rome controlled all Italy, most of the Iberian peninsula, sections of the southern Mediterranean littoral (Carthage, Cyrenaica), Macedonia, and Greece.

Asia Minor and Syria were added by 66 BCE and after Caesar's conquest of Gallia (it ended in 51 BCE) the republic controlled slightly more than

2 million km². During the next 65 years that total grew by two-thirds as it added Egypt (in 30 BCE), virtually all the southern coast of the Mediterranean, today's Belgium and Netherlands, and parts of Germany, and as it extended its Balkan border eastward until it reached the Black Sea. When Augustus died in 14 CE the empire (he became the first emperor in 27 BCE) controlled about 3.5 million km² and subsequent additions (including Britain, Dacia, Armenia, Mesopotamia) led to a peak of about 4.3 (perhaps 4.5) million km² by the beginning of the 2nd century CE under Trajan.

The growth trajectory of the maximum area controlled from the republic's foundation until the greatest extent under Trajan has an excellent logistic fit—but that is an expected course typical of so many organisms, simple or complex, and the Roman example illustrates how useless such quantitative models are as predictive tools. If a Greek mathematician in Roman employ during Trajan's rule at the beginning of the 2nd century CE (the emperor died in 117) knew how to calculate a logistic curve of the empire's territorial growth (starting in 509 BCE with the republic's foundation), and if the high degree of fit led him to believe that it must be an excellent forecasting method, then he would have foreseen not any growth ad infinitum but a comforting plateau at about 5 million km² (figure 5.11).

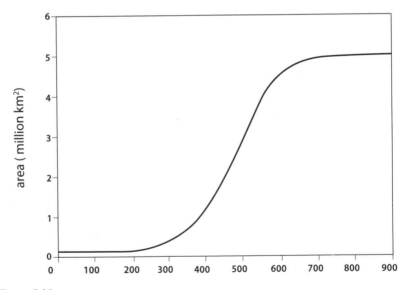

Figure 5.11
Growth of the Roman republic and empire, 509 BCE–117 CE and the implied future trajectory based on a logistic fit. Data from Taagepera (1979) and author's area measurements based on Talbert (2000). Year zero is 509 BCE.

Despite many challenges, by 390 CE the empire still controlled, albeit much more precariously along many borders, the territory amounting to nearly 90% of its maximum extent under Trajan. Then external pressures and internal discords led to a rapid unraveling and the demise of Roman imperial rule in 476 in the West. The eastern empire (where the imperial capital was relocated from Rome in 330) not only survived but by the middle of the 6th century (under Justinian and his leading general, Flavius Belisarius) even regained temporary control over Italy, Dalmatia, and parts of North Africa and Spain (Gregory 2010). After that brief expansion, Byzantium retreated but continued to rule over large (but shifting) parts of the eastern Mediterranean region for nearly 1,000 years after Romulus was deposed in Rome in 476: Constantinople was occupied by Ottoman invaders only in May 1453. When we replot the trajectory of the Roman expansion and retreat starting in 509 BCE with the republic's foundation and ending in 1453 with the fall of Constantinople, we get a relatively close approximation of a normal curve with a prolonged right tail, suggesting that the Byzantine empire was living on borrowed time for at least 700 years, that is for most of its existence (figure 5.12).

In contrast, the territorial expansion of the Chinese empire does not fit closely a sigmoidal curve (Tan 1982–1988). The first dynasty (Xia, 2070–1600

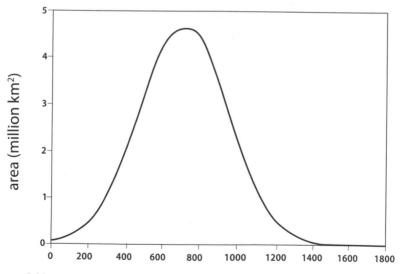

Figure 5.12
Growth of the Roman republic and empire and the gradual retreat of Byzantium, 509 BCE–1453 CE. Data from Taagepera (1979) and author's area measurements based on Talbert (2000). Year zero is 509 BCE.

BCE) was limited to about 100,000 km^2. The Shang dynasty (1600–1046 BCE) had expanded to about 1.25 million km^2 by 1100 BCE, the short-lived Qin (221–206 BCE) reached about 2 million km^2, and the Han dynasty, its successor and the Roman contemporary (206 BCE–220 CE), actually surpassed the Roman reach with about 6.5 million km^2 by 100 CE. Reverses under the Sui dynasty (581–618) more than halved that extent to 3 million km^3, under Tang (618–907) the renewed expansion reached 5.4 million km^2, and another short-lived dynasty, the Mongol-led Yuan (1271–1368), attached large parts of the Asian nomadic interior to the empire, enlarging it briefly to as much as 11.5 million km^2.

Return to Chinese rule under the Ming dynasty (1368–1644) also meant a return to essentially Han dynasty borders, while the westward push of the Manchu dynasty (Qing, China's last imperial rulers, 1644–1912) conquered territories whose total area surpassed the Mongolian maximum, peaking at about 13.1 million km^2 in 1790 and still encompassing about 11.5 million km^2 by 1880. That imperial longevity—more than 3.5 millennia of continuous governance over a fluctuating territory which had nearly always included the core area along the middle and lower Huang He and most of whose population always spoke the same language—is unparalleled in history. Even more remarkable is how this enduring configuration survived into the 21st century.

After almost four decades of post-imperial turmoil (including prolonged civil war and Japanese aggression), the Communist state established in October 1949 quickly integrated all traditional non-Han territories (Tibet, Xinjiang, Inner Mongolia, Manchuria), and only Taiwan (lost in 1895 to Japan) remained under Nationalist control. Then, after 27 years of Maoist orthodoxy and economic misery, Deng Xiaoping set China on a reformist course that boosted GDP (in constant 2010 dollars) from about $0.3 trillion to $10.2 trillion between 1980 and 2017 (World Bank 2018), making the country the world's largest economy in terms of purchasing power parity and leading to the adoption of many policies strongly resembling ancient imperial practices (Frank 1998; Bergsten et al. 2009; Morrison 2017). China, once again, has strong and unyielding central control over 9.6 million km^2 (slightly larger than the US) and its leadership, once again, refers to millennia of imperial history in superlative terms.

And it does not tolerate any real dissent, it exercises pervasive social control, it pressures its smaller neighbors, it exhibits territorial ambitions that run counter to international norms (claiming sovereignty over virtually the entire South China Sea), and its grandiose plans of a new Silk Road are to put many nearby and more distant Asian (and African) economies firmly within Beijing's economic control: Qing dynasty strategists would approve.

And (in an unmistakably symbolic way) the leaders still run the new empire from the Forbidden City. They just moved a few hundred meters southwest from those drafty imperial halls that became a mass tourist trap to walled-off Zhongnanhai, a former imperial garden that houses the headquarters of the Communist Party, the State Council, and the President. But China's ascent will be, inevitably, self-limiting: as its economic growth moderates and as its population continues to age faster in the coming two generations than the EU has done since 1970, the dynamics of the world's longest surviving empire will soon enter a new phase of gradual retreat.

The long-term adaptation of empires is thus a far more fascinating subject to study than trying to find the closest mathematical fit for their expansive period, and the contrast between Rome and China offers some revealing specificities. Both empires had to face protracted barbarian pressures—but while Rome succumbed to them, China was eventually able to absorb them. Although both empires had to rely on large armies to defend their vulnerable borders, the institutions for doing so were different: Rome delegated power to its military and that made the Roman generals both kingmakers and contenders for the supreme power, while China's governance relied on top-down bureaucracy that checked the authority of generals (Zheng 2015). These realities are illustrated by comparing the transfer of power in the Roman Empire and in the Qin and Han dynasties: 62% of Roman changes of power involved military accession, while in China hereditary successions accounted for 87% of changes.

Both empires had to reckon with new religions making bids for dominance, but the victorious Christianity did not prevent the Roman Empire's demise (it may have actually accelerated it), while in China Buddhism (and later also Islam and Christianity) never rose to such prominence. The history of language is another key difference: although Latin survived for more than a millennium after the fall of the Western Roman Empire as the language of church, laws, chronicles, and serious writing, in everyday use it was gradually displaced by its successor Romance languages, while the Chinese language and ideographic writing system remained remarkably constant until the 1950s, when the Communists instituted just a minor change of character simplification. Clearly, the amalgam of China's cultural forces was strongly centripetal, that of the Roman ways steadily more centrifugal.

Economies

As already noted, no adjective has been combined in modern writings more frequently with the noun that is the subject of this book than economic, and while economic growth is no more as ascendant a term as it was during the 1960s, it remains exceedingly common. Public concerns come and go, but preoccupation with economic growth persists and news items and studies concerning its most common measure, GDP, are inescapable. And (as already noted) in the affluent Western economies they are now almost always tinged with a bit of anxiety: it seems that GDP growth could (should?) be always higher in order for the economists, politicians, and informed citizenry to feel a bit better.

Most of this section will be devoted to a systematic examination of economic growth. The coverage will start by describing some key problems with GDP, an aggregate measure that is as convenient and as revealing as it is misleading. Then I will trace the long-term trajectories of national and global economic growth expressed in annual rates (total or, for revealing comparisons, per capita) and in actual (usually inflation-adjusted) monies. I will close this examination by focusing on the dynamics of economic growth, on its roots, preconditions, causes, enablers, promoters, and retarders. But before doing so I will look at the fundamental physical necessities and outcomes of growth, that is at energy and material flows that are now commonly overlooked (or deliberately ignored) as if the process could be only about energy-free, dematerialized changes of abstract aggregates quantified so imperfectly in such an inadequate measure of real value as money.

Although economists have a long history of ignoring energy, all economic activities are, in fundamental physical (thermodynamic) terms, simple or sequential energy conversions aimed at producing specific products or services. That is why I will trace the global expansion of primary energy use (all fuels and all forms of primary, that is nonthermal, electricity converted to a common denominator, multiples of joule in scientific units), as well as the growth of major fuels (coals, crude oils, natural gases) and electricity generation, whose level is one of the best physical proxy measures for the overall level of economic activity. Food is, of course, the most fundamental of all energy inputs and I will review such basic processes of agricultural growth as the expansion of croplands and grasslands and output of grain and meat.

As for the basic material inputs, their increasing variety has been one of the quintessential marks of economic modernization. During the early modern era (1500–1800) even the best performers (18th-century England and Qing China) had overwhelmingly wooden economies (wooden houses, ships, carriages, and tools) supplemented by considerable (but highly variable) masses of stone and bricks in construction (common in Europe, rare in East Asia) and by very limited number of metallic, glass, and ceramic objects, ranging from armor to fine porcelain. Only the 19th century saw the introduction of affordable steel and cement and the first production of aluminum, and only the 20th century brought the synthesis of ammonia (the base of all nitrogenous fertilizers) and plastics, and later of solid-state electronics based on silicon. I will trace just the most notable trends of this material diversification by looking at global consumption of wood, steel, aluminum, cement, ammonia, plastics, and silicon.

Energy Inputs

Traditional economies were energized overwhelmingly by biomass fuels (wood, charcoal, straw, dung) and by animate power (human labor, draft animals), with very small shares of inanimate power derived from flowing water and wind. Aggregate per capita use of these inputs changed very slowly during the 1,000 years that elapsed between Rome's greatest imperial expansion and Europe's late medieval era. My calculations indicate that annual use of all forms of energy averaged at least 18 GJ/capita during the height of imperial rule (Smil 2010c)—while Galloway et al. (1996) estimated London's average fuel consumption at about 25 GJ/capita in 1300. Waterwheels and windmills became gradually more important in the early modern Europe during the 16th and 17th centuries, and England was the first country where coal had already become the dominant fuel by the middle of the 17th century. The rest of Europe, Asia, and the newly created US remained overwhelmingly wooden economies until the 19th century (Smil 1017a).

Traditional economies broke free from the constraints imposed on their growth by reliance on annual products of photosynthesis supplemented by relatively small contributions of wind and flowing water (Wrigley 2010; Smil 2017a). Wrigley (2011, 2) sees an intriguing paradox in the fact that this liberation was done "by gaining access to the products of photosynthesis stockpiled over a geological time span. It was the steadily increasing use of coal as an energy source which provided the escape route." Global consumption of all primary energies (all traditional biomass and all fossil fuels) slightly more than doubled during the 19th century, from just 20 EJ in 1800 to about 44 EJ in 1900, with coal's share rising from less than 2% in 1800 to 47% in 1900 (Smil 2017a).

During the 20th century, global consumption of all primary energies— all fuels as well as all forms of primary electricity (hydro, nuclear, wind, solar) and all modern biofuels (logging residues, bioethanol, biodiesel)— grew almost exactly ninefold, to 391 EJ, and fossil fuels (with crude oil in the lead but with coal and natural gas not far behind) supplied about 80% of the total. By 2015, largely thanks to China's extraordinary economic expansion, the global total rose by another 34%. The growth rates of global energy production have followed predictable trajectories, diminishing from high values during the early decades of fossil fuel extraction or electricity generation (when they were commonly on the order of 10%/year and displayed considerable year-to-year fluctuations) to recent gains of generally less than 4% as aggregate outputs increased and as fluctuations became less wide-ranging (Höök et al. 2012).

The share of traditional biomass energies fell from just over 50% in 1900 to less than 8% by the year 2015, but because their supply cannot be accurately monitored, standard international statistics leave them out and count only modern fossil fuels and biofuels and primary electricity. Consumption of those commercial energies rose from less than 0.5 EJ in 1800 to about 22 EJ in 1900. Rounded global multiples for 1900–2000 were as follows: all primary energy (including traditional biomass) ninefold; traditional biomass twofold; commercial energy 16-fold; fossil fuels 14-fold; coal 4.7-fold; crude oil 138-fold; natural gas 375-fold; electricity (as well as thermal generation) roughly 500-fold; hydroelectricity nearly 300-fold.

Post-1800 global consumption of all primary energy (including all traditional phytomass fuels) fits closely a symmetrical four-parameter logistic curve with the inflection point in the year 1992 and indicating a total of about 690 EJ in 2100, very close to the asymptotic level (figure 5.13, top image). The post-1800 global supply of all fossil fuels and primary electricity forms another logistic curve with the inflection point in the year 2000 and indicating total consumption of about 655 EJ in 2050 (figure 5.13, bottom image). For comparison, both ExxonMobil and International Energy Agency forecasts for the year 2040 are higher than the logistic trajectory based on 215 years of global consumption: the logistic trend points to 617 EJ in 2040, the ExxonMobil projection goes as high as 740 EJ (ExxonMobil 2016). A closer look at the trajectories of the three principal fossil fuels (for coal since 1800, for crude oil since 1870, for natural gas since 1890) shows close logistic fits but none of the predictions based on these equations seems to be close to the recent assessments of the most likely performance.

Commercial extraction of crude oil began in 1846 in Russia (the Baku fields) and in 1856 in the US (in Pennsylvania), and during the 20th century global output rose almost exactly 200-fold, with the bulk of the gain taking place between 1950 and 1973 when low oil prices encouraged rising demand driven by post-WWII modernization in Europe, North America, and Japan (Smil 2017a). Two rounds of OPEC-driven oil price increases (quintupling in 1973–1974, near-quadrupling in 1979–1980) led to stagnating or slowly rising demand: by the year 2000 output was less than 20% above 1980s

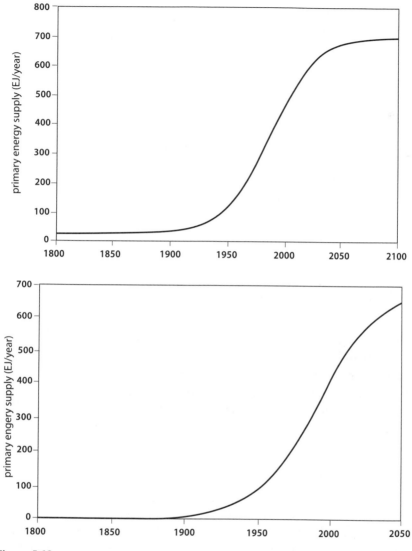

Figure 5.13
Growth of global primary energy supply (including traditional biomass fuels) and
fossil fuel and primary electricity supply since 1800. Data from Smil (2017b).

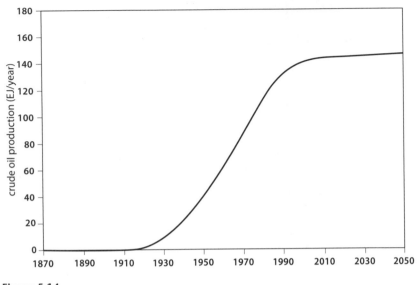

Figure 5.14
Growth of global crude oil production since 1870. Data from Smil (2017b).

level but by 2015 it had risen by another 20% thanks to growing demand in rapidly modernizing China. The logistic trajectory based on 1870–2015 extraction indicates the inflection point in 1969 and no further long-term expansion (figure 5.14). That contrasts with all standard long-term projections: for example, the new policies scenario of the International Energy Agency sees a 12% increase by 2040 and Exxon forecasts an additional 20% in the same year, and reduced demand is envisaged only with adherence to policies that would limit atmospheric CO_2 concentrations to 450 ppm by 2050 (IEA 2018; ExxonMobil 2016).

Pre-WWII extraction of natural gas was overwhelmingly an American affair, but between 1950 and 2000 global output grew 11-fold as the Soviet Union surpassed US production and as Canada, the North Sea, Netherlands, and Australia emerged as major producers (Smil 2015b). The logistic fit of post-1870 global gas extraction has its inflection point in 1994 and output in 2050 only 25% above the 2015 level (figure 5.15). This looks like an underestimate of the most likely extraction. Horizontal drilling and hydraulic fracturing made the US, once again, the world's largest natural gas producer, and moreover one with long-term aspirations to become also the world's largest exporter of LNG. The growth of Russian and Chinese production, increased LNG exports from Qatar and Australia, and the entry of Iran into the global LNG market will combine to lift output considerably:

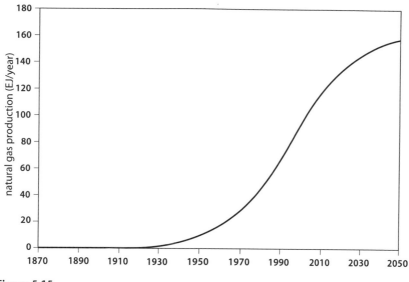

Figure 5.15
Growth of global natural gas extraction since 1870. Data from Smil (2017b).

as a result, Exxon forecasts a 50% rise between 2015 and 2040 and the new policies scenario of the International Energy Agency had a similar target, with a 46% rise by 2040.

In contrast, protracting the 1800–2015 logistic curve for global coal extraction (whose trajectory has been distorted by the recent quadrupling of Chinese production) results in a large overestimate of the most likely output: there is a very low probability that the world will produce about 75% more coal in 2050 than it did in 2015 (figure 5.16). Forecasts for China, by far the world's greatest coal producer (responsible for half of the total in 2016) range from a slight gain to a significant decline, and while India will rely on coal as its principal fuel at least until 2047 (Government of India 2017), elsewhere the concerns about global warming and the fuel's rapid substitution by natural gas in electricity generation will constrain its future use. Coal is the most carbon-intensive fuel, releasing about 90 g CO_2/MJ, while natural gas emits 25% less, or only about 68 g CO_2/MJ; because in the US coal generated nearly half of all electricity in 2005 and only 30% by 2016, the country achieved a faster reduction of its CO_2 emissions during that period than any other high-income economy, including Germany with its heavily subsidized PV and wind electricity generation.

After a wartime peak, American production was in decline by 1945 but its subsequent loss of two major markets, household heating and railroad

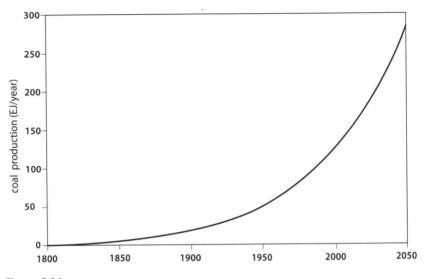

Figure 5.16

Growth of global coal production since 1800. While the two logistic curves for crude oil and natural gas provide a highly plausible indication of future development, coal's indicated trajectory will almost certainly diverge from the indicated trend. Data from Smil (2017b).

transportation, was more than compensated by the rising demand for steam coal to generate electricity that resulted in six decades of rising extraction, with peak annual production at just over 1 Gt (1.063) in 2008. But given the just noted ascent of natural gas, as well as weakening opportunities for export, it is almost certain that that was the all-time peak: by 2016 the output was down to 660.5 Mt, a 38% drop in just eight years (USEIA 2017a). China's coal extraction peaked in 2013 at 3.97 Gt, by 2016 it was down by nearly 15% but then rose again in 2017 and 2018. As the major economies attempt to accelerate the transition from coal to fuel that is less carbon intensive and to renewables, the long-term fate of US, Chinese, Indian, or Australian coal mining remains uncertain, but British coal production has already run its full course (see chapter 6).

Commercial electricity generation began in 1882 and remained limited until the first decade of the 20th century. During the earliest decades of electricity generation, the aggregate output of still fairly small hydro projects was nearly as important as production in coal-fired plants, but by the 1920s thermal generation had become dominant: it produced nearly two-thirds of all electricity by 1950 and almost exactly 66% in 2015. Total generation grew more than sevenfold between 1920 and 1950 (from 0.13 to

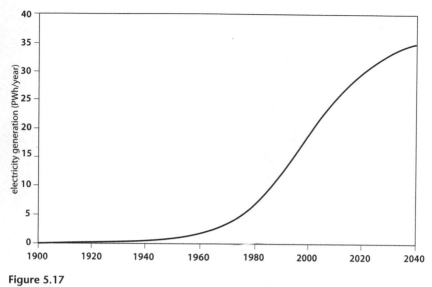

Figure 5.17
Growth of global electricity generation since 1900. Data from Smil (2017b) and BP (2017).

0.858 PWh) and then it duplicated that growth rate between 1950 and 1980 (to 7.069 PWh). Post-1980 growth has been slower as a logistic curve began to form (inflection point in 2005) and as global generation reached about 24 PWh in 2015 (figure 5.17). The logistic trajectory points to about 35 PWh in 2050, a gain of about 45% in 35 years.

Hydroelectric generation nearly quintupled between 1950 and 1980, when large dams were prominent components of modernization. Later they came to be seen as environmentally risky but China, India, and Brazil kept on building and worldwide output almost exactly doubled between 1980 and 2010. The logistic trajectory has its inflection point only in 2009 and it points to a nearly 50% increase by 2050 (figure 5.18). Nuclear generation had much faster penetration than either thermal or hydro; after its slow beginning (starting in October 1956 in the UK), it grew more than 200-fold between 1960 and 1980 and it nearly tripled during the 1980s as the plants ordered during the 1970s were finally completed. That was the period of impressive exponential growth, with generation increasing annually by nearly 29% between 1957 and 1980 and averaging still a very high rate of 23% between 1957 and 1990.

Expectations of the global expansion of nuclear generation were affected by the Three Mile Island accident in the US (in 1979) and by the catastrophic release of radiation from the Soviet reactor in Chornobyl (in 1985)

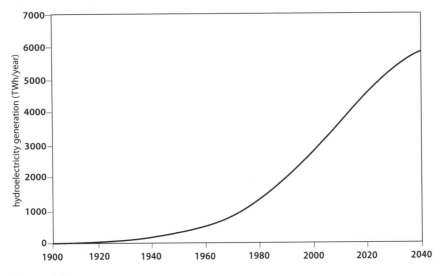

Figure 5.18
Growth of global hydroelectricity generation since 1900. Data from Smil (2017b) and BP (2017).

but these events were not the most decisive factors in moderating the long-term outlook. In the case of Three Mile Island, no radiation was released from the plant and the Chornobyl catastrophe would have had a different outcome if the Soviet reactor had had what all Western designs mandated: a confinement structure. Cost overruns in building new plants and reduced growth of electricity demand were the most important factors behind the weakened Western prospects, but Japan, China, India, South Korea, and even Russia did not abandon their considerable expansion plans and kept on building. In the new century a substantial share of increased generation came from much-improved capacity factors but by 2010 output was only about 7% above the 2000 level, and the total for 2015 was actually down (affected by the closing of all Japanese stations in the aftermath of the Fukushima Dai-ichi disaster in 2011).

Early expectations for the growth of nuclear power turned out to be overly optimistic and as a result the International Atomic Energy Agency (IAEA) lowered its 1980 forecast (for more than 700 GW in 2000) to 503 GW in 2005 (Semenov et al. 1989). In reality, the 2015 total came only to 376 GW—and using a logistic curve derived from the 1956–1990 expansion of global nuclear generation to forecast the 2015 total would have ended up with a projection that turned out to be only about 7% lower than the power actually generated in that year, an excellent result for a 25-year

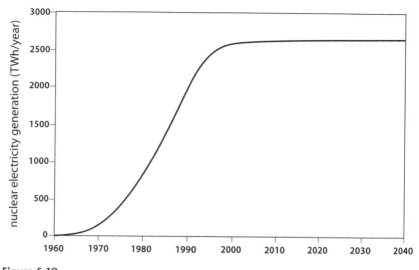

Figure 5.19

Growth of global nuclear generation since 1960. Data from Smil (2017b) and BP (2017).

forecast. Repeating the exercise based on the 1956–2015 trajectory produces another well-fitting logistic curve with the inflection point in 1985 that forecasts only a 4% gain in generation by 2030, indicating that nuclear development reached its saturation (figure 5.19).

That conclusion, affected by recent decline and stagnation, might look too pessimistic—but the outlook may be even poorer as there are only marginal prospects in the EU and North America (where all older reactors will cease operating well before 2050) and as the continuing expansion in Asia may not offset that decline. In 2017 about 60 reactors in 15 countries were under construction but more than 130 of the 440 reactors operating in 2017 will be closed down by 2035 (WNA 2017). In contrast, the IAEA's latest long-term forecast puts 2030 generation at least at 24% (low estimate) and as much as 86% (high estimate) above the 2015 level (IAEA 2016). The higher estimate can be easily dismissed as yet another instance of the IEAE's chronic wishful thinking, and the chances are high that the eventual outcome might be, once again, closer to the logistic forecast.

Translating the advances in total primary energy use or total electricity generation into growth trajectories of per capita supply is easy but the resulting rates require careful interpretation. Because of a highly skewed global distribution of energy use, there is an order-of-magnitude difference between high- and low-income countries in annual per capita rates: the US at 285 GJ/capita, Germany at 160 GJ, China at 95 GJ, India at 27 GJ, Ethiopia at 21 GJ (World Bank 2018). The worldwide mean of about 80 GJ/capita in 2015 (compared to just 27 GJ/capita in 1900) is far above the supply available to billions of inhabitants of Asia and Africa, and far below the level enjoyed by about 1.5 billion affluent people (including the richest groups in China, India, Indonesia, and Brazil). There are substantial intranational differences, with wealthy urban families consuming far more than poor rural ones.

Food Production

Food is, of course, the most indispensable form of energy but it is never treated as such in modern economic studies. Growth of staple crop yields and changes in productivity of domestic animals were traced in some detail in chapter 2, and here I will concentrate on the growth of key inputs that have made it possible not only to feed the expanding global population but to do so at a gradually improving level, that is with greater supply reserves and with higher quality average diets (more protein and micronutrients). Despite the previously described advances in typical yields, the overall population increases could not have been adequately fed from productivity increases alone and the world has seen substantial expansion of both cultivated land and grasslands used for the grazing of domesticated animals, mostly cattle.

The reconstructed trajectories of post-1700 global cropland and grassland areas (PBL 2010) show excellent logistic fits, both with inflection points during the 1920s. Global cropland (arable land and land used for permanent crops) increased from about 260 Mha in 1700 to nearly 1.5 Gha in the year 2000 and the trajectory indicates expansion of at least another 10%, to about 1.65 Gha, by 2050 (figure 5.20). Rapid expansion of the cultivated area during the latter half of the 19th century was the result of large-scale conversions of grasslands in the US and Canada, as well as in Argentina, Russia, and parts of China: the trajectory of the US cropland area is the best illustration of this process (figure 5.21). Grassland expansion was a much more extensive process, with the total rising from 500 Mha in 1700 to 3.5 Gha by the year 2000: takeoff also began during the 19th century but the expansion continued at relatively high rates during the 20th century due to large-scale conversion of forests to pastures in Asia, Africa, and particularly in Latin America, and the logistic trend indicates a further relatively minor extension by 2050 (figure 5.22).

But the decisive factor in the growth of modern food production has been its transformation from a totally solar-driven system to a hybrid that is now critically dependent on rising inputs of energies produced by modern

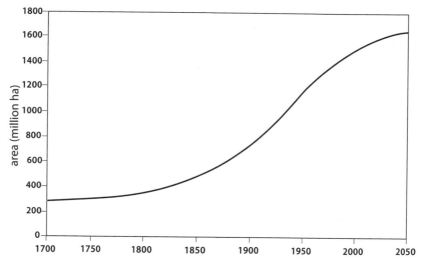

Figure 5.20
Growth of global cropland, 1700–2050. Logistic curve had its inflection point in 1876 and the total is now less than 5% below the asymptote. Data from PBL (2010) and FAO (2018).

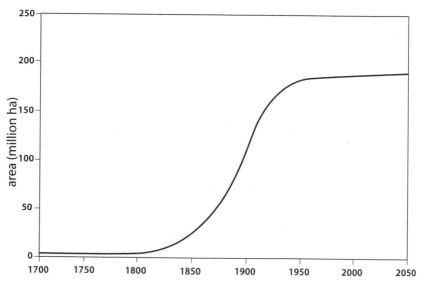

Figure 5.21
Growth of US cropland, 1700–2050. Inflection point came already in 1876 and the recently cultivated area is very close to the asymptotic level. Data from PBL (2010) and FAO (2018).

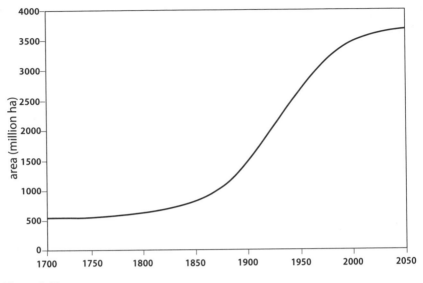

Figure 5.22
Growth of global grasslands. The inflection year was in 1923 and the total area is now less than 10% from the asymptotic level. Data from PBL (2010) and FAO (2018).

anthropogenic conversions. All traditional agricultures shared the same energetic foundation as they were powered solely by the photosynthetic conversion of solar radiation. Crop photosynthesis produced all food and all animal feed, which, in turn, sustained human labor and animal draft used in agriculture; recycling of plant matter and of animal and human wastes replenished soil fertility; and iron tools used in farming (sickles, scythes, plow shares) were made from the metal smelted in charcoal-fueled blast furnaces (Smil 2017a).

In contrast, modern farming complements the indispensable sun-driven photosynthetic conversion by a multitude of anthropogenic energy inputs derived mostly from fossil fuels and also from primary electricity. We might think of them as direct and indirect external energy subsidies, with the first category including all fuels and electricity used to operate the field and processing machinery of modern farming, and the second category composed of many fossil energy inputs used to produce agricultural machinery and chemicals (coke for iron smelting, hydrocarbons for the synthesis of ammonia, pesticides and herbicides). In comparison to these major flows, the energies required to develop new crops (supporting basic breeding research and field work) add up to a relatively minor—but now absolutely indispensable—requirement.

My reconstruction of energy inputs into modern farming indicates that during the 20th century—when the global population increased 3.7-fold and the total harvested area expanded by only about 40%—these anthropogenic subsidies increased nearly 130-fold, from just 0.1 to almost 13 EJ (Smil 2017a). They come in a wide variety of energy sources used by many industries and services that support cropping and animal production. The largest direct uses of energy in agriculture are liquid fuels (diesel oil and gasoline) and electricity to energize field and crop-processing machinery (mostly tractors and combines) and trucks, to power irrigation pumps and sprinklers, and to dry grain.

The two largest indirect energy inputs are natural gas and electricity to produce fertilizers (to synthesize ammonia and to extract and process phosphates and potassium) and various energies required to produce farm machinery and components (from tractors to irrigation pipes) and to synthesize pesticides and herbicides. Mechanization of modern agriculture is now nearly complete, with all field tasks performed by machines. The irrigated area is still expanding: its global total roughly quintupled during the 20th century, increasing from less than 50 Mha to more than 250 Mha, and then rising to 275 Mha by 2015 (FAO 2018). As a result, in 2015 about 18% of the world's harvested cropland was irrigated (most of it in Asia), about half of it relying on water pumped mostly from wells but also from rivers and lakes. Drawing water from deep aquifers is commonly the single largest energy cost in cropping.

Nitrogen is the most important macronutrient required to support increasing crop yields and in traditional agricultures its supply was limited by the recycling of organic matter (crop residues and human and animal waste). Chilean nitrates (discovered in 1809) provided the first inorganic option, but the road to inexpensive nitrogen fertilizers was opened only in 1909 with Fritz Haber's discovery of ammonia synthesis, which was commercialized under the leadership of Carl Bosch in 1913 (Smil 2001). Global production of nitrogen fertilizers took off slowly, with major gains coming only after WWII when energy costs of the synthesis were greatly reduced by new production techniques (from more than 100 GJ/t of ammonia in 1913 to less than 30 GJ/t during the 1990s).

Global consumption reached 85 Mt of nitrogen in 2000 and 115 Mt of nitrogen in 2015 and the complete (1913–2015) trajectory closely fits a symmetrical logistic curve with the inflection point in 1982 that has come very close to its asymptote (figure 5.23). The payoff of this high-energy input has been extremely rewarding. Synthesis of ammonia requires just 1% of global energy use but the application of nitrogen fertilizers has enabled us to grow

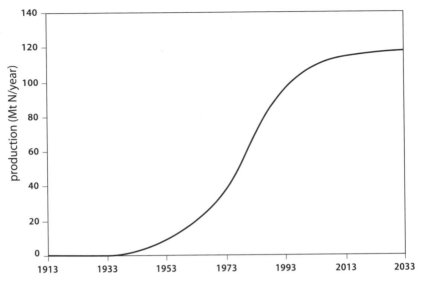

Figure 5.23
Worldwide production of nitrogenous fertilizers since 1913. Another logistic curve
that is very close to its asymptote. Data from Smil (2001) and FAO (2018).

about 40% of the current global food supply, and about 50% of China's
crop harvest. Stated inversely, two out of every five people alive (and every
second person in China) is now adequately fed thanks to the Haber-Bosch
synthesis of ammonia.

The growth of direct and indirect anthropogenic energy inputs has revolutionized food production: it has made it possible to realize most of the
growth potential inherent in new hybrids and short-stalked cereal varieties (see chapter 2 for the growth of their yields). The best indicator of
the progress of food production is the aggregate harvest of staple grain
crops (wheat, rice, corn, barley, rye, oats, sorghum). Its global total quintupled during the 20th century (rising from less than 400 Mt to 1.86 Gt)
and it reached a new record of 2.51 Gt in 2015 (Smil 2013a; FAO 2018).
The post-1900 growth trajectory shows a very close logistic fit with the
inflection point in 1992 and with about 3 Gt forecast for the year 2050
(figure 5.24). And when expressed in energy terms, the total food crop harvest (staple grains, legumes, tubers, sugar crops, oil crops, vegetables, and
fruits) increased sixfold during the 20th century, staying well ahead of the
3.7-fold increase in the world's total population.

In 1900 the global crop harvest prorated to an average per capita diet
that was barely above the mean for basic needs. Obviously, this limited the

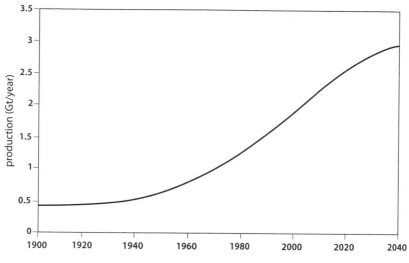

Figure 5.24

Global harvest of staple grain crops since 1900. Data from Smil (2013a) and FAO (2018).

diversion of crops to feed animals and, given the unequal access to food, it resulted in widespread malnutrition and in some regions in recurrent famines. Because of the sextupling of the crop harvest, the average per capita availability of food energy amounted to about 2,800 kcal/day and as the total includes infants, small children, and the elderly (whose energy needs are far lower than those of working adults), the average for adults was above 3,000 kcal/day, with the mean rates even higher in high-income countries, leading to enormous (on the order of 40%) food waste. In contrast, the declining share of people in low-income countries who remain undernourished are deprived because of their limited access to food, not because of inadequate food supply.

Larger harvests have also made it possible to divert more crops into animal feed (about 35% globally, 50–60% in affluent countries) and resulted in rising consumption of meat, eggs, and dairy products (Smil 2013a). Global meat output (red meat and poultry) rose from less than 50 Mt in 1950 to 230 Mt in the year 2000 and by 2015 it had surpassed 300 Mt (FAO 2018). The trajectory indicates a logistic curve still in its early phase and output of 600 Mt by 2050. FAO expects this doubling to take place but I would argue that this might be yet another case of a mechanistic forecast that will run into new consumption realities. Average meat intakes have either stagnated or declined in nearly all affluent countries, are close to saturation in China, are unlikely to reach Chinese levels in India, and may be rising slower than anticipated in Africa.

Material Inputs

Even a diligent reader of economic news may go for days without seeing any reference to materials that form the physical foundation of modern civilization. Yet their annual global flows add up to tens of millions (many industrial chemicals), hundreds of millions (plastic, and, as already explained, ammonia used largely for fertilizers) and even billions of tonnes (steel, cement). This neglect of the world's material foundations has further intensified with the widely held belief that dematerialization has been on the march, an impression created by the relentless crowding of more components on a microchip, the process captured by Moore's law underpinning the miniaturization and hence the not only relative but even absolute dematerialization of the modern e-world.

Whenever a new product relies on improving microprocessors, the growth of its performance, or decline of its cost, will proceed at rates closely resembling Moore's law. This is obviously true about the processing speed of computers (instructions per second), while the cost of computing has been declining even faster (about 50%/year since the late 1970s), the cost of camera chips (pixels/$) has been dropping nearly as fast, and the capacities of magnetic storage (the recording density of storage media) have been growing by more than 50%/year since the early 1990s. Other advances associated with silicon and semiconductors have seen rapid doublings of performances or declines in cost: the efficacy of light-emitting diodes (lumens per watt) has been rising by about 30%/year since the late 1970s, doubling every 3.3 years) and the cost of photovoltaic cells (dollars per peak watt) has recently been declining at an annual rate of about 20%.

These advances have led to the unintended effect of raising general expectations regarding the pace of technical progress. This is a clear *pars pro toto* mistake or, as I have called it, Moore's curse (Smil 2015a). Rapid progress is now assumed to improve everything from the energy density of batteries to 3D printing of living organs in short periods of time. These advances have also raised unrealistic expectations about the general progress of dematerialization. Thanks to Moore's law, that trend has been quite impressive as far as computation is concerned, with the mass per unit of RAM ratio having been cut by nine orders of magnitude since 1981 (Smil 2014a). But this example is also quite exceptional, as trends from the e-world are not readily copied in the world of mass material demands. There has not been (because there cannot be) any Moore's law-like progression in building essential infrastructures, expanding megacities, and manufacturing vehicles, airplanes or household appliances where even reductions of an order of magnitude (that is maintaining the performance with only a tenth of the original mass) are uncommon.

While many of these investments and acquisitions have benefited from relative dematerialization (thanks to stronger steels, the adoption of new composite materials, or better overall designs), there has been no absolute dematerialization on a macro level:

> Progressively lower mass (and hence decreased cost) of individual products, be they common consumer items or powerful prime movers, has contributed to their increased use as well as to their deployment in heavier (more powerful, larger, more comfortable) machines. Inevitably, this has resulted in a very steep rise in demand for the constituent materials—even after making an adjustment for increased populations or for a greater numbers of businesses. (Smil 2014b, 131)

American cars are an excellent illustration of these trends. Advances in design have made the engines prime examples of relative dematerialization, with a rising power/mass ratio. In the early 1920s the dominant Ford Model T had a mass/power ratio of 15.3 g/W, while nearly 100 years later the best Ford engines have a mass/power ratio of less than 1 g/W, a very impressive 94% reduction in less than a century. But this gain has been negated by the growing average power and average mass of American cars. As already shown (see chapter 3), average power ratings have seen a linear increase. The Model T had power of 15 kW, but the average power of new US vehicles has been above 150 kW since 2003 and in 2015 it reached a new record of 171 kW, making the average car of the second decade of the 20th century nearly 12 times as powerful as the Model T—and erasing all relative dematerialization gains from the reduced mass/power ratio (Smil 2014b; USEPA 2016b).

And the average vehicle got heavier. In 1908 the original Model T weighed just 540 kg, three decades later another best-selling Ford Model 74 weighed 1,090 kg, and in 1975, when the US Environmental Protection Agency began to monitor key parameters of newly sold cars, it reached 1,842 kg. The rise of gasoline prices during the 1970s led to an average weight decline that proved to be only temporary: the trend toward heavier vehicles resumed during the late 1980s with the introduction of SUVs and with the rising popularity of light trucks; by 2004 the average new US passenger vehicle weighed slightly more than in 1975 and by 2015 the weight had decreased only by about 2% (USEPA 2016b).

As a result, in 2015 the average US vehicle was 3.6 times heavier than the Model T, and any intervening dematerialization of engine and car design (including substitution of steel by lighter aluminum, magnesium, and plastics) would not have resulted in absolute dematerialization even if annual car sales had remained unchanged for more than a century. In reality, they rose by three orders of magnitude, from just 4,000 to about 19 million units, resulting in massive new requirements for materials, and a century later the American experience is now being repeated in China, the world's largest automotive market since 2009, with more than 20 million passenger vehicles sold annually since 2013 (NBS 2016).

Steel has always been, and remains, the key car-building metal and it is also the indispensable structural and reinforcing material in the construction of buildings (particularly of high-rises and skyscrapers), roads, tunnels, bridges, railroads, airports, ports, and a wide range of industrial and transportation machinery and household products (Smil 2016b). The metal's primacy is recent. In preindustrial societies steel was a rare and expensive material made mostly by laborious carburization of wrought iron and reserved for weapons and high-quality utensils. Even by 1870 its global output had not surpassed 500,000 t, and the production of iron was itself limited as long as the smelting was energized by charcoal.

Centuries of charcoal-based smelting brought gradual efficiency gains (from as many as 20 units of charcoal per unit of hot metal in medieval Europe to just eight units during the late 18th century) but the fundamental change that opened the way to modern mass-scale iron production was the replacement of charcoal by coke that began in England in 1709 but that took off only after 1750 (Smil 2016b). The age of inexpensive steel arrived only with the introduction of Bessemer convertors (introduced in 1856) and not long afterwards with the widespread adoption of open-hearth furnaces that remained the dominant mode of steelmaking until the 1950s, when basic oxygen furnaces began their relatively rapid conquest of the market (figure 5.25).

Worldwide production of steel approached 30 Mt by 1900, reached about 140 Mt at the beginning of WWII, and afterwards the postwar demand for infrastructural, construction, transportation, and appliance steel pushed the total to more than 700 Mt by 1980. This was followed by two decades of stagnation and slow growth that ended with the extraordinary expansion of China's steel industry: by 2010 the total had surpassed 1.4 Gt, and by 2015 it was over 1.6 Gt, with two-thirds made in China (figure 5.26). A logistic fit is fairly good but its future trajectory (output of 4 Gt by 2050, and no inflection point for centuries to come) indicates impossible achievements. Steel demand has been stagnating or declining in all high-income countries, is now close to saturation in China and although there are large

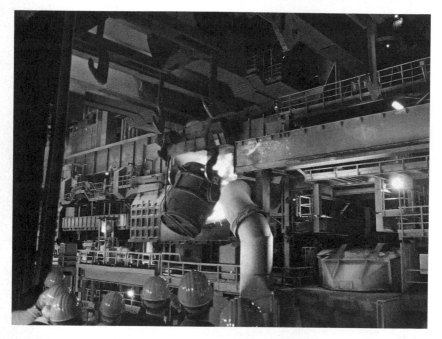

Figure 5.25
Basic oxygen furnaces, such as this one at ThyssenKrupp steelworks in Duisburg, dominate the global production of steel. Photo available at wikimedia.

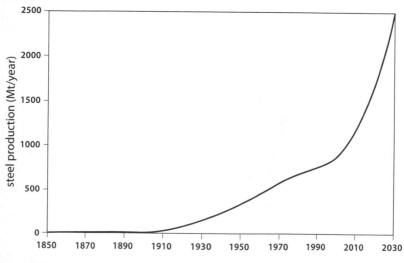

Figure 5.26
Worldwide steel production since 1850. Data from Smil (2016b).

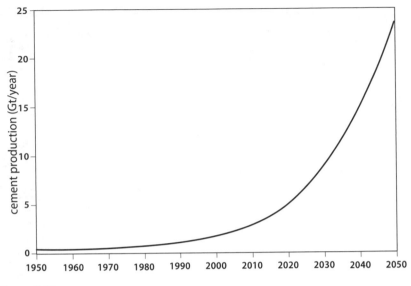

Figure 5.27
Worldwide cement production since 1950. Data from Smil (2014b).

unmet needs in India and sub-Saharan Africa they will not result, at most, in another doubling of the global steel output by 2050 (Smil 2016b).

Annual steel output is now roughly equaled by the production of stone (with about 90% of it being crushed stone and 10% dimension stone) and surpassed only by the production of construction sand (US total about 1 Gt in 2016, with no reliable global aggregate available but likely to be on the order of 4 Gt), cement (4.1 Gt in 2015), and bricks (estimated to be on the order of 4.5 Gt). Global cement production rose from about 130 Mt in 1950 (dominated by the US) to 1.8 Gt by the year 2000 and to 4.1 Gt in 2017 (USGS 2017b; figure 5.27). China became the largest producer in 1986 and it now accounts for nearly 60% of the global total (2.4 Gt in 2017).

Historical perspective provides the best appreciation of China's soaring growth of cement consumption. While the US consumption of cement added up to about 4.56 Gt during the entire 20th century, China emplaced more of it, 4.9 Gt, in just three years between 2008 and 2010 and used even more of it (5.5 Gt) to make concrete between the years between 2009 and 2011 (NBS 2016). The global trajectory of cement production conforms to a logistic curve in its early stage of growth but the implied expansion to more than 20 Gt by the year 2050 is most unlikely as the rapid post-1990 growth was driven by China's exceptional demand stimulated by the country's high economic growth and further potentiated by delayed urbanization and by excessive infrastructural investment, a combination of growth factors not likely to be repeated either in India or in sub-Saharan Africa, the major regions for a potentially large expansion of cement production.

Modern economic growth has required not only much expanded extraction of mineral elements and compounds but also the creation of new, synthetic materials. Aggregate extraction of many elements amounts to a small fraction of producing iron, aluminum or copper but their uses (such as tantalum in microelectronics capacitors and neodymium in tiny powerful magnets) have become indispensable. And a case could be made that another element whose extraction is negligible compared to major metal mining might lend a suitable name to the post-1950 era. To the sequence of Stone, Bronze and Iron Ages, first proposed by Christian Thomsen (1836), we might add the Silicon Age starting in 1954 when Texas Instruments released the first silicon transistor, soon followed by integrated circuits and then by microprocessors (see the electronics section in chapter 4).

Silicon is abundant because silica (SiO_2) is the most important mineral element in the Earth's crust. Traditional uses of the mineral in glassmaking (where it accounts for about 70% of all raw materials) were joined by metallurgical applications, above all the production of ferrosilicon alloys (with 15–90% Si) and by chemical syntheses, above all the production of silicones. The metallurgical market claims about 80% of the element's annual global production, which rose from 1 Mt in 1950 to 7.6 Mt in 2015 (USGS 2017b). Only a small share ends up as high-grade metal. In the year 2000, global production of electronic grade polycrystalline silicon was just over 18,000 t and by 2012 it rose to about 28 000 t, and after crystallization and cutting about a third of this mass ended up as wafers used for microchip fabrication.

Producing silicon of high purity is a challenge. The metal, used in solar PV cells and in semiconductors, accounts for a small share of the total use but for the PV applications the required purity is 99.9999–99.999999% (6–8 N), while electronic-grade silicon for microchips has purity levels of 9–11 N, that is up to 99.999999999% pure. Silicon wafer shipments for semiconductors rose from just over 3.5 Mm^2 in the year 2000 to 6.9 Mm^2 in 2016 (SEMI 2017), and global accounts show the value of these shipments rising from less than $4 billion in 1976 (the first years for which worldwide data are available) to about $200 billion in the year 2000 and reaching about $340 billion in 2016 (SIA 2017). Since 1996 the annual growth rate has averaged 4.8% and the complete 1976–2016 trajectory of global shipments has a good logistic fit, with the inflection point in 1997 and appearing to be very close to saturation (figure 5.28).

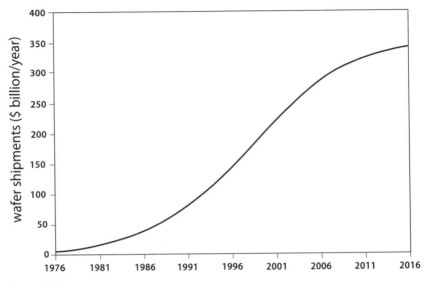

Figure 5.28
Logistic curve of worldwide semiconductor sales, 1976–2016. Plotted from data in
SIA (2017).

Semiconductor silicon is also an excellent example of the very high
energy costs of some new materials (composites used to make the latest
aircraft are another example of this shift). Electricity accounts for most of
energy used along the complicated production chain, which starts with Si
made from quartz and ends with microchip wafers and requires at least 2.1
MWh/kg. Even if using only hydroelectricity, this would be equivalent to
7.6 GJ/kg, but electricity generated from fossil fuels would nearly triple the
total for finished wafers to more than 20 GJ/kg. In comparison, primary
steel (made from pig iron smelted from iron ore) needs about 25 MJ/kg and
about 200 MJ/kg are needed for primary aluminum, which means that pure
silicon costs 100 times more than aluminum and 800 times more than steel;
as a result, even small quantities of new highly energy-intensive materials
can create substantial energy demand.

Opening the section on economic growth by three brief reviews on
the physical inputs of energies, food, and materials has been a deliberate
choice. I intended to stress the first-things-first principle that is now so
often ignored in the world of economic abstractions, and also to emphasize how imperfectly those complex physical realities get appraised in
monetary terms. Food production is by far the best example of this skewed
valuation. As the entire agricultural sector now contributes less than 2% to

national gross domestic products in every G7 country, economists see it as an entirely marginal undertaking even as they obsess about the latest valuation of Google (Alphabet) or Facebook.

They need to be reminded that it is perfectly possible to have affluent, productive economies without any of these would-be masters of the universe (as was the case before, respectively, 1998 or 2004)—but that even the richest economies with extensive food storage capacities would literally die in a matter of months without ongoing food production. Similarly, they may dismiss the steel industry as an old industrial undertaking and as a largely spent low-value-added activity—but no segment of the modern economy (including all services, electronics, and data management) could exist without a constant and affordable supply of many varieties of high-quality steel (Smil 2016b).

In tracing the trajectories of abstract economic growth—reduced to aggregate measures, above all to GDP and GDP/capita, or expressed in annual growth rates, a metric particularly worshipped by modern economists—I will start with large-scale, long-term perspectives, including past global estimates and more accurate recent worldwide aggregates, and the longest available reconstructions of national trends for some of the world's major economies. Only then will I proceed to an examination of key growth factors and growth correlations by examining the roles of such diverse drivers as population growth, demographic transition, investment, energy inputs, education, technical innovation, and overall political setting.

Quantifying Economic Growth

Given the complexity of modern economies, only a broad aggregate measure can capture their growth. This measure, now universally deployed, is gross domestic product. Its oft-repeated definition seems straightforward: GDP expresses the monetary value of all final goods and services that are produced or provided within the borders of a country during a specified period of time (monthly or quarterly in national reports, per year for international comparisons). But measuring GDP growth, and hence ascertaining its disappointing or satisfactory rates, is an inherently difficult matter and one whose systematic practice is quite recent.

Its origins go back to the 1930s when Simon Kuznets was asked by the US Congress to estimate the country's national income (Kuznets 1934). Its scope was defined by John Maynard Keynes, the measure became a key tool for the international financial institutions set up by the Bretton Woods agreement in 1944, and it was widely applied for the first time to the growing post-WWII economies (Coyle 2014). Before too long it became obvious that, like every aggregate measure, GDP has many drawbacks—but despite suggested adjustments and proposals for alternative accounts, it has become only more entrenched as the dominant yardstick for appraising the achievements and assessing the growth of national economies.

Problems begin with the choice of currency. In order to derive comparable values required for calculating long-term growth rates it is necessary to express GDP in constant monies, that is in inflation-adjusted terms, but that requires continuous, reliable, and broadly based monitoring of price changes. Not doing so may make only a small difference when inflation remains low (as it has been, generally, in the West since the beginning of the 21st century) but comparing costs in current monies during periods of higher inflation rates (in the West they reached double digits during the 1980s) could lead to major distortions.

Even in countries with capable statistical services, this results in often considerable uncertainties, as is best illustrated by the frequency and extent of GDP revisions. Zwijnenburg (2015) found that between 1994 and 2013 the mean absolute revision of year-on-year quarterly growth (the growth rate of a quarter compared to the same quarter of the previous year) for 18 countries in the Organisation for Economic Co-operation and Development (OECD) was 0.36% after one year, 0.5% after two years, and 0.61% after three years, with the average three-year value as high as 0.93% for Japan. As the originally assessed growth rates during that period were on the order of 1–3%, such revisions clearly matter.

On the most basic level, proper GDP accounting requires a definition of the economy, that is, putting the boundaries on what gets counted. Because GDP accounting was established at a time when manufacturing was a leading sector of the economy (with shares of 30–40% during the 1950s), its output continues to be monitored in a relatively more disaggregated manner than the contributions of the now-dominant service sector (in itself a highly heterogeneous group of activities) which make up 70–80% of GDP in affluent countries. Counting all final goods and services may seem to be a fairly comprehensive definition of economic activity—but it is not.

Even if we knew with great certainty the size of a country's economy defined by monetary transactions, it would be still difficult to make a proper adjustment for calculating real long-term growth unless we also knew the trend of nonmonetary exchanges or activities, whose share of the overall economy may remain fairly stable for decades but may rise or decline as economies advance or falter. As it is structured, the GDP concept cannot capture nonmonetary exchanges (the barter economy) and unpaid work (such as household chores or child care provided by members of a family or by relatives and friends) or those financial transactions that take place out-side the monitored flows of modern economies, deliberately avoiding them or being hidden, a sector known as the informal, shadow, underground, or black economy.

The barter economy, common in all preindustrial societies, has been largely eliminated in modern economies, while unpaid services are as important as ever and unreported transactions are thriving. Housework has been always excluded from GDP, and although it can be argued that most household chores became easier over time, care of the elderly will be tak-ing more unpaid time in all affluent societies with aging populations and rising life expectancies. Interestingly, Britain's Office for National Statistics estimated that in 2014, when the country's GDP reached £1.8 trillion, the value of unpaid labor was £1 trillion (Athow 2016). And counting only what is sold and bought leaves out many important activities, particularly in modern economies with their rising shares of electronic information and digital production: Internet providers charge a monthly fee that includes virtually unlimited access to almost any conceivable category of informa-tion, with the marginal cost of searching for news or participating in social media being very close to nothing, and hence excluded from the standard GDP accounts.

The size of the black economy can be only estimated but its share of total production was growing during the last decades of the 20th century (Lippert and Walker 1997), and at the beginning of the 21st century its size was put at about 15% of official GDP in affluent nations and at one-third in low-income countries, with shares as high as 40% or more in Mexico, the Philippines, and Nigeria (Schneider 2003). The best available studies show it to be far from negligible even in some of the world's most affluent coun-tries with generally good governance and with low levels of corruption. A comprehensive study of the shadow economy in the European Union put the average for all member states at 18.3% in 2015, with the range from 8.3% in Luxembourg to 30.6% in Bulgaria, and with Germany and France nearly identical at, respectively, 12.2% and 12.3% (Schneider 2015). In an older study of 162 countries, Schneider et al. (2010) put the mean at 31% in 2007, with the extremes ranging between 8.2% for Switzerland to 62.6% for Bolivia.

How uncertain these estimates are can be illustrated by many compari-sons. In a closer study of Germany's black economy, Schneider and Buehn (2016) compared the outcomes of eight studies using different methods (including discrepancies between expenditure and income and between official and actual employment, a currency demand approach, and surveys) and found that between 2000 and 2005 estimates of the country's shadow economy were as small as 1% and as large as 15–16% of official GDP. And while Schneider et al. put India's shadow economy at 21% of official GDP in 2006, a confidential report commissioned by the Indian government (and leaked to the press) put the size of the country's black economy at nearly 75% of the official GDP (Mehra 2014). And Statistics Canada (2016) claimed that in 2013 the country's shadow economy was just 2.4% of official GDP and that this share had remained unchanged since 2002, a remarkable fact (if true)—while Schneider (2015) put Canada's 2015 share at 10.3%, identical to the Australian rate.

And then there is GDP's almost utter inability to capture qualitative improvements. For decades Bell offered American consumers one model of its standard black rotary-dial phone, and then came push-button dialing, a variety of electronic phones, and eventually cellular phones and smartphones. Successive outlays spent on acquiring these items or paying rental fees tell us nothing about the fundamentally different qualities embodied by changing designs. The same is, of course, true about cars—a rising share of their value is now in electronic components and hence they are mechatronic devices, not simply mechanical machines—and, to different degrees, also about housing and long-distance travel, in terms of both speed and comfort: compare what the same price bought in 1955 with a seat in a propeller-driven Constellation and in 2015 in a Boeing 787.

GDP is not a reliable measure of the total economic product, and it is an outright inferior measure as far as the quality of life and real prosperity are concerned. From a long-term perspective, the most fundamental failure of GDP accounts is to ignore diverse forms of environmental degradation caused by economic activities and treat the depletion of finite resources as current income that adds to wealth. These are, of course, utterly unsustainable premises as no society can exist without adequate support provided by natural capital stored in biodiversity and in photosynthesizing species and maintained by many indispensable environmental services ranging from soil renewal to water retention by forests and wetlands (Smil 1994, 2013a).

Remarkably, economists call these critical omissions "environmental externalities": the very choice of the noun is telling because historically they were not an integral part of the cost of doing business and their still far from adequate pricing has been making slow progress. Most major gains have come only since the 1950s, with most of the externalities far from getting internalized. Reducing air pollution is an excellent example of this internalization of former externalities, that is paying higher prices in exchange for a cleaner environment. One of the first large-scale instances of this effort was the elimination of visible particulate air pollution from the combustion of coal in large electricity-generating plants, due to the post-1950 installation of electrostatic precipitators that remove more than 99% of all particles (USEPA 2016a). The next step, starting during the 1970s, was a large-scale adoption of flue gas desulfurization that greatly reduced the risk of acid precipitation, first in Europe and North America, later also in China. Removal of particulates and sulfur raises the cost of electricity generation by about 10%.

But most externalities remain entirely unaccounted for. Among the most widespread negative impacts whose costs are completely ignored in product pricing are the declining yields caused by the universally increased rates of soil erosion in intensive row-crop cultivation (of corn or soybeans, two leading grain and legume species); the formation of dead zones in coastal waters caused by excessive runoff of nitrogenous fertilizers causing eutrophication of aquatic environments; the health effects and material damage caused by the photochemical smog that is now common in all megacities; and the rapid loss of biodiversity caused by such diverse actions as mass-scale monocropping and tropical deforestation.

The largest externality that remains unaccounted for is the undoubtedly very large cost of relatively rapid global warming (that would increase average tropospheric temperature by more than 2°C) attributable to anthropogenic combustion of fossil fuels and land-use changes (IPCC 2014). But in this case there is, at least, a reasonable excuse, as the complexities, interactions, and feedbacks of change attributable to rising concentrations of greenhouse gases are extremely difficult to monetize, especially as some regions, some countries, and some economic sectors will also derive various benefits from rising temperatures and from an accelerated water cycle, and as many of these impacts will not be seen in force for decades to come (and hence will be steeply discounted by today's valuations).

As a result, the carbon tax favored by many environmentalists and by some economists would be nothing but a largely arbitrary (and also a very crude) form of internalizing an unknown fraction of the unfolding and future effects of global warming. These are not new concerns. Kuznets was fully aware of these deficiencies (obviously not of the effects of global warming but of environmental externalities in general and of other ignored inputs). He asked who could place a value on the country's rivers or on the skills and capacities of housewives and his suggested subtraction of disservices from national income estimates was far more radical than most of the recent calls for GDP redefinition.

His preference is worth quoting at length.

This writer, for one, would like to see work begun on national income estimates that would not be based upon the acceptance, prevailing heretofore, of the market place as the basis of social productivity judgments. It would be of great value to have national income estimates that would remove from the total the elements which, from the standpoint of a more enlightened social philosophy than that of an acquisitive society, represent dis-service rather than service. Such estimates would subtract from the present national income totals all expenses on armament, most of the outlays on advertising, a great many of the expenses involved in financial and speculative activities, and what is perhaps most important, the outlays that have been made necessary in order to overcome difficulties that are, properly speaking, costs implicit in our economic civilization. All the gigantic outlays on our urban civilization, subways, expensive housing, etc., which in our usual estimates we include at the value of the net product they yield on the market, do not really represent net services to the individuals comprising the nation but are, from their viewpoint, an evil necessary in order to be able to make a living (i.e., they are largely business expenses rather than living expenses). Obviously the removal of such items from national income estimates, difficult as it would be, would make national income totals much better gauges of the volume of services produced, for comparison among years and among nations. (Kuznets 1937, 37)

Economists have suggested fixing many inadequacies of GDP with suggestions ranging from using comparable market rates to value household chores (or shadow pricing measured by time devoted to a task) to quantifying environmental deterioration, and many critics have called for more radical redesigns or for abandoning the measure and adopting an entirely new valuation (Nordhaus and Tobin 1972; Zolotas 1981; Daly and Cobb 1989; Costanza et al. 2009; World Economic Forum 2017). In all cases, the goal is to quantify the extent to which economic development meets society's needs (for adequate nutrition, shelter, personal freedoms, environmental quality) rather than measuring the magnitude of market transactions.

For example, Daly and Cobb (1989) introduced a per capita index of sustainable economic welfare that included the costs of commuting, car accidents, urbanization, water, air and noise pollution, loss of farmland and wetlands, depletion of nonrenewable resources, and an estimate of long-term environmental damages. Their calculations showed that between 1976 and 1986 their index fell by 10% even as per capita GDP rose by just over 20%. Proceeding in an analogical way (quantifying all key economic and health burdens), my quantification of the annual costs of China's environmental degradation and pollution during the early 1990s put them, conservatively, at 6–8% of the country's GDP during those years, erasing most of the officially claimed growth (Smil 1996). And the World Bank now argues that measuring wealth is a superior approach and their comprehensive study for the period between 1995 and 2014 does so by quantifying both natural and human capital as well as net foreign assets (Lange et al. 2018).

Natural capital includes valuations of forests, farmland, pastures, and subsoil assets. But human capital, measured as total earnings over a person's lifetime (and based on numerous household surveys), is the most important component of this wealth index. Not surprisingly, estimates of human capital wealth are closely correlated with GDP per capita. The new metric is thus a clone of the old one and it indicates that between 1995 and 2014 the global average of total per capita wealth was increasing by 1% a year and by 4% a year in upper middle-income countries. All of these attempts to fix GDP's shortcomings have one thing in common: their valuations of natural capital or environmental services would be very different if they could monetize such fundamental changes as the loss of biodiversity and the biospheric impacts of anthropogenic climate change.

As already noted in chapter 1, there is also a debate about replacing GDP with a measure assessing well-being, happiness, or subjective satisfaction with life, with Bhutan actually using its Gross National Happiness index. Easterlin's (1974) initial examination of the link between GDP and happiness correctly noted that the happiness differences between rich and poor countries that might be expected on the basis of within-country differences based on economic status are not supported by international comparisons. In the US richer people are happier than people with lower incomes, but citizens of many low-income countries are happier than those in many affluent nations. Many subsequent and recent studies have confirmed that there are no strong links between per capita levels of GDP and personal happiness (Diener et al. 1997; Bruni and Porta 2005), and the top 25 countries of the 2017 *World Happiness Report* (Helliwell et al. 2017) include not only affluent Switzerland, Canada, and Sweden but also Costa Rica, Brazil, and Mexico, with Uruguay ahead of France and Japan behind Nicaragua.

And, clearly, while GDP is a construct that can keep on increasing, happiness (or satisfaction with life) is a variable with an obvious upper limit that cannot keep on showing correlations with ever higher per capita levels of income or wealth. Evidence from 32 countries shows that as better education and higher incomes diffuse through a society, they enhance fewer people's subjective well-being (Zagórski et al. 2010). But the two variables are strongly linked, just not proportionately (Coyle 2011) and it is hard to imagine that overwhelming shares of people, be they very happy or rather unhappy, would welcome the substantial cuts in consumption and levels of employment brought by zero-growth economies or by deliberate reductions of economic activity. Consequently, it appears that all that the replacement of GDP by a universal index of happiness might do would be to introduce another questionable metric.

Finally, replacing money-based valuations by energy-based valuations has been advocated for more than a century (Ostwald 1909; Soddy 1926; Odum 1971). The choice is unassailable from a fundamental energetic point of view, but in practice it brings its own set of shortcomings. All single-item theories of value suffer from what Rose (1986) called selective inattention to the complexity of civilizations and to the interconnectedness of things, and "treating all non-energy entities merely as energy transformations and pricing everything according to embodied energy content is forcing the multifaceted reality into dubious one-dimensional confines" (Smil 2008, 344). GDP is clearly a flawed concept but while some proposed alternatives offer better insights, so far none can be seen as decisively superior.

Economic Growth in Long-Term Perspective

Any problems we might have with modern GDP accounts get only magnified when we try to reconstruct long-term trends of economic growth. The obvious question to ask is what it really means when we apply the GDP concept to those societies where a large share of labor (if not most) was provided by enslaved or indentured adults and children, or to societies where a significant share of income was repeatedly earned through armed aggression, pillage, and confiscation. And even after moving into the early modern era, we face the absence of any standardized performance monitoring of readily measured agricultural and industrial outputs (a practice that began in earnest only during the 19th century). Moreover, we also have either a complete lack of information or only some irregular questionable numbers for population growth, crop harvests, food availability, extraction of minerals, and artisanal manufactures, the key proxy measures that could be used as a scaffolding for building up reasonable estimates of economic performance.

But economists, used to abstracts and to their aggregates, have not been dissuaded by these realities and many studies in economic history use the GDP concept almost as easily as do assessments of modern economic progress. Moreover, they do so without trying to alert the readers to fundamental uncertainties involved in such retrospective exercises and to the inherently unreliable outcome of any generalizations based on these highly questionable quantifications. Perhaps the best that can be expected from these efforts is to get the feel for the correct magnitudes of change and for the long-term direction of economic activities, that is labeling them as declining, stagnant, slowly growing, or exceptional given the time and place.

Nothing illustrates the perils of reconstructing economic performance in the past better than the comparison of modern Europe (or, more specifically, of its most advanced economies) with the imperial China (or with Jiangnan, its best-off region south of the Yangzi). Thanks to the work of Andre Gunder Frank (1998) and Kenneth Pomeranz (2000), it has been widely accepted that China was richer than, or at least as rich as western Europe until the end of the 18th century, and that only the advancing European industrialization of the early 19th century took away that long primacy and explained the subsequent great divergence. Frank (1998) argued that contrary to a generally held view, there was a global economy between 1400 and 1800, and that there is only one conclusion after discarding the Eurocentric bias of late medieval and early modern history: that the economy was centered on Asia in general and on Chinese trade, goods, and marketplaces in particular, and hence the post-1980 return to China's global economic primacy is nothing but a ReOrient, to echo Frank's book title.

Pomeranz (2000, 49) aimed to refute "the common claim that Europe was already richer than the rest of the world before industrialization," because "it seems likely that average incomes in Japan, China, and parts of southeast Asia were comparable to (or higher than) those in western Europe even in the late eighteenth century." He also stressed that the vastly more equal distribution of land in China suggests greater income equality, that a typical farm family spent about the same share of its income on food in the 17th century as peasants and artisans did in late 18th-century England, and that Europe overcame the developmental constraints thanks to its external expansion (by exploiting the New World's resources), not by anything internal.

But Maddison's (2007) reconstruction of average per capita GDPs presents a very different sequence: it has the Chinese rate about 20% behind Europe at the beginning of the common era, only about 7% ahead at the end of the first millennium, just 4% ahead by 1300, and already 35% behind in 1700, with the gap opening to about 80% by 1949 when China became reunified (Taiwan excepted) after generations of civil war and Japanese aggression. And a more recent evaluation, based on a large amount of Chinese historical literature, makes the case for an even earlier divergence of economic performance.

Broadberry et al. (2014) reconstructed per capita GDPs for China, England (UK), Holland (Netherlands), Italy, Spain, and Japan between the late

10th century and 1850, and concluded that China's average was highest during the Northern Song dynasty (960–1126) when the country led the world in living standards. Subsequently, China's average per capita GDP declined during the Ming (1368–1644) and Qing (1644–1912) dynasties. By 1300 China's living standards had fallen behind Italy (although in the Yangzi delta, conditions might still have been similar to the richest parts of Europe), by 1400 they were behind England and Holland, by 1750, when China's average per capita GDP was no higher than in Japan, the rate was only about 40% of the UK's level, and 100 years later that gap increased to about 80%.

Such contradictory conclusions make it questionable to view historical GDP reconstructions even as just approximate trend indicators. But there is one conclusion that these studies share: preindustrial growth of GDP was very slow, with annual per capita rates measured in fractions of 1%. The best available historic reconstructions imply average annual growth rates of 0.18% for England between 1090 and 1850, 0.2% for Holland between 1348 and 1850 (van Zanden and van Leeuwen 2012), and a vanishingly small gain of 0.03% a year for Spain between 1270 and 1850. Central and northern Italy did not experience virtually any per capita growth between 1300 and 1913 (Malanima 2011), and the Chinese economy saw an average decline of 0.1% between 1020 and 1850 (Broadberry et al. 2014). Similarly, Maddison's (2007) widely quoted quantification of the world economy between 1 and 2030 lists no European country with per capita GDP growth surpassing 0.2% between 1500 and 1820, but subsequently western Europe averaged growth of 0.98% between 1820 and 1870 and 1.33% growth between 1870 and 1913; analogical rates for the US were 1.34% and 1.82%, and they were 0.19% and 1.48% for Japan, whose economic modernization began shortly after the Meiji restoration in 1868.

Taking a really long view, made possible by the exceptional amount of historical information and by the country's pioneering nature in economic modernization, Broadberry et al. (2015) reconstructed six centuries of English and British economic growth, and Crafts and Mills (2017) extended the series to 2013 and offered additional interpretations. The conclusions of their work can be summarized as follows. Long-term growth was a segmented trend-stationary process, with random fluctuations always reverting back to the trend line. There was essentially no per capita GDP growth before the 1660s (annual mean of 0.03% before 1663), but two accelerations came afterwards as the rate rose to about 0.8% during the late 17th century, declined to less than 0.3% during the 18th century, and rose to about 1% after 1822. Remarkably, there was an absence of any growth reversals. The industrial revolution, the country's signature economic breakthrough, significantly elevated the trend growth of real GDP per person but it had an even more impressive impact on the growth of industrial output.

The traditional view of the British industrial revolution as a broad-based advance generating relatively impressive growth rates underwent substantial revision during the 1980s (C. Harley 1982; Crafts 1985). The latest views see a gradual acceleration with rapid technical advances and productivity growth confined to relatively few sectors. The contradiction of rapid industrialization but relatively modest growth is explained by the early adoption of capitalist farming and, for decades, the limited impact of steam on productivity growth (Crafts 2005). Reconstruction of annual real GDP growth rates shows a steady acceleration from 0.7% between 1700 and 1760 to 1% between 1760 and 1801, 1.9% during the next 30 years, and 2.4% between 1831 and 1873. More than half of the contribution came from total factor productivity, just over 20% from capital deepening, and nothing from agriculture.

The early decades of the British industrial revolution were closely connected with the invention and improvement of steam engines but Crafts (2004) demonstrated that the machine contributed little to the country's pre-1830 economic growth, and that its potential was realized only with a widespread adoption of high-pressure designs after 1850. Consequently, the steam engine had its greatest impact on productivity growth only during the second half of the 19th century, a century after Watt's famous patent. The invention, initial deployment, improvements, and eventual economic benefits of the steam engine raise a more fundamental question that has preoccupied many historians for generations: why did Britain lead?

Allen's (2009, 2) simple explanation—"The Industrial Revolution, in short, was invented in Britain in the eighteenth century because it paid to invent it there"—is convincing because he shows that (unlike across the Channel) in Britain cheap capital and even cheaper energy coexisted with relatively high wages, a combination that made it possible to bear the high fixed costs of developing such fundamental inventions as steam engines and coke-based iron ore smelting. In contrast, Mokyr (2009, 122) refutes Allen's arguments and concludes that the country became the industrial leader because it took advantage of its physical endowment "thanks to the great synergy of the Enlightenment: the combination of the Baconian program in useful knowledge and the recognition that better institutions created better incentives."

To simplify, this sets profit motivation vs. knowledge and the institutional environment as the principal agent of change. Allen sees the Enlightenment, at best, as a marginal factor, for Mokyr the Enlightenment rules. But Crafts (2010) is closer to the real explanation: those two perspectives are not mutually exclusive and they might be seen eventually as complementary. In any case, profit and enlightenment, however important, are still only two factors whose study could be used to explain growth. Specific historical circumstances going beyond profit and not critically affected by enlightened innovations may point national trajectories (at least temporarily) in different directions. Different paths to modernity in two related countries are perhaps best illustrated by contrasting the British and the Dutch trajectories (de Vries 2000).

Before 1800 both countries benefited from agricultural productivity that was far above other European nations, and both also had only small productivity gaps between the agricultural and nonagricultural sectors. Subsequently, the structure of the British economy underwent a radical shift from farming to industrial production, while the Dutch economy changed very slowly during the 19th century. The roots of this difference are in population growth. The British population doubled between 1720 and 1815, and doubled again by 1870, and the country, a net food importer since 1760, financed its rising food imports by industrial exports. As de Vries (2000, 462) put it, "It is in this setting that industrial exports rose—had to rise, one might say."

While population pressure pushed the British economy away from farming, that stimulus was missing in the Netherlands where the early 19th-century population grew slowly and where the agricultural sector continued to increase, becoming a major exporter to Britain. The combination of farming, commerce, and some industries sufficed to produce what became known as the surreptitious growth of the 19th century—but a country that had established an essentially modern economy by the 17th century did not join the other creators of the modern industrial world. That took place only during the 20th century, when the Netherlands also experienced very rapid population growth. De Vries (2000, 464) uses this important example to stress the unsuitability of the model of sustained, linear economic growth and how necessary it is "to advocate a model of modern growth that is more historical and shorn of its modernist rigidities."

These reminders should be kept in mind when judging Rostow's supposedly universal sequence of economic growth stages as a society progresses from traditional arrangements to the preconditions for economic takeoff, and as the eventual takeoff is followed by the drive to maturity and finally into the era of high mass consumption. Not surprisingly, Rostow (1960) chose British history as his universal template for national economic development, but a close reading reveals a more nuanced portrayal than using the country's experience as the model of a rigid sequence to be followed by all developing states (Ortolano 2015). British economic progress was, and was not, a paradigmatic case of modern economic growth, as there are always significant national idiosyncrasies and as late-starting rapid modernizers, particularly in post-WWII East Asia, do not so easily fit into a model based on the gradual industrialization of the world's first modern economy.

As the quality of available information improved during the 19th century, reconstructed GDP trends tracing the great economic takeoff in western European nations and in the US (soon joined also by Russia and Japan) became more reliable. Between 1913 and 1950 per capita GDP growth slowed down to 0.76% in western Europe and 1.61% in the US, but between 1950 and 1973 it reached records highs of 4.05% in western Europe, 2.45% in the US and, most impressively, 8.06% in Japan (Maddison 2007). During the remainder of the 20th century, economic growth declined in all affluent countries, with per capita rates averaging just below 2% in both western Europe and the US, and just above 2% in Japan. In contrast, the world's two most populous countries experienced unprecedented periods of growth, about 3% a year per capita in India and more than 5% in China as the country embarked on rapid modernization following Mao Zedong's death in 1976.

Tracing per capita GDP growth in constant monies allows us to gauge a country's ascent along the continuum from poverty to a modicum of prosperity and eventually to various degrees of affluence. Average US per capita GDP (calculated in constant $2009) quadrupled during the 19th century (to about $6,000), then it grew nearly 7.5 times during the 20th century to $44,750, and it added a further 15% during the first 15 years of the 21st century (Johnston and Williamson 2017). Multiples during the 50 years between 1960 and 2010 ranged from less than threefold (about 2.8 times to more than $48,000/capita) for the US as the country moved to mass (but unequally shared) prosperity. The multiple was more than fourfold for Japan (to ¥3.9 million) as the country rose from post-WWII destruction to the world's second-largest economy, before it yielded that spot to China. And China's gain was 24-fold (increase to nearly 39,000 renminbi) as the country became the world's second-largest economy.

As expected, long-term trajectories of national GDP growth (expressed in constant monies) conform very closely to symmetrical logistic curves, but their inflection points range widely, reflecting country-specific conditions and different stages of economic development. Both French and

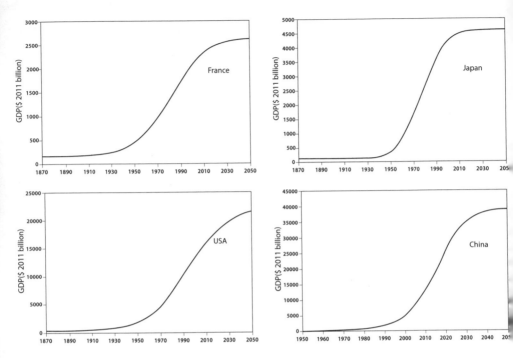

Figure 5.29
Growth and logistic outlook of GDP (expressed in international $2011) in four major economies—France, Japan, and the US since 1870, and China since 1950. Data from World Bank (2018).

Japanese trajectories had inflection points nearly four decades ago (Japan in 1979, France in 1981) and both imply only restrained growth by 2050 (figure 5.29). US trajectory had its inflection point in 1996 but compared to 2015 it indicates roughly a further 30% gain by 2050, while China's inflection point came in 2016 and by 2050 the country's inflation-adjusted GDP could be twice as large as it was in 2015 (figure 5.29).

In order to appraise actual standards of living, international comparisons of these achievements are now commonly done in values converted to purchasing power parity (PPP). If comparisons based on exchange rates mislead (they may work well for financial flows but not for food or non-traded goods), those based on PPP—relating one currency to another by buying the same amount of goods and services—are far from perfect either. In order to be meaningful, a comparative basket must be fairly capacious but that means that it cannot be made identical: if so, it would ignore, or at least greatly distort, too many specific and qualitative differences that reflect national dietary and consumption peculiarities, expectations, and preferences.

Staple grains of one country are almost never eaten in another (sorghum and teff, common in Nigeria and Ethiopia, respectively, are not consumed in Spain or Japan). The preferred meat in one economy (beef in the US) may be proscribed in another (in Hindu India). The education component of the basket must include the cost of postsecondary schooling in the US (it now enrolls more than half of all people in that age group and it has become steadily more expensive, leading to often burdensome loans), but getting a university degree remains a rare expectation in Niger or Malawi. On the other hand, because of low wages, labor-intensive services are often cheaper in low-income countries even when adjusted for PPP.

The obvious general conclusion is that the PPP comparison should work best for countries with similar habits and expectations and with similar economic structures: no country pair is perfect but the US and Canada or France and Germany are good examples of this comparative proximity— but even the comparison of rather similar economies is not easy. Obviously, comparing the US and China, and even more so the US and Ethiopia, remain uncertain and fallible endeavors. When the World Bank adjusted its methodology in 2005, it cut China's PPP-based GDP by 40%. In any case, derivations of detailed PPP-based comparisons require vast price data collections that need to be constantly upgraded (Callen 2017). The expected outcome is that the differences between market and PPP-based rates are relatively small for affluent countries but could be very large for some low-income nations, even exaggerating their actual average quality of life.

Keeping these realities in mind, here are a few absolute (slightly rounded) per capita PPP GDP values for 2016 (in international dollars) together with multiples for 1990 to 2016: US $56,500, up 2.4 times; EU $39,600, up 2.6 times; China $15,500, up nearly 16 times; India $6,600, up nearly sixfold; and Nigeria $5,900, up just threefold (World Bank 2018). Notably, in 1990 both India's and Nigeria's per capita PPP GDP rates were higher than China's, with Nigeria's value twice as high! The worldwide mean in 2016 was virtually identical with the Chinese average, and, largely thanks to China's economic rise, the worldwide distribution f average per capita income has been getting less skewed.

Moatsos et al. (2014) traced the changes in global income since 1820, when it was fairly normally distributed, while most the world's population lived below what we now define as the extreme poverty line. The latest reevaluation of global income, in terms of 2011 PPPs, puts it at $1.90/day or about $700/year (Ferreira et al. 2015). As economic development proceeded, the mean of income distribution has kept rising but so has the income inequality and by 1975 global income distribution was distinctly bimodal, with the first mode below the poverty line and the second mode (capturing the income in affluent nations) almost an order of magnitude higher. Then, with advances in Asia in general and China in particular, the pattern shifted again to a near-normal distribution whose mode was well above the poverty line.

But the growth rate that is of the greatest interest and that is often reported by the media is not a per capita value but simply either the nominal or real (inflation-adjusted) quarterly or annual GDP gain: this is the rate that makes economists worried whenever they judge it to be too low or ecstatic when they see it rising. This adulation of a simple quotient seen in isolation is irrational. As I already noted in chapter1, when the average annual growth of the US economy (calculated by using real monies) averaged almost 5% during the early 1950s, that cumulative gain added about $3,500 for every one of 160 million citizens. The cumulative gain during the first half of the 2010s, when annual growth averaged 2%, added $4,800 for every one of 317 million people—which means that the recent "slow" growth has been greatly superior to the past "fast" growth, an inevitable consequence of the expanding principal.

But prevailing perceptions seem to be immune to this algebraic truism, the best proof being the admiration expressed by economists and by news media when Chinese official statistics kept announcing yet another year of near 10% GDP growth. According to the National Bureau of Statistics, China's annual GDP growth (at constant prices) averaged 9.92% during the 1990s, and reached 11.6% during the first decade of the 21st century (NBS 2016). Inevitably, such an expansive pace cannot be supported for long, and between 2010 and 2015 the annual growth rate slowed down to about 7.6%. I hasten to add that in reality China's economy was not averaging double-digit decadal growth during the early years of the 21st century, the simple explanation being that China's economic statistics in general, and its GDP figures in particular, are not as reliable as those produced in the US, Japan, and the EU (Koch-Weser 2013; Owyang and Shell 2017).

Chronically inflated nature of the country's economic statistics has been repeatedly admitted by the Chinese themselves. This is due to incomplete survey coverage, deliberate manipulation (formerly even outright falsification), secretive ways used to derive and weigh key indexes, and efforts to mask data volatility, and the result is many inconsistencies and contradictory claims. For example, Rawski (2001) pointed out that between 1997 and 2000 official GDP growth totaled 24.7% while energy consumption

declined by 12.8%, a most unlikely combination for a rapidly industrializing economy with high energy intensity, and an outcome that would be
an unprecedented departure from the pattern followed by all of East Asia's
rapid modernizers (Japan, Taiwan, South Korea).

But perhaps the most revealing way (because of its objectivity and its
immunity to falsification) to illustrate the likely magnitude of China's
exaggerated reporting of GDP growth is based on long-term observation of
night-light intensity that has been measured by satellites since the 1970s.
This luminosity turns out to be a good proxy for measuring economic
activity and (after controlling for population density) it is well correlated
with income. Henderson et al. (2012) used national aggregates of changing luminosity to estimate changes in economic activity for 188 countries.
When they compared the official GDP growth rates with the increase in
night-light intensity, they discovered that between 1992 and 2006 China's
reported GDP grew nearly twice as fast as did the luminosity. In contrast,
the gap for India was smaller and other countries with economic data of
questionable quality (Brazil, Russia) showed even lower differences, confirming the exceptional unreliability of Chinese statistics.

Japanese statistics have been always much more credible and before
China's post-Mao rise, Japan was the paragon of rapid economic growth: it
reached the pre-WWII level of its GDP only in 1953, and although it had
peak performance years above 10% its annual growth rates (in real terms)
averaged 8.3% between 1955 and 1965, 7.9% between 1965 and 1975, and
then only 4.3% between 1975 and 1985 as the country (importing virtually 100% of its crude oil and natural gas) was affected by two rounds of
OPEC-driven price increases. South Korea tried to emulate its great antago-
nist (and its former colonizer) by embarking on rapid economic expansion:
between 1966 and 1999 its annual GDP surpassed 10% but decadal means
stayed below 10% (World Bank 2018).

DeLong (2002) cites an exceptional commitment to education, an extraordinarily large market size, and a similarly extraordinary natural resource
endowment, particularly the country's energy riches, as the three main
factors explaining America's technical and economic leadership during the
20th century. The first reality produced more high school and university
graduates than in any other affluent nation, and until the emergence of a
more integrated European Union there was no open-market economic unit
whose size came close to the US and allowed similar economies of scale.
As for energy supply, the US was the world's largest producer of coal until
1983 (when China became the leader), the world's largest producer of crude
oil until 1976 (when the Soviet Union assumed the lead), and the world's

largest producer of natural gas until 1983 (due to the Soviet advances). I must add that the latter two lost primacies were recently regained as a result of widespread deployment of horizontal drilling and hydraulic fracturing.

US statistics allow us to reconstruct more than two centuries of economic growth. Average annual growth of real (inflation-adjusted, with GDP deflator set to 2009 US$) US GDP rose from 3.88% during the first half of the 19th century to 4.31% during the second half, with corresponding per capita rates at 0.85% and 1.89% (Johnston and Williamson 2017). During the slowdown in the first four decades of the 20th century, the average was 2.85% (1.2%/capita) between 1901 and 1929, and the 1930s (with steep economic decline during the decade's first half) still ended up with an expanded economy and with annual growth averaging 2.08% and 1.38% per capita.

Post-WWII real growth averaged 3.25% (1.73%/capita) between 1945 and 1973 when the Western economies were affected by OPEC's quintupling of crude oil prices. Even so, the next decade maintained annual growth at just above 3%, and this was followed by a notable slowdown to 2.55% (1.54%/capita) between 1986 and 2016, and annual growth averaged just 1.86% (and 1.01%/capita) during the first 16 years of the 21st century. These longer-term averages hide considerable shorter-term fluctuations, including recurrent business cycles. Between 1854 and 2009 the US experienced 33 cycles, that is averaging one every 4.7 years, but the frequency has been declining: between 1854 and 1919 there was a business cycle recurring every four years, the frequency between 1919 and 1945 was 4.3 years, and between 1945 and 2009 it lengthened to 5.8 years. Average peak-to-trough contraction for all cycles lasted 17.5 months and expansion from their troughs to a new peak averaged nearly 39 months (NBER 2017).

Given the fact that the US continues to be the world's largest economy (when the comparison is done by using exchange rates), it is not surprising that the country's declining growth rate has been reflected by the global trend. This is well conveyed by following decadal peak growth rates of the worldwide economic product: they declined from 6.66% during the 1960s to 5.35% during the 1970s, 4.65% during the 1980s and 3.67% during the century's last decade (World Bank 2018). A high of 4.32% in 2010 was an exception due to the recovery from the world's greatest post-WWII downturn, and the post-2011 rates stayed below 3%.

Examinations of the importance of historical events for long-term economic development are surprisingly recent, with the most important contributions focusing on the impact of colonial rule (the difference between former Spanish and British colonies providing the most obvious contrasts) and on the origins of current institutions, above all the legal arrangements that affect financial affairs (Engerman and Sokoloff 1994; Acemoglu et al. 2002). Nunn's (2009) summary of these studies emphasized the contrast between an undeniable conclusion that history matters and a continued inability to describe exact channels of causality through which it matters, leaving us with black boxes that still wait to be unpacked.

At the same time, the role of the basic sociopolitical setting on economic growth and individual prosperity was perfectly illustrated by comparing the outcomes in countries controlled for decades by Communist parties with the achievements of neighboring nations. These contrasts are even more telling because some of the comparisons involve countries with identical nationalities (East and West Germany, North and South Korea, China, and Taiwan) or countries whose standard of living prior to Communist take-over were not only very similar but even higher than that of their neighbors (Czechoslovakia and Austria are perhaps the best instance of the latter reality).

Economic growth may mean, as it did in the Soviet Union, overfulfilling the goals set by five-year plans but leaving the population only marginally better off. Instead, it should produce higher standards of life and should reduce, rather than exacerbate, the income inequality that was characteristic of traditional societies. Living standards can be measured in many ways. They can be reduced to single-variable proxies or traced by indexes. Proxies can be monetary (such as average per capita income or average disposable income), physical (such as infant mortality, whose falling rates are closely connected to rising quality of life, or average life expectancy), or they can reflect individual perception (satisfaction with life, happiness). As already noted, the Human Development Index has been the most widely used measure of improving quality of life. No matter which measure of standard of living is chosen, national averages of Western countries show long periods of steady gains (with takeoffs during the late 19th century) as well as some notable post-1950 improvements.

Reliable post-WWII data show that per capita income in affluent countries conforms to symmetrical logistic curves that reflect specific national circumstances. Between 1950 and 2016 US income quadrupled, the inflection point came only in 1995, and a further 20% rise could be expected by 2050. In contrast, during the same period Japanese income rose 16-fold, inflection came already in 1982, and further growth may be less than 10% by 2050 (figure 5.30). Surprisingly, China's per capita income also shows a near-perfect logistic fit, with a 20-fold rise since 1950, inflection point in 2012 (coinciding with the onset of the country's rising dependency ratio),

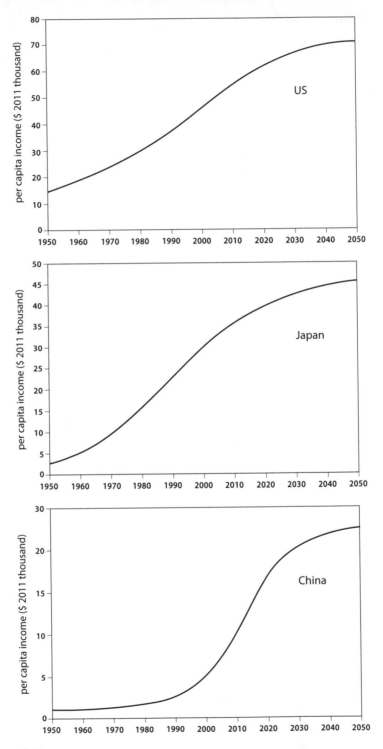

Figure 5.30
Growth of per capita income in the US, Japan, and China since 1950. Data from World Bank (2018).

and although a further 60% gain is indicated by 2050, in absolute terms that would imply income of $22,500, equal to roughly a third of the US level expected by the mid-21st century. This would indicate a negative answer to the question of whether China can become truly rich before it becomes old.

Any review of long-term economic growth would be incomplete without noting the long-term annualized gains of equity markets. Long perspectives are necessary because these markets undergo repeated fluctuations resulting in extended periods of minimum growth. Since 1900 America's Dow Jones has had its two longest stagnating periods between 1905 and 1925 and between the late 1960s and the late 1980s (Macrotrends 2017; FedPrimeRate 2017). During the 20th century, real annualized returns of major equity markets ranged from 2.1% in Italy and 2.8% in Germany to 5.9% in Canada. 6.3% in the US, and 7.4% in Australia (Dimson 2003). French returns averaged 3.1%, Japanese 4.1%, and British 5.2%, and in the long run markets in all countries greatly outperformed bonds or bills.

Sources of Economic Growth

Explaining the sources of economic growth and identifying the key factors required for its durability has turned out to be no less challenging than coming up with a quantification of aggregate economic growth that would be sufficiently accurate (representative might be a better adjective) to construct revealing long-term trajectories. This is, of course, hardly uncommon as there are many analogies of failing to pinpoint the causes of complex phenomena. Historians have tried to explain the fall of Roman Empire by suggesting such diverse reasons as military overextension (imperial overreach), debasement of currency, barbarian invasions, and moral decay, and an entire book was devoted to listing scores of such factors (Rollins 1983). Modern nutritional advice is so bewildering because the supposedly most efficacious diets to reduce disease and premature mortality are completely antithetical, ranging from high carbohydrate to no carbohydrate intakes, and from taking no supplementary micronutrients (vitamins, minerals) to administrating daily megadoses.

More fundamentally, we now know that in such instances any search for a limited number of causes amounts to a preordained failure. Nobody with a background in the study of complex systems (be they natural ecosystems or productive anthropogenic agricultural and industrial assemblages) would try to reduce the explanation of their roots, preconditions, and causes to a few dominant drivers. But economists have been trying to do precisely that for more than two centuries. Their search for the roots of economic growth might be conveniently divided into identifying proximate causes and finding the ultimate reasons, but neither approach has all the answers.

Their traditional explanations have been indefensibly narrow as they have focused on just a few proximate causes. The neoclassical version of growth theory is a perfect example of this reductionism. Its explanations rest on idealized models that have largely ignored the physical setting of economic activities—most prominently by leaving out energy use, the most fundamental physical variable—and that have not paid enough attention to history and to a multitude of technical, social, legal, and political factors that are involved in complex interactions. In the theory's advanced version, economic output is a function of capital, labor, and a measure that gauges the level of available technology (Solow 1957). The model emphasizes how economic growth arises from the accumulation of capital, and the rate of saving depends on the rate of population growth, growth in technology, and the rate of capital depreciation, with all of these variables taken as exogenous.

One of the big surprises resulting from the early studies of economic growth accounting that were published during the 1950s was that a high share of output growth could not be explained by the level of inputs used in production, that is by labor (hours worked) and capital used (Abramovitz 1956; Solow 1957; Kendrick 1961). The unexplained residual must reflect advances in production techniques and it has become known as total factor productivity (TFP) or (more accurately, because the studies do not capture all the factors contributing to economic growth, but less frequently) as multifactor productivity growth.

In modern economies, gains in TFP—subsuming the effect of innovation and technical advances or, most fundamentally, the level of deployed knowledge—have contributed more to the measured growth of labor productivity than the growth in capital invested per worker, and they have often (but not always) accounted for the single largest share among the trio of key growth factors (Shackleton 2013). A new wave of growth studies began during the 1980s and it has been distinguished by its focus on endogenous growth factors, above all on technical advances and improvements in human capital (education, health), but also on diffusion of innovations, government policies (affecting the ease of doing business, taxation, infrastructural upgrading or maintenance), and population changes (demographic transition, dependency ratios, aging).

America's rise from a marginal power in 1800 to the world's economic leader by 1900 is a perfect illustration of how the quest for higher profits, innovation based not just on empirical improvements but on an unprecedented advanced in new fundamental technical and scientific understandings, and historical peculiarities (the pre-1865 dominance of slavery in the

South, an extraordinarily rich energy endowment, and urban-based growth in the North) all combined to determine the country's unique growth trajectory. The increasing importance of knowledge-based technical advances can be traced by comparing the sources of growth calculated for different periods. During the first half of the 19th century, capital and labor explained about 95% of American annual growth and total factor productivity accounted for just 5%. American TFP remained low during the Civil War decade but Kendrick's (1961) reconstruction shows that annual TFP growth in manufacturing amounted to 0.86% during the 1870s, 1.94% during the 1880s, and 1.12% during the 1890s.

These levels were higher than the means for the last three decades of the 20th century, providing clear proofs of the late 19th century's knowledge-based progress (Smil 2005; Field 2009). Overall nonfarm private-sector TFP growth during the 250 years after the Civil War averaged 1.6–1.8%/year, and the most notable 20th-century surge did not come as a result of post-1970 information and communication advances: it began early in the 19th century and it peaked during the Great Depression (with effects reaching into the 1970s), with mass adoption of electricity, telephones, automobiles, and new chemicals being the main sources of growth. During the first half of the 20th century (1913–1950), US TFP accounted for half of overall growth, and between 1950 and 1973 there was only a minor change (Crafts and O'Rourke 2013). And, contrary to the widespread perception of unprecedented advances, TFP growth was no higher than 1–1.5% during the 1990s and the first decade of the 21st century, a historically unexceptional range.

Abramovitz (1956) has shown that since 1870 the combination of labor and capital accounted for just 10% of the growth of net per capita output in the US economy and just 20% of labor productivity growth. Solow (1957) concluded that between 1909 and 1949, when the US economy doubled its gross output per hour of work, 88% of that increase should be attributed to technical advances. Denison (1985) came up with the following allocation for US economic growth between 1929 and 1982: 55% due to advances in knowledge, 16% due to improved resource allocation (labor shift from farming to industry), and 18% due to economies of scale. Because the latter two components are largely functions of technical advances, Denison's findings attributed at least three-quarters of economic growth to technical innovation. Solow (1987) generalized these realities in his Nobel Prize lecture by concluding that "the permanent rate of growth of output per unit of labor input…depends entirely on the rate of technological progress in the broadest sense."

The appraisal by Crafts (1999) of the economic growth of major economies during the 20th century stressed several major generalizations. There were substantial per capita gains in average GDP: more than tripling in Russia; quadrupling in China, from a very low level, and in the UK; nearly sextupling in the US; and multiplying about 17 times in Japan (with TFP share increasing from 32% in 1913–1950 to 39% between 1950 and 1973 and then declining to 26% between 1973 and 1999). Post-WWII annual GDP growth was exceptionally rapid between 1950 and 1973 (average rates of about 2.5% in the US and UK, 5% in West Germany, and 8% in Japan), with TFP as its main component (capital contribution was dominant before 1950). During the subsequent slowdown, TFP became less important but there were impressive gains in living standards (measured by the HDI), particularly in Japan where the index grew about 2.5-fold to match the US and UK levels.

All early studies of TPF treated technical advances as an exogenous variable (innovations coming from outside to be eventually adopted by enterprises), an indefensibly unidirectional interpretation that ignores ongoing learning processes and feedbacks within enterprises. Arrow (1962) was the first economist to posit endogenous models of economic growth with technical change deriving from previous actions within an economy and with a continuing increase of resources devoted to innovation. This notion became standard during the 1980s (Romer 1990), but Jones (1995) pointed out that a substantial increase in the number of US scientists deployed in research and development (used as a proxy of technical innovation) had not produced a comparable gain in economic growth during the previous four decades.

De Loo and Soete (1999) tried to explain this lack of correlation by the fact that research and development efforts were increasingly concerned with product differentiation rather than with product (or process) innovation, a focus that improved consumers' welfare but did little for economic growth. And David (1990) noted a historical analogy between the apparent failure of microprocessor-driven innovations to create a surge in US productivity during the 1980s and the limited impact of pre-1920 electrification, decades after the commissioning of the first power plants. US productivity growth, below 1.5%/year between 1973 and 1995, was reversed during the late 1990s when its rate of 2.5%/year was nearly as high as it was between 1960 and 1973.

In his series of studies, culminating in a comprehensive book, Gordon (2000, 2012, 2016) questioned the fundamental Solowian assumption of economic growth as a continuous process that will persist forever, and demonstrated, contrary to the prevailing impression of unprecedented progress, that in many respects the much-touted "New Economy"—based on exploiting computing, information processing, and telecommunication advances made possible by the growth of microprocessor capabilities (conforming to Moore's law)—does not measure up to the great inventions of the past.

A long-term perspective shows virtually no growth of major economies before 1750, and accelerated growth in the frontier (that is the richest Western) economies, in the UK after 1750 and the US a century later. This growth reached its peak in the middle of the 20th century and it has been declining ever since, raising an unorthodox question about how much further the frontier growth rate could decline. Gordon (2016) concludes that the second industrial revolution of 1870–1900 (with its introduction of electricity, internal combustion engines, running water, indoor toilets, communications, entertainment, launching of oil extraction and chemical industries) was far more consequential than both the first revolution (1750–1830, introducing steam and railroads) and the third (begun in 1960 and still unfolding, with computers, the Web and mobile phones as its icons).

The second revolution was largely responsible for eight decades of relatively rapid productivity growth between 1890 and 1972, and once the post-1945 spin-off from its previous fundamental advances (ranging from air conditioning and jetliners to interstate highways) had run their course, productivity growth slowed down after 1973, save for a brief growth revival between 1996 and 2004. By taking a close look at the nature and impacts of technical innovations, I made very similar arguments in my twin books on creating and transforming the 20th century (Smil 2005, 2006b). My periodization was slightly different as I concluded that the period between 1860 and 1913 was a unique historical phenomenon that may have no similar follow-up.

We may never again see such a concatenation of technical advances (electricity, internal combustion engines, automobiles, powered flight, chemical syntheses) as we experienced during the 50 years preceding WWI. As Gordon (2016) points out, the post-2000 years have centered on entertainment and communication devices whose enthusiastic adoption and widespread deployment does not fundamentally change either labor productivity (in fact, it may reduce it due to addictive distractions created by "social media") or the standard of living in ways comparable to transformations brought by such fundamental innovations as electricity, internal combustion engines, and modern health care. Again, I stressed the same facts viewed from historical and technical perspectives (Smil 2006b).

The latest statistics make it clear that the declining trend of productivity growth in general, and of US productivity in particular, is all too real. Between 1987 and 2004, US labor productivity growth averaged 2.1%, between 2004 and 2014 it was just 1.2%, and its post-2011 mean has been a mere 0.6%, including three quarters of actual decline between the end of 2015 and the first half of 2016 (BLS 2017). This is a worrisome trend because during the coming 50 years the second major component of growth, the expansion of the labor supply, will decline substantially (by as much as 80%) in all mature economies with aging populations. Some economists have argued that productivity in modern service-dominated economies is increasingly difficult to measure and that our data are failing to capture its real progress. Others believe that shortage of demand and (despite low interest rates) investment opportunities is the main constraint on growth. Yet another explanation sees the slowdown primarily as a lag in realizing productivity benefits following the adoption of new techniques (Manyika et al. 2017). All of these explanations may be partially, or largely, valid.

Looking ahead, Gordon (2016) sees six headwinds that will reduce long-term growth even if innovation were to continue at rates similar to the recent past: a changing population structure, changing education, rising inequality, impacts of globalization, challenges of energy and the environment, and the burdens of consumer and government debt. Gordon's provocative "exercise in subtraction" concludes that, except for the richest 1%, the future growth of annual per capita consumption could fall below 0.5% for many years, even decades, to come. Inevitably, these interpretations and concerns have been criticized (particularly by the promoters of a sweeping artificial intelligence revolution) but we will have to wait for another decade or so (a few years do not make a trend) before concluding that the new e-world has been a disappointment as far as labor productivity is concerned—or finding that its delayed impacts are making an enormous difference and ushering in a new era of productivity growth.

The most persistent inquest into the ultimate causes of economic growth has been carried out by Joel Mokyr. He has stressed the importance of knowledge as the key reason behind the Western economic rise (Mokyr 2002) and in his latest book he traces the origins of the modern economy to what is known as the "Republic of Letters" (Mokyr 2017). Its market for ideas flourished in early modern Europe between 1500 and the end of the Enlightenment, with political fragmentation supporting intellectual inquiries, a precondition that was absent at that time anywhere else, including technically adept China. According to Mokyr, the origins of economic growth have to do more with enlightened reasoning (Desiderius Erasmus,

Francis Bacon, and Isaac Newton) than with any distinct technical or business practices. Again, other interpretations of those European origins are available (notably Allen 2009) but there can be no doubt that reducing the moving forces to machines and profits would be a grossly reductionist view.

Growth Interactions

I agree with Grossman and Helpman (1991) that it is better not to draw any specific inferences about the underlying causes of economic growth because the factors involved are dynamically linked within a complex system, making the exogenous-endogenous dichotomy largely an artificial construct. Broad qualitative conclusions explaining the roots of economic growth and the sources of productivity are thus preferable to allocations of shares attributable to specific causes. Unfortunately, the most common approach to studying the roots of growth has been to treat the key factors as exogenous inputs into single-equation regressions.

Kibritcioglu and Dibooglu (2001, 1) are correct when they point out that these approaches "consider *one-way* causalities running from selected economic (and recently, non-economic) regressors to per-capita real output growth ignoring the possible endogeneity of most factors" and when they conclude that "the nature of economic growth is too complex to be captured by estimating single-equation regressions." They presented a helpful graphic summary of possible interactions in the economic growth process by aggregating the set of factors into nine groups (capital and labor; technology; demography; geography (including climate); culture; institutions; income distribution; government policies; macroeconomic stability and economic growth) and by interpreting long-run growth as a net outcome of multilateral interactions among these sets and the economic growth itself.

Of the possible 55 interactions, 23 are strongly and five are weakly bidirectional, while 23 are unidirectional, and only four cells show weak or negligible interactions. This matrix provides a useful tool for mapping the explanatory approaches. Neoclassical theory explains growth by focusing on the linkages of capital and labor, Keynes saw nearly all of the action confined to government policies. Geographic determinism is concerned with interactions of climate and soils, even the shape of continents, and population growth. Endogenous growth theory concentrates above all on how technical advances interact with economic growth, and yet other theories see institutional arrangements (including the rule of law and low levels of corruption) as preeminent drivers of economic growth.

There are too many theories investigating in detail these specific links between individual factors and economic growth to present their systematic review. Instead, I have chosen several key factors—including energy, education, health, demographic shifts, trade, income inequality, and corruption—for brief appraisals of their importance. Each of them plays important and yet also restricted roles in promoting or impeding economic growth. Seeing them as pieces in a mosaic of factors helps to explains why some nations have done so much better than others, and why some economies have enjoyed long growth runs while others are still waiting for takeoffs even though some of their preconditions for vigorous economic development are actually superior when compared to other countries that have joined the ranks of well-off societies.

Energy's fundamental role in economic growth is obvious: all productive activities require its conversions. But the mainstream economists have never seen it that way, and Robert Ayres has done more than anybody else to expose the fundamental weaknesses of their understanding.

> Economic concepts…lack any systematic awareness of the implications of the Laws of Thermodynamics for the physical process of production. A corollary, almost worthy of being a separate bad idea on its own, is that energy doesn't matter (much) because the cost share of energy in the economy is so small that it can be ignored…as if output could be produced by labor and capital alone—or as if energy is merely a form of man-made capital that can be produced (as opposed to extracted) by labor and capital…The essential truth missing from economic education is that energy is the stuff of the universe, that all matter is also a form of energy, and that the economic system is essentially a system for extracting, processing and transforming energy as resources into energy embodied in products and services. (Ayres 2017, 40)

Ayres showed convincingly that since the onset of the industrial revolution economic growth has been driven largely by declining energy costs resulting from the discovery and extensive exploitation of relatively inexpensive and highly energy-dense fossil fuels (Ayres and Warr 2009; Ayres and Voudouris 2014; Ayres 2016). And Schumpeter's (1939) classical account of Western business cycles, based on Kondratiev (1926), showed how new energy sources and prime movers led to cyclically accelerated investment. As identified by Kondratiev, the first upswing (1787–1817) coincided with the rising extraction of coal and with the initial adoption of stationary steam engines. The second upswing (1844–1875) was driven by the deployment of steam engines on railroads and in steamships and by advances in iron metallurgy (Bessemer steel). The third upswing (1890–1920) was governed by the widespread adoption of commercial electricity generation and by the replacement of steam-powered mechanical drives by electric motors in industrial production.

Center points of these upturns were about 40–56 years apart, and post-WWII research confirmed the existence of these approximately 50-year pulsations and of the recurrence of economic cycles tied to technical inventions in particular (Marchetti 1986a; Vasko et al. 1990; Allianz 2010; Bernard et al. 2013). Post-Kondratiev cycles had upswings between 1939 and 1974 (the fourth cycle), and 1984 and 2008 (the fifth, electronic cycle) and they were dominated by computing, information and telecommunication techniques (Grinin et al. 2016). The initial stages of adopting new primary energies have correlated well with the starts of major innovation periods. Moreover, in a fascinating feedback, it appears that economic depressions acted as triggers of innovative activity (Mensch 1979): the last deep global downturn during the 1930s brought us such fundamental advances as gas turbines (jet engines), fluorescent lights, radar, and nuclear energy.

Other waves have been identified—ranging from Kitchin cycles of 3–5 years to Kuznets cycles (average 15–25 years)—but Kondratiev cycles (with average duration of 40–60 years, often reduced to 55–56 years) have been both the most often invoked and the most frequently doubted. Theodore Modis maintains that a wide range of anthropogenic and natural phenomena (ranging from bank failures and homicides to hurricanes and sunspot activity) resonate with this cycle—but a closer look at his presentation shows correlations ranging from significant to tenuous, and he correctly concludes that "all quantitative confidence levels involved in these observations are poor by scientific standards and permit critics to question the very existence of this phenomenon" (Modis 2017, 63).

Focacci (2017) confirmed this conclusion by analyzing both Kondratiev's original data (never before processed by harmonic analysis in their whole dataset) and the latest and longest available economic series. He concluded that it seems very difficult to sustain the original hypothesis and that "this device could be considered more a 'technical fitting procedure' than an explanatory marked and prominent evidence of a real phenomenon" (Focacci 2017, 281). The verdict is convincing: there are cyclical patterns with amplitudes of 40–60 years but in the absence of any strong evidence for greater regularity and the lack of any unifying explanation, it is best not to elevate Kondratiev cycles to predictable mirrors of reality.

Trends of GDP growth and energy consumption and trends in the energy intensity of economies (J/$) have been analyzed on a national level for many economies but careful interpretations are required to explain the results. During the 20th century, global primary energy use (excluding all processing losses and nonfuel uses) increased nearly eightfold while the world economic product rose more than 18-fold, implying energy/product elasticity of less than 0.5, but national specificities produced substantially different elasticities: very close to 1 for Japan, 0.6 for China, and less than 0.4 for the US. Historical analyses confirm a universal trend of declining energy intensities. The UK's energy intensity rose before 1850 with the adoption of steam engines and railways, and Canadian and US intensities experienced a similar rise 60–70 years later, with the US rate peaking before 1920. Japan's energy intensity was rising until 1970, China's until 1980.

The declining energy intensity of modern economies has been due to the decreasing importance of energy-intensive capital inputs required to build basic infrastructures during the earlier stages of economic development, to rising efficiencies of fuel combustion and electricity conversions, and to higher shares of less energy-intensive services (retail, education, finance) in total GDPs. According to Kaufmann (1992), most of the post-1950 decline of energy intensities in modern economies was due mainly to the changing compositions of energy use and of the type of dominant goods and services rather than to technical advances.

A close link between energy and GDP growth is further confirmed by very high (in excess of 0.9) correlations between per capita GDP and energy use when all countries are included for any given year—but the link weakens considerably once we examine more homogeneous groups of countries. To become rich necessitates a substantial increase in energy use but energy consumption among affluent nations (be it per GDP unit or per capita) varies widely, producing very low correlations. There is simply no fixed (or even very similar) amount of energy required to produce identical (or very similar) per capita GDPs. For example, in 2016 German and Australian per capita GDPs were nearly identical ($48,100 and $48,900 in PPP terms) but Australia's per capita energy use was nearly 45% higher. Conversely, Australia's and South Korea's per capita energy use was nearly identical but Australia's per capita GDP was nearly 30% higher.

Even more importantly, while average per capita energy use of primary energy has been flat in many affluent countries for two to three decades, their real per capita GDPs have been rising. In the US, per capita energy consumption in 2016 was about 15% below its 1979 peak, while real per capita GDP rose by nearly 80% during the same period (FRED 2017). Similarly, decoupling of per capita primary energy use and GDP growth has taken place since the 1980s in other affluent countries. At the same time, it must be noted that these decades of relative energy-GDP decoupling coincided with extensive offshoring of energy-intensive industries from affluent countries to Asia in general and to China in particular and that this shift reduces the extent of the observed energy-GDP decoupling.

The role of education in fostering modern economic growth seems to be self-evident. Not surprisingly, Galor (2011) concluded that during the last three decades of the 19th century investment in education was the most important factor in reducing the fertility of western European countries. The rising share of children (6–14 years of age) in school correlates strongly with the falling birth rate (Wrigley and Schofield 1981). And Galor and Moav (2002) traced the onset of the western European transition to the rise in demand for human capital, a shift that favored quality (fewer children) over quantity and that was reinforced by other complementary trends, above all by rising life expectancy. In practice, the shift took the form of educational reforms (compulsory elementary school attendance), a rising wage differential between parental and child labor, and laws restricting and abolishing child labor. In contrast, in Asian countries the transition was delayed due to a lack of demand for skilled labor and slow gains in life expectancy.

DeLong (2002, 144) stresses the role of education for later modernizers and of research for advanced economies:

A follower economy with a higher level of educational attainment is likely to have a much more successful time at adapting to local conditions inventions and innovations from the industrial core of the world economy. Thus education appears to be a key policy for successful economic growth outside the industrial core. Inside the industrial core, without better technology increases in the capital stock produced by investment rapidly run into diminishing returns. One-fifth of total gross investment is research and development. More than half of net investment is…investments in knowledge, as opposed to investments in machinery, equipment, structures, and infrastructure.

Health is, obviously, a direct source of human welfare and also a critical factor in raising income levels as it affects labor productivity and savings for retirement and determines prevailing life spans. The interaction between health and economic growth was first examined by Ehrlich and Lui (1991) and it has become clear that health status (measured by life expectancy or by various indicators) is an important contributor to subsequent growth (Barro 2013). But Bloom and Canning (2008) found that the macroeconomic evidence for health's effect on economic growth is mixed and it is possible that, until a fertility transition takes place, gains from health may be outweighed by the consequences of increased survival. And Bhargava et al. (2001) identified only a relatively small effect of the adult survival rate on the economic growth rate in low-income countries, with every 1% change of the former associated with an approximate 0.05% increase in the latter, but this should be compared with their finding that a 1% increase in the investment/GDP ratio was associated with a 0.014% increase in GDP growth.

The demographic transition eventually had a threefold effect on economic growth (Galor 2011). Declining population growth reduced the dilution of the growing stock of capital and of the burden imposed on infrastructures, resulting in a higher per capita allocation of resources and services. Reduced fertility led to a highly consequential reallocation of resources from quantity (large numbers of children destined to remain poor and uneducated) to quality (small number of children receiving much better care and always basic, and increasingly more advanced, forms of education). Finally, a shift in the age distribution caused by declining fertility produced a temporarily higher fraction of the economically active population, which translated into higher productivity per capita.

The search for the causal factors of the demographic transition led to some obvious conclusions and to some mistaken claims. Becker (1960) believed that the reduction of fertility was a consequence of higher incomes generated during industrialization, but that was not the case throughout western Europe, where fertility rates began to decline noticeably during the same time (during the 1870s) in countries with significantly different per capita incomes. The best estimates for 1870 show German per capita GDP at only about 60% of the British value, with the Swedish and Finnish rates at, respectively, just 40% and 30% (Maddison 2007). During the opening decades of their demographic transitions, the growth rates of income per capita were similar (ranging between 1.2 and 1.6%) in western European countries despite the just noted substantial differences in the income level.

An important consequence of the demographic transition has become known as the demographic dividend, first identified in the East Asian economies (Bloom et al. 2000). The boost to economic growth is provided by a combination of improved child health (higher survival rates in the first benefiting cohort followed by fewer children in the next), increased human capital resulting from better health and better education of the surviving children, and an increased labor supply as low fertility allows higher female labor participation.

If this new bulge cohort can be productively employed, there will be notable gains in economic performance, as was demonstrated in Japan after 1950, then in South Korea, and in China after 1990. Conversely, the effects of population aging on economic growth are overwhelmingly negative (McMorrow and Roeger 2004). Aged populations provide a smaller taxation base and lower per capita state revenues, create a higher average tax burden, and raise dependency ratios. These ratios will commonly double in affluent countries during the first half of the 21st century, threatening to bankrupt the existing pension plans unless higher contributions or lower payments are enacted soon; and there will be unprecedented demand for geriatric health care.

The modern pursuit of economic globalization owes a great deal to a widely held conviction that open trade promotes economic growth while trade restrictions dampen it. The role of international trade in economic growth has been obvious. Its rise started around 1870 and it was cut short by WWI, but only a new analysis by Klasing and Milionis (2014) that included 62 countries representing 90% of global GDP between 1870 and 1948 showed how dramatic that rise and fall was. They found that trade shares were nearly 40% higher than previously documented, that they rose from about 18% in 1870 to 30% in 1913, collapsed to 10% by 1932, and recovered to only 16% by 1949—and it was not until 1974 that the world's level of trade openness reached again the record of 1913. The subsequent rise led to the peak 60.93% in 2008 (World Bank 2018) and a logistic curve with the inflection point in 1988 provides the best (moderately good) fit for the long-term trajectory (1870–2015) of the measure, and it indicates that hardly any further growth lies ahead (figure 5.31).

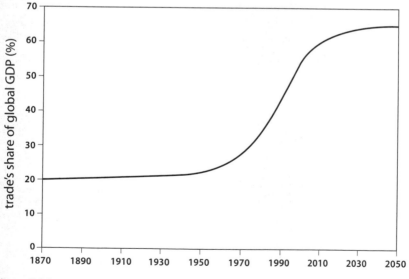

Figure 5.31
Growing shares of international trade in the world economic product since 1870. Data from Klasing and Milionis (2014) and World Bank (2018).

The benefits of open markets are among the key tenets of the European Union, the world's largest economy that is also highly outward-oriented. The EU has no doubt that open markets (including foreign direct investment) generate more economic growth and more and better jobs for Europe and its partners, and the European Commission concluded that if all free trade talks that were underway in 2014 were completed, the new arrangements would increase the EU's GDP by more than 2%, the equivalent of adding an economy like Austria or Denmark (European Commission 2014). The choice of measures affects the conclusions. Busse and Königer (2012) showed that the impact of trade on GDP per capita growth is not adequately captured by using the trade-to-GDP (trade openness) ratio, and that using the volume of exports and imports as a share of lagged total GDP is a better measure to reveal trade's positive and significant impact on growth.

Perhaps the best summary of trade's effects on economic growth can be gained from a closer look at the evidence published by Rodriguez and Rodrik (2000). They found that greatly overstating the systematic evidence in favor of trade openness helps to generate exaggerated expectations and to interfere with institutional reforms which might have potentially greater payoffs. Their conclusion:

> The effects of trade liberalization may be on balance beneficial on standard comparative-advantage grounds; the evidence provides no strong reason to dispute this. What we dispute is the view, increasingly common, that integration into the world economy is such a potent force for economic growth that it can effectively substitute for a development strategy. (Rodriguez and Rodrik 2000, 318)

The neoclassical model of economic growth implies long-term convergence of per capita GDP only if all economies were intrinsically identical or very similar: nations with lower starting levels would grow at faster rates while affluent countries would experience diminishing returns to capital. In reality, this convergence is conditional because the economic performance depends on variables ranging from fertilities to saving rates and from government policies to access to innovation, and these factors vary widely across economies. As a result, poor and war-devastated South Korea, copying the Japanese model of targeted-sector development (first light manufactures and shipbuilding, then cars and electronics), grew rapidly while Nigeria presents a case of exceptional decline and stagnation.

When Kuznets (1955) made the first systematic attempt to address the linkage between economic growth and income equality he stressed "the meagerness of reliable information presented. The paper is perhaps 5 per cent empirical information and 95 per cent speculation, some of it possibly tainted by wishful thinking" (Kuznets 1955, 26). Still, his general conclusion (or as he put it, a preliminary informed guess) based on his scant sample of the United States, England, and Germany was that the relative distribution of income had been moving toward equality, with the trend most likely beginning before WWI but particularly noticeable since the 1920s. Subsequent availability of more reliable statistics and diligent efforts to reconstruct historical data series made the assessment of income inequality both more accurate and more nuanced, but the outcomes of these studies still depend on data quality and on analytical techniques.

The most conspicuous trend from the global perspective is how North America and western Europe continued to pull ahead of the rest of the world during the entire 20th century and how even China's rapid post-1980 growth (which put the country far ahead of its former peers, including India and Nigeria) did not narrow the income gap between the West and the rest to a significant extent. The extent of global inequality (unweighted by population) appeared to change little between 1950 and 1975 but increased during the last quarter of the 20th century (Milanovic 2012); while the population-weighted trend showed a significant convergence of national incomes from the late 1960s, nearly all of it was attributable to China's post-1980 rise and without its gains global inequality showed little change between 1950 and 2000.

At the same time, there was an increase in the number of downwardly mobile countries. While in 1960 only 25 countries had per capita GDPs lower than a third of the rate in the poorest Western nation, by the year 2000 their count rose to almost 80, with Africa accounting for most of this undesirable gain, but with urban slums, the markers of modern inequality, expanding also in Asia and Latin America (figure 5.32). The most remarkable consequence of this rising inequality was the emergence of what Milanovic (2002, 92) called "the emptiness in the middle." By the end of the 20th century, fewer than 4% of all people lived in countries whose average per capita income would qualify them as "middle class" ($(PPP)8,000–20,000), while 80% were below the lower threshold.

The growth of inequality, and its causes and consequences, has attracted a great deal of recent attention (Milanovic 2012; Piketty 2014; Zucman 2014; Dabla-Norris et al. 2015; Alvaredo et al. 2017; Scheidel 2017). US data were used to identify three stages of inequality shifts during the 20th century. First, the economic crisis of the 1930s and WWII combined to more than halve the concentration of incomes at the top. In 1928 the richest 1% of households claimed 28% of all income, by 1950 it was just above 10%. The second stage lasted just over 30 years: widely shared prosperity further

Figure 5.32
Petare slum in Caracas, Venezuela, is an example of a fairly orderly slum development. Photo available at wikimedia.

lowered the top 1% share to below 10% by the late 1970s and income gaps did not widen. Finally, that changed as economic growth slowed down and as the incomes of households in the middle and lower brackets slowed appreciably while those of households at the top continued to rise. Piketty et al. (2018) concluded that in the US the top 1% share increased by two-thirds since 1960 and that it had doubled since 1980.

This widely reported conclusion was based on using individual tax returns but Auten and Splinter (2018) argued that those estimates are biased because of tax base changes, missing income sources, and major social changes, and their adjusted estimates present a very different outcome. While the top federal individual income tax rate declined from 91% to 39.6% between 1960 and 2015, base-broadening reforms and the reduced use of tax shelters had actually boosted effective tax rates of the top 1% from 14% to 24% while the taxes of the bottom 90% fell, suggesting an increase in overall tax progressivity and resulting in only a small gain in the top 1% income shares in the US.

At the same time, trends similar to those estimated by Piketty for the US—pre-WWII inequality decline, a relatively stable post-WWII distribution until the 1980s, and a subsequent rise in inequality—have been also reported in Canada, the UK, Italy, and in Russia where the post-Soviet rise in inequality has been especially steep (WWID 2018). And compared to income, distribution of wealth (total net value of a household's property and financial assets) is far more skewed. By 2016 no more than 3% of all US households held more than half of the nation's wealth, the top 1% claimed 39%, and the top 0.5% owned about 33%—while the bottom 90% had 23% (Stone et al. 2017). Economic globalization has been one of the contributing factors: while open trade raises aggregate income, it also increases income inequality (Antràs et al. 2017).

Corruption—practiced in many ways as bribery, theft of public assets, and patronage, and ranging from a ubiquitous low level to exceptional looting of state treasuries—increases the cost of doing business, results in waste of resources and inefficiency, perpetuates poverty, erodes public trust, undermines the rule of law, and delegitimizes the state. World Bank and World Economic Forum estimates put its global cost at more than 5% of the world economic product and (in bribes alone) more than $1 trillion a year (OECD 2014). Even modest estimates of the reduction in output growth, when cumulated over time, imply massive output losses due to corruption that in many developing countries may exceed 100% of current GDP. But there is no simple universal link between corruption and economic growth, and a rational argument might see a low incidence of corruption useful if it acts to circumvent cumbersome bureaucratic rules.

High post-1990 rates of GDP growth in China have been clearly compatible with high levels of corruption: Transparency International (2017) puts China, with a score of 40, in 79th place among 176 compared countries with extreme scores ranging from the least corrupt Denmark at 90 to 10 for Somalia. Other East Asian countries a with relatively high incidence of corruption (Japan, South Korea, Taiwan) have also experienced high rates of growth, leading some economists to suggest the prevalence of an East Asian paradox that belies the common assumption of a negative correlation between corruption and GDP growth.

But East Asian growth and corruption may have more to do with the stage of economic development than with any cultural/regional peculiarities. According to Ramirez (2014), corruption in the US in the early 1870s—when the country's real per capita income was about $2,800 in terms of 2005 dollars—was seven to nine times higher than in China in 1996, when the country reached the corresponding level of per capita income, and by 1928—when the US per capita income was at $7,500 and equal to China's 2009 rate—corruption was similar in both countries. If Ramirez is correct this would imply that China's recent corruption has not been alarmingly high compared to the US historical experience and that it is bound to decline with further development.

After restricting their sample of studied countries only to those who are considered to be free (hence excluding economies ranging from China to Saudi Arabia), Méndez and Sepúlveda (2006) found that the growth-maximizing level of corruption is significantly greater than zero, with the practice beneficial for economic growth at low levels of incidence and detrimental at high levels of incidence. Mo (2001) offered some insight into the effects of higher levels of corruption. His regression suggested that a 1% increase in the corruption level reduces the growth rate by about 0.72% or that a 1 unit increase in the corruption index reduces the growth rate by about 0.5%, with corruption-induced political instability accounting for most of the effect. We must concede that in some circumstances or at some stages of economic development a certain level of corruption may be mitigated by other factors and may be associated with satisfactory GDP growth. At the same time, I would maintain that corrupt ways cannot offer the best path to stable economic development, social justice, and legitimate state power.

Finally, in one of the more unusual analyses, Bjørnskov and Kurrild-Klitgaard (2014) evaluated a conventional hypothesis that republics should experience faster economic growth than monarchies and that they should also experience lower transitional costs following reforms. But their study of regressing decadal growth rates of 27 countries between 1820 and 2000 showed no significant growth differences between the two regimes, as well as no differences as far as incremental reforms were concerned. On this evidence, republics do not appear more conducive to economic growth than monarchies.

Civilizations

Paradoxically, my coverage of the growth of the world's most complex anthropogenic systems will not be a long examination because in this chapter I have been progressing from easily and revealingly measurable developments to changes that cannot be satisfactorily captured (regardless of the requisite availability of primary information) either by a small set of quantifiable variables or by more complicated indexes and composite valuations. Growth of populations, although subject to many driving forces, can be followed quite accurately by focusing on key vital statistics and on survival rates (life expectancies). For cities, tracing the trajectories of just two variables—their populations and their areas—provides us with the most revealing determinants of their physical growth, and in more recent history this could be supplemented by data capturing their economic power.

Measuring the growth of national economies remains, as I have shown in some detail, an enormous challenge. This is not only because the most frequently used variable (GDP) provides partial and questionable coverage but also because the very meaning of national economies has become questionable in an increasingly integrated global economic system. Moreover, there is no obviously superior, universally acceptable, and readily quantifiable alternative to replace the unsatisfactory GDP standard. Even so, it is incomparably easier to quantify modern economic growth than to assess the growth of extinct civilizations or to quantify the multifaceted progress of globalization.

As in all cases of complex concepts, the difficulties start with the definition of the analyzed subject. The ancient Latin *civilitas* served originally as the equivalent of an even older *Greek* politiké, civil government, which meant the governance of city affairs. French enlightenment pioneered that master-word, but definitions offered by French thinkers have ranged widely. The first printed mention was in Mirabeau's *L'ami des hommes* (1756, 192) when he noted that "La religion est sans contredit le premier et le plus utile frein de l'humanité: c'est le premier ressort de la civilisation" (religion is unquestionably the first and most useful brake of humanity: it is the first spring of civilization). Even if we were to agree with such an arguable statement, how would we use it to trace the growth of civilization?

In 1771 the *Dictionnaire de Trévoux* defined civilization as a term of jurisprudence, an act of justice, a judgment that makes a criminal trial civil. This puts civilization into a long historical perspective by contrasting it with barbarism and primitivity, but how we do translate that concept into an indicator of secular civilizational growth—particularly given the total of casualties that could be ascribed to the perverted judicial processes of the 20th century? Stalin and Hitler, as well as Mao, used staged and widely publicized as well as swift and secret courts and trials to legitimize the enormity of crimes they committed against their own people.

Eventually the term has become used widely, to describe both an outcome (in the broadest possible terms, the way of life of specific societies, extinct and extant) and a process (as civilization diffuses and evolves toward more complex social, economic, and technical arrangements). Morin (1854, 3), impressed by the process, noted that "civilization has in itself an expansive force which disseminates through the populations. It is communicated by the books, by trade, by attendance: it spreads like heat by contact." This singular view is one of unity and universal adoption— and it is in sharp contrast with a plural view of different, incompatible, or outright adversarial civilizations. Switching to the plural forces us to come up with (inevitably arbitrary) criteria used to separate simple societies from more complex civilizations and requires us to be prepared for arguments about suitable subdivisions. Clearly, such labels as Christian or Muslim civilization mask complex realities, ignoring the legacies of abiding hatred and mass-scale violence (Catholics vs. Protestants, *Sunni* vs. *Shi'i*).

But historians keep on trying and there is no shortage of truly modern, seemingly comprehensive definitions. Fernand Braudel, France's best known 20th-century historian, opted for a broad description of specific outcomes:

> A civilization is first of all a space, a "cultural area," as the anthropologists would say, a locus. Within the locus…you must picture a great variety of "goods," of cultural characteristics, ranging from the form of its houses, the material of which they are built, their roofing, to skills like feathering arrows, to a dialect or a group of dialects, to tastes in cooking, to a particular technology, a structure of beliefs, a way of making love, and even to the compass, paper, and the printing press. (Braudel 1982, 202)

But Braudel left out, as do most historians, the key ingredient, the energy needed to make all of those goods and activities a reality. Houses, roofs, arrows or paper do not arise *ex nihilo*, nor do the beliefs that must be nurtured by food and celebrated in places of worship. Bertrand Binoche—who edited an entire book devoted to the ambiguities of the term civilization (*Les équivoques de la civilisation*)—offered a crisper definition: "In the current sense, civilization is the set of traits that characterize the state of a given society, from the technical, intellectual, political and moral point of view, without making any value judgment" (Binoche 2005, 57).

But the unhelpful diversity of French definitions should not be singled out. Tainter (1988) plunged into his discourse of collapsing civilizations without defining the term, while in my book on the biospheric cycles and civilization I opted for the most fundamental biophysical approach, describing civilizations as intricate subsystems of the biosphere, dependent on its multitude of goods and services, with the modern high-energy civilization being highly successful in substituting, modifying, and manipulating its demands for environmental goods but remaining as dependent on biospheric services as any of its less elaborate predecessors (Smil 1997). That might be a fairly comprehensive biophysical definition but we would still have to decide which of many constituent variables describing this reality we would wish to quantify in order to assess long-term growth, stagnation, or decline.

At this point a persevering reader of this book will have seen the growth of many of these constituent parts of modern civilization (ranging from its population and food production to energy use and a variety of technical constructs and artifacts) covered in preceding chapters. Could the key indicators, seen as a series of advances, be combined by constructing a compounded measure that would gauge the growth of human civilization? Ideally, this should be done by quantifying the progressing complexity of civilization that has defined the evolution of our species and its recent history. This should trace trajectories from hominins to *Homo sapiens*, from foragers surviving in small cooperative groups to the first crop growers and city dwellers, from long-lasting ancient civilizations energized overwhelmingly by human and animal muscle and by burning of biomass fuels to industrial societies concentrating progressively in cities and finally to a highly networked global civilization. Could social development be measured and charted through time and space?

Measuring Advances

One way to do that would be to trace the increasing number of roles (a constantly advancing division of labor) in evolving societies. The sociology of roles, be they stable gender and cultural roles or those acquired through social differentiation, became a notable research subject with pioneering works by Mead (1934), Linton (1936), Moreno (1951), and Parsons (1951). But the measure is highly problematic: how does one meaningfully quantify the proliferation of occupational niches or how does one assess success in moving up an ever-changing social ladder? By using detailed job descriptions to discriminate among marginally different roles, by rising incomes, or by gauging personal satisfaction?

And is such occupational/social differentiation a sign of real progress? Does society truly benefit by seemingly ever-increasing occupational specialization? Creation of these new roles is accompanied by the loss of such valuable, flexible skills as the ability to grow one's own food or to repair a range of small machines. And, obviously, the rise of complexity measured simply by the multiplication of occupational roles is not always desirable. One could name scores of occupations whose existence proves a regrettable dysfunctionality of modern civilization rather than its admirable accomplishments. Entire firms of lawyers specialized in defending criminal organizations and large sums spent on training and equipping specialized SWAT teams to be deployed during terrorist attacks are just two of many prominent examples.

Whatever the merits and drawbacks of specific indicators, it appears that the most revealing (also the most defensible) measure of social development must combine a number of components; it must be a composite index. Ian

Morris—in a follow-up volume to his *Why the West Rules—For Now* (Morris 2011)—tried to achieve precisely that but in order to capture this growth in a more nuanced manner he calculated two sets of developmental advances for the West and for the East (Morris 2013). His division follows a historical progression, with the leading edge of Western development moving from southwestern Asia (Mesopotamia) to the Mediterranean, Europe, and eventually to North America, while the Eastern domain began in the Yellow River valley and eventually extended to all of eastern and southeastern Asia, with the latest frontier areas in Japan and east China.

Morris's index of social development "is the bundle of technological, subsistence, organizational, and cultural accomplishments through which people feed, clothe, house, and reproduce themselves, explain the world around them, resolve disputes within their communities, extend their power at the expense of other communities, and defend themselves against others' attempts to extend power" or, more concisely, it is "a measure of communities' abilities to get things done in the world" (Morris 2013, 15). Its four components are total energy capture, social organization (measured as the growth of cities), war-making capability, and information technology (measured as advances in skills and as speed and reach of information means). He calculated their specific scores and combined totals in intervals of every millennium since 14,000 BCE and then every 100 years since 1,500 BCE.

Even the best-conceived index is open to questions about its composition, and, more importantly, quantifying historic trends will be always challenging, often impossible. To anybody even remotely familiar with the availability and reliability of information required to quantify these four variables going back 17 millennia, it is immediately obvious that all but a few pre-1800 entries are largely guesses based on the best available (but frequently indirect) supporting evidence. Morris readily acknowledges these constraints and explains the limits of his quantifications but, even so, I would argue that the final numbers are even more uncertain, and much more contestable, than he concedes. I will illustrate this by looking just at energy capture because until 1800 this single component accounted for more than 80% of the value of his final social development indexes.

Morris based his energy capture estimate on a simplified framework proposed by Cook (1971), but Cook had greatly overestimated Western energy consumption before the 19th century. Consequently, Morris put the average daily per capita energy capture in 100 CE at 31,000 kcal, that is about 47 GJ/year—while the global annual mean in the year 2000 was no more than 65 GJ. That would imply a gain of less than 40% in in 19 centuries, or a vanishingly small annual increase of 0.07%. Much more realistically, my best estimate for the Roman Empire of the 2nd century CE is no more than 20 GJ/year (Smil 2010c). Morris has the daily per capita Western energy capture at 38,000 kcal in 1800 (58 GJ/year)—while the most reliable examination of energy needs in early modern Europe put the mean (including food and fodder) at about 17 GJ/capita in 1800, or 70% lower (Kander et al. 2013). A weighted mean including higher US consumption moves the Western total for 1800 to no more than about 25 GJ.

And Morris puts the average daily per capita Western energy capture at 230,000 kcal in the year 2000 but that total (about 350 GJ/year) is representative only of the US, where the aggregate per capita supply of food, animal feed, and all commercial fuels and electricity reached about 239,000 kcal/day (365 GJ/year). In Europe the daily mean was only 111,000 kcal/capita and the weighted daily average for the West was thus about 160,000 kcal/capita (244 GJ/year), or 30% lower than Morris's rate. And these are the entries for a component that can be, if data are available, calculated rather accurately, and is fundamentally more revealing than the largest city size (is Lagos a sign of desirable development?) or dividing populations into skill categories—to say nothing about the highly arguable inclusion of war-making capability as a key ingredient of a social development index.

In any case, as constructed by Morris (2013), the aggregate Western index rises from 4.36 in 14,000 BCE to 43.3 by 100 CE, then it fluctuates between roughly 28 and 41 until 1700 before it quadrupled by 1900 (170.24) and reached 906.37 in the year 2000. Energy capture, war-making capacity, and information technology each contributed 250 points, and organization added 156 points. The Eastern index differs little until 1800 but it remains at only 71 in 1900 and rises to 564.83 by the year 2000 (Morris 2013). To sum up, Morris's social development scores rise by an order of magnitude from prehistory to the Roman or Han empires, then mark nearly two millennia of stagnation followed by roughly a 20-fold post-1700 gain in the West and 13-fold gain in the East.

Other aggregate developmental indicators are available but their historical reconstruction would be even more questionable or outright impossible. As already noted, the Human Development Index, published annually since 2010, could be extended backwards by assuming plausible life expectancies and indicators of education and literacy (with, obviously, little differentiation until the recent centuries, as mass illiteracy was the norm) and (as already stressed) by deploying highly questionable estimates (guesses would be a better term) of equivalent per capita GDPs going back millennia.

And calculating meaningful historic values of the Social Progress Index introduced in 2013 is not at all realistic. This index measures 16 out of 17 of the UN's Sustainable Development Goals and reflects 131 out of 169 targets in the categories of basic human needs (nutrition, water, sanitation), foundations of well-being (access to knowledge, environmental quality), and opportunities, including personal rights and freedoms (SPI 2018). The index is designed to monitor the progress of individual countries rather than to gauge advances of leading civilizations in the past or to provide an informative and properly weighted indicator of the global situation.

And even if we were able to calculate a fairly accurate index of average civilizational progress, we would still face another challenging task: making it more meaningful by adjusting to disparities in standards of living, and later in income, that have marked any settled society. Recent interest in the prevalence of economic inequalities has not only confirmed their persistence and ubiquity but also demonstrated their prehistoric origins—Kohler et al. (2017) traced them to post-Neolithic wealth disparities created by agriculture—and exposed their tendency to increase during most of the periods of economic growth and to decline only during violent times (Scheidel 2017). Even in some of the world's most equitable societies, differences in group and personal outcomes are far from negligible, making all aggregate average markers meaningful only in comparison with other similarly undifferentiated approximations.

Specific Multiples

Measuring civilizational advances by constructing more or less elaborate composite indexes may not be the best solution to the challenge. The main reason is that the growth rates of individual components included in any wide-ranging index attempting to measure civilizational advances have been vastly different, with long-term gains often separated by orders of magnitude. Calculating composite indexes on the basis of such heterogeneous variables is questionable—especially as there is no unbiased way to weigh their importance. How should we weigh relatively small but existentially all-important gains in average daily per capita food availability compared to enormous increases of many orders of magnitude in the destructive power of explosive weapons? Assigning equal weights to food supply and weapons is as questionable as weighing communication advances more heavily than progress in reducing income inequality—but there is no readily available justification for deploying different weights.

That is why I think that the most revealing way to appraise the growth of civilizational achievements and capabilities is simply to compare a wide range of those critical multiples that can be quantified with acceptable reliability. Presenting long-term growth in terms of multiples has, of course, a major disadvantage in that it does not inform us about the intervening trajectories of specific processes (with some of the gains being relatively gradual, others concentrated in the recent past). But it allows us to use the same metric when comparing many variables whose detailed trajectories cannot be reconstructed due to the missing intervening observations but whose starting and ending points are known with sufficient, or perfect, accuracy. And, of course, all of these specific trajectories were traced in relevant chapters of this book.

I will review these critical multiples in ascending order, starting with those variables where long-term gains were necessarily marginal or relatively restricted because they have been limited by biophysical imperatives: body heights, animate exertions, crop yields, per capita food supply, and average size of living areas belong to this category of constrained multiples. I will conclude by reviewing a number of advances whose gains have been essentially infinitely large when measured across the civilization's life span, with calculating and telecommunication capabilities being the most obvious examples, and with the destructive power of weapons not far behind.

But before I begin, more caveats are in order. When comparing technical and productive advances, the multiples convey accurate impressions as they refer to the growth of indicated peak capabilities (such as the maximum speed of long-distance transportation) or typical (characteristic) performances (such as average yield of staple grains). When dealing with economic matters and consumption, the use of per capita rates is, inevitably, not as revealing because it refers to averages—but incomes, energy supply, access to food, or living conditions have usually skewed as well as bimodal distributions, and in such instances calculated or assumed means (although routinely used) are not representative, particularly in countries with high degrees of socioeconomic inequality.

The smallest relative gains concern human growth and performance, staple crop harvests, and daily supply of food. A comparison of average heights can be only approximate because we do not have sufficiently representative samples for premodern eras. According to Hermanussen (2003), during the pre-glacial maximum (Upper Paleolithic, before 16,000 BCE) European males were slim and tall (mean height 179 cm) and subsequently their heights declined to less than 165 cm during the Neolithic period and then remained between 165 and 170 cm until the end of the 19th century. A century later, means of European male height increased to 175–180 cm (Marck et al. 2017), resulting in a small multiple of about 1.06 during the past century.

During the 20th century (there are no comparable data for earlier periods), male athletic performances had improved by just 16% in running

800 m, about 30% in high jump, and about 75% in shot put, while gains for females were considerably larger (Marck et al. 2017). Approximate multiples for human physical performance since the beginning of organized international competitions (the first modern Olympiad was held in Athens in 1896) have thus ranged (depending on the discipline) between 1.15 and 1.75 for men and 1.35 and 2.5 for women, and (as already noted), since the 1980s they have established clear plateaus.

The first harvests of wild wheat were just a few hundred, and at best about 500 kg/ha. Even during the closing decades of the 19th century, yields on the Great Plains averaged just 1 t/ha, and the recent worldwide mean has been about 3.5 t/ha, 4 t/ha in Europe, and 6 t/ha in western Europe (FAO 2018). This means that the multiple since the time of the first cultivated plants to modern varieties has been roughly an order of magnitude (7–12 times). Harvests of unimproved corn varieties in precontact American societies practicing gardening and shifting cultivation were around 1 t/ha, compared to the recent Central American mean of less than 3.5 t/ha and the North American average of about 11 t/ha (FAO 2018), resulting in multiples ranging roughly between three and ten, again, at best an order of magnitude. Early Chinese rice cultivation (during the Han dynasty) produced mostly 0.9–1.3t/ha and recent yields range between 6 and 7 t/ha, resulting in multiples between five and seven.

Population-wide food requirements in traditional societies where most adults engaged daily in moderate to heavy work averaged between 2,300 and 2,600 kcal/day, while actual supplies at best met that need but were commonly 10–20% lower, resulting in widespread malnutrition, stunting, and premature mortality. Improved crop varieties, fertilizers, pesticides, irrigation, and mechanization of field work lifted yields, while the shift from primary and secondary economic activities to much less strenuous services lowered average food needs. As a result, modern affluent societies (with the notable exception of Japan) have wasteful surpluses of food, with daily per capita availability in Europe and North America in excess of not just 3,000 but even 3,500 kcal—while the population-wide per capita intakes compatible with good health (and lowered by rising shares of the elderly) range mostly between 2,000 and 2,300 kcal/day. Food-related multiples have thus gone the opposite way: average needs declined by 10–20% (multiples 0.9–0.8) compared to preindustrial means, while average supply in affluent countries rose by 30–40% (multiples 1.3–1.4).

The best values for annual energy supply rates are as follows. Prehistoric rates, including food and fuel for open-fire cooking, were 5–6 GJ/capita. Roman energy capture for all uses was around 20 GJ/capita. Western

(European and North American) means were no more than 25 GJ by 1800, and the population-weighted mean for all affluent countries was 240 GJ by the year 2000 (Smil 2010c, 2017a; Kander 2013). Using this progression to gauge the advance of Western civilization (a choice justifiable by energy's fundamental importance) would get us roughly a quintupling of average energy capture until the onset of the industrial era, and then roughly an order-of-magnitude increase by the year 2000, altogether an almost 50-fold gain in per capita energy supply since prehistory.

But this sequence is misleading because it measures gross energy inputs, not the rates of actual useful energy conversions. Higher conversion efficiencies have been one of the key hallmarks of human progress. An open fire may convert less than 5% of wood energy into useful heat for cooking, but household gas-fueled heating furnaces are now more than 95% efficient. Draft animals or hard-working humans convert 15–20% of feed or food into useful mechanical energy, large diesel engines are 50% efficient, electric motors exceed 90%. My best estimates are that average conversion efficiencies of the total energy supply (aggregated across the entire use spectrum) rose from no more than 10% in antiquity to 20% by 1900 and then close to 50% by the year 2000 (Smil 2017a). After taking this quintupling of average conversion efficiency into account, the overall gain of useful Western energy capture would be about 250-fold since prehistory. This result, obtained via a much easier calculation route, coincides with Morris's overall Western social index multiple.

Economic gain across two millennia can be derived from Goldsmith's (1984) estimate of Roman per capita income that was supported by Frier's (1993) analysis of subsistence annuities. The mean per capita expenditure of some 380 sestercii was adjusted and converted by Maddison (2007) to a GDP equivalent of about 570 international (1990) dollars in PPP terms or roughly $1,000 in 2015 monies. Compared to 2015 PPP per capita GDPs of $57,000 in the US and $36,000 in Italy, it indicates roughly 40- to 60-fold gain. A different approach to long-term gains in wealth can be derived by approximating the total mass of family possessions, including dwellings. A photographic documentary by Menzel (1994) offers an excellent visual guide to this simplified (considering merely total masses without any reference to improving qualities and durabilities of materials) but revealing metric.

Possessions of prehistoric cave-dwelling foragers amounted often to less than 10 and rarely more than 20kg/capita (clothes, bowls, tools, weapons). For a rural family of five people in Tokugawa Japan living in a wooden *minka* and engaged in rice and barley farming, per capita possessions (house, sheds, tools, clothes, mats, bedding, kitchen equipment) added up to about 1 t/capita, more than for a poor Haitian rural family of the 1990s shown in Menzel's book. In contrast, materials claimed by an American family of four living in an average-sized furnished house equipped with expected electrical and electronic appliances and devices (air conditioning, TVs, stove, refrigerator) and having two commonly sized vehicles will prorate to about 10 t/capita, with the house and its contents accounting for 80–85% of the total. Typical per capita material multiples have been thus three orders of magnitude since prehistory and an order of magnitude from the pre-industrial (subsistence farming) era.

Increasing personal mobility has been a key marker of modern growth, and in terms of common travel speeds on land the multiple for the fastest standard performances—from walking (5 km/h) to high-speed trains (300 km/h)—has been 60-fold. For all commercially available means of transport (from coaches at 6 km/h to jetliners at 900 km/h) it has been 150-fold. But typical travel speeds experienced by masses of daily commuters (using cars, buses, and peri-urban trains) average mostly between 50 and 100 km/h, reducing the overall multiple to just 10- to 20-fold and, as explained in chapter 4, the effective speed of automotive commuting in many American cities may now be as low, or even lower, than unimpeded walking.

But all of these multiples appear modest in comparison with two classes of advances: the growth of destructive power and of our communication, information, and calculation capabilities. The extraordinary growth of war-making capabilities is a regrettable testament to the civilization's priorities (Smil 2017a). The kinetic energy of a killing arrow shot in an ancient battle was about 15 J, a sword expertly wielded by a Tokugawa samurai had kinetic energy of 75 J—but a depleted uranium shell fired by an Abrams tank has kinetic energy of 6 MJ, a difference of five orders of magnitude (100,000-fold). And the multiple in total destructive energy released by explosives has amounted to seven orders of magnitude: the Nagasaki nuclear bomb released 92.4 TJ compared to 2 MJ for a hand grenade, a multiple of 46.7 million. And if we were to compare the grenade to the most powerful never-used hydrogen bomb in the Soviet arsenal (Tsar Bomba tested above Novaya Zemlya on October 30, 1961 with power of 209 PJ), the difference would be 11 orders of magnitude (multiple of 100 billion).

But the largest multiples apply to access to information, textual and visual. Multiples from prehistoric foragers or from illiterate slaves of Mediterranean antiquity who possessed no textual or illustrative information to the era of the Internet and mass mobile phone ownership are obviously infinite.

Ancient Rome had some impressive libraries, the largest of them housing a few thousand scrolls. But even if we make liberal assumptions—3,000 hand-copied scrolls with 1 MB/scroll—a major Roman library would contain some 3 GB of information. A correct order-of-magnitude estimate for worldwide information storage (overwhelmingly hand-copied texts) at the beginning of the common era was in tens of GB, unlikely more than 50 GB.

Lesk (1997) put the book holdings of the Library of Congress at 20 TB and photo collections, maps, and movie and audio recordings would increase the total storage to about 3 PB. All analog information stored worldwide by the end of the 20th century was at least 1,000 times larger, or 3 EB, that is eight orders of magnitude more (100 million times) than two millennia ago. Even in 1997 the comparison was incomplete because the shift of information from analog to digital storage was underway, with the Web growing by an order of magnitude every year. Lesk thought that the number of Internet users might grow eventually to 1 billion ("but not more") and the total storage might increase to 800 TB.

Two decades later these are risible underestimates. The number of Internet hosts first surpassed 1 billion in 2014, by 2005 aggregate information reached 100 EB (five orders of magnitude higher than Lesk's eventual total), by 2007 the civilization was able to store (when optimally compressed) 290 EB with 94% of it being in digital form (Hilbert and López 2011), and by 2016 the worldwide supply of storage surpassed 16 ZB, rising 11 orders of magnitude (320 billion times) above the total reached 2000 years ago (Seagate 2017). Once we reach multiples of 10^9 to 10^{11}, making a mistake of one or two orders of magnitude in estimating such totals seems almost irrelevant for illustrating long-term advances. Our knowledge base may now be actually a trillion times, rather than "just" hundreds of billion times, larger than at the beginning of the common era, and, in any case, by 2025 the total is expected to go up by another order of magnitude (Seagate 2017).

This might be perhaps the simplest single-paragraph summation of civilizational advances, a concise summary of growth that matters most. Our ability to provide a reliable, adequate food supply thanks to yields an order of magnitude higher than in early agricultures has been made possible by large energy subsidies and it has been accompanied by excessive waste. A near-tripling of average life expectancies has been achieved primarily by drastic reductions of infant mortality and by effective control of bacterial infections. Our fastest mass-travel speeds are now 50–150 times higher than walking. Per capita economic product in affluent countries is roughly 100 times larger than in antiquity, and useful energy deployed per capita is up to 200–250 times higher. Gains in destructive power have seen multiples of many (5–11) orders of magnitude. And, for an average human, there has been essentially an infinitely large multiple in access to stored information, while the store of information civilization-wide will soon be a trillion times larger than it was two millennia ago.

And this is the most worrisome obverse of these advances: they have been accompanied by a multitude of assaults on the biosphere. Foremost among them has been the scale of the human claim on plants, including a significant reduction of the peak post-glacial area of natural forests (on the order of 20%), mostly due to deforestation in temperate and tropical regions; a concurrent expansion of cropland to cover about 11% of continental surfaces; and an annual harvest of close to 20% of the biosphere's primary productivity (Smil 2013a). Other major global concerns are the intensification of natural soil erosion rates, the reduction of untouched wilderness areas to shrinking isolated fragments, and a rapid loss of biodiversity in general and within the most species-rich biomes in particular. And then there is the leading global concern: since 1850 we have emitted close to 300 Gt of fossil carbon to the atmosphere (Boden and Andres 2017). This has increased tropospheric CO_2 concentrations from 280 ppm to 405 ppm by the end of 2017 and set the biosphere on a course of anthropogenic global warming (NOAA 2017).

These realities clearly demonstrate that our preferences have not been to channel our growing capabilities either into protecting the biosphere or into assuring decent prospects for all newborns and reducing life's inequalities to tolerable differences. Judging by the extraordinary results that are significantly out of line with the long-term enhancements of our productive and protective abilities, we have preferred to concentrate disproportionately on multiplying the destructive capacities of our weapons and, even more so, on enlarging our abilities for the mass-scale acquisition and storage of information and for instant telecommunication, and have done so to an extent that has become not merely questionable but clearly counterproductive in many ways.

6   What Comes After Growth: or demise and continuity

What comes after growth? The answers are determined by its subject and by the time spans under consideration. The fan of possibilities that opens with the end of growth is wider than one might think before trying to come up with a typology of postgrowth trajectories. In the biosphere, the extremes range from the nearly instant death of individual ephemeral microorganisms (and only a slightly deferred demise of many short-lived invertebrates) to the collective perpetuation of life. Apoptosis, the programmed death of cells, and obliteration on the individual organismic level (decomposition of bodies and recycling of compounds and elements) is just a part of astonishingly long perpetuations of species across long evolutionary time spans. In the case of bacterial and archaeal colonies, this span is of a near-planetary age. The ancestry of today's microbes can be traced perhaps as far back as 3.95 billion years old to the sedimentary rocks in Labrador in which Tashiro et al. (2017) discovered traces of biogenic graphite.

And in cases of some higher animals this perpetuation has proceeded in such a conservative manner that the living species look and function very much as they did hundreds of millions years ago. The horseshoe crab (*Limulus polyphemus*, now on the list of vulnerable species) is one of the few well-known examples of this conservative evolution (IUCN 2017a). Few vertebrates live longer than humans. Long-lived animals include a few species of fish, sharks and whales and the giant tortoise, while the Greenland shark (*Somniosus microcephalus*) is most likely the longest-living vertebrate: the largest known animal was found to be 392 ± 120 years old (Nielsen et al. 2016). But the evolutionary direction of vertebrates in general, and mammals in particular, has been not only toward advanced behavior but also toward a longer life span, with our species achieving particularly impressive gains (Neill 2014).

The life cycles of many energy conversions, artifacts, and manufacturing techniques have normal distributions, ranging from nearly perfect bell-shaped fits to asymmetrical (or interrupted) declines whose progress is accelerated or slowed down by historical or national specificities. What comes after these instances of growth peaks is thus a fairly orderly decline whose rates closely mirror the gains that prevailed during the (sometimes not-so-distant) ascent. I will describe some notable example of both completed trajectories (when the product or practice has ceased to exist) as well unfolding declines in different stages.

Not too many people are interested in the demise of traditional wheat-harvesting processes or old steelmaking techniques. In contrast, studies of the decline and demise of populations, cities, societies, empires, economies, and civilizations are never out of fashion. Sudden or violent endings—including the Thera eruption (affecting ancient Minoan culture), the end of classical Maya states during the 8th and 9th centuries, or the collapse of the Romanov empire in 1917—attract particular fascination. The collapse of power structures has been a historical constant as long-enduring empires disappear or as artificially assembled states cease to exist—but the term economic collapse is a modern hyperbolic statement. Unlike empires and states, modern economies do not cease to exist, but they can experience periods of severely reduced output that causes hardships, starvation, and deaths, and that may require long periods of recovery.

In chapter 1, I cautioned against indiscriminate use of logistic curves in forecasting growth trajectories of artifacts, processes, and systems, and here is the apposite place to do the same as far as the forecasting of decline and demise based on a normal distribution is concerned. Given the ubiquity of life-cycle distributions that not only resemble a bell shape but often show a near-perfect correspondence between the actual numbers and ideal mathematical expressions, it is not surprising that this regularity seems to offer an excellent forecasting tool. The fate of compact cassettes or CDs could have been very accurately predicted by charting their future course right after their sales reached their peak. But caution is advisable even in those cases where the downslope of a normal curve has been well established and where further, and highly predictable, decline appears inevitable: following that trajectory could lead to some spectacular failures.

Perhaps the most consequential recent example of making this (understandable) error has been the mechanistic application of a normal distribution trajectory to US crude oil extraction. That application was made famous by M. King Hubbert (1956), who predicted, correctly, the peak of American crude oil output in 1970, and his forecast seemed to be of enduring value. If in 1980 you entered the US crude oil extraction data for the entire 20th century and calculated the total annual output expected in

2008 you would have made only about a 6% error as US crude oil extraction continued its long-predicted decline (figure 6.1, top). But the year 2008 turned out to be a turning point as subsequent output began to rise rapidly thanks to the innovative combination of horizontal drilling and hydraulic fracturing of America's plentiful hydrocarbon-bearing shales.

In 2015—when output, if it were to follow the normal curve decline, was due to be back to the level reached in 1940—US crude oil production rose nearly 90% above the 2008 low and missed the 1970 extraction record by only about 2%, resulting in a new bimodal extraction curve (figure 6.1, bottom). This great reversal of US oil-producing fortunes led not only to much-reduced imports but also (in December 2015) to the lifting of the 40-year-old ban on crude oil exports from the US (Harder and Cook 2015). Already by far the world's largest exporter of refined oil products, the US has ramped up its sales of crude oil to such an extent that by November 2018 its exports surpassed its crude oil imports and put the country ahead of all OPEC exporters except of Saudi Arabia and Iraq. The US, seen just a decade ago as a steadily declining producer, would now qualify to join the organization of crude oil exporters!

And I will cite just another excellent example of the perils of forecasting based on a seemingly preordained normal curve, the growth of Greater London's population, which can be charted reliably thanks to decennial censuses since 1801 (Morrey 1978; GLA 2015). Fitting the best trend to these data since their inception in 1801 to 1981 produces a near-perfect Gaussian curve ($R^2 = 0.991$), peaking in the 1940s at less than 9 million people and indicating only some 2.1 million people by 2050 (figure 6.2, top). Adding three decades of population data to the trajectory (the era of great immigration and internationalization of the global city) changes the best fit to a four-parameter logistic curve with the inflexion point in 1877 and population stabilizing at about 8 million people during the first half of the 21st century (figure 6.2, bottom).

Answers to the question of what comes after growth fall along a continuum ranging from fairly generic and highly regular outcomes (that are also readily quantifiable and, to a great extent, predictable) to many idiosyncratic, highly space- and time-specific results that present concatenations of many uncertainties and unknowns. Many growth phenomena belong to the first category and this allows us to make highly accurate forecasts, be they typical weights of mature domestic animals heading for slaughter, yields of staple grains to be harvested from intensively cultivated croplands, or heights of schoolchild cohorts. Uncertain outcomes are more common than is generally believed, and (as the recent US hydrocarbon revolution demonstrates)

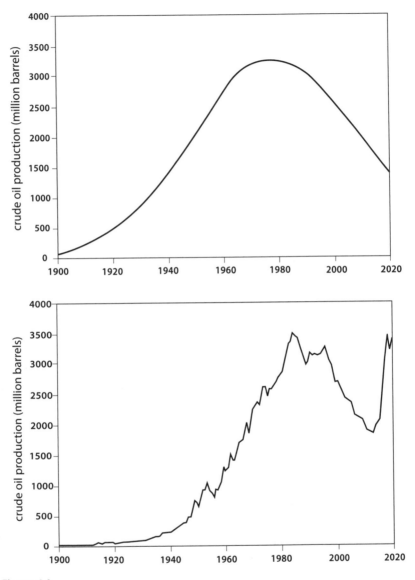

Figure 6.1
US crude oil extraction forecast based on the 1900–1980 trajectory, and actual 1900–2018 performance. Data from USBC (1975) and USEIA (2019).

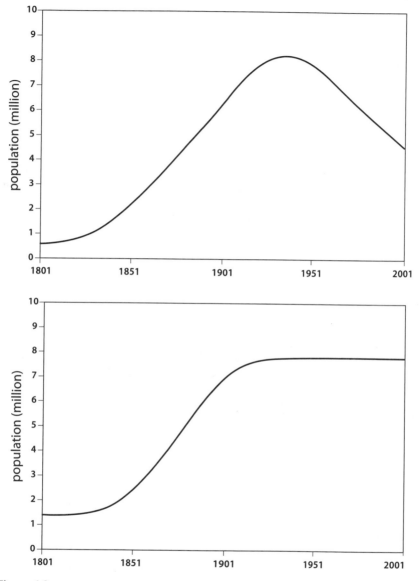

Figure 6.2
Population of Greater London: best fits based on 1801–1981 and 1801–2001 totals.
Data from Morrey (1978) and GLA (2015).

they can be encountered even after decades of consensus have pointed in the opposite direction and can have momentous consequences.

On the global level, there is no greater what-comes-after-growth uncertainty than the very fate of modern high-energy civilization with its still continuing population growth, high material requirements, and commensurately high environmental impacts. All of these long-lasting trends will have to end, deliberately or involuntarily. There is no possibility that we will be "saved" by an early coming of the Singularity or by an early terraforming of Mars. Such fictions make great news headlines but are worthless for dealing with civilizational challenges. Dealing with them is further complicated by continued profound uncertainties as we still have only approximate ideas about tolerable biospheric boundaries (Steffen et al. 2015) and hence of the timing of deliberate epochal shifts onto a new existential plane. If the biosphere is already in an overstressed mode, can we carry on for another five generations before correcting the course, or is the mid-21st century the latest time to act? Will we be able to come close to a genuine planetary equilibrium that would protect the biosphere from any global unraveling, or will our transformations come too late?

We have no way to predict the actual course, not only because of our imperfect understanding of complex interactions but above all because a wide range of future options has not been (yet) foreclosed. What will happen a generation or a century from now remains contingent on our intervening actions. Wrong decisions can accelerate decline and demise, while proceeding cautiously could greatly limit most (if not all) undesirable biospheric and social outcomes. Acting in radical ways could open new prospects for global civilization. What comes after the growth our civilization has experienced during the past two centuries will determine if we will prosper as a species not only during the next two centuries but perhaps for millennia to come.

Life Cycles of Organisms

For the simplest creatures—single-celled organisms without a nucleus (prokaryotes), including bacteria and archaea, another ancient domain present in many terrestrial and aquatic environments—rapid division perpetuates the species but is followed by the swift death of individual cells (excepting those that can remain cryptobiotic for extended periods of time). All prokaryotes divide rapidly (with division cycles measured often in minutes) and grow rapidly and hence the notion of their life span is fundamentally different from the existence of plants and animals. Most single-cell organisms live only briefly. The most abundant single-celled photosynthesizing organisms in the ocean, cyanobacteria belonging to the genus Prochlorococcus, live, on average, less than two days.

Pelagibacter ubique is an even more abundant microbe but it is a chemoheterotroph, it survives by consuming dead organic matter dissolved in the ocean, and it also has the smallest genome known for a free-living microorganism (Giovannoni et al. 2005). The aggregate mass (usually known as standing biomass) of single-celled photosynthesizers present in the ocean at any time averages only about 3 Gt C. But the rapid turnover of these phytoplanktonic cells means that the annual net primary productivity of marine photosynthesis (at 48 Gt C) is almost as high as that of terrestrial ecosystems (56 Gt C) that store perhaps as much as 200 times more phytomass (Houghton and Goetz 2008). Moreover, many prokaryotes—and a few other microorganisms, including Tardigrada, those remarkable miniature (0.1–1.5 mm) water bears (Jönsson and Bertolani 2001)—can enter cryptobiotic states where the capacity for life can be preserved for extended periods of time (up to 10^8 years) and in extreme environments as all metabolic processes get suspended inside protective spores (Clegg 2001; Wharton 2002; figure 6.3).

The after-growth trajectory of many archaea and bacteria could be thus succinctly described as prompt postdivision death of individual cells but an unequaled longevity of species or communities (microbial communities often include complex assemblages of many archaeal and bacterial species, commonly also in extreme environments). The rapid regeneration of prokaryotes has preserved, in some cases in almost unchanged forms, the world's oldest living species that appeared for the first time more than 3 billion years ago. The life cycles of photosynthesizing macroorganisms are very different. As already explained (in chapter 2), several tree species survive for more than 1,000 years but these oldest-living terrestrial organisms achieve that feat by being largely dead.

Most of the tree phytomass is locked as cellulose and lignin in structural polymers and in cell walls—but these tissues, indispensable for support, protection, and conduction of water and dissolved nutrients, are not alive. The radial extent of the cambial zone (where the tree growth is generated) is not easy to delimit due to the gradual transition between living tissues (phloem) and dead tissues (xylem). While some parenchymatic cells may remain alive for many months, years, and even decades, the share of living phytomass in the total standing forest mass is almost certainly no higher than 15% (Smil 2013a). The growth trajectory of trees could be thus succinctly described as a mass-scale production of short-lived cells required to

Figure 6.3
Tardigrada, one of the near-indestructible forms of life capable of cryptobiotic existence. Photo available at wikimedia.

ensure structural integrity of the organism and the extraordinary height and longevity of some species.

In plants, animals, and in humans, regenerating cells keep organs and organisms alive for extended periods of time even after the cessation of overall growth in mass or height—but some key organs have cells that last a lifetime and either are not renewed by any subsequent growth or have only a minimal renewal rate. The life span of cells in human tissues can now be accurately determined by measuring ^{14}C levels in modern DNA (Spalding et al. 2005). Cells lining the gut last no longer than five days, red blood cells last four months—but the average age of an adult body's cell is 7–10 years, and skeletal cells average about 15 years. Cellular regeneration keeps organs and organisms alive, and that includes many brain tissues—but analysis of brain cells taken from the adult occipital cerebral cortex showed ^{14}C levels of their genomic DNA corresponding to the individual's age and hence indicating the absence of postnatal cortical neurogenesis in humans.

[14]C studies have also made it possible to establish the age of cardiac muscle cells (cardiomyocytes) in humans (Bergmann et al. 2009, 2015). Nearly all cardiomyocytes were already generated *in utero*, their final number $(3.2 \times 10^9 \pm 0.75 \times 10^9)$ is reached just one month after birth and it remains constant during the entire human life span. The cells have a very low turnover that decreases with age, from the highest rate of 0.8% during the first decade of life to just 0.3% at age 75, and about 80% of the cardiomyocytes will never change after 10 years of age, no matter what the ultimate life span might be. In contrast, endothelial and mesenchymal cells increase into adulthood. The growth trajectory of heart muscle cells could be thus succinctly described as a near-complete acquisition of their total number before birth followed by growth in size until the end of puberty and then a steady decades-long functioning accompanied by very limited, and declining, regeneration before eventual death.

Jones et al. (2014) collected data on relative mortality and standardized the age axis to start at the mean age of reproductive maturity and to end at a terminal age when only 5% of adults are still alive. Their most surprising finding is that the predictable pattern of increasing mortality (and declining fertility) with age after maturity is not the norm, and that the relative mortalities follow a range of trajectories that include not only the predicted increasing trend, but also constant, humped, bowed, and even decreasing patterns for both long- and short-lived species. A barely rising trend during early maturity followed by a steep increase of relative mortality with advanced age is characteristic of humans (figure 6.4), and other species with a relatively steep mortality rise in the later stages of life include water fleas, guppies, mynahs, and lions.

Trajectories for baboons and deer are far less steep, and mortality of 8–20 years old chimpanzees rises only slightly above the linear trajectory. Near-linear but much less steep increases also characterize mature mortality trends for the freshwater crocodile and common lizards, while relative mortalities for such different species as hydra (*Hydra magnipapillata*), red abalone, collared flycatcher, and the great rhododendron follow flat, or nearly flat, trajectories with increasing age. And those for red gorgonian, netleaf oak, desert turtle, and white mangrove show slight to pronounced mortality declines with age (figure 6.4). Lack of data for most species as well as for quantifying intraspecific variation precludes making any grand generalizations.

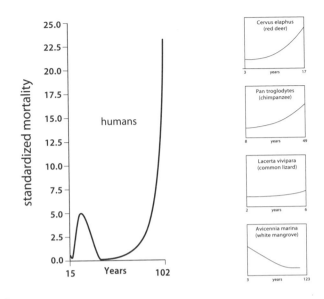

Figure 6.4
Mortality curves for various species as functions of age. Simplified from Jones et al. (2014).

Animal growth is often followed not by any extended period of maturity but by sudden death. That is, of course, the norm for large numbers of animals whose life is cut short by predation and by the billions of birds and mammals we kill annually for meat. Recent annual global totals have been on the order of 60 billion chickens, 1.5 billion pigs, and 300 million heads of cattle (FAO 2018). Some animals are slaughtered long before they reach maturity. The life expectancy of wild pigs is as long as two decades, their typical natural lifespan is 10–12 years, and even in ecosystems with high rates of predation they can average half a dozen years—but animals reared for meat by intensive feeding are now slaughtered at 5–6 months of age, suckling pigs (to be roasted whole, *cochinillo asado* being a great Spanish favorite) commonly at just 4–5 weeks (Frayer 2013).

In contrast to the much-shortened life spans of domestic animals, the quest for longer human life expectancy has achieved some notable results. Humans are exceptionally long-lived when compared to animals of a similar body mass or to other primates. Pigs can live for up to 20 years, chimpanzee females almost 40 years, orangutans in captivity more than 60 years but the mean is about 40 years—but in 2015 the highest nationwide means for humans were 83.7 years in Japan and 83.4 years in Switzerland (WHO 2016), and in 2015 Japan had more than 60,000 centenarians (Japan Times

2015). What is remarkable about increasing human life expectancies is that once the vigorous organismic growth is over, the period of maturity in healthy individuals can now span decades with little apparent deterioration of basic mental and physical functions.

Some individuals can also maintain their mature weight (within small fluctuating bounds) for more than half a century, and extremes of physical exertion keep rising: 80 years for the oldest climber to reach the peak of Mount Everest, 85 years for completing a marathon in less than four hours (Longman 2016), 92 years for finishing it in less than six hours. The span of mental achievements has been also lengthening: using a large sample of Quebec professors, Gingras et al. (2008) showed that the average annual number of papers by active (publishing) professors declined only minimally between 50 and 70 years of age, and since 1950 the average age of all Nobel laureates rose by 13 years.

But long life after growth is far from universal. Combined life expectancies are below 60 years in at least 25 African countries, and Russian males have a shorter average life expectancy at birth not only when compared with males in China but even with males in India: between 2010 and 2015 the respective means were 64.6, 74.2, and 66.2 years (UN 2017). And every year, death still comes prematurely to tens of millions, preventing them from accomplishing their growth. Too many babies still die in the first year of their life: infant mortalities are nearly 100 per 1,000 live births in some countries of Saharan and sub-Saharan Africa (Mali, Chad, Niger, Angola), about 40 in India, and 20 in Egypt. In only one large populous country, Japan, there are now below 2, about the lowest level attainable in a modern society (PRB 2016). Nearly 5 million children now die every year before reaching their first year of life. And even in the richest countries there are hundreds of deaths among young adults (20–24) who had just reached their maturity, with the US male rate on the order of 1,400/million due mostly to accidents, overdoses, or suicides (Blum and Qureshi 2011).

Even without any specific diseases, lifelong stress on vital organs is particularly high. Normalized entropy stress (with rest of the body equal to 1) is 37 for the heart, 34 for the kidneys, 17 for the brain and 15 for the liver (Annamalai and Silva 2012). The heart is thus under the most severe stress and, not surprisingly, heart disease is the leading cause of death for both men and women (in the US accounting for roughly one in four deaths), with coronary heart disease being the most common type (CDC 2017). For these reasons and also due to other limits (already outlined in chapter 2), it is unlikely that we will see any further substantial increases in the human life span in the near future. One of the most convincing images supporting this conclusion was published by Marck et al. (2017). They plotted maximal ages at death of the oldest women and men, as well as maximal ages for the oldest male and female Olympians since the beginning of the 20th century. The first two trends have shown hardly any change during the 20th century, strongly suggesting that a plateau of around 115–120 years is the upper limit for human longevity (Marck et al. 2017). Maximal life spans of the oldest Olympians showed notable gains until the 1970s but have since leveled off at around 100 years.

Retreat of Artifacts and Processes

Although they attract no media attention and there are no new publications devoted to extolling their indispensability, we rely on a very large number of artifacts that have seen no fundamental change—be it in terms of their basic design or their outward appearance—ever since their optimized forms conquered their respective markets. Similarly, there are many industrial and manufacturing processes whose efficient operation relies on deploying such ancient inventions as sawing, grinding, polishing, casting, annealing, and welding. These periods of remarkable stability are often measured not only in generations (for example, electric current transformers) but in centuries (mass-produced screws) and even millennia; belt buckles are a good quotidian example in that enduring category—the lost wax casting process for metals has been known for more than 5,000 years. Of course, there have been many upgradings of materials and production processes but basic designs and sequences have endured because of their capability and reliable performance.

Many of these necessities of life are durable products with many of their market segments being quite limited (how many hammers will an average family buy in half a century?); others need to be made in vastly expanded quantities in order to meet new market needs. One of the best (and completely hidden) examples of new output growth of an old artifact has been created by the explosion of portable electronic devices that have to be charged. As a result, we have seen an unprecedented growth of the global stock of tiny transformers that step down the AC grid voltage (100 V in Japan, 120 V in North America, 220 V in China, 230 V in Germany) to 5 V DC for mobile phones and tablets and to 12 V–19 V DC for laptops: by 2017 their annual production was about 2 billion units (Smil 2017d).

This impressive growth did not require any change of the artifact's basic design but it necessitated ongoing miniaturization—while many other long-established artifacts have seen only quantitative (output) growth and no qualitative changes. The long-term trajectories of such artifacts often have a fluctuating growth rate—for example, think of new waves of consumer products creating new demand for screws and other fasteners—but no annual peak of their output is imminent as irregular gradual slow growth is the norm. In contrast, many postgrowth trajectories of technical advances follow one of two similar courses of extended performance plateaus.

First, for decades or generations after reaching the limit of its growth, the upper asymptote can remain horizontal with hardly any attendant changes. The classic black Bakelite hard-wired rotary dial telephone combining the transmitter and receiver in the same unit was introduced during the late 1920s and the long rule of telephone monopolies ensured that hundreds of millions of its copies were added during the next four decades (figure 6.5). Push-button dialing was introduced only in 1963 and during the 1960s phones also began to change color and be available in many new shapes (Smil 2006b). The telephone was thus on an extended no-growth plateau, but once it left it, its development has seen some of the fastest sequential growth waves (portable phones, cellphones, smartphones) in modern industry.

Figure 6.5
Black bakelite phone. Image available at oldphoneworks.com.

Second, performances can dip a bit from the highest level and settle at somewhat lower ratings, as happened with oil tankers or with the capacities of largest commonly installed steam turbogenerators. The largest crude oil tanker was *Seawise Giant*, built in 1979, then enlarged to more than 560,000 dwt and relaunched after war damage as *Jahre Viking* (1991–2004), used as an off-loading unit off Qatar, and in 2009 sold to Indian ship-breakers (Konrad 2010). Building a tanker of 1 million dwt was technically possible but *Seawise Giant* remained an oddity and in 2015 there were only two ultra-large crude carriers (441,000 dwt) in operation. For a variety of reasons—docking and off-loading options, passages through canals, insurance costs, rerouting flexibility—most of the world's oil is transported in very large crude carriers (160,000–320,000 dwt) that can take onboard between 1.9 and 2.2 million barrels of crude oil (USEIA 2014).

Similarly, after years of vigorous post-WWII growth, by 1965 the installed capacity of America's largest steam turbogenerators reached 1,000 MW (Driscoll et al. 1964) and with electricity demand doubling every decade many utilities began to order units of 600–800 MW. But the subsequent slow-down of electricity demand and system considerations (as a rule, in order to maintain system stability in case of a sudden outage, the largest unit should not be more than 5% of overall capacity) led to declining modal ratings, with most post-1970 installations being in turbogenerators and gas turbines with capacities between 50 and 250 MW (Smil 2003).

New developments can sometimes bring very abrupt ends to further growth of well-established but suddenly outdated techniques, but in many cases the retreat of established artifacts and processes has followed normal-distribution curves. I will note here just a few important examples illustrating the Gaussian fate of energy extraction (coal mining), prime movers (farm horses and steam locomotives), mass-produced artifacts (music recordings), and industrial processes (open-hearth furnaces in American steelmaking). And to bring in entirely different, indeed the world's most destructive man-made products, I will look at the rise and decline of nuclear warhead stockpiles in the Soviet Union/Russia.

We now have two completed coal production trajectories, with the end of the Dutch one preceding the British one by four decades (figure 6.6). WWII disruption aside, the Dutch trajectory resembles a blunted normal curve with a steeper decline resulting from a fairly rapid closure of the country's coal mines once the abundant and inexpensive natural gas from the giant Groningen field became available during the 1960s (Smil 2017a). The complete British extraction curve (with accurate data going back to the beginning of the 18th century) reflects many national specificities of the

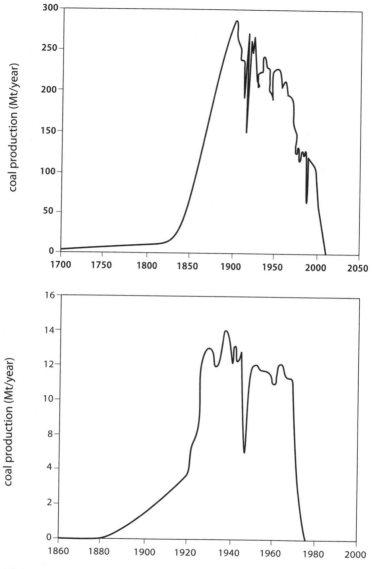

Figure 6.6

Complete trajectories of British and Dutch coal extraction. Plotted from data in de Jong (2004) and DECC (2015).

world's pioneering large-scale coal extraction. Major oscillations between the extraction peak in 1913 (when 1.1 million miners produced about 290 Mt from more than 3,000 mines) and the mid-1950s were the result of wars, strikes, and economic downturns.

Nationwide output was still above 200 Mt during the 1950s and 130 Mt in 1980, but a protracted coal miners' strike in 1984 and switch to natural gas accelerated the fuels demise and by the year 2000 the total fell to only 31 Mt and 11,000 workers. The last British deep mine (Kellingley pit in North Yorkshire) was shut down in December 2015, ending more than half a millennium of British coal extraction (Hicks and Allen 1999; DECC 2015; Moss 2015). If it were not for assorted disruptive factors, the completed trajectory would be close to a slightly asymmetrical bell-shaped curve with the bulk of the output extracted between 1860 and the year 2000 (figure 6.6). Unlike British coal, British steel remains a going concern but its annual output has been reduced to around a third of the peak value and the trajectory conforms (with many expected fluctuations caused by economic downturns and wars) to a normal distribution (figure 6.7).

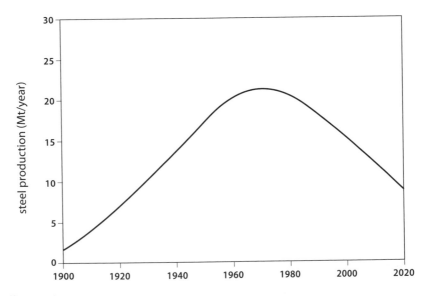

Figure 6.7
British steel output, 1900–2020. Fluctuating output reflects economic downturns, expansions, and wars and hence the normal curve is not a particularly close fit (R^2 of 0.79). The production peak came in 1970, with the 2015 output below the level attained first in 1936. Data from https://visual.ons.gov.uk/the-british-steel-industry-since-the-1970s/.

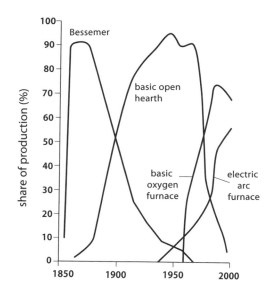

Figure 6.8
Steelmaking transitions in the US, 1850–2000. From Smil (2005) and WSA (2017).

Innovation waves in steelmaking resulted in the formation of two asymmetrical bell-shaped curves: Bessemer furnaces (the first modern method of steelmaking introduced during the 1870s) quickly conquered the market by 1880 and, in turn, they were rapidly displaced by open-hearth steelmaking, which dominated the US industry until the 1960s (Smil 2016b). Departures from the normally distributed trajectories of their American output (fast expansion between 1910 and 1930, fast post-1970 decline) reflect the extraordinarily high demand for steel in early 19th-century America and the belated introduction of basic oxygen furnaces during the 1960s (figure 6.8). That displacement was completed in all Western countries as there are no operating open-hearth furnaces anywhere in North America, the EU, or Japan (WSA 2017).

No animate prime mover has made a greater historical difference than the horse, and American historical data allow us to follow the rise of draft horses from fewer than 2 million animals in 1850 to the peak of 21.5 million in 1915 (in addition there were also some 5 million mules), followed by an expected decline to 10 million by 1940 and to just over 3 million by 1960 (USBC 1975; figure 6.9). Steam locomotives were introduced to the US soon after their English debut during the early 1830s. Their total reached 30,000 just before 1890 and then doubled in just two decades; the descent began during the late 1920s with the adoption of diesel engines,

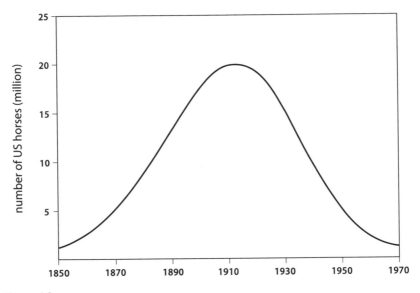

Figure 6.9
Number of American draft horses between 1850 and 1970 conforms closely to the normal curve trajectory. Data from USBC (1975).

and by 1960 there were fewer than 400 operating machines (USBC 1975; figure 6.10).

Car ownership continues to grow rapidly in all low- and medium-income Asian countries, but the total number of US passenger cars shows clear signs of saturation. If the trajectory were to follow the projected Gaussian fit, the country would have no more than about 65 million vehicles by the year 2100 compared to nearly 190 million in 2015 (figure 6.11). This decline could be further accelerated by convenient on-demand availability of future autonomous vehicles but I suspect that this innovation will make a substantial difference much later than is now widely assumed. But it is certain that car ownership declines will be much steeper in countries experiencing relatively fast population decline, above all in Japan.

Turning to small consumer products, detailed US data make it possible to follow the waves of music recordings. Sales of vinyl records (singles and long-playing records (LPs) introduced in 1948) reached their peak in 1978 with 531 million units, declined to less than 10 million units by 1999 and 5 million units by 2004, but then revived a bit to 17.2 million records in 2016 (RIAA 2017). Cassette tapes were introduced in 1963 in Europe and in 1964 in the US; their sales peaked in 1988 and essentially ceased by 2005. Compact disc (CD) sales began in 1984, peaked in 1999, and by 2016 were

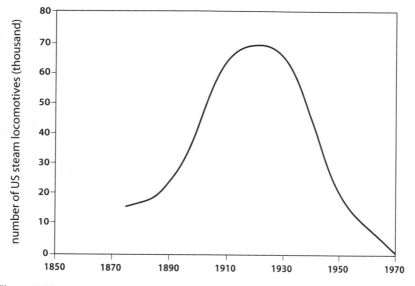

Figure 6.10

Number of US steam locomotives: a very good Gaussian fit for the nine decades between 1876 and 1967. Data from USBC (1975).

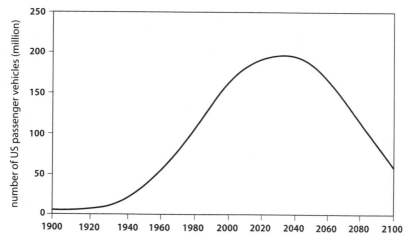

Figure 6.11

The historical growth of the US passenger car fleet can be fitted quite well into a normal curve peaking around 2030. Data from USBC (1975) and from subsequent volumes of the US *Statistical Abstract*.

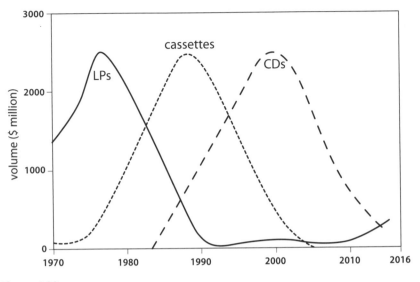

Figure 6.12
Successive normal curves chart the US sales of recorded music: vinyl records were displaced by cassette tapes, cassettes were displaced by CDs, and those were largely eliminated by music downloading and then by streaming. Plotted from data in RIAA (2017).

below 100 million units as the last one of these three successive audio techniques, whose rise and retreat followed normal curves, became dwarfed by music downloading (figure 6.12). But its dominance was even more fleeting. American downloads peaked at over 1.5 billion units in 2012 before retreating to just over 800 million by 2016. Another unmistakable Gaussian trajectory has formed rapidly as downloading was replaced by streaming: by 2016 streaming revenues were more than twice as high than for downloading (RIAA 2017).

But in some cases commercial demise does not mean the absolute end of old techniques, processes, or machines: techniques linger, forming very long but barely noticeable asymmetrical right tails of normal distribution. Most surviving steam locomotives are now in museums—but some are still used for a few vacation fun rides. Even in affluent Western countries, some small- farms still use horses. And while the last open-hearth furnaces were shut down in Japan in 1980 and have been absent from the Western mills for a generation, the outdated process has lingered in the post-Soviet Ukraine, whose open-hearth furnaces still produced nearly half of all steel in the year 2000 and nearly 23% even in 2015 (WSA 2017).

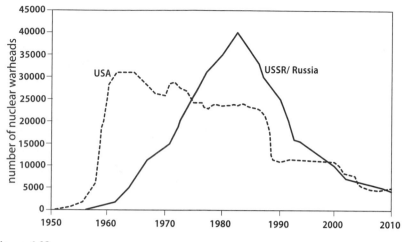

Figure 6.13
Totals of US and Soviet/Russian nuclear warheads, 1953–2010. Norris and Kristensen (2006) and Arms Control Association (2017).

The growth and decline of warhead numbers in the two nuclear superpowers shows two different patterns (Norris and Kristensen 2006). The Soviet/Russian trajectory forms a nearly perfect and pointed normal curve with a peak total of 40,000 warheads in 1986. Thanks to the dissolution of the Soviet Union, this was followed by an almost instant retreat to levels agreed upon by bilateral treaties. In contrast, the initial US growth during the 1950s was much faster than in the Soviet Union (reaching a peak of 32,040 warheads in 1967) and it was followed by stepwise reductions resulting in a highly asymmetrical distribution (figure 6.13). Of course, unlike open-hearth furnaces or steam locomotives, nuclear warheads are still around in large numbers. In 2017 the combined total of deployed American and Russian warheads was nearly 4,000 and, barring a most unlikely global nuclear disarmament, the right-hand tail stretches as far as we can see.

Depending on how things get counted, long right-side tails are common with many once-ubiquitous artifacts. The demise of commercial wind-powered shipping has been absolute as there are no sail ships used for intercontinental trade and hence no shipyards fashioning sleek and fast clippers. But sail ships are still used by navies for training and they are increasingly popular for small-capacity warm-ocean cruising. And there is a long list of practices and products that have ceased to have any economic importance but survive as archaic exceptions: some people still make swords by hand in forges, there are still farriers—but how many people could now explain the meaning of such words (still very common at the beginning of the 20th century) as hames, martingale, or crupper?

Finally, before leaving the world of artifacts and processes, a paragraph about the end of Moore's law. Its progress has been kept alive by steady advances in microchip design but it was always clear that this process has its physical and economic limits: at 5 nm the width of transistors in the latest IBM design is only about 20 silicon atoms, and new fabrication facilities now cost on the order of $10 billion (Rupp and Selberherr 2011; Rojas 2012; IBM 2017; Dormehl 2018). But this does not mean any abrupt end to Moore's law, just notable deceleration of growth whose pace will depend on other adjustments we can make: introducing better algorithms and software, relying on more specialized chips, introducing new materials and new (3D) configurations and, more distant possibilities, deploying photonic and quantum computing. Feynman's (1959) famous dictum of having plenty of room at the bottom remains in force.

Populations and Societies

Many low-density pastoral societies disappeared without leaving any long-lasting marks on the landscape where they herded their cattle, horses, or sheep. The demise of traditional agricultures—many based on deforestation (often, as in the Mediterranean and North China, on a very large scale), extensive terracing, and sophisticated irrigation arrangements, and producing increasing densities of permanent settlements—has been easier to follow. While carbon-dating of crops and artifacts may be fairly reliable and the times of decline or disappearance may be narrowly constrained, correctly identifying the reasons for gradual retreat or sudden collapse remains challenging. Controversies about the collapse of Mayan societies (Culbert 1973; Webster 2002) are an excellent example of these continuing uncertainties. In contrast, most sizable cities of early antiquity left at least some archaeological evidence, and during late antiquity and the Middle Ages the material record can be augmented by increasingly abundant written records, making an accurate reconstruction of urban trajectories possible.

Populations

While global projections remain uncertain, we are on much more solid ground in forecasting the long-term trajectories of many nations with very low fertility whose populations are not only rapidly aging but actually already declining. This demographic shift has many social and economic consequences. The emerging demographic deficit is expressed either as the overall dependency ratio—the quotient of the economically active population, usually aged 15–64 but in many countries now more accurately 20–69, and all dependents (0–15 and 65+)—or as the elderly dependency ratio (16–56/65+). In the EU the elderly dependency ratio will rise to 51% by 2050 as the number of economically active per people older than 65 years is halved from four to two. For the OECD countries as a group, the trends of incoming (20–24) and outgoing (60–64) working-age cohorts crossed in 2016.

Leaving aside the unlikely resurgence of fertilities, there are only two ways to reverse this demographic deficit and lower the dependency ratios: large-scale immigration of young people ready to join the labor force (a condition that is not necessarily met by some indiscriminate mass movement of refugees with disproportionate shares of small children, and women without skills and education) and working longer. The economic and social implications of aging societies and depopulating regions and countries will combine universal concerns with country- and region-specific challenges, and we cannot anticipate all possible outcomes.

The first category includes security of pensions, provision of adequate health care, coping with unprecedented numbers of mentally ill old people, and maintenance of expansive infrastructures, while more specific concerns arise from exceptionally rapid regional aging exacerbated by rising income inequality. Some of today's assumption may turn out to be wrong. Working longer may not be enough to prevent the collapse of pension systems. And even if most people were willing to work past their normal retirement age, there would still be shortages of labor in health services as well as in occupations that (even if highly mechanized) will always require some demanding physical exertions. And a world dominated by the elderly may not be necessarily more peaceful (Longman 2010).

Declining fertility rather than changing mortality is the dominant factor in contemporary population aging (Lee and Zhou 2017) and in a concurrent rise of old age dependency ratios. But forecasts are also complicated by uncertainties associated with aging. For example, forecasts of the western European population above the age of 80 have 95% probability intervals of 5.5–20.7% by 2050 and 5–4.8% by 2100, a surprisingly large difference (Lutz et al. 2008). Japan has been at the leading edge of the massive aging wave that has begun to engulf nearly all affluent nations. Its average fertility fell from the post-WWII peak of 2.75 in the early 1950s to below the replacement level by the late 1970s, and the total population peaked at 128.08 million in 2008 and had declined to 127.7 million by October 2017.

This trend could be reversed only by turning to large-scale, Canadian- or Australian-style, immigration and admitting annually many hundreds of thousands of newcomers, still a highly unlikely choice but one whose adoption cannot be excluded in a more distant future. Forecasts of a future depopulation of Japan keep changing. At the beginning of the 21st century the official forecasts were for about 121 million by 2025 and only about 100 million people by the year 2050 (NIPSSR 2002). In 2012, the forecast was for 86.74 million by 2060 (with 40% of all people above 65), and in 2017 it was changed to 88.08 million by 2065 (NIPSSR 2017).

Using these projections to plot Japan's population trajectory between 1872 and 2065 produces a good Gaussian fit ($R^2 = 0.965$) and the protraction of that normal curve points to about 58 million people in 2100, equal to the total of the early 1920s. The aggregate decline is only a part of the aging-and-declining progression: the share of people 65 years and older will rise from less than 20% in the year 2000 to 35% by 2050 as Japan's age-sex population structure will rest on a much-narrowed foundation and its cudgel-like profile will contrast with a barrel-shaped form by the end of the 20th century and with the classic broad-based pyramid of the 1930s and the early 1950s (figure 6.14).

Perhaps the most astonishing outcome of Japan's population aging is that by 2050 the country is likely to have more people 80 years and older than children up to 14 years of age and become the world's first truly geriatric society (UN 2017). That would be the first time such a lopsided ratio had been experienced by any population during the long span of human evolution. A cascade of socioeconomic consequences resulting from these new demographic realities is self-evident—but no society is prepared to deal with it, particularly not one that still continues to reject any substantial immigration.

The European Union's population is expected to grow until 2025 before it begins to decline, but populations of several member states, including Estonia, Latvia, Hungary, Bulgaria, and Romania, had already peaked in the 1980s or 1990s and (compared to 2015) they and other EU nations will see large aggregate declines by 2050. Populations are projected to decrease by 28% in Bulgaria, 22% in Romania, 14% in Poland and Estonia, 11% in Greece and Portugal, and by 8% in Germany (UN 2017). As Demeny (2003) noted, the fate of a depopulating and aging Europe could be contemplated with equanimity only if it were an island and not a continent under enormous population pressure from its high-fertility neighbors. The EU's southern and southeastern hinterland includes 27 exclusively or predominantly Muslim states situated between the Atlantic Ocean and India. In 2015 their population was about 800 million compared to the EU's 508 million, but their total fertility rate was 2.8 compared to the EU's 1.6 (World Bank 2017).

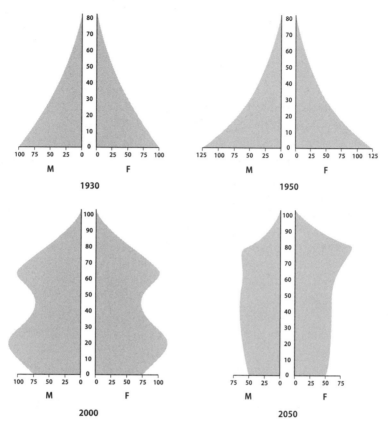

Figure 6.14
Age-sex structures of the Japanese population, 1930, 1950, 2000, and 2050. Simplified from Smil (2007).

Recent immigration from Europe's Muslim hinterland is already adding up to the greatest influx of people the continent has experienced in more than a thousand years (Smil 2010a). And as shown by the sudden mass influx of migrants to Germany in 2016, by their inflow from North Africa to Italy and Spain, and by their record numbers in Sweden (in relative terms), this migration is already having major social and political consequences. Some EU member countries have refused to share the refugee burden and attitudes to immigration have hardened even in previously relative welcoming Germany, Italy, and France. But this might be only a prelude. By 2080 the EU's population (without immigration) is forecast to fall by about 60 million people to less than 450 million (Eurostat 2015) while the total population of the continent's Muslim hinterland will rise to more than 1.3 billion.

Notable population decline is also forecast for Russia (almost 10% drop between 2015 and 2050). Russia's total fertility rate declined, with a temporary uptick during the 1980s, from about 2.8 during the early 1950s to only 1.25 at the beginning of the 21st century, and by 2016 it had risen only marginally to 1.46. When the Soviet Union disintegrated in late 1991, Russia's population was about 140 million, by 2017 the total had risen to about 144 million (largely due to immigration from former Soviet republics), and the UN's medium-variant forecast is for 132.7 million in 2050 (UN 2017). The most remarkable component of this process has been Russia's dismal male life expectancy.

By the late 1960s belated health and nutrition improvements raised Russia's combined life expectancy to within about four years of the EU's average, but by the century's end the gap widened to more than 12 years due to dismal male prospects. Between 2000 and 2005 Russia's male life expectancy at birth was less than 59 years and although it rose to nearly 64 years between 2010 and 2015 it was (as already noted) still below not only the Chinese mean (slightly over 73 years) but even lower than in India (UN 2017). China's challenges are different, as the country's population prospects are rooted in what I called an uncommonly twisted foundation (Smil 2010a).

The traditionally excessive preference for sons in China became more intense due to the one-child policy and the country now has a highly aberrant sex ratio at birth, much higher than in other Asian countries with a high preference for boys. While the normal ratio of newborns is 1.06 (106 boys for 100 girls, as in Nigeria or Indonesia) and the global mean between 2010 and 2015 was 1.07, China's ratio was 1.16 compared to India's 1.11 and Pakistan's 1.09 (UN 2017). In some Chinese provinces the ratios have been above 1.2, and a study found 20 rural townships in Anhui province with an incredible ratio of 1.52 (Wu et al. 2006). The consequences of this twisted growth are obvious even when the fundamental moral question of the mass-scale abortion of girls is ignored. The ensuing sex disparity prevents large numbers of men from ever marrying, and creates the well-known challenges of unattached lives, more crime- and violence-prone males and more common female abductions.

While populations will decline, their old age dependency ratios will grow. Between 1960 and 2015 the ratio rose from 15% to 22% in the US (4.5 workers for every old person), but it soared from just 9% to 43% in Japan, where it could reach (depending on demographic assumptions) at least 60% and as much as 82% (just 1.2 people working for every retiree) by 2050 (UN 2017). And thanks to China's rapid aging, the 2050 old age dependency ratio may surpass 40% compared to just 13% in 2015, a shift for which the country's economy is unprepared.

But, once again, these aggregates do not tell the whole story because the depopulation process in every nation is characterized by large regional disparities. Perhaps the two best examples of regional depopulation in affluent countries are the recent histories of the former East Germany (German Democratic Republic, the state which existed between 1949 and 1990), and Tohoku, the northeastern portion of Honshu, Japan's largest island. With the exception of the capital and its surroundings, every region of the former German Democratic Republic is expected to lose people in the coming decades even as some of the country's western regions keep on having slight overall gains. Japan's Tohoku has seen migration of young people to the capital and other large southern cities for decades, and the region's depopulation and aging were accelerated by the Fukushima nuclear disaster in March 2011.

And how will the trajectory of the global population look when seen in a very long-term perspective? When choosing a 16,000-year scale—from 8,000 BCE (roughly since the beginnings of agriculture and sedentary existence) to 8,000 CE—we know that the trajectory of human population will be a nearly flat pre-1500 line followed by a slow rise and then a rapid post-1850 ascent. But we do not know if there will be a partial or a similarly rapid (though not necessarily symmetrical) descent to a rate that could be sustained for millennia of a new, postgrowth civilization or if humanity will destroy itself or if it will be terminated by planetary or cosmic forces.

Cities

The history of cities after they reach their apogee falls into many categories distinguished by the longevity of post-peak existence and by the manner of demise (gradual decline vs. collapse or violent disbanding). Many ancient cities—including such famous early mud-brick and stone settlements as Mesopotamian Eridu, Uruk, and Lagash—continued to exist for millennia before their complete, or near-complete, destruction. Uruk and Lagash are now just mounds of rubble, Nineveh had some excavated walls rebuilt, and under Saddam Hussein's regime Babylon had extensive reconstruction atop its ruins but then suffered further damage when the site was occupied by the US troops (AP 2006).

Some cities had managed to survive many successive waves of invaders before they almost completely disappeared. Merv (in today's Turkmenistan) is an outstanding example of this endurance: it survived ancient Greek, Arabs, Turks, Mongols, and Uzbeks before it was razed by the Emir of Bokhara in 1789 (WHS 2017). Other cities had only relatively brief periods of glory followed by destruction or abandonment: Old and New Sarai, the successive capitals of the Mongol Golden Horde on the Akhtuba River (northeast of Astrakhan in the lower Volga watershed), are perhaps the best examples of this ephemeral existence, with the latter one razed in 1556.

The death of some cities begat instantly the existence of very different successors: invading Spaniards erased most of the Aztec culture and transformed Tenochtitlán to their image. But the city was left in the same place, with the same physical vulnerabilities, being too close to two volcanoes, Popocatépetl and Iztaccíhuatl, and prone to repeated major earthquakes whose impact is made worse by the quake-induced liquefaction of lacustrine soils left behind by Lake Texcoco (Tenochtitlán was on an island in the lake, which was later drained by Spaniards). The modern megalopolis (metropolitan area of more than 21 million people in 2017) in the Valley of Mexico is thus a direct descendant of Moctezuma's lake city (Calnek 2003).

There are many examples of once-great cities that, after losing their dominance or formerly great importance within their respective nations, survived as major settlements, even continued to prosper within the new constraints. Two great eastern capitals are outstanding examples of that trajectory: Xi'an (ancient Chang'an), capital of 10 dynasties (between Qin, 9221–206 BCE, and Tang, 705–904), and Kyoto, capital of the Tokugawa shogunate that ruled Japan between 1600 and 1868 (Stavros 2014). With some 14 million people, Xi'an, the capital of Shaanxi province, is China's ninth-largest metropolitan area, and besides its cultural riches it is now the country's leader in the aerospace and software industries. Kyoto is Japan's seventh-largest city, almost as large as Kobe, and although it remains famous for its temples, gardens and crafts, it also has headquarters of such major companies as Kyocera (electronics), Nintendo (games), and Omron (automation).

But some cities also offer excellent examples of growth followed first by protracted decline (even coming close to a complete unraveling) and, many centuries later, by a remarkable resurrection. Rome is certainly the most outstanding case in this revival category (Hibbert 1985). The steady urban rise of republican Rome during the five centuries up to the beginning of the common era was followed by three centuries of imperial dominance over the Mediterranean world. After the imperial capital was moved east (in 330), Rome entered a long period (more than a thousand years) of marginalized existence (Krautheimer 2000). A slow reversal of this long stagnation began only with the transformation of the city into the great capital of the Renaissance and Baroque architecture, but Rome's population remained far below even the late imperial count until the late 19th century, when the city became the capital of the unified Italian state in 1870. Subsequent exponential growth brought its population to just above 2.8 million people by the early 1980s and after a temporary slight decline that total was reached again by 2016.

And at the beginning of the 21st century urban decline is, once again, a major European concern as it affects large regions of the continent, above all in the entire southeast (especially in Romania, Bulgaria, and Albania), in the Baltic States, in northwestern Spain and in Portugal, and in most parts of Germany. A remarkable interactive map provides a high-resolution record of this decline (and some continuing growth) between 2001 and 2011 for all EU countries as well as for Turkey (Berliner Morgenpost 2015). Cities and towns in Latvia, Lithuania, and Bulgaria are in particularly rapid retreat (some with annual population losses of more than 2%), while in the former German Democratic Republic only some suburbs of the capital (Berlin) have seen some expansion while depopulation has been affecting not only cities with less than 100,000 people and some industrialized urban centers with more than 200,000 people (Chemnitz, Halle) but even such old prominent cities as Leipzig and Dresden whose 2016 population totals were, respectively, about 20% and 12% below their pre-WWII counts.

Japanese depopulation (in some places going back to the 1970s) has been fastest among smaller municipalities, but Osaka, the country's second-largest city, now has (within its designated boundaries) about 15% fewer people than in 1960, and Kitakyushu, the most prominent industrial city in the southern part of the country, had its population peak in 1980. The Russian population will decline by a quarter by 2050 compared to the early post-Soviet era (148 million in 1991, 111 million expected in 2050). And in 2015 the country had 319 single-industry towns established or expanded during the Soviet era that are now at risk of economic collapse, which would bring massive social dislocation as they contain about 10% of Russia's population (Moscow Times 2015). Even some of the major cities have seen recent population declines, including Nizhny Novgorod and Samara, respectively the fourth- and fifth-largest urban areas in the country.

Societies, States, and Empires
The postgrowth typology of simpler societies that were not organized in states, of states (small and large), and empires (when the word is understood in its wider, sociocultural, meaning, not as a specific political entity)

resembles that of cities. Not a few societies, states, and empires reached their apogees and then unraveled rapidly. Other polities lingered on after they ceased growing and their periods of decline became eventually much longer than the periods of their ascent. Others yet ceased to exist because of political intrigues and military conquest or survived as greatly diminished and largely impotent entities only to be restored or resurrected as circumstances changed in their favor and as they embarked on yet another territorial or economic expansion.

There is no shortage of examples of rapid societal demise, ranging from small islands to expansive empires. Rapa Nui (Easter Island) has presented perhaps the most persistent case of postgrowth mysteries. Why was a society that erected hundreds of *moai*, impressively sized stone sculptures, reduced to a small number of inhabitants? In a much-cited explanation, Diamond (2011) attributed this societal collapse to reckless deforestation of the island. This might have satisfied uncritical readers and TV audiences but Hunt (2006) identified the introduced Polynesian rats as the leading destructors of the *Jubaea* palm forests, and Puleston et al. (2017) estimated that dryland sweet potato cultivation could have supported more than 17,000 people. The eventual population collapse was not triggered by deforestation or starvation but by the introduction of infectious diseases (following the first contact with Europeans in 1722) and by enslavement. Middleton (2017) reviews this history among other modern myths of ancient collapses.

And sudden disintegration of states creating smaller national entities has been relatively common in recent history, often violent (Bangladesh seceding from Pakistan in 1971, the breakup of Yugoslavia, which started in June 1991 and resulted in the formation of five new states), sometimes peaceful (the dissolution of Czechoslovakia in 1993). But large size (of territory or population) has been no protection against sudden (or relatively sudden) unraveling, and histories of rising and collapsing empires and civilizations have had a prominent place in Western narratives. This interest is exemplified by the popularity and durability of such famous works as Gibbon's influential analysis of the decline and fall of the Roman Empire (Gibbon 1776–1789), writings on the long-lost glories of imperial China, with its apogee under the emperor Kangxi (Spence 1988), and the unraveling of Western civilization narrated first in an influential fashion by Spengler (1918). Gibbon's history and the demise of the *imperium Romanum* resonated strongly in late 19th- and early 20th-century Europe as the British and French empires reached their apogees.

Tainter's (1988, 193) definition of collapse embraces all essential aspects of a sudden loss of existing arrangements:

Collapse is fundamentally a sudden, pronounced loss of an established level of sociopolitical complexity. A complex society that has collapsed is suddenly smaller, simpler, less stratified, and less socially differentiated. Specialization decreases and there is less centralized control. The flow of information drops, people trade and interact less, and there is overall lower coordination among individuals and groups. Economic activity drops to a commensurate level, while the arts and literature experience such a quantitative decline that a dark age often ensues. Population levels tend to drop, and for those who are left the known world shrinks.

Some inevitable exceptions aside, this definition describes well a variety of recent collapses. When applied to the collapse of the Russian Empire in 1917, the definition is almost perfect in all respects, except for the statement about less centralized control (true only in the earliest chaotic postrevolutionary months) and about a dark age ushered in by a decline in the arts (there was no shortage of new creative activities). In contrast, while the collapse of the Soviet Union (a highly centralized *de facto* empire of continental proportions) led to a large decline in economic activity and to population decrease, it ended the era of Communist control and propaganda and it brought personal freedoms and (despite continued centralizing tendencies) a much freer flow of information.

Popular as it has been, the idea of the death of a civilization that formed a powerful state or a long-lasting empire often does not correspond to reality as languages may survive: for example, even as the original states were obliterated centuries ago, Central America still has a million Maya speakers. More generally, as outlined by a leading proponent of social history, many cultural specificities and beliefs continue to exercise their influence (Sorokin 1957). Indeed, Pitirim Sorokin's place of birth (the czarist empire) is an excellent illustration of these continuities. Russia's Eastern Orthodox civilization appeared to be wiped out by the Communist revolution and by subsequent mass-scale persecution of that ancient religion, but today's Russia abounds with symbols of its prerevolutionary past, state power is allied with the old religion (with its new magnificently restored, and rebuilt, churches), and the continuity of old concerns and fears is unmistakable.

Roman civilization, the foremost and an unceasing subject of collapse studies, is an even better example of remarkable continuity as some of its features were preserved by the Holy Roman Empire for nearly a millennium (962–1806). After a prolonged period of decentralizing turmoil and of two world wars, the gradual unification returned in the form of the

European Union, set up symbolically by the Treaty of Rome (March 25, 1957) and eventually extending to every part of Europe that used to belong to the Roman Empire with the sole exception of Switzerland. More than a millennium and a half after the empire's gradual takeover by outsiders, its enduring components range from governance and legal structures (the parliamentary systems of many countries include senates and powerful senators and are influenced by Roman civil law) to architectural styles, and from an immense linguistic heritage (not only in all Romance languages, as more than half of English words are Latin or Greek-via-Latin) to many cultural commonalities and shared attitudes.

In contrast, there is no shortage of historically ephemeral, albeit in the meantime enormously destructive, expansions that lasted only a few decades, or just a few years. Imperial demise can be swift and powers that appeared to be invincible may be returned to their pre-expansion borders, be severely curtailed, or even cease to exist in a matter of years. Napoleon's European empire is among the best examples: it reached its territorial apogee before the invasion of Russia in July 1812 (directly controlling most of the western half of the continent, and indirectly much of the rest all the way to the western borders of the Russian and Ottoman empires). The empire suffered an enormous setback with the catastrophic retreat from Moscow—in December 1812 only about 10,000 men of the initial army of 422,000 crossed the Neman River of Lithuania—and then came the defeat at Waterloo; by March 31, 1814, Russian troops had occupied Paris (Leggiere 2007) and just three years after escaping from Russia Napoleon began awaiting his death on St. Helena.

Another prominent 19th-century example is that of the Taiping rebellion led by Hong Xiuquan. Starting in 1850 the followers of this self-styled Heavenly Son conquered a large area of South China, but by 1864 the rebellion was over (Spence 1996). And while British India had been in retreat for decades (perhaps even for nearly a century counting from the Mutiny in 1857), its final territorial unraveling in 1947 took place too fast, resulting in the enormous human suffering of hasty partition (Khan 2007). Japanese and German aggressions are the best modern examples of this short-lived (yet immensely destructive) growth-and-collapse sequence.

Japan's quest for an empire began with the attack on Qing China in 1894–1895 (resulting in the annexation of Taiwan). The next step came with the annexation of Korea in 1905, in 1933 Japanese armies occupied Manchuria, and just four years later they began their conquest of eastern China. The attack on Pearl Harbor in December 1941 (figure 6.15) and

Figure 6.15
The beginning of the end of Japan's short-lived empire: USS *West Virginia* sinking in Pearl Harbor on December 7, 1941, after the Japanese torpedo and bomb attack. Photo from the Library of Congress.

occupation of most of Southeast Asia extended imperial control from Burma to the tropical atolls in the Pacific and from the cold and foggy Aleutians to New Guinea. The empire's territorial peak was reached in early 1942, and Japan still controlled most of the conquered lands by the end of 1944—but devastating defeat came swiftly and Japan's capitulation was signed on September 2, 1945: the imperial adventure thus lasted almost exactly 50 years (Jansen 2000).

And Hitler's Thousand Year Reich lasted just 12 years, with its collapse proceeding much faster than its ascent (Shirer 1990; Kershaw 2012). Hitler became Chancellor in January 1933, German troops occupied Austria in March 1938, Czechoslovakia was dismembered in September 1938, and Poland was invaded in August 1939—but the territorial limits of German conquest came just three years later, in October1942, when the Reich controlled territory from the French Atlantic shores to the Caucasus and from

Norway to Greece. All of that was gone within 30 months, by May 1945. That was both a precipitous and a complete collapse involving the demise of an initially powerful political entity as well as of the social attitudes and cultural norms dictated by its leadership as it tried to realize its pernicious vision of a new Germany.

And, quite remarkably, the demise of a vastly more extensive and incomparably more powerful Soviet empire was accomplished—aside from an aborted coup staged by the Communist old guard in August 19–21, 1991, by removing Gorbachev from power, when just three people died—without any violence. The Soviet Union's European possessions (under *de facto* control since the end of WWII) regained their independence during a domino-like sequence that started in Poland in April 1989 and ended in late 1989: the Berlin Wall fell on November 9, the end of the Communist regimes in Sofia and Prague came on, respectively, November 10 and 28, and in Bucharest on December 22 (Fowkes 1995).

The Communist Party's control within the Soviet Union had weakened steadily during 1990. Russia declared sovereignty with a limited application of Soviet laws in June 1990 and the inevitable unraveling was made legal on December 8, 1991 at a meeting in one of the most unlikely places to dissolve an empire, in a state hunting lodge in one the continent's last primeval forests, in Belarus near the Polish border (Plokhy 2014). In contrast, as detailed in chapter 5, the much-studied fall of the Roman Empire was an affair that spanned centuries if we look at just the western part, or roughly a millennium when we include the prolonged weakening of the eastern (Byzantine) empire.

Given this range of outcomes, Arbesman's (2011) analysis is an expected quantitative confirmation of the fact that imperial survival is remarkably idiosyncratic and distinct, and that the aggregate distribution of imperial lifetimes (including the entities whose rule spanned more than three millennia) follows an exponential distribution, with the rate of collapse of an empire independent of its age. Empires thus behave much like species whose probability of extinction is independent of their age but remains constant over the evolutionary span (Van Valen 1973). Thanks to the eponymous queen in Lewis Carroll's *Through the Looking Glass* (who explained "Now, *here*, you see, it takes all the running you can do, to keep in the same place"), this reality is known as the Red Queen effect: longevity confers no advantage, survival demands constant adaptation, evolution, and proliferation merely to maintain one's place against the onslaught of competing species—or adversarial groups, be they upstart nomadic marauders, neighboring, or even distant, states, or other already established empires.

The Ottoman Empire is perhaps the best example of protracted retreat and Poland is one of the most famous cases of national resurrection. The Ottoman Empire reached most of its peak extent of about 4.3 million km^2 after about three centuries of logistic growth that followed the dynasty's founding in 1299, but its subsequent decline lasted more than three centuries before its dissolution in 1922 (Gündüz 2002; Barkey 2008). Polish statehood was established during the 10th century and the territory controlled by the country's rulers eventually expanded (after the Peace of Deulino in 1619, in the form of the Polish-Lithuanian commonwealth) from the Baltic to southern Ukraine and from Silesia to Smolensk (Zamoyski 2012). Less than two centuries later the country ceased to exist after three rounds of partitioning (1772–1795) among Russia, Prussia, and Austria but it was reconstituted after WWI and reemerged from the occupation and destruction of WWII in a much-changed territorial form after Stalin took away its eastern territories and rewarded it with new lands taken from Germany in the west.

But China provides by far the most notable example of a modern resurrection trajectory. After millennia of territorial expansion, it became the world's second-largest state (surpassed only by imperial Russia) and during the early modern era (until the end of the 18th century) it was also the world's largest economy. China's retreat from this great power position began in 1842 with the British victory in the First Opium War. The country, unwilling to modernize along Japanese lines, was defeated in 1895 by Japan less than four decades after Japan began its modernization. Its last imperial dynasty unraveled in 1911 and that left the country adrift until 1949, when the Communist Party reconstituted unitary rule. Misrule is the correct term, as its policies caused the greatest famine in human history (1959–1961) that was preceded and followed by a madness of violence of many purges in the 1950s and the grotesquely mislabeled Cultural Revolution of the late 1960s and early 1970s (Schoppa 2010).

Only in 1979, with Deng Xiaoping's rise to power, did China begin to reclaim its great power status and in 2014, when its GDP is expressed in purchasing power parity, it became, once again, the world's largest economy (World Bank 2017). But the Chinese leadership should not ignore the lessons of post-WWII Japanese history: there is no comparable example of a country whose global standing was transformed so swiftly from a much admired socially dynamic paragon of rapid economic growth, manufacturing skills, and export superpower to a chronically underperforming economy and a fraying society beset by a multitude of challenges that have no readily deployable solutions. And Japan's trajectory is of universal interest.

We can forecast and assemble alternative scenarios but we will not truly understand the new dynamics of very low or no-growth economies with declining populations until they have existed for some time. Post-1989 Japan offers the earliest glimpse of the challenges of a new, postgrowth, society as the country's new economic realities have become conflated with an apparently irreversible demographic retreat.

Japan as a Study in Retreat

Japan is thus the first major modern, affluent society to deal with unprecedented adjustments following high-growth decades of its economy and of its population. Many European countries will soon follow, but given the size of its economy, and of its importance for global trade, Japan is a particularly noteworthy case for studying what follows after reaching the peak of economic performance as well as the peak of population. In chapter 1 (in dealing with exponential growth) I noted the admiration that accompanied Japan's rapid economic progress once it had recovered from WWII destruction. By the mid-1980s the country's prestige and universal recognition of its technical excellence and economic dynamism appeared to bring ever closer Ezra Vogel's forecast of Japan as the world's number one (Vogel 1979).

The achievements of this new economic superpower elicited strong—and, predictably, quite opposite—sentiments on both sides of the Pacific. Perhaps most outspokenly, in 1989 a book entitled provocatively *The Japan That Can Say No* was published by Akio Morita, the co-founder and chairman of Sony Corporation, and Shintaro Ishihara, a prominent politician and that year's candidate for the leadership of the country's ruling Liberal Democratic Party (Morita and Ishihara 1989). Their book described the world dependent on Japan's innovation in general and on its semiconductors in particular, scolded America's inferior business practices, and praised Japan's superior morals and behavior. And Americans did not confront this with determined defiance, as the country seemed to lose its collective nerve and as too many of its leaders began to believe that Japan could really become the world's economic leader (Smil 2013b).

This fear found expression in reactions ranging from puerile smashing of Toshiba electronics by a few US congressmen to congressional demands that the Japanese automakers adopt "voluntary" export restraints. The US had also imposed 100% tariff on Japan's electronic exports ranging from TV sets to computer disks, and in 1987 Congress began to fund Sematech, a new industry-government consortium uniting the 14 largest US semiconductor companies in a bid to prevent what appeared to be an inevitable

Japanese dominance of that critical economic sector. But even a disinterested observer had to agree that Japan's economic growth and dynamism of the 1980s were real enough, evident in the country's large trade surpluses gained from selling a growing variety of high-quality manufactures, in its extraordinarily high saving rates, appreciating currency, and clean, safe and well-functioning cities.

As I wrote on the 20th anniversary of the Nikkei's peak (Smil 2009, 6):

> I will never forget the feel of Japan during the late 1980s, the peak of its power and, even more so, of its confidence and arrogance. In 1988 and 1989 there was no other place on the planet like Tokyo's Ginza. One could see such congregations of polished large Mercedes SEs and SELs, such elegantly dressed crowds, and such free spending, driven by the worldwide profits of Japan, Inc. and the soaring purchasing power of its currency. The notion that in just a few years this time of shining opulence and unlimited prospects would become known as the time of deluded *baburu ekonomi* was not on anybody's mind.

The fall was even more spectacular than the rise. During the 1960s Japan's GDP grew nearly 2.5-fold, during the 1970s it expanded by another 50%, and during the 1980s, even as Japan became the world's second-largest economy, it managed another 50% rise. And on December 29, 1989, Japan's leading stock market index, Nikkei 225, reached its historic peak of 38,915.87 points, concluding a decade that saw it rising nearly six-fold, and almost quadrupling during the preceding six years. When the bubble economy began to deflate, the retreat was first mistaken for a temporary correction. The Nikkei fell below 30,000 in March 1990, then it recovered in just two months before a long slide set in. The index lost nearly 40% in 1990, fell below 15,000 in January 1995 and below 10,000 in September 2001 (Nikkei 225 2017; figure 6.16). As McCormack (1996) noted (hyperbolically, contrasting the previous adulation with new realities), it had taken less than a decade for Japan to move from number one to number zero.

A new century brought no fundamental relief. Before the global economic downturn, the Nikkei 225 managed to rise to more than 17,000 by July 2007, then it fell and after a fluctuating recovery it stood just above 20,000 at the beginning of 2019, still considerably lower than its peak of three decades ago! And the falling Nikkei was not an exceptional marker of retreat. During the first half of the 1990s, urban land prices in the country's six largest cities dropped by 50% and by 2005 they were just 25% of the bubble-era level. Japanese manufacturing began shifting to China; Intel, not Hitachi or Mitsubishi, remained the world's largest semiconductor maker and the industry's global leader, and in 2016 the US companies dominated with 48% of the global market while Japanese production, the

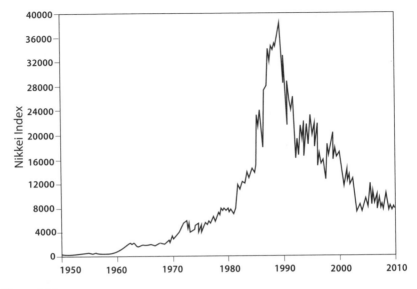

Figure 6.16
Nikkei 225 average, 1950–2010. Graph based on data available at https://fred.stlouisfed
.org/series/NIKKEI225.

world's largest during the late 1980s, was just 11% of worldwide shipments (SIA 2017).

Moreover, some Japanese companies have been failing to deliver the quality that has become expected for products coming from the country that based its economic ascent during the 1970s and 1980s on reliable, high-quality manufactures, a wave led by cars and electronics (Smil 2013b). Since the year 2000 a growing number of Japanese companies have sold substandard, even dangerous, products (millions of Takata airbags are perhaps the most notable entry in the latter category) and admitted to falsifying inspection data. These companies have included Toray Industries (textiles and chemicals), automakers Nissan and Subaru, and most notably Kobe Steel and Mitsubishi Materials, whose parts and equipment are used worldwide in airplanes, trains, cars, and electricity generation plants (Wells 2017). GDP growth fell sharply, adding less than 12% during the 1990s and less than 8% during the first decade of the 21st century (World Bank 2017).

And the long-term (1870–2015) logistic fit of GDP growth (values in PPP in 2011 international dollars; see figure 5.29) indicates that the country faces a long period of minimal or no economic growth. Japan's economic weakness soon translated into notable social shifts, including an obvious rise in homelessness, widespread loss of previously standard lifelong employment, and a decline in labor participation among young workers. And just as the worst post-WWII global economic crisis was coming to its end, Japan was hit by the Tohoku earthquake, a massive tsunami, and a catastrophic failure of three nuclear reactors in the Fukushima Dai-ichi plant in March 2011. This was a setback with enormous social and economic consequences for the region, where even before those catastrophic events the only local employment in many small villages in the interior of Fukushima and Iwate provinces was to grow some vegetables, produce artisanal charcoal, and make small wooden manufactures.

Rapidly changing governments, whose promises of reforms keep falling far short of Japan's enormous challenges, have not offered any effective solutions. The unique combination of competitive advantages that propelled the country during the 1980s will never return and, perhaps most importantly, the post-1989 economic retreat lasted for so long that it became conflated with Japan's demographic decline (figure 6.17). Not only

Figure 6.17
In a photo taken in April 2009 an old man looks from the top floor of Tokyo's municipal building on the sprawling city: during his lifetime the country rose from defeat and devastation to become a respected, even feared, economic superpower but almost immediately began its gradual economic and demographic retreat. Author's photo.

is the country aging rapidly—now clearly on its way to becoming the most geriatric society (NIPSSR 2002)—but after a decade of minimal growth its population began to decline and, as already noted, by the fall of 2017 it was down to 127.7 million people, a loss of nearly 1.3 million in six years (SB 2017b), and in 2018 the population loss reached a new record of 449,000 people.

The Japanese population, the 11th-largest in 2017, might just squeeze into the top 30 by 2100 (UN 2017). The long-term impact of this demographic retreat may have a relatively limited impact on Japan's manufacturing. Cohorts of young people best suited for this work will be declining, but significant shares of production capacities have been already moved offshore as Japan followed (with the lag of 10–20 years) the deindustrialization trend so evident in the EU and the US, and further progress of robotization should keep productivity rising: Japan has pioneered this automation trend, it already deploys by far the largest number of industrial robots, and several companies remain among the leading global enablers of plant automation.

But there will be no way to avoid adverse effects on Japan's admirable infrastructure of public transportation, on the country's food production, and on its health care. Japan's dense but aging transportation network will continue to experience high rates of use and hence it will require meticulous maintenance, an imperative perhaps best illustrated by the fact that during peak travel times rapid trains, traveling at up to 300 km/h, leave Tokyo's main station at intervals as brief as three minutes, and have been doing so with an annually averaged delay of less than one minute (Smil 2014a). Maintenance and reconstruction of transportation networks has become highly mechanized but it still entails plenty of physical exertion not suited for an aging workforce.

The average age of Japanese farmers has surpassed 67 years, nearly all rural areas have been experiencing progressive depopulation (with only a handful of elderly residents left in many villages), the small sizes of typical farms are not suitable for mechanized operations deploying large field machinery, and the country already has the lowest food self-sufficiency rate among all major economies. When measured in terms of overall dietary energy supply, Japan's self-sufficiency rate (more than 70% in 1965) is now just 38%, lower than in such import-dependent countries as Switzerland or South Korea) and in an entirely different category than more than self-sufficient US, Canada, or Australia (Smil and Kobayashi 2012; Japan Press Weekly 2018). And the shortages of health-care personnel and other workers, bound to get more acute as the population ages, seem to have no easy solution. A new bill passed in 2018 opened the way for the formal acceptance of foreign workers but getting permanent residency will remain difficult.

The aftermath of Japan's ascent has been so poignant because it was preceded by a vertiginous rise and because the contrast between before and after became so stark within a single decade. Akio Morita died in 1999, spared from seeing his Sony falling from a globally dominant maker of admired electronics to a troubled underperformer. In early 2019 its stock value was only about a third of its peak level of February 2000; the company has cut its labor force repeatedly, lost its high credit rating, and has not had a globally successful product for more than a decade. Ishihara became a long-serving governor of Tokyo (1999–2012), lost his re-election bid as a member of parliament, and kept making provocative statements. But the notion of an assertive Japan dictating its own terms and saying no to the world in general, and to the US in particular, seems now quite risible.

And yet it is not easy to answer the question of what has come after growth in Japan, and what will follow. Many labels—stagnation, chronic retreat, gradual unravelling, creeping decay, spreading shabbiness, return to more realistic expectations—could be used to describe the post-1989 economic, social, and demographic trajectories, but such descriptions do not amount to the complete verdict. At the time when the country was greatly admired for its high economic growth and manufacturing prowess, its housing conditions remained poor in comparison to other affluent nations. That situation has actually improved a bit during the last generation even as a new concern—rising numbers of abandoned properties—becomes a common reality: about 10 million houses and apartments were empty in 2018, and the total is expected to rise to 20 million by 2030.

Looking back, what stands out above all is not any particular statistic of decline but the contrast with the past and expected performance. French or British economic problems seem unremarkable because during the 1980s nobody thought about France or the UK as the future #1, nobody saw Italy as the paragon of economic dynamism and astonishing inventiveness. And although it may now be seen as an economic and demographic has-been, Japan still remains the world's third-largest economy (no matter if the total is expressed in nominal or purchasing power parity monies) and its per capita (PPP-adjusted) GDP is about the same as in France or the UK (World Bank 2018).

This is what I wrote on the 20th anniversary of the Nikkei 225 (Smil 2009, 5–6):

Nations rise and fall, and they stay in positions of strategic dominance or economic ascendance for different (and unpredictable) periods of time…Japan's quest for the leading role in the global economy lasted roughly 40 years…and in its final phase it involved an economic confrontation with the United States that engendered a great deal of exaggerated confidence in Japan and deep concern and self-doubt about the nature of America's resilience and the effectiveness of its response…As it moves into its new (and truly uncharted) demographic and economic era, Japan will not implode and turn into a dysfunctional polity. If the past two decades are any guide, it may not manage its retreat brilliantly, but I believe it will find ways to deal with its new challenges without causing any grave perturbations on the global scene…and without losing its deserved status as a well-functioning society.

Coming decades will show to what extent I got it wrong.

Economies

Temporary setbacks—often relatively short-lived, sometimes lingering for many years—have been recurrent features of modern economic growth. Among the major economies the greatest output declines of the 20th century have included a 26% reduction of US GDP (in constant monies) between 1929 and 1933 caused by the global recession; a 51% decline of Japan's gross national product (again, in constant monies) between the pre-WWII peak in 1939 and the postwar low in 1946; and Germany's 29% drop between 1944 and 1945 (Harrison 2000). Recoveries from such declines took years: the US regained the 1929 GDP level in 1936; Japan surpassed its prewar economic performance only in 1953.

But no modern economy has gone into such a long, uninterrupted decline that it could be seen as a new unprecedented trend, and even stagnating economies had their poor performances interspersed with periods of growth. When measured in national currency, Japan's economy more than tripled between 1975 and 1995 (from ¥153 trillion to ¥512.5 trillion) while between 1995 and 2015 it grew by less than 4% (to ¥535.5 trillion), an enormous downturn from a steep linear rise to a generation-long stagnation (World Bank 2017). But even during those two decades Japan's stagnating and fluctuating economy declined during nine years and grew slightly in 11 years, avoiding uninterrupted protracted retreat.

What lies ahead for major countries and for the world economy? Some economists reconstruct historic trajectories and see a logistic curve forming—but are content to leave it at that. For example, Boretos (2009) fitted global economic growth into a logistic curve whose full life cycle is about two centuries, eventually reaching saturation level by the beginning of the 22nd century. But there is no talk about saturation in mainstream economic publications, which all assume that the future will not be that different from the past as endless human ingenuity will be able to support many generations of growth.

For decades economists have been engaged in constant forecasting, and global, regional and national versions are now offered by all leading international organizations, including the International Monetary Fund, OECD, United Nations, and the World Bank. Near-term forecasts (1–4 years) of national GDP and of regional and global economic product are the most common, but some forecasts now extend to mid-term (5–10 years), and a few of them look ahead for more than a generation. The World Bank offers short-term GDP forecasts for all of its member countries, while the OECD's latest forecast is simply the continuation of an exponential curve with an annual growth rate of 2.5%: starting with the global economic product of about US$11 trillion (in 2010 PPP monies) and reaching about $76 trillion in 2018, it brings the total to US$221 trillion by 2060.

How long will a similar trajectory hold: for another decade, another century, or another millennium? Of course, most economists have a ready answer as they see no after-growth stage: human ingenuity will keep on driving economic growth forever, solving challenges that may seem insurmountable today, especially as the techno-optimists firmly anticipate wealth creation progressively decoupling from additional demand for energy and materials. Mokyr (2014) has nearly unlimited confidence about the coming flood of near-miraculous transformations ranging from genetically modified crops (that will withstand rising global temperatures, manufacture their own nutrients, and protect themselves against insects) to a revolution in material science "that may make the synthetic substances of the twentieth century look like the Stone Age by comparison." In June 2018 a special innovation issue of *Spectrum* gathered some of these accounts of coming near-miracles—but it also carried my critical (not so fast!) riposte (Smil 2018b).

Such cornucopian views have been further potentiated by many claims about the impending arrival of omnipotent artificial intelligence. A growth of computerization, robotization, and the rising capabilities of artificial intelligence are expected to bring a massive elimination of existing jobs— with the share of occupations at risk of such a takeover as high as 50% (Frey and Osborne 2015)—but to allow continued economic growth. But how will the robots secure the raw materials for their production, how will they be energized? Will the robots organize their own supply infrastructures, their extraction of metals and minerals? Will they design and put in place their own generation of renewable electricity and its long-distance high-voltage transmission, transformation, and distribution?

We are already near global saturation with devices that are essentially powerful portable mini-robots: every mobile phone is a computer whose processing power is orders of magnitude higher than that of the stationary devices of two generations ago—but its ownership is now in billions and more than 1.5 billion of these complex artifacts (built of aluminum, plastics, glass, and precious metals) are now discarded every year. Obviously, such trends cannot continue on a planet that is expected to accommodate some 10 billion people before the end of this century, and hence looking at what might come after the economic growth is not just a matter of fascinating speculations, it should be a key concern as we think about extending the life span of modern civilization.

Decoupling economic growth from energy and material inputs contradicts physical laws: basic needs for food, shelter, education, and employment for the additional billions of people to be added by 2100 will alone demand substantial energy flows and material inputs. True, those inputs will have lower relative intensities (energy/mass, mass/mass) than today's average rates—but the absolute totals will keep rising (with continued population growth) or will moderate but remain substantial. Ward et al. (2016, 10) confirmed this truism when they used historical data and modeled projections to conclude "that growth in GDP ultimately cannot plausibly be decoupled from growth in material and energy use, demonstrating categorically that GDP growth cannot be sustained indefinitely." This makes it highly misleading to advocate any growth-oriented policies assuming that such a decoupling, and continued GDP growth, is possible.

And it is similarly misleading to talk about any imminent practice of circular economy. Modern economies are based on massive linear flows of energy, fertilizers, other agrochemicals, and water required to produce food, and on even more massive energy and material flows to sustain industrial activities, transportation, and services. Circularization of the two key flows is impossible (reusing spent energy would require nothing less than abolishing entropy; reusing water used in cropping would require the capture of all evapotranspiration and field runoff), and (with the exception of a few metals in some countries) high-intensity (>80% of total flows), mass-scale recycling of materials (above all construction waste, plastics, and electronic waste) remains elusive.

Daly (2009) summed up the three conditions that would allow continuous economic growth on the Earth: if the economy were not an open subsystem of a finite and nongrowing biophysical system; if the economy were growing in a nonphysical dimension; and if the laws of thermodynamics did not apply. But none of these realities can be evaded, circumvented, or substituted by other arrangements—and hence it is easy to side with Kenneth Boulding who noted (not sparing his fellow economists) that "Anyone who believes in indefinite growth in anything physical, on a physically finite planet, is either mad or an economist" (quoted in US Congress 1973, 248).

Boulding was also one of the early proponents of new economic thinking when he introduced his distinction between the "cowboy economy" and the "spaceman economy":

> the cowboy being symbolic of the illimitable plains and also associated with reckless, exploitative, romantic, and violent behavior, which is characteristic of open societies. The closed economy of the future might similarly be called the "spaceman" economy, in which the earth has become a single spaceship, without unlimited reservoirs of anything, either for extraction or for pollution, and in which, therefore, man must find his place in a cyclical ecological system which is capable of continuous reproduction of material form even though it cannot escape having inputs of energy.
>
> The difference between the two types of economy becomes most apparent in the attitude towards consumption. In the cowboy economy, consumption is regarded as a good thing and production likewise...By contrast, in the spaceman economy, throughput is by no means a desideratum, and is indeed to be regarded as something to be minimized rather than maximized...This idea that both production and consumption are bad things rather than good things is very strange to economists...(Boulding 1966, 7–8)

Questions about the costs of economic growth and its further desirability and arguments in favor of a steady-state economy began to appear during the 1960s and 1970s (Boulding 1964, 1966; Mishan 1967; Daly 1971) and the period's most widely publicized, and the most influential analysis of what will come after economic growth was *The Limits to Growth* (Meadows et al. 1972). This short study was a slightly modified version of Jay Forrester's work on dynamic systems (Forrester 1971) and it modeled global interactions of population, resources (including energy), industrial and food output, pollution, investment, and health based on historical values for the period between 1900 and 1970. The "standard" world model run assumed no major changes in the existing world system and it predicted that both food supply per capita and industrial output per capita would peak shortly after the year 2000.

This was to be followed by fairly steep declines

> as resource prices rise and mines are depleted, more and more capital must be used for obtaining resources, leaving less to be invested for future growth. Finally investment cannot keep up with depreciation, and the industrial base collapses, taking with it the service and agricultural systems, which have become dependent on industrial inputs (such as fertilizers, pesticides, hospital laboratories, computers, and especially energy for mechanization). For a short time the situation is

especially serious because population, with the delays inherent in the age structure and the process of social adjustment, keeps rising. Population finally decreases when the death rate is driven upward by lack of food and health services. (Meadows et al. 1972, 124)

Overshoot and collapse caused by nonrenewable resource depletion were inevitable outcomes and while the report concluded that the exact timing of these events was not meaningful, it was certain that growth would stopped well before the year 2100 if no major adjustments were made. Because I knew the programming language used to build the model (Forrester's DYNAMO) I deconstructed the model line by line (not a very difficult task, as their model of the world fit into fewer than 150 lines) and quickly realized the number of indefensible simplifications and misleading assumptions. I still remember my surprise when I saw such key variables as *Nonrenewable Resources* and *Pollution*—as if it were possible to lump together the enormous variety of mineral resources (ranging from relatively abundant and highly substitutable minerals to unsubstitutable and fairly rare elements) and all forms of pollution (lumping short-lived atmospheric gases with long-lived radioactive wastes) into single bundles interacting with other complex variables.

A 30-year update of the report (Meadows et al. 2004) left the basic finding unchanged: humanity is in overshoot and the ensuing damage and suffering could be greatly reduced through wise policies. Another retrospective analysis found the standard model to be on track after 30 years (Turner 2008)—but how that can be asserted by actually quantifying the just noted disparate bundles of variables is hard to understand. The original report, as well as all sequels inspired by it, emphasized the obvious (exponential growth is impossible, biospheric flows and capacities are finite), but the grossly simplified modeling approach is not a nuanced realistic analysis of new global complexities—but essentially an exhortation, a call for change based on some solid evidence and some dubious assumptions. As a result, some of its conclusions are unexceptional, and others are questionable.

The report was followed by many kindred inquiries into the capacity of the biosphere and the availability of natural resources to support further economic growth: some were of a cornucopian nature, seeing few limits to further growth (Simon 1981; Simon and Kahn 1984); others, reflecting concerns about the Earth's carrying capacity, led to the rise of a new discipline of ecological economics (Daly 1980; Costanza 1997; Daly and Farley 2010; Martínez-Alier 2015). This has eventually led to advocacy of not just economies without any growth but ones deliberately trying to reduce overall economic output, a shift awkwardly labeled as de-growth. Book titles convey these sentiments: *Living within Limits* (Hardin 1992); *Beyond Growth* (Daly 1996); *Prosperity without Growth* (Jackson 2009); *From Bioeconomics to Degrowth* (Georgescu-Roegen and Bonaiuti 2011); *The Economics of Enough* (Coyle 2011); *Degrowth: A Vocabulary for a New Era* (D'Alisa et al. 2014). In reality, there are no economies embarking on such paths.

As already noted, since the 1990s there have been also many studies of the limits to the growing extraction of mineral resources in general and to an imminent arrival of peak global oil production in particular (Deffeyes 2003)—and, given oil's importance in the global economy, of inevitable and permanent economic downturn. I labeled this wave a new catastrophist cult, and wrote that the proponents of imminent peak oil "resort to deliberately alarmist arguments as they mix incontestable facts with caricatures of complex realities and as they ignore anything that does not fit their preconceived conclusions in order to issue their obituaries of modern civilization" (Smil 2006a, 22). More than a decade later, the global output of oil keeps on slowly rising and world oil prices remain relatively low.

And all of these concerns have been made more pressing by new forecasts of continued population growth that have not confirmed the earlier conclusions that the global population was unlikely to surpass 9 billion, and predicted a total of 9.7 billion by 2050 (UN 2017). A much-publicized approach to address these matters focused on the notion of sustainable development. The term entered the public discourse with the release of the *Report of the World Commission on Environment and Development: Our Common Future*, widely known as the Bruntland Report after the former Norwegian prime minister who chaired the commission that prepared it (WCED 1987).

Ever since, the adjective has become one of the most misused descriptors of desirable human actions. The report's definition of the process is exceedingly loose:

> Sustainable development is development that meets the needs of the present without compromising the ability of future generations to meet their own needs. It contains within it two key concepts: the concept of "needs," in particular the essential needs of the world's poor, to which overriding priority should be given; and the idea of limitations imposed by the state of technology and social organization on the environment's ability to meet present and future needs. (WCED 1987, 41)

This leaves all key variables undefined: what are "the needs of the present"? Do they correspond to American, EU, Japanese, Bangladeshi, or Congolese expectations or to some average concocted by a committee? Even essential needs are arguable: they may be easily defined in terms of the nutrition required to meet adequate physical and mental growth (so much of total energy, so many grams of the three macronutrients, and so many fractions of a gram of micronutrients), but it is much more difficult to define them in terms of rewarding employment, adequate living conditions, widely available education, and opportunities for personal development and leisure.

Moreover, the report made it clear that its goals are global:

> Thus the goals of economic and social development must be defined in terms of sustainability in all countries—developed or developing, market-oriented or centrally planned. Interpretations will vary, but must share certain general features and must flow from a consensus on the basic concept of sustainable development and on a broad strategic framework for achieving it.

But given the existing disparities between affluent, middle-income and low-income countries, it is difficult to see any universal agreement either on "certain general features" or on "a broad strategic framework" for achieving sustainable development.

Concerns about excessive global warming (a rise in the average tropospheric temperature surpassing 2°C) further strengthened the arguments in favor of limited or "sustainable" growth, and to many it appeared that the deepest post-WWII economic crisis in 2008 and 2009 was the unplanned but unsurprising beginning of global economic retreat. Heinberg (2010, xv), argued that "a good case can now be made that the year 2007…was indeed the year, if not of 'peak of everything,' then at least of 'peak of many things'" and subtitled his book *Waking Up to the Century of Declines*. He explicitly listed the "zeniths" of worldwide economic activity and global energy consumption, and peaks of crude oil output and of worldwide shipping.

But all of those zeniths have been already much surpassed, with most increases following the temporary economic downturn of 2008 and 2009 being actually fairly impressive. By 2017 global economic product was 60% higher than in 2007 (IMF 2017), by 2016 global primary energy consumption was 14% higher than in 2007, crude oil supplies rose by 11%, and the total of all seaborne cargoes was 25% higher (UNCTAD 2017). Obviously, this cannot be taken as a firm indicator of prospective achievements—but it is yet another proof of the futility of quantitative forecasting of complex affairs. At the same time, there is no doubt that since 1973 (when the unprecedented period of rapid post-WWII growth ended) the world economy has become impressively more energy efficient and relatively less material-intensive—while continuing population growth, further increases of consumption in affluent countries, and fast economic advances in Asia in general, and in China in particular, have translated into relatively strong absolute global growth in both energy and material requirements.

In relative terms (per unit of economic product) the global economy has shifted in the direction of greater sustainability but in absolute terms it has shown no tendency toward deliberately slower growth, and degrowth remains a cherished topic for ecological economists, not a guiding principle for any companies or governments. As a result, we can only speculate when and how we might be able to put an end to material growth and forge a new society that would survive without worshipping the impossible god of continuously increasing consumption: no country has committed to following such a path. Two generations after the concerns entered the public domain, the economic orthodoxy still does not have any more rational model to follow than the one of continuous growth, with special admiration reserved for high rate-gains such as those recorded by China during the first decade of the 21st century. Indeed, the worship of eternal growth has in some ways intensified because we are now promised that truly miraculous solutions will be provided by technological change that will soon reach the unimaginable Singularity, the result of an "exponential growth in the rate of exponential growth."

A persevering reader of this book—replete with facts and arguments about confined growth, constraints and limits—might have some doubts regarding the likelihood of this specific outcome and hence it might be in order to repeat the key conclusions of Kurzweil's forecast that were cited in this book's preface:

> An analysis of the history of technology shows that technological change is exponential... we won't experience 100 years of progress in the 21st century—it will be more like 20,000 years of progress (at today's rate)... There's even exponential growth in the rate of exponential growth. Within a few decades, machine intelligence will surpass human intelligence, leading to The Singularity... a rupture in the fabric of human history. The implications include the merger of biological and nonbiological intelligence, immortal software-based humans, and ultra-high levels of intelligence that expand outward in the universe at the speed of light. (Kurzweil 2001, 1).

If this were true, writing this book would have been a monumental blunder, as we would soon get growth at the speed of light (I urge those with a modicum of scientific education to pause and think what this would mean in reality). And the author of these forecasts is swallowing daily scores of pills in order to ensure that he will live to see the Singularity's arrival: his latest forecasts see machines achieving human levels of intelligence in 2029 and the Singularity still on track for 2045 (Kurzweil 2017). Modis (2006, 112) put it well as he closed his review of Kurzweil's book by writing that "as science fiction goes... I prefer more literary prose... and less of this science." I believe that, acting as risk minimizers, we must assume that there will be no singularity-driven technical salvation because there will not be any speed-of-light growth of our knowledge. I agree that "on today's evidence, technologizing our way out of this does not look likely...the only solution left to us is to change our behavior, radically and globally, on every level. In short, we urgently need to consume less. A lot less." (Emmott 2013, 184–186).

Hence back to square one: no modern society has been taking any thoughtful, effective steps to find its way toward deliberately very low or no growth even in settings where a relatively high level of average affluence and obviously excessive levels of consumption and waste are all too evident. This means that I can answer the question of what comes after economic growth only by making it scale-specific and contingent on the time spans under consideration. The answers would then range from more growth during periods of years to decades for most of the world's economies to a nonnegligible probability of some kind of involuntary global retreat—that is substantial prolonged worldwide retrenchment, followed, at best, by greatly diminished rates during a halting recovery, at worst by further gradual decline, that is degrowth not by choice but as a reaction to cumulative (economic, extraction, consumption, environmental) excesses.

Modern Civilization

After millennia of slow and unsteady progress, the two centuries of unprecedented growth—of populations, food production, infrastructures, and of extractive, manufacturing, transportation, and communication techniques—have brought changes that were truly unimaginable at the outset of this transformational process. Modernity has been synonymous with growth and its rewards have been immense and all-encompassing. This achievement is even more impressive given the fact that Malthus did more than greatly underestimate our capacities to provide for growing populations: he also underestimated the future growth of the global population.

Its total, at about 900 million in 1800, not only kept on increasing exponentially during the 19th century, taking 110 years to double to 1.8 billion, but (as already explained) the growth rates accelerated during the 20th century as hyperbolic growth resulted in the next doubling, to 3.6 billion, in only 60 years; and, after the growth rates moderated, the next doubling, to 7.2 billion, was accomplished in not even 45 years, with the 2017 total at 7.3 billion in 2017. And yet never in history has there been such a high proportion of the global population that is adequately fed, well-schooled, lives in a modicum of comfort, and has such a long average life expectancy. Moreover, we have the technical means to eliminate the remaining malnutrition and to raise the living standards of the poorest segments in any society.

But scientific understanding offers no clear grasp of what lies ahead. Utopianism (now in its techno-optimistic-electronic-artificial-intelligence garb) and catastrophism (updated Malthusianism concerned with exhaustion of natural resources and destruction of the biosphere's capacity to support continued economic growth) are not just labels for contradictory opinions and sentiments of uninformed commentators. The terms correctly describe divergent views that coexist within the mainstream of modern scientific research. Long-established scholarly journals considered to be the most reliable sources of information in their fields have been carrying these contradictory messages for decades, and I have not discerned any toning down of extreme claims in the 21st century.

Are we to look forward to the coming age of plenty where "farmers could feed the world indefinitely" (Fuglie 2013, 26), where "economic and environmental outcomes can be decoupled" (Hatfield-Dodds et al. 2015), and where people using abundant, infinitely malleable materials "will conjure objects as easily as we now play music or movies" (Ball 2014, 40)? Or do we agree that waste production must begin to decline during this century (Hoornweg et al. 2013) and that we should contemplate the peak of everything due to the imminent depletion of many mineral resources (Heinberg 2010; Klare 2012)? Should we then view the future of mass consumption with equanimity or with increasing foreboding? Or, to rephrase it by reusing the labels chosen for the title of a recent book examining the two polar positions, should we listen to prophets of environmental perils or ignore them because the salvation will come from inventive wizards (Mann 2018)?

Growth has brought a number of obvious benefits, from making life easier (including the ownership of all machines and gadgets that make running a household incomparably less onerous that a century ago) to (however ephemeral) feelings of satisfaction and enjoyment by displaying (often almost instantly disposable) pieces of manufactured junk. Compared to these, losses of individual comforts and intangible benefits are of a minor importance, although many individuals value them very highly. For myself, they might include walking on a quiet forest path, looking at a starry sky bisected by the Milky Way, standing alone in front of *Las Meninas*...The first experience is still common in remote boreal forests and those are also the best places to avoid light pollution. But unless you get a private, after-hours, tour of the Museo del Prado, standing alone front of Velázquez's astonishing *Las Meninas* is now, briefly, possible only if you are the first one in the morning lineup and walk fast directly to room 12 on the first floor: in minutes it will fill up with guided masses from Shanghai or Osaka.

Any meaningful cost-benefit analysis of these (real and perceived) personal gains and burdens inherent in mass consumption is impossible as the two effects have no common metric. The judgment falls largely into the realm of value. But (as challenging as it may be) appraising the collective gains and losses of global economic growth and mass consumption raises indisputable concerns, above all because of intergenerational obligations arising from the need to maintain a habitable biosphere. Again, techno-optimists are not perturbed and cite the recent dematerialization trend as a key shift promised to make a new world possible.

But while relative dematerialization, particularly in consumer electronics, has helped to maintain some high growth rates, absolute dematerialization is a different matter. Mass consumption (measured by numbers of people acquiring an item) is also always increased consumption of mass (be it measured by inputs of energy or raw materials). Arguments about the impressive miniaturization (and hence dematerialization) of modern electronics are based on faulty assumptions. Smartphones may be small and light but their energy and material footprints are surprisingly large. Here are my calculations of respective embodied energies in the year 2015 based on the best available data (Smil 2016a).

Inevitably, in absolute terms, a car with a mass 10,000 times that of a smartphone (1.4 t vs. 140 g) embodies considerably more energy, but global aggregates tell a very different story. In 2015 worldwide sales reached 1.9 billion mobile phones, 60 million laptops, and 230 million tablets (Gartner 2017). Their total mass was about 550,000 t, and with conservative assumptions of average embodied energies of 0.25 GJ/phone, 4.5 GJ/laptop, and 1 GJ for a tablet (Wu et al. 2010; Anders and Andersen 2010), making these devices required about 1 EJ of primary energy.

A passenger car (steel, aluminum, and plastics make most of its mass) needs nearly 100 GJ to produce (Volkswagen 2010), which means that the 72 million vehicles sold in 2015 embodied about 7 EJ of energy in about 100 million t of machines. The mass of newly sold cars was thus 180 times that of all portable electronics—but their production required only seven times as much energy. Moreover, portable electronic devices have short life spans (averaging just two years) and their production thus embodies globally about 0.5 EJ per year of use—while passenger cars last a decade and their worldwide production embodies about 0.7 EJ per year of use—that is only 40% more than making all portable electronic devices! This makes for a stunning conclusion: even if my approximate aggregate calculations were to err by 50% in opposite directions (i.e., cars embodying more and electronics requiring less energy than I assume), the global totals would be still of the same order of magnitude and, most likely, they would not differ by more than a factor of two.

Of course, operating energy costs are vastly different. A compact American passenger car consumes about 500 GJ of gasoline during a decade of its service, five times its embodied energy cost. A smartphone consumes annually just 4 kWh of electricity, less than 30 MJ during its two years of service, or just 3% of its embodied energy cost if the electricity is from nuclear fission or from a PV cell, and about 8% if it comes from burning coal. But the cost of electrifying the net is already high and it continues to rise. In 2013 US data centers consumed about 91 TWh of electricity (2.2% of all generation) and are projected to use about 3.5% by 2020. In global terms, the aggregate demand of information and communications networks claimed nearly 5% of worldwide electricity generation in 2012 and it will approach 10% by 2020. In aggregate, tiny phones leave a not-so-tiny energy—and hence environmental—footprint.

And there are no even remotely comparable dematerialization shifts where the basic modern infrastructures, structures, and now indispensable artifacts (ranging from fertilizers to turbines) are concerned. Two key factors militate against any early decline of global energy demand and material consumption. The first is the continuing growth of the global population with its obvious implications for higher food and energy outputs and expanded industrial production. But the more important reality is that the demand for higher material per capita consumption is still far from saturated even in the world's most affluent societies and that their achievements act as powerful attractors for all societies on the lower rungs of economic development: the recent quest of China's *nouveaux riches* to out-American America in ostentatious consumption is a perfect example of this effect.

Hopes for an early end to this demand are unrealistic because the growth of material consumption is a universal and durable phenomenon: objects of desire change, desire remains. Mukerji (1983) showed that among wealthy merchants and aristocrats the growth of personal consumption began at the very beginning of the early modern era. During the 16th century their homes began to fill with paintings, imported rugs, tea services, and upholstered chairs—and even before the 17th century a growing array of consumer goods found its way to the homes of peasants and laborers. Rugs and tea services may be low on the list of modern desires but far more energy-intensive products requiring rare minerals and elaborate industrial processes and handled by transportation-intensive global production chains have taken their place. In any case, how likely is it that in the future our ingenuity could feed growth that could be embodied solely in immaterial achievements?

Techno-optimists are convinced that technical fixes (those already emerging and those to come in the future in response to critical problems) will solve even seemingly intractable challenges. Anticipations of technical progress have been always affected by unrealistic expectations belonging to several categories of distinct errors. The combination of the early hype and of the replacement hype error is perhaps the most common, with recent cases including the claims of extraordinarily rapid decarbonization of global energy use and, perhaps most notably, the promise of a fourth industrial revolution "that will fundamentally alter the way we live, work, and relate to one another. In its scale, scope, and complexity, the transformation will be unlike anything humankind has experienced before" (Schwab 2016, 1). Impact errors are also common, as economic, environmental, and social aspects of new techniques and processes are underestimated or are naively portrayed as innocuous and easily manageable.

But historical perspectives demand skepticism. I stand by my conclusion that the two generations preceding WWI were the most exceptional innovative period in history and that its contributions have been far more consequential than the advances of the last two generations (Smil 2005). Similarly, Ferguson (2012, 2) based his refusal to believe in the techno-optimistic hype on contrasting recent achievements with past accomplishments and by offering "simple lessons from history: More and faster information is not good in itself. Knowledge is not always the cure. And network effects are not always positive." In contrast, Mokyr (2016) stresses that progress is not a natural phenomenon but a relatively recent human invention and that the alternative to technical progress "is always worse." Ultimately, it comes down to the biosphere's capacity to support an expanding population consuming at higher rates.

And yet, the biosphere's indispensability and degradation are not among the concerns of those introducing ever-larger information flows and ever-faster communication and they are never mentioned in the Kurzweilian promise of infinite growth. In contrast, half a century after his first apocalyptic warnings, Ehrlich still predicts the bleakest planetary future due to the insurmountable environmental problems: "Environmental problems have contributed to numerous collapses of civilizations in the past. Now, for the first time, a global collapse appears likely. Overpopulation, overconsumption by the rich and poor choices of technologies are major drivers; dramatic cultural change provides the main hope of averting calamity" (Ehrlich and Ehrlich 2013, 1).

In contrast, it is not difficult to offer a **very** different scenario that, while not highly likely, is not implausible. African fertilities decline much faster than expected. Indian population growth decelerates rapidly. Rest of the world sees population stagnations and declines. Aging populations consume less and this, in combination with relative dematerialization, eases the burdens imposed on the biosphere. Economic growth moderates while advances in energy conversion and storage usher in affordable all-electric or hydrogen economies. Natural ecosystems begin their comeback, as forests have already done in Europe and parts of North America. I wish all of this came to pass as rapidly as possible—but acting as responsible risk minimizers we cannot simply hope for low-probability outcomes.

There is no need to be a catastrophist in order to see what I call the great obverse: all that we have lost as a result of growth in general and mass consumption of artifacts and experiences in particular, the extent to which we have already imperiled the life on Earth, and the potential for further damage resulting from a growing population and rising aspirations. The overall environmental cost of growth is still going up as it spans an enormous range of impacts. Some of them are largely matters of sentiment and preference, some have brought regrets and inconvenience and affected our perception and enjoyment of some aspects of our existence, even our collective health, but have not imperiled civilization's survival.

As already noted, the loss of darkness (light pollution) is a foremost example in this category: it not only ruins astronomical observations and prevents hundreds of millions of people from ever seeing the great band of our galaxy, it also affects ecosystems and animal and human health (due to the disruption of circadian cycle) and, obviously, it increases energy consumption in a particularly wasteful manner (IDA 2017; figure 6.18). But if it were the only anthropogenic disturbance of our biosphere, our lives would be negatively affected but the future of our civilization would not be fundamentally compromised. Unfortunately, there are too many anthropogenic transformations whose increasing intensity and combined effect have been doing precisely that, and while two or three generations ago the same actions had overwhelmingly local or regional consequences, their impacts are now truly global.

These effects have been abundantly documented by increasingly comprehensive monitoring of the biosphere. Thanks to sensors mounted on

Figure 6.18
Few nighttime images from space illustrate the extent of anthropogenic light pollution as stunningly as the view of the most densely populated parts of Western and Central Europe. NASA image.

orbiting Earth-observation satellites, we now have (adequate to outstanding) knowledge of the anthropogenic insults to the integrity of both terrestrial and aquatic ecosystems. No major biome (be it tropical or temperate grasslands and forest, tundras or wetlands) has escaped extensive destruction or at least modification, with some of these transformations going back thousands of years, others remaining relative subdued but growing at unprecedented rates since the 1950s. Oceans have been affected by changes ranging from gradual storage of heat generated by the tropospheric warming (Wang et al. 2018) to massive accumulation of microplastics (GESAMP 2015) and by declining oxygen content in both open and coastal waters (Breitburg et al. 2018).

The capacity of fresh water resources to deliver reliable supplies, particularly in densely populated Asia where cropping relies heavily on irrigation and where Himalayan glaciers are a key source of runoff, has been reduced, in some regions to a worrisome degree. Changes in the Earth's gravity measured by satellites indicate large-scale mass losses of groundwater in northern India caused by excessive withdrawals (Tiwari et al. 2009); the Aral Sea has almost entirely disappeared (Usmanova 2013); groundwater levels in the Ogallala Aquifer, underlying the world's most productive farmland in the US Corn Belt, continue to decline (USGS 2017a); and too many aquifers around the world are polluted with pesticide and herbicide residues, nitrates, and heavy metals.

There is no need to resort to exaggerated claims about species loss to realize that the decline of global biodiversity has been proceeding at rates that, on geological time scales, may already amount to the Earth's sixth mass extinction wave (Barnosky et al. 2011). I have calculated that during the 20th century the mass of wild mammals was halved (and the mass of elephants was reduced by 90%), while the mass of domesticated animals more than tripled and the global mass of humanity more than quadrupled (Smil 2013a). People and their animals have been steadily marginalizing all wild species. And Darimont et al. (2015), after analyzing a database of 2,125 exploited wild animal populations, found that humans take up to 14 times as much adult zoomass (that is the reproductive capital of animal species) as do other predators, functioning as an unsustainable "super predator." Some insects are also in retreat: most importantly, some wild and managed pollinators (bees) have been in decline in several regions, a shift with potentially enormous consequences for many crops (Potts et al. 2016).

Losses of high-quality arable land in alluvial regions and destruction of natural coastlands—both done in order to accommodate growing cities, factories, and transportation links—do not make urgent headlines but their extent clearly imperils our capacity to feed ourselves. China now has less arable land per capita than Bangladesh and yet its population is too large to be ever fed by imports. There is not enough grain on the global market to satisfy China's annual need for rice, wheat, and corn even if China were the only importer: in 2017–2018 worldwide trade in milled rice, wheat, and corn was about 380 Mt while China's annual grain harvest is now around 570 Mt (FAO 2018; USDA 2017b). The expanding human footprint has greatly reduced areas of contiguous wilderness, with the largest remaining intact forests concentrated overwhelmingly in just three countries, Russia, Canada, and Brazil (Potapov et al. 2008).

All of these concerns, some going back many generations, have been recently both intensified and overshadowed by the worries about the impact of anthropogenic warming, an environmental change with truly global effects. Worldwide emissions from the combustion of fossil fuels (and, a minor addition, from the production of cement) have been reconstructed starting with just 3 Mt C in the middle of the 17th century; 100 Mt C was reached by 1863 and the first billion by 1927; 50 years later the total surpassed 5 Gt C and in 2015 it was just a bit below 10 Gt C, or more than 36 Gt CO_2 (Marland et al. 2017). The trajectory fits very closely a symmetric logistic curve with the inflection point in 2010 and yielding values of

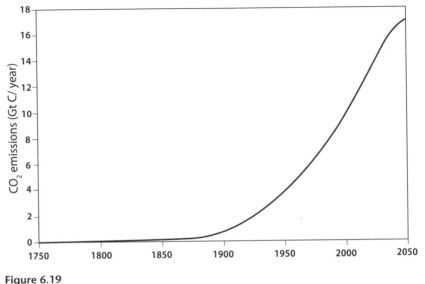

Figure 6.19
Global CO_2 emissions, 1750–2050. Data from Marland et al. (2017).

about 17 Gt C in 2050 (figure 6.19). US post-1800 emissions show some significant temporary departures from a logistic trend but they reached their inflection point in 1967 and it appears most likely that they will not rise significantly above the recent level.

The logistic trend indicating slightly rising global CO_2 emissions is in contrast with the worldwide effort to reduce CO_2 emissions in order, as the 2015 Paris Agreement called for, to keep average global warming to no more than 2°C above the preindustrial level (UNFCCC 2015). Indeed, US energy-related emissions have already seen some declines and global emissions barely changed between 2014 and 2016—but resumed their growth in 2017 and 2018 (IEA 2018). The long-term outlook is unclear; after all, a key conclusion of the Paris meeting was that "the estimated aggregate greenhouse gas emission levels…resulting from the intended nationally determined contributions do not fall within least-cost 2°C scenarios but rather lead to a projected level of 55 Gt in 2030" (UNFCCC 2015, 3). As a result, 2030 emissions would be more than 50% above the 2015 level and higher (at almost exactly 15 Gt C) than the logistic forecast for 2050!

Many of these concerns led to a renewed call (the first one was issued in 1992) to curtail environmental destruction (Ripple et al. 2017). The appeal cited increases in population, ruminant livestock numbers, CO_2 emissions, and tropospheric temperature, and declines in freshwater resources, in marine catches, in forested areas, and in the abundance of vertebrate species as the key trends that pose a growing risk to sustaining biospheric conditions compatible with the long-term survival of humanity In contrast, Nielsen (2018, 1) assures us that "anthropogenic signatures are characterised by the Great Deceleration in the second half of the 20th century. The second half of the 20th century does not mark the beginning of the Anthropocene but most likely the beginning of the end of the strong anthropogenic impacts, maybe even the beginning of a transition to a sustainable future."

This is, of course, both expected (as all high growth rates must eventually moderate) and not at all reassuring as far as the state of the biosphere is concerned. To use a key example, growth of global primary energy consumption has been decelerating since 1950, but between 1900 and 1950 (when the growth rate was hyperbolic) annual use of all energy grew 2.3 times while during the century's second half the decelerated growth increased the annual energy use nearly four-fold. Growth rates are lower than two generations ago but absolute annual use of energy (or materials, food, or water) is considerably higher, a combination that does not reduce the burdens imposed on the biosphere.

At the same time, there are no simple, single-value thresholds that would indicate crossing the lines from worrisome but acceptable levels of deterioration of the biosphere to the realm of catastrophic outcomes. But our understanding of the dynamic links between the state of the biosphere and the fortunes of our civilization makes it clear that all of the trends that have been moving in undesirable directions will have to be, sooner rather than later, curtailed if not reversed. Good life within planetary boundaries is possible even if the global population continues to grow—but not without fundamentally restructured provisioning systems, a shift that would entail substantial challenge to current economic strategies (O'Neill et al. 2018).

There is no possibility of reconciling the preservation of a well-functioning biosphere with the standard economic mantra that is akin to positing a *perpetuum mobile* machine as it does not conceive any problems of sustainability in relation to resources or excessive stress on the environment. Most economists are either unaware or dismissive of the advances that took place in our understanding of the synergistic functioning of civilization and the biosphere—and yet they maintain a monopoly on supplying their physically impossible narratives of continuing growth that guide decisions made by national governments and companies.

And, as if this economic growth *perpetuum mobile* were not enough, those who believe in imminent singularity make an even more improbable claim as they envisage acceleration of perpetual growth based on electronics. A small minority of economists, and many historians, environmentalists, and students of complex systems disagree: they recognize the obvious, the impossibility of infinite growth on a finite planet, but the steps we have taken so far have been insignificant and largely ineffective compared to the ubiquity and the scale of the required temporary remedies and eventual long-lasting solutions.

Coda

Natural growth taking place on the Earth is always limited. The universe may be expanding—and may be doing so (or not) at an accelerated rate (Nielsen et al. 2016)—but the planet has finite amounts of elements, it receives and processes a finite amount of energy, and it can support only a finite amount of anthropogenic intervention. The old ocean crust is subducted in deep trenches into the mantle in order to make space for the new crust created by magmatic upwelling at spreading ridges. Orogenic (mountain-forming) uplift is limited by tectonic forces and kept in check by erosion. Organisms differ in their rate of growth and they follow different trajectories from their origin to their death: some species follow confined exponential curves, the growth of others fits various S-curves, from symmetrical logistic to more complex functions. The growth of most organisms culminates in mature masses and dimensions: indeterminate growth ended by an organism's demise is much less common.

Maturity plateaus of organic growth range from minutes to days for microbes and marine plankton, and from months for annual plants to decades, centuries, even several thousand years for long-lived trees. Growth of heterotrophs is generally more restricted, with humans outliving all but a few animal species. And while some animals, and many large trees, continue to grow after they reach maturity, their lives end due to predation, infestation, or environmental hazards. Similarly, entire ecosystems gradually evolve the greatest species complexity and the highest photosynthetic productivity to reach their climax status, which may be maintained for extended periods of time (10^3 to 10^6 years) before it is destroyed or transformed by climate change (resulting in droughts, fires, or floods), geotectonic upheavals (continental uplift, megavolcanic eruptions, massive earthquakes, tsunami), or impacts of asteroids.

There is no unlimited growth of individual organisms and, *in extenso*, of all supra-organismic assemblies that range from spatially restricted plant and animal communities (a meadow, a pond) to biomes (boreal forest, tropical rain forest, savanna) covering large parts of continents. And the same confined trajectories (often following near-perfect logistic curves) have marked the growth of inanimate artifacts, be they simple tools or complex machines, energy converters, or cities. But the human population seemed to defy this expected pattern: for generations its growth was hyperbolic—but this phase had to end and since the late 1960s a new S-curve has been forming.

In contrast, modern civilization has been engaged in a range of activities, and it has institutionalized an array of behaviors, that are driven by the notion of continued growth, be it of specific technical performances, average per capita incomes, or the entire global economy. Growth of individual devices or systems follows confined trajectories but we are assured that there is no need to worry because perpetual streams of innovations initiate new ascents and keep the escalator rising. A disproportionate share of people in charge of national policies are economists, lawyers, and techno-optimists who do not doubt this narrative and who rarely think about the biosphere's indispensability for the survival of human societies. Not surprisingly, no government has ever made policies with the biosphere in mind. No government has advocated moderate, subdued economic growth as its priority, even in the world's most affluent countries no major political party has been serious about re-considering the pace of economic growth.

Given these realities, how strong and how persuasive are the constituencies clamoring to see the moderation, if not the end, of growth, that is, at least, maintenance of unmistakable performance plateaus? The recent ubiquity of sustainability mantras is not the same thing: sustainability remains so poorly defined (what are its spatial and temporal scales?) that in too many specific cases we could not be sure if we have already reached it or if it will remain elusive. But what if today's best-defined stable plateaus are utterly inadequate, what if maintaining many (perhaps most) outputs at today's level may be quite insufficient to make human existence sustainable for at least as long as we have been around as civilized societies, that is on the order of thousands of years? How can we be sure that the techno-optimistic escalator will never stop ascending?

How many people are taking seriously an even more unthinkable goal, one that aims not only at setting limits but having deliberately declining levels and performances (or, in inelegant and inaccurate newspeak, "negative growth" or "degrowth") as its widely accepted and broadly pursued way of regress. This noun alone illuminates our predicament: using regress as a qualifier of civilizational achievement, after a long-lasting addiction to progress, seems unreal. This creates an irreconcilable conflict or, more accurately, a challenge for which we have yet to find an effective solution (assuming that one exists).

Continuous material growth, based on ever greater extraction of the Earth's inorganic and organic resources and on increased degradation of the biosphere's finite stocks and services, is impossible. Dematerialization—doing more with less—cannot remove this constraint. So far, it has been only a relative phenomenon: we are using less steel or less energy per unit of final product or per desired performance, but as the global population has grown from 1 billion in the first decade of the 19th century to 7.5 billion in 2018, and as rising standards of living have elevated average demand, the aggregate claim on the Earth's materials and on the biosphere's resources has grown alongside many phenomena of relative dematerialization (Smil 2013a). Recognition of these realities leads to decidedly non-Kurzweilian conclusions, although forecasting the timing and the specifics of any possible protracted global economic stagnation, uncontrollable social decline, or a truly catastrophic change remains elusive and counterproductive.

The outlook would be very different if our concerns were limited to just a few kinds of environmental degradation that could be readily managed by technical fixes, that is by measures akin to our post-1950 successes in treating urban wastewater, preventing emissions of particulates and sulfur dioxide from large stationary sources and, perhaps most notably, arresting the further rise of stratospheric ozone levels by outlawing chlorofluorocarbons (The Ozone Hole 2018). Unfortunately, concerns are legion, and after decades of efforts we have yet to arrest the growth of all kinds of the most widespread environmental degradations, the first necessary step before reversing such undesirable trends.

That is as true of the depletion of deep aquifers (whose water is withdrawn for mostly highly inefficient crop irrigation) and deforestation in wet tropics (the harbors of the biosphere's greatest species diversity) as it is of the globally excessive soil erosion that is, slowly but steadily, diminishing the productive capacity of crop fields; as true of the continuing losses of biodiversity (be it due to deforestation, spreading urbanization, or demand for traditional medicines) as it is of a multifaceted assault on the oceans that ranges from overfishing at the top of the marine food chain to the now ubiquitous presence of microplastics in seawater (GESAMP 2015).

Concerns about rapid global warming—now generally seen as an average tropospheric temperature increase of more than 2°C above the pre-1850 mean—are only the latest, and the most prominent, expression of that irreconcilable conflict between the quest for continuous economic growth and the biosphere's limited capacity to deal with its environmental burdens (IPCC 2014). And they are also an excellent demonstration of the limits of readily adopted and affordable technical fixes: even if the world's nations fulfilled all of their targets for reducing greenhouse gas emissions to which they agreed in Paris in late 2015, the average increase of tropospheric temperature would still rise well above 2°C by 2050 (UNFCCC 2015)—and the latest IPCC goal is to keep the anthropogenic rise to no more than 1.5°C (IPCC 2018), the target that is almost certainly beyond our technical and economic means. But global warming is not the only overarching concern. We do not know how much more of natural land cover and what share of biodiversity we can lose with relative impunity, and if the global population were to survive in relatively large numbers for much longer than its recorded period (that is, longer than 5,000 years), it would almost certainly run into some material restrictions. And we may not succeed in this unprecedented effort to reconcile planetary constraints with human aspirations (or should it be delusions?). "Perhaps the destiny of man is to have a short, but fiery, exciting and extravagant life rather than a long, uneventful and vegetative existence. Let other species—the amoebas, for example—which have no spiritual ambitions inherit an earth still bathed in plenty of sunshine" (Georgescu-Roegen 1975, 379). But we must try, and for that we need new visions. "Where there is no vision, the people perish" (Proverbs 29:18) is an ancient statement that is as hyperbolic as it is insightful. A later admonition puts the need for action in moral terms: "So whoever knows the right thing to do and fails to do it, for him it is sin" (James 4:17).

We may not know every detail of doing the right thing, but the direction of the required actions is clear: to ensure the habitability of the biosphere while maintaining human dignity. And sin can be easily left out and doing the right thing could be motivated by the quest (moral imperative?) to preserve our species while inflicting the least possible damage on other organisms with whom we share the biosphere. Given the scope of our challenges, adjectives such as radical and bold, to describe the needed vision, and such terms as fundamental shifts and unprecedented adjustments, to characterize the many required changes of policies and everyday practices, are self-evident. This book contains many growth trajectories that may be useful indicators of unfolding processes but, as I stressed repeatedly, they should never be mistaken for specific forecasts. Forecasting the state of modern civilization for generations or centuries to come remains an impossible exercise. Even relatively near-term forecasts are bound to fail: no matter how assiduously assembled, a 2018 construct of the world as it might be in

2100 would be, almost certainly, even more misleading than the construct of the year 2018 made in 1936.

But we are on a much firmer ground when concluding that the past practices—pursuit of the highest possible economic growth rates, extending the culture of excessive consumption to additional billions of people, and treating the biosphere as a mere assembly of goods and services to be exploited (and used as a dumping ground) with impunity—must change in radical ways. There is nothing new in this perception. This is what Horace wrote two millennia ago in his *Satires*: "Est modus in rebus, sunt certi denique fines quos ultra citraque nequit consistere rectum" (There is a mean in things, there are, lastly certain limits on either side of which right cannot be found). But two millennia later this is not merely a moral exhortation.

The long-term survival of our civilization cannot be assured without setting such limits on the planetary scale. I believe that a fundamental departure from the long-established pattern of maximizing growth and promoting material consumption cannot be delayed by another century and that before 2100 modern civilization will have to make major steps toward ensuring the long-term habitability of its biosphere.

Abbreviations

A	(ampere)
AC	(alternating current)
bhp	(break horsepower)
BMI	(body mass index)
C_3	(molecule with three carbon atoms)
C_4	(molecule with four carbon atoms)
cd	(candela)
CD	(compact disc)
CIMMYT	(International Maize and Wheat Improvement Center)
cm	(centimeter)
CO_2	(carbon dioxide)
DC	(direct current)
dwt	(deadweight ton)
EB	(exabyte)
EJ	(exajoule)
ETOPS	(Extended-range Twin-engine Operational Performance Standards)
EU	(European Union)
FAO	(Food and Agriculture Organization)
FBL	(feedback loop)
flops	(floating point operations per second)
g	(gram)
GB	(gigabyte)
GDP	(gross domestic product)
GE	(General Electric)
Gha	(gigahectare)
GHz	(gigahertz)
GJ	(gigajoule)
Gm	(gigameter)

GPP	(gross primary productivity)
GPS	(global positioning system)
Gt	(gigatonne)
Gt C	(gigatonne of carbon)
Gt C/year	(gigatonne of carbon per year)
Gt CO₂	(gigatonne of carbon dioxide)
GW	(gigawatt)
GWₑ	(gigawatt electric)
GWₚ	(gigawatt peak)
h	(hour)
ha	(hectare)
HDI	(Human Development Index)
hp	(horsepower)
Hz	(hertz)
IAEA	(International Atomic Energy Agency)
IDI	(Inclusive Development Index)
IRRI	(International Rice Research Institute)
ISA	(impervious surface area)
J	(joule)
K	(kelvin)
kB	(kilobyte)
kcal	(kilocalorie)
kg	(kilogram)
kHz	(kilohertz)
kJ	(kilojoules)
km	(kilometer)
kN	(kilonewton)
kPa	(kilopascal)
kW	(kilowatt)
kWh	(kilowatt hour)
L	(liter)
lbs	(pounds)
lbs/in²	(pounds per square inch)
LED	(light emitting diode)
lm/W	(lumens per watt)
LNG	(liquified natural gas)
LP	(long-playing record)
m	(meter)
μm	(micrometer)
MB	(megabyte)

Mha	(megahectare)
Mhz	(megahertz)
MIPS	(million instructions per second)
MJ	(megajoule)
mL	(milliliter)
mm	(millimeter)
Mm^2	(million square meters)
Mm^3	(million cubic meters)
mol	(mole)
MPa	(megapascal)
mph	(miles per hour)
MSOPS	(million standardized operations per second)
Mt	(million tonnes)
Mt C	(million tonnes of carbon)
MVA	(megavolt amperes)
MW	(megawatt)
MW_e	(megawatt electric)
MW_p	(megawatt peak)
N	(nitrogen)
NEP	(net ecosystem productivity)
NH_3	(ammonia)
NPP	(net primary productivity)
O_2	(oxygen)
OECD	(Organisation for Economic Co-operation and Development)
OLED	(organic light emitting diode)
OPEC	(Organization of the Petroleum Exporting Countries)
ops	(operations per second)
PB	(petabyte)
PDCAAS	(protein digestibility corrected amino acid score)
pH	(measure of acidity)
pkm	(passenger-kilometers)
ppm	(parts per million)
PPP	(purchasing power parity)
PV	(photovoltaic)
P&W	(Pratt & Whitney)
PWh	(petawatthour)
R_A	(autotrophic respiration)
R_H	(heterotrophic respiration)
RAM	(random access memory)
rpm	(revolutions per minute)

s	(second)
SAD	(species-abundance distribution)
Si	(silicon)
SI	(International System of Units)
SUV	(sport-utility vehicle)
t	(tonne, metric ton)
t C/ha	(tonne of carbon per hectare)
TB	(terabyte)
TFP	(total factor productivity)
TFR	(total fertility rate)
TJ	(terajoule)
T/W	(thrust-to-weight ratio)
TWh	(terawatthour)
TWh/year	(terawatthour per year)
UK	(United Kingdom)
UN	(United Nations)
US	(United States)
V	(volt)
VPD	(vapor pressure deficit)
W	(watt)
W/m²	(watts per square meter)
Wh	(watthour)
WH/kg	(watthours per kilogram)
WHO	(World Health Organization)
WWI	(First World War)
WWII	(Second World War)
ZB	(zettabyte)

Scientific Units and Their Multiples and Submultiples

Basic SI units

Quantity	Name	Symbol
Length	meter	m
Mass	kilogram	kg
Time	second	s
Electric current	ampere	A
Temperature	kelvin	K
Amount of substance	mole	mol
Luminous intensity	candela	cd

Other units used in the text

Quantity	Name	Symbol
Area	hectare	ha
	square meter	m^2
Electric potential	volt	V
Energy	joule	J
Force	newton	N
Mass	gram	g
	tonne	t
Power	watt	W
Pressure	pascal	Pa
Temperature	degree Celsius	$^{\circ}C$
Volume	cubic meter	m^3

Multiples used in the International System of Units

Prefix	Abbreviation	Scientific notation
deka	da	10^1
hecto	h	10^2
kilo	k	10^3
mega	M	10^6
giga	G	10^9
tera	T	10^{12}
peta	P	10^{15}
exa	E	10^{18}
zetta	Z	10^{21}
yotta	Y	10^{24}

Submultiples used in the International System of Units

Prefix	Abbreviation	Scientific notation
deci	d	10^{-1}
centi	c	10^{-2}
milli	m	10^{-3}
micro	μ	10^{-6}
nano	n	10^{-9}
pico	p	10^{-12}
femto	f	10^{-15}
atto	a	10^{-18}
zepto	z	10^{-21}
yocto	y	10^{-24}

References

Aarestrup, F. 2012. Get pigs off antibiotics. *Nature* 486:465–466.

ABB. 2016. ABB wins orders of over $300 million for world's first 1,100 kV UHVDC power link in China. http://www.abb.ca/cawp/seitp202/f0f2535bc7672244c1257ff5 0025264b.aspx.

Abraham, T. 2005. *Twenty-First Century Plague: The Story of SARS.* Baltimore, MD: Johns Hopkins University Press.

Abramovitz, M. 1956. Resource and output trends in the United States. *American Economic Review Papers and Proceedings* 46:5–23.

ABS (American Bureau of Shipping). 2014. Guide for propulsion systems for LNG carriers. https://preview.eagle.org/eagleExternalPortalWEB/ShowProperty/BEA%20 Repository/Rules&Guides/Current/112_PropulsionSystemsforLNGCarriers/Pub112 _LNG_Propulsion_GuideDec05.

Acemoglu, D., et al. 2002. Reversal of fortune: Geography and institutions in the making of the modern world income distribution. *Quarterly Journal of Economics* 117:1231–1294.

Adame, P., et al. 2014. Diameter growth performance of tree functional groups in Puerto Rican secondary tropical forests. *Forest Systems* 23:52–63.

Adamic, L. A. 2000. Zipf, power-laws, and Pareto—a ranking tutorial. http://www .hpl.hp.com/research/idl/papers/ranking/ranking.html.

Adams, H. [1904] 1919. A law of acceleration. In H. Adams, *The Education of Henry Adams.* New York: Houghton Mifflin, ch. 34.

Adams, H. [1909] 1920. The rule of phase applied to history. In H. Adams and B. Adams, *The Degradation of the Democratic Dogma.* New York: Macmillan, pp. 267–311.

Adams, J. 1993. *Ocean Steamers: A History of Ocean-Going Passenger Steamships 1820–1970.* London: New Cavendish Books.

Adams, R., et al. 2016. *Are CEOs Born Leaders? Lessons from Traits of a Million Individuals.* Helsinki: Aalto School of Business.

AHDB (Agriculture and Horticulture Development Board). 2015. ADAS final 2015 harvest summary. https://cereals.ahdb.org.uk/markets/market-news/2015/october /09/adas-final-harvest-summary-report-2015.aspx.

Aiello, L. C., and P. Wheeler. 1995. The expensive-tissue hypothesis. *Current Anthropology* 36:199–221.

Airbus. 2014. EASA certifies A350 XWB for up to 370-minute ETOPS. http://www .airbus.com/newsevents/news-events-single/detail/easa-certifies-a350-xwb-for-up-to -370-minute-etops/.

Alcock, S. E., et al., eds. 2001. *Empires, Perspectives from Archaeology and History.* Cambridge: Cambridge University Press.

Alessio, D. 2013. '… territorial acquisitions are among the landmarks of our history': The buying and leasing of imperial territory. *Global Discourse* 3:74–96.

Alexander, B. T. 2000. *The U.S. Homebuilding Industry: A Half-Century of Building the American Dream.* Cambridge, MA: Harvard University Press.

Allen, R. 1978. *Pictorial History of KLM.* Worthington: Littlehampton Book Services.

Allen, R. C. 2005. English and Welsh agriculture, 1300–1850: Output, inputs, and income. https://www.nuffield.ox.ac.uk/users/Allen/unpublished/AllenEandW.pdf.

Allen, R. C. 2009. *The British Industrial Revolution in Global Perspective.* Cambridge: Cambridge University Press.

Allianz. 2010. *The Sixth Kondratieff—Long Waves of Prosperity.* Frankfurt am Main: Allianz. https://www.allianz.com/content/dam/onemarketing/azcom/Allianz_com /migration/media/press/document/other/kondratieff_en.pdf.

Allianz. 2015. *The Megacity State: The World's Biggest Cities Shaping Our Future.* Munich: Allianz.

Alroy, J. 1998. Cope's rule and the dynamics of body mass evolution in North American mammals. *Science* 280:731–734.

Alstom. 2013. Alstom commissions world's most powerful hydroelectric units at Xiangjiaba hydro power plant, in China. http://www.alstom.com/press-centre/2013 /7/alstom-commissions-worlds-most-powerful-hydroelectric-units-at-xiangjiaba -hydro-power-plant-in-china/.

Alvaredo, F., et al. 2017. *Global Inequality Dynamics: New Findings from WID.world.* Cambridge, MA: National Bureau of Economic Research.

Ambrose, S. H. 1998. Late Pleistocene human population bottlenecks: Volcanic winter, and the differentiation of modern humans. *Journal of Human Evolution* 34:623–651.

Ambrose, S. H. 2003. Did the super-eruption of Toba cause a human population bottleneck? Reply to Gathorne-Hardy and Harcourt-Smith. *Journal of Human Evolution* 45:231–237.

AMSC (American Superconductor Corporation). 2012. SeaTitan™ 10 MW wind turbine. http://www.amsc.com/documents/seatitan-10-mw-wind-turbine-data-sheet/.

Amthor, J. S. 1998. Perspective on the relative insignificance of increasing atmospheric CO2 concentration to crop yield. *Field Crops Research* 58:109–127.

Amthor, J. S., and D. D. Baldocchi. 2001. Terrestrial higher plant respiration and net primary production. In J. Roy et al., eds., *Terrestrial Global Productivity*. San Diego: Academic Press, pp. 33–59.

Anders, S. G., and O. Andersen. 2010. Life cycle assessments of consumer electronics—Are they consistent? *International Journal of Life Cycle Assessment* 15:827–836.

Anderson, B. D. 2003. *The Physics of Sailing Explained*. Dobbs Ferry, NY: Sheridan House.

Andrews, A., and M. Pascoe. 2008. *Clifton Suspension Bridge*. Bristol: Broadcast Books.

Anglaret, P. 2013. Nuclear power plants: The Turbine Island. http://www.sfen.org/sites/default/files/public/atoms/files/2013-philippe_anglaret_alstom_the_turbine_island.pdf.

Angus, J. 2011. The remarkable improvements in Australian mixed farming. http://www.ioa.uwa.edu.au/__data/assets/pdf_file/0006/1519566/John-Angus-Presentation.pdf.

Annamalai, K., and C. Silva. 2012. Entropy stress and scaling of vital organs over life span based on allometric laws. *Entropy* 14:2550–2577.

Antão, L. H., et al. 2017. Prevalence of multimodal species abundance distributions is linked to spatial and taxonomic breadth. *Global Ecology and Biogeography* 26:203–215.

Anthony, D. W. 2007. *The Horse, the Wheel, and Language: How Bronze-Age Riders from the Eurasian Steppes Shaped the Modern World*. Princeton, NJ: Princeton University Press.

Antràs, P., et al. 2017. Globalization, inequality and welfare. *Journal of International Economics* 108:387–412.

AP (Associated Press). 2006. U.S. admits military damaged Babylon ruins. http://www.nbcnews.com/id/12316998/ns/world_news-mideast_n_africa/t/us-admits-military-damaged-babylon-ruins/#.Whsk7zGWx9A.

AquaBounty. 2017. Our salmon. http://aquabounty.com/our-salmon/.

Arbesman, S. 2011. The life-spans of empires. *Historical Methods* 44:127–129.

Arms Control Association. 2017. Nuclear weapons: Who has what at a glance. https://www.armscontrol.org/factsheets/Nuclearweaponswhohaswhat.

Armstrong, R. 1969. *The Merchantmen*. London: Ernest Benn.

Arnold, D. 2002. Fitting a logistic curve to data. https://www.math.hmc.edu/~depillis/PCMI2005WEBSITE/logistic_REDWOODS.pdf.

Arrow, K. 1962. Economic Welfare and the Allocation of Resources for Invention. In: *The Rate and Direction of Inventive Activity: Economic and Social Factors*, Princeton University Press, pp. 609–626.

Asao, S., et al. 2015. Variation in foliar respiration and wood CO_2 efflux rates among species and canopy layers in a wet tropical forest. *Tree Physiology* 35:148–159.

ASCE (American Society of Civil Engineers). 2017. *2017 Report Card for America's Infrastructure*. https://www.infrastructurereportcard.org/wp-content/uploads/2016/10/2017-Infrastructure-Report-Card.pdf.

Ashby, T. 1935. *The Aqueducts of Ancient Rome*. Oxford: Oxford University Press.

ASME (American Society of Mechanical Engineers). 1980. The Pioneer Zephyr. https://www.asme.org/wwwasmeorg/media/ResourceFiles/AboutASME/Who%20We%20Are/Engineering%20History/Landmarks/58-Pioneer-Zephyr-1934.pdf.

ASME. 1988. *The World's First Industrial Gas Turbine Set at Neuchâtel (1939)*. New York: ASME. http://www.asme.org/history/brochures/h135.pdf.

ASME. 2017. Philo 6 steam-electric generating unit. https://www.asme.org/about-asme/who-we-are/engineering-history/landmarks/228-philo-6-steam-electric-generating-unit.

Asseng, S., et al. 2014. Rising temperatures reduce global wheat production. *Nature Climate Change* 5:143–147.

Assmann, E. 1970. *The Principles of Forest Yield Study: Studies in the Organic Production, Structure, Increment and Yield of Forest Stands*. Oxford: Pergamon Press.

ATAG (Air Transport Action Group). 2010. *Beginner's Guide to Aviation Efficiency*. Geneva: ATAG.

Athow, J. 2016. Economics revision. *The Economist*, May 24, 2016, p. 12. https://www.economist.com/letters/2016/05/14/letters-to-the-editor.

Atlas Historique de Paris. 2016. *La croissance de Paris*. http://paris-atlas-historique.fr/8.html.

Auerbach, F. 1913. Das Gesetz der Bevölkerungskonzentration. *Petermanns Geographische Mitteilungen* 59:73–76.

Ausloos M., and R. Cerqueti. 2016. A universal rank-size law. *PLoS ONE* 11(11): e0166011. doi:10.1371/journal.pone.0166011.

Auten, G., and D. Splinter. 2018. Income inequality in the United States: Using tax data to measure long-term trends. http://davidsplinter.com/AutenSplinter-Tax_Data_and_Inequality.pdf.

Aviagen. 2014. *Ross Broiler Management Handbook.* http://en.aviagen.com/assets/Tech_Center/Ross_Broiler/Ross-Broiler-Handbook-2014i-EN.pdf.

Axelsen, J. B., et al. 2014. Multiannual forecasting of seasonal influenza dynamics reveals climatic and evolutionary drivers. *Proceedings of the National Academy of Sciences of the USA* 111:9538–9542.

Ayres, R. 2016. *Energy, Complexity and Wealth Maximization.* Cham: Springer.

Ayres, R. 2017. Gaps in mainstream economics: Energy, growth, and sustainability. In S. Shmelev, ed., *Green Economy Reader: Lectures in Ecological Economics and Sustainability.* Berlin: Springer, pp. 39–54.

Ayres, R., and V. Voudouris. 2014. The economic growth enigma: Capital, labour and useful energy? *Energy Policy* 64:16–28.

Ayres, R., and B. Warr. 2009. *The Economic Growth Engine: How Energy and Work Drive Material Prosperity.* Cheltenham: Edward Elgar.

Babcock & Wilcox. 2017. 150 years of industry firsts. https://www.babcock.com/en/about/history.

Bacaër, N. 2011. *A Short History of Mathematical Population Dynamics.* London: Springer.

Bagnall, R. S., and B. W. Frier. 1994. *The Demography of Roman Egypt.* Cambridge: Cambridge University Press.

Bai, J., et al. 2014. *Does Economic Growth Reduce Corruption? Theory and Evidence from Vietnam.* Boston: National Bureau of Economic Research.

Bain, R. 2015. The 7 graphs that tell you everything you need to know about lighting. http://luxreview.com/article/2015/07/7-graphs-that-tell-you-everything-you-need-to-know-about-lighting.

Bak, P. 1996. *How Nature Works: The Science of Self-Organized Criticality.* New York: Copernicus.

Baldridge, E., et al. 2016. An extensive comparison of species-abundance distribution models. *PeerJ* 4: e2823. doi.10.7717/peerj.2823.

Baldwin, G. C. 1977. *Pyramids of the New World.* New York: G. P. Putnam's Sons.

Ball, P. 2014. Infinitely malleable materials. *IEEE Spectrum* (June):40–44.

Ballal, D., and J. Zelina. 2003. Progress in aeroengine technology (1939–2003). *Journal of Aircraft* 41:43–50.

Banavar, J. R., et al. 2010. A general basis for quarter-power scaling in animals. *Proceedings of the National Academy of Sciences of the USA* 107:15816–15820.

Banks, R. B. 1994. *Growth and Diffusion Phenomena: Mathematical Frameworks and Applications*. Berlin: Springer.

Baranyi, J. 2010. *Modelling and Parameter Estimation of Bacterial Growth with Distributed Lag Time*. Szeged, Hungary: University of Szeged.

Barfield, T. J. 2001. The shadow empires: Imperial state formation along the Chinese-Nomad frontier. In S. E. Alcock et al., eds., *Empires: Perspectives from Archaeology and History*, Cambridge: Cambridge University Press, pp. 10–41.

Barker, G. 2009. *The Agricultural Revolution in Prehistory: Why Did Foragers Become Farmers?* Oxford: Oxford University Press.

Barkey, K. 2008. *Empire of Difference: The Ottomans in Comparative Perspective*. Cambridge: Cambridge University Press.

Barnosky, A. D., et al. 2011. Has the Earth's sixth mass extinction already arrived? *Nature* 471:51–57.

Barro, R. J. 2013. Health and economic growth. *Annals of Economics and Finance* 14-2(A):305–342.

Barrow, J. D. 2012. How Usain Bolt can run faster—effortlessly. *Significance* 9:9–12.

Barry, J. M. 2005. *The Great Influenza*. New York: Penguin.

Bashford, A. 2014. *Global Population: History, Geopolitics, and Life on Earth*. New York: Columbia University Press.

Bassham, J. A., and M. Calvin. 1957. *The Path of Carbon in Photosynthesis*. Englewood Cliffs, NJ: Prentice Hall.

Bassino, J. 2006. The growth of agricultural output, and food supply in Meiji Japan: Economic miracle or statistical artifact? *Economic Development and Cultural Change* 54:503–521.

Baten, J., and M. Blum. 2012. Growing tall but unequal: New findings and new background evidence on anthropometric welfare in 156 countries, 1810–1989. *Economic History of Developing Regions* 27:sup1, S66–S85. http://dx.doi.org/10.1080/20780389.2012.657489.

Baten, J., and M. Blum 2014. Human height since 1820. In J. L. van Zanden et al., eds., *How Was Life? Global Well-Being since 1820*, Paris: OECD, pp. 117–137.

Bates, K. T., et al. 2015. Downsizing a giant: Re-evaluating *Dreadnoughtus* body mass. *Biology Letters* 11:20150215.

Batt, R. A. 1980. *Influences on Animal Growth and Development*. London: Edward Arnold.

Batty, M. 2006. Rank clocks. *Nature* 444:592–596.

Batty, M. 2013. An outline of complexity theory. http://www.spatialcomplexity.info /files/2013/02/Complexity-Lecture-1.pdf.

Bazzaz, F., and W. Sombroek, eds. 1996. *Global Climate Change and Agricultural Production*. Chichester: Wiley.

BCRC (Beef Cattle Research Council). 2016. Optimizing feedlot feed efficiency. http://www.beefresearch.ca/research-topic.cfm/optimizing-feedlot-feed-efficiency-8.

Beard, A. S., and M. J. Blaser. 2001. The ecology of height. *Perspectives in Biology and Medicine* 45:475–498.

Beard, M. 2007. *The Roman Triumph*. Cambridge, MA: Belknap Press.

Beard, M. 2015. *SPQR: A History of Ancient Rome*. New York: Liveright Books.

Beaver, P. 1972. *A History of Tunnels*. Secaucus, NJ: Citadel Press.

Bebar, J. 1999. Wall Street's record century. *CNN Money*, December 31. http://money .cnn.com/1999/12/31/markets/markets_newyork/.

Becker, G. S. 1960. An economic analysis of fertility. In Universities-National Bureau, ed., *Demographic and Economic Change in Developed Countries*. Princeton, NJ: Princeton University Press. pp. 209–240.

Behar, D. M., et al. 2008. The dawn of human matrilineal diversity. *American Journal of Human Genetics* 82: 1130–1140.

Behrens, K., et al. (2014. Productive cities: Sorting, selection, and agglomeration. *Journal of Political Economy* 122:507–553.

Behrman, R. E., and A. S. Butler, eds. 2007. *Preterm Birth: Causes, Consequences, and Prevention*. Washington, DC: National Academy Press.

Belmont Stakes. 2017. Past winners. https://www.belmontstakes.com/history/past -winners/.

Beloch, K.1886. *Die Bevölkerung der griechischen-römischen Welt*. Leipzig: Duncker & Humblot.

Benford, F. 1938. The law of anomalous numbers. *Proceedings of the American Philosophical Society* 78:551–572.

Bengtsson, B., and G. Johansson. 2000. The treatment of growth hormone deficiency in adults. *Journal of Clinical Endocrinology & Metabolism* 85:933–937.

Bennett, M. K. 1935. British wheat yield per acre for seven centuries. *Economic History* 3(10):12–29.

Benson, R. B. J., et al. 2014. Rates of dinosaur body mass evolution indicate 170 million years of sustained ecological innovation on the avian stem lineage. *PLoS Biology* 12(5):e1001853.

Benton, M. J. 1979. Ectothermy and the success of dinosaurs. *Evolution* 33: 983–997.

Bergman, B. 2013. Trichodesmium—a widespread marine cyanobacterium with unusual nitrogen fixation properties. *FEMS Microbiology Reviews* 37:286–302.

Bergmann, O., et al. 2009. Evidence for cardiomyocyte renewal in humans. *Science* 324:98–102.

Bergmann, O., et al. 2015. Dynamics of cell generation and turnover in the human heart. *Cell* 161:1566–1575.

Bergsten, F., et al. 2009. *China's Rise: Challenges and Opportunities*. Washington, DC: Peterson Institute for International Economics.

Berliner Morgenpost. 2015. Where the population of Europe is growing—and where it's declining. https://interaktiv.morgenpost.de/europakarte/#5/47.857/15.688/en.

Bernard, L., et al. 2013. *Time Scales and Mechanisms of Economic Cycles*. Amherst: University of Massachusetts Press.

Berndt, E. R., and N. J. Rappaport. 2001. Price and quality of desktop and mobile personal computers: A quarter-century historical overview. *American Economic Review* 91:268–273.

Berry, P. M., et al. 2015. Historical analysis of the effects of breeding on the height of winter wheat (*Triticum aestivum*) and consequences for lodging. *Euphytica* 203:375–383.

Bertillon, J. 1894. *Essai de statistique comparée du surpeuplement des habitations à Paris et dans les grandes capitales européennes*. Paris: Imprimerie Chaix.

Besselink, I. J. M., et al. 2011. Evaluation of 20000 km driven with a battery electric vehicle. European Electric Vehicle Congress, Brussels, Belgium, October 26–28, 2011.

Bettencourt, L. M. A., and J. Lobo. 2016. Urban scaling in Europe. *Journal of the Royal Society Interface* 13:20160005. doi.org/10.1098/rsif.2016.0005.

Betz, A. 1926. *Wind-Energie und ihre Ausnutzung durch Windmühlen*. Göttingen: Vandenhoeck & Ruprecht.

Bhargava, A., et al. 2001. Modeling the effects of health on economic growth. *Journal of Health Economics* 20:423–440.

Bhatta, B. 2010. *Analysis of Urban Growth and Sprawl from Remote Sensing Data*. Berlin: Springer.

Binoche, B. 2005. *Les équivoques de la civilisation*. Paris: Champ Vallon.

Biraben, J.-N. 2003. The rising numbers of humankind. *Population et Sociétés* 394:1–4.

Birch, C. P. D. 1999. A new generalized logistic sigmoid growth equation compared with the Richards growth equation. *Annals of Botany* 83:713–723.

Bjørnskov, C., and P. Kurrild-Klitgaard. 2014. Economic growth and institutional reform in modern monarchies and republics: A historical cross-country perspective 1820–2000. *Journal of Institutional and Theoretical Economics* 170:453–481.

Blanchard, Y., et al. 2013. The cavity magnetron: Not just a British invention. *IEEE Antennas and Propagation Magazine* 55:244–254.

Blanken, L. J. 2012. *Rational Empires: Institutional Incentives and Imperial Expansion*. Chicago: University of Chicago Press.

Blatchford, R. A., et al. 2012. Contrast in light intensity, rather than day length, influences the behavior and health of broiler chickens. *Poultry Science* 91:1768–1774.

Blaxter, K. 1986. Bioenergetics and growth: The whole and the parts. *Journal of Animal Science* 63(suppl. 2): 1–10.

Bliss, C. I. 1935. The calculation of the dosage mortality curve. *Annals of Applied Biology* 22:134–167.

Blöchl, E., et al. 1997. *Pyrolobus fumarii*, gen. and sp. nov., represents a novel group of archaea, extending the temperature limit for life to 113°C. *Extremophiles* 1:14–21.

Block, L. 2003. *To Harness the Wind: A Short History of the Development of Sails*. Annapolis, MD: Naval Institute Press.

Bloom, D. E., et al. 2000. Population dynamics and economic growth in Asia. *Population and Development Review* 26(suppl.):257–290.

Bloom, D. E., and D. Canning. 2008. *Population Health and Economic Growth*. Washington, DC: World Bank.

BLS (Bureau of Labor Statistics). 2017. Labor productivity growth since the Great Recession. https://www.bls.gov/opub/ted/2017/labor-productivity-growth-since-the -great-recession.htm.

Blue, L., and T. J. Espenshade. 2011. Population momentum across the demographic transition. *Population and Development Review* 37:721–747.

Blum, R. W., and F. Qureshi. 2011. *Morbidity and Mortality among Adolescents and Young Adults in the United States*. https://www.jhsph.edu/research/centers-and -institutes/center-for-adolescent-health/_images/_pre-redesign/az/US%20Fact%20 Sheet_FINAL.pdf.

Blumberg, A. A. 1968. Logistic growth rate functions, *Journal of Theoretical Biology* 21:42–44.

Bocquet-Appel, J. P. 2011. When the world's population took off: The springboard of the Neolithic demographic transition. *Science* 333:560–561.

Bocquet-Appel, J. P., and O. Bar-Yosef. 2008. *The Neolithic Demographic Transition and Its Consequences*. New York: Springer Science and Business Media.

Boden, T., and B. Andres. 2017. Global CO_2 emissions from fossil-fuel burning, cement manufacture, and gas flaring: 1751–2014. http://cdiac.ess-dive.lbl.gov/ftp /ndp030/global.1751_2014.ems.

Boeing. 2013. World class supplier quality. http://787updates.newairplane.com/787 -Suppliers/World-Class-Supplier-Quality.

Bogin, B. 1999. Evolutionary perspective on human growth. *Annual Review of Anthropology* 28:109–153.

Bokma, F. 2004. Evidence against universal metabolic allometry. *Functional Ecology* 18:184–187.

Bokma, F., et al. 2016. Testing for Depéret's rule (body size increase) in mammals using combined extinct and extant data. *Systematic Biology* 65:98–108.

Bonan, G. B. 2008. Forests and climate change: Forcings, feedbacks, and the climate benefits of forests. *Science* 320:1444–1449.

Bongaarts, J. 2006. How long will we live? *Population and Development Review* 32:605–628.

Bongaarts, J., and R. A. Bulatao, eds. 2000. *Beyond Six Billion: Forecasting the World's Population*. Washington, DC: NRC.

Bonneuil, N. 2005. History and dynamics: Marriage or *mésalliance*? *History and Theory* 44:265–270.

Bono, P., and C. Boni. 1996. Water supply of Rome in antiquity and today. *Environmental Geology* 27:126–134.

Bontemps, J.-D., et al. 2012. Shifts in the height-related competitiveness of tree species following recent climate warming and implications for tree community composition: The case of common beech and sessile oak as predominant broadleaved species in Europe. *Oikos* 21:1287–1299.

Boom Technology. 2017. The future is supersonic. https://boomsupersonic.com/.

Boretos, G. P. 2009. The future of the global economy. *Technological Forecasting and Social Change* 76:316–326.

Borlaug, N. 1970. *The Green Revolution, Peace, and Humanity*. Nobel lecture, December 11. https://www.nobelprize.org/prizes/peace/1970/borlaug/lecture/.

Boteler, R., and J. Malinowski. 2015. The impact of the integral horsepower amended rule. http://www.nema.org/Communications/Documents/NEMA-Integral-HP-Rule-Webinar.pdf.

Boukal, D. S., et al. 2014. Life-history implications of the allometric scaling of growth. *Journal of Theoretical Biology* 359:199–207.

Boulding, K. E. 1964. in *The Meaning of the 20th Century: The Great Transition*. New York: Harper & Row.

Boulding, K. 1966. The economics of the coming spaceship Earth. In H. Jarrett, ed., *Environmental Quality in a Growing Economy*, Baltimore, MD: Resources for the Future/Johns Hopkins University Press, pp. 3–14.

Bourgeon, L., et al. 2017. Earliest human presence in North America dated to the last glacial maximum: New radiocarbon dates from Bluefish Caves, Canada. *PLoS ONE* 12(1):e0169486. doi:10.1371/journal.pone.0169486.

Bourneuf, G. 2008. *Workhorse of the Fleet*. Houston: American Bureau of Shipping.

Bowditch, H. P. 1891. The growth of children studied by Galton's percentile grades. In *22nd Annual Report of the State Board of Health of Massachusetts*. Boston: Wright & Potter, pp. 479–525.

Bowersock, G. W. 1983. *Roman Arabia*. Cambridge, MA: Harvard University Press.

Bowman, D. M. J. S., et al. 2013. Detecting trends in tree growth: Not so simple. *Trends in Plant Science* 18:11–17.

Boyd, W. 2003. Making meat: Science, technology, and American poultry production. *Technology and Culture* 42:631–664.

BP (British Petroleum). 2017. *BP Statistical Review of World Energy*. London: BP.

Brandstetter, T. 2005. 'The most wonderful piece of machinery the world can boast of': The water-works at Marly, 1680–1830. *History and Technology* 21:205–220.

Braudel, F. 1982. *On History*. Chicago: University of Chicago Press.

Brazier, M. A. B., ed. 1975. *Growth and Development of the Brain: Nutritional, Genetic, and Environmental Factors*. New York: Raven Press.

Breitburg, D., et al. 2018. Declining oxygen in the global ocean and coastal waters. *Science* 359:eaam7240. doi:10.1126/science.aam7240.

Brendon, P. 2008. *The Decline and Fall of the British Empire, 1781–1997*. New York: Vintage Books.

Brice, G. 1752. *Description de la Ville de Paris, et de tout ce qu'elle contient de plus remarquable*. Paris: Librairies Associés.

Bridgemeister, 2017. Suspension bridges of USA. http://www.bridgemeister.com/list.php?type=country&country=usa.

Brissona, N., et al. 2010. Why are wheat yields stagnating in Europe? A comprehensive data analysis for France. *Field Crops Research* 119:201–212.

Bristow, D., and C. Kennedy 2015. Why do cities grow? Insights from nonequilibrium thermodynamics at the urban and global scales. *Journal of Industrial Ecology* 19:211–221. http://www2.lse.ac.uk/economicHistory/whosWho/profiles/sbroadberry.aspx.

Broadberry, S., et al. 2014. *China, Europe and the Great Divergence: A Study in Historical National Accounting, 980–1850*. London: London School of Economics. http://eh.net/eha/wp-content/uploads/2014/05/Broadberry.pdf.

Broadberry, S., et al. 2015. *British Economic Growth, 1270–1870*. Cambridge: Cambridge University Press.

Brody, S. 1945. *Bioenergetics and Growth*. New York: Reinhold.

Bronson, D. R., and S. T. Gower. 2010. Ecosystem warming does not affect photosynthesis or aboveground autotrophic respiration for boreal black spruce. *Tree Physiology* 30:441–449.

Brown, D. 1998. The Sulzer diesel engine centenary. *Schip & Werf de Zee* (November):57–60.

Brown, J. H., and G. B. West, eds. 2000. *Scaling in Biology*. Oxford: Oxford University Press.

Brown, J. H., et al. 2004. Toward a metabolic theory of ecology. *Ecology* 85:1771–1789.

Bruneau, B. G., ed. 2012. *Heart Development*. Cambridge, MA: Academic Press.

Bruni, L., and P. L. Porta. 2005. *Economics and Happiness*. New York: Oxford University Press.

Brunt, L. 2015. *Weather Shocks and English Wheat Yields, 1690–1871*. Bergen, Norway: Institutt for Samfunnsøkonomi.

Bryc, W. 1995. *The Normal Distribution: Characterizations with Applications*. Berlin: Springer.

BTS (Bureau of Transportation Statistics). 2017. National transportation statistics. https://www.rita.dot.gov/bts/sites/rita.dot.gov.bts/files/publications/national_transportation_statistics/index.html.

Buan, P., and Y. Wang. 1995. Comparison of the modified Weibull and Richards growth function for developing site index equations. *New Forests* 9:147–155.

Buchanan, R. L., et al. 1997. When is simple good enough: A comparison of the Gompertz, Baranyi, and three-phase models for fitting bacterial growth curves. *Food Microbiology* 14:313–326.

Bulliet, R. W. 1975. *The Camel and the Wheel*. Cambridge, MA: Harvard University Press.

Burbank. J., and F. Cooper. 2012. *Empires in World History: Power and the Politics of Difference.* Princeton, NJ: Princeton University Press.

Burchfiel, B. C., and E. Wang, eds. 2008. *Investigations into the Tectonics of the Tibetan Plateau.* Boulder, CO: Geological Society of America.

Burkhart, H. E., and M. Tomé. 2012. *Modeling Forest Trees and Stands.* Berlin: Springer.

Burness, G. P., et al. 2001. Dinosaurs, dragons, and dwarfs: The evolution of maximal body size. *Proceedings of the National Academy of Sciences of the USA* 98:14518–14523.

Burns, B. 2018. Edison's electric pen. http://electricpen.org/ep.htm.

Burstall, A. F. 1968. *Simple Working Models of Historic Machines.* Cambridge, MA: MIT Press.

Busse, M., and J. Königer. 2012. *Trade and Economic Growth: A Re-examination of the Empirical Evidence.* Hamburg: Hamburg Institute of International Economics.

Butler, T. 2014. Plague history: Yersin's discovery of the causative bacterium in 1894 enabled, in the subsequent century, scientific progress in understanding the disease and the development of treatments and vaccines. *Clinical Microbiology and Infection* 20:202–209.

Butt, N., et al. 2014. Relationships between tree growth and weather extremes: Spatial and interspecific comparisons in a temperate broadleaf forest. *Forest Ecology and Management* 334:209–216.

Butzer, K. W. 1976. *Early Hydraulic Civilization in Egypt.* Chicago: University of Chicago Press.

Cactus Feeders. 2017. Feeding a hungry world. http://www.cactusfeeders.com/.

Cailleux, A. 1951. L'homme en surexpansion. *Bulletin de la Société Préhistorique Francaise* 48(1–2):62–70.

Cailliet, G. M., et al. 2006. Age and growth studies of chondrichthyan fishes: The need for consistency in terminology, verification, validation, and growth function fitting. *Environmental Biology of Fishes* 77:211–228.

Calderini, D. F., and G. A. Slafer.1998. Changes in yield and yield stability in wheat during the 20th century. *Field Crops Research* 57:335–347.

Caldwell, J. C. 2006. *Demographic Transition Theory.* Dordrecht: Springer.

Callen, T. 2017. Purchasing power parity: Weights matter. http://www.imf.org/external/pubs/ft/fandd/basics/ppp.htm.

Calnek, E. 2003. Tenochtitlan-Tlatelolco: The natural history of a city. In W. T. Sanders et al., eds., *El Urbanismo en Mesoamérica/Urbanism in Mesoamerica*, vol. 1. Mexico City: Instituto Nacional de Antropología e Historia, pp. 149–202.

Calow, P. 1977. Conversion efficiencies in heterotrophic organisms. *Biological Reviews* 52:385–409.

Calvin, M. 1989. Forty years of photosynthesis and related activities. *Photosynthesis Research* 211:3–16.

Cameron, N., and B. Bogin. 2012. *Human Development and Growth*. Cambridge, MA: Academic Press.

Cames, M., and E. Helmers. 2013. Critical evaluation of the European diesel car boom—global comparison, environmental effects and various national strategies. *Environmental Sciences Europe* 25. https://doi.org/10.1186/2190-4715-25-15.

Campbell, B. M. S. 2000. *English Seigniorial Agriculture, 1250–1450*. Cambridge: Cambridge University Press.

Campbell, B M. S., and M. Overton. 1993. A new perspective on medieval and early modern agriculture: Six centuries of Norfolk farming c.1250–c.1850. *Past and Present* 141:38–105.

Campbell, I. C. 1995. The lateen sail in world history. *Journal of World History* 6: 1–23.

Campbell, J. E., et al. 2017. Large historical growth in global terrestrial gross primary production. *Nature* 544:784–787.

Campion, D. R., et al., eds. 1989. *Animal Growth Regulation*. Berlin: Springer.

Canadell, J. G., et al. 2007. Saturation of the terrestrial carbon sink. In J. G. Canadell et al., eds., *Terrestrial Ecosystems in a Changing World*. Berlin: Springer, pp. 59–78.

Canalys. 2007. 64 million smart phones shipped worldwide in 2006. https://www .canalys.com/static/press_release/2007/r2007024.pdf.

Canning, D., et al. 2015. *Africa's Demographic Transition: Dividend or Disaster?* Washington, DC: World Bank.

Canton, J. 2011. The extreme future of megacities. *Significance* (June):53–56.

CARC (Canadian Agri-Food Research Council). 2003. *Recommended Code of Practice for the Care and Handling of Farm Animals: Chickens, Turkeys and Breeders from Hatchery to Processing Plant*. Ottawa: CARC.

Carder, A. 1995. *Forest Giants of the World: Past and Present*. Markham, ON: Fitzhenry & Whiteside.

Carneiro, R. L., and D. F. Hilse. 1966. On determining the probable rate of population growth during the Neolithic. *American Anthropologist* 68:177–181.

Carroll, C. 1982. National city-size distributions: What do we know after 67 years of research? *Progress in Human Geography* 6:1–43.

Carroll, J. 2007. Most Americans "very satisfied" with their personal lives. http://news.gallup.com/poll/103483/most-americans-very-satisfied-their-personal-lives.aspx.

Carr-Saunders, A. M. 1936. *World Population: Past Growth and Present Trends*. Oxford: Clarendon Press.

Carter, R. A. 2000. *Buffalo Bill Cody: The Man behind the Legend*. New York: John Wiley.

Carter, R. A. 2006. Boat remains and maritime trade in the Persian Gulf during the sixth and fifth millennia BC. *Antiquity* 80:52–63.

Cartier, M. 2002. La population de la Chine au fil des siècles. In I. Attané, ed., *La Chine au seuil de XXIe siècle: Questions de population, questions de société*. Paris: Institut National d'Études Démographiques, pp. 21–31.

Casciato, D. A., et al. 1975. Growth curves of anaerobic bacteria in solid media. *Applied Microbiology* 29:610–614.

Case, A., and C. Paxson. 2008. Stature and status: Height, ability, and labor market outcomes. *Journal of Political Economy* 116:499–532.

Case, T. J. 1978. On the evolution and adaptive significance of postnatal growth rates in the terrestrial vertebrates. *Quarterly Review of Biology* 53:243–282.

Casella, R. M., and I. Wuebber. 1999. *War Emergency Pipeline (Inch Lines)*. HAER No. TX-76. Washington, DC: Historic American Engineering Record. http://lcweb2.loc.gov/master/pnp/habshaer/tx/tx0900/tx0944/data/tx0944data.pdf.

Casson, L. 1951. Speed under sail of ancient ships. *Transactions and Proceedings of the American Philological Association* 82:136–148.

Casson, L. 1971. *Ships and Seamanship in the Ancient World*. Princeton, NJ: Princeton University Press.

Casterline, J. B., and J. Bongaarts. 2017. *Fertility Transition in Sub-Saharan Africa*. New York: Population Council.

Çatalhöyük Research Project. 2017. History of the excavations. http://www.catalhoyuk.com/project/history.

Cavaleri, M. A., et al. 2006. Wood CO_2 efflux in a primary tropical rain forest. *Global Change Biology* 12:2442–2458.

Cavallini, F. 1993. Fitting a logistic curve to data. *College Mathematics Journal* 24:247–253.

CDC (Centers for Disease Control and Prevention). 2010. Growth charts. https://www.cdc.gov/growthcharts/.

CDC. 2011. Life expectancy at birth, at age 65, and at age 75, by sex, race, and Hispanic origin: United States, selected years 1900–2010. https://www.cdc.gov/nchs /data/hus/2011/022.pdf.

CDC. 2012. Body measurements. http://www.cdc.gov/nchs/fastats/body-measure ments.htm.

CDC. 2013. *Antibiotic Resistance Threats in the United States, 2013*. https://www.cdc .gov/drugresistance/pdf/ar-threats-2013-508.pdf.

CDC. 2016. Developmental milestones. http://www.cdc.gov/ncbddd/actearly/mile stones/.

CDC. 2017. Leading causes of death. https://www.cdc.gov/nchs/fastats/leading -causes-of-death.htm.

CEHA (Canadian Environmental Health Atlas). 2016. SARS outbreak in Canada. http://www.ehatlas.ca/sars-severe-acute-respiratory-syndrome/case-study/sars -outbreak-canada.

Chambers, J. Q., et al. 2004. Respiration from a tropical forest ecosystem: Partitioning of sources and low carbon use efficiency. *Ecological Applications* 14: S72-S88.

Chan, M. 2009. World now at the start of 2009 influenza pandemic. http://www.who .int/mediacentre/news/statements/2009/h1n1_pandemic_phase6_20090611/en/.

Chanda, A., et al. 2008. Convergence (and divergence) in the biological standard of living in the USA, 1820–1900. *Cliometrica* 2:19–48.

Chandler, T. 1987. *Four Thousand Years of Urban Growth: An Historical Census*. Lewiston, NY: St. David's University Press.

Chang, S., et al. 2003. Infection with vancomycin-resistant *Staphylococcus aureus* containing the *vanA* resistance gene. *New England Journal of Medicine* 348:1342–1347.

Chaplain, M. A. J., et al. 1999. *On Growth and Form: Spatio-temporal Pattern Formation in Biology*. New York: John Wiley.

Chapuis, A., and E. Gélis. 1928. *Le monde des automates: Étude historique et technique*. Paris: E. Gélis.

Chase-Dunn, C., and T. D. Hall. 1994. The historical evolution of world-systems. *Sociological Inquiry* 64:257–280.

Chase-Dunn, C., et al. 2006. *Upward Sweeps of Empire and City Growth since the Bronze Age*. Riverside, CA: Institute for Research on World-Systems.

Chauvin, J. P., et al. 2017. What is different about urbanization in rich and poor countries? Cities in Brazil, China, India and the United States. *Journal of Urban Economics* 98:17–49.

Chen, W., et al. 2015. Air quality of Beijing and impacts of the new ambient air quality standard. *Atmosphere* 6:1243–1258.

Chen, Y. 2015. Power-law distributions based on exponential distributions: Latent scaling, spurious Zipf's law, and fractal rabbits. *Fractals*, 23. https://doi.org/10.1142/S0218348X15500097.

Chen, Y. 2016. The evolution of Zipf's law indicative of city development. *Physica A* 443:555–567.

Chesnais, J.-C. 1992. *The Demographic Transition: Stages, Patterns, and Economic Implications*. Oxford: Oxford University Press.

Chesner, C. A., et al. 1991. Eruptive history of Earth's largest Quaternary caldera (Toba, Indonesia) clarified. *Geology* 19:200–203.

Chiba, L. I. 2010. *Swine Production Handbook*. http://www.ag.auburn.edu/~chibale/swineproduction.html.

Chilvers, B. L., et al. 2007. Growth and survival of New Zealand sea lions, *Phocarctos hookeri*: Birth to 3 months. *Polar Biology* 30:459–469.

Ching, F. D. K., et al. 2011. *A Global History of Architecture*. Hoboken, NJ: John Wiley & Sons.

Chongqing Municipal Government. 2017. Comprehensive market situation. http://en.cq.gov.cn/.

Chorley, G. P. H. 1981. The agricultural revolution in Northern Europe, 1750–1880: Nitrogen, legumes, and crop productivity. *Economic History* 34:71–93.

Chu, W., et al. 2016. A survey analysis of energy use and conservation opportunities in Chinese households. In B. Su and E. Thomson, eds., *China's Energy Efficiency and Conservation*. Berlin: Springer, pp. 5–22.

Chumlea, W. C., et al. 2009. First seriatim study into old age for weight, stature and BMI: The Fels longitudinal study. *Journal of Nutrition, Health & Aging* 13:3–5.

Churkina, G., et al. 2010. Carbon stored in human settlements: The coterminous United States. *Global Change Biology* 16:135–143.

CIA (Central Intelligence Agency). 2017. The world factbook. ttps://www.cia.gov/library/publications/the-world-factbook/ https://www.cia.gov/library/publications/resources/the-world-factbook/index.html.

Ciccone, A., and R. E. Hall. 1996. Productivity and the density of economic activity. *American Economic Review* 86:54–70.

CISCO. 2017. The zettabyte era: Trends and analysis. https://webobjects.cdw.com/webobjects/media/pdf/Solutions/Networking/White-Paper-Cisco-The-Zettabyte-Era-Trends-and-Analysis.pdf.

Clark, D., and D. B. Clark, 1999. Assessing the growth of tropical rain forest trees. *Ecological Applications* 9:981–997.

Clark, G. 1991. Yields per acre in English agriculture, 1250–1850: Evidence from labour inputs. *Economic History Review* 44:445–460.

Clark, G. 2008. *A Farewell to Alms: A Brief Economic History of the World.* Princeton, NJ: Princeton University Press.

Clark, G. T. 2009. Advanced construction techniques: Tunnels and shafts. http://courses.washington.edu/cm510/tunneling.pdf.

Clarke, A. 2014. The thermal limits to life on Earth. *International Journal of Astrobiology* 13:141–154.

Clarkson, C., et al. 2017. Human occupation of northern Australia by 65,000 years ago. *Nature* 547:306–310.

Clauset, A., et al. 2009. Power-law distributions in empirical data. *SIAM Review* 51:661–703.

Clavering, E. 1995. The coal mills of Northeast England: The use of waterwheels for draining coal mines, 1600–1750. *Technology and Culture* 36:211–241.

Clegg, J. S. 2001. Cryptobiosis—a peculiar state of biological organization. *Comparative Biochemistry and Physiology B* 128:613–624.

Clerk, D. 1909. *The Gas, Petrol, and Oil Engine.* London: Longmans, Green.

Clio Infra. 2017. Height. https://clio-infra.eu/Indicators/HeightGini.html.

CNI (Confederação Nacional da Indústria). 2012. *Forest Plantations: Opportunities and Challenges for the Brazilian Pulp and Paper Industry on the Path of Sustainability.* Brasília: CNI.

Cochran, P. H. 1979. *Site Index and Height Growth Curves for Managed Even-Aged Stands of Douglas-Fir East of the Cascades in Oregon and Washington.* Portland, OR: US Department of Agriculture.

Cohen, J. E. 1995. *How Many People Can the Earth Support?* New York: Norton.

Cole, T. J. 2012. The development of growth references and growth charts. *Annals of Human Biology* 39:382–394.

Comin, D., and B. Hobijn. 2004. Cross-country technology adoption: Making the theories face the facts. *Journal of Monetary Economics* 51:39–83.

Compoundchem. 2015. Recycling rates of smartphone metals. http://www.compoundchem.com/wp-content/uploads/2015/09/Recycling-Rates-of-Smartphone-Elements.pdf.

Conder, J. 2016. fit_logistic (t,Q). *MathWorks.* https://www.mathworks.com/matlabcentral/fileexchange/41781-fit-logistic-t-q-.

Congdon, J. D., et al. 2013. Indeterminate growth in long-lived freshwater turtles as a component of individual fitness *Evolutionary Ecology* 27:445–459.

Conner, M. 2001. *Hans von Ohain: Elegance in Flight*. Reston, VA: American Institute of Aeronautics and Astronautics.

Connor, P. 2011. Railway passenger vehicle capacity. http://www.railway-tech nical.com/Infopaper%202%20Railway%20Passenger%20Vehicle%20Capacity %20v1.pdf.

Cook, E. 1971. The flow of energy in an industrial society. *Scientific American* 225(3): 135–142.

Coomes, D. A., and R. B. Allen, 2009. Testing the metabolic scaling theory of tree growth. *Journal of Ecology* 97:1369–1373.

Coren. L. R. 1998. *The Evolutionary Trajectory: The Growth of Information in the History and Future of Earth*. Boca Raton, FL: CRC Press.

Corner, E. J. H. 1964. *The Life of Plants*. London: Weidenfeld & Nicolson.

Costanza, R., et al. 1997. *An Introduction to Ecological Economics*. Boca Raton, FL: St. Lucie Press and International Society for Ecological Economics.

Costanza, R., et al. 2009. *Beyond GDP: The Need for New Measures of Progress*. Boston: Boston University Press.

Cotterell, B., and J. Kamminga. 1990. *Machines of Pre-industrial Technology*. Cambridge: Cambridge University Press.

Cox, M. M., and J. R. Battista 2005. Deinococcus radiodurans—the consummate survivor. *Nature Reviews. Microbiology* 3:882–892.

Coyle, D. 2011.*The Economics of Enough*. Princeton, NJ: Princeton University Press.

Coyle, D. 2014. *GDP: A Brief but Affectionate History*. Princeton, NJ: Princeton University Press.

Crafts, N. F. R. 1985. *British Economic Growth during the Industrial Revolution*. Oxford: Clarendon Press.

Crafts, N. 1999. Economic growth in the twentieth century. *Oxford Review of Economic Policy* 15:18–34.

Crafts, N. 2004. Steam as a general purpose technology: A growth accounting perspective. *Economic Journal* 114:338–351.

Crafts, N. 2005. The first industrial revolution: Resolving the slow growth/ rapid industrialization paradox. *Journal of the European Economic Association* 3:525–534.

Crafts, N. F. R. 2010. Explaining the first Industrial Revolution: Two views. *European Review of Economic History* 15:153–168.

Crafts, N., and T. Mills. 2017. Six centuries of British economic growth: A time-series perspective. *European Review of Economic History* 21:141–159.

Crafts, N., and K. H. O'Rourke. 2013. Twentieth century growth. https://www.economics.ox.ac.uk/materials/papers/12884/Crafts%20O%27Rourke%20117.pdf.

Cramer, J. S. 2003. *Logit Models from Economics and Other Fields.* Cambridge: Cambridge University Press.

Cristelli, M., et al. 2012. There is more than a power law in Zipf. *Scientific Reports* 2:812. doi:10.1038/srep00812.

Croft, T., ed. 1922. *Steam-Engine Principles and Practice.* New York: McGraw-Hill.

Croizé, J.-C. 2009. Politique et configuration du logement en France (1900–1980). Paris: Sciences de l'Homme et Société, Université Paris Nanterre.

Croppenstedt, A., and C. Muller. 2000. The impact of farmers' health and nutritional status on their productivity and efficiency: Evidence from Ethiopia. *Economic Development and Cultural Change* 48:475–502.

Crosby, A. W. 1989. *America's Forgotten Pandemic: The Influenza of 1918.* Cambridge: Cambridge University Press.

Crow, J. F. 1998. 90 years ago: The beginning of hybrid maize. *Genetics* 148:923–928. doi:10.1126/science.132.3436.1291.

CSO (Central Statistical Office). 1975. *The Population of Finland.* http://www.cicred.org/Eng/Publications/pdf/c-c15.pdf.

CTBUH (Council on Tall Buildings and Human Habitat). 2011a. The tallest 20 in 2020: Entering the era of the megatall. http://www.ctbuh.org/TallBuildings/HeightStatistics/BuildingsinNumbers/TheTallest20in2020/tabid/2926/language/en-US/Default.aspx.

CTBUH 2011b. What do you think is the single biggest limiting factor that would prevent humanity creating a mile-high tower or higher? http://www.ctbuh.org/TallBuildings/VideoLibrary/VideoInterviews/VideoInterviews2011AwardsSymposium/CompilationInterviewQuestion1/tabid/3027/language/en-GB/Default.aspx.

CTBUH. 2018. Height & statistics. http://www.ctbuh.org/TallBuildings/HeightStatistics/tabid/1735/language/en-US/Default.aspx.

Cuenot, F. 2009. CO_2 emissions from new cars and vehicle weight in Europe: How the EU regulation could have been avoided and how to reach it? *Energy Policy* 37:3832–3842.

Culbert, T. P., ed. 1973. *The Classic Maya Collapse.* Albuquerque: University of New Mexico Press.

Cuntz, M. 2011. A dent in carbon's gold standard. *Science* 477:547–548.

Curtis, M., ed. 2005. *The Mongol Empire: Its Rise and Legacy.* London: Routledge.

Dabla-Norris, E., et al. 2015. *Causes and Consequences of Income Inequality: A Global Perspective*. Washington, DC: International Monetary Fund.

Dalby, W. E. 1920. *Steam Power*. London: Edward Arnold.

D'Alisa, G., et al., eds. 2014. *Degrowth: A Vocabulary for a New Era*. London: Routledge.

Dalrymple, D. G. 1986. *Development and Spread of High-Yielding Rice Varieties in Developing Countries*. Washington, DC: USAID.

Daly, H. E., ed. 1971. *Toward a Stationary-State Economy*. San Francisco: W. H. Freeman.

Daly, H. 1980. *Economics, Ecology, Ethics: Essays Toward a Steady-State Economy*. San Francisco: W. H. Freeman.

Daly, H. 1996. *Beyond Growth*. Boston: Beacon Press.

Daly, H. E. 2009. From a failed growth economy to a steady-state economy. United States Society for Ecological Economics lecture, June 1. http://ppc.uiowa.edu/sites /default/files/sites/default/files/uploads/daly_failed_growth_economy.pdf.

Daly, H. E., and J. B. Cobb Jr. 1989. *For the Common Good: Redirecting the Economy Toward Community, the Environment, and a Sustainable Future*. Boston: Beacon Press.

Daly, H., and J. Farley. 2010. *Ecological Economics: Principles and Applications*. Washington, DC: Island Press.

Damuth, J. 2001. Scaling of growth: Plants and animals are not so different. *Proceedings of the National Academy of Sciences of the USA* 98:2113–2114.

Darimont, C. T., et al. 2015. The unique ecology of human predators. *Nature* 349: 858–860.

Darling, K. 2004. *Concorde*. Marlborough: Crowood Aviation.

Darwin, C. 1861. *On the Origin of Species by Means of Natural Selection*. New York: D. Appleton.

Darwin, J. 2008. *After Tamerlane: The Rise and Fall of Global Empires, 1400–2000*. New York: Bloomsbury.

Daugherty, C. R. 1927. The development of horse-power equipment in the United States. In C. R. Daugherty et al., *Power Capacity and Production in the United States*. Washington, DC: US Geological Survey, pp. 5–112.

Davenport, C. B. 1926. Human growth curve. *Journal of General Physiology* 10(2): 205–216.

David, P. 1990. The dynamo and the computer: An historical perspective on the modern productivity paradox. *American Economic Review* 80:355–361.

David, S. 2003. *The Indian Mutiny*. New York: Penguin.

Davis, J. 2011. Mercedes-Benz history: Diesel passenger car premiered 75 years ago. http://www.emercedesbenz.com/autos/mercedes-benz/classic/mercedes-benz-history -diesel-passenger-car-premiered-75-years-ago/.

Davis, J., et al. 2018. *Transportation Energy Data Book*. Oak Ridge, TN: Oak Ridge National Laboratory.

Davis, K. 1945. The world demographic transition. *Annals of the American Academy of Political and Social Science* 237:1–11.

Davis, K. 1955. The origin and growth of urbanization in the world. *American Journal of Sociology* 60:429–437.

Davis, K. 1967. Population policy: Will current programs succeed? *Science* 158:730–739.

Davis, S. C., et al. 2016. *Transportation Energy Data Book: Edition 35*. Oak Ridge, TN: Oak Ridge National Laboratory. http://cta.ornl.gov/data/tedb35/Edition35 _Full_Doc.pdf.

Day, T., and P. D. Taylor. 1997. Von Bertalanffy growth equation should not be used to model age and size at maturity. *American Naturalist* 149:381–393.

Dean, R., et al. 2012. The top 10 fungal pathogens in molecular plant pathology. *Molecular Plant Pathology* 13:414–430.

de Beer, H. 2004. Observations on the history of Dutch physical stature from the late-Middle Ages to the present. *Economics and Human Biology* 2:45–55.

de Beer, H. 2012. Dairy products and physical stature: A systematic review and meta-analysis of controlled trials. *Economics and Human Biology* 10:299–309.

de Beer, J. 2013. *Transparency in Population Forecasting: Methods for Fitting and Projecting Fertility, Mortality and Migration*. Chicago: University of Chicago Press.

de Buffon, G.-L. L., Comte. 1753. *Histoire naturelle. Supplément: Tome quatrième*. Paris: Imprimerie Royale.

DECC (Department of Energy & Climate Change). 2015. Historical coal data, 1853–2014. https://www.gov.uk/government/statistical-data-sets/historical-coal-data-coal -production-availability-and-consumption-1853-to-2014.

Deffeyes, K. S. 2001. *Hubbert's Peak: The Impending World Oil Shortage*. Princeton, NJ: Princeton University Press.

De Gans, H. A. 1999. *Population Forecasting 1895–1945: The Transition to Modernity*. Dordrecht: Kluwer Academic.

De Graaf, G., and M. Prein. 2005. Fitting growth with the von Bertalanffy growth function: A comparison of three approaches of multivariate analysis of fish growth in aquaculture experiments. *Aquaculture Research* 36:100–109.

de Jong, T. P. R. 2004. Coal mining in the Netherlands: The need for a proper assessment. *Geologica Belgica* 7:231–243.

DeLong, B. 2002. *Macroeconomics*. Burr Ridge, IL: McGraw-Hill Higher Education.

De Long, B., and A. Shleifer. 1993. *Princes and Merchants: European City Growth before the Industrial Revolution*. Cambridge, MA: National Bureau of Economic Research.

De Loo, I., and L. Soete. 1999. *The Impact of Technology on Economic Growth: Some New Ideas and Empirical Considerations*. Tokyo: UNU-MERIT Research.

Demandt, A. 1984. *Der Fall Roms: Die Auflösung des römischen Reiches im Urteil der Nachwelt*. Munich: C. H. Beck.

Demeny, P. 2003. Population policy dilemmas in Europe at the dawn of the twenty-first century. *Population and Development Review* 29:1–28.

Demeny, P. 2004. Population futures for the next three hundred years: Soft landing or surprises to come? *Population and Development Review* 30(3):507–517.

Demographia. 2001. Greater London, Inner London and Outer London: Population and density history. http://demographia.com/dm-lon31.htm.

de Moivre, A. 1738. *The Doctrine of Chances*. London: H. Woodfall.

Denison, E. F. 1985. *Trends in American Economic Growth 1929–1982*. Washington, DC: Brookings Institution.

Denny, M. 2007. *Ingenium: Five Machines That Changed the World*. Baltimore, MD: Johns Hopkins University Press.

Denny, M. W. 2008. Limits to running speed in dogs, horses and humans. *Journal of Experimental Biology* 211:3836–3849.

de Onis, M., et al. 2011. Prevalence and trends of stunting among pre-school children,1990–2020. *Public Health Nutrition*. doi:10.1017/S1368980011001315.

Depéret, C. J. J. 1907. *Les transformations du monde animal*. Paris: Flammarion.

des Cars, J. 1988. *Haussmann: La gloire du second Empire*. Paris: Perrin.

Desgorces, F.-D., et al. 2012. Similar slow down in running speed progression in species under human pressure. *Journal of Evolutionary Biology* 25:1792–1799.

Devezas, T. C., et al. 2005. The growth dynamics of the Internet and the long wave theory. *Technological Forecasting and Social Change* 72:913–935.

Devine, W. D. 1983. From shafts to wires: Historical perspective on electrification. *Journal of Economic History* 43:347–372.

de Vries, J. 2000. Dutch economic growth in comparative-historical perspective, 1500–2000. *De Economist* 148:443–467.

Dewey, C. 1993. *Anglo-Indian Attitudes: The Mind of the Indian Civil Service*. London: Bloomsbury.

Diamond, J. 2011. *Collapse: How Societies Choose to Fail or Succeed*. New York: Penguin Books.

Dickey, P. S. 1968. *Liberty Engine 1918–1942*. New York: Random House.

Dickinson, H. W. 1939. *A Short History of the Steam Engine*. Cambridge: Cambridge University Press.

Dickmann, D. I. 2006. Silviculture and biology of short-rotation woody crops in temperate regions: Then and now. *Biomass and Bioenergy* 30:696–705.

Dieffenbach, E. M., and R. B. Gray. 1960. The development of the tractor. In US Department of Agriculture, *Power to Produce: 1960 Yearbook of Agriculture*, Washington, DC: USDA, pp. 24–45.

Diener, E., et al. 1997. Recent findings on subjective well-being. *Indian Journal of Clinical Psychology* 24:25–41.

Diesel, E. 1937. *Diesel: Der Mensch, das Werk, das Schicksal*. Hamburg: Hanseatische Verlagsanstalt.

Diesel, R. 1893. *Theorie und Konstruktion eines rationellen Wärmemotors zum Ersatz der Dampfmaschinen und der heute bekannten Verbrennungsmotoren*. Berlin: Julius Springer.

Diesel, R. 1903. *Solidarismus: Natürliche wirtschaftliche Erlösung des Menschen*. Munich. Reprint Augsburg: Maro, 2007.

Diesel, R. 1913. *Die Entstehung des Dieselmotors*. Berlin: Julius Springer.

Di Giorgio, C., et al. 1996. Atmospheric pollution by airborne microorganisms in the city of Marseilles. *Atmospheric Environment* 30:155–160.

Dillon, M. E., and M. R. Frazier. 2013. Thermodynamics constrains allometric scaling of optimal development time in insects. *PLoS ONE* 8(12):e84308. doi:10.1371/journal.pone.0084308.

Dimson, E. 2003. Triumph of the optimists. (Lecture following E. Dimson et al., *Triumph of the Optimists*, Princeton, NJ: Princeton University Press, 2002.) Arrowstreet Capital, London.

Dinda, S., et al. 2006. Height, weight and earnings among coalminers in India. *Economics and Human Biology* 4:342–350.

Dodds, P. S., et al. 2001. Re-examination of the "3/4-law" of metabolism. *Journal of Theoretical Biology* 209:9–27.

Doe, H. 2017. *The First Atlantic Liner: Brunel's SS Great Western*. Stroud: Amberley.

Dolan, B., ed. 2000. *Malthus, Medicine and Morality: Malthusianism after 1798.* Amsterdam: Rodopi.

Dolgonosov, B. M. 2010. On the reasons of hyperbolic growth in the biological and human world systems. *Ecological Modelling* 221:1702–1709.

Donald C. M., and J. Hamblin. 1976. The biological yield and harvest index of cereals as agronomic and plant breeding criteria. *Advances in Agronomy* 28:361–405.

Dong, X., et al. 2016. Evidence for a limit to human lifespan. *Nature* 538:257–259.

Dormehl, L. 2018. Computers can't keep shrinking, but they'll keep getting better. *Digital Trends.* https://www.digitaltrends.com/computing/end-moores-law-end-of -computers/.

Drewry, C. S. 1832. *A Memoir of Suspension Bridges: Comprising The History of Their Origin and Progress.* London: Longman.

Driscoll, J. M., et al. 1964. Design of 1000-MW steam turbine-generator unit for Ravenswood No 3. *Journal of Engineering for Power* 86(2):209–218.

Duan-yai, S., et al. 1999. Growth data of broiler chickens fitted to Gompertz equation. *Asian-Australian Journal of Animal Science* 12:1177–1180.

Duddu, P. 2013. The 10 biggest hydroelectric power plants in the world. http://www .power-technology.com/features/feature-the-10-biggest-hydroelectric-power-plants -in-the-world/.

Dumpleton, B., and M. Miller. 1974. *Brunel's Three Ships.* Melksham: Colin Venton.

Duncan-Jones, R. 1990. *Structure and Scale in the Roman Economy.* Cambridge: Cambridge University Press.

Dunsworth, H. M., et al. 2012. Metabolic hypothesis for human altriciality. *Proceedings of the National Academy of Sciences of the USA* 109:15212–15216.

Durand, J. D. 1974. *Historical Estimates of World Population: An Evaluation.* Philadelphia: University of Pennsylvania, Population Center.

Duranton, G., and W. R. Kerr. 2015. *The Logic of Agglomeration.* Cambridge, MA: Harvard Business School. http://www.hbs.edu/faculty/Publication%20Files/16-037 _eb512e96-28d6-4c02-a7a9-39b52db95b00.pdf.

Dyson, T., et al., eds. 2005. *Twenty-First Century India: Population, Economy, Human Development, and the Environment.* Oxford: Oxford University Press.

Easterlin, R. A. 1974. Does economic growth improve the human lot? Some empirical evidence. In P. A. David and M. W. Reder, eds., *Nations and Households in Economic Growth: Essays in Honor of Moses Abramovitz.* New York: Academic Press, pp. 89–125.

Economist. 2016. The immigration paradox. *The Economist*, July 16, p. 48.

Edison, T. A. 1884. *Electrical Indicator: Specification Forming Part of Letters Patent No. 307,031, Dated October 21, 1884*. Washington, DC: US Patent Office.

Edmonds, R. L., ed. 1982. *Analysis of Coniferous Forest Ecosystems in the Western United States*. New York: Van Nostrand Reinhold.

Edwards, N. T., and P. J. Hanson. 2003. Aboveground autotrophic respiration. In P. J. Hanson and S. D. Wullschleger, eds., *North American Temperate Deciduous Forest Responses to Changing Precipitation Regimes*. New York: Springer, pp. 48–66.

Eeckhout, J. 2004. Gibrat's law for (all) cities. *American Economic Review* 94: 1429–1451.

Ehrlich, I., and F. T. Lui, 1991. Intergenerational trade, longevity, and economic growth. *Journal of Political Economy* 99:1029–1059.

Ehrlich, P. 1968. *The Population Bomb*. New York: Ballantine Books.

Ehrlich, P. R., and A. H. Ehrlich. 2013. Can a collapse of global civilization be avoided? *Proceedings of the Royal Society B* 280:20122845. http://dx.doi.org/10.1098/rspb.2012 .2845.

EIU (Economist Intelligence Unit). 2011. *Building Rome in a Day: The Sustainability of China's Housing Boom*. London: EIU. http://www.excellentfuture.ca/sites/default /files/Building%20Rome%20in%20a%20Day_0.pdf.

Ejsmond, M. J., et al. 2010. How to time growth and reproduction during the vegetative season: An evolutionary choice for indeterminate growers in environments. *American Naturalist* 175:551–563.

Elias, D. 2000. *The Dow 40,000 Portfolio: The Stocks to Own to Outperform Today's Leading Benchmark*. New York: McGraw Hill.

Ellis, H. 1977. *The Lore of the Train*. New York: Crescent Books.

Ellison, G., and E. Glaeser. 1997. Geographic concentration in U.S. manufacturing industries: A dartboard approach. *Journal of Political Economy* 105: 889–927.

Elphick, P. 2001. *Liberty: The Ships That Won the War*. Annapolis, MD: Naval Institute Press.

Elvidge, C. D., et al. 2007. Global distribution and density of constructed impervious surfaces. *Sensors* 7:1962–1979.

Ely, C. 2014. Life expectancy of electronics. https://www.cta.tech/News/Blog/Articles /2014/September/The-Life-Expectancy-of-Electronics.aspx.

eMarketer. 2017. eMarketer updates US time spent with media figures. https://www .emarketer.com/Article/eMarketer-Updates-US-Time-Spent-with-Media-Figures /1016587.

Emmott, S. 2013. *Ten Billion*. New York: Vintage Books.

Emporis. 2017. Cities with most skyscrapers. https://www.emporis.com/statistics/most-skyscraper-cities-worldwide.

Enberg, K., et al. 2008. *Fish Growth*. Bergen, Norway: University of Bergen.

Enders, J. C., and M. Remig. 2014. *Theories of Sustainable Development*. London: Routledge.

Engerman, S. L., and K. L. Sokoloff. 1994. *Factor Endowments: Institutions, and Differential Paths of Growth among New World Economies: A View from Economic Historians of the United States*. Boston: National Bureau of Economic Research.

Enquist, B. J., et al. 1998. Allometric scaling of plant energetics and population density. *Nature* 395:163–165.

Enquist, B., et al. 1999. Allometric scaling of production and life-history variation in vascular plants. *Nature* 401:907–911.

Enquist, B. J., et al. 2007. A general integrative model for scaling plant growth, carbon flux, and functional trait spectra. *Nature* 449:218–222.

Erdkamp, P. 2005. *The Grain Market in the Roman Empire*. Cambridge: Cambridge University Press.

Erickson, G. M., et al. 2004. Gigantism and comparative life-history parameters of tyrannosaurid dinosaurs. *Nature* 430:772–775.

Erlande-Brandenburg, A. 1994. *The Cathedral: The Social and Architectural Dynamics of Construction*. Cambridge: Cambridge University Press.

Eshed, V., et al. 2004. Has the transition to agriculture reshaped the demographic structure of prehistoric populations? New evidence from the Levant. *American Journal of Physical Anthropology* 124:315–329.

Espe, M. B., et al. 2016. Estimating yield potential in temperate high-yielding, direct-seeded US rice production systems. *Field Crops Research* 193:123–132.

Estoup, J. 1916. *Les gammes stenographiques*. Paris: Gauthier-Villars.

Eugster, E. 2015. Gigantism. *Endotext*. http://www.ncbi.nlm.nih.gov/books/NBK279155/.

Euler, L. 1748. *Introductio in analysin infinitorum*. Lausanne: Marcum-Michaelem Bosquet & Socios.

European Commission. 2014. *Trade and Investment 2014*. Brussels: EC. http://trade.ec.europa.eu/doclib/docs/2014/january/tradoc_152062.pdf.

European Commission. 2016. Hormones in meat. http://ec.europa.eu/food/safety/chemical_safety/meat_hormones/index_en.htm.

Eurostat. 2015. Demographic balance, 1 January 2015–1 January 2080 (thousands) PF15.png. http://ec.europa.eu/eurostat/statistics-explained/index.php/File:Demographic _balance,_1_January_2015_%E2%80%93_1_January_2080_(thousands)_PF15.png.

Eurostat. 2017a. Population on 1 January. http://ec.europa.eu/eurostat/tgm/table.do ?tab=table&init=1&language=en&pcode=tps00001&plugin=1.

Eurostat. 2017b. Total fertility rate, 1960–2015 (live births per woman). http://ec .europa.eu/eurostat/statistics-explained/index.php/File:Total_fertility_rate,_1960 %E2%80%932015_(live_births_per_woman)_YB17.png.

Evans, D. S. 2004. The growth and diffusion of credit cards in society. *Payment Card Economics Review* 2:59–76.

EWEA (European Wind Energy Association). 2016. *Wind Power 2015 European Statistics.* http://www.ewea.org/fileadmin/files/library/publications/statistics/EWEA-Annual -Statistics-2015.pdf.

ExxonMobil. 2016. The outlook for energy: A view to 2040. http://corporate .exxonmobil.com/en/energy/energy-outlook.

Facebook. 2018. Stats. https://newsroom.fb.com/company-info/.

Fairbairn, W. 1860. *Useful Information for Engineers.* London: Longmans.

Fairchild, B. D. 2005. Broiler production systems: The ideal stocking density? http:// www.thepoultrysite.com/articles/322/broiler-production-systems-the-ideal-stocking -density/.

Falchi, F., et al. 2016. The new world atlas of artificial night sky brightness. *Science Advances* 2:1–25.

Falk, M., et al. 2008. Flux partitioning in an old-growth forest: Seasonal and interannual dynamics. *Tree Physiology* 28:509–20.

FAO (Food and Agriculture Organization). 2015a. *Global Forest Resources Assessment 2015.* Rome: FAO. http://www.fao.org/3/a-i4793e.pdf.

FAO. 2015b. *The State of Food Insecurity.* Rome: FAO. http://www.fao.org/hunger/en/.

FAO. 2015c. *Yield Gap Analysis of Field Crops: Methods and Case Studies.* Rome: FAO.

FAO. 2018. Faostat. http://www.fao.org/faostat/en/#data.

Faraday, M. 1839. *Experimental Researches in Electricity.* London: Richard and John Edward Taylor.

Faure, A. 1998. Les couches nouvelles de la propriété: Un peuple parisien à la conquête du bon logis à la veille de la Grande Guerre. *Le Mouvement Social* 182: 53–78.

FedPrimeRate. 2017. Dow Jones Industrial Average history. http://www.fedprimerate .com/dow-jones-industrial-average-history-djia.htm.

Fekedulegn, D., et al. 1999. Parameter estimation of nonlinear growth models in forestry. *Silva Fennica* 33:327–336.

Felton, N. 2008. Consumption spreads faster today. http://www.nytimes.com/imagepages/2008/02/10/opinion/10op.graphic.ready.html.

Ferguson, N. 2004. *Empire: How Britain Made the Modern World*. London: Penguin.

Ferguson, N. 2012. Don't believe the techno-utopian hype. *Newsweek*, July 30. http://www.newsweek.com/niall-ferguson-dont-believe-techno-utopian-hype-65611.

Fernández-González, F. 2006. *Ship Structures under Sail and under Gunfire*. Madrid: Universidad Politécnica de Madrid.

Ferreira, A. A. 2012. Evaluation of the growth of children: Path of the growth charts. *Demetra* 7:191–202.

Ferreira, F. H. G., et al. 2015. *A Global Count of the Extreme Poor in 2012: Data Issues, Methodology and Initial Results*. Washington, DC: World Bank Group.

Ferrer, M. L., and T. Navarra. 1997. *Levittown: The First 50 Years*. Mount Pleasant, SC: Arcadia.

Feynman, R. 1959. There's plenty of room at the bottom. https://pdfs.semanticscholar.org/1bc8/21e55e3b381eaba62bb02c861b9cb5273309.pdf.

Field, A. J. 2009. US economic growth in the Gilded Age. *Journal of Macroeconomics* 31:173–190.

Fields, N. 2005. *Rome's Northern Frontier AD 70–235*. Wellingborough: Osprey.

Finarelli, J. A., and J. J. Flynn. 2006. Ancestral state reconstruction of body size in the Caniformia (Carnivora, Mammalia): The effects of incorporating data from the fossil record. *System Biology* 55:301–313.

Finucane, M. M., et al. 2011. National, regional, and global trends in body mass index since 1980: Systematic analysis of health examination surveys and epidemiological studies with 960 country-years and 9.1 million participants. *Lancet* 377:557–567. doi:10.1016/S0140-6736(10)62037-5.

Fish, J. L., and C. A. Lockwood. 2003. Dietary constraints on encephalization in primates. *American Journal of Physical Anthropology* 120:171–181.

Fisher, J. C., and R. H. Pry. 1971. A simple substitution model of technological change. *Technological Forecasting and Social Change* 3:75–88.

Fleming, J. A. 1934. *Memories of a Scientific Life*. London: Marshall, Morgan & Scott.

Flichy, P. 2007. *Understanding Technological Innovation: A Socio-Technical Approach*. Northampton, MA: Edward Elgar.

Flink, J. J. 1988. *The Automobile Age*. Cambridge, MA: MIT Press.

Floud, R., et al. 2011. *The Changing Body: Health, Nutrition, and Human Development in the Western World since 1700*. Cambridge: Cambridge University Press.

Fluschnik, T., et al. 2016. The size distribution, scaling properties and spatial organization of urban clusters: A global and regional percolation perspective. *International Journal of Geo-Information* 5: 110. doi:10.3390/ijgi5070110.

Flying Scotsman. 2017. British train national treasure. http://www.flyingscotsman .org.uk/.

FNAIM (Fédération National de l'Immobilier). 2015. *Le logement en France*. Paris: FNAIM.

Focacci, A. 2017. Controversial curves of the economy: An up-to-date investigation of long waves. *Technological Forecasting and Social Change* 116:271–285.

Fogel, R. W., 2004. *The Escape from Hunger and Premature Death, 1700–2100*. New York: Cambridge University Press.

Fogel, R. W. 2012. *Explaining Long-Term Trends in Health and Longevity*. Cambridge: Cambridge University Press.

Foley, R. A., and P. C. Lee. 1991. Ecology and energetics of encephalization in hominid evolution. *Philosophical Transactions of the Royal Society of London, B* 334:223–232.

Forbes. 2017. The world's billionaires. https://www.forbes.com/billionaires/#623b 87b2251c.

Forrester, J. 1971. *World Dynamics*. Cambridge, MA: Wright-Allen Press.

Foster. D. R., ed. 2014. *Hemlock: A Forest Giant on the Edge*. New Haven, CT: Yale University Press.

Foster, D. R., and J. D. Aber. 2004. *Forests in Time: The Environmental Consequences of 1,000 Years of Change in New England*. New Haven CT: Yale University Press.

Fouquet, R. 2008. *Heat, Power and Light: Revolutions in Energy Services*. London: Edward Elgar.

Fowkes, B. 1995. *Rise and Fall of Communism in Eastern Europe*. London: Palgrave Macmillan.

Fraas, L. M. 2014. *Low-Cost Solar Electric Power*. Berlin: Spinger.

Frank, A. G. 1998. *ReOrient: Global Economy in the Asian Age*. Berkeley, CA: University of California Press.

Franke. J. 2002. The Benson boiler turns 75: The success story of a steam generator. *Siemens Power Journal Online* (May). https://www.energy.siemens.com/nl/pool/hq /power-generation/power-plants/steam-power-plant-solutions/benson%20boiler/The _Benson_Boiler_Turns_75.pdf.

Franke, J., and R. Kral. 2003. Supercritical boiler technology for future market conditions. https://www.energy.siemens.com/hq/pool/hq/power-generation/power-plants/steam-power-plant-solutions/benson%20boiler/Supercritical_Boiler_Technology_for_Future_Market_Conditions.pdf.

Frayer, L. 2013. A farm-to-table delicacy from Spain: Roasted baby pig. https://www.npr.org/sections/thesalt/2013/09/04/218959923/a-farm-to-table-delicacy-from-spain-roasted-baby-pig.

Fréchet, M. 1941. Sur la loi de répartition de certaines grandeurs géographiques. *Journal de la Societé de Statistique de Paris*, 82:114–122.

FRED. 2017. Gross domestic product. https://fred.stlouisfed.org/series/GDP.

Freer-Smith, P., et al. 2009. *Forestry and Climate Change*. Wallingford: CABI.

Frey, C., and M. Osborne. 2015. *Technology at Work: The Future of Innovation and Employment*. Oxford: Citi and Oxford Martin School.

Frier, B. W. 1993. Subsistence annuities and per capita income in the early Roman Empire. *Classical Philology* 88:222–230.

Frier, B. W. 2000. Demography. In A. K. Bowman et al., eds., *The Cambridge Ancient History*, vol. 11: *The High Empire, A.D. 70–192*, 2nd ed. Cambridge: Cambridge University Press, pp. 787–816.

Frillmann, K. 2015. Call the mega-plumbers: The world's longest pipe needs fixing. http://www.wnyc.org/story/call-mega-plumbers-fixing-longest-pipe-world-/.

Fu, Q., and C. Land. 2015. The increasing prevalence of overweight and obesity of children and youth in China, 1989–2009: An age–period–cohort analysis. *Population Research Policy Review* 34:901–921.

Fuglie, K. 2013. Why the pessimists are wrong. *IEEE Spectrum* (June):26–30.

Future Beef. 2016. Feed consumption and liveweight gain. https://futurebeef.com.au/knowledge-centre/feedlots/beef-cattle-feedlots-feed-consumption-and-liveweight-gain/.

Gaastra, F. S. 2007. *The Dutch East India Company*. Zutpen: Walburg Press.

Gabaix, X. 1999. Zipf's law for cities: An explanation. *Quarterly Journal of Economics* 114:739–767.

Gabaix, X., and R. Ibragimov. 2011. Rank -1/2: A simple way to improve the OLS estimation of tail exponents. *Journal of Business & Economic Statistics* 29:24–39. http://dx.doi.org/10.1198/jbes.2009.06157.

Galleon, D., and C. Reedy. 2017. Kurzweil claims that the singularity will happen by 2045. *Futurism*, October 5. https://futurism.com/kurzweil-claims-that-the-singularity-will-happen-by-2045/.

Galloway, J. A., et al. 1996. Fuelling the city: Production and distribution of fire-wood and fuel in London's region, 1290–1400. *Economic History Review* 49:447–472.

Galor, O. 2011. *The Demographic Transition: Causes and Consequences*. Cambridge, MA: National Bureau of Economic Research.

Galor, O., and O. Moav. 2002. Natural selection and the origin of economic growth. *Quarterly Journal of Economics* 117:1133–1191.

Galton F. 1876. On the height and weight of boys aged 14, in town and country public schools. *Journal of Anthropological Institute of Great Britain and Ireland* 5:174–181.

Galton, F. 1879. The geometric mean, in vital and social statistics. *Proceedings of the Royal Society* 29:365–367.

Gao, C. Q., et al. 2016. Growth curves and age-related changes in carcass characteristics, organs, serum parameters, and intestinal transporter gene expression in domestic pigeon (*Columba livia*). *Poultry Science* 95:867–877.

Gardiner, R., and R. W. Unger, eds. 2000. *Cogs, Caravels, and Galleons: The Sailing Ship 1000–1650*. Oxford: Oxford University Press.

Garnsey, P. 1988. *Famine and Food Supply in the Graeco-Roman World*. Cambridge: Cambridge University Press.

Gaston, K., et al. 2005. The structure of global species–range size distributions: Raptors and owls. *Global Ecology and Biogeography* 14:67–76.

Gaudart, J., et al. 2010. Demography and diffusion in epidemics: Malaria and Black Death spread. *Acta Biotheoretica* 58:277–305.

Gauss, C. F. 1809. *Theoria motus corporum coellestium*. Hamburg: F. Perthes & I. H. Besser.

GE (General Electric). 2017a. Arabelle steam turbines for nuclear power plants. https://www.gepower.com/steam/products/steam-turbines/arabelle.html.

GE. 2017b. Evolution series locomotives. https://www.getransportation.com/locomotive-and-services/evolution-series-locomotive.

GE. 2017c. 9HA.01/.02 gas turbine (50 Hz). https://www.gepower.com/gas/gas-turbines/9ha.

Geddes, P. 1915. *Cities in Evolution: An Introduction to the Town Planning Movement and to the Study of Cities*. London: Williams & Norgate.

Gelband, H., et al. 2015. *The State of the World's Antibiotics*. Washington, DC: Center for Disease Dynamics, Economics and Policy.

Gell-Mann, M. 1994. *The Quark and the Jaguar: Adventures in the Simple and the Complex*. New York: W. H. Freeman.

Georgescu-Roegen, N. 1975. Energy and economic myths. *Southern Economic Journal* 41:347–381.

Georgescu-Roegen, N., and M. Bonaiuti, eds. 2011. *From Bioeconomics to Degrowth: Georgescu-Roegen's 'New Economics' in Eight Essays.* London: Routledge.

Gerhold, D., ed. 1996. *Road Transport in the Horse-Drawn Era.* Aldershot: Scholar Press.

Gerland, P., et al. 2014. World population stabilization unlikely this century. *Science* 346:234–237.

Gerrard, D. E., and A. L. Grant. 2007. *Principles of Animal Growth and Development.* Dubuque, IA: Kendall Hunt.

GESAMP (Joint Group of Experts on Scientific Aspects of Marine Environmental Protection). 2015. *Microplastics in the Ocean.* http://web.tuat.ac.jp/~gaia/item/GESAMP.pdf.

Gewin, V. 2003. Genetically modified corn—environmental benefits and risks. *PLoS Biology* 1:15–19.

Gewirtz, D. A., et al. 2007. *Apoptosis, Senescence and Cancer.* Totowa, NJ: Humana Press.

Gibbon, E. 1776–1789. *The History of the Decline and Fall of the Roman Empire.* London: Strahan & Cadell.

Gibbon, R. 2010. *Stephenson's Rocket and the Rainhill Trials.* London: Shire.

Gibrat, R. 1931. *Les inégalités économiques.* Paris: Librairie du Recueil Sirey.

Giegling, F., et al., eds. 1964. *Chronologisch-thematisches Verzeichnis sämtlicher Tonwerke Wolfgang Amade Mozarts.* Wiesbaden: Breitkopf & Härtel.

Gies, F., and J. Gies. 1995. *Cathedral Forge and Waterwheel: Technology and Invention in the Middle Ages.* New York: Harper.

Gignoux, C. R., et al. 2011. Rapid, global demographic expansions after the origins of agriculture. *Proceedings of the National Academy of Sciences of the USA* 108:6044–6049.

Gillespie, S. 2002. Evolution of drug resistance in *Mycobacterium tuberculosis*: Clinical and molecular perspective. *Antimicrobial Agents and Chemotherapy* 46:267–274.

Gilliver, M. A., et al. 1999. Antibiotic resistance found in wild rodents. *Nature* 401:233–234.

Gingras, Y., et al. 2008. The effects of aging on researchers' publication and citation patterns. *PLoS ONE* 3(12):e4048. doi:10.1371/journal.pone.0004048.

Giovannoni, S. J., et al. 2005. Genome streamlining in a cosmopolitan oceanic bacterium. *Science* 309:1242–1245.

GLA (Greater London Authority). 2015. *Population Growth in London, 1939–2015*. London: GLA.

Glaeser, E. L., ed. 2010. *Agglomeration Economics*. Chicago: University of Chicago Press.

Glaeser, E. L. 2011. *Triumph of the City: How Our Greatest Invention Makes Us Richer, Smarter, Greener, Healthier, and Happier*. New York: Penguin.

Glaeser, E. L., et al. 1992. Growth in cities. *Journal of Political Economy* 100:1126–1152.

Glancey, J. 2016. *Concorde: The Rise and Fall of the Supersonic Airliner*. London: Atlantic Books.

Glazier, D. S. 2006. The 3/4-power law is not universal: Evolution of isometric, ontogenetic metabolic scaling in pelagic animals. *BioScience* 56:325–332.

Glazier, D. S. 2010. A unifying explanation for diverse metabolic scaling in animals and plants. *Biological Reviews* 85:111–138.

Gliozzi, A. S., et al. 2012. A novel approach to the analysis of human growth. *Theoretical Biology and Medical Modelling* 9:1–15.

Global Footprint Network. 2017. Global Footprint Network. https://www.footprint network.org/.

Glynn, J. 1849. *Rudimentary Treatise on the Construction of Cranes and Machinery for Raising Heavy Bodies, for the Erection of Buildings, and for Hoisting Heavy Goods*. London: John Weale.

GNH Centre. 2016. The story of GNH [Gross National Happiness]. http://www .gnhcentrebhutan.org/what-is-gnh/the-story-of-gnh/.

Godwin, W. 1820. *Of Population: An Enquiry Concerning the Power of Increase in the Numbers of Mankind, Being an Answer to Mr. Malthus's Essay on That Subject*. London: Longman, Hurst, Rees, Orme & Brown.

Gog, J. R., et al. 2014. Spatial transmission of 2009 pandemic influenza in the US. *PLoS Computational Biology* 10(6):e1003635. doi:10.1371/journal.pcbi.1003635.

Gold, S. 2003. *The Development of European Forest Resources, 1950 to 2000*. Geneva: United Nations. https://www.unece.org/fileadmin/DAM/timber/docs/efsos/03-sept /dp-d.pdf.

Gold, T. 1992. The deep, hot biosphere. *Proceedings of the National Academy of Sciences of the USA* 89:6045–6049.

Goldsmith, R. W. 1984. An estimate of the size and structure of the national product of the early Roman Empire. *Review of Income and Wealth* 30:263–288.

Goldstein, E., et al. 2011. Estimating incidence curves of several infections using symptom surveillance data. *PLoS ONE* 6(8):e23380. doi:10.1371/journal.pone.0023380.

Goldstein, J. R., and G. Stecklov. 2002. Long-range population projections made simple. *Population and Development Review* 28:123–141.

Golitsin, Y. N., and M. C. Krylov. 2010. *Cell Division: Theory, Variants and Degradation.* Hauppauge, NJ: Nova Science.

Golley, J., and F. Whittle. 1987. *Whittle: The True Story.* Washington, DC: Smithsonian Institution Press.

Gómez, J. M., and M. Verdú. 2017. Network theory may explain the vulnerability of medieval human settlements to the Black Death pandemic. *Scientific Reports* 7:43467. doi:10.1038/srep43467.

Gómez-García, E., et al. 2013. A dynamic volume and biomass growth model system for even-aged downy birch stands in south-western Europe. *Forestry* 87:165–176. http://forestry.oxfordjournals.org/content/early/2013/11/26/forestry.cpt045.full.pdf.

Gompertz, B. 1825. On the nature of the function expressive of the law of human mortality, and on a new mode of determining the value of life contingencies. *Philosophical Transactions of the Royal Society of London* 123:513–585.

Gordon, R. J. 2000. Does the "New Economy" measure up to the great inventions of the past? *Journal of Economic Perspectives* 14:49–74.

Gordon, R. J. 2012. *Is U.S. Economic Growth Over? Faltering Innovations Confront the Six Headwinds.* Cambridge, MA: National Bureau of Economic Research.

Gordon, R. J. 2016. *The Rise and Fall of American Growth.* Princeton, NJ: Princeton University Press.

Gottmann, J. 1961. *Megalopolis: The Urbanized Northeastern Seaboard of the United States.* New York: Twentieth Century Fund.

Government of India. 2017. Draft national energy policy. http://niti.gov.in /writereaddata/files/new_initiatives/NEP-ID_27.06.2017.pdf.

Gowin, E. B. 1915. *The Executive and His Control of Men.* New York: Macmillan.

Grady, J. M., et al. 2014. Evidence for mesothermy in dinosaurs. *Science* 344: 1268–1272.

Graf, R. J. 2013. Crop yield and production trends in Western Canada. http://www .pgdc.ca/pdfs/wrt/Crop%20Yield%20Trends%20FINAL.pdf.

Granatstein, V. L., et al. 1999. Vacuum electronics at the dawn of the twenty-first century. *Proceedings of the IEEE* 87:702–716.

Granéli, E., and J. T. Turner, eds. 2006, *Ecology of Harmful Algae.* Berlin: Springer.

Grassini, P., et al. 2013. Distinguishing between yield advances and yield plateaus in historical crop production trends. *Nature Communications* 4:2918 doi:10.1038 /ncomms3918.

Green, D. 2011. *Means to an End: Apoptosis and Other Cell Death Mechanisms*. Cold Spring Harbor, NY: Cold Spring Harbor Laboratory Press.

Greenpeace Canada. 2008. *Turning Up the Heat: Global Warming and the Degradation of Canada's Boreal Forest*. Toronto, ON: Greenpeace Canada.

Gregory, P. J., and S. Nortcliff, eds. 2013. *Soil Conditions and Plant Growth*. Hoboken, NJ: Wiley-Blackwell.

Gregory, T. E. 2010. *A History of Byzantium*. Oxford: Wiley-Blackwell.

Griebeler, E. M. 2013. Body temperatures in dinosaurs: What can growth curves tell us? *PLoS ONE* 8(10):e74317. doi:10.1371/journal.pone.

Grinin, L., et al. 2016. *Kondratieff Waves in the World System Perspective*. Cham: Springer International.

Gross, J. 2004. *A Normal Distribution Course*. Bern: Peter Lang.

Grossman, G. M., and E. Helpman. 1991. Trade, knowledge spillovers, and growth. *European Economic Review* 35:517–526.

Groth, H., and J. F. May, eds. 2017. *Africa's Population: In Search of a Demographic Dividend*. Berlin: Springer.

Grübler, A. 1990. *The Rise and Fall of Infrastructures: Dynamics of Evolution and Technological Change in Transport*. Heidelberg: Physica.

GSMArena. 2017. All mobile phone brands. http://www.gsmarena.com/makers .php3.

Gündüz, G. 2002. The nonlinear and scaled growth of the Ottoman and Roman empires. *Journal of Mathematical Sociology* 26:167–187.

Gunston, B. 1986. *World Encyclopedia of Aero Engines*. Wellingborough: Patrick Stephens.

Gunston, B. 2006. *The Development of Jet and Turbine Aero Engines*. Sparkford: Haynes.

Guo, D., et al. 2015. Multi-scale modeling for the transmission of influenza and the evaluation of interventions toward it. *Scientific Reports* (March). doi:10.1038/srep08980.

Gust, I. D., et al. 2001. Planning for the next pandemic of influenza. *Review in Medical Virology* 11:59–70.

Gutenberg, B., and C. F. Richter. 1942. Earthquake magnitude, intensity, energy and acceleration. *Bulletin of the Seismological Society of America* 32:163–191.

GYGA (Global Yield Gap and Water Productivity Atlas). 2017. *Global Yield Gap Atlas*. http://www.yieldgap.org/.

Haensch, S., et al. 2010. Distinct clones of *Yersinia pestis* caused the Black Death. *PLoS Pathogens* 6(10):e1001134. doi:10.1371/journal.ppat.1001134.

Halévy, D. 1948. *Essai sur l'accélération de l'histoire*. Paris: Self.

Hall, E. C. 1996. *Journey to the Moon: The History of the Apollo Guidance Computer*. Washington, DC: American Institute of Aeronautics and Astronautics.

Hall, M., et al. 2004. *Cell Growth: Control of Cell Size*. Cold Spring Harbor, NY: Cold Spring Laboratory Press.

Hameed, Z., and J. Vatn. 2012. Important challenges for 10 MW reference wind turbine from RAMS perspective. *Energy Procedia* 24:263–270.

Hamilton, B. 2000. East African running dominance: What is behind it? *British Journal of Sports Medicine* 34:391–394.

Hamilton, N. R. S., et al. 1995. In defense of the –3/2 boundary rule: A re-evaluation of self-thinning concepts and status. *Annals of Botany* 76:569–577.

Hampton, J. 1991. Estimation of southern bluefin tuna Thunnus maccoyii growth parameters from tagging data using von Bertalanffy models incorporating individual variation. *Fishery Bulletin U.S.* 89:577–590.

Hanley, S. B. 1987. Urban sanitation in preindustrial Japan. *Journal of Interdisciplinary History* 18:1–26.

Hanley, S. B. 1997. *Everyday Things in Premodern Japan*. Berkeley: University of California Press.

Harder, A., and L. Cook. 2015. Congressional leaders agree to lift 40-year ban on oil exports. *Wall Street Journal*, December 16. https://www.wsj.com/articles/congressional-leaders-agree-to-lift-40-year-ban-on-oil-exports-1450242995.

Hardin, G. 1992. *Living within Limits: Ecology, Economics and Population Taboos*. New York: Oxford University Press.

Hardy, G., and A. B. Kinney. 2005. *The Establishment of the Han Empire and Imperial China*. Westport, CT: Greenwood Press.

Hargrove, T., and W. R. Coffman. 2006. *Rice Today* (October–December):35–38. http://www.goldenrice.org/PDFs/Breeding_History_Sept_2006.pdf.

Harley, C. K. 1982. British industrialization before 1841: Evidence of slower growth during the Industrial Revolution. *Journal of Economic History* 42:267–289.

Harley, E. T. 1982. *Pennsy Q Class*. Hicksville, NY: N.J. International.

Harpending, H. C., et al. 1993. The genetic structure of ancient human populations. *Current Anthropology* 34:483–496.

Harris, K., and R. Nielsen 2017. Where did the Neanderthals go? *BMC Biology* 15:73 doi:10.1186/s12915-017-0414-2.

Harrison, M., ed. 2000. *The Economics of World War II: Six Great Powers in International Comparison*. Cambridge: Cambridge University Press.

Hart, E. B., et al. 1920. The nutritional requirements of baby chicks. *The Journal of Biological Chemistry* 52:379–386.

Hart, H. 1931. *The Technique of Social Progress*. New York: Henry Holt.

Hart, H. 1945. Logistic social trends. *American Journal of Sociology* 50:337–352.

Hassan, A., ed. 2017. Food security and child malnutrition: The impact on health, growth and well-being. Toronto, ON: Apple Academic Press.

Hassen, A. T., et al. 2004. Use of linear and non-linear growth curves to describe body weight changes of young Angus bulls and heifers. *Animal Industry Report*: AS 650, ASL R1869. http://lib.dr.iastate.edu/ans_air/vol650/iss1/28.

Hatch, M. D. 1992. C_4 photosynthesis: An unlikely process full of surprises. *Plant Cell Physiology* 4:333–342.

Hatfield-Dodds, S., et al. 2015. Australia is 'free to choose' economic growth and falling environmental pressures. *Nature* 527:49–53.

Haub, C. 1995. How many people have ever lived on Earth? *Population Today* (February):5.

Hauspie, R., et al. 2004. *Methods in Human Growth Research*. Cambridge: Cambridge University Press.

Havenstein, G. B. 2006. Performance changes in poultry and livestock following 50 years of genetic selection. *Lohmann Information* 41:30–37.

Hawks, J., et al. 2000. Population bottlenecks and Pleistocene human evolution. *Molecular Biology and Evolution* 17:2–22.

He, L., et al. 2012. Relationships between net primary productivity and forest stand age in U.S. forests. *Global Biogeochemical Cycles* 26(3). doi:10.1029/2010GB003942.

Heather, P. 2006. *The Fall of Roman Empire: A New History of Rome and the Barbarians*. New York: Oxford University Press.

Hecht, G. 2009. *The Radiance of France*. Cambridge, MA: MIT Press.

Hecht, J. 2018. Undersea data monster. *IEEE Spectrum* 55:36–39.

Hector, K. L., and S. Nakagawa. 2012. Quantitative analysis of compensatory and catch-up growth in diverse taxa. *Journal of Animal Ecology* 81:583–593.

Heeren, F. 2011. Rise of the titans. *Nature* 475:159–161.

Heim, N. A., et al. 2015. Cope's rule in the evolution of marine animals. *Science* 347:867–870.

Heinberg, R. 2010. *Peak Everything: Waking Up to the Century of Declines*. Gabriola Island, BC: New Society.

Helliwell, J. F., et al., eds. 2017. *World Happiness Report 2017*. New York: Center for Sustainable Development.

Henderson, J., et al. 2012. Measuring economic growth from outer space. *American Economic Review* 102:994–1028.

Hendricks, B. 2008. WP1B4 Up-scaling. Paper presented at EWEC2008. www.upwind .eu/.../EWEC2008%20Presentations/Ben%20Hendriks.pdf.

Henig, R. M. 2001. *The Monk in the Garden: The Lost and Found Genius of Gregor Mendel, the Father of Genetics*. Boston: Houghton Mifflin Harcourt.

Herbert R. A., and R. J. Sharp, eds. 1992. *Molecular Biology and Biotechnology of Extremophiles*. Glasgow: Blackie.

Hermansen, G. 1978. The populations of Rome: The regionaries. *Historia* 27:129–168.

Hermanussen, M. 2003. Stature of early Europeans. *Hormones* 2(3):175–178.

Hern, W. M. 1999. How many times has the human population doubled? Comparison with cancer. *Population and Environment* 21:59–80.

Hertz, H. 1887. Über sehr schnell elektrische Schwingungen. *Annalen der Physik* 21:421–448.

Hibbert, C. 1985. *Rome: The Biography of a City*. London: Penguin Books.

Hicks, J., and G. Allen. 1999. *A Century of Change: Trends in UK Statistics since 1900*. London: House of Commons Library. http://www.parliement.uk/commons/lib /research/rp99/rp99-111.pdf.

Hilbert, M., and P. López. 2011. The world's technological capacity to store, communicate, and compute information. *Science* 332:60–65.

Hill, D. 1984. *A History of Engineering in Classical and Medieval Times*. La Salle, IL: Open Court.

History of Bridges. 2017. The world's longest bridge—Danyang–Kunshan Grand Bridge. http://www.historyofbridges.com/famous-bridges/longest-bridge-in-the-world/.

Hjelm, B., et al. 2015. Diameter–height models for fast-growing poplar plantations on agricultural land in Sweden. *Bioenergy Research* 8:1759–1768.

HKTDC (Hong Kong Trade Development Council). 2017. PRD economic profile. http://china-trade-research.hktdc.com/business-news/article/Facts-and-Figures/PRD -Economic-Profile/ff/en/1/1X000000/1X06BW84.htm.

Hobara, S., et al. 2014. The roles of microorganisms in litter decomposition and soil formation. *Biogeochemistry* 118:471–486.

Hochberg, Z. 2011. Developmental plasticity in child growth and maturation. *Frontiers in Endocrinology* 2:41 doi:10.3389/fendo.2011.00041.

Hodge, A. T. 2001. *Roman Aqueducts and Water Supply*. London: Duckworth.

Hoegemeyer, T. 2014. *History: Corn Breeding and the US Seed Industry*. Lincoln: University of Nebraska Press. http://imbgl.cropsci.illinois.edu/school/2014/11_THOMAS_HOEGEMEYER.pdf.

Hogan, W. T. 1971. *Economic History of the Iron and Steel Industry in the United States*. 5 vols. Lexington, MA: Lexington Books.

Hone, D. W., and M. J. Benton. 2005. The evolution of large size: How does Cope's Rule work? *Trends in Ecology and Evolution* 20:4–6.

Höök, M., et al. 2012. Descriptive and predictive growth curves in energy system analysis. *Natural Resources Research* 20:103–116.

Hoornweg, D., et al. 2013. Waste production must peak this century. *Nature* 502: 615–617.

Hoppa, R. D., and C. M. Fitzgerald. 1999. *Human Growth in the Past: Studies from Bones and Teeth*. Cambridge: Cambridge University Press.

Horikoshi, K. 2016. *Extremophiles: Where It All Began*. Tokyo: Springer.

Horikoshi, K., and W. D. Grant, eds. 1998. *Extremophiles: Microbial Life in Extreme Environments*. New York: Wiley-Liss.

Hossner, K. L. 2005. *Hormonal Regulation of Farm Animal Growth*. Wallingford: CABI.

Houghton, R. A., and S. J. Goetz. 2008. New satellites help quantify carbon sources and sinks. *Eos* 89:417–418.

Howard, B., et al. 2012. Spatial distribution of urban building energy consumption by end use. *Energy and Buildings* 45:141–151.

HSBEC (Honshu-Shikoku Bridge Expressway Company). 2017. Akashi Kayoko Bridge. http://www.jb-honshi.co.jp/english/bridgeworld/bridge.html.

HSCIC (Health and Social Care Information Centre). 2015. *Statistics on Obesity, Physical Activity and Diet England 2015*. London: HSCIC.

Hu, M., et al. 2010. Dynamics of urban and rural housing stocks in China. *Building Research & Information* 38:301–317.

Huang, L. 2013. Optimization of a new mathematical model for bacterial growth. *Food Control* 32:283–288.

Hubbert, M. K. 1956. Nuclear energy and the fossil fuels. (Paper presented at the Spring Meeting of the Southern District Division of Production, American Petroleum Institute, San Antonio, March 7–9.) http://www.hubbertpeak.com/hubbert/1956/1956.pdf.

Hughes, A. 2006. *Electric Motors and Drives*. Oxford: Elsevier.

Hughes, D. E. 1899. Researches of Professor D. E. Hughes, F.R.S., in electric waves and their application to wireless telegraphy, 1879–1886. In J. J. Fahie, *A History of Wireless Telegraphy*. London: Blackwood, Appendix D, pp. 305–316.

Humphreys, W. F. 1979. Production and respiration in animal communities. *Journal of Animal Ecology* 48:427–453.

Humphries, M. O. 2013. Paths of infection: The First World War and the origins of the 1918 influenza pandemic. *War in History* 21:55–81.

Hunt, R. J. 2011. *The History of the Industrial Gas Turbine (Part 1 The First Fifty Years 1940–1990)*. Bedford: Institution of Diesel and Gas Turbine Engineers. http://www .idgte.org/IDGTE%20Paper%20582%20History%20of%20The%20Industrial%20 Gas%20Turbine%20Part%201%20v2%20%28revised%2014-Jan-11%29.pdf.

Hunt, T. L. 2006. Rethinking the fall of Easter Island. *American Scientist* 94:412–419.

Hunter, L. C., and L. Bryant. 1991. *A History of Industrial Power in the United States, 1780–1930*, vol. 3: *The Transmission of Power*. Cambridge, MA: MIT Press.

Hurnik, F., et al. 1991. *Recommended Code of Practice for the Care and Handling of Farm Animals: Beef Cattle*. Ottawa: Agriculture and Agri-Food Canada.

Hutchinson, J. R., et al. 2011. A computational analysis of limb and body dimensions in Tyrannosaurus rex with implications for locomotion, ontogeny, and growth. *PLoS ONE* 6(10):e26037.

Hwang, K., and M. Chen. 2017. *Big-Data Analytics for Cloud, IoT and Cognitive Computing*. New York: John Wiley & Sons.

Hydrocarbon Technology. 2017. West-East Gas Pipeline Project. https://www .hydrocarbons-technology.com/projects/west-east/.

Hydro-Québec. 2017. Power transmission in Québec. http://www.hydroquebec.com /learning/transport/grandes-distances.html.

IAEA (International Atomic Energy Agency). 2016. *Energy, Electricity and Nuclear Power Estimates for the Period up to 2050*. Vienna: IAEA. http://www-pub.iaea.org /MTCD/Publications/PDF/RDS-1-36Web-28008110.pdf.

IATA. 2016. IATA forecasts passenger demand to double over 20 years. http://www .iata.org/pressroom/pr/Pages/2016-10-18-02.aspx.

IBM. 2017. 5 nanometer transistors inching their way into chips. https://www.ibm .com/blogs/think/2017/06/5-nanometer-transistors/.

ICAO (International Civil Aviation Organization). 2016. *Annual Report 2016*. https:// www.icao.int/annual-report-2016/Pages/default.aspx.

ICCT (International Council on Clean Transportation). 2016. *European Vehicle Market Statistics*. Berlin: ICCT.

Ichihashi, R., and M. Tateno. 2015. Biomass allocation and long-term growth patterns of temperate lianas in comparison with trees. *New Phytologist* 207:604–612.

ICOLD (International Commission on Large Dams). 2017. *World Register of Dams.* http://www.icold-cigb.net/GB/world_register/world_register_of_dams.asp.

IDA (International Dark-Sky Association). 2017. Light pollution. http://www.darksky .org/light-pollution/.

IEA (International Energy Agency). 2018. *Global Energy and CO2 Status Report, 2017.* Paris: IEA. http://www.iea.org/geco/.

Iizumi, T., and N. Ramankutty. 2016. Changes in yield variability of major crops for 1981–2010 explained by climate change. *Environment Research Letters* 11:034003.

Illich, I. 1974. *Energy and Equity.* New York: Harper & Row.

IMF (International Monetary Fund). 2017. IMF data mapper. http://www.imf.org /external/datamapper/PPPGDP@WEO/OEMDC/ADVEC/WEOWORLD.

Imre, A., and J. Novotný. 2016. Fractals and the Korcak-law: A history and a correction. *European Physical Journal H* 41:69–91.

Inoue, H., et al. 2012. Polity scale shifts in world-systems since the Bronze Age: A comparative inventory of upsweeps and collapses. *International Journal of Comparative Sociology* 53:210–229.

INSEE (Institut National de la Statistique et des Études Économiques). 1990. *Annuaire rétrospectif de la France: 1948–1988.* Paris: INSEE.

Intel. 2017. Intel's first microprocessor. https://www.intel.com/content/www/us/en /history/museum-story-of-intel-4004.html.

Intel. 2018a. Moore's law and Intel innovation. http://www.intel.com/content/www /us/en/history/museum-gordon-moore-law.html.

Intel. 2018b. Intel chip performs 10 trillion calculations per second. https://newsroom .intel.com/news/intel-chip-performs-10-trillion-calculations-per-second/#gs .FLHXhMuI.

International Poplar Commission. 2016. *Poplars and Other Fast-Growing Trees— Renewable Resources for Future Green Economies.* Rome: FAO.

IPCC (Intergovernmental Panel on Climate Change). 2014. *Climate Change 2014: Synthesis Report.* Geneva: IPCC. http://www.ipcc.ch/report/ar5/syr/.

IPCC. 2018. *Global Warming of 1.5 °C.* https://www.ipcc.ch/sr15/.

IRRI (International Rice Research Institute). 1982. *IR36: The World's Most Popular Rice.* Los Baños: IRRI. http://books.irri.org/IR36.pdf.

Isaac, B. 1992. *The Limits of Empire: The Roman Army in the East.* Oxford: Oxford University Press.

ISC (Internet System Consortium). 2017. ISC Internet domain survey. https://www.isc.org/network/survey/.

ISD (Information Services Department, Hong Kong). 2015. Population. https://www.gov.hk/en/about/abouthk/factsheets/docs/population.pdf.

Ishimoto, M., and K. Iida. 1939. Observations sur les séismes enregistrés par le micro-séismographe construit dernièrement. *Bulletin of the Earthquake Research Institute, University of Tokyo* 17:443–478.

Islam, M. D., et al. 2009. Measurement of solar energy radiation in Abu Dhabi, UAE. *Applied Energy* 86:511–515.

ITTO (International Tropical Timber Organization). 2009. *Encouraging Industrial Forest Plantations in the Tropics*. Yokohama: ITTO.

IUCN (International Union for the Conservation of Nature). 2017a. Limulus poly-phemus. http://www.iucnredlist.org/details/11987/0.

IUCN. 2017b. Mellisuga helenae. http://www.iucnredlist.org/details/22688214/0.

Jackson, T. 2009. *Prosperity without Growth: Economics for a Finite Planet*. London: Earthscan.

Jacobs, J. 1970. *The Economy of Cities*. New York: Vintage.

Jamison, D. T., et al., eds. 2006. *Disease Control Priorities in Developing Countries*. Washington, DC: World Bank.

Jang, J., and Y. H. Jang. 2012. Spatial distributions of islands in fractal surfaces and natural surfaces. *Chaos, Solitons & Fractals* 45:1453–1459.

Jansen, M. 2000. *The Making of Modern Japan*. Cambridge, MA: Belknap Press.

Jansen, T., et al. 2002. Mitochondrial DNA and the origins of the domestic horse. *Proceedings of the National Academy of Sciences of the USA* 99:10905–10910.

Japan Press Weekly. 2018. Japan's food self-sufficiency rate remains below 40%. http://www.japan-press.co.jp/modules/news/index.php?id=11673.

Japan Times. 2015. Japan's centenarian population tops 60,000 for first time. http://www.japantimes.co.jp/news/2015/09/11/national/japans-centenarian-population-tops-60000-first-time/#.V4-SDjFTGUk.

Japan Today. 2013. The 51 busiest train stations in the world—all but 6 located in Japan. https://japantoday.com/category/features/travel/the-51-busiest-train-stations-in-the-world-all-but-6-located-in-japan.

Jaskelioff, M., et al. 2011. Telomerase reactivation reverses tissue degeneration in aged telomerase deficient mice. *Nature* 469:102–106.

JBS Five Rivers Cattle Feeding. 2017. JBS Five Rivers Cattle Feeding LLC. https://fiveriverscattle.com/pages/default.aspx.

Jedwab, R., and D. Vollrath. 2014. Urbanization without growth in historical perspective. *Explorations in Economic History* 58:1–21.

Ji, C., and T. Chen. 2008. Secular changes in stature and body mass index for Chinese youth in sixteen major cities, 1950s–2005. *American Journal of Human Biology* 20:530–537.

Jiang, B., et al. 2015. Zipf's law for all the natural cities around the world. *International Journal of Geographical Information Science* 29:498–522.

Johnson, A. M. 1956. *The Development of American Pipelines 1862–1906*. Westport, CT: Greenwood Press.

Johnson, N. P., and J. Mueller. 2002. Updating the accounts: Global mortality of the 1918–1920 "Spanish" influenza pandemic. *Bulletin of the History of Medicine* 76:105–115.

Johnson. W., et al. 2012. Eighty-year trends in infant weight and length growth: The Fels Longitudinal Study. *Journal of Pediatrics* 160:762–768.

Johnston, L., and S. H. Williamson. 2017. What was the U.S. GDP then? Measuring worth. http://www.measuringworth.org/usgdp/.

Jones, C. I. 1995. R&D-based models of economic growth. *Journal of Political Economy* 103:759–784.

Jones, H. 1973. *Steam Engines*. London: Ernest Benn.

Jones, O. R., et al. 2014. Diversity of ageing across the tree of life. *Nature* 505: 169–173.

Jones, R. C. 2011. *Crossing the Menai: An Illustrated History of the Ferries and Bridges of the Menai Strait*. Wrexham: Bridge Books.

Jönsson, K. I., and R. Bertolani. 2001. Facts and fiction about long-term survival in tardigrades. *Journal of Zoology* 255:121–123.

Jordan, E. O. 1927. *Epidemic Influenza: A Survey*. New York: American Medical Association.

Joyner, M. J., et al. 2011. The two-hour marathon: Who and when? *Journal of Applied Physiology* 110:275–277.

JR Central. 2017. About the shinkansen. https://global.jr-central.co.jp/en/company/about_shinkansen.

Kadlec, C. W., and R. J. Acampora. 1999. *Dow 100,000: Fact or Fiction*. New York: New York Institute of Finance.

Kahm, M., et al. 2010. Grofit: Fitting biological growth curves with r. *Journal of Statistical Software* 33:1021.

Kander, A. 2013. The second and third industrial revolutions. In A. Kander et al., *Power to the People: Energy in Europe over the Last Five Centuries.* Princeton, NJ: Princeton University Press, pp. 249–386.

Kander, A., et al. 2013. *Power to the People: Energy in Europe over the Last Five Centuries.* Princeton, NJ: Princeton University Press.

Kaneda, T., and C. Haub. 2011. How many people have ever lived on Earth? http://www.prb.org/Publications/Articles/2002/HowManyPeopleHaveEverLivedonEarth.aspx.

Kantar World Panel. 2015. Apple's replacement opportunity is far from over. https://www.kantarworldpanel.com/global/News/Apples-Replacement-Opportunity-is-Far-From-Over.

Kapitsa, S. P. 1992. Matematicheskaya model' rosta naseleniya mira.. *Matematicheskoye Modelirovaniye* 4(6):65–79.

Karkach, A. S. 2006. Trajectories and models of individual growth. *Demographic Research* 15:347–400.

Kaspari, M., et al. 2008. Multiple nutrients limit litterfall and decomposition in a tropical forest. *Ecology Letters* 11:35–43.

Kato, C., et al. 1998. Extremely barophilic bacteria isolated from the Mariana Trench, Challenger Deep, at a depth of 11,000 meters. *Applied and Environmental Microbiology* 64:1510–1513.

Katsukawa, Y., et al. 2002. Indeterminate growth is selected by a trade-off between high fecundity and risk avoidance in stochastic environments. *Population Ecology* 44:265–272.

Kaufmann, R. K. 1992. A biophysical analysis of the energy/real GDP ratio: Implications for substitution and technical change. *Ecological Economics* 6:35–56.

Kawashima, C. 1986. *Minka: Traditional Houses of Rural Japan.* Tokyo: Kodansha.

Keay, J. 1994. *The Honourable Company: A History of the English East India Company.* London: Macmillan.

Keith, D. 2013. *A Case for Climate Engineering.* Cambridge, MA: MIT Press.

Keith, H., et al. 2009. Re-evaluation of forest biomass carbon stocks and lessons from the world's most carbon-dense forests. *Proceedings of he National Academy of Sciences of the USA* 106:11635–11640.

Keller, J. D. 1946. Growth curves of nations. *Human Biology* 18:204–220.

Kelly, J. 2006. *The Great Mortality: An Intimate History of the Black Death, the Most Devastating Plague of All Time.* New York: Harper Perennial.

Kelly, M., and C. Ó Gráda. 2018. *Speed under Sails during the Early Industrial Revolution*. London: Center for Economic Policy Research.

Kempf, K. 1961. *Electronic Computers within the Ordnance Corps*. Aberdeen Proving Ground, MD: US Army Ordnance Corps.

Kendrick, J. W. 1961. *Productivity Trends in the United States*. Princeton, NJ: Princeton University Press.

Kennedy, C. A., et al. 2015. Energy and material flows of megacities. *Proceedings of the National Academy of Sciences of the USA* 112:5985–5990.

Kentucky Derby. 2017. Kentucky Derby winners. https://www.kentuckyderby.com/history/kentucky-derby-winners.

Kershaw, I. 2012. *The End: The Defiance and Destruction of Hitler's Germany, 1944–1945*. New York: Penguin.

Keyfitz, N., and W. Flieger. 1971. *Population: Facts and Methods of Demography*. San Francisco: W. H. Freeman.

Keyfitz, N., and W. Flieger. 1991. *World Population Growth and Aging: Demographic Trends in the Late Twentieth Century*. Chicago: University of Chicago Press.

Khan, Y. 2007. *The Great Partition: The Making of India and Pakistan*. New Haven, CT: Yale University Press.

Khodaee, G. H., and M. Saeidi. 2016. Increases of obesity and overweight in children: An alarm for parents and policymakers. *International Journal of Pediatrics* 4:1591–1601.

Kibritcioglu, A., and S. Dibooglu. 2001. *Long-Run Economic Growth: An Interdisciplinary Approach*. Urbana-Champaign: University of Illinois at Urbana-Champaign Press.

Kiewit. 2017. Verrazano narrows bridge dehumidification. http://www.kiewit.com/projects/transportation/bridge/verrazano-narrows-bridge-dehumidification.

Kilbourne, E. D. 2006. Influenza pandemics of the 20th century. *Emerging Infectious Diseases* 12:9–14.

Killen, S. S., et al. 2010. The intraspecific scaling of metabolic rate with body mass in fishes depends on lifestyle and temperature. *Ecology Letters* 13:184–193.

Killingray, D., and H. Phillips. 2003. *The Spanish Influenza Pandemic of 1918–19: New Perspectives*. London: Routledge.

Kimura, D., ed. 2008. *Cell Growth Processes: New Research*. New York: Nova Biomedical Books.

Kingsley, M. C. S. 1979. Fitting the von Bertalanffy growth equation to polar bear age-weight data. *Canadian Journal of Zoology* 57:1020–1025.

Kingsolver, J. G., and D. W. Pfennig. 2004. Individual-level selection as a cause of Cope's Rule of phyletic size increase. *Evolution* 58:1608–1612.

Kint, J., et al. 2006. Pierre-François Verhulst's final triumph. In M. Ausloos and M. Dirickx, eds., *The Logistic Map and the Route to Chaos: From the Beginnings to Modern Applications*. Berlin: Springer, pp. 3–11.

Kirk, D. 1996. Demographic transition theory. *Population Studies* 50:361–387.

Kitterick, R., et al., eds. 2013. *Old Saint Peter's, Rome*. Cambridge: Cambridge University Press.

Klare, M. 2012. The end of easy everything. *Current History* 111(741):24–28.

Klasing, M. J., and P. Milionis. 2014. Quantifying the evolution of world trade, 1870–1949. *Journal of International Economics* 92:185–197.

Kleiber, M. 1932. Body size and metabolism. *Hilgardia* 6: 315–353.

Kleiber, M. 1961. *The Fire of Life*. New York: John Wiley.

Klein, H. A. 1978. Pieter Bruegel the Elder as a guide to 16th-century technology. *Scientific American* 238(3):134–140.

Kludas, A. 2000. *Record Breakers of the North Atlantic: Blue Riband Liners 1838–1952*. London: Chatham.

Klümper, W., and M. Qaim. 2014. A meta-analysis of the impacts of genetically modified crops. *PLoS ONE* 9(11):e111629. doi:10.1371/journal.pone.0111629.

Knizetova, H., et al. 1995. Comparative study of growth curves in poultry. *Genetics Selection Evolution* 27:365–375.

Koch, G. W., et al. 2004. The limits to tree height. *Nature* 428:851–854.

Koch, G. W., et al. 2015. Growth maximization trumps maintenance of leaf conductance in the tallest angiosperm. *Oecologia* 177:321–331.

Koch-Weser, J. N. 2013. *The Reliability of China's Economic Data: An Analysis of National Output*. https://www.uscc.gov/sites/default/files/Research/TheReliabilityof China%27sEconomicData.pdf.

Koehler, H. W., and W. Oehlers. 1998. 95 years of diesel-electric propulsion: From a makeshift solution to a modern propulsion system. (Paper presented at the 2nd International Diesel Electric Propulsion conference, Helsinki, April 26–29, 1998.)

Koepke, N., and J. Baten. 2005. The biological standard of living in Europe during the last two millennia. *European Review of Economic History* 9:61–95.

Koepke, N., and J. Baten. 2008. Agricultural specialization and height in ancient and medieval Europe. *Explorations in Economic History* 45:127–146.

Kohler, H.-P., et al. 2002. The emergence of lowest-low fertility in Europe during the 1990s. *Population and Development Review* 28:641–680.

Kohler, T. A., et al. 2017. Greater post-Neolithic wealth disparities in Eurasia than in North America and Mesoamerica. *Nature* doi:10.1038/nature24646.

Komlos, J. 1995. *The Biological Standard of Living in Europe and America, 1700–1900*. Aldershot: Variorum.

Komlos, J. 2001. On the biological standard of living of eighteenth-century Americans: Taller, richer, healthier. *Research in Economic History* 20:223–248.

Kondratiev, N. D. 1926. Die langen Wellen der Konjunktur. *Archiv für Sozialwissenschaft und Sozialpolitik* 56:573–609.

Konrad, T. 2010. MV Mont, Knock Nevis, Jahre Viking—world's largest supertanker. *gCaptain*, July 18. http://gcaptain.com/mont-knock-nevis-jahre-viking-worlds-largest -tanker-ship/#.Vc3zB4dRGM8.

Kooijman, S. A. L. M. 2000 *Dynamic Energy and Mass Budgets in Biological Systems*. Cambridge: Cambridge University Press.

Korčák, J. 1938. Deux types fondamentaux de distribution statistique. *Bulletin de l'Institut International de Statistique* 3:295–299.

Korčák, J. 1941. Přírodní dualita statistického rozložení. *Statistický Obzor* 22:171–222.

Körner, C., et al. 2007. CO_2 fertilization: When, where, how much? In J. G. Canadell et al., eds., *Terrestrial Ecosystems in a Changing World*, Berlin: Springer, pp. 9–21.

Korotayev, A., et al. 2006. *Introduction to Social Macrodynamics: Compact Macromodels of the World System Growth*. Moscow: URSS.

Koyama, K., et al. 2017. A lognormal distribution of the lengths of terminal twigs on self-similar branches of elm trees. *Proceedings of the Royal Society B* 284(1846):20162395. doi:10.1098/rspb.2016.2395.

Kozłowski, J., and M. Konarzewski. 2004. Is West, Brown and Enquist's model of allometric scaling mathematically correct and biologically relevant? *Functional Ecology* 18:283–289.

Kozłowski, J., and A. T. Teriokhin. 1999. Allocation of energy between growth and reproduction: The Pontryagin Maximum Principle solution for the case of age- and season-dependent mortality. *Evolutionary Ecology Research*, 1: 423–441.

Kraikivski, P. 2013. *Trends in Biophysics: From Cell Dynamics Toward Multicellular Growth Phenomena*. Waretown, NJ: Apple Academic Press.

Krautheimer, R. 2000. *Rome: Profile of a City, 312–1308*. Princeton, NJ: Princeton University Press.

Kremer, M. 1993. Population growth and technological change: One million BC to 1990. *Quarterly Journal of Economics* 108:681–716.

Kretschmann, H. J., ed. 1986. *Brain Growth*. Basel: S. Karger.

Krøll Cranes. 2017. K10000: The most profitable solution for heavy lifts. http://www.krollcranes.dk/media/k-10000.pdf.

Kron, G. 2005. Anthropometry, physical anthropology, and the reconstruction of ancient health, nutrition, and living standards. *Historia* 54:68–83.

Krugman, P. 1991. *Geography and Trade*. Cambridge, MA: MIT Press.

Kruse, T. N., et al. 2014. Speed trends in male distance running. *PLoS ONE* 9(11): e112978. doi:10.1371/journal.pone.0112978.

Kuczmarski, R. J., et al. 2002. 2000 CDC growth charts for the United States: Methods and development. *Vital and Health Statistics* 11(246):1–190.

Kullinger, K. 2009. High-megawatt electric drive motors. https://www.nist.gov/sites/default/files/documents/pml/high_megawatt/4_2-Approved-Kullinger.pdf.

Kunsch, P. L. 2006. Limits to success. The Iron Law of Verhulst. In M. Ausloos and M. Dirickx, eds., *The Logistic Map and the Route to Chaos: From the Beginnings to Modern Applications*. Berlin: Springer, pp. 29–51.

Kurtz, M. J., and A. Schrank. 2007. Growth and governance: Models, measures, and mechanisms. *Journal of Politics* 69:538–554.

Kurzweil, R. 2001. The law of accelerating returns. http://www.kurzweilai.net/the-law-of-accelerating-returns.

Kurzweil, R. 2005. *The Singularity Is Near*. New York: Penguin.

Kurzweil, R. 2017. Kurzweil Accelerating Intelligence. http://www.kurzweilai.net/.

Kushner, D. 2009. *Levittown: Two Families, One Tycoon, and the Fight for Civil Rights in America's Legendary Suburb*. New York: Walker.

Kuznets, S. 1934. *National Income 1929–1932*. (A report to the U.S. Senate, 73rd Congress, 2nd session.) Washington, DC: US Government Printing Office.

Kuznets, S. 1937. National income and capital formation, 1919–1935. In M. Friedman, ed., *Studies in Income and Wealth*. Washington, DC: National Bureau of Economic Research, vol. 1, pp. 35–48.

Kuznets, S. 1955. Economic growth and income inequality. *American Economic Review* 65:1–28.

Kyoto-machisen. 2017. Kyo-machiya (Kyoto traditional townhouses). http://kyoto-machisen.jp/fund_old/english/pdf/machiya_design.pdf.

Lagercrantz, H. 2016. *Infant Brain Development: Formation of the Mind and the Emergence of Consciousness*. Berlin: Springer.

Laherrère, J., and D. Sornette. 1998. Stretched exponential distributions in nature and economy: "Fat tails" with characteristic scales. *European Physical Journal B* 2:525–539.

Laird, A. K. 1967. Evolution of the human growth curve. *Growth* 31:345–355.

Lamb, J. P. 2007. *Evolution of the American Diesel Locomotive*. Bloomington: Indiana University Press.

Lampl, M. 2009. Human growth from the cell to the organism: Saltations and integrative physiology. *Annals of Human Biology* 36:478–495.

Lampl, M., et al. 1992. Saltation and stasis: A model of human growth. *Journal of Science* 28:801–803.

Landau, S. B., and C. W. Condit. 1996. *Rise of the New York Skyscraper, 1865–1913*. New Haven, CT: Yale University Press.

Landry, A. 1934. *La révolution démographique: Études et essais sur les problèmes de la population*. Paris: INED-Presses Universitaires de France.

Lange, G.-M., et al., eds. 2018. *The Changing Wealth of Nations*. Washington, DC: World Bank Group.

Laplace, P. S. 1774. Mémoire sur la Probabilité des Causes par les évènemens. *Mémoires de Mathematique et de Physique*, Presentés à l'Académie Royale des Sciences, Par Divers Savans & Lus Dans ses Assemblées, Tome Sixième, 1774, pp. 621–656.

Laplace, P. S. 1812. *Théorie analytique des probabilités*. Paris: Courcier.

Larson, A. 2017. World's most-efficient combined cycle plant: EDF Bouchain. *Power*, September 1, pp. 22–23.

Lartey, A. 2015. What would it take to prevent stunted growth in children in sub-Saharan Africa? *Proceedings of the Nutrition Society* 74:449–453.

Laurin, M. 2004. The evolution of body size, Cope's rule and the origin of amniotes. *Systematic Biology* 53:594–622.

Lavery, B. 1984. *The Ship of the Line*, vol. 2: *Design, Construction and Fittings*. Annapolis, MD: Naval Institute Press.

Lavoie, M., and E. Stockhammer. 2013. *Wage-Led Growth: An Equitable Strategy for Economic Recovery*. London: Palgrave Macmillan.

Lawrence, D., et al. 2016. Long term population, city size and climate trends in the Fertile Crescent: A first approximation. *PLoS ONE* 11(3):e0152563. doi:10.1371/journal.pone.0152563.

Lawrence, T. L., et al., eds. 2013. *Growth of Farm Animals*. Wallingford: CABI.

Lefebvre, L. 2012. Primate encephalization. *Progress in Brain Research* 195:393–412.

Lee, J., and J. Mo. 2011. Analysis of technological innovation and environmental performance improvement in aviation sector. *International Journal of Environmental Research and Public Health* 8:3777–3795.

Lee, R. D., and D. S. Reher, eds. 2011. *Demographic Transition and Its Consequences*. New York: Population and Development Review.

Lee, R., and Y. Zhou. 2017. Does fertility or mortality drive contemporary population aging? The revisionist view revisited. *Population and Development Review* 43:285–301.

Lee, S., and N. Wong. 2010. Reconstruction of epidemic curves for pandemic influenza A (H1N1) 2009 at city and sub-city levels. *Virology Journal* 7:321. http://www.virologyj.com/content/7/1/321.

Lees, A. 2015. *The City: A World History*. Oxford: Oxford University Press.

Leggiere, M. V. 2007. *The Fall of Napoleon: The Allied Invasion of France, 1813–1814*. Cambridge: Cambridge University Press.

Lehner, M. 1997. *The Complete Pyramids*. London: Thames & Hudson.

Leigh, S. R. 1996. Evolution of human growth spurts. *American Journal of Physical Anthropology* 101:455–474.

Leigh, S. R. 2001. Evolution of human growth. *Evolutionary Anthropology* 10:223–236.

Lelieveld, J., et al. 2016. Strongly increasing heat extremes in the Middle East and North Africa (MENA) in the 21st century, *Climatic Change* 137:245–260. doi:10.1007/s10584-016-1665-6.

Leonard, W. R., et al. 2007. Effects of brain evolution on human nutrition and metabolism. *Annual Review of Nutrition* 27:311–327.

Lepre, J. P. 1990. *The Egyptian Pyramids*. Jefferson, NC: McFarland.

Le Quéré, C., et al. 2013. The global carbon budget 1959–2011. *Earth System Science Data* 5:165–185.

Lesk, M. 1997. How much information is there in the world? https://courses.cs.washington.edu/courses/cse590s/03au/lesk.pdf.

Lesthaeghe, R. 2014. The second demographic transition: A concise overview of its development. *Proceedings of the National Academy of Sciences of the USA* 111:18112–18115.

Lesthaeghe, R., and L. Neidert. 2006. The second demographic transition in the United States: Exception or textbook example? *Population and Development Review* 32:669–698.

Lesthaeghe R., and D. van de Kaa. 1986. Twee demografische transities? In D. van de Kaa and R. Lesthaeghe, eds., *Bevolking: Groei en krimp*, Deventer: Van Loghum Slaterus, pp. 9–24.

Leyzerovich, A. S. 2008. *Steam Turbines for Modern Fossil-Fuel Power Plants*. Lilburn, GA: Fairmont Press.

Li, H., et al. 2005. Lack of evidence for 3/4 scaling of metabolism in terrestrial plants. *Journal of Integrative Plant Biology* 47:1173–1183.

Li, N., et al. 2009. Functional mapping of human growth trajectories. *Journal of Theoretical Biology* 261:33–42.

Li, X., et al. 2015 Which games are growing bacterial populations playing? *Journal of the Royal Society Interface* 12:20150121.

Li, X., et al. 2016. Patterns of cereal yield growth across China from 1980 to 2010 and their implications for food production and food security. *PLoS ONE* 11(7):e0159061. doi:10.1371/journal.pone.0159061.

Liebherr. 2017. Products. https://www.liebherr.com/en/dnk/products/construction -machines/tower-cranes/top-slewing-cranes/top-slewing-cranes.html.

Lifson, N., and R. McClintock. 1966. Theory of use of the turnover rates of body water for measuring energy and material balance. *Journal of Theoretical Biology* 12:46–74.

Lima-Mendez, G., and J. van Helden. 2009. The powerful law of the power law and other myths in network biology. *Molecular Biosystems* 5:1482–1493.

Limpert, E. 2001. Log-normal distributions across the sciences: Keys and clues. *Bio-Science* 51:341–352.

Lin, M., and P. Huybers. 2012. Reckoning wheat yield trends *Environmental Research Letters* 7:1–6.

Linton, R. 1936. *The Study of Man*. New York: Appleton Century Crofts.

Lintott, A. 1981. What was the 'Imperium Romanum'? *Greece & Rome* 28:53–67.

Lippert, O., and M. Walker, eds. 1997. *The Underground Economy: Global Evidence of Its Size and Impact*. Vancouver: Fraser Institute.

Lippi, G., et al. 2008. Updates on improvement of human athletic performance: Focus on world records in athletics. *British Medical Bulletin* 87:7–15.

Litton, C. M., et al. 2007. Carbon allocation in forest ecosystems. *Global Change Biology* 13: 2089–2109.

Liu, J., et al. 2005. China's changing landscape during the 1990s: Large-scale land transformation estimated with satellite data. *Geophysical Research Letters* 32:L02405. doi:10.1029/2004GL021649.

Liu, T., et al. 2001. *Asian Population History*. Oxford: Oxford University Press.

Livi-Bacci, M. 2000. *The Population of Europe*. Oxford: Wiley-Blackwell.

Livi-Bacci, M. 2012. *A Concise History of World Population*. Oxford: Wiley-Blackwell.

Lloyd, J., and G. D. Farquhar. 2008. Effects of rising temperatures and [CO_2] on the physiology of tropical forest trees. *Philosophical Transactions of the Royal Society B* 363:1811–1817.

Lloyd-Smith, J. O., et al. 2005. Superspreading and the effect of individual variation on disease emergence. *Nature* 438:355–359.

Lobell, D. B., et al. 2014. Greater sensitivity to drought accompanies maize yield increase in the U.S. Midwest. *Science* 344:516–519.

Longman, J. 2016. 85-year-old marathoner is so fast that even scientists marvel. *New York Times*, December 28. https://www.nytimes.com/2016/12/28/sports/ed-whitlock -marathon-running.html.

Longman, P. 2010. Think again: Global aging. *Foreign Policy* (November):52–58.

Lonsdale, W. M. 1990. The self-thinning rule: Dead or alive? *Ecology* 71:1373–1388.

Lotka, A. J. 1926. The frequency distribution of scientific productivity. *Journal of the Washington Academy of Sciences* 16:317–324.

Lubbock J. 1870. *The Origin of Civilisation and the Primitive Condition of Man*. London: Longmans, Green.

Luckstead, J., and S. Devadoss. 2014. Do the world's largest cities follow Zipf's and Gibrat's laws? *Economics Letters* 125:182–186.

Ludy, L. V. 1909. *A Practical Treatise on Locomotive Boiler and Engine Design, Construction, and Operation*. Chicago: American Technical Society.

Luknatsskii, N. N. 1936. Podnyatie Aleksandrovskoi kolonny v 1832. *Stroitel'naya Promyshlennost'* (13):31–34.

Lumpkin, T. A. 2015. How a gene from Japan revolutionized the world of wheat: CIMMYT's quest for combining genes to mitigate threats to global food security. In Y. Ogihara et al., eds., *Advances in Wheat Genetics: From Genome to Field*. Berlin: Springer, pp. 13–20.

Lundborg, P., et al. 2014. Height and earnings: The role of cognitive and noncognitive skills. *Journal of Human Resources* 49:141–166.

Luo, J., et al. 2015. Estimation of growth curves and suitable slaughter weight of the Liangshan pig. *Asian Australian Journal of Animal Science* 28:1252–1258.

Lutz, W., et al. 2001. The end of world population growth. *Nature* 412:543–545.

Lutz, W., et al. 2004. *The End of World Population Growth in the 21st Century: New Challenges for Human Capital Formation and Sustainable Development*. London: Earthscan.

Lutz, W., et al. 2006. The low-fertility trap hypothesis: Forces that may lead to further postponement and fewer births in Europe. *Vienna Yearbook of Population Research* 4:167–192.

Lutz, W., et al. 2008. The coming acceleration of global population aging. *Nature* 451:716–719.

Luyssaert, S., et al. 2007. CO_2 balance of boreal, temperate, and tropical forests derived from a global database. *Global Change Biology* 13:2509–2537.

Luyssaert, S., et al. 2008. Old growth forests as global carbon sinks. *Nature* 455:213–215.

Lyon, A. 2014. Why are normal distributions normal? *British Journal for the Philosophy of Science* 65:621–649.

Ma, J., et al. 2015. Gross primary production of global forest ecosystems has been overestimated. *Scientific Reports* 5:10820. doi:10.1038/srep10820.

MacArthur, R. H., and E. O. Wilson. 1967. *The Theory of Island Biogeography*. Princeton, NJ: Princeton University Press.

Macieira-Coelho, A., ed. 2005. *Developmental Biology of Neoplastic Growth*. Berlin: Springer.

Macrotrends. 2017. Dow Jones—100 year historical chart. http://www.macrotrends.net/1319/dow-jones-100-year-historical-chart.

Maddison, A. 2007. *Contours of the World Economy, 1–2020 AD*. Oxford: Oxford University Press.

Magurran, A. E. 1988. *Ecological Diversity and Its Measurement*. London: Croom Helm.

Mahaffey, J. A. 2011. *The History of Nuclear Power*. New York: Facts on File.

Mahmoud, K. M. 2013. *Durability of Bridge Structures*. Boca Raton, FL: CRC Press.

Maino, J. L., et al. 2014. Metabolic constraints and currencies in animal ecology: Reconciling theories for metabolic scaling. *Journal of Animal Ecology* 83:20–29.

Maitra, A., and K. A. Dill. 2015. Bacterial growth laws reflect the evolutionary importance of energy efficiency. *Proceedings of the National Academy of Sciences of the USA* 112:406–411.

Malanima, P. 2011. The long decline of a leading economy: GDP in Central and Northern Italy, 1300–1913. *European Review of Economic History* 15:169–219.

Malthus, T. 1798. *An Essay on the Principle of Population*. London: J. Johnson. http://www.esp.org/books/malthus/population/malthus.pdf.

Malthus, T. R. 1807. *An Essay on the Principle of Population*. London: J. Johnson.

Malyshev, D. A., et al. 2014. A semi-synthetic organism with an expanded genetic alphabet. *Nature* 509:385–388.

Manary, M., et al. 2016. Protein quality and growth in malnourished children. *Food and Nutrition Bulletin* 37:S29–S36.

Mandelbrot, B. 1967. How long is the coast of Britain? Statistical self-similarity and fractional dimension. *Science* 156:636–638.

Mandelbrot, B. 1975. Stochastic models for the Earth's relief, the shape and the fractal dimension of the coastlines, and the number-area rule for islands. *Proceedings of the National Academy of Sciences of the USA* 72:3825–3828.

Mandelbrot, B. 1977. *Fractals: Form, Chance and Dimension*. San Francisco: Freeman.

Mandelbrot, B. B. 1982. *The Fractal Geometry of Nature*. New York: Freeman.

MAN Diesel. 2007. MAN Diesel Sets New World Standard. https://pdfs.semanticscholar .org/b85a/f0ad9b92e1ff3797672805dadce123e2a6cf.pdf.

MAN Diesel. 2018. *Two-stroke Low Speed Engines*. https://powerplants.man-es.com /products/two-stroke-low-speed-engines.

Mann, C. C. 2018. *The Wizard and the Prophet: Two Remarkable Scientists and Their Dueling Visions to Shape Tomorrow's World*. New York: Knopf.

Mansfield, J., et al. 2012. Top 10 plant pathogenic bacteria in molecular plant path. *Molecular Plant Pathology* 13:614–629.

Manyika, J., et al. 2017. *The Productivity Puzzle: A Close Look at the United States*. New York: McKinsey Global Institute.

Marc, A., et al. 2014. Marathon progress: Demography, morphology and environment. *Journal of Sports Sciences* 32:524–532.

Marchetti, C. 1977. Primary energy substitution models: On the interaction between energy and society. *Technological Forecasting and Social Change* 10:345–356.

Marchetti, C. 1985. *Action Curves and Clockwork Geniuses*. Laxenburg: International Institute for Applied Systems Analysis. http://pure.iiasa.ac.at/2627/1/WP-85-074.pdf.

Marchetti, C. 1986a. Fifty-year pulsation in human affairs. *Futures* 18:376–388.

Marchetti, C. 1986b. *Stable Rules in Social and Economic Behavior*. Laxenburg: International Institute for Applied Systems Analysis. http://www.cesaremarchetti.org /archive/scan/MARCHETTI-066.pdf.

Marchetti, C., and J. H. Ausubel. 2012. Quantitative dynamics of human empires. *International Journal of Anthropology* 27:1–62.

Marchetti, C., and N. Nakicenovic. 1979. *The Dynamics of Energy Systems and the Logistic Substitution Model*. Laxenburg: International Institute for Applied Systems Analysis.

Marck, A., et al. 2017. Are we reaching the limits of *Homo sapiens*? *Frontiers in Physiology* 8 doi:10.3389/fphys.2017.00812.

Marfan Foundation. 2017. What is Marfan syndrome? http://www.marfan.org/about/marfan.

Marine Log. 2017. *Selandia* (1912). http://www.marinelog.com/docs/cen2.html.

Marković, D., and C. Gros. 2014. Power laws and self-organized criticality in theory and nature. *Physics Reports* 536:41–74.

Marks, E. C. R. 1904. *The Construction of Cranes and Other Lifting Machinery*. Manchester: Technical Publishing Company.

Marland, G., et al. 2017. Global, regional, and national fossil-fuel CO_2 emissions. http://cdiac.ess-dive.lbl.gov/trends/emis/overview.html.

Marquet, P. A., et al. 2005. Scaling and power-laws in ecological systems. *Journal of Experimental Biology* 208:1749–1769.

Marshall, A. 1890. *Principles of Economics*. London: Macmillan.

Martin, P. 1991. *Growth and Yield Prediction Systems*. Victoria, BC: Ministry of Forests.

Martin, T. C. 1922. *Forty Years of Edison Service, 1882–1922: Outlining the Growth and Development of the Edison System in New York City*. New York: New York Edison Company.

Martínez-Alier, J., ed. 2015. *Handbook of Ecological Economics*. Cheltenham: Edward Elgar.

Martin-Silverstone, E., et al. 2015. Exploring the relationship between skeletal mass and total body mass in birds. *PLoS ONE* 10(10):e0141794. doi:10.1371/journal.pone.0141794.

Martorell, R., and F. Haschke. 2001. *Nutrition and Growth*. Philadelphia: Lippincott Williams & Wilkins.

Maruyama, S., and S. Nakamura. 2015. The decline in BMI among Japanese women after World War II. *Economics and Human Biology* 18:125–138.

Mather, A. S. 2005. Assessing the world's forests. *Global Environmental Change* 15:267–280.

Mathews, J. D., et al. 2007. A biological model for influenza transmission: Pandemic planning implications of asymptomatic infection and immunity. *PLoS ONE* 2(11):e1220. doi:10.1371/journal.pone.0001220.

Mathews, T. J., and B. E. Hamilton. 2014. First births to older women continue to rise. *NCHS Data Brief* 152:1–8.

Matthies, A. L. 1992. Medieval treadwheels: Artists' views of building construction. *Technology and Culture* 33:510–547.

Mattison, J. A., et al. 2012. Impact of caloric restriction on health and survival in rhesus monkeys: The NIA study. *Nature* 489:318–321.

Maxwell, J. C. 1865. A dynamical theory of the electromagnetic field. *Philosophical Transactions of the Royal Society London* 155:495–512.

Maxwell, J. C. 1873. *A Treatise on Electricity and Magnetism.* Oxford: Clarendon Press.

May, R. M. 1981. Patterns in multi-species communities. In R. M. May, ed., *Theoretical Ecology: Principles and Applications.* Oxford: Blackwell, pp. 197–227.

Mayer, S., and P. Mayer. 2006. Connections to World War I. In D. A. Herring, ed., *Anatomy of a Pandemic: The 1918 Influenza in Hamilton.* Hamilton, ON: Allegra, pp. 18–30.

Mazor, S. 1995. The history of the microcomputer—Invention and evolution. *Proceedings of the IEEE* 83:1601–1608.

McAdam, J. L. 1824. *Remarks on the Present System of Road Making; With Observations, Deduced from Practice and Experience.* London: Longman.

McAlister, D. 1879. The law of geometric mean. *Proceedings of the Royal Society* 29:367–376.

McAllister, B. 2010. *DC-3: A Legend in Her Time: A 75th Anniversary Photographic Tribute.* Boulder, CO: Roundup Press.

McCormack, G. 1996. *The Emptiness of Japanese Affluence.* Armonk, NY: M. E. Sharpe.

McCullough, M. E. 1973. *Optimum Feeding of Dairy Animals: For Milk and Meat.* Athens: University of Georgia Press.

McEvedy, C., and R. Jones. 1978. *Atlas of World Population History.* London: Allen Lane.

McGowan, A. P. 1980. *The Century before Steam: The Development of the Sailing Ship, 1700–1820.* London: Stationary Office.

McGranahan, G., et al. 2005. Urban systems. In R. Hassan et al., eds., *Ecosystems and Human Well-Being: Current Status and Trends.* Washington DC: Island Press, pp. 795–825.

McIver, D. J., and J. S. Brownstein. 2014. Wikipedia usage estimates prevalence of influenza-like illness in the United States in near real-time. *PLoS Computational Biology* 10(4):e1003581. doi:10.1371/journal.pcbi.1003581.

McKay, R. C. 1928. *Some Famous Sailing Ships and Their Builder, Donald McKay*. New York: G. P. Putnam's Sons.

McKechnie, A. E., and B. O. Wolf. 2004. The allometry of avian basal metabolic rate: Good predictions need good data. *Physiological and Biochemical Zoology* 77:502–521.

McKendrick, A. G., and M. Kesava Pai. 1911. The rate of multiplication of microorganisms: A mathematical study. *Proceedings of the Royal Society of Edinburgh* 31:649–655.

McMahon, S. M., et al. 2010. Evidence for a recent increase in forest growth. *Proceedings of the National Academy of Sciences of the USA* 107:3611–3615. www.pnas.org/cgi /doi/10.1073/pnas.0912376107.

McMahon, T. 1973. Size and shape in biology. *Science* 179:1201–1204.

McMahon, T., and J. T. Bonner. 1983. *On Size and Life*. New York: W. H. Freeman.

McMorrow, K., and W. Roeger. 2004. *The Economic and Financial Market Consequences of Global Aging*. New York: Springer.

McNab, B. K. 2009. Resources and energetics determined dinosaur maximal size. *Proceedings of the National Academy of Sciences of the USA* 106:12184–12188.

Mead, D. J. 2005. Forests for energy and the role of planted trees. *Critical Reviews in Plant Sciences* 24:407–421.

Mead, G. H. 1934. *Mind, Self, and Society*. Chicago: University of Chicago Press.

Meadows, D. J., et al. 1972. *The Limits to Growth*. New York: Universe Books.

Meadows, D., et al. 2004. *Limits to Growth: The 30-Year Update*. White River Junction, VT: Chelsea Green.

Meeker, M. 2017. Internet trends 2017—code conference. http://www.kpcb.com /internet-trends.

Mehra, P. 2014. Black economy now amounts to 75% of GDP. http://www.thehindu .com/news/national/black-economy-now-amounts-to-75-of-gdp/article6278286.ece ?homepage=true#lb?ref=infograph/0/.

Mehrotra, S., and E. Delamonica. 2007. *Eliminating Human Poverty: Macroeconomic and Social Policies for Equitable Growth*. London: Zed Books.

Melhem, Z. 2013. *Electricity Transmission, Distribution and Storage Systems*. Sawston: Woodhead.

Méndez, F., and F. Sepúlveda. 2006. Corruption, growth and political regimes: Cross-country evidence. *European Journal of Political Economy* 22:82–98.

Mensch, G. 1979. *Stalemate in Technology*. Cambridge, MA: Ballinger.

Menzel, P. 1994. *Material World: A Global Family Portrait*. San Francisco: Sierra Club.

Menzes, M., et al. 2003. Annual growth rings and long-term growth patterns of mangrove trees from the Bragança peninsula, North Brazil. *Wetlands Ecology and Management* 11:233–242.

Metrocosm. 2017. The history of urbanization, 3700 BC–2000 AD. http://metrocosm .com/history-of-cities/.

Meyer, F. 1947. *l'Accélération évolutive*. Paris: Librairie des Sciences et des Arts.

Meyer, F., and J. Vallee. 1975. The dynamics of long-term growth. *Technological Forecasting and Social Change* 7:285–300.

Meyer, P. S., et al. 1999. A primer on logistic growth and substitution: The mathematics of the Loglet Lab software. *Technological Forecasting and Social Change* 61:247–271.

Meynen, P. G. 1968. *Thomas Robert Malthus, His Predecessors and Contemporary Critics*. New York: New York University Press.

Michaletz, S. T., et al. 2014. Convergence of terrestrial plant production across global climate gradients. *Nature* 512:39–43.

Michelet, J. 1872. *Histoire du XIXe siècle*. Paris: G. Baillière.

Middleton, G. D. 2017. *Understanding Collapse: Ancient History and Modern Myths*. Cambridge: Cambridge University Press.

Mihhalevski, A., et al. 2010. Growth characterization of individual rye sourdough bacteria by isothermal microcalorimetry. *Journal of Applied Microbiology* 110:529–540.

Milanovic, B., ed. 2012. *Globalization and Inequality*. Cheltenham: Edward Elgar.

Millar, F. 1993. *The Roman Near East 31 BC–AD 337*. Cambridge, MA: Harvard University Press.

Millward, D. J. 2017. Nutrition, infection and stunting: The roles of deficiencies of individual nutrients and foods, and of inflammation, as determinants of reduced linear growth of children. *Nutrition Research Reviews* 30:50–72.

Minetti, A. E. 2003. Efficiency of equine express postal systems. *Nature* 426:785–786.

Ministry of Forestry. 1999. *How to Determine Site Index in Silviculture*. Victoria, BC: Ministry of Forestry.

Mirabeau, V. R. 1756. *L'ami des hommes, ou Traité de la population*. Avignon.

Miranda, L. C. M., and C. A. S. Lima. 2012. Trends and cycles of the internet evolution and worldwide impacts. *Technological Forecasting and Social Change* 79:744–765.

Mishan, E. F. 1967. *Costs of Economic Growth*. New York: Praeger.

Mitchell, B., ed. 1998. *International Historical Statistics*. London: Palgrave Macmillan.

Mitzenmacher, M. 2004. A brief history of generative models for power law and lognormal distributions. *Internet Mathematics* 1:226–251.

Miyamoto, M. 2004. Quantitative aspects of Tokugawa economy. In A. Hayami, O. Satō and R.P. Toby, eds., *Emergence of Economic Society in Japan, 1600–1859*, vol. 1 of *The Economic History of Japan: 1600–1990*. Oxford: Oxford University Press, pp. 36–84.

Mo, P. H. 2001. Corruption and economic growth. *Journal of Comparative Economics* 29:66–79.

Moatsos, M., et al. 2014. Income inequality since 1820. In J. L. van Zanden et al., eds., *How Was Life? Global Well-Being since 1820*. Paris: OECD, pp. 199–215.

Modelski, G. 2003. *World Cities: −3000 to 2000*. Washington, DC: FAROS 2000.

Modern Power Systems. 2010. Full steam ahead for Flamanville 3 EPR turbine island construction. http://www.modernpowersystems.com/features/featurefull-steam-ahead -for-flamanville-3-epr-turbine-island-construction/.

Modis, T. 1992. *Predictions: Society's Telltale Signature Reveals the Past and Forecasts the Future*. New York: Simon & Schuster.

Modis, T. 2005. The end of the internet rush. *Technological Forecasting and Social Change* 72:938–943.

Modis, T. 2006. The singularity is near: When humans transcend biology-Discussions. *Technological Forecasting and Social Change* 73:104–112.

Modis, T. 2017. A hard-science approach to Kondratieff's economic cycle. *Technological Forecasting and Social Change* 122:63–70.

Mohler, C. L., et al. 1978. Structure and allometry of trees during self-thinning of pure stands. *Journal of Ecology* 66:599–614.

Mokyr, J. 2002. *The Gifts of Athena: Historical Origins of the Knowledge Economy*. Princeton, NJ: Princeton University Press.

Mokyr, J. 2009. *The Enlightened Economy: An Economic History of Britain 1700–1850*. New Haven, CT: Yale University Press.

Mokyr, J. 2014. The next age of invention: Technology's future is brighter than pessimists allow. *City Journal* 24:12–21. https://www.city-journal.org/html/next-age -invention-13618.html.

Mokyr, J. 2016. Progress isn't natural. *The Atlantic*, November 17. https://www .theatlantic.com/business/archive/2016/11/progress-isnt-natural-mokyr/507740/.

Mokyr, J. 2017. *A Culture of Growth: The Origins of the Modern Economy*. Princeton, NJ: Princeton University Press.

Monaco, A. 2011. Edison's Pearl Street Station recognized with milestone. http:// theinstitute.ieee.org/tech-history/technology-history/edisons-pearl-street-station -recognized-with-milestone810.

Monecke, S., et al. 2009. Modelling the black death. A historical case study and implications for the epidemiology of bubonic plague. *International Journal of Medical Microbiology* 299:582–593.

Monod, J. 1949. The growth of bacterial cultures. *Annual Review of Microbiology* 3:371–394.

Monroe, M., and F. Bokma. 2010. Little evidence for Cope's Rule from Bayesian phylogenetic analysis of extant mammals. *Journal of Evolutionary Biology* 23: 2017–2021.

Moore, G. E. 1965. Cramming more components onto integrated circuits. *Electronics* 38(8):114–117.

Moore, G. E. 1975. Progress in digital integrated electronics. *Technical Digest, IEEE International Electron Devices Meeting*, 11–13.

Moore, G. E. 2003. No exponential is forever: But "Forever" can be delayed! (Paper presented at IEEE International Solid-State Circuits Conference, San Francisco.) http://ieeexplore.ieee.org/document/1234194/.

Mora, C., et al. 2011. How many species are there on Earth and in the ocean? *PLoS Biology* 9(8):e1001127. doi:10.1371/journal.pbio.1001127.

Moravec, H. 1988. *Mind Children*. Cambridge, MA: Harvard University Press.

Moreno, J. L. 1951. *Sociometry, Experimental Method and the Science of Society: An Approach to a New Political Orientation*. Boston: Beacon House.

Morens, D. M., and A. S. Fauci. 2007. The 1918 influenza pandemic: Insights for the 21st century. *Journal of Infectious Diseases* 195:1018–1028.

Morgan, D. O. 2007. *The Cell Cycle: Principles of Control*. London: New Science Press.

Morin, R. 1854. *Civilisation*. Saumur: P. Godet.

Morison, S. E. 1951. *Aleutians, Gilberts and Marshalls, June 1942—April 1944*. New York: Little, Brown.

Morita, A., and S. Ishihara. 1989. *"No" to ieru Nihon* (The Japan That Can Say No). Tokyo: Konbusha. English translation: http://mohsen.banan.1.byname.net/content /republished/doc.public/politics/japan/publication/japanSaysNo/japanSaysNo.pdf.

Moritz, L. A. 1958. *Grain-Mills and Flour in Classical Antiquity*. Oxford: Clarendon Press.

Morrey, C. R. 1978. *The Changing Population of the London Boroughs*. London: Greater London Council.

Morris, I. 2005. *The Growth of Greek Cities in the First Millennium BC*. Stanford, CA: Stanford University Press.

Morris, I. 2011. *Why the West Rules—For Now: The Patterns of History, and What They Reveal about the Future.* New York: Picador.

Morris, I. 2013. *The Measure of Civilization: How Social Development Decides the Fate of Nations.* Princeton, NJ: Princeton University Press.

Morrison, J. L., and M. D. Morecroft, eds. 2006. *Plant Growth and Climate Change.* Oxford: Blackwell.

Morrison, W. M. 2017. *China's Economic Rise: History, Trends, Challenges, and Implications for the United States.* Washington, DC: Congressional Research Service. https://fas.org/sgp/crs/row/RL33534.pdf.

Moscow Times. 2015. Russian single-industry towns face a crisis. *Moscow Times*, July 22. https://themoscowtimes.com/articles/russian-single-industry-towns-face-crisis-48457.

Moss, A. 2015. Kellingley mining machines buried in last deep pit. *BBC News*, December 18. http://www.bbc.com/news/uk-england-york-north-yorkshire-35063853.

Mukerji, C. 1983. *From Graven Images: Patterns of Modern Materialism.* New York: Columbia University Press.

Muller, G., and K. Kauppert. 2004. Performance characteristics of water wheels. *Journal of Hydraulic Research* 42:451–460.

Müller, W. 1939. *Die Wasserräder.* Detmold: Moritz Schäfer.

Muller-Landau, H. C., et al. 2006. Testing metabolic ecology theory for allometric scaling of tree size, growth and mortality in tropical forests. *Ecology Letters* 9:575–588.

Mumby, H. S., et al. 2015. Distinguishing between determinate and indeterminate growth in a long-lived mammal. *BMC Evolutionary Biology* 15:214.

Munich Re. 2004. Megacities—megarisks: Trends and challenges for insurance and risk management. http://www.preventionweb.net/files/646_10363.pdf.

Murphy, G. I. 1968. Patterns in life history phenomena and the environment. *American Naturalist* 102:52–64.

Murray, T. 2011. *Rails across Canada: The History of Canadian Pacific and Canadian National Railways.* Minneapolis, MN: Voyageur Press.

Myhrvold, N. P. 2013. Revisiting the estimation of dinosaur growth rates. *PLoS ONE* 8(12):e81917.

Myhrvold, N. P. 2015. Comment on "Evidence for mesothermy in dinosaurs." *Science* 348:982.

Nafus, M. G. 2015. Indeterminate growth in desert tortoises. *Copeia* 103:520–524.

NAHB (National Association of Home Builders). 2017. New single-family home size trends lower. http://eyeonhousing.org/2017/08/new-single-family-home-size-trends -lower/.

Naito, A. 2003. *Edo, the City That Became Tokyo: An Illustrated History*. Tokyo: Kodansha.

Nakicenovic, N., and A. Grübler, eds. 1991. *Diffusion of Technologies and Social Behavior*. Berlin: Springer-Verlag.

Nasdaq. 2017. Nasdaq Composite Index. http://www.nasdaq.com/markets/nasdaq -composite.

Natale, V., and A. Rajagopalan. 2014. Worldwide variation in human growth and the World Health Organization growth standards: A systematic review. *British Medical Journal Open* 4:e003735. doi:10.1136/bmjopen-2013–003735.

Natanson, L. J., et al. 2006. Validated age and growth estimates for the shortfin mako, *Isurus oxyrinchus*, in the North Atlantic ocean. *Environmental Biology of Fishes* 77:367–383.

Naudts, K., et al. 2016. Europe's forest management did not mitigate climate warming. *Science* 351:597–600.

Nautical Magazine. 1854. Rapid sailing. In *The Nautical Magazine and Naval Chronicle for 1854: A Journal of Papers on Subjects Connected with Maritime Affairs*. London: Simpkins, Marshall, pp. 399–400.

Navigant. 2015. *Adoption of Light-Emitting Diodes in Common Lighting Applications*. https://energy.gov/sites/prod/files/2015/07/f24/led-adoption-report_2015.pdf.

NBA (National Basketball Association). 2015. NBA starting lineups ranked by height. http://nba-teams.pointafter.com/stories/8626/nba-starting-lineups-ranked-height.

NBER (National Bureau of Economic Research). 2017. US business cycle expansions and contractions. http://www.nber.org/cycles.html.

NBS (National Bureau of Statistics of China). 2000. *China Statistical Yearbook 2000*. Beijing: NBS.

NBS. 2016. *China Statistical Yearbook 2016*. Beijing: NBS. http://www.stats.gov.cn/tjsj /ndsj/2016/indexeh.htm.

NCBA (National Cattlemen's Beef Association). 2016. Growth promotant use in cattle production. http://www.explorebeef.org/cmdocs/explorebeef/factsheet_growthpromo tantuse.pdf.

NCC (National Chicken Council). 2018 *US Broiler Performance*. https://www.national chickencouncil.org/about-the-industry/statistics/u-s-broiler-performance/.

NCD Risk Factor Collaboration (NCD-RisC). 2016. A century of trends in adult human height. *eLife* 5:e13410. doi:10.7554/eLife.13410.

Needham, J. 1965. *Science and Civilization in China*, vol. 4: *Physics and Physical Technology*, part 2: *Mechanical Engineering*. Cambridge: Cambridge University Press.

Neill, D. 2014. Evolution of lifespan. *Journal of Theoretical Biology* 358:232–245.

Nesteruk, F. Y. 1963. *Razvitie gidroenergetiki SSSR* (Development of Hydroenergy in the USSR). Moscow: Academy of Sciences of the USSR.

Newall, P. 2012. *Cunard Line: A Fleet History*. Longton: Ships in Focus.

Newbold, K. B. 2006. *Six Billion Plus: World Population in the Twenty-First Century*. Lanham, MD: Rowman & Littlefield.

Newcomb, S. 1881. Note on the frequency of use of the different digits in natural numbers. *American Journal of Mathematics* 4:39–40.

Newman, M. E. J. 2005. Power laws, Pareto distributions and Zipf's law. *Contemporary Physics* 46(5):323–351. doi:10.1080/00107510500052444.

Newson, L., and P. J. Richerson. 2009. Why do people become modern: A Darwinian mechanism. *Population and Development Review* 35:117–158.

NGA (National Gallery of Art). 2007. *Painting in the Dutch Golden Age: A Profile of the Seventeenth Century*. Washington, DC: NGA.

Nguimkeu, P. 2014. A simple selection test between the Gompertz and Logistic growth models. *Technological Forecasting and Social Change* 88:98–105.

Nichol. K. L., et al. 2010. Modeling seasonal influenza outbreak in a closed college campus: Impact of pre-season vaccination, in-season vaccination and holidays/breaks. *PLoS ONE* 5(3):e9548. doi:10.1371/journal.pone.0009548.

Niel, F. 1961. *Dolmens et menhirs*. Paris: Presses Universitaires de France.

Nielsen, J., et al. 2016. Eye lens radiocarbon reveals centuries of longevity in the Greenland shark (*Somniosus microcephalus*). *Science* 353:702–704.

Nielsen, R., et al. 2017. Tracing the peopling of the world through genomics. *Nature* 541:302–310.

Nielsen, R. W. 2015. Hyperbolic growth of the world population in the past 12,000 years. http://arxiv.org/ftp/arxiv/papers/1510/1510.00992.pdf.

Nielsen, R. W. 2018. Mathematical analysis of anthropogenic signatures: The Great Deceleration, https://arxiv.org/pdf/1803.06935.

Nikkei 225. 2017. Historical data (Nikkei 225). http://indexes.nikkei.co.jp/en/nkave/archives/data.

Niklas, K. J., and B. J. Enquist. 2001. Invariant scaling relationships for interspecific plant biomass production rates and body size. *Proceedings of the National Academy of Sciences of the USA* 98:2922–2927.

NIPSSR (National Institute of Population and Social Security Research). 2002. *Population Projections for Japan: 2001–2050. With Long-Range Population Projections: 2051–2100.* http://www.ipss.go.jp/pp-newest/e/ppfj02/ppfj02.pdf.

NIPSSR. 2017. Projection: Population and household. http://www.ipss.go.jp/site-ad/index_english/population-e.html.

NOAA (National Oceanic & Atmospheric Administration). 2017. Recent monthly average Mauna Loa CO_2. https://www.esrl.noaa.gov/gmd/ccgg/trends/.

Noguchi, T., and T. Fujii. 2000. Minimizing the effect of natural disasters. *Japan Railway & Transport Review* 23:52–59.

Nordhaus, W. D. 1998. *Do Real-Output and Real-Wage Measures Capture Reality? The History of Lighting Suggests Not.* New Haven, CT: Cowless Foundation for Research in Economics at Yale University.

Nordhaus, W. D. 2001. *The Progress of Computing.* New Haven, CT: Yale University Press. http://www.econ.yale.edu/~nordhaus/homepage/prog_083001a.pdf.

Nordhaus, W., and J. Tobin. 1972. Is growth obsolete? In National Bureau of Economic Research, *Economic Growth.* New York: Columbia University Press, pp. 1–80.

Noren, S. R., et al. 2014. Energy demands for maintenance, growth, pregnancy, and lactation of female Pacific walruses (*Odobenus rosmarus divergens*). *Physiological and Biochemical Zoology* 87:837–854.

Norris, R. S., and H. M. Kristensen. 2006. Global nuclear stockpiles, 1945–2006. *Bulletin of the Atomic Scientists* 62(4):64–66.

Norwich, J. J. ed. 2009. *The Great Cities in History.* London: Thames & Hudson.

Notestein, F. W. 1945. Population—The long view. In T. W. Schultz, ed., *Food for the World.* Chicago: University of Chicago Press, pp. 36–57.

Novák, L., et al. 2007. Body mass growth in newborns, children and adolescents. *Prague Medical Report* 108:155–166.

NRC (National Research Council). 1994. *Nutrient Requirements of Poultry*, 9th rev. ed. Washington, DC: NRC.

NRC. 1998. *Nutrient Requirements of Swine*,10th rev. ed. Washington, DC: NRC.

NRC. 1999. *The Use of Drugs in Food Animals: Benefits and Risks.* Washington, DC: NRC.

NRC. 2000a. *Beyond Six Billion: Forecasting the World's Population.* Washington, DC: National Academies Press.

NRC. 2000b. *Nutrient Requirements of Beef Cattle: Seventh Revised Edition: Update 2000.* Washington, DC: NRC.

NREL (National Renewable Energy Laboratory). 2018. Research cell efficiency records. https://www.nrel.gov/pv/assets/pdfs/pv-efficiency-chart.20181221.pdf.

Nsoesie, E. O., et al. 2014. A Dirichlet process model for classifying and forecasting epidemic curves. *BMC Infectious Diseases* 14:1–12.

Nunn, N. 2009. The importance of history for economic development. *Annual Review of Economics* 1:65–92.

NXP Semiconductors. 2016. Window lift and relay based DC motor control reference design using the S12VR. https://www.nxp.com/docs/en/reference-manual/DRM 160.pdf.

O'Dea, J. A., and M. Eriksen. 2010. *Childhood Obesity Prevention: International Research, Controversies and Interventions*. Oxford: Oxford University Press.

Odum, H. T. 1971. *Environment, Power, and Society*. New York: John Wiley.

OECD (Organisation for Economic Co-operation and Development). 2014. The rationale for fighting corruption. https://www.oecd.org/cleangovbiz/49693613.pdf.

OECD. 2016. *The Governance of Inclusive Growth*. Paris: OECD.

OECD. 2018. GDP long-term forecast. https://data.oecd.org/gdp/gdp-long-term-forecast.htm.

Oeppen, J., and J. W. Vaupel. 2002. Broken limits to life expectancy. *Science* 296: 1029–1031.

Ogden, C. L., et al. 2012. Prevalence of obesity and trends in body mass index among US children and adolescents, 1999–2010. *Journal of the American Medical Association* 307:483–490.

Ogden, C. L., et al. 2016. Trends in obesity prevalence among children and adolescents in the United States, 1988–1994 through 2013–2014. *Journal of the American Medical Association* 315:2292–2299.

Okamura, S. 1995. *History of Electron Tubes*. Amsterdam: Ios Press.

Oliveira, F. F., and M. A. Batalha. 2005. Lognormal abundance distribution of woody species in a cerrado fragment. *Revista Brasileira Botanica* 28:39–45.

Olshansky, S. J. 2016. Measuring our narrow strip of life. *Nature* 538:175–176.

Ombach, G. 2017. Challenges and requirements for high volume production of electric motors. http://www.sae.org/events/training/symposia/emotor/presentations /2011/GrzegorzOmbach.pdf.

O'Neil, D. W., et al. 2018 A good life for all within planetary boundaries. *Nature Sustainability* 1:88–95.

Onge, J. M. S., et al. 2008. Historical trends in height, weight, and body mass: Data from U.S. Major League Baseball players, 1869–1983. *Economics and Human Biology* 6:482–488.

Onoda, S. 2015. Tunnels in Japan. *Japan Railway & Transport Review* 66:38–51.

Onywera, V. O. 2009. East African runners: Their genetics, lifestyle and athletic prowess. *Medicine and Sport Science* 54:102–109.

Ormrod, D. 2003. *The Rise of Commercial Empires: England and the Netherlands in the Age of Mercantilism,1650–1770*. Cambridge: Cambridge University Press.

Ort, D. R., and S. P. Long. 2014. Limits on yields in the Corn Belt. *Science* 344:484–485.

Ortolano, G. 2015. The typicalities of the English? Walt Rostow, the stages of economic growth, and modern British history. *Modern Intellectual History* 12:657–684.

Osepchuk, J. M. 2015. Births of technologies do not always occur at times of invention or discovery. *IEEE Microwave Magazine* (May):150–160.

Osram Sylvania. 2009. Light source efficacy over time comparison. https://www.slideshare.net/sodhi/ArchLED2008SSLEnergyLegislative2.

Ostwald, W. 1890. Über Autokatalyse. *Berichte über die Verhandlungen der Königlich-Sächsischen Gesellschaft der Wissenschaften zu Leipzig, Mathematisch-Physische Classe* 42:189–19.

Ostwald, W. 1909. *Energetische Grundlagen der Kulturwissenschaften*. Leipzig: Alfred Kröner.

Overton. M. 1984. Agricultural productivity in eighteenth-century England: Some further speculations. *Economic History Review* 37:244–251.

Owens, J. N., and H. G. Lund. 2009. *Forests and Forest Plants*. Oxford: EOLSS.

Owyang, M. T., and H. Shell. 2017. China's economic data: An accurate reflection, or just smoke and mirrors? https://www.stlouisfed.org/~/media/Publications/Regional-Economist/2017/Second_quarter_2017/China.pdf.

Ozone Hole. 2018. http://www.theozonehole.com/.

Pardo, S. A., et al. 2013. Avoiding fishy growth curves. *Methods in Ecology and Evolution*. doi:10.1111/2041-210x.12020.

Pareto, V. 1896. *Cours d'Économie Politique: Professé à l'Université de Lausanne*, vol. 1. Lausanne: F. Rouge.

Parikh, V., and J. Shukla. 1995. Urbanization, energy use and greenhouse effects in economic development: Results from a cross-national study of developing countries. *Global Environmental Change* 5:87–103.

Parkin, T. G. 1992. *Demography and Roman Society*. Baltimore, MD: Johns Hopkins University Press.

Parks, J. R. 2011. *A Theory of Feeding and Growth of Animals*. Berlin: Springer.

Parson, T. H. 2010. *The Rule of Empires: Those Who Built Them, Those Who Endured Them, and Why They Always Fall*. Oxford: Oxford University Press.

Parsons, C. A. 1911. *The Steam Turbine*. Cambridge: Cambridge University Press.

Parsons, R. H. 1936. *The Development of Parsons Steam Turbine*. London: Constable.

Parsons, T. 1951. *The Social System*. London: Routledge & Kegan Paul.

Pasciuti, D., and C. Chase-Dunn. 2002. *Estimating the Population Sizes of Cities*. Riverside, CA: Institute for Research on World-Systems. http://irows.ucr.edu/research/citemp/estcit/estcit.htm.

Pastijn, H. 2006. Chaotic growth with the logistic model of P.-F. Verhulst. In M. Ausloos and M. Dirickx, eds., *The Logistic Map and the Route to Chaos: From the Beginnings to Modern Applications*. Berlin: Springer, pp. 13–28.

PBL (Planbureau voor de Leefomgeving). 2010. Land use data. http://themasites.pbl.nl/tridion/en/themasites/hyde/landusedata/index-2.html.

PCA. 2017. Highways. http://www.cement.org/concrete-basics/paving/concrete-paving-types/highways.

Pearl, R. 1924. *Studies in Human Biology*. Baltimore, MD: Williams & Wilkins.

Pearl, R., and L. J. Reed. 1920. On the rate of growth of the population of the United States since 1790 and its mathematical representation. *Proceedings of the National Academy of Sciences of the USA* 6:275–288.

Pearson, K. 1924. Historical note on the origin of the normal curve of errors. *Biometrika* 16:402–404.

Peeringa, J., et al. 2011. Upwind 20MW Wind Turbine PreDesign. https://www.ecn.nl/publicaties/PdfFetch.aspx?nr=ECN-E--11-017.

Pekkonen, M., et al. 2013. Resource availability and competition shape the evolution of survival and growth ability in a bacterial community. *PLoS ONE* 8(9):e76471. doi:10.1371/journal.pone.0076471.

Peláez-Samaniegoa, M. R. 2008. Improvements of Brazilian carbonization industry as part of the creation of a global biomass economy. *Renewable and Sustainable Energy Reviews* 12:1063–1086.

Peleg, M., and M. G. Corradini. 2011. Microbial growth curves: What the models tell us and what they cannot. *Critical Reviews in Food Science and Nutrition* 51:10 917–945. doi:10.1080/10408398.2011.570463.

Peñuelas, J., et al. 2011. Increased water-use efficiency during the 20th century did not translate into enhanced tree growth. *Global Ecology and Biogeography* 20:597–608.

Pepper, I. L., et al. 2011. *Environmental Microbiology*. Boston: Academic Press.

Perdue, P. C. 2005. *China Marches West: The Qing Conquest of Central Eurasia*. Cambridge, MA: Belknap Press.

Perrin, L., et al. 2016. Growth of the coccolithophore *Emiliania huxleyi* in light- and nutrient-limited batch reactors: Relevance for the BIOSOPE deep ecological niche of coccolithophores. *Biogeosciences* 13:5983–6001.

Perry, J. S. 1945. The reproduction of the wild brown rat (*Rattus norvegicus* Erxleben). *Journal of Zoology* 115:19–46.

Petruszewycz, M. 1973. L'histoire de la loi d'Estoup-Zipf: Documents. *Mathématique et Science Humaines* 44:41–56.

Pew Research Center. 2015. Americans' Internet access: 2000–2015. http://www.pewinternet.org/2015/06/26/americans-internet-access-2000-2015/.

PHAC (Public Health Agency of Canada). 2004. *Renewal of Public Health in Canada*. http://www.phac-aspc.gc.ca/publicat/sars-sras/naylor/index-eng.php.

Phillips, J. D. 1999. *Earth Surface Systems: Complexity, Order and Scale*. Malden, MA: Blackwell.

Phys.org. 2015. Unveiling of the world's smallest and most powerful micro motors. https://phys.org/news/2015-05-unveiling-world-smallest-powerful-micro.html.

Piketty, T. 2014. *Capital in the 21st Century*. Cambridge, MA: Harvard University Press.

Piel, G. 1972. *The Acceleration of History*. New York: Random House.

Pietrobelli, A., et al. 1998. Body Mass Index as a measure of adiposity among children and adolescents: A validation study. *Journal of Pediatrics* 132:204–210.

Pietronero, L., et al. 2001. Explaining the uneven distribution of numbers in nature: The laws of Benford and Zipf. *Physica A* 293:297–304. https://www.researchgate.net/publication/222685079_Explaining_the_uneven_distribution_of_numbers_in_nature_The_laws_of_Benford_and_Zipf.

Pinto, C. M. A., et al. 2012. Double power law behavior in everyday phenomena. *Chaotic Modeling and Simulation* 4:695–700.

Pioneer. 2017. Corn seeding rate considerations. https://www.pioneer.com/home/site/us/agronomy/library/corn-seeding-rate-considerations/.

Pittman, K. J., et al. 2016. The legacy of past pandemics: Common human mutations that protect against infectious disease. *PLoS Pathogens* 12(7):e1005680. doi:10.1371/journal.ppat.1005680.

Plank, L. D., and J. D. Harvey. 1979. Generation time statistics of *Escherichia coli* B measured by synchronous culture techniques. *Journal of General Microbiology* 115:69–77.

Plasson, R., et al. 2011. Autocatalysis: At the root of self-replication. *Artificial Life* 17:219–236.

Plokhy, S. 2014. *The Last Empire: The Final Days of the Soviet Union.* London: Oneworld.

Plutarch. 1917. *Lives*, vol. 5. Trans. B. Perrin. Cambridge, MA: Harvard University Press.

Pokorný, M. 2014. *Pražský hrad.* Bratislava: Slovart.

Polly, P. D., and J. Alroy. 1998. Cope's Rule. *Science* 282:50–51.

Pomeranz, K. 2000. *The Great Divergence: China, Europe, and the Making of the Modern World Economy.* Princeton, NJ: Princeton University Press.

Pontzer, H., et al. 2009. Biomechanics of running indicates endothermy in bipedal dinosaurs. *PLoS ONE* 4(11):e7783.

Pontzer, H., et al. 2016. Metabolic acceleration and the evolution of human brain size and life history. *Nature* 533:190192.

Poot, J., and M. Roskruge, eds. 2018. *Population Change and Impacts in Asia and the Pacific.* Berlin: Springer.

Pope, F. L. 1891. The inventors of the electric motor. *Electrical Engineer* 11(140): S. 1–5; (141): S. 33–39.

Poston, D. L., and D. Yaukey, eds. 1992. *The Population of Modern China.* Berlin: Springer.

Potapov, P. A., et al. 2008. Mapping the world's intact forest landscapes by remote sensing. *Ecology and Society* 13(2):51. htttp://www.ecologyandsociety.org/vol13/iss2/art51/.

Potter, C., et al. 2008. Storage of carbon in U.S. forests predicted from satellite data, ecosystem modeling, and inventory summaries. *Climatic Change* 90:269–282.

Potts, S. G., et al. 2016. Safeguarding pollinators and their values to human well-being. *Nature* 540:220–228.

Pratt & Whitney. 2017. JT9D Engine. http://www.pw.utc.com/JT9D_Engine.

PRB (Population Reference Bureau). 2016. Life expectancy at birth, by gender, 1970 and 2014. http://www.prb.org/DataFinder/Topic/Rankings.aspx?ind=6.

Prentice, M. B., and L. Rahalison. 2007. Plague. *Lancet* 369(9568):1196–207.

Preston, F. W. 1948. The commonness and rarity of species. *Ecology* 29:254–283.

Pretzsch, H. 2006. Species-specific allometric scaling under self-thinning: Evidence from long-term plots in forest stands. *Oecologia* 146:572–583.

Pretzsch, H. 2009. *Forest Dynamics, Growth and Yield: From Measurement to Model.* Berlin: Springer.

Price, C. A., et al. 2012. Testing the metabolic theory of ecology. *Ecology Letters* 15:1465–1474.

Price, D. J. de S. 1963. *Little Science, Big Science.* New York: Columbia University Press.

Price, T. D., and O. Bar-Yosef. 2011. The origins of agriculture: New data, new ideas. *Current Anthropology* 52(S4):S163–S174.

Prost, A. 1991. Public and private spheres in France. In A. Prost and G. Vincent, eds., *A History of Private Life*, vol. 5. Cambridge, MA: Belknap Press, pp. 1–103.

Psenner, R., and B. Sattler. 1998. Life at the freezing point. *Science* 280:2073–2074.

Puleston, C. O., et al. 2017. Rain, sun, soil, and sweat: A consideration of population limits on Rapa Nui (Easter Island) before European contact. *Frontiers in Ecology and Evolution* 5:69. doi: 10.3389/fevo.2017.00069.

Quetelet, A. 1835. *Sur l'homme et le développement de ses facultés*, vol. 2. Paris: Bachelier.

Quetelet, A. 1846. *Lettres a S. A. R. le duc régnant de Saxe-Cobourg et Gotha: Sur la théorie des probabilités.* Brussels: M. Hayez.

Quince, C., et al. 2008. Biphasic growth in fish, I: Theoretical foundations. *Journal of Theoretical Biology* 254:197–206.

Radford, P. F., and A. J. Ward-Smith. 2003. British running performances in the eighteenth century. *Journal of Sports Sciences* 21:429–438.

Radiomuseum. 2017. Radiola Superheterodyne AR-812 "Semi-Portable." http://www .radiomuseum.org/r/rca_superheterodyne_ar812.html.

Raftery, A. E., et al. 2012. Bayesian probabilistic population projections for all countries. *Proceedings of the National Academy of Sciences of the USA* 109:13915–13921.

Raimi, R. A. 1976. The first digit problem. *American Mathematical Monthly* 83:521–538.

Ramankutty, N., and J. A. Foley. 1999. Estimating historical changes in global land cover: Croplands from 1700 to 1992. *Global Biogeochemical Cycles* 13:997–1027.

Ramirez, C. D. 2014. Is corruption in China "out of control"? A comparison with the US in historical perspective. *Journal of Comparative Economics* 42:76–91.

Rankine, W. J. M. 1866. *Useful Rules and Tables Relating to Mensuration, Engineering Structures and Machines.* London: G. Griffin.

Raoult, D., et al. 2013. Plague: History and contemporary analysis. *Journal of Infection* 66:18–26.

Rawski, T. G. 2001. What is happening to China's GDP statistics? *China Economic Review* 12:347–354.

Rea, M. S., ed. 2000. *IESNA Handbook*. New York: Illuminating Engineering Society of North America.

Recht, R. 2008. *Believing and Seeing: The Art of Gothic Cathedrals*. Chicago: University of Chicago Press.

Reed, H. S., and R. H. Holland. 1919. The growth rate of an annual plant Helianthus. *Proceedings of the National Academy of Sciences of the USA* 5:135–144.

Reed, L. J., and J. Berkson. 1929. The application of the logistic function to experimental data. *Journal of Physical Chemistry* 33:760–779.

Reich, P. B., et al. 2006. Universal scaling of respiratory metabolism, size and nitrogen in plants. *Nature* 439:457–461.

Reid, A. H., et al. 1999. Origin and evolution of the 1918 "Spanish" influenza virus hemagglutinin gene. *Proceedings of the National Academy of Sciences of the USA* 96:1651–1656.

Reineke, L. H. 1933. Perfecting a stand density index for even-aged forests. *Journal of Agricultural Research* 46:627–638.

Reinhard. M. R., et al. 1988. *Histoire générale de population mondiale*. Paris: Montchrestien.

Reinsel, D., et al. 2018. *The Digitization of the World: From Edge to Core*. https://www.seagate.com/files/www-content/our-story/trends/files/idc-seagate-dataage-whitepaper.pdf.

Reisner, A. 2017. Speed of animals: Horse. http://www.speedofanimals.com/animals/horse.

Reitz, L. P., and S. C. Salmon. 1968. Origin, history and use of Norin 10 wheat. *Crop Science* 8:686–689.

Reymer, A., and G. Schubert. 1984. Phanerozoic addition rates to the continental-crust and crustal growth. *Tectonics* 3:63–77.

Reynolds, J. 1970. *Windmills and Watermills*. London: Hugh Evelyn.

Reynolds, T. S. 2002. *Stronger Than a Hundred Men: A History of the Vertical Water Wheel*. Baltimore, MD: Johns Hopkins University Press.

Rhodes, J. 2017. Steam vs. diesel: A comparison of modern steam and diesel in the Class I railroad environment. http://www.internationalsteam.co.uk/trains/newsteam/modern50.htm.

RIAA (Recording Industry Association of America). 2017. U.S. sales database. https://www.riaa.com/u-s-sales-database/.

Richards, D. C. 2010. *Relationship between Speed and Risk of Fatal Injury: Pedestrians and Car Occupants*. London: Department of Transport.

Richards, F. J. 1959. A flexible growth function for empirical use. *Journal of Experimental Botany* 10(29):290–300.

Richardson, J. 1886. *The Compound Steam Engine*. Birmingham: British Association for the Advancement of Science.

Richardson, L. F. 1948. Variation of the frequency of fatal quarrels with magnitude. *Journal of the American Statistical Association* 43:523–46.

Richerson, P. J., et al. 2001. Was agriculture impossible during the Pleistocene but mandatory during the Holocene? A climate change hypothesis. *American Antiquity* 66:387–411.

Richter, C. F. 1935. An instrumental earthquake magnitude scale. *Bulletin of the Seismological Society of America* 25(1–2):1–32.

Ricklefs, R. E. 2010. Embryo growth rates in birds and mammals. *Functional Ecology* 24:588–596.

Rickman, G. 1971. *Roman Granaries and Store Buildings*. Cambridge: Cambridge University Press.

Rickman, G. E. 1980. The grain trade under the Roman Empire. *Memoirs from the American Academy in Rome* 36:261–276.

Rinehart, K. E. 1996. Environmental challenges as related to animal agriculture—Poultry. In E. T. Kornegay, ed., *Nutrient Management of Food Animals to Enhance and Protect the Environment*. Boca Raton, FL: Lewis, pp. 21–28.

Ringbauer, J. A., et al. 2006. Effects of large-scale poultry farms on aquatic microbial communities: A molecular investigation. *Journal of Water and Health* 4:77–86.

Ripple, W. J., et al. 2017. World scientists' warning to humanity: A second notice. *BioScience* 67:1026–1028. https://doi.org/10.1093/biosci/bix125.

Rivera, M., and E. Rogers. 2006. Innovation diffusion, network features, and cultural communication variables. *Problems and Perspectives in Management* 2:126–135.

Rizzo, C., et al. 2008. Scenarios of diffusion and control of an influenza pandemic in Italy. *Epidemiology & Infection* 136:1650–1657.

Robert, L., et al. 2008. Rapid increase in human life expectancy: Will it soon be limited by the aging of elastin? *Biogerontology* 9:119–133.

Robertson, T. B. 1908. On the normal rate of growth of an individual, and its biochemical significance. *Archiv für Entwicklungsmechanik der Organismen* 25:581–614.

Robertson, T. B. 1923. *The Chemical Basis of Growth and Senescence*. Montreal: J. B. Lippincott.

Roche, A. F., and S. S. Sun. 2003. *Human Growth: Assessment and Interpretation*. Cambridge: Cambridge University Press.

Roche, D. 2000. *A History of Everyday Things: The Birth of Consumption in France, 1600–1800*. Cambridge: Cambridge University Press.

Rodriguez, F., and D. Rodrik. 2000. Trade policy and economic growth: A skeptic's guide to the cross-national evidence. https://drodrik.scholar.harvard.edu/files/dani -rodrik/files/trade-policy-economic-growth.pdf.

Roff, D. A. 1980. A motion for the retirement of the von Bertalanffy function. *Canadian Journal of Fisheries and Aquatic Science* 37:127–129.

Rogers, E. 2003. *Diffusion of Innovations*. New York: Free Press.

Rogin, L. 1931. *The Introduction of Farm Machinery*. Berkeley: University of California Press.

Rojas, R. 2012. Gordon Moore and his law: Numerical methods to the rescue. *Documenta Mathematica* · Extra Volume ISMP 2012: 401–415.

Rollins, A. 1983. *The Fall of Rome: A Reference Guide*. Jefferson, NC: McFarland.

Rolt, L. T. C., and J. S. Allen. 1997. *The Steam Engine of Thomas Newcomen*. Cedarburg, WI: Landmark.

Romaní, A. M., et al. 2006. Interactions of bacteria and fungi on decomposing litter: Differential extracellular enzyme activities. *Ecology* 87(10):2559–69.

Romer, P. M. 1986. Increasing returns and long run growth. *Journal of Political Economy* 94:1002–1037.

Romer, P. M. 1990. Endogenous technological change. *Journal of Political Economy* 98:S71–S102.

Rosen, W. 2007. *Justinian's Flea: Plague, Empire, and the Birth of Europe*. New York: Viking.

Rosenthal, N., and R. P. Harvey, eds. 2010. *Heart Development and Regeneration*. Cambridge, MA: Academic Press.

Roser, M. 2017. Human height. https://ourworldindata.org/human-height/.

Ross, B. 2016. *The Madoff Chronicles: Inside the Secret World of Bernie and Ruth*. Burbank, CA: Kingswell.

Ross, D. G. 2012. *The Era of the Clipper Ships: The Legacy of Donald McKay*. Lexington, KY: Create Space.

Rostow, W. W. 1960. *The Stages of Economic Growth: A Non-communist Manifesto*. Cambridge: Cambridge University Press.

Rubin, H. 2011. *Future Global Shocks: Pandemics*. Paris: OECD.

Rubner, M. 1883. Über den einfluss der Körpergrösse auf Stoff- und Kraftwechsel. *Zeitschrift für Biologie* 19:535–562.

Ruff, C. 2002. Variation in human body size and shape. *Annual Review of Anthropology* 31:211–32.

Rupp, K., and S. Selberherr. 2011. The economic limit to Moore's law. *IEEE Transactions on Semiconductot Manufacturing* 24(1):1–4.

Russell, N. 2002. The wild side of human domestication. *Society & Animals* 10:285–302.

Rüst, C. A., et al. 2013. Analysis of performance and age of the fastest 100-mile ultramarathoners worldwide. *Clinics* 68:605–611.

Ruttan, V. W. 2000. *Technology, Growth, and Development: An Induced Innovation Perspective*. Oxford: Oxford University Press.

Ryan, M. G., et al. 1996. Comparing models of ecosystem function for temperate conifer forests. In A. I. Greymeyer et al. eds., *Global Change: Effects on Coniferous Forests and Grasslands*. New York: John Wiley, pp. 313–361.

Ryder, H. W., et al. 1976. Future performance in footracing. *Scientific American* 224(6):109–119.

Saichev, A. I., et al. 2010. *Theory of Zipf's Law and Beyond*. Berlin: Springer.

Santarelli, E., et al. 2006. Gibrat's Law: An overview of the empirical literature. In E. Santarelli, ed., *Entrepreneurship, Growth, and Innovation: The Dynamics of Firms and Industries*. New York: Springer, pp. 41–73.

Sapkota, A. R., et al. 2007. What do we feed to food-producing animals? A review of animal feed ingredients and their potential impacts on human health. *Environmental Health Perspectives* 115:663–668.

Saunders-Hastings, P. R., and D. Krewski. 2016. Reviewing the history of pandemic influenza: Understanding patterns of emergence and transmission. *Pathogens* 5(4):66; doi:10.3390/pathogens5040066.

Savage, C. I. 1959. *An Economic History of Transport*. London: Hutchinson.

Savery, T. 1702. *Miner's Friend; Or, An Engine to Raise Water by Fire*. London: S. Crouch.

SB (Statistics Bureau, Japan). 1996. *Historical Statistics of Japan*. http://www.stat.go.jp/english/data/chouki/.

SB. 2006. Stature by age and sex. http://www.stat.go.jp/english/data/chouki/24.htm.

SB. 2017a. *Japan Statistical Yearbook*. Tokyo: SB. http://www.stat.go.jp/english/data/handbook/pdf/2017all.pdf.

SB. 2017b. Monthly report: June 1, 2017 (final estimates), November 1, 2017 (provisional estimates). http://www.stat.go.jp/english/data/jinsui/tsuki/index.htm.

SBB (Schweizerische Bundesbahnen). 2017. "Switzerland through and through" The north-south Gotthard corridor. https://company.sbb.ch/content/dam/sbb/de/pdf

/sbb-konzern/medien/hintergrund-dossier/Gotthard/Basispraesentation_Gotthard _TP_KOM_PONS_en_2016.pdf.

Scanes, C. G., ed. 2003. *Biology of Growth of Domestic Animals*. Ames: Iowa State Press.

Scaruffi, P. 2008. Highest mountains in the world. http://www.scaruffi.com/travel /tallest.html.

Scheidel, W. 2007. *Roman Population Size: The Logic of the Debate*. Stanford, CA: Princeton/Stanford Working Papers in Classics.

Scheidel, W. 2017. *The Great Leveler: Violence and the History of Inequality from the Stone Age to the Twenty-First Century*. Princeton, NJ: Princeton University Press.

Scherbov, S., et al. 2011. The uncertain timing of reaching 8 billion, peak world population, and other demographic milestones. *Population and Development Review* 37:571–578.

Schmandt, J., and C. H. Ward. 2000. *Sustainable Development: The Challenge of Transition*. Cambridge: Cambridge University Press.

Schmidt-Nielsen, K. 1984. *Scaling: Why Is Animal Size So Important?* Cambridge: Cambridge University Press.

Schneider, F. 2003. The development of the shadow economies and shadow labour force of 21 OECD and 22 transition countries. *CESifo DICE Report* 1:17–23.

Schneider, F. 2015. Size and development of the shadow economy of 31 European and 5 other OECD countries from 2003 to 2015: Different developments. http://www.econ.jku.at/members/Schneider/files/publications/2015/ShadEc Europe31.pdf.

Schneider, F., and A. Buehn. 2016. *Estimating the Size of the Shadow Economy: Methods, Problems and Open Questions*. Bonn: IZA.

Schneider, F., et al. 2010. *Shadow Economies All over the World: New Estimates for 162 Countries from 1999 to 2007*. Washington, DC: World Bank.

Schneider, G. E. 2014. *Brain Structure and Its Origins: In Development and in Evolution of Behavior and the Mind*. Cambridge, MA: MIT Press.

Schoch, T., et al. 2012. Social inequality and the biological standard of living: An anthropometric analysis of Swiss conscription data, 1875–1950. *Economics and Human Biology* 10:154–173.

Schoppa, R. K. 2010. *Twentieth Century China*. Oxford: Oxford University Press.

Schram, W. 2017. Green and Roman siphons. http://www.romanaqueducts.info /siphons/siphons.htm.

Schroeder, P. 2003. Is the U.S. an empire? *History News Network https://historynewsnetwork.org/article/1237*.

Schtickzelle, M. 1981. Pierre-François Verhulst (1804–1849). *Population* 3:541–555.

Schumpeter, J. A. 1939. *Business Cycles: A Theoretical, Historical, and Statistical Analysis of the Capitalist Process*. New York: McGraw–Hill.

Schurr, S. H. 1984. Energy use, technological change, and productive efficiency: An economic-historical interpretation. *Annual Review of Energy* 9:409–425.

Schurr, S. H., and B. C. Netschert. 1960. *Energy in the American Economy 1850–1975*. Baltimore, MD: Johns Hopkins University Press.

Schurr, S. H., et al. 1990. *Electricity in the American Economy: Agent of Technological Progress*. New York: Greenwood Press.

Schwab, K. 2016. The Fourth Industrial Revolution: What it means, how to respond. *World Economic Forum*, January 14. https://www.weforum.org/agenda/2016/01/the-fourth-industrial-revolution-what-it-means-and-how-to-respond/.

Schwartz, J. J., et al. 2005. Dating the growth of oceanic crust at a slow-spreading ridge. *Science* 310:654–657.

Schwarz, G. R. 2008. *The History and Development of Caravels*. College Station: Texas A&M University Press.

Scommegna, P. 2011. U.S. megalopolises 50 years later, http://www.prb.org/Publications/Articles/2011/us-megalopolises-50-years.aspx.

Scotti, R. A. 2007. *Basilica: The Splendor and the Scandal: Building St. Peter's*. New York: Plume.

Seagate. 2017. Data Age 2025: The evolution of data to life-critical. https://itupdate.com.au/page/data-age-2025-the-evolution-of-data-to-life-critical.

Sedeaud, A., et al. 2014. Secular trend: Morphology and performance. *Journal of Sports Sciences* 32:1146–1154. doi: 10.1080/02640414.2014.889841.

Seebacher, F. 2003. Dinosaur body temperatures: The occurrence of endothermy and ectothermy. *Paleobiology* 29:105–122.

Sellers, W. I., et al. 2013. March of the titans: The locomotor capabilities of sauropod dinosaurs. *PLoS ONE* 8(10):e78733.

Semenov, B., et al. 1989. Growth projections and development trends for nuclear power. *IAEA Bulletin* 3:6–12.

Semenzato, P., et al. 2011. Growth prediction for five tree species in an Italian urban forest. *Urban Forestry & Urban Greening* 10:169–176.

SEMI. 2017. Silicon shipment statistics. http://www.semi.org/en/MarketInfo/Silicon ShipmentStatistics.

Shackell, N. L., et al. 1997. Growth of cod (*Gadus morhua*) estimated from mark-recapture programs on the Scotian Shelf and adjacent areas. *ICES Journal of Marine Science* 54:383–398.

Shackleton, R. 2013. *Total Factor Productivity Growth in Historical Perspective.* Washington, DC: Congressional Budget Office.

Shaman, J., et al. 2010. Absolute humidity and the seasonal onset of influenza in the continental United States. *PLOS Biology* https://doi.org/10.1371/journal.pbio .1000316.

Shapiro, A.-L. 1985. *Housing the Poor of Paris 1850–1902.* Madison: University of Wisconsin Press.

Sharif, M. N., and K. Ramanathan. 1981. Binomial innovation diffusion models with dynamic potential adopter population, *Technological Forecasting and Social Change* 20:63–87.

Sharif, M. N., and K. Ramanathan. 1982. Polynomial innovation diffusion models. *Technological Forecasting and Social Change* 21:301–323.

Shestopaloff, Y. K. 2016. Metabolic allometric scaling model: Combining cellular transportation and heat dissipation constraints. *Journal of Experimental Biology* 219:2481–2489.

Shi, P. J., et al. 2014. On the 3/4-exponent von Bertalanffy equation for ontogenetic growth. *Ecological Modelling* 276:23–28.

Shinbrot, M. 1961. Doomsday. (Letter to the editor.) *Science* 133:940–941.

Shipman, P. 2013. Why is human childbirth so painful? *American Scientist* 101:426–429.

Shirer, W. L. 1990. *The Rise and Fall of the Third Reich.* New York: Simon & Schuster.

Shockley, W., and H. J. Queisser. 1961. Detailed balance limit of efficiency of p-n junction solar cells. *Journal of Applied Physics* 32:510–519.

Shortridge, R. W. 1989. Francis and his turbine. *Hydro Power* (February):24–28.

Shugart, H., et al. 2003. *Forests & Global Climate Change: Potential Impacts on U.S. Forest Resources.* Arlington, VA: Pew Center on Global Climate Change.

Shull, C. M. 2013. *Modeling Growth of Pigs Reared to Heavy Weights.* Urbana-Champaign: University of Illinois at Urbana-Champaign Press.

Shyklo, A. E. 2017. Simple explanation of Zipf's mystery via new rank-share distribution, derived from combinatorics of the ranking process. https://ssrn.com/abstract =2918642.

SIA (Semiconductor Industry Association). 2017. *2017 Factbook.* http://go.semicon ductors.org/2017-sia-factbook-0-0-0.

Sibly, R. M., and J. H. Brown. 2009. Mammal reproductive strategies driven by offspring mortality-size relationships. *American Naturalist* 173:E185–E199.

Siegel, K. R., et al. 2014. Do we produce enough fruits and vegetables to meet global health need? *PLOS ONE* 9(8):e10405.

Siemens. 2017a. Pioneering and proven: H-Class Series power plants. https://www .energy.siemens.com/hq/en/fossil-power-generation/power-plants/h-class-series/h -class-series-power-plants.htm.

Siemens. 2017b. SGT5–8000H heavy-duty gas turbine (50 Hz). https://www.siemens .com/global/en/home/products/energy/power-generation/gas-turbines/sgt5-8000h .html#!/.

Sillett, S. C., et al. 2010. Increasing wood production through old age in tall trees. *Forest Ecology and Management* 259:976–994.

Sillett, S. C., et al. 2015. Biomass and growth potential of *Eucalyptus regnans* up to 100 m tall. *Forest Ecology and Management* 348:78–91.

Silva, L. C. R., and M. Anand. 2013. Probing for the influence of atmospheric CO_2 and climate change on forest ecosystems across biomes. *Global Ecology and Biogeography* 22:83–92.

Silver, C. 1976. *Guide to the Horses of the World.* Oxford: Elsevier Phaidon.

Simon, H. A. 1955. On a class of skew distribution functions. *Biometrika.* 42: 425–440.

Simon, J. 1981. *The Ultimate Resource.* Princeton, NJ: Princeton University Press.

Simon, J., and H. Kahn, eds. 1984. *The Resourceful Earth.* Oxford: Basil Blackwell.

Simonsen, L., et al. 2013. Global mortality estimates for the 2009 influenza pandemic from the GLaMOR project: A modeling study. *PLoS Medicine* 10:e1001558.

Sims, L. D., et al. 2002. Avian influenza in Hong Kong 1997–2002. *Avian Diseases* 47:832–838.

Singularity.com. 2017. Resources. http://www.singularity.com/charts/page17.html.

Sitwell, N. H. 1981. *Roman Roads of Europe.* New York: St. Martin's Press.

Sivak, M., and O. Tsimhoni. 2009. Fuel efficiency of vehicles on US roads: 1936–2006. *Energy Policy* 37:3168–3170.

Šizling, A. L., et al. 2009. Invariance in species-abundance distributions. *Theoretical Ecology* 2:89–103.

Skyscraper Center. 2017. 100 tallest completed buildings in the world by height to architectural top. https://www.skyscrapercenter.com/buildings.

Smayda, T. J. 1997. Harmful algal blooms: Their ecophysiology and general relevance to phytoplankton blooms in the sea. *Limnology and Oceanography* 42:1137–1153.

Smeaton, J. 1759. An experimental enquiry concerning the natural power of water and wind to turn mills, and other machines, depending on a circular motion. *Philosophical Transactions of the Royal Society of London* 51:100–174.

Smil, V. 1994. *Global Ecology*. London: Routledge.

Smil, V. 1996. *Environmental Problems in China: Estimates of Economic Costs*. Honolulu, HI: East-West Center.

Smil, V. 1997. *Cycles of Life*. New York: Scientific American Library.

Smil, V. 1999. Crop residues: Agriculture's largest harvest. *BioScience* 49:299–308.

Smil, V. 2000. *Feeding the World*. Cambridge, MA: MIT Press.

Smil, V. 2001. *Enriching the Earth*. Cambridge, MA: MIT Press.

Smil, V. 2002. *The Earth's Biosphere*. Cambridge, MA: MIT Press.

Smil, V. 2003. *Energy at the Crossroads*. Cambridge, MA: MIT Press.

Smil, V. 2005. *Creating the Twentieth Century*. New York: Oxford University Press.

Smil, V. 2006a. Peak oil: A catastrophist cult and complex realities. *World Watch* 19:22–24.

Smil, V. 2006b. *Transforming the Twentieth Century*. New York: Oxford University Press.

Smil, V. 2007. The unprecedented shift in Japan's population: Numbers, age, and prospect. *Japan Focus* 5(4). http://apjjf.org/-Vaclav-Smil/2411/article.html.

Smil, V. 2008. *Energy in Nature and Society*. Cambridge, MA: MIT Press.

Smil, V. 2009. Two decades later: Nikkei and lessons from the fall. *The American*, December 29.

Smil, V. 2010a. *Global Catastrophes and Trends*. Cambridge, MA: MIT Press.

Smil, V. 2010b. *Prime Movers of Globalization*. Cambridge, MA: MIT Press.

Smil, V. 2010c. *Why America Is Not a New Rome*. Cambridge, MA: MIT Press.

Smil, V. 2013a. *Harvesting the Biosphere*. Cambridge, MA: MIT Press.

Smil, V. 2013b. *Made in the USA*. Cambridge, MA: MIT Press.

Smil, V. 2013c. *Should We Eat Meat?* Chichester: Wiley Blackwell.

Smil, V. 2014a. Fifty years of the *Shinkansen*. *Asia-Pacific Journal: Japan Focus*, December 1. http://apjjf.org/2014/12/48/Vaclav-Smil/4227.html.

Smil, V. 2014b. *Making the Modern World*. Chichester: Wiley.

Smil, V. 2015a. Moore's curse. *IEEE Spectrum* (April):26.

Smil, V. 2015b. *Natural Gas*. Chichester: Wiley.

Smil, V. 2015c. *Power Density*. Cambridge, MA: MIT Press.

Smil, V. 2016a. Embodied energy: Mobile devices and cars. *Spectrum IEEE* (May):26. http://ieeexplore.ieee.org/stamp/stamp.jsp?arnumber=7459114.

Smil, V. 2016b. *Still the Iron Age*. Oxford: Elsevier.

Smil, V. 2017a. *Energy and Civilization*. Cambridge, MA: MIT Press.

Smil, V. 2017b. *Energy Transitions*. Santa Barbara, CA: Praeger.

Smil, V. 2017c. *Oil: A Beginner's Guide*. London: Oneworld.

Smil, V. 2017d. Transformers, the unsung technology. *Spectrum IEEE* (August):24.

Smil, V. 2018a. February 1878: The first phonograph. *Spectrum IEEE* (February):24.

Smil, V. 2018b. It'll be harder than we thought to get the carbon out. *Spectrum IEEE* (June):72–75.

Smil, V., and K. Kobayashi. 2012. *Japan's Dietary Transition and Its Impacts*. Cambridge, MA: MIT Press.

Smith, D. R. 1987. The wind farms of the Altamont Pass. *Annual Review of Energy* 12:145–183.

Smith, F. A., et al. 2016. Body size evolution across the Geozoic. *Annual Review of Earth and Planetary Sciences* 44:523–553.

Smith, K. 1951. *The Malthusian Controversy*. London: Routledge.

Smith, N. 1980. The origins of the water turbine. *Scientific American* 242(1):138–148.

Smith, R. D., and J. Coast. 2002. Antimicrobial resistance: A global response. *Bulletin of the World Health Organization* 80:126–133.

Smock, R. 1991. Gas turbine, combined cycle orders continue. *Power Engineering* 95(5):17–22.

Snacken, R., et al. 1999. The next influenza pandemic: Lessons from Hong Kong, 1997. *Emerging Infectious Diseases* 5:195–203.

Sobotka, T. 2008. The diverse faces of the Second Demographic Transition in Europe. *Demographic Research* 19:171–224.

Soddy, F. 1926. *Wealth, Virtual Wealth and Debt: The Solution of the Economic Paradox.* London: George Allen & Unwin.

Sohn, K. 2015. The value of male height in the marriage market. *Economics and Human Biology* 18:110–124.

SolarInsure. 2017. Top 5 largest solar power plants of the world. https://www .solarinsure.com/largest-solar-power-plants.

Solow, R. M. 1957. Technical change and the aggregate production. *Review of Economics and Statistics* 39:313–320.

Solow, R. M. 1987. Growth theory and after. http://nobelprize.org/nobel_prizes /economics/laureates/1987/solow-lecture.html.

Soo, K. T. 2005. Zipf's Law for cities: A cross-country investigation. *Regional Science and Urban Economics* 35:239–263.

Sorokin, P. 1957. *Social and Cultural Dynamics.* Oxford: Porter Sargent.

Spalding, K. L., et al. 2005. Retrospective birth dating of cells in humans. *Cell* 122: 133–143.

Speakman, J. R. 1997. *Doubly Labelled Water: Theory and Practice.* Berlin: Springer.

Speer, J. H. 2011. *Fundamentals of Tree Ring Research.* Tucson: University of Arizona Press.

Spence, J. D. 1988. *Emperor of China: Self-Portrait of K'ang-Hsi.* New York: Vintage.

Spence, J. D. 1996. *God's Chinese Son: The Taiping Heavenly Kingdom of Hong Xiuquan.* New York: W. W. Norton.

Spengler, O. 1918. *Der Untergang des Abendlandes.* Vienna: Braumüller.

SPI (Social Progress Imperative). 2018. Index to action to impact. https://www .socialprogress.org/.

Spillman, W. J., and E. Lang. 1924. *The Law of Diminishing Returns,* part 1: *The Law of the Diminishing Increment.* Chicago: World Book.

Spurr, S. H. 1956. Natural restocking of forests following the 1938 hurricane in Central New England. *Ecology* 37:443–451.

Stanhill, G. 1976. Trends and deviations in the yield of the English wheat crop during the last 750 years. *Agro-Ecosystems* 3:1–10.

Stanton, W. 2003. *The Rapid Growth of Human Populations 1750–2000.* London: Multi-Science.

The State of Obesity. 2017. Adult obesity in the United States. http://stateofobesity .org/adult-obesity/.

Statistics Canada. 2016. Statistics Canada Study on the Underground Economy in Canada, 1992–2013. https://www.canada.ca/en/revenue-agency/news/newsroom/fact -sheets/fact-sheets-2016/statistics-canada-study-on-underground-economy-canada -1992-2013.html.

Staub, K., et al. 2011. Edouard Mallet's early and almost forgotten study of the average height of Genevan conscripts in 1835. *Economics & Human Biology* 9:438–442.

Staub, K., and F. J. Rühli. 2013. "From growth in height to growth in breadth": The changing body shape of Swiss conscripts since the late 19th century and possible endocrine explanations. *General and Comparative Endocrinology* 188:9–15.

Stavros, M. 2014. *Kyoto: An Urban History of Japan's Premodern Capital*. Honolulu: University of Hawaii Press.

SteamLocomotive.com. 2017. The "largest" steam locomotives. http://www.steam locomotive.com/misc/largest.php.

Steckel, R. H. 2004. New light on the "Dark Ages": The remarkably tall stature of northern European men during the medieval era. *Social Science History* 28: 211–229.

Steckel, R. H. 2007. A pernicious side of capitalism: The care and feeding of slave children. https://www.researchgate.net/publication/228923215_A_Pernicious_Side _of_Capitalism_The_Care_and_Feeding_of_Slave_Children.

Steckel, R. H. 2008. Biological measures of the standard of living. *Journal of Economic Perspectives* 22:129–152.

Steckel, R. H. 2009. Heights and human welfare: Recent developments and new directions. *Explorations in Economic History* 46:1–23.

Steffen, W., et al. 2015. Planetary Boundaries: Guiding human development on a changing planet. *Science* 347(6223):1259855.

Steinhoff, M. 2007. *Influenza: Virus and Disease, Epidemics and Pandemics*. Baltimore, MD: Johns Hopkins University Press.

Stephenson, N. L., et al. 2014. Rate of tree carbon accumulation increases continuously with tree size. *Nature* 507:90–93.

Stetter, K. O. 1998. Hyperthermophiles: Isolation, classification, and properties. In K. Horikoshi and W. D. Grant, eds., *Extremophiles: Microbial Life in Extreme Environments*. New York: Wiley-Liss, pp. 1–24.

Stewart, I. D. 2011. A systematic review and scientific critique of methodology in modern urban heat island literature. *International Journal of Climatology* 31:200–217.

Stoler, A. L., et al., eds. 2007. *Imperial Formations*. Santa Fe, NM: SAR Press.

Stone, C., et al. 2017. *A Guide to Statistics on Historical Trends in Income Inequality*. Washington, DC: Center on Budget and Policy Priorities. https://www.cbpp.org

/research/poverty-and-inequality/a-guide-to-statistics-on-historical-trends-in
-income-inequality.

Stravitz, D. 2002. *The Chrysler Building: Creating a New York Icon, Day by Day*. Princeton, NJ: Princeton Architectural Press.

Studzinski, G. P. 2000. *Cell Growth, Cell Differentiation and Senescence: A Practical Approach*. Oxford: Oxford University Press.

Stumpf, M. P. H., and M. A. Porter. 2012. Critical truths about power laws. *Science* 335:665–666.

Subramaniam, A., et al. 2002. Detecting Trichodesmium blooms in SeaWiFS imagery. *Deep-Sea Research: Part II* 49:107–121.

Svefors, P., et al. 2016. Stunted at 10 years: Linear growth trajectories and stunting from birth to pre-adolescence in a rural Bangladeshi cohort. *PLoS ONE*. doi:10.1371 /journal.pone.0149700.

Swain, G. F. 1885. General introduction. In *Reports on the Water-Power of the United States*. Washington, DC: USGPO, pp. xi–xxxix. https://babel.hathitrust.org/cgi/pt?id =uc1.c2532640;view=1up;seq=7.

Szreter, S. 1993. The idea of demographic transition and the study of fertility change: A critical intellectual history. *Population and Development Review* 19:659–701.

Taagepera, R. 1968. Growth curves of empires. *General Systems* 13:171–176.

Taagepera, R. 1978. Size and duration of empires: Growth-decline curves, 3000 to 600 B.C. *Social Science Research* 7:180–196.

Taagepera, R. 1979. Size and duration of empires: Growth-decline curves, 600 B.C. to 600 A.D. *Social Science History* 3:115–138.

Taagepera, R. 2014. A world population growth model: Interaction with Earth's carrying capacity and technology in limited space. *Technological Forecasting and Social Change* 82:34–41.

Tainter, J. 1988. *The Collapse of Complex Societies*. Cambridge: Cambridge University Press.

Talbert, R. J. A., ed. 2000. *Barrington Atlas of the Greek and Roman World*. Princeton, NJ: Princeton University Press.

Tallgrass Energy. 2017. Rockies Express Pipeline. http://www.tallgrassenergylp.com /Operations_REX.aspx.

Tan, Q. 1982–1988. *Zhōngguó lìshǐ dìtú jí* (*The Historical Atlas of China*). Beijing: China Cartographic.

Tanner, J. M. 1962. *Growth and Adolescence*. Oxford: Blackwell Scientific.

Tanner, J. M. 2010. *A History of the Study of Human Growth.* Cambridge: Cambridge University Press.

Tashiro, T., et al. 2017. Early trace of life from 3.95 Ga sedimentary rocks in Labrador, Canada. *Nature* 549:516–518.

Tate, K. 2012. NASA's Mighty Saturn V Moon Rocket Explained. https://www.space.com/18422-apollo-saturn-v-moon-rocket-nasa-infographic.html.

Taubenberger, J. K., and D. M. Morens. 2006. 1918 influenza: The mother of all pandemics. *Emerging Infectious Diseases* 12:15–22.

Taylor, B. 2017. Charles E. Taylor: The man aviation history almost forgot. https://www.faa.gov/about/office_org/field_offices/fsdo/phl/local_more/media/CT%20Hist.pdf.

Taylor, P., et al. 2006. Luxury or necessity? Things we can't live without: The list has grown in the past decade. http://www.pewsocialtrends.org/files/2010/10/Luxury.pdf.

Taylor, S. 2016. *The Fall and Rise of Nuclear Power in Britain.* Cambridge: Cambridge University Press.

Techradar.com. 2017. Best CPUs and processor deals from AMD and Intel in 2017. http://www.techradar.com/news/computing-components/processors/best-cpu-the-8-top-processors-today-1046063.

Teck, R. M., and D. E. Hilt. 1991. *Individual-Tree Diameter Growth Model for the Northeastern United States.* Radnor, PA: Northeastern Forest Experiment Station.

Teir, S. 2002. *The History of Steam Generation.* Helsinki: Helsinki University of Technology.

Teixeira, C. M. G. L., et al. 2014. A new perspective on the growth pattern of the wandering albatross (*Diomedea exulans*) through DEB theory. *Journal of Sea Research* 94:117–127.

Temin, P. 2001. A market economy in the early Roman empire. *The Journal of Roman Studies* 91:169–181.

Tesla, N. 1888. *Electro-magnetic Motor. Specification forming part of Letters Patent No. 391,968, dated May 1, 1888.* Washington, DC: US Patent Office. http://www.uspto.gov.

Thaxton, J. P., et al. 2006. Stocking density and physiological adaptive responses of broilers. *Poultry Science* 85:344–351.

Thomlinson, R. 1975. *Demographic Problems: Controversy over Population Control.* Encino, CA: Dickenson.

Thompson, D. W. 1917. *On Growth and Form.* Cambridge: Cambridge University Press.

Thompson, D. W. 1942. *On Growth and Form: A New Edition*. Cambridge: Cambridge University Press.

Thompson, M. 2010. Corliss centennial engine. http://newsm.org/steam-e/corliss -centennial-engine/.

Thompson, W. S. 1929. Population. *American Journal of Sociology* 34:959–975.

Thomsen, C. J. 1836. *Ledetraad til nordisk oldkyndighed, udg. af det Kongelige nordiske oldskrift-selskab*. Copenhagen: S. L. Møllers.

Thomsen, P. M., ed. 2011. *The U.S. EU Beef Hormone and Poultry Disputes*. New York: Nova Science.

Thurston, R. H. 1886. *History of the Steam Engine*. New York: D. Appleton.

Tiwari, V. M., et al. 2009. Dwindling groundwater resources in northern India, from satellite gravity observations. *Geophysical Research Letters* doi:10.1029/2009GL039401 12(6):e0178691. https://doi.org/10.1371/journal.pone.0178691.

Tjørve, K. M. C. and E. Tjørve. 2017. The use of Gompertz models in growth analyses, and new Gompertz-model approach: An addition to the Unified-Richards family. *PLoS ONE* 12(6):e0178691. https://doi.org/10.1371/journal.pone.0178691.

TMG (Tokyo Metropolitan Region). 2017. The structure of the Tokyo Metropolitan Government (TMG). http://www.metro.tokyo.jp/ENGLISH/ABOUT/STRUCTURE /structure02.htm.

Tobler, W. 1970. A computer movie simulating urban growth in the Detroit region. *Economic Geography*, 46(Supplement): 234–240.

Tollefson, J. 2014. Tree growth never slows. *Nature* (January). doi:10.1038 /nature.2014.14536.

Tollenaar, M. 1985. What is the current upper limit of corn productivity? In *Proceedings of the Conference on Physiology, Biochemistry and Chemistry Associated with Maximum Yield Corn, St. Louis, MO*. http://www1.biologie.uni-hamburg.de/b-online /library/maize/www.ag.iastate.edu/departments/agronomy/yield.html.

Top 500. 2017. The list. https://www.top500.org/lists/2017/06/.

Toselli, S., et al. 2005. Growth of Chinese Italian infants in the first 2 years of life. *Annals of Human Biology* 32: 15–29.

Transneft'. 2017. Istoria. http://www.transneft.ru/about/story/.

Transparency International. 2017. *Corruption Perceptions Index 2016*. https://www .transparency.org/news/feature/corruption_perceptions_index_2016.

Trautman, J. 2011. *Pan American Clippers: The Golden Age of Flying Boats*. Boston: Boston Mills Press.

Trumbore, S. 2006. Carbon respired by terrestrial ecosystems—recent progress and challenges. *Global Change Biology* 12:141–153.

Tsoularis, A. 2001. Analysis of logistic growth models. *Research Letters in the Information and Mathematical Sciences* 2:23–46.

Tumanovskii, A. G., et al. 2017. Review of the coal-fired, over-supercritical and ultra-supercritical steam power plants. *Thermal Engineering* 64(2):83–96.

Tupy, M. L. 2012. Why iPhone 5 and Siri are good for capitalism. http://www.cato .org/blog/miracle-iphone-or-how-capitalism-can-be-good-environment.

Turchin, P. 2009. A theory for formation of large empires. *Journal of Global History* 4:191–217.

Turnbough, B. 2013. 12 Billion electric motors to be shipped in consumer products by 2018. https://technology.ihs.com/485065/12-billion-electric-motors-to-be -shipped-in-consumer-products-by-2018.

Turner, G. 2008. *A Comparison of Limits to Growth with Thirty Years of Reality.* Canberra: CSIRO.

Turner, J., et al. 2005. *The Welfare of Broiler Chickens in the European Union.* Petersfield: Compassion in World Farming Trust. http://www.ciwf.org.uk/includes/documents /cm_docs/2008/w/welfare_of_broilers_in_the_eu_2005.pdf.

Turner, M. E., et al. 1976. A theory of growth. *Mathematical Biosciences* 29:367–373.

Turner, M. J., et al. 1998. *Fractal Geometry in Digital Imaging.* San Diego: Academic Press.

UCS (Union of Concerned Scientists). 2001. *Hogging It: Estimates of Antimicrobial Use in Livestock.* Washington, DC: UCS.

Ulijaszek, S. J., et al., eds. 1998. *The Cambridge Encyclopedia of Human Growth and Development.* Cambridge: Cambridge University Press.

Ulrich, W., et al. 2010. A meta-analysis of species–abundance distributions. *Oikos* 119:1149–1155.

UN (United Nations). 1969. *Growth of the World's Urban and Rural Population, 1920–2000.* New York: UN.

UN. 1990. *The World at Six Billion.* New York: UN.

UN. 2000. *Forest Resources of Europe, CIS, North America, Australia, Japan and New Zealand (Industrialized Temperate\Boreal Countries).* Geneva: UN.

UN. 2001. *World Population Prospects The 2000 Revision.* http://www.un.org/esa /population/publications/wpp2000/highlights.pdf.

UN. 2004. *World Population to 2300.* New York: UN. http://www.un.org/esa /population/publications/longrange2/WorldPop2300final.pdf.

UN. 2014. *World Urbanization Prospects*. New York: UN. https://esa.un.org/unpd/wup /publications/files/wup2014-highlights.Pdf.

UN. 2016. *The World's Cities in 2016*. http://www.un.org/en/development/desa /population/publications/pdf/urbanization/the_worlds_cities_in_2016_data _booklet.pdf.

UN. 2017. *World Population Prospects: 2017 Revision*. https://esa.un.org/unpd/wpp/.

UNCTAD (United Nations Conference on Trade and Development). 2017. *Review of Maritime Transport 2017*. Geneva: UNCTAD. http://unctad.org/en/PublicationsLibrary /rmt2017_en.pdf.

UNDP (United Nations Development Programme). 2016. *Human Development Report 2016*. New York: UNDP. http://hdr.undp.org/sites/default/files/2016_human _development_report.pdf.

UNESCO (United Nations Educational, Scientific and Cultural Organization). 2016. Harmful Algal Bloom Programme. http://hab.ioc-unesco.org/index.php?option=com _content&view=article&id=5&Itemid=16.

UNESCO. 2018. UIS statistics. http://data.uis.unesco.org/.

UNFCCC (United Nations Framework Convention on Climate Change). 2015. *Adoption of the Paris Agreement*. https://unfccc.int/resource/docs/2015/cop21/eng/l09r01.pdf.

Unsicker, K., and K. Krieglstein, eds. 2008. *Cell Signaling and Growth Factors in Development: From Molecules to Organogenesis*.Weinheim: Wiley-VCH.

USAID (United States Agency for International Development). 2010. *Desired Number of Children: 2000–2008*. https://dhsprogram.com/pubs/pdf/CR25/CR25.pdf.

USBC (United States Bureau of the Census). 1975. *Historical Statistics of the United States: Colonial Times to 1970*. Washington, DC: USBC.

USBR (US Bureau of Reclamation). 2016. Grand Coulee Dam. https://www.usbr.gov /pn/grandcoulee/.

USCB (United States Census Bureau). 2013. Crowding. Housing characteristics in the U.S.—tables. https://www.census.gov/hhes/www/housing/census/histcensushsg.html.

USCB. 2016a. Highlights of annual 2015 characteristics of new housing. https:// www.census.gov/construction/chars/highlights.html.

USCB. 2016b. World population: Historical estimates of world population. https:// www.census.gov/population/international/data/worldpop/table_history.php.

USCB. 2017. Median and average square feet of floor area in new single-family houses completed by location: Built for sale. https://www.census.gov/construction/chars/pdf /medavgsqft.pdf.

US Congress. 1973. *Energy Reorganization Act of 1973: Hearings, Ninety-Third Congress, First Session, on H.R. 11510*. Washington, DC: US Government Printing House.

USDA (US Department of Agriculture). 2010. *Wood Handbook*. Madison, WI: USDA.

USDA. 2015. Overview of the United States hog industry. http://usda.mannlib.cornell .edu/usda/current/hogview/hogview-10-29-2015.pdf.

USDA. 2016a. *Kansas Wheat History*. Manhattan, KS: USDA. https://www.nass.usda .gov/Statistics_by_State/Kansas/Publications/Crops/whthist.pdf.

USDA. 2016b. Recent TRENDS in GE adoption. https://www.ers.usda.gov/data -products/adoption-of-genetically-engineered-crops-in-the-us/recent-trends-in-ge -adoption.aspx.

USDA. 2017a. Crop production historical track records. http://usda.mannlib.cornell .edu/MannUsda/viewDocumentInfo.do?documentID=1593.

USDA. 2017b. Grain: World markets and trade. https://apps.fas.usda.gov/psdonline /circulars/grain.pdf.

USDA. 2017c. *2016 Agricultural Statistics Annual*. https://www.nass.usda.gov/Publica tions/Ag_Statistics/2016/index.php.

USDC (US Department of Commerce). 2012. New York-Newark, NY-NJ-CT-PA Combined Statistical Area. https://www2.census.gov/geo/maps/econ/ec2012/csa/EC2012 _330M200US408M.pdf.

USDI (US Department of Interior). 2017. Grand Coulee Dam statistics and facts. https://www.usbr.gov/pn/grandcoulee/pubs/factsheet.pdf.

USDOE. 2017. The history of solar. https://www1.eere.energy.gov/solar/pdfs/solar _timeline.pdf.

USDOT (US Department of Transportation). 2017a. The Dwight D. Eisenhower System of Interstate and Defense Highways. https://www.fhwa.dot.gov/interstate /finalmap.cfm.

USDOT. 2017b. Table 1–50: U.S. ton-miles of freight (BTS special tabulation). https:// www.bts.gov/archive/publications/national_transportation_statistics/table_01_50.

USEIA (US Energy Information Administration). 2000. *The Changing Structure of the Electric Power Industry 2000: An Update*. http://webapp1.dlib.indiana.edu/virtual_disk _library/index.cgi/4265704/FID1578/pdf/electric/056200.pdf.

USEIA. 2014. Oil tanker sizes range from general purpose to ultra-large crude carriers on AFRA scale. http://www.eia.gov/todayinenergy/detail.cfm?id=17991.

USEIA. 2016. Average operating heat rate for selected energy sources. https://www .eia.gov/electricity/annual/html/epa_08_01.html.

USEIA. 2017a. What is U.S. electricity generation by energy source? https://www.eia
.gov/tools/faqs/faq.php?id=427&t=3.

USEIA. 2017b. U.S. product supplied of finished motor gasoline. https://www.eia
.gov/dnav/pet/hist/LeafHandler.ashx?n=pet&s=mgfupus2&f=a.

USEIA. 2019. U.S. Field Production of Crude Oil. https://www.eia.gov/dnav/pet/hist
/LeafHandler.ashx?n=PET&s=MCRFPUS1&f=M.

USEPA. 2016a. Air pollution control technology fact sheets. https://www3.epa.gov
/ttncatc1/cica/atech_e.html#111.

USEPA. 2016b. *Light-Duty Vehicle CO2 and Fuel Economy Trends*. Washington, DC:
USEPA. https://www.epa.gov/fuel-economy-trends/report-tables-and-appendices-co2
-and-fuel-economy-trends.

US Forest Service. 2018. Growing stock trees. https://www.definedterm.com/growing
_stock_trees.

US FPC (US Federal Power Commission). 1965. *Northeast Power Failure, November 9
and 10, 1965: A Report to the President*. Washington, DC: US FPC.

USGS (United States Geological Survey). 2000. National land cover dataset: U.S.
Geological Survey fact sheet 108–00. https://pubs.usgs.gov/fs/2000/0108.

USGS. 2017a. High Plains aquifer groundwater levels continue to decline. https://
www.usgs.gov/news/usgs-high-plains-aquifer-groundwater-levels-continue
-decline.

USGS. 2017b. National Minerals Information Center. https://minerals.usgs.gov
/minerals/.

Usmanova, R. M. 2013. Aral Sea and sustainable development. *Water Science and
Technology* 47(7–8):41–47.

Vaganov, E. A., et al. 2006. *Growth Dynamics of Conifer Tree Rings: Images of Past and
Future Environments*. Berlin: Springer.

Van Bavel, J., and D. S. Reher. 2013. The Baby Boom and its causes: What we know
and what we need to know. *Population and Development Review* 39:257–288.

van den Bergh, J. C. J. M., and P. Rietveld. 2003. *"Limits to World Population" Revisited: Meta-analysis and Meta-estimation*. Amsterdam: Free University.

Van der Spiegel, J., et al. 2000. The ENIAC: History, operation and reconstruction in
VLSI. In R. Rojas and U. Hashagen, eds., *The First Computers: History and Architectures*.
Cambridge, MA: MIT Press, pp. 121–178.

van Geenhuizen, M. T., et al. 2009. *Technological Innovation across Nations: Applied
Studies of Coevolutionary Development*. Berlin: Springer.

van Hoof, T. B., et al. 2006. Forest re-growth on medieval farmland after the Black Death pandemic: Implications for atmospheric CO_2 levels. *Palaeogeography, Palaeoclimatology, Palaeoecology* 237:396–411.

van Ijselmuijden, K., et al. 2015. Study for a suspension bridge with a main span of 3700 m. In *Structural Engineering: Providing Solutions to Global Challenges*, International Association for Bridge and Structural Engineering, ABSE Symposium Report, pp. 1–8.

Van Valen, L. 1973. A new evolutionary law. *Evolutionary Theory* 1:1–30.

van Zanden, J. L., and B. van Leeuwen. 2012. Persistent but not consistent: The growth of national income in Holland, 1347–1807. *Explorations in Economic History* 49:119–130.

Vasko, T., et al., eds. 1990. *Life Cycles and Long Waves*. Berlin: Springer.

Vasudevan, A. 2010. *Tonnage Measurement of Ships: Historical Evolution, Current Issues and Proposals for the Way Forward*. Malmö: World Maritime University.

Verbelen, J.-P., and K. Vissenberg, eds. 2007. *The Expanding Cell*. Berlin: Springer.

Verhulst, P. F. 1838. Notice sur la loi que la population suit dans son accroissement. *Correspondance Mathématique et Physique* 10:113–121.

Verhulst, P. F. 1845. Recherches mathématiques sur la loi d'accroissement de la population. *Nouveaux Mémoires de l'Académie Royale des Sciences et Belles-Lettres de Bruxelles* 18:1–42.

Verhulst, P. F. 1847. Deuxième mémoire sur la loi d'accroissement de la population. *Mémoires de l'Académie Royale des Sciences, des Lettres et des Beaux-Arts de Belgique* 20:1–32.

Vermeij, G. J. 2016. Gigantism and its implications for the history of life. *PloS ONE* 11:e0146092. doi:10.1371.

Vernadsky, V. I. 1929. *Le biosphere*. Paris: Librairie Felix Alcan.

Vestas. 2017a. Three new turbines rating up to 4.2 MW. https://www.vestas.com/en/products/turbines#!.

Vestas. 2017b. World's most powerful wind turbine once again smashes 24 hour power generation record as 9 MW wind turbine is launched. http://www.mhivestasoffshore.com/new-24-hour-record/.

Vieira, S., and R. Hoffmann. 1977. Comparison of the logistic and Gompertz growth functions considering additive and multiplicative error terms. *Applied Statistics* 26:143–148.

Ville, S. P. 1990. *Transport and the Development of European Economy, 1750–1918*. London: Macmillan.

Villermé, L. R. 1829. Mémoire sur la taille de l'homme en France. *Annales d'Hygiène Publique et de Médecine Légale*, pp. 51–396.

Vincek, D., et al. 2012. Modeling of pig growth by S-function—least absolute deviation. *Archiv für Tierzucht* 55:364–374.

Virgo, N., et al. 2014. Self-organising autocatalysis. In *ALIFE 14: Proceedings of the Fourteenth International Conference on the Synthesis and Simulation of Living Systems*. https://mitpress.mit.edu/sites/default/files/titles/content/alife14/978-0-262-32621-6 -ch080.pdf.

Visscher, P. M. 2008. Sizing up human height variation. *Nature Genetics* 40:489–490.

Vogel, E. F. 1979. *Japan as Number One: Lessons for America*. Cambridge, MA: Harvard University Press.

Vogel, O. 1977. Semidwarf wheats increase production capability and problems. https://www.ars.usda.gov/pacific-west-area/pullman-wa/whgq/history/orville-vogel -speech-on-semidwarf-wheats/.

Vogels, M., et al. 1975. P. F. Verhulst "Notice sur la loi que la population suit dans son accroissement" from Correspondance Mathématique et Physique. Ghent, Vol. X, 1838. *Journal of Biological Physics* 3:183–192.

Voith. 2017. Generators. http://www.voith.com/en/products-services/hydro-power /generators-557.html.

Volkswagen. 2010. *The Golf Environmental Commendation Background Report*. Wolfsburg: Volkswagen.

von Bertalanffy, L. 1938. A quantitative theory of organic growth. *Human Biology* 10:181–213.

von Bertalanffy, L. 1957. Quantitative laws in metabolism and growth. *Quarterly Review of Biology* 32:217–231.

von Bertalanffy, L. 1960. Principles and theory of growth. In W. N. Nowinski, ed., *Fundamental Aspects of Normal and Malignant Growth*. Amsterdam: Elsevier, pp. 137–259.

von Bertalanffy, L. 1968. *General Systems Theory*. New York: George Braziller.

von Foerster, H., et al. 1960. Doomsday: Friday, 13 November, A.D. 2026. *Science* 132:1291–1295.

von Hoerner, S. J. 1975. Population explosion and interstellar expansion. *Journal of the British Interplanetary Society* 28:691–712.

von Thünen, J. H. 1826. *Der isolierte Staat in Beziehung auf Landwirtschaft und Nationalökonomie*. Hamburg: Perthes. Republished Jena: Gustav Fischer, 1910. https:// archive.org/details/derisoliertestaa00thuoft.

von Tunzelmann, G. N. 1978. *Steam Power and British Industrialization to 1860.* Oxford: Clarendon Press.

Wackernagel, M., and W. Rees. 1996. *Our Ecological Footprint: Reducing Human Impact on the Earth.* Gabriola Island, BC: New Society.

Wackernagel, M., et al. 2002. Tracking the ecological overshoot of the human economy. *Proceedings of the National Academy of Sciences of the USA* 99:9266–9271.

Waliszewski, P., and J. Konarski. 2005. A mystery of the Gompertz function. In G. A. Losa et al., eds., *Fractals in Biology and Medicine.* Basel: Birkhäuser, pp. 278–286.

Wallerstein, I. M. 2004. *World-Systems Analysis: An Introduction.* Durham, NC: Duke University Press.

Wallis, M. 2001. *Route 66.* New York: St. Martin's Griffin.

Walsh, J. J., et al. 2006. Red tides in the Gulf of Mexico: Where, when, and why? *Journal of Geophysical Research* 111(C11003):1–46. doi:10.1029/2004JC002813.

Walsh, T. R., and R. A. Howe. 2002. The prevalence and mechanisms of vancomycin resistance in Staphylococcus aureus. *Annual Review of Microbiology* 56:657–675.

Walton, S. A., ed. 2006. *Wind and Water in the Middle Ages: Fluid Technologies from Antiquity to the Renaissance.* Tempe: Arizona Center for Medieval and Renaissance Studies.

Walz, W., and H. Niemann. 1997. *Daimler-Benz: Wo das Auto Anfing.* Konstanz: Stadler.

Wang, G., et al. 2018. Consensuses and discrepancies of basin-scale ocean heat content changes in different ocean analyses. *Climate Dynamics* 50:2471–2487. https://doi.org/10.1007/s00382-017-3751-5.

Warburton, R. 1981. A history of the development of the steam boiler, with particular reference to its use in the electricity supply industry. (Master's thesis, Loughborough University, Loughborough.) https://dspace.lboro.ac.uk/2134/10498.

Ward, J. D., et al. 2016. Is decoupling GDP growth from environmental impact possible? *PLoS ONE* 11(10):e0164733. doi:10.1371/journal.pone.0164733.

Waring, R. H., et al. 1998. Net primary production of forests: A constant fraction of gross primary production? *Tree Physiology* 18:129–1343.

Wärtsilä. 2006. *Emma Maersk.* https://www.wartsila.com/resources/customer-references/view/emma-maersk.

Wärtsilä. 2009. Wärtsilä RT-flex96C and Wärtsilä RTA96C technology review. http://wartsila.com.

WaterAid. 2015. *Undernutrition and Water, Sanitation and Hygiene.* London: WaterAid.

Watkins, G. 1967. Steam power—an illustrated guide. *Industrial Archaeology* 4:81–110.

Watt, J. 1769. *Steam Engines, &c. 29 April 1769.* Patent reprint by G. E. Eyre and W. Spottiswoode, 1855. https://upload.wikimedia.org/wikipedia/commons/0/0d /James_Watt_Patent_1769_No_913.pdf.

Watts, P. 1905. *The Ships of the Royal Navy as They Existed at the Time of Trafalgar.* London: Institution of Naval Architects.

WBCSD (World Business Council for Sustainable Development). 2004. *Mobility 2030: Meeting the Challenges of Sustainability.* Geneva: WBCSD.

WCED (World Commission on Environment and Development). 1987. *Report of the World Commission on Environment and Development: Our Common Future.* http://www .un-documents.net/our-common-future.pdf.

Webster, D., ed. 2002. *Fall of the Ancient Maya: Solving the Mystery of the Maya Collapse.* London: Thames & Hudson.

Wei, W., et al. 2013. A calibrated human Y-chromosomal phylogeny based on resequencing. *Genome Research* 23:388–395.

Weibull, W. 1951. A statistical distribution function of a wide applicability. *Journal of Applied Mechanics* 18:293–297.

Weiner, J., et al. 2001. The nature of tree growth and the "age-related decline in forest productivity." *Oikos* 94:374–376.

Weishampel. J. F., et al. 2007. Forest canopy recovery from the 1938 hurricane and subsequent salvage damage measured with airborne LiDAR. *Remote Sensing of Environment* 109:142–153.

Weiskittel, A. R., et al. 2011. *Forest Growth and Yield Modeling.* Chichester: Wiley Blackwell.

Wells, P. 2017. Mitsubishi Materials admits to product data falsification. *Financial Times,* November 23. https://www.ft.com/content/a023d962-d03c-11e7-b781-794ce 08b24dc.

Welp, L., et al. 2011. Interannual variability in the oxygen isotopes of atmospheric CO_2 driven by El Niño. *Nature* 477:579–582.

Wenzel, S., et al. 2016. Projected land photosynthesis constrained by changes in the seasonal cycle of atmospheric CO_2. *Nature* 538:499–501.

Werner, J., and E. M. Griebeler. 2014. Allometries of maximum growth rate versus body mass at maximum growth indicate that non-avian dinosaurs had growth rates typical of fast growing ectothermic sauropsids. *PLoS ONE* 9(2):e88834.

Wescott, N. P. 1936. *Origins and Early History of the Tetraethyl Lead Business.* Wilmington, DE: Du Pont.

Wesson, R. 2016. *RF Solid State Cooking White Paper.* Nijmegen: Ampleon.

West, G. 2017. *Scale: The Universal Laws of Growth, Innovation, Sustainability, and the Pace of Life in Organisms, Cities, Economies, and Companies.* New York: Penguin.

West, G. B., and J. H. Brown. 2005. The origin of allometric scaling laws in biology from genomes to ecosystems: Towards a quantitative unifying theory of biological structure and organization. *Journal of Experimental Biology* 208:1575–1592.

West, G. B., et al. 1997. A general model for the origin of allometric scaling laws in biology. *Science* 276:122–126.

West, G. B., et al. 1999. A general model for the structure and allometry of plant vascular systems. *Nature* 400:664–667.

West, G. B., et al. 2001. A general model for ontogenetic growth. *Nature* 413: 628–631.

Weyand, P. G., et al. 2000. Faster top running speeds are achieved with greater ground forces not more rapid leg movements. *Journal of Applied Physiology* 89: 1991–1999.

Wharton, D. A. 2002. *Life at the Limits: Organisms in Extreme Environments.* Cambridge: Cambridge University Press.

Whipp, B. J., and S. A. Ward. 1992. Will women soon outrun men? *Nature* 355:25.

White, C. R., and R. S. Seymour. 2003. Mammalian basal metabolic rate is proportional to body mass$^{2/3}$. *Proceedings of the National Academy of Sciences of the USA* 100:4046–4049.

White, C. R., et al. 2007. Allometric exponents do not support a universal metabolic allometry. *Ecology* 88:315–323.

White, L. 1978. *Medieval Religion and Technology.* Berkeley: University of California Press.

White, O., et al. 1999. Genome sequence of the radioresistant bacterium *Deinococcus radiodurans* R1. *Science* 286:1571–1577.

White, W., and D. Culver. 2012. *Encyclopedia of Caves.* Cambridge, MA: Academic Press.

Whitman, W. B., et al. 1998. Prokaryotes: The unseen majority. *Proceedings of the National Academy of Sciences of the USA* 95:6578–6583.

Whittemore, C. T., and I. Kyriazakis. 2006. *Science and Practice of Pig Production.* Chichester: Wiley-Blackwell.

WHO (World Health Organization). 2000. *Obesity: Preventing and Managing the Global Epidemic. Report of a WHO Consultation.* Geneva: WHO.

WHO. 2006. *Child Growth Standards.* Geneva: WHO.

WHO. 2016. Life expectancy increased by 5 years since 2000, but health inequalities persist. http://www.who.int/mediacentre/news/releases/2016/health-inequalities -persist/en/.

WHO. 2017. Obesity. http://www.who.int/topics/obesity/en/.

WHS (World Heritage Site). 2017. Ancient Merv. http://www.worldheritagesite.org /list/Ancient+Merv.

Wier, S. K. 1996. Insight from geometry and physics into the construction of Egyptian Old Kingdom pyramids. *Cambridge Archaeological Journal* 6:150–163.

Williams, M. 2006. *Deforesting the Earth: From Prehistory to Global Crisis*. Chicago: University of Chicago Press.

Williamson, J. A. 1916. *The Foundation and Growth of the British Empire*. London: Macmillan.

Williamson, M., and K. J. Gaston. 2005. The lognormal distribution is not an appropriate null hypothesis for the species–abundance distribution. *Journal of Animal Ecology* 74:409–422.

Willis, S. 2003. The capability of sailing warships. Part 1: Windward performance. *Northern Mariner/Le marin du nord* 13(4):29–39.

Wilson, A., and J. Boehland. 2005. Small is beautiful: U.S. house size, resource use, and the environment. *Journal of Industrial Ecology* 9:277–287.

Wilson, A. I. 2008. Machines in Greek and Roman technology. In J. P. Oleson, ed., *The Oxford Handbook of Technology in the Classical World*. New York: Oxford University Press, pp. 337–366.

Wilson, A. M. 1999. Windmills, cattle and railroad: The settlement of the Llano Estacado. *Journal of the West* 38(1):62–67.

Wilson, C. 2011. Understanding global demographic convergence since 1950. *Population and Development Review* 37:375–388.

Winsor, C. P. 1932. The Gompertz curve as a growth curve. *Proceedings of the National Academy of Sciences of the USA* 18:2–8.

Winter, J., and M. Teitelbaum. 2013. *The Global Spread of Fertility Decline: Population, Fear and Uncertainty*. New Haven, CT: Yale University Press.

Winter, T. N. 2007. The *Mechanical Problems* in the corpus of Aristotle. (Classics and Religious Studies Department, University of Nebraska.) https://digitalcommons.unl .edu/cgi/viewcontent.cgi?article=1067&context=classicsfacpub.

Wiser, R., and M. Bollinger. 2016. *2015 Wind Technologies Market Report*. Oak Ridge, TN: USDOE. https://energy.gov/sites/prod/files/2016/08/f33/2015-Wind-Technologies -Market-Report-08162016.pdf.

WNA. 2017. Plans for new reactors worldwide. http://www.world-nuclear.org /information-library/current-and-future-generation/plans-for-new-reactors -worldwide.aspx.

Woese, C. R., and G. E. Fox. 1977. Phylogenetic structure of the prokaryotic domain: The primary kingdoms. *Proceedings of the National Academy of Sciences of the USA* 74:5088–5090.

Woese, C. R., et al. 1990. Towards a natural system of organisms: Proposal for the domains Archaea, Bacteria, and Eucarya. *Proceedings of the National Academy of Sciences of the USA* 87:4576–4579.

Wong, K. V., et al. 2013. Review of world urban heat islands: Many linked to increased mortality. *Journal of Energy Resources Technology* 135:022101–11.

Wood, A. R., et al. 2014. Defining the role of common variation in the genomic and biological architecture of adult human height. *Nature Genetics* 46:1173–86.

Woodall, F. P. 1982. Water wheels for winding. *Industrial Archaeology* 16:333–338.

Woodbridge, R., et al. 2016. *Atlas of Household Energy Consumption and Expenditure in India*. Chennai: Centre for Development Finance.

Woodward, H. N., et al. 2011. Osteohistological evidence for determinate growth in the American alligator. *Herpetology* 45:339–342.

World Bank. 2018. DataBank. http://databank.worldbank.org/data/home.aspx.

World Economic Forum. 2017. *The Inclusive Growth and Development Report.* http:// www3.weforum.org/docs/WEF_Forum_IncGrwth_2017.pdf.

Wrangham, R. 2009. *Catching Fire*. New York: Basic Books.

Wright, Q. 1942. *A Study of War*. Chicago: University of Chicago Press.

Wright, S. 1926. *The Biology of Population Growth* by Raymond Pearl; *The Natural Increase of Mankind* by J. Shirley Sweeney (book reviews). *Journal of the American Statistical Association* 21:493–497.

Wrigley, E. A. 2010. *Energy and the English Industrial Revolution*. Cambridge: Cambridge University Press.

Wrigley, E. A. 2011. Opening Pandora's box: A new look at the industrial revolution. http://voxeu.org/article/industrial-revolution-energy-revolution.

Wrigley, E. A., and R. Schofield. 1981. *The Population History of England, 1541–1871: A Reconstruction*. Cambridge: Cambridge University Press.

WSA (World Steel Association). 2017. *Steel Statistical Yearbook 2016*. https://www .worldsteel.org/en/dam/jcr:37ad1117-fefc-4df3-b84f-6295478ae460/Steel+Statistical +Yearbook+2016.pdf.

Wu, J., et al. 2010. Analysis of material and energy consumption of mobile phones in China. *Energy Policy* 38:4135–4141.

Wu, Z., et al. 2006. Determinants of high sex ratio among newborns: A cohort study from rural Anhui province, China. *Reproductive Health Matters* 14:172–180.

WWID (World Wealth and Income Data Base). 2018. World Inequality Database. https://wid.world/.

Xinhua. 2016. China's high-speed rail track exceeds 20,000 km. http://news.xinhua net.com/english/2016-09/10/c_135678132.htm.

Yakovenko, V. M., and J. B. Rosser. 2009. Colloquium: Statistical mechanics of money, wealth, and income. *Review of Modern Physics* 81:1703–1725.

Yang, R. C., et al. 1978. The potential of Weibull-type functions as flexible growth curves. *Canadian Journal of Forestry Research* 8:424–431.

Yang, W., et al. 2014. The 1918 influenza pandemic in New York City: Age-specific timing, mortality, and transmission dynamics. *Influenza and Other Respiratory Viruses* 8:177–188.

Yang, Z., et al. 2015. Comparison of the China growth charts with the WHO growth standards in assessing malnutrition of children. *BMJ Open* 5:e006107. doi:10.1136 /bmjopen-2014–006107.

Yaroshenko, T. Y. et al. 2015. Wavelet modeling and prediction of the stability of states: The Roman Empire and the European Union. *Communications in Nonlinear Science and Numerical Simulation* 26(1–3):265–275.

Yayanos, A. A., et al. 1981. Obligately barophilic bacterium from the Mariana Trench. *Proceedings of the National Academy of Sciences of the USA* 78:5212–5215.

Yoda, K. T., et al. 1963. Self-thinning in overcrowded pure stands under cultivated and natural conditions. *Journal of the Institute of Polytechnics* 14:107–129.

Yoneyama, T., and M. S. Krishnamoorthy. 2012. Simulating the spread of influenza pandemic of 2009 considering international traffic. *Simulation: Transactions of the Society for Modeling and Simulation International* 88(4):437–449.

Young, G. K. 2001. *Rome's Eastern Trade: International Commerce and Imperial Policy, 31 BC-AD 305.* London: Routledge.

Yu, X., et al. 2015. A review of China's rural water management. *Sustainability* 7:5773–5792.

Yuan, Y., and J. Wang. 2012. China's stunted children. *China Dialogue,* May 15. https://www.chinadialogue.net/article/show/single/en/4927-China-s-stunted-children.

Yule, G. U. 1925a. The growth of population and the factors which control it. *Journal of the Royal Statistical Society* 88:1–58.

Yule, G. U. 1925b. A mathematical theory of evolution, based on the conclusions of Dr. J. C. Willis, F.R.S. *Philosophical Transactions of the Royal Society of London. Series B* 213:21–87.

Zagórski, K., et al. 2010. Economic development and happiness: Evidence from 32 nations. *Polish Sociological Review* 1(169):3–20.

Zahid, H. J., et al. 2016. Agriculture, population growth, and statistical analysis of the radiocarbon record. *Proceedings of the National Academy of Sciences of the USA.* 113:931–935.

Zamoyski, A. 2012. *Poland: A History.* New York: Hippocrene Books.

Zeder, M. 2008. Domestication and early agriculture in the Mediterranean Basin: Origins, diffusion, and impact. *Proceedings of the National Academy of Sciences of the USA* 105:11597–11604.

Zeller, T. 2007. *Driving Germany: The Landscape of the German Autobahn, 1930–1970.* New York: Berghahn.

Zhang, D., et al. 2008. Rates of litter decomposition in terrestrial ecosystems: Global patterns and controlling factors. *Journal of Plant Ecology* 1:85–93.

Zhang, Q., and W. A. Dick. 2014. Growth of soil bacteria, on penicillin and neomycin, not previously exposed to these antibiotics. *Science of the Total Environment* 493:445–453.

Zhang, W. 2006. *Economic Growth with Income and Wealth Distribution.* London: Palgrave Macmillan.

Zhao, Y., and S. Wang. 2015. The relationship between urbanization, economic growth and energy consumption in China: An econometric perspective analysis. *Sustainability* 7:5609–5627.

Zheng, C. Z. 2015. *Military Moral Hazard and the Fate of Empires.* http://economics .uwo.ca/people/zheng_docs/empire.pdf.

Zheng, H., et al. 2012. MtDNA analysis of global populations support that major population expansions began before Neolithic time. *Scientific Reports* 2:745. doi:10.1038 /srep00745.

Zhou, Y., et al. 2012. Options of sustainable groundwater development in Beijing Plain, China. *Physics and Chemistry of the Earth, Parts A/B/C* 47–48:99–113.

Zijdeman, R. L., and F. R. de Silva. 2014. Life expectancy since 1820. In J. L. van Zanden et al., eds., *How Was Life? Global Well-Being since 1820.* Paris: OECD, pp. 101–116.

Zipf, G. K. 1935. *The Psycho-Biology of Language.* Boston, MA: Houghton-Mifflin.

Zipf, G. K. 1949. *Human Behavior and the Principle of Least Effort.* Boston: Addison-Wesley Press.

Zohary, D., et al. 2012. *Domestication of Plants in the Old World*. Oxford: Oxford University Press.

Zolotas, X. 1981. *Economic Growth and Declining Social Welfare*. New York: New York University Press.

Zong, X., and H. Li. 2013. Construction of a new growth references for China based on urban Chinese children: Comparison with the WHO growth standards. *PLoS ONE* 8(3):e59569. doi:10.1371/journal.pone.0059569.

Zu, C., and H. Li. 2011. Thermodynamic analysis on energy densities of batteries. *Energy and Environmental Science* 4:2614–2625.

Zucman, G. 2014. Wealth inequality in the United States since 1913: Evidence from capitalized income tax data. *Quarterly Journal of Economics* 131:519–578.

Zuidhof, M. J. et al. 2014. Growth, efficiency, and yield of commercial broilers from 1957, 1978, and 2005. *Poultry Science* 93:2970–2982.

Zullinger, E. M., et al. 1984. Fitting sigmoidal equations to mammalian growth curves. *Journal of Mammalogy* 65:607–636.

Zupan, Z., et al. 2017. Wine glass size in England from 1700 to 2017: A measure of our time. *British Medical Journal* 359:j5623 doi:10.1136/b.

Zwijnenburg, J. 2015. Revisions of quarterly GDP in selected OECD countries. *OECD Statistics Brief* 22. Paris: OECD.

Index